CASE-BASED REASONING

Proceedings of a Workshop on
Case-Based Reasoning

Edited by Janet Kolodner

Holiday Inn, Clearwater Beach, Florida
May 10-13, 1988

Sponsored by:

Defense Advanced Research Projects Agency
Information Science and Technology Office

This document contains copies of reports prepared for
the DARPA Case-Based Reasoning Workshop. Included are
reports from both DARPA/ISTO sponsored programs and
from other researchers active in the field.

APPROVED FOR PUBLIC RELEASE
DISTRIBUTION UNLIMITED

The views and conclusions contained in this document are those of the authors and should not be
interpreted as necesarily representing the official policies, either expressed or implied, of the Defense
Advanced Research Projects Agency or the United States Government.

Distributed by

Morgan Kaufmann Publishers, Inc.

2929 Campus Drive

San Mateo, California 94403

ISBN 0-934613-93-1

Printed in the United States of America

ACKNOWLEDGMENTS

This workshop was organized at the direction of LTC Robert L. Simpson, Program Manager for Machine Intelligence in the Information Science and Technology Office of the Defense Advanced Research Projects Agency (DARPA). The purpose of the workshop is to review progress of research being conducted by organizations sponsored by the DARPA program on Case-Based Reasoning, to share research issues and results with other academic, industrial and government research personnel, and to provide a forum for the advancement of the state-of-the-art in Case-Based Reasoning.

The technical chair for the selection of papers for the workshop and organization of the program was handled by Professor Janet Kolodner of the Georgia Institute of Technology. Dr. Kolodner was assisted by a program committee composed of:

Luda Kopeikina, GTE Labs
William Mark, Lockheed AI Center
Chris Riesbeck, Yale University and Cognitive Systems
Edwina Rissland, University of Massachusetts, Amherst
Kris Hammond, University of Chicago
Dave Waltz, Thinking Machines and Brandeis University

Local arrangements were coordinated by Ms. Ruth Nelson of Cognitive Systems. Arrangement and editing of this proceedings was done by Janet Kolodner of Georgia Institute of Technology.

DARPA Workshop on Case-Based Reasoning
Contents

1	**Contents**	i
2	**Subject Index**	iii
3	**Author Index**	xii
4	**Background Papers**	
	1. Schank, Roger C., Reminding and Memory, from *Dynamic Memory*, Chapter 2, 1982.	1
	2. Hammond, Kristian, Case-Based Planning: Viewing Planning as a Memory Task, position paper written for the DARPA Workshop on Planning, Santa Cruz, CA, 1987.	17
	3. Kolodner, Janet L., Extending Problem Solving Capabilities Through Case-Based Inference, from *Proceedings of the 4th Annual International Machine Learning Workshop*, 1987.	21
	4. Ashley, Kevin & Rissland, Edwina, Compare and Contrast, a Test of Expertise, from *Proceedings of AAAI-87*, 1987.	31
5	**Contributed Papers**	
	1. Alterman, Richard, An Adaptive Planner, from *Proceedings of AAAI-86*.	37
	2. Barletta, Ralph & Mark, William, Explanation-Based Indexing of Cases.	50
	3. Birnbaum, Lawrence & Collins, Gregg, The Transfer of Experience Across Planning Domains Through the Acquisition of Abstract Strategies.	61
	4. Bradtke, Steven & Lehnert, Wendy G., Some Experiments with Case-Based Search.	80
	5. Branting, L. Karl, The Role of Explanation in Reasoning from Legal Precedent.	94
	6. Carbonell, Jaime & Velose, Manuela, Integrating Derivational Analogy into a General Problem Solving Architecture.	104
	7. Dupuy, Trevor, Military History and Case-Based Reasoning.	125

8. Farrell, Robert, Facilitating Self-Education by Questioning Assumptive Reasoning using Paradigm Cases. 136

9. Hammond, Kristian J., Opportunistic Memory: Storing and recalling suspended goals. 154

10. Hammond, Kristian J. & Hurwitz, Neil, Extracting Diagnostic Features from Explanations. 169

11. Hendler, James A., Refitting Plans for Case-Based Reasoning. 179

12. Hinrichs, Thomas R., Towards an Architecture for Open World Problem Solving. 182

13. Kass, Alex M. & Leake, David B., Case-Based Reasoning Applied to Constructing Explanations. 190

14. Klein, Gary A. & Calderwood, Roberta, How do People use Analogues to Make Decisions? 209

15. Klein, Gary A., Whitaker, Leslie A., & King, James A., Using Analogues to Predict and Plan. 224

16. Kolodner, Janet L., Retrieving Events from a Case Memory: A Parallel Implementation. 233

17. Kopeikina, Ludmila, Bandau, Richard, & Lemmon, Alan, Case-Based Reasoning for Continuous Control. 250

18. Koton, Phyllis, Reasoning about Evidence in Causal Explanations. 260

19. Marks, Mitchell, Hammond, Kristian A., & Converse, Tim, Planning in an Open World: A Pluralistic Approach. 271

20. Navinchandra, D., Case-Based Reasoning in CYCLOPS, a Design Problem Solver. 286

21. Owens, Christopher, Domain-Independent Prototype Cases for Planning. 302

22. Riesbeck, Christopher K., An Interface for Case-Based Knowledge Acquisition. 312

23. Rissland, Edwina L. & Ashley, Kevin D., Credit Assignment and the Problem of Competing Factors in Case-Based Reasoning. 327

24. Ruby, David & Kibler, Dennis, Exploration of Case-Based Problem Solving. 345

25. Seifert, Colleen M., Goals in Reminding. 357

26. Shinn, Hong S., Abstractional Analogy: A Model of Analogical Reasoning. 370

27. Simmons, Reid G., A Theory of Debugging. 388

28. Stanfill, Craig, Learning to Read: A Memory-Based Model. 402

29. Stanfill, Craig & Waltz, David L., The Memory-Based Reasoning Paradigm. 414

30. Sycara, Katia, Using Case-Based Reasoning for Plan Adaptation and Repair. 425

31. Turner, Roy M., Organizing and Using Schematic Knowledge for Medical Diagnosis. 435

32. Wall, Rajendra S., Donahue, Dan, & Hill, Stan, The Use of Domain Semantics for Retrieval and Explanation in Case-Based Reasoning. 447

33. Williams, Robert S., Learning to Program by Examining and Modifying Cases. 463

6 Appendix: Bibliography on Case-Based Reasoning and Related Topics

A-1

DARPA Workshop on Case-Based Reasoning
Subject Index

1 Adaptation and Repair

1. Alterman, Richard, An Adaptive Planner, from *Proceedings of AAAI-86*. — 37
2. Ashley, Kevin & Rissland, Edwina, Compare and Contrast, a Test of Expertise, from *Proceedings of AAAI-87*, 1987. — 31
3. Carbonell, Jaime & Velose, Manuela, Integrating Derivational Analogy into a General Problem Solving Architecture. — 104
4. Hammond, Kristian, Case-Based Planning: Viewing planning as a memory task. — 17
5. Hendler, James A., Refitting Plans for Case-Based Reasoning. — 179
6. Kass, Alex M. & Leake, David B., Case-Based Reasoning Applied to Constructing Explanations. — 190
7. Kolodner, Janet L., Extending Problem Solving Capabilities Through Case-Based Inference, from *Proceedings of the 4th Annual International Machine Learning Workshop*, 1987. — 21
8. Kopeikina, Ludmila, Bandau, Richard, & Lemmon, Alan, Case-Based Reasoning for Continuous Control. — 250
9. Koton, Phyllis, Reasoning about Evidence in Causal Explanations. — 260
10. Shinn, Hong S., Abstractional Analogy: A Model of Analogical Reasoning. — 370
11. Simmons, Reid G., A Theory of Debugging. — 388
12. Sycara, Katia, Using Case-Based Reasoning for Plan Adaptation and Repair. — 425

2 Applications

2.1 Legal Reasoning and Mediation

1. Ashley, Kevin & Rissland, Edwina, Compare and Contrast, a Test of Expertise, from *Proceedings of AAAI-87*, 1987. — 31
2. Branting, L. Karl, The Role of Explanation in Reasoning from Legal Precedent. — 94
3. Rissland, Edwina L. & Ashley, Kevin D., Credit Assignment and the Problem of Competing Factors in Case-Based Reasoning. item Sycara, Katia, Using Case-Based Reasoning for Plan Adaptation and Repair. — 327

2.2 Manufacturing

1. Barletta, Ralph & Mark, William, Explanation-Based Indexing of Cases. … 50
2. Klein, Gary A., Whitaker, Leslie A., & King, James A., Using Analogues to Predict and Plan. … 224
3. Kopeikina, Ludmila, Bandau, Richard, & Lemmon, Alan, Case-Based Reasoning for Continuous Control. … 250
4. Navinchandra, D., Case-Based Reasoning in CYCLOPS, a Design Problem Solver. … 286

2.3 Medical Reasoning

1. Koton, Phyllis, Reasoning about Evidence in Causal Explanations. … 260
2. Turner, Roy M., Organizing and Using Schematic Knowledge for Medical Diagnosis. … 435

2.4 Military Applications

1. Dupuy, Trevor, Military History and Case-Based Reasoning. … 125
2. Klein, Gary A., Whitaker, Leslie A., & King, James A., Using Analogues to Predict and Plan. … 224
3. Wall, Rajendra S., Donahue, Dan, & Hill, Stan, The Use of Domain Semantics for Retrieval and Explanation in Case-Based Reasoning. … 447

2.5 Instruction

1. Farrell, Robert, Facilitating Self-Education by Questioning Assumptive Reasoning using Paradigm Cases. … 136

3 Applications Support

1. Riesbeck, Christopher K., An Interface for Case-Based Knowledge Acquisition. … 312

4 Background

1. Ashley, Kevin & Rissland, Edwina, Compare and Contrast, a Test of Expertise, from *Proceedings of AAAI-87*, 1987. … 31
2. Hammond, Kristian, Case-Based Planning: Viewing planning as a memory task. … 17
3. Klein, Gary A. & Calderwood, Roberta, How do People use Analogues to Make Decisions? … 209
4. Kolodner, Janet L., Extending Problem Solving Capabilities Through Case-Based Inference, from *Proceedings of the 4th Annual International Machine Learning Workshop*, 1987. … 21
5. Schank, Roger C., Reminding and Memory, from *Dynamic Memory*, Chapter 2, 1982. … 1
6. Stanfill, Craig & Waltz, David L., The Memory-Based Reasoning Paradigm. … 414

5 Design Problem Solving

See "Tasks for a Case-Based Reasoner".

6 Diagnosis

See "Tasks for a Case-Based Reasoner".

7 Domain-Independent Inferences

1. Owens, Christopher, Domain-Independent Prototype Cases for Planning. — 302
2. Birnbaum, Lawrence & Collins, Gregg, The Transfer of Experience Across Planning Domains Through the Acquisition of Abstract Strategies. — 61

8 Explanation-Based Case-Based Reasoning

1. Birnbaum, Lawrence & Collins, Gregg, The Transfer of Experience Across Planning Domains Through the Acquisition of Abstract Strategies. — 61
2. Branting, L. Karl, The Role of Explanation in Reasoning from Legal Precedent. — 94
3. Carbonell, Jaime & Velose, Manuela, Integrating Derivational Analogy into a General Problem Solving Architecture. — 104
4. Hammond, Kristian J. & Hurwitz, Neil, Extracting Diagnostic Features from Explanations. — 169
5. Kass, Alex M. & Leake, David B., Case-Based Reasoning Applied to Constructing Explanations. — 190
6. Koton, Phyllis, Reasoning about Evidence in Causal Explanations. — 260
7. Navinchandra, D., Case-Based Reasoning in CYCLOPS, a Design Problem Solver. — 286
8. Rissland, Edwina L. & Ashley, Kevin D., Credit Assignment and the Problem of Competing Factors in Case-Based Reasoning. — 327

9 Exploratory Programs

1. Ashley, Kevin & Rissland, Edwina, Compare and Contrast, a Test of Expertise, from *Proceedings of AAAI-87*, 1987. — 31
2. Barletta, Ralph & Mark, William, Explanation-Based Indexing of Cases. — 50
3. Carbonell, Jaime & Velose, Manuela, Integrating Derivational Analogy into a General Problem Solving Architecture. — 104

4. Farrell, Robert, Facilitating Self-Education by Questioning Assumptive Reasoning using Paradigm Cases. 136

5. Hammond, Kristian J., Opportunistic Memory: Storing and recalling suspended goals. 154

6. Hammond, Kristian J. & Hurwitz, Neil, Extracting Diagnostic Features from Explanations. 169

7. Hinrichs, Thomas R., Towards an Architecture for Open World Problem Solving. 182

8. Kass, Alex M. & Leake, David B., Case-Based Reasoning Applied to Constructing Explanations. 190

9. Kolodner, Janet L., Extending Problem Solving Capabilities Through Case-Based Inference, from *Proceedings of the 4th Annual International Machine Learning Workshop*, 1987. 21

10. Kolodner, Janet L., Retrieving Events from a Case Memory: A Parallel Implementation. 233

11. Koton, Phyllis, Reasoning about Evidence in Causal Explanations. 260

12. Kopeikina, Ludmila, Bandau, Richard, & Lemmon, Alan, Case-Based Reasoning for Continuous Control. 250

13. Navinchandra, D., Case-Based Reasoning in CYCLOPS, a Design Problem Solver. 286

14. Owens, Christopher, Domain-Independent Prototype Cases for Planning. 302

15. Shinn, Hong S., Abstractional Analogy: A Model of Analogical Reasoning. 370

16. Simmons, Reid G., A Theory of Debugging. 388

17. Stanfill, Craig, Learning to Read: A Memory-Based Model. 402

18. Stanfill, Craig & Waltz, David L., The Memory-Based Reasoning Paradigm. 414

19. Sycara, Katia, Using Case-Based Reasoning for Plan Adaptation and Repair. 425

20. Turner, Roy M., Organizing and Using Schematic Knowledge for Medical Diagnosis. 435

21. Wall, Rajendra S., Donahue, Dan, & Hill, Stan, The Use of Domain Semantics for Retrieval and Explanation in Case-Based Reasoning. 447

22. Williams, Robert S., Learning to Program by Examining and Modifying Cases. 463

10 Feasibility and Uses of Case-Based Reasoning

1. Branting, L. Karl, The Role of Explanation in Reasoning from Legal Precedent. 94

2. Dupuy, Trevor, Military History and Case-Based Reasoning. 125

3. Farrell, Robert, Facilitating Self-Education by Questioning Assumptive Reasoning using Paradigm Cases. 136

4. Hammond, Kristian, Case-Based Planning: Viewing planning as a memory task. 17

5. Klein, Gary A. & Calderwood, Roberta, How do People use Analogues to Make Decisions? 209

6. Klein, Gary A., Whitaker, Leslie A., & King, James A., Using Analogues to Predict and Plan. 224

7. Marks, Mitchell, Hammond, Kristian A., & Converse, Tim, Planning in an Open World: A Pluralistic Approach. 271

8. Owens, Christopher, Domain-Independent Prototype Cases for Planning. 302

11 Indexing and Retrieval

1. Hammond, Kristian, Case-Based Planning: Viewing planning as a memory task. — 17
2. Kolodner, Janet L., Retrieving Events from a Case Memory: A Parallel Implementation. — 233
3. Riesbeck, Christopher K., An Interface for Case-Based Knowledge Acquisition. — 312
4. Schank, Roger C., Reminding and Memory, from *Dynamic Memory*, Chapter 2, 1982. — 1
5. Stanfill, Craig, Learning to Read: A Memory-Based Model. — 402
6. Stanfill, Craig & Waltz, David L., The Memory-Based Reasoning Paradigm. — 414
7. Wall, Rajendra S., Donahue, Dan, & Hill, Stan, The Use of Domain Semantics for Retrieval and Explanation in Case-Based Reasoning. — 447
8. Williams, Robert S., Learning to Program by Examining and Modifying Cases. — 463

11.1 Analysis of Indexing Methods

1. Bradtke, Steven & Lehnert, Wendy G., Some Experiments with Case-Based Search. — 80
2. Ruby, David & Kibler, Dennis, Exploration of Case-Based Problem Solving. — 345

11.2 Choosing Indices Using Explanation-Based Methods

1. Barletta, Ralph & Mark, William, Explanation-Based Indexing of Cases. — 50
2. Hammond, Kristian J. & Hurwitz, Neil, Extracting Diagnostic Features from Explanations. — 169

11.3 Choosing the Best from Many Retrieved Cases

1. Ashley, Kevin & Rissland, Edwina, Compare and Contrast, a Test of Expertise, from *Proceedings of AAAI-87*, 1987. — 31
2. Koton, Phyllis, Reasoning about Evidence in Causal Explanations. — 260
3. Kopeikina, Ludmila, Bandau, Richard, & Lemmon, Alan, Case-Based Reasoning for Continuous Control. — 250
4. Rissland, Edwina L. & Ashley, Kevin D., Credit Assignment and the Problem of Competing Factors in Case-Based Reasoning. — 327

11.4 Intentional Retrieval

1. Farrell, Robert, Facilitating Self-Education by Questioning Assumptive Reasoning using Paradigm Cases. — 136
2. Schank, Roger C., Reminding and Memory, from *Dynamic Memory*, Chapter 2, 1982. — 1
3. Seifert, Colleen M., Goals in Reminding. — 357

11.5 Organizing General Knowledge and Cases

1. Alterman, Richard, An Adaptive Planner, from *Proceedings of AAAI-86*.   37
2. Kass, Alex M. & Leake, David B., Case-Based Reasoning Applied to Constructing Explanations.   190
3. Kolodner, Janet L., Retrieving Events from a Case Memory: A Parallel Implementation.   233
4. Owens, Christopher, Domain-Independent Prototype Cases for Planning.   302
5. Rissland, Edwina L. & Ashley, Kevin D., Credit Assignment and the Problem of Competing Factors in Case-Based Reasoning.   327
6. Schank, Roger C., Reminding and Memory, from *Dynamic Memory*, Chapter 2, 1982.   1
7. Shinn, Hong S., Abstractional Analogy: A Model of Analogical Reasoning.   370
8. Turner, Roy M., Organizing and Using Schematic Knowledge for Medical Diagnosis.   435

12 Integrating Case-Based and Other Problem Solving Methods

1. Barletta, Ralph & Mark, William, Explanation-Based Indexing of Cases.   50
2. Carbonell, Jaime & Velose, Manuela, Integrating Derivational Analogy into a General Problem Solving Architecture.   104
3. Hammond, Kristian J., Opportunistic Memory: Storing and recalling suspended goals.   154
4. Hammond, Kristian J. & Hurwitz, Neil, Extracting Diagnostic Features from Explanations.   169
5. Hendler, James A., Refitting Plans for Case-Based Reasoning.   179
6. Hinrichs, Thomas R., Towards an Architecture for Open World Problem Solving.   182
7. Kolodner, Janet L., Extending Problem Solving Capabilities Through Case-Based Inference, from *Proceedings of the 4th Annual International Machine Learning Workshop*, 1987.   21
8. Koton, Phyllis, Reasoning about Evidence in Causal Explanations.   260
9. Marks, Mitchell, Hammond, Kristian A., & Converse, Tim, Planning in an Open World: A Pluralistic Approach.   271
10. Sycara, Katia, Using Case-Based Reasoning for Plan Adaptation and Repair.   425
11. Turner, Roy M., Organizing and Using Schematic Knowledge for Medical Diagnosis.   435

13 Integrating Execution and Planning

1. Alterman, Richard, An Adaptive Planner, from *Proceedings of AAAI-86*.   37
2. Hammond, Kristian J., Opportunistic Memory: Storing and recalling suspended goals.   154
3. Marks, Mitchell, Hammond, Kristian A., & Converse, Tim, Planning in an Open World: A Pluralistic Approach.   271
4. Turner, Roy M., Organizing and Using Schematic Knowledge for Medical Diagnosis.   435

14 Learning from Cases

1. Birnbaum, Lawrence & Collins, Gregg, The Transfer of Experience Across Planning Domains Through the Acquisition of Abstract Strategies. — 61
2. Carbonell, Jaime & Velose, Manuela, Integrating Derivational Analogy into a General Problem Solving Architecture. — 104
3. Farrell, Robert, Facilitating Self-Education by Questioning Assumptive Reasoning using Paradigm Cases. — 136
4. Hammond, Kristian J., Opportunistic Memory: Storing and recalling suspended goals. — 154
5. Hammond, Kristian J. & Hurwitz, Neil, Extracting Diagnostic Features from Explanations. — 169
6. Kolodner, Janet L., Extending Problem Solving Capabilities Through Case-Based Inference, from *Proceedings of the 4th Annual International Machine Learning Workshop*, 1987. — 21
7. Schank, Roger C., Reminding and Memory, from *Dynamic Memory*, Chapter 2, 1982. — 1
8. Shinn, Hong S., Abstractional Analogy: A Model of Analogical Reasoning. — 370
9. Stanfill, Craig, Learning to Read: A Memory-Based Model. — 402
10. Stanfill, Craig & Waltz, David L., The Memory-Based Reasoning Paradigm. — 414
11. Williams, Robert S., Learning to Program by Examining and Modifying Cases. — 463

15 Mapping

1. Branting, L. Karl, The Role of Explanation in Reasoning from Legal Precedent. — 94
2. Shinn, Hong S., Abstractional Analogy: A Model of Analogical Reasoning. — 370

16 Open Worlds

1. Hinrichs, Thomas R., Towards an Architecture for Open World Problem Solving. — 182
2. Marks, Mitchell, Hammond, Kristian A., & Converse, Tim, Planning in an Open World: A Pluralistic Approach. — 271

17 Opportunistic Problem Solving

1. Hammond, Kristian J., Opportunistic Memory: Storing and recalling suspended goals. — 154
2. Hinrichs, Thomas R., Towards an Architecture for Open World Problem Solving. — 182
3. Marks, Mitchell, Hammond, Kristian A., & Converse, Tim, Planning in an Open World: A Pluralistic Approach. — 271
4. Turner, Roy M., Organizing and Using Schematic Knowledge for Medical Diagnosis. — 435

18 Planning

See "Tasks for a Case-Based Reasoner".

19 Psychological Investigations

1. Klein, Gary A. & Calderwood, Roberta, How do People use Analogues to Make Decisions?   209
2. Klein, Gary A., Whitaker, Leslie A., & King, James A., Using Analogues to Predict and Plan.   224
3. Seifert, Colleen M., Goals in Reminding.   357

20 Representing Cases

1. Carbonell, Jaime & Velose, Manuela, Integrating Derivational Analogy into a General Problem Solving Architecture.   104
2. Hendler, James A., Refitting Plans for Case-Based Reasoning.   179
3. Kass, Alex M. & Leake, David B., Case-Based Reasoning Applied to Constructing Explanations.   190
4. Kolodner, Janet L., Extending Problem Solving Capabilities Through Case-Based Inference, from *Proceedings of the 4th Annual International Machine Learning Workshop*, 1987.   21
5. Kolodner, Janet L., Retrieving Events from a Case Memory: A Parallel Implementation.   233
6. Kopeikina, Ludmila, Bandau, Richard, & Lemmon, Alan, Case-Based Reasoning for Continuous Control.   250
7. Koton, Phyllis, Reasoning about Evidence in Causal Explanations.   260
8. Navinchandra, D., Case-Based Reasoning in CYCLOPS, a Design Problem Solver.   286
9. Owens, Christopher, Domain-Independent Prototype Cases for Planning.   302
10. Riesbeck, Christopher K., An Interface for Case-Based Knowledge Acquisition.   312
11. Shinn, Hong S., Abstractional Analogy: A Model of Analogical Reasoning.   370

21 Tasks for a Case-Based Reasoner

21.1 Design Problem Solving

1. Hinrichs, Thomas R., Towards an Architecture for Open World Problem Solving.   182
2. Navinchandra, D., Case-Based Reasoning in CYCLOPS, a Design Problem Solver.   286
3. Shinn, Hong S., Abstractional Analogy: A Model of Analogical Reasoning.   370

21.2 Diagnosis

1. Hammond, Kristian J. & Hurwitz, Neil, Extracting Diagnostic Features from Explanations. — 169
2. Koton, Phyllis, Reasoning about Evidence in Causal Explanations. — 260
3. Turner, Roy M., Organizing and Using Schematic Knowledge for Medical Diagnosis. — 435

21.3 Explanation

1. Branting, L. Karl, The Role of Explanation in Reasoning from Legal Precedent. — 94
2. Kass, Alex M. & Leake, David B., Case-Based Reasoning Applied to Constructing Explanations. — 190
3. Owens, Christopher, Domain-Independent Prototype Cases for Planning. — 302

21.4 Planning

1. Alterman, Richard, An Adaptive Planner, from *Proceedings of AAAI-86*. — 37
2. Carbonell, Jaime & Velose, Manuela, Integrating Derivational Analogy into a General Problem Solving Architecture. — 104
3. Dupuy, Trevor, Military History and Case-Based Reasoning. — 125
4. Hammond, Kristian, Case-Based Planning: Viewing planning as a memory task. — 17
5. Hammond, Kristian J., Opportunistic Memory: Storing and recalling suspended goals. — 154
6. Hendler, James A., Refitting Plans for Case-Based Reasoning. — 179
7. Kolodner, Janet L., Extending Problem Solving Capabilities Through Case-Based Inference, from *Proceedings of the 4th Annual International Machine Learning Workshop*, 1987. — 21
8. Marks, Mitchell, Hammond, Kristian A., & Converse, Tim, Planning in an Open World: A Pluralistic Approach. — 271
9. Simmons, Reid G., A Theory of Debugging. — 388
10. Turner, Roy M., Organizing and Using Schematic Knowledge for Medical Diagnosis. — 435

21.5 Precedent-Based Reasoning

1. Ashley, Kevin & Rissland, Edwina, Compare and Contrast, a Test of Expertise, from *Proceedings of AAAI-87*, 1987. — 31
2. Branting, L. Karl, The Role of Explanation in Reasoning from Legal Precedent. — 94
3. Rissland, Edwina L. & Ashley, Kevin D., Credit Assignment and the Problem of Competing Factors in Case-Based Reasoning. — 327
4. Sycara, Katia, Using Case-Based Reasoning for Plan Adaptation and Repair. — 425
5. Wall, Rajendra S., Donahue, Dan, & Hill, Stan, The Use of Domain Semantics for Retrieval and Explanation in Case-Based Reasoning. — 447

21.6 Process Control

1. Kopeikina, Ludmila, Bandau, Richard, & Lemmon, Alan, Case-Based Reasoning for Continuous Control. — 250

CASE-BASED REASONING WORKSHOP

AUTHOR INDEX

Alterman, Richard	37
Ashley, Kevin D.	31, 327
Barletta, Ralph	50
Birnbaum, Lawrence	61
Bradtke, Steven	80
Brandau, Richard	250
Branting, L. Karl	94
Calderwood, Roberta	209
Carbonell, Jamie	104
Collins, Gregg	61
Converse, Tim	271
Donahue, Dan	447
Dupuy, Trevor N.	125
Farrell, Robert	136
Hammond, Kristian J.	17, 154, 169, 271
Hendler, James A.	179
Hill, Stan	447
Hinrichs, Thomas R.	182
Hurwitz, Neil	169
Kambampati, Subbarao	179
Kass, Alex M.	190
Kibler, Dennis	345
Klein, Gary A.	209, 224
Kolodner, Janet L.	21, 233
Kopeikina, Ludmila	250
Koton, Phyllis	260
Leake, David B.	190
Lehnert, Wendy G.	80
Lemmon, Alan	250
Mark, William	50

AUTHOR INDEX
Page 2

Marks, Mitchell	271
Navinchandra, D.	286
Owens, Christopher	302
Riesbeck, Christopher	312
Rissland, Edwina L.	31, 327
Ruby, David	345
Seifert, Colleen M.	357
Schank, Roger C.	1
Shinn, Hong S.	370
Simmons, Reid G.	388
Stanfill, Craig	402, 414
Sycara, Katia	425
Turner, Roy M.	435
Velose, Manuela	104
Wall, Rajendra S.	447
Waltz, David L.	414
Whitaker, Leslie A.	224
Williams, Robert S.	463

BACKGROUND PAPERS

REMINDING AND MEMORY

DYNAMIC MEMORY
A Theory of Reminding and Learning
in Computers and People
(Chapter 2)

Roger C. Schank
Yale University

Cambridge University Press
Cambridge, England (1982)

Reminding

What are the issues a theory of memory must account for? What should any memory structure, in principle, be?

The human memory system, and hence any sensibly designed computer model of that memory system must have the ability to cope with new information in a reasonable way. Any new input that is to be processed by a memory system should cause some adjustment in that system. A dynamic memory system is one that is altered in some way by every experience it processes. A memory system that fails to learn from its experiences is unlikely to be very useful.

In addition, any good memory system must be capable of finding what it has in it. This seems to go without saying, but the issue of what to find can be quite a problem. With respect to episodic memory, that is the part of the memory system concerned with memory for events that are part of personal experience, we wish to find particular episodes in memory that are closely related to the input we are processing. But how do we define relatedness? And how do we know where to look for related episodes?

One phenomenon that sheds light on both the problem of retrieval and our ability to learn is the phenomenon of reminding. Reminding is a crucial aspect of human memory that has received little attention from researchers on memory. (For example, in a highly regarded recent book that attempts to catalog research by psychologists on memory, Crowder (1976), **reminding** does not even appear in the index as a subject that is mentioned.) Yet reminding is an everyday occurrence, a common feature of memory. We are reminded of one person by another, of one building by another and so on. But, more significant than the reminding that a physical object can cause of another physical object, is the reminding that occurs across situations. One event can remind you of another.

Why does this happen? Far from being an irrelevant artifact of memory, reminding is at the root of how we understand. It is also at the root of how we learn.

From Dynamic Memory - A Theory of Reminding and Learning in Computers and People, by Roger C. Schank. Copyright 1982. Cambridge University Press, Reprinted with Permission.

At the outset, it is important to distinguish the following broad classes of reminding since they tend to have different effects in an understanding system and must be accounted for in different ways.

1. Physical objects can remind you of other physical objects.
2. Physical objects can remind you of events.
3. Events can remind you of physical objects.
4. Events can remind you of events in the same domain.
5. Events can remind you of events in different domains.

For our purposes here, we will be concerned with the last two of these (4 and 5), because we are primarily interested in event memory. To the extent that reminding can tell us about the nature and organization of the episodic memory system, the most interesting cases would be those where, in the normal course of attempting to understand an event, we are able to find a particular event in memory that in some way relates to the processing of that event. That is, the organization of a dynamic episodic memory system depends upon the use of that system in understanding. Reminding occurs as a natural part of the process of understanding new situations in terms of previously processed situations (although it is not always obvious to us as processors exactly why a given reminding has occurred). Exactly how human memory controls processing and naturally gets reminded is the question we must address.

Why one experience reminds you of another is of primary importance to any theory of human understanding and memory. If people are reminded of things during the natural course of a conversation, or while reading, or when seeing something, then this tells us something of importance about the understanding process. Given the assumption that understanding an event means finding an appropriate place for a representation of that event in memory, reminding would indicate that a specific episode in memory has been excited or **seen** during the natural course of processing the new input. To be reminded of something we must have come across it while we were processing the new input. But, to have done this we either had to be **looking** for this reminded event or else we must have **run into it accidently**. In either case, reminding reveals something significant about the nature of memory structures and the understanding process.

If we found an episode because we were looking for it, we must ask ourselves how we knew of that episode's existence so that we were able to look for it.

If the explanation of reminding is that we **accidently run into an episode**, we must ask why that **accident** occurs, and whether that accident has relevance to our processing.

We will argue here that it is an amalgamation of these two explanations that provides us with the method by which reminding takes place. We are not consciously looking for a particular episode in memory during processing, because we do not explicitly know of that episode's existence. We do, however, know where episodes like the one we are currently processing are likely to be stored. Further, our method of processing new episodes is to utilize memory structures that contain episodes that are the most closely related to that new episode. Thus, reminding occurs when we have found the most appropriate structure in memory that will help in processing a new input. When no one episode is that closely related to an input, we can still process it, but no reminding occurs.

One thing that is obvious about reminding is that the more you know about a subject, the more you can be reminded of, within the course of processing inputs related to that subject. Thus, experts in particular fields might be expected to have reminding experiences directly tied in with their expertise. For certain people, we might expect reminding experiences corresponding to:

1. known chess patterns
2. known political patterns
3. previously encountered similar situations
4. patterns of behavior of a particular individual
5. relatedness of scientific theories
6. types of football plays
7. kinds of music or paintings

Why is it that some people are reminded of a famous chess game upon viewing another game and some people are not? The answer, obviously, is that not everyone has knowledge of famous chess games. Obvious as this may be, it says something very important about memory. We use what we know to help us process what we receive. We would be quite surprised if a chess expert were **not** reminded of a famous chess game upon seeing one just like it. We expect an expert to have categorized his experiences in such a way as to have them available for aid in processing new experiences. (An interesting problem here is that people can be reminded of something on occasion but can fail to evoke the same memory in a similar circumstance. This is a property of a dynamic memory, its changeability makes people's memory systems function differently in apparently similar situations.)

Thus, reminding is not a phenomenon that just happens to occur to some people at some times. It is a phenomenon that must occur, that as human understanders we expect to occur, in an individual who has a certain set of knowledge organized in a fashion that is likely to bring that knowledge to bear at a certain time.

This implies that an expert is constantly receiving new inputs and evaluating them and understanding them in terms of previously processed inputs. We understand in terms of what we already understood. But, trite as this may seem, this view of understanding has not been seriously pursued either by psychologists interested in understanding or by Artificial Intelligence (AI) researchers interested in understanding or in expert systems. To build an expert system, two possible avenues are open. One is to attempt to get at the compiled knowledge of the expert, that is, the rules he uses when he makes the decisions that reflect his expertise (see Buchanan et al., 1976; Davis, 1976; and Feigenbaum, 1977) for examples of this work). This approach has the advantage of being orderly and methodical. Its disadvantage is that such a system would not be able to reorganize what it knew. It would thus have a difficult time learning.

An alternative is to attempt to model the raw memory of the expert. This would involve creating a set of categories of subdomains of the expertise in question and equipping the system with rules for the automatic modification of those categories. Such a system would attempt to process new experiences in terms of the most closely related old experiences available. Upon finding an episode that strongly related, whatever that might turn out to mean, a reminding would occur. The new episode would then be indexed in terms of the old episode. New categories would be built as needed when old categories turned out to be useless from either under-utilization or over-utilization, or because the expectations contained within them were too often wrong.

An expert then is someone who gets reminded of just the right prior experience to help him in processing his current experiences. But, in a sense, we are all experts. We are experts on our own experiences. We all must utilize some system of categories, and rules for modifying those categories to help us find what we know when we need to know it.

Some things to consider are:

1. What is it that we do to new inputs while processing them that seems to automatically make conscious the most relevenmt old information?

2. How have prior experiences been categorized or labeled such that they will show up (i.e., be called to mind) at precisely the right moment)?

There is one other point to be made here. We are not always reminded of our most relevant prior experience in processing a new input. Thus, another question must also be put:

3. How can we have (mis)classified an experience so as to not bring it to mind at an appropriate time?

So, how do we get reminded? This problem is clearly strongly related to the problem of how we process new inputs at all. If reminding naturally occurs during processing by a dynamic memory system, how we get reminded and how we process ought to amount to different views of the same mechanism.

Let's consider an example of reminding. There is an otherwise ordinary table-service restaurant in Boston, Legal Seafood, where you are asked to pay the check before the food comes. Going to another table-service restaurant where one paid after ordering should normally cause one to be reminded of Legal Seafood if one had been to Legal Seafood. How is such reminding likely to take place?

A script-based view of the processing involved here has the restaurant script being called into play to help process any restaurant experience. In attempting to account for reminding within the natural course of script-based processing, it becomes clear that scripts must be **dynamic memory structures**. That is, given the phenomenon of reminding and what we said above about the relatedness of reminding and processing, a script cannot be a static (that is, unchangeable) data structure. Rather, the restaurant script must actually contain particular memories, such as the experience in Legal Seafood, and must be capable of accumulating new episodes that it has helped to process.

Let's consider this point more carefully. We are arguing that a script is a collection of specific memories organized around common points. Part of the justification for this modification of our old view of scripts is that it really is not possible to say **exactly** what is and what is not part of any script. Particular experiences invade our attempts to make generalizations. To put this another way, we do not believe in the script as a kind of semantic memory data structure, apart from living, breathing, episodic memories. What we know of restaurants is compiled from a multitude of experiences with them, and these experiences are stored with what we have compiled.

A script is built up over time by repeated encounters with a situation. When an event occurs for the first time it is categorized uniquely. (Actually things are rarely seen as being entirely unique.) Repeated encounters with similar events cause an initial category to contain more and more episodes. Elements of those episodes that are identical are treated as a unit, a script. But, subsequent episodes that differ from the script partially are attached to the part of a script that they relate to. The differing parts of the episode are stored in terms of their difference from the script. In this way, such episodes can be found when similar differences are encountered during processing.

Thus, we want to consider a script as an active memory organizer. It is this view of a script that is relevant in the Legal Seafood example. When we hit a deviation from our normal expectations in a script, and a previously processed episode is relevant to that deviation, we can expect to be reminded of that episode, so that that entire episode can help us in processing the current experience.

One thing that we are arguing against here is the notion of a track that we put forth previously (Schank and Abelson, 1977). A track was a script-like substructure that in form was just like any other script piece. It was called into play when some deviation from the norm was encountered. But, what really seems to happen is that, rather than finding new script pieces to help us when our expectations foul up, we find actual, real live memories. We then use these memories to help us in processing. That is, we formulate new expectations from these experiences that help us to understand our new experience in terms of the relevant old one that has been found.

Thus we are arguing that scripts actually have a stronger role than we had previously supposed. One of their primary functions is as organizers of information in memory. The restaurant script, for example, organizes various restaurant experiences such that when a deviation from the normal flow of the script occurs, the most relevant experience (the one that has been indexed in terms of that deviation) comes to mind. It comes to mind so that expectations can be derived from it about what will happen next in the new experience. Thus, reminding, in a sense, forces us to make use of prior knowledge to form expectations.

One important consequence of the reminding phenomenon is that it alters our view of what it means to understand. For example, when we enter Burger King, having before been to McDonald's but never having been to Burger King, we are confronted with a new situation which we must attempt to **understand**. We can say that a person understands such an experience (i.e., he understands Burger King in the sense of being able to operate in it) when he says "Oh I see, Burger King is just like McDonald's," and then begins to use his information about McDonald's to help him in processing what he encounters at Burger King.

To put this another way, we might expect that at some point during a trip to eat at a Burger King, a person might be **reminded** of McDonald's. Understanding means being reminded of the closest previously experienced phenomenon. That is, when we are reminded of some event or experience in the course of undergoing a different experience, this reminding behavior is not random. We are reminded of a particular experience because the structures we are using to process the new experience are the same structures we are using to organize memory. We cannot help but pass through the old memories while processing a new input.

Finding the **right** one (that is, the one that is most specific to the experience at hand) is what we mean by understanding. Does this mean that episodic memory structures and processing structures are the same thing? The answer is yes. It follows then that there is no permanent (i.e., unchangeable) data structure in memory that exists solely for processing purposes. Scripts, plans, goals, and any other structures that are of use in understanding must be useful as organizing storage devices for memories. These structures exist to help us make sense of what we have seen and will see. Thus, memory structures for storage and processing structures for analysis of inputs are exactly the same structures.

According to this view, it is hardly surprising that we are reminded of similar events. Since memory and processing structures are the same, sitting right at the very spot most relevant for processing will be the experience most like the current one. Thus, the discovery of a coherent set of principles governing what is likely to remind one of what is a crucial step, not only in research on the organization of memory, but also for natural language processing in general. We will now consider reminding in more detail.

Types of Reminding

The word **remind** is used in English to mean a great many different things. Joe can **remind you of** Fred. You can ask someone to **remind you to**

do something. We get reminded of a good joke, of past experiences, of things we intended to do and so on.

The type of reminding that we have been discussing is what we call **processing-based reminding**. This is the kind of reminding that occurs during the normal course of understanding or processing some new information as a natural consequence of the processing of that information.

In a broad categorization of reminding, two other types of reminding come up that bear superficial similarity to processing-based reminding but which are not relevant for our purposes here. The first of these is what we term **dictionary-based reminding**. Often when we look up a word in our **mental dictionaries**, we find an entire episode from our experience located with the definition, almost as if it were a part of that definition. Such dictionary-based reminding clearly cannot occur for words that are in great use in our daily lives. But for words, concepts, or objects that we use infrequently, such reminding is likely to occur. Thus, **Toyota** can bring to mind a particular Toyota and an experience associated with it. Similarly, phrases, such as "I am not a crook," or "I am the greatest," bring to mind particular episodes. Dictionary-based reminding is easily accounted for. Our mental dictionaries do not look like Webster's. Information about how to use a word or phrase, what circumstances it first appeared in for you, who uses it, the classes of things it can be applied to, feelings associated with it, and so on, are part of our mental entry for a word. In a sense, the less that is there, the more we notice it. As we gather a great deal of information about a word, the particular memories that we have associated with it tend to lose their connection to the word. Only the essential user-definition remains.

Thus, dictionary-based reminding is a phenomenon that helps to define a word for us in terms of a particular memory. This is not very useful in the long run. In fact, if we treated every word like that, we would find it very difficult to actually process anything in a reasonable amount of time. Such reminding is an important part of initial concept formation, however. Thus, there is a sense in which when such reminding does not occur, we may well have understood better, since the concept is more universally, that is, less particularly, defined.

Actually, dictionary-based reminding is a processing type of reminding too, namely one having to do with the processing of words (and sometimes objects). But, dictionary-based reminding is not very relevant to the operation of a dynamic episodic memory.

The second kind of reminding that is irrelevant to our discussion here is **visually-based reminding**. Sometimes one thing just looks like another. Since our minds organize perceptual cues and find items in memory based on such cues, it is hardly surprising that such reminding should occur. In processing-based reminding, the best reminding that should occur is the one we are least likely to notice. When we enter a restaurant we have been to before, the order of processing, that is, our expectations about the events in that restaurant, and their sub-sequent realization, should remind us of that restaurant. In other words, we process to what we perceive to be the closest fitting memory structure. If there is an exact fit, we are processing to the structure that contains the episode that fits. We do not feel that we have been reminded because reminding occurs when the fit is approximate, not exact. Nonetheless, in the strict sense of reminding we have been reminded of exactly the right thing.

The same thing occurs in perceptual processing. In processing John's face, the best fit is the memory piece that contains the perceptual features for John's face. We do not feel reminded by this, we simply feel that we have recognized the set of perceptual features. We feel reminded there too, when the fit is approximate. A new person can physically remind us of one we already have features in our mind for, because there is a partial match.

It is easy to confuse visually-based reminding with processing-based reminding. Visual processing is a kind of processing of course, so they are quite close. Moreover, frequently, after an approximate perceptual match has been made, an episode from memory comes to mind that is associated with that approximate perceptual match. This is the visual analogue of dictionary-based reminding. Associated with the perceptual features of an object that has not been accessed a great many times will be one or more experiences connected to that object. Once the input has triggered a structure in memory that defines the input, memory is not overly concerned with whether the input was the perception of sights or sounds. However, the kind of reminding that we are interested in is situation-based, not perception-based. That is, in processing a situation, when one is reminded of another situation, the new situation should be quite relevant to our understanding of the original situation.

Types of Processing-Based Reminding

We can now discuss the kinds of processing-based reminding that there are. If we can determine some of the kinds of reminding experiences (from here on, when we say reminding, we shall mean processing-based situational reminding) that there are, then we will have, at the same time, determined some of the possible organizational strategies that there are in memory. Reminding is the result of similar organization, after all. Thus, one can help in the discovery of the other.

Reminding Based Upon Event Expectations

The first type of reminding that we shall discuss is the kind we were referring to in the Legal Seafood example. This reminding is based on the assumptions about processing that were captured by the notion of scripts as presented in Schank and Abelson (1977). (The definition of a script that we shall use in this book is considerably more restricted than our old definition. But, the particulars of what is and is not a script need not concern us at this point. We shall return to this issue in Chapter 5.)

The assumption that is relevant is that, given an action, it is reasonable to expect that another particular action will follow. In other words, it seems to be true that, as processors of the world around us, we make assumptions about what will happen next. Such assumptions are often based upon what we know about the situation we are in.

Whatever structural entities actually have the responsibility for encoding such expectations should serve both as memory organizers and as data structures used in processing. Such structures contain predictions and expectations about the normal flow of events in some standardized situation.

In such a structure, whenever an expectation derived from that structure fails, its failure is marked. Thus, any deviation from the normal flow of events, in a structure whose task it is to encode expectations about the normal flow of events, is remembered by indexing that structure with a pointer to the episode that caused the expectation failure. That index is placed at the point of deviation. Thus, if ordering in a restaurant is handled by expectations derived from a restaurant structure, then the Legal Seafood experience would cause an expectation failure in that structure. In that case, the Legal Seafood experience would be stored in memory in terms of a failed expectation about ordering in a standard restaurant.

Thus, reminding that is based upon expectations about events occurs when the structure that was directing processing produces an expectation that does not work the way it was supposed to. This kind of reminding occurs whenever a deviation occurs in the normal flow of events in a structure. At the end of these deviations are indices that characterize the nature of the deviation. A match on the index brings to light the memory stored there.

Consider a script we might call **ride in airplane**. Under the event of serving drinks we might find memories about **drinks spilled on lap, free drinks, drunken party in next seat**, and so on. Each of these are potential indices, based on expectation failures from one's own experience, under which actual memories are found.

We would expect then, that all of one's experiences inside an airplane are organized by some airplane structure (as well as by other structures that might also be relevant). These particular memories are indexed according to their peculiar attributes with respect to the event in the relevant script piece.

According to this view there are two key questions:

1. What are the categories or classes of memory structure?

2. How are indices formed and used in memory organization within a structure?

In addition there is a third question. Not all reminding is neatly restricted within a given memory structure that reflects one particular context (such as restaurants and airplanes). Sometimes reminding can occur across such structures. Thus we have the question:

1. How does a memory organized in one memory structure remind you of something that would naturally be classed in a different structure?

The answer to this last question is a key problem before us in this book. It is important to understand why it is a key question within the bounds of processing-based reminding.

Recall that in studying processing-based reminding we are trying to discover how an extremely relevant memory can be brought to the fore in the natural course of processing. In the kind of reminding we just discussed, we suggested that one way such reminding occurs is this: In attempting to make predictions about what will happen next in a sequence of events, a relevant structure is brought in. In the course of applying the expectations derived from that structure, we attempt to get the most specific expectations to apply. Often these must be found by using an actual memory which has been stored under a failure of one of the expectations that is part of that structure. Thus, to get reminded in this way, there must have been an initial match on the basis of an identity between the structure now active and the one originally used to process the recalled episode (i.e., the one you were reminded of).

Now, the question is, can we ever get reminded of something that is not from a close match in an identical structure? It is obvious that people do get reminded across contextually-bounded structures of the type we have been using for illustration here. That is, a reminded event can have something in common with the initial event, but that common element does not have to be its physical or societal situation. But how can such reminding occur, if all memories are stored in terms of structures such as the scripts of Schank and Abelson (1977)?

It is obvious that it cannot. As we said in that book, many different types of structures govern processing. We made distinctions between plan application, goal tracking, and script application, often seeming to suggest that the **correct level of processing** flitted from one to the other. What seems clear now is that memories are stored at all levels and that processing of inputs must take place on each level.

That is, at the same time that we are applying a script-like structure, we are also processing the same input in a number of different ways. To find out what those other ways are, we must take a look at other kinds of reminding.

Goal-Based Reminding

In processing an input we are not only attempting to understand each event that happens as an event itself. We are also attempting to get a larger picture, to see the forest for the trees so to speak. We not only want to know what happened but why it happened. Thus we must track goals.

An example here will serve to illustrate goal-based reminding. Someone told me about an experience of waiting on a long line at the post office and noticing that the person ahead had been waiting all that time to buy one stamp. This reminded me of people who buy a dollar or two of gas in a gas station.

What could be the connection? One possibility is that I had characterized such motorists as **people who prefer to do annoying tasks over and over when they could have done them less often if they had purchased larger quantities in the first place.** Now such a category is extremely bizarre. That is, it is unlikely that there is such a structure in memory. The existence of so complex a structure would imply that we are simply creating and matching categories in our heads in order to be reminded. As this seems rather unreasonable, we must look for some more realistic way of explaining such a reminding.

Recall that processing considerations are intimately connected with memory categorizations. If we ask what kind of processing issues might be in common between the post office experience and the gas station experience, we find that in the **goal-based** analysis of the kind we have proposed in Schank and Abelson (1977), there is a very obvious similarity here. Both stories related to goal subsumption failures (Wilensky, 1978). In processing any story we are trying to find out why the actor did what he did. Questions about the motivations of an actor are made and answered until a level of goal-based or theme-based explanation is reached. In this story, why the person bought a stamp is easy, as is why he stood in line. But good goal-based processing should note that the story is without point if only those two goals are tracked (Schank & Wilensky, 1977). The **point** of the story is that the actor's behavior was somehow unusual. This unusualness was his failure to think about the future. In particular, he could have saved himself future effort by buying more stamps either before now or at this time. But he failed to **subsume** this goal. Thus the story is telling us about a goal-subsumption failure of a particular kind. Understanding this story involves understanding the kind of goal-subsumption failure that occurred.

Thus there are a set of memories organized by **goal-subsumption failure** in much the same way as script-like structures organized memories earlier. Here too, there are a set of indices on particular kinds of goal-subsumption failures. One of these has to do with waiting in line for service. That is where the gas station experience sits in memory. The new post office experience is processed using structures that track goals. At the same time, it is being processed using structures that carry expectations based upon particular contexts. As it happens there are no relevant processing predictions that come from the script-like structures here. The contexts in the reminding are quite different. But the goal tracking causes a reminding that can have potentially useful consequences if it is desirable to attempt to understand the motivations of the actor in the events that were described. Our assertion is that, as processors we always seek an understanding of why people do what they do. Reminding that occurs in response to our questioning ourselves about why an actor did what he did can be useful for making significant generalizations (i.e., learning). In other words, attempting to understand at the level of goals can lead to a generalization that may be valid in future processing.

Consider another example of goal-based reminding. Recently my secretary took a day off because her grandmother died. My previous secretary had had a great many relatives die and was gone a great deal because of it. It is not surprising that one experience reminded me of the other. Furthermore, I could not help but make predictions based upon the first secretary's subsequent behavior with respect to the second's future behavior. Consciously, I knew that these predictions were useless since there was no similarity between the two people, but the reminding occurred nevertheless.

What could a memory structure be like in which both these experiences would be stored? Again, we do not want to have static nodes in memory much as **employee's relative dies** (the hierarchical superset in both cases). Our memory connections must have processing relevance which may or may not be semantic superset relevance. (In this example, I had had other employee's relatives dies, but I was not reminded of those experiences.)

Here again goal-tracking causes a recognition that goal subsumption failure has occurred. One method of goal subsumption is to hire a secretary. I had processed both of these situations with respect to how they related to him. They both caused a particular goal-subsumption of mine (the same one) to be temporarily blocked. The temporary blocking of secretarial work due to the death of a relative is an index under goal-subsumption failure. The reminding that occurred, again had the possibility of applying what occurred in the first situation to the understanding of the second. In this instance, that application was deemed to be irrelevant by X. But the recognition of like patterns from which generalizations (and thus predictions about the future) can be made, is very important for a knowing system. The fact that the particular reminding was of no use here does not obviate the general significance of such goal-based remindings.

One key issue in the reminding and memory storage problem, then, is the question of what higher level memory structures are used in processing a new input. We have already worked with some of these structures in Schank and Abelson (1977), Wilensky (1978), and Carbonell (1979). We have recognized such structures as Goal-Blockage, Goal-Failure, Goal-Replacement, and Goal-Competition, not to mention the various structures associated with satisfying a goal. Each time one of these goal-based structures is accessed during normal processing, that structure becomes a source of predictions that are useful for future processing and learning via reminding. Structures based upon goal-tracking are thus likely to be of significance in a memory that can get reminded.

Plan-Based Reminding

It follows that if goals are being tracked, then so are the plans that are created to satisfy these goals. If we are to learn from our remindings, and that does seem to be one of the principal uses of reminding, then we must learn at every level for which we have knowledge. It follows then, that there should be a reminding that is plan-based. Such remindings should facilitate our construction of better plans.

Consider the following example. Recently my daughter was diving in the ocean looking for sand dollars. I pointed out where a group of them were, yet she proceeded to dive elsewhere. I asked why and she told me that the water was shallower where she was diving. This reminded me of the old joke about the drunk searching for his lost ring under the lamppost where the light was better.

People quite commonly undergo such reminding experiences, jokes or funny stories being common types of things to be reminded of. What types of processing does such a reminding imply?

The implication is that, just as script-like structures must be full of indices to particular episodes that either justify various expectations or that codify past failed expectations, so are plans used as memory structures as well. How would this work in this case? Here, the similarity in these two stories is that they both employed some plan that embodied the idea of **looking where it is convenient**. But it is not the plan itself that is the index here. One could correctly pursue that plan and not be reminded of the drunk and the lamppost. The reminding occurs because this plan has occurred in a context where that plan should have been known by the planner to be a bad plan. We shall discuss the difficulties involved in this example and what they imply later on. For now, the main point is that memories are stored in terms of plans too. Hence, reminding can also be plan-based.

Reminding Across Multiple Contexts

There is no reason why reminding must be limited to the kinds of structures and processing that we have previously worked on, and indeed it is not. Reminding can take place in terms of high level structural patterns that cut across a sequence of events, as opposed to the reminding that we have been discussing thus far -- reminding that occurs at particular points in the processing of individual events. This kind of reminding occurs when a pattern of events, as analyzed in broad, goal-related terms, is detected and found to be similar to a previously perceived pattern from another context.

To consider an example: We can imagine a head of state on a state visit getting into an argument that disrupts the visit. Hearing about this could remind you of arguments with your mother on a visit. It could also remind you of a rainstorm during a picnic. Recall that any given input is processed on many different levels simultaneously. Imagine a context in which our supposed head of state visit took a great deal of planning, went smoothly at the outset, was expected to have great ramifications for future efforts at consummating an important deal, and then went awry because of some capricious act under the control of no one in particular that caused the argument and the subsequent diplomatic rift. The same sort of thing could be happening at a well-planned picnic that was intended to have important personal or business ramifications and then got fouled up because of the weather that in turn permanently ruined the pending deal.

A less fanciful example of the same phenomenon occurs in watching a play or movie. If you have seen **Romeo and Juliet** and are watching **West Side**

Story for the first time, it is highly likely that at some point in the middle of **West Side Story** you will notice that it is the **Romeo and Juliet** story in a modern-day New York, with music. Such a realization is a reminding experience of the classic kind. That is, this reminding represents true understanding of the kind we mentioned earlier between McDonald's and Burger King. Here again the reminding matches the most relevant piece of memory and that brings with it a great many expectations that are both relevant and valid.

But the complexity in matching **West Side Story** to **Romeo and Juliet** is tremendous. In the Burger King example, it was only necessary to be in some sort of **fast food** script and proceed merrily down that script. But in this example, everything is superficially different. The city is New York, there is a gang warfare, there are songs. To see **West Side Story** as an instance of **Romeo and Juliet** one must be not only processing the normal complement of scripts and goals. One must also be, in a sense, summarizing the overall plot to oneself, because that is where the match occurs.

Thus, we have yet another level of analysis that people must be engaged in, in understanding, that of making an overall assessment of events in terms of their goals, the conditions that obtain during the pursuit of those goals, the events of their actions, the interpersonal relationships that are affected, and the eventual outcome of the entire situation.

Morals

When a new input is received, in addition to all the other analyses we have suggested, we also tend to draw conclusions from what we have just processed. Often these conclusions themselves can remind us of something. A moral derived from a story, the realization of the **point** of the story, and so on, can each serve as an index to memories that have been stored in terms of the points they illustrate or the messages they convey.

Such reminding depends, of course, on our having made the actual categorization of index for the prototypical story. In other words, unlike the other kinds of reminding that we have so far discussed, here we would have had to pre-analyze the prototypical story in terms of its moral message or point. Indeed, we probably do just that. Why else would we choose to remember a joke or story unless it had a point we were particularly fond of?

But here the problem is one of finding the adage or joke that is relevant. We found the **drunk** joke mentioned earlier because the plans being used were the same. Similarly, we can find morals when physical or situational structures such as scripts are the same. But what do we do when the only similarity is the moral itself? To find memories that way implies that there are higher level structures in memory that correspond to such morals. This also involves being reminded across contexts. We shall have to come up with structures that can account for such remindings.

Intentional Reminding

The last type of reminding we shall discuss is what we label intentional reminding. Sometimes one can get reminded of something by just the right mix of ingredients, by the right question to memory, so to speak. In these circumstances, reminding is not directly caused by the kind of processing that we are doing at the time. Rather, the processing is directed by the desire to call a relevant past experience to mind. It is as if we were trying to be reminded. We, as processors, know that if only we were to be reminded of something here, it would help us in our processing. We thus try to get reminded. If we are trying to answer a question, then reminding is a form of getting the answer. In other words, we try to remind ourselves of the answer. But, even if what we are doing is simply trying to understand a situation, intentional reminding represents our attempt to come up with a relevant experience that will help us to understnad our current situ-ation. Not all intentional reminding is consciously intended, however. Much of it comes from just thinking about what is happening to us at a given time, without any conscious feeling that we wish we were reminded of something. Our thinking of a way to solve a particular problem often causes us to be reminded.

On a walk on the beach, I was asked by the person whom I was walking with if he should take his dog along. This reminded me of the last time I had been visiting someone and had gone for a walk and had taken the resident dog along. I had objected, but my host said that we had to take it, and with good reason (protecting us from other dogs), it turned out. This reminding experience caused me to ask myself if we would **need** the dog on the beach in the same way. I thought not and said so.

The above is an example of intentional reminding. Had I not been reminded at all, I would have simply responded that I didn't want to take the dog, since I don't especially like dogs. Instead I posed a problem to myself. Knowing how and when to pose that problem (here, finding the possible advantages of taking the dog) is a complex problem which is discussed in Chapter 4 and in Schank (1981). To solve this problem, I attempted to be reminded of a relevant experience, if there was one.

Intentional reminding is extremely common. It forms the basis of a good deal of our conversation and of our thought. We try to get reminded by narrowing the contexts that we are thinking about until a memory item is reached. This narrowing is effected by a series of indices. Often these indices are provided by the input, but sometimes they must be provided by the person doing the thinking in an attempt to concsciously narrow the context.

In the situation above, two contexts were active: **visiting a colleague at his home** and **taking a walk**. Each of these contexts alone had too many experiences in it to come up with any actual memories. But the index of **dog** changes things. The **dog** index is what is necessary to focus the search. Here **taking the dog** was a sufficient cue for me because I so rarely did it.

The process of searching memory depends upon having a set of structures that adequately describe the contents of memory and a set of indices that point out the unusual features of the structures. Given such entities, it is then possible to search memory for intentional reminding.

As another example, my wife referred to the fact that we had eaten a pineapple in Hawaii when we were last there. I couldn't recall it. I asked where we had eaten it. She said the beach. That didn't help. I tried to imagine the beach belonging to the hotel we stayed at, but remembered that it didn't have a beach. I tried to imagine eating a pineapple in other contexts around the hotel in case she was mistaken, but couldn't. Finally I took myself mentally around the island, looking for beaches, that is, setting cues of unique scenes for myself. Finally I found a beach that set up a scene that did have pineapple eating in it (along with a picture of everything else that happened at that beach).

The point here is that memory search is constrained by the organization of memory. In order to search effectively we must attempt to **remind** ourselves of what we are looking for. To do this means locating the memory/processing structure that was used to understand the material being searched for in the first place. This requires **putting yourself** in the original processing situation. That is, if we can get ourselves to process the right kind of input, we can find what we are looking for in memory.

A Perspective on Reminding

Reminding, then, is a highly significant phenomenon that has much to say to us about the nature of memory. It tells us about how memory is organized. It also tells us about learning and generalization. If memory has within it a set of structures, it seems obvious that these structures cannot be immutable. As new information enters memory, the structures adapt. Adapting initially means storing new episodes in terms of old expectations generated by existing structures. Eventually expectations that used to work will have to be invalidated. Indices that were once useful will cease to be of use because the unique instances they indexed are no longer unique. New structures will have to be built.

Reminding serves as the start of all this. As a result, looking at reminding gives a snapshot of memory at an instant of time. After that snapshot has been taken, memory must adjust by somehow combining the old reminded episode with the newly processed episode to form a generalization that will be of future use in processing. Thus, reminding not only tells us about memory organization, it also signals memory that it will have to adapt to the current episode. Reminding is the basis for learning.

CASE-BASED PLANNING[1]

Kristian J. Hammond
Department of Computer Science
The University of Chicago
Chicago, IL 60637

"Those who cannot remember the past are condemned to repeat it." — Santayana

The central idea of Case Based Planning is that planning is done from memory rather than from rules or "first principles." Complete plans for conjunctive goals are stored in memory for later use. Memories of plan failures are stored so that they can be recalled and thus avoided in later planning. Specific repairs are stored and reapplied when the problems that they solve are anticipated. And specific techniques for conjoining plans are saved. In general, planning is a matter of recalling what has worked in the past rather than projecting what could work in the future.

The ideas behind CBP rise out of a simple principle:

If it worked, use it again.

and a corollary

If it works, don't worry about it.

The refinements of the basic idea come out of a second, equally simple, principle:

If it didn't work, remember not to do again.

to which is added

If it doesn't work, fix it.

CBP suggests that the way to deal with the combinatorics of planning and projection and is to let experience tell the planner when and where things work and don't work. Rather than replanning, reuse plans. Rather than projecting the effects of actions into the future, recall what they were in the past. Rather than simulating a plan to tease out problematic interactions, recall and avoid those that have cropped up before.

There are two ways to view CBP:

---

[1] This paper was written for the Planning Paradigms Panel of 1987 DARPA Workshop on Planning, Santa Cruz, CA.

PLANNING IS REMEMBERING. The control of a planner should be guided by traces of past planning. This means different things to different planners. In Carbonell's derivational analogy it means that traces of past search, success and deadends, are used to guide present search when problem-solving. In SOAR it means that "chunks" built in response to sub-goaling are used to plan for new situations. In CHEF it means that memories of past failures are used to guide the search for existing plans that avoid those failures. In each of these planners, the search for a plan or solution is heavily influenced by the experiences that the planner has had in the past. In effect, the structure of the external world imposes itself on the space that is searched.

PLANS ARE REMEMBERED. Plans have to be saved. I can think of no reasonable argument against this. I can think of reasons why it is hard, but nothing to indicate that indexing and retrieving plans is a harder task than that of "first principle" planning itself. Further, by working from existing plans, a planner is able to plan in absence of a complete model of its domain... or even a model of all of the operators in the plan it is running. But more on that later.

There are certain assumptions that we make in CBP:

> The first assumption is that we do not have a closed world. This limits the usefulness of preplanning and projection.

> Second, we have an incomplete and imperfect model of the world. This is assumed of not just the domain in general but also of the steps in plans that we use on a regular basis.

> The third is that we are not producing analyses or proofs of a plan's soundness. We are producing plans. This is forced on us by our second assumption.

> Fourth, we cannot do projection. That is, we cannot run simulations of our plans in order to tease out problems due to step interactions. This is forced on us by our first and second assumptions.

We do not make these assumptions because we want to. We make them because we have been forced to. It is what we have to assume of real world domains and the knowledge we can have of them. But we have observed that human planners are able to plan in complex domains, often with little knowledge of the true physics of those domains. This allows us to believe that it is possible for a planner to plan and do where it cannot understand.

But we still need to produce plans. How do we do this without projection? Without the pre- and post- condition information how do we string together operators? How do we build plans if we don't have perfect knowledge of our operators?

- New plans are built from old plans. But the internal effects of these plans need not be known and need not be analyzed by the planner.

- Projection is replaced with ANTICIPATION, which is based on experience rather than simulation. A CBP associates actual failures with the features that, to the best of its knowledge, predict them and is "reminded" of those failures when the same features arise again. Whatever causal knowledge is available to the planner is used to determine what those features are.

- Plans are selected on the basis of the goals that they satisfy, the problems that they avoid and the features in the world that have been associated with them in the past. This is a somewhat reactive approach, but, instead of associating features in the world with "concrete operators", we associate them with abstract plans. Also, the planner's causal knowledge is again used to determine which associations between features and plans will be most useful in later planning.

- Knowledge of individual operators is not used in planning itself. It is used instead to explain failed plans in order to repair them and discover the features that can be used later to anticipate and thus avoid the problems in later planning.

- To deal with conjunctive goals plans from memory have to be modified. But plan modification has to be done in the absence of full knowledge of the effects of that modification. This can lead to faulty plans.

- Any planning problems due to bad modification of existing plans, however, can be repaired and the repairs can be added to the set of changes that have to be made when adding the goals planned for to other existing plans.

This framework suggests six basic CBP processes:

1. An ANTICIPATOR that predicts planning problems on the basis of the failures that have been caused by the interaction of goals similar to those in the current input. Often the "anticipation" is just part of the retrieval process in that features that predict a problem are often directly associated with the plan that avoids it.

2. A RETRIEVER that searches a plan memory for a plan that satisfies as many of the current goals as possible while avoiding the problems that the ANTICIPATOR has predicted.

3. A MODIFIER that alters the plan found by the RETRIEVER to achieve any goals from the input that it does not satisfy.

4. A STORER that places new plans in memory, indexed by the goals that they satisfy and the problems that they avoid.

5. A REPAIRER that is called if a plan fails. It is here that we argue that causal knowledge is applied – if it is applied at all.

6. An ASSIGNER that uses the causal explanation built during repair to determine the features which will predict this failure in the future. This knowledge is used to index the failure for later anticipation. As in repair, causal knowledge is useful in anticipation but not essential.

Now let's make this concrete with an example based on a problem suggested by Bob Wilensky. The planner wants a newspaper. It searches for and finds its fetch paper plan. The plan is simple: go outside; pick up paper; go inside. Unfortunately it's raining—so the planner gets wet, the violation of one of its preservation goals.

But this is easy to solve: one of the preconditions of picking up the paper, that the robot is near the paper, enables the violation of a preservation goal, staying dry, in the presence of rain. As a result of this reasoning it can conclude that an in-place repair is to dry itself off. Further, it can conclude that a long range repair, aimed at later use, would be to block the effects of the rain even in the presence of the enabling condition. That is, use an umbrella.

But when should the planner use the umbrella? Should it use it when it notices rain, projects its actions forward in time, encounters the failure again, engenders a new preservation goal to avoid being wet and then counter-plans against this state by grabbing an umbrella? This seems like a bit much. Why not just associate the plan with going out in the rain?

This is what we do. Once this new plan is in hand, it is placed in memory, indexed by the features which predict its usefulness. The choice of features is made using the rules that explained the failure in the initial plan. In this case, rain and the goal of getting something that is outside predict the problem, so the "umbrella" version of fetch is indexed by those features. So in a later situation in which rain is present, the modified plan is recalled.

The connection between feature and plan is direct, even though the decision to make that connection was made on the basis of a deep causal model of the domain. What we avoid in doing this is the problem of constantly rederiving the problems that will occur when the planner goes out in the rain. The umbrella variation is not used because the planner has once again figured out the being outside in the rain will make it wet. It is used because it is raining.

The decisions concerning repair and indexing are made using a knowledge base of rules that would normally be associated with plan generation. But it is used less often than in plan generation, and once it is used, the planner can avoid using it again in planning for situations that it has already handled.

This is only a sketch of CBP and there are still many arguments within the group of CBP researchers about even the rough design I have outlined here. But there is agreement on one basic point: memory of the actual is more important than rules that outline the possible.

Extending Problem Solver Capabilities Through Case-Based Inference

JANET L. KOLODNER (KOLODNER@GATECH.EDU)

School of Information and Computer Science, Georgia Institute of Technology,
Atlanta, GA 30332 U.S.A.

Abstract

In case-based reasoning, the problem solver makes its inferences based directly on previous cases rather than by the more traditional approach of using general knowledge. Case-based reasoning results in several enhancements to problem solving behavior over time. First, recall of previous failures warns the problem solver of potential for failure and allows the problem solver to avoid making mistakes made previously. Second, previous decisions that have been made previously are suggested to the problem solver so that its decisions do not have to all be made from scratch. This lessens the search space and also is a way of shortcutting the constraint satisfaction process. Third, if abstract schemata can be derived from cases that have been seen previously, generalized knowledge can be augmented. This allows real shortcuts in problem solving. Decisions that previously took several reasoning steps to make may be possible through application of a generalized schema.

1. Introduction

Much of the problem solving people do from day to day involves consideration of previous similar situations. Access to previous experiences helps the problem solver anticipate and avoid repeating mistakes and aids in the derivation of reasoning shortcuts. The work reported in this paper is an investigation of the processes involved in making inferences based on individual past experiences. The set of processes that are employed to do this are called *case-based reasoning processes*. Our goals in this endeavor are manifold. First, we wish to understand the processes involved in doing this type of problem solving analogy. Apparently, it comes easily and naturally to people. But it is not a process that is normally employed in problem solving or learning systems. Our second goal parallels the first. As a result of learning about the processes involved in case-based reasoning, we want to be able to specify what an automatic reasoning system needs to employ these processes and under what circumstances they ought to be applied.

To illustrate case-based reasoning, we give two examples from the meal planning domain. Case-based reasoning, in these examples, is in the context of problem solving. While attempting to solve the problem of deriving an appropriate meal for a client, the caterer, who is the problem solver, is reminded of several previous meals and uses those to aid the problem solving, first to anticipate and avoid a problem she had previously when she did not know to plan for vegetarians attending a dinner party. In this case, case-based reasoning directs her to find out the information that she had been missing the last time that had caused a problem in the previous meal. In the second instance of case-based reasoning, the previous case is used to make suggestions about cuisine and what to serve at the meal. Taking the constraints set up by the current problem into account, the caterer is reminded of a meal in which some of the same constraints were active and begins planning the new meal based on that. Taking into account the differences between the two situations, the caterer comes up with a plan appropriate to the current meal. Without the previous cases, the problem solver would have repeated its previous mistake of not planning for vegetarians when it was possible some would be at the party, and it would have had to derive a meal for the party from scratch. Previous cases thus give the caterer a chance to improve her performance in two ways.

Kolodner, J. L., Extending Problem Solving Capabilities Through Case-Based Inference. (Proc. 4th Annual Int'l Machine Learning Workshop (1987). Reprinted with permission of Morgan Kaufmann, Publishers.

> Client: I'm having a party for my research group next Saturday. There will be about 20 people.
>
> ...
>
> Caterer: *(Remembering another party with graduate students, where there was no adequate provision for the one vegetarian in the group)* Are there any vegetarians in the group?
>
> Client: Yes, ...
>
> ...
>
> Caterer: *Last time you had a buffet dinner and were on a limited budget, you served a combination of Indian and Chinese dishes. We could do that again, but substitute several vegie dishes for some of the meat ones.*

Over the past several years, we have investigated case-based reasoning in a variety of domains, some common-sense and some expert. Our most recent endeavors are in the domains of labor mediation (Sycara, 1985), meal planning (Cullingford & Kolodner, 1986; Kolodner, in press), and planning for acquisition of household products (Turner, 1986). Our illustrations in this paper will come from the meal planning domain. Our program, called JULIA (Cullingford & Kolodner, 1986; Kolodner, in press) employs a combination of case-based reasoning, constraint propagation, and problem reduction problem solving to derive menus for meals. It uses its remindings of past failures to warn it of the potential for error and to suggest means of avoiding errors made in the past. It uses its remindings of past successes to derive suggestions as it is planning a meal. Previous cases can suggest whole meals, parts of meals, or attributes of meals, depending on the problem solver's focus at the time reminding happens.

2. Making a Case-Based Inference

Making a case-based inference, in the simplest case, includes the following set of steps:

1. Recall a previous case
2. Focus on appropriate parts of that case
3. Use those parts of the previous case to derive an appropriate decision for the new case

2.1. Recalling a previous case

Recall of a previous case is done by probing the memory. According to Schank's (1982) MOPs theory, understanding of a new input (case) includes finding the best knowledge in memory that can be used to make predictions from it. Finding this knowledge is equivalent to integrating the new case with what is already in the memory. As reasoning is going on, according to this theory, memory is constantly being probed and updated, the case is getting better integrated, and better knowledge to use in making predictions about the case is being derived.

According to the same theory, generalized knowledge and individual cases are organized together in the same memory (see Kolodner, 1984; Lebowitz, 1983 for means of implementing such a memory). As a result, as a case is being understood and integrated into memory, both generalized knowledge and individual cases become available to use in further processing it. The case is integrated to the most specific possible place in memory. It may closely fit a generalized category or may be most similar to a specific previous case. When it closely fits a generalized category, the generalized knowledge associated with that category is used for problem solving. When it most closely fits a case, that case becomes available for case-based reasoning. Because the current case can be better integrated into memory as more is derived about it, new cases not previously considered are encountered in memory and become available for case-based reasoning as problem solving progresses. Usually, cases encountered later in problem solving are similar to the current case in more specific ways than the ones recalled earlier in problem solving. The problem solver thus may use several cases in coming up with a problem solution, each related more specifically to the current case than the one that came before.

In JULIA, recall is realized by a memory process running concurrently with the problem solver. A global knowledge structure (called a blackboard) holds the representation of the current problem situation, including the problem statement and the evolving solution. The memory prober uses the problem representation to derive its cues for searching memory. As the problem statement is filled out in more detail, the memory prober has additional cues available to it, and as a result new cases may become available for case-based reasoning as problem solving progresses. Because several cases may be available at once, JULIA needs a way to choose from among the available cases. It focusses first on those that share the most goals with the current case. To choose the best of those, it chooses those that share the most and most important constraints. Other features are taken into account only after that.

2.2. Focussing on appropriate parts of the recalled case

Any particular case that is recalled could be quite large. The entire case is not necessary for making a case-based inference. In fact, the whole case with all of its details is too cumbersome to work with. Rather, the parts of the case that have relevance to the new case are the ones to focus on. There are two ways this can be done. If the previous case was successfully resolved, the problem solver's current reasoning goals determine focus. If the previous case resulted in failure, focus is on those parts of the previous case that were responsible for the failure.

Let us examine the case where the previous problem was successfully resolved first. In this case, it is the problem solver's current reasoning goals that determine which parts of the previous case to focus on. In general, problem solving involves achieving a number of goals that are often reduced to subgoals. A reasoner that has to plan a meal will have subgoals associated with finding a cuisine, finding an appetizer, finding a main course, finding a dessert, etc. Each of these subgoals may itself be reduced to several subgoals. Finding an appetizer, for example, may require coming up with a main ingredient, coming up with a preferred preparation method or flavor enhancer, and then finding a recipe. Given the current goal of the reasoner, focus is directed to those parts of the previous case that are relevant to fulfilling that goal. Thus, when a caterer is reminded of a case while trying to determine cuisine, it will focus on the cuisine of the previous meal and the reasons it was a good choice in that case to see if the cuisine chosen previously is appropriate for the current case. When it is trying to come up with a dessert, it will focus on the dessert served in a previous case it is reminded of and the reasons that dessert was a good choice.

Where do these reasoning goals come from? One can think of a general purpose reasoner that is at least initially in charge of reasoning goals. As a problem is being reasoned about, the goals and subgoals that must be achieved to resolve it are derived by that reasoner. In Carbonell (1983, 1986), that reasoner is a means-ends analysis problem solver and therefore derives its subgoals by comparing the current and goal states, deriving their differences, and setting up subgoals of reducing those differences. After a case is recalled, the progression of subgoals that were used in solving that case are used to complete processing of the current case. Another method, used by Hammond (1986), Kolodner (1985), Kolodner, Simpson, & Sycara (1985), and Simpson (1985), is to set the sequence of goals a priori. The problem solver progresses through the sequence of goals, attempting to achieve each one. If a case is available when a goal is encountered, that case is used to achieve the goal, otherwise from-scratch methods are used. After one goal is achieved, the next in the set sequence is attempted.

JULIA is implemented yet another way. The case-based reasoner runs in conjunction with a constraint satisfier, problem reduction problem solver, constraint propagator, and conversational controller. A goal scheduler keeps track of the current goals of the system. Goals are posted on the global blackboard for all processes to see, and any that have the potential to achieve a posted goal attempt it. Any time one of those processes needs information, it posts its goals with the goal scheduler. This means that the case-based reasoner can take its direction from any of the processes requiring inferences to be made.

The goal scheduler initially takes its direction from a problem reduction problem solver. The problem reduction problem solver knows, for example, that to plan a meal, one must first derive meal constraints and descriptors, then plan the main course, then plan the salad, appetizer, and dessert. When memory returns a case, the case-based reasoner attempts to achieve the system's current most specific goals by using the case. When that goal is achieved, it may use the same case to attempt to achieve other active goals. The case-based reasoner itself might also need to achieve a set of subgoals that cannot immediately be achieved by the current case. When this happens, it posts those goals with the goal scheduler.

Suppose, for example, that the current most specific posted goals are "choose main dish", "choose side dish (veg)", and "choose side dish (starch)", all subordinate to "choose main course". If the memory returns a case at this point, the case-based reasoner will first focus on the main dish of the previous course to see if anything can be adopted from it. If, after suggesting the main dish used previously, no new cases are returned from memory, it will use the same case to attempt to achieve its side dish (veg) goal. In general, case-based inference can be used to achieve goals at any level of detail or abstraction, and when this happens, full problem reduction is shortcutted.

When the previous case resulted in failure, focus is directed to those parts of the previous case that were responsible for that failure. In essence, when a failed case is recalled, the current goals of the problem solver are put on hold and focus is on avoiding the error made previously. In the dialog above, for example, the caterer was trying to fill in meal descriptors (constraints) before beginning the job of choosing dishes for the meal. Meal descriptors include finding out cost, deriving cuisine, finding out how serving might be done, and finding out how many people will be in attendance. In the course of attempting to achieve these subgoals, she was reminded of a previous failed case in which vegetarians were not accounted for in the planning. The case-based reasoner focuses on that failure and attempts to find out if it is possible for that failure to happen in the current case, and, if so, attempts to prevent it. We explain the processing necessary for this task below. After dealing with a failed case, focus may revert back to the goals that were active before finding the failure, or the problem statement might be sufficiently changed by the process of preventing the failure that problem solving goals must be rederived using the new problem statement.

2.3. Making the case-based inference

At this point, we have an old case and a problem solver goal, we have focused on a part of the old case that is to be used in achieving that goal, and we have the case we are currently working on. When the previous case was successful, the purpose of the case-based inference is to achieve the goal for the new case based on the old one. For example, if the current goal is to choose a cuisine, and a previous case is available with similar meal constraints and meal description, the case-based reasoner examines the choice of cuisine from the old case (the way the cuisine goal was achieved in the previous case) to derive a way of achieving that goal in the new case. When the previous case resulted in failure or failed expectations, the purpose of case-based inference is to judge whether the same error is possible in the current case and to avoid repeating it.

Let us consider first the processes of case-based inference when the previous case was successfully resolved. There are several processes available for making such case-based inferences:

1. Transfer the solution that achieved the goal in the previous case.
2. Transfer the solution that achieved the goal and modify it based on differences between the current and previous case.
3. Transfer the inference method by which the previous goal was achieved.
4. Create an abstraction of the problem descriptions from the two cases, extend it to fit the solution to the previous case, and apply it to the new case to create a solution.

The process to be used depends on a number of considerations: Is there a value that, when derived, will achieve the goal, and if so, is that value available in the old case? Do we know how that value was derived for the old case? Was it by an "easy" or a "complex" set of reasoning steps? Do we know why the value from the previous case was appropriate? Do we know why the method of deriving that value previously was appropriate? If achievement of the goal is not done by simple derivation of a value, do we have a generalized schema that explains how the goal was achieved previously? If no schema, do we have the set of steps? Is our goal to derive a plan or is it to derive a feature value? Is the problem solution easily decomposable into non-overlapping parts? Or is the previous solution one that integrates the achievement of several goals simultaneously?

When the goal to be achieved can be achieved by choosing a single value or fully-instantiated frame, Method (1) is the one of choice. This method is the simplest, and is the one employed by Carbonell (1983), Hammond (1986), Kolodner, et al. (1985), and Simpson (1985). It requires a lookup of the solution to the active goal in the previous case and then consideration of whether that solution will work in the current case. Suppose, for example, that JULIA has the goal of choosing a main dish. It is appropriate, in this case, to recall the main dish used previously and consider whether it is appropriate for the current case. This method is also appropriate when the inferences necessary for achieving the goal were quite complex and only the solution itself is necessary as a hypothesis. This might happen in meal planning if there was a lot of trial and error reasoning that went into choosing a particular dish for a previous meal. Only the dish need be considered. The long reasoning chain followed previously does not have to be repeated.**

When the solution transferred from a previous case does not fit the new case, Methods (2) or (3) are necessary. We consider Method (3) first and consider Method (2) later since it is used in other cases also. According to Method (3), the chain of inference used to derive a solution to the current goal in the previous case is repeated in the new case. When the goal is a high-level one and the task is planning, Method (3) is equivalent to Carbonell's (1986) derivational analogy. Let us consider, however, the case where the goal is a fairly specific one: "choose main dish (vegetarian)". One way this can be done is to choose a dish that normally has meat but to use the vegetarian version of it.* If, when the problem solver is trying

---

** This is also the case in medical diagnosis. A previous diagnosis acts as a hypothesis that must be confirmed, and at least initially, direct transfer of the solution (diagnosis) from the previous case is all that is necessary.

* We are not considering the ins and outs of the planning necessary to do this. See Hammond (1986) for a description of that. Considered Hammond's way, this goal would be a fairly complex one. We are assuming that the system is not deriving the recipe, but rather is choosing from among recipes it has

to achieve this goal, it is reminded of a meal in which vegetarian lasagne was chosen as the main dish in this way, it might attempt the same inference method: choose a dish central to the chosen cuisine, then search the set of vegetarian recipes for a version of it that does not have meat. In essense, using this method, the conditions under which a previous decision was made are taken into account, and the case-based inference tends to be a transfer of the method of decision making or the inference rules used previously rather than the solution. Because this method is more time-consuming than the transfer method (1), JULIA uses it only if transfer has been ruled out or if solutions require different features.

When the previous solution is not easily decomposable into non-overlapping parts, when it integrates the achievement of several goals simultaneously, when a high level goal with a routine achievement method provides the current focus, or when a high level goal that cannot easily be decomposed provides the current focus, Method (2), sometimes called *comparison-based reasoning*,** is the one of choice. Using this case-based reasoning method, the solution that achieved the goal previously is transferred from the previous case and modified based on differences between the current and previous case. While this method has not been implemented in JULIA, we have found it useful for the task of labor mediation (Sycara, 1985), in which the previous solution integrates partial fulfillment of many simultaneous competing and conflicting goals and cannot be easily decomposed into parts. We (Turner, 1986) and others (Alterman, in press) have also found it useful in achieving goals with a routine method of achievement when a case the specializes that routine is available.

Method (4) is more schema-based (see, e.g., Holyoak (1984)). In this method, the current and previous cases are compared and a schema describing the similarities of the problem statements is described.*** The schema must be such that it can be used to describe both problem statements. The schema is then broadened to describe the solution to the previous problem, and the new problem is solved by applying the schema to that problem. In principle, it should be possible through this method to derive real problem solver shortcuts by storing the derivations of the reasoning steps in the schema where they do not have to be considered during later problem solving except when something goes wrong. This is not possible with any of the other methods by themselves.

While these four methods are the ones that are applicable when the previous case resulted in success, additional reasoning must go on when the previous case resulted in failure (Carbonell, 1986, Kolodner, in press). In this case, the conditions under which previous values were computed and the set of steps used to make decisions are checked against the new case to see if the same potential for failure exists. The previous case may also provide suggestions to the problem solver of how to proceed. In essense, the reasoning that goes on here is a special case of derivational analogy.

In short, the steps that must be followed to capitalize on a previous failure are*: (1) determine what was responsible for the previous failure, if possible (this may already be recorded, and if not, some short amount of time is spent attempting to derive it), (2) direct reasoning focus to the decision in the new problem that is analogous to the one that caused the failure in the previous one (this may be the one currently being focussed on or one that its correct solution is dependent on), (3) check for the potential for the same failure in the new case, either by seeing if the explanation of the previous failure holds in the new case or by checking the reasons why the previous decision was made and seeing if the same

---

available.
** Term due to Gary Klein.
*** Work being done by Hong Shinn.
*Of course, it is more complex than the set of steps shown here, but these steps form the core of the processing. See Kolodner (in press) for more detail.

justifications might apply in the new case (this step may require additional information gathering), (4) if not, potential for error is not there, so return to the interrupted step and keep going, (5) if so, rule out the previous errorful decision as a possibility for the current case, and if the previous case was finally resolved correctly, determine if the decision made when it was resolved correctly is applicable to the new case, (6) if so, use it as a suggestion for a case-based inference, (7) if step 2 redirected focus, then redo whatever decisions must be redone as a result (i.e., follow dependencies) and return to the reasoning step that was interrupted.

This is the procedure used by the caterer in the example in Section 1 to determine the need to ask if any guests were vegetarians. After the errorful situation was encountered, the first step was to determine what was responsible for it. In this case, the problem was that the vegetarian constraint was missing from the problem description when problem solving was going on. Focus is directed to constraints on food selection. Checking for the potential for failure in the new case, we find that we do not have any food constraints listed. Since the previous case failed because of lack of knowledge and we are missing the same knowledge in this case, there is a potential for error, and the information necessary to avoid the error is gathered by asking if there are any vegetarians.

2.4. Representational support

Because this processing requires knowing why previous decisions were made, what other decisions previous decisions were dependent on, and what was responsible for previous failures, there must be both a representational system and a bookkeeping system that keep track of this knowledge. Our solution to the representational problem is to have "value frames" (Kolodner, 1986) associated with each value recorded by the system**. Each time the problem solver makes a decision, it records its decision in the value slot of the value frame and also records what led it to that decision. Value frames include facets for a value, other values that were suggested as alternatives, ruled out values, conditions that were considered in choosing the value, and the inference rule or method or set of steps used to make the decision. Each inference rule that is recorded has three parts to it: the rule body, the bindings that were used in this instance, and the source of those bindings (i.e., where in the problem description can the values used in the bindings be found). The knowledge kept in value frames supports both derivation-type case-based inference (i.e., Method (3)) and avoidance of previous mistakes.

While value frames keep the justifications for each decision, pointers in the other direction are needed when the problem solver needs to retract an already-made decision. Our solution has been to integrate a truth-maintenance type system with our problem solver (Kolodner, in press).

3. Implementations

The earliest implementation of a case-based reasoner to come out of our group is the MEDIATOR (Simpson, 1985, Kolodner, et al., 1985), a program that uses case-based reasoning to understand and resolve disputes in a common-sense way. There are several major points illustrated by the MEDIATOR project. First, it showed that case-based inference is appropriate for any kind of inference that needs to be made, provided the appropriate previous cases are available. Second, it showed how at least some reasoning shortcuts are allowed with case-based reasoning. Third, the MEDIATOR illustrated that if the reasoning process keeps its reasoning goals explicit, then the case-based reasoning process can be

---
**Value frames hold essentially the same things Carbonell (1986) claims are necessary for derivational analogies.

directed by those goals.

Our most current implementation of the processes described in this paper is JULIA (Cullingford & Kolodner, 1986, Kolodner, in press), an attempt to design an automated colleague that acts as a caterer's assistant. JULIA integrates several processes, as described above. In the following example of JULIA solving a problem, we see some of the processing JULIA does.

The dialog begins with JULIA introducing herself and the user stating her problem.*

```
<JULIA> Hello. I'm JULIA, a Caterer's Advisor. May I help you?
USER =>
  I'm having a dinner next week for my research group.
  There is no room for all of them in the dining room.
<JULIA>
*** The initial problem is:
***** Frame #<FRAME 34502032> *****
Name: M-MEAL774
  Isa: (<M-MEAL>)
  Category: INDIVIDUAL
  Slots:
    ACTUAL-RESULT: NIL
    CHARACTERS: (?HOST ?GUESTS ?PARTICIPANTS)
    CONSTRAINTS: (<C-LIMITED-SPACE778>)
    DEFINED-SLOTS: NIL
    DESCRIPTOR: NIL
    EXPECTED-RESULT: NIL
    FOLLOW-UP: NIL
    GOALS: (<E-EAT776> <S-HUNGER777>)
    GUESTS: <*JLK*S-GROUP>
    HOST: <*JLK*>
    ORDER: NIL
    PARTICIPANTS: (?HOST ?GUESTS)
    SETTING: <*JLK*S-HOUSE>
    STEPS: NIL
    TIME: NIL
```

JULIA's problem reduction problem solver starts out in charge. It assumes that its goal is to instantiate a meal, and it adds the appropriate task and goal to the task tree and goal chain. It then immediately reduces that task to its component parts and begins working on the first of them, the meal descriptor task. Meal descriptors include the meal's cuisine, the style of presentation, and the placement of the guests when they eat.

```
***** Planning for the task MEAL-TASK775 .......
  TASK-TREE = (((<MEAL-TASK775>))
  The active goal chain is  ( M-MEAL )
  Reducing the task MEAL-TASK775 to subtasks (<MEAL-DESCRIPTOR-TASK>
     <MAIN-COURSE-TASK> <APPETIZER-TASK> <SALAD-TASK> <DESSERT-TASK>)
***** Planning for the task MEAL-DESCRIPTOR-TASK .......
```

---

* When JULIA is complete, all input will be in natural language. At the moment, JULIA's natural language component is not yet connected, so input to JULIA is a conceptual representation and output is canned phrases. We show the English equivalent to the input here.

```
TASK-TREE = ((<MEAL-DESCRIPTOR-TASK> <MAIN-COURSE-TASK> <APPETIZER-TASK>
      <SALAD-TASK> <DESSERT-TASK>) (<MEAL-TASK775>))
```
The active goal chain is   (MEAL-DESCRIPTOR <= M-MEAL)

JULIA works on some of the meal descriptors and gets to the point where it needs to formulate a cuisine, but it has no information to go on. So it asks.

Constraint Satisfaction ......
   Checking constraints for slot CUISINE of MEAL-DESCRIPTOR783 ...
   instantiating slot CUISINE of frame MEAL-DESCRIPTOR783 ...
<JULIA> What cuisine would you like?
USER => mexican
<JULIA>
Constraint Satisfaction ......
   Checking constraints for slot CUISINE of MEAL-DESCRIPTOR783 ...
   instantiating slot CUISINE of frame MEAL-DESCRIPTOR783 ...
   --> The value is MEXICAN-CUISINE
   ...
The meal descriptor is:
       The CUISINE is MEXICAN-CUISINE
       The EATING-CONFIG is STANDING
       The PRESENTATION is BUFFET
       The FORMALITY is INFORMAL

JULIA goes on to its next task, choosing a main course, and suggests chili for the main course (we leave out the way it did that). At that point, it is reminded of a meal in which chili was served. If this meal had been a successful one, the reminding would provide suggestions about other parts of the meal. In this case, however, some guests, who did not eat hot food, were left unsatisfied.

***** Planning for the task MAIN-COURSE-TASK ....
```
   TASK-TREE = ((<MAIN-COURSE-TASK> <APPETIZER-TASK> <SALAD-TASK>
         <DESSERT-TASK>) (<MEAL-TASK775>))
```
   The active goal chain is   (SC-MAIN-COURSE <= M-MEAL)
<JULIA> What about CHILI791 for the main course?
USER => ok
<JULIA>
***** Reminded of MEAL80, where chili was the main course
***** Case-based reasoning with the case MEAL80

***** Frame #<FRAME 27067331> *****
Name: MEAL80
   Isa: (<M-MEAL>)
   Category: INDIVIDUAL
   Slots:
       ACTUAL-RESULT: <ACTUAL-RESULT80>
       CHARACTERS: (?HOST ?GUESTS ?PARTICIPANTS)
       CONSTRAINTS: (<C-COST11>)
       DEFINED-SLOTS: NIL
       DESCRIPTOR: <MEAL-DESCRIPTOR80>
       EXPECTED-RESULT: <EXPECTED-RESULT80>
       FOLLOW-UP: NIL

```
             GOALS: (<S-HUNGER80> <E-EAT80>)
             GUESTS: (<*JLK*S-PARENTS>)
             HOST: <*JLK*>
             ORDER: ((<SC-SALAD80> <SC-MAIN-COURSE80>))
             PARTICIPANTS: (?HOST ?GUESTS)
             SETTING: <*JLK*S-HOUSE>
             STEPS: (<SC-SALAD80> <SC-MAIN-COURSE80>)
```

*** Trying to do analogy-mapping the case MEAL80 ...
Checking if the previous plan for goals S-HUNGER80 E-EAT80 was successful ......
Previous plan execution failure found
***** Frame #<FRAME 27070771> *****
Name: ACTUAL-RESULT80
  Isa: (<ACTUAL-RESULT>)
  Category: PROTOTYPE
  Slots:
    DEFINED-SLOTS: NIL
    GOALS-ACHIEVED: NIL
    GOALS-FAILED: (<S-HUNGER20> <E-EAT20>)
The set of goals failed was S-HUNGER80 E-EAT80
It was because ((NOT EVERY ONE ATE SPICY DISH))

JULIA will try to avoid making this mistake again. The previous failure was because of a missing constraint about spices, and JULIA seeks to find out if this constraint should be taken into account in the current case. JULIA therefore asks if any of the participants don't eat spicy food, finds out there are some, and creates a "non-spicy-food" constraint for the current case. It propagates that constraint and checks it against what it has already decided. It finds out that Mexican food is spicy. It therefore rules out Mexican as a cuisine, and because choosing a main course is dependent on having a value for cuisine, deletes the choose-a-main-course task from the task network, and reschedules the meal-descriptor task and the choose-a-main-course task. It then goes on from there.

*** Attempting to avoid the previous plan failure......
The assigned blame was that C-NON-SPICY-PREF80 had not been considered.
To avoid previous plan failure ...
Asking the user of a missing constraint C-NON-SPICY-PREF
<JULIA> Is there anyone who doesn't like spicy food? (How many?)
USER => 3
<JULIA>
Trying to propagate the constraint C-NON-SPICY-PREF793 ....
  --> Generating a new constraint C-NON-SPICY-CUISINE794
  --> Generating a new constraint C-NON-SPICY-DISH795
Trying to propagate the constraint C-NON-SPICY-CUISINE794 ....
  --> No constraint has been generated from C-NON-SPICY-CUISINE794
Trying to propagate the constraint C-NON-SPICY-DISH795 ....
  --> No constraint has been generated from C-NON-SPICY-DISH795
Applying constraint C-NON-SPICY-PREF793
  --> One of the characteristics of MEXICAN-CUISINE is spicy
    --> Aborting MEXICAN-CUISINE
  --> Killing the current task MAIN-COURSE-TASK ......
  --> Rescheduling MEAL-DESCRIPTOR-TASK MAIN-COURSE-TASK into the task network ..

Compare and Contrast, A Test of Expertise [1]

Kevin D. Ashley and Edwina L. Rissland[2]
Department of Computer and Information Science
University of Massachusetts
Amherst, MA 01003

Abstract

In this paper we present three key elements of case-based reasoning ("CBR") and describe how these are realized in our *HYPO* program which performs legal reasoning in the domain of trade secret law by comparing and contrasting cases. More specifically, the key elements involve how prior cases are used for: (1) Credit assignment of factual features; (2) Justification; and (3) Argument in domains that do not necessarily have strong causal theories or well-understood empirical regularities. We show how HYPO uses "dimensions", "case-analysis-record" and "claim lattice" mechanisms to perform indexing and relevancy assessment of past cases dynamically and how it compares and contrasts cases to come up with the best cases pro and con a decision.

I. Introduction

It is one thing for an expert to analyze a problem situation and another to compare it to similar situations and explain why they are the same or different. If a human expert could perform only the former task, we might well doubt his level of expertise. Critically comparing a situation to other cases – showing why they are the same or pointing out the crucial differences – is an important component of explaining, arguing and planning. One could not reason analogically without it. Only by focussing on important differences, as well as similarities, can one choose the best cases, avoid the worst cases or extrapolate from cases not so on point. Despite the importance of this crucial intellectual skill, most expert systems do not represent cases or have the control structure to facilitate comparing cases. Research in Case-Based Reasoning ("CBR") focusses on that deficit and how to correct it.

---

[1] This work was supported (in part) by: the Advanced Research Projects Agency of the Department of Defense, monitored by the Office of Naval Research under contract no. N00014-84-K-0017, and an IBM Graduate Student Fellowship.

[2] Copyright ©1986. Kevin D. Ashley & Edwina L. Rissland All rights reserved.

Kevin D. Ashley & Edwina L. Rissland, Compare and Contrast, A Test of Expertise, (American Association for Artificial Intelligence - 1986). Reprinted with Permission

II. CBR Involves Critically Comparing Cases

A case-based approach to reasoning has three basic elements:

1. Credit Assignment: A decision-maker decides a case because of some factual features and inspite of others. In other words, the decider assigns credit or blame to some of the case's factual features. In effect, the decision of a case: (a) *Selects* certain features that are important enough for purposes of credit assignment (Not all facts make a difference to the outcome.); (b) *Clusters* the selected features; and (c) "*Weights*" them. Features in the cluster that favor the decision are ranked higher than those against it. In this way a prior case represents "experience".

2. Precedential Justifications: That a prior case (i.e., a *precedent*) had a certain cluster of features, and that its decision was made because of some of those features and inspite of others, is treated as a basis for a *justification* for coming to the same conclusion in a future case with a similar combination of features. By assumption, a precedential justification is *a* reason for coming to a decision in a subsequent case (and in fact prior cases will be cited in support of an argument that the new case should be decided, or that conflicting vfeatures should be resolved, in the same way as in the prior case.) Since the experience represented by prior cases matters for future decision-making, those cases need to be accessible for analyzing future cases.

3. Arguments: CBR is inherently adversarial; there seldom is one right answer. Instead there are arguments based on prior cases. CBR generates arguments presenting the possibly inconsistent alternative justifications. Although there are criteria for preferring some justifications over others, for telling good arguments from bad, and for making decisions accordingly, CBR's recommendations always must be viewed as presenting alternatives.

Given its elements, it is essential that a CBR system facilitate comparing new cases against old. Searching for justifications for deciding a new case is like searching through a space of prior cases for relevant precedents where the criterion for assessing relevance must take into account how useful a prior case will be in an argument about the new case. To make the search feasible, a CBR system must represent and record cases and organize them for efficient selection and comparison. In a word, this means *indexing*. The cases in the CKB should be indexed by the same features that are involved in credit assignment.

With its emphasis on comparing a new situation to prior cases and comparing prior cases among themselves to find those that make the best justifications, CBR yields some important advantages: *First*, it is useful in domains that do not have a strong model. In domains like law, strategic planning, philosophical inquiry and historical political analysis, experts make reasoned decisions in spite of the facts that the rules are incomplete, use predicates whose meanings are not well defined (the *open textured* problem) or lead to inconsistent results. In these domains the expertise is simply organized differently along case-based lines. To the outsider, legal decision-making may seem arbitrary and chaotic, but, with its doctrine of case precedent, the law is an organized chaos. See [Levi, 1949]. *Second*, even in domains with strong models, case-based approaches are better-suited for a number of reasoning tasks involving explanation, persuasion and planning. We expect experts to be able to: 1. Explain their analysis of a situation by giving examples and posing hypotheticals to demonstrate the critical features, which if different, would have lead to a different conclusion; 2. Persuade us to believe the conclusion by: comparing the current situation approvingly to previous cases; extrapolating from less-similar cases (e.g., by pointing out differentiating features of the current situation that warrant the desired conclusion even more strongly); and posing hypotheticals to illustrate the dire consequences if the proposed conclusion is not adopted. 3. Plan for contingencies by posing hypothetical scenarios (worst, best, most recent, most likely cases, etc.) that illustrate the consequences of and alternatives to a given course of action.

Of course, a CBR approach has costs: 1. Constructing and maintaining the index; 2. dealing with the combinatorics of large numbers of cases and the depth of inferencing necessary to invoke the index; and 3. coming up with evaluation criteria for assessing justifications and arguments. For examples of recent research on these issues, see [Kolodner, 1983, Kolodner, Simpson and Sycara-Cyranski, 1985, Hammond, 1986a, Hammond, 1986b, Carbonell, 1983a, Carbonell, 1983b].

III. The HYPO Program and its Domain

HYPO is a case-based reasoning program which operates in the domain of trade secret law [Rissland, Valcarce and Ashley, 1984, Rissland and Ashley, 1986, Rissland and Ashley, 1987]. HYPO accepts a fact situation from its user, analyzes it, retrieves other relevant cases from its Case-Knowledge-Base ("CKB"), considers various assignments of importance to facts, "positions" the retrieved cases with respect to the curent case, selects important most-on-point and most-dangerous cases, suggests interesting or critical hypotheticals, proposes the skeleton of an argument, and justifies this argument with case citations in the form demanded in legal scholarship [Ashley, 1986, Ashley and Rissland, 1987].

In HYPO, the main sources of legal knowledge are contained in HYPO's CKB and its library of dimensions. Dimensions represent the legal relationship between various clusters of operative facts and the legal conclusion they support or undermine. Dimensions provide not only indices into lines of cases and their attendant analyses and arguments but also a mechanism by which to judge the strength, or weakness, of a fact situation with respect to that line of reasoning. For instance, one line of trade secret cases focusses on the degree to which the "cat (i.e., secret) has been let out of the bag", even by the complaining plaintiff, himself: that is, how many disclosures of the putative secret were there and of what kind? This way of looking at a trade secret case (captured by the *Disclose-Secret* dimension) provides one approach to resolving a misappropriation dispute and was used in the *Data General* and *Midland Ross* cases discussed below. Another approach might emphasize the competitive advantage gained by the defendant at the plaintiff's expense or the switching of key employee from the plaintiff to the defendant [Rissland and Ashley, 1986]. Each dimension has: *prerequisites*, expressed in terms of *factual predicates*, that tell whether dimension applies to a case or not; *focal slots* that single out the particular facts making a case stronger or weaker along the dimension and range information that tells how a change in the focal slot affects that strength (e.g., for *Disclose-Secrets*, the focal slot is the number of disclosees. Increasing that number weakens the plaintiff's position. See generally [Ashley, 1986].

IV. HYPO's Reasoning Process

Here is how HYPO reasons about a new fact situation (call it the **current fact situation** or **cfs**, for short). *First*, in analyzing a new cfs, HYPO runs through the library of dimensions and produces a **case-analysis-record** that contains: (1) applicable factual predicates; (2) applicable dimensions; (3) near-miss dimensions; (4) potential claims and (5) relevant cases from the CKB. Near-miss dimensions are those for which some, but not all, of the prerequisites are satisfied. The combined list of applicable and near-miss dimensions is called the **D-list**. Figure 1 describes a cfs based, for purposes of illustration, on *Crown Industries, Inc. v. Kawneer Co.*, 335 F.Supp. 7 (N.D.Ill., 1971). Figure 2 shows the case-analysis-record for the cfs.

Second, HYPO uses the case-analysis-record to construct the **claim lattice**, which is a lattice such that: the root is the cfs together with its D-list; and (2) successor nodes contain pointers to cases that share a subset, usually proper, of the dimensions in the cfs's D-list. Figure 3 shows the claim lattice actually generated by the HYPO program for analyzing the cfs of Figure 1 from the viewpoint of a trade secrets misappropriation claim. (There is a separate claim lattice for each possible claim.)

From 1962 to 1964, Crown Industries, Inc., the plaintiff (π), developed a hydraulic power pack, PX-121, for automatic door openers. Crown complained that defendant (δ) Kawneer Co. developed a competing product, PX-125, by misappropriating π's trade secrets. Crown's power packs had been sold to and installed in five public retail establishments. Crown made disclosures about the power pack to a third party, and in 1963 and 1965 a Crown employee made disclosures concerning the pack to Kawneer. PX-121 did not have any unique features not generally known to the prior art. It took Kawneer six years to develop PX-125, from 1962 to 1968.

Figure 1: Current Fact Situation (cfs) based on *Crown Industries, Inc. v. Kawneer Co.*

The ordering scheme enables claim lattices to capture a sense of closeness to the cfs of cases in the CKB. Those sharing more dimensions are nearer to the cfs. Those nodes closest to the root whose subsets of the cfs's D-list do not contain near-miss dimensions can be considered most-on-point-cases "mopc's" to the cfs; leaf nodes are the least-on-point. All of the cases displayed are relevant to the cfs because they all share some legally important strengths or weaknesses with the fact situation as represented by the dimensions shared with the cfs.

Third, HYPO uses the claim lattice to identify the competing parties' mopc's. There are two pro-defendant ("δ") mopc's in Figure 3 (a): *Midland-Ross* and *Yokana*. Since mopc's share the most legally important strengths and weaknesses with the cfs (i.e., mopc's are the closest analogies to the cfs), *Midland Ross* and *Yokana* are the most persuasive cases HYPO could cite for the defendant. (*Crown Industries* is also a mopc, but that is the very case on which the cfs is based. Eventhough it would be silly to cite a case in an argument about itself, it makes sense that HYPO regards a case as most on point to itself.)

<u>Applicable Factual Predicates</u>:
exists-corporate-claimant,
exists-confidential-info, exists-disclosures ...

<u>Applicable Dimensions</u>: *Disclose-Secrets*

<u>Near-Miss Dimensions</u>:
Restricted-Disclose,
Competitive-Advantage,
Vertical-Knowledge

<u>Potential Claims</u>: Trade Secrets Misappropriation

<u>Relevant CKB cites</u>: See claim lattice, Figure 3 (a)

Figure 2: Case-Analysis-Record for CFS

There are no pro-plaintiff ("π") mopc's in Figure 3 (a). *Data General*, for example, is not a mopc because, although it is very close to the root, the *Restricted-Disclose* dimension, which applies to *Data General*, and which would help π if it applied to the cfs, is only a near-miss for the cfs.(*Restricted-Disclose* is a near-miss because the cfs does not have the prerequisite factual predicate that some disclosees agreed to keep π's secrets confidential. Note that *Restricted-Disclose* is *'d in Figure 3 (a).) Although not a mopc, the *Data General* case is potentially a mopc for π. A **potential mopc** is very similar to the cfs, except that some dimensions that apply to it are near-misses with respect to the cfs; Potential mopc's reside in nodes closest to the root. As shown below, if it were true that the disclosees had agreed to keep π's confidential information secret, *Data General* would become a very important case to the plaintiff.

Fourth, HYPO uses the cases in the claim lattice to make and respond to precedent-citing arguments about the cfs. Different major branches of the lattice indicate different ways to argue the case, effectively one way for each group of mopc's. HYPO a three-ply argument starting with a **point** for *side 1*, a **response** for *side 2* and, possibly a **rebuttal** for *side 1* again.

HYPO, for instance, can argue the case for *side 1*, the defendant ("δ") in the cfs, by *citing* a pro-defendant mopc, as in Figure 4 [a]. Recall that in Figure 3 (a) there are two such mopc's, *Midland Ross* and *Yokana*. HYPO justifies the point expressly by drawing the analogy between the cfs and the cited cases by reciting the facts associated with dimension they have in common, *Disclose-Secrets*, namely that in both cases, plaintiff disclosed its secrets to some outsiders.

HYPO responds to points like that of Figure 4 [a] by *distinguishing* the cited case using three basic methods: (1) Comparing the strengths of cfs and cited case along the dimensions they share in common; (2) Finding strengths or weaknesses, represented by dimensions, that the cfs and cited case do *not* share. (3) Finding other cases that are more on point than the cited case. Figure 4 [b] is an example of the first method. HYPO distinguishes *Midland-Ross* on behalf of *side 2*, the plaintiff, by comparing values in the cfs and cited case of the focal slots of the shared dimension. HYPO knows from the claim lattice and the range information about the *Disclose-Secrets* dimension, that *Midland-Ross* presents a stronger case for δ because π disclosed the confidential information to 100 outsiders; in the cfs, Crown disclosed to only five. HYPO supports the response by citing the *Data General* case where the plaintiff won despite having made many more disclosures than in *Midland-Ross*.

For a rebuttal, HYPO distinguishes any case cited in the response, as in Figure 4 [c]. Using the second method of distinguishing HYPO points out the pro-π strength whose absence from the cfs makes *Data General* only a *potential* mopc, namely that the disclosures were subject to restrictions to maintain confidentiality (a feature captured by the *Restricted-Disclose* dimension that applies to *Data*

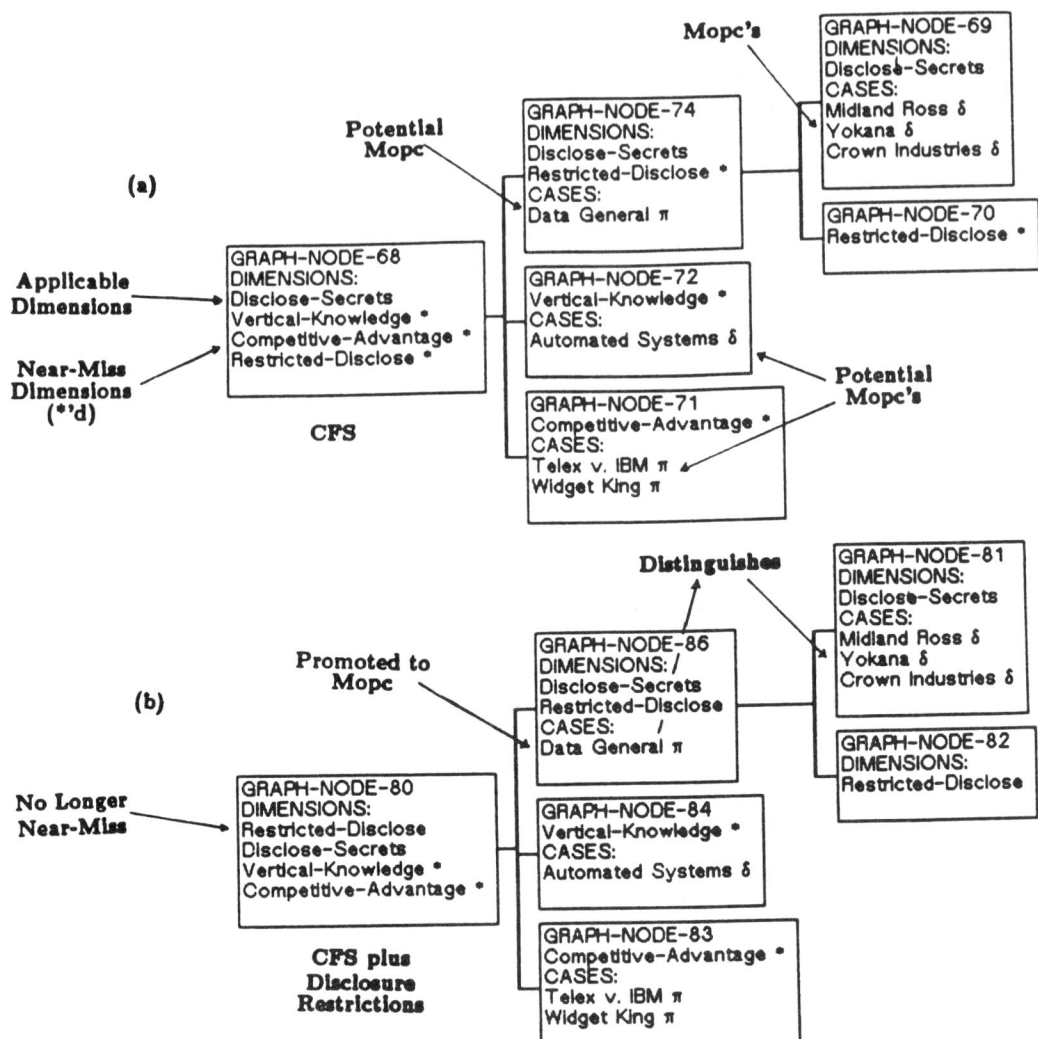

The root node of claim lattice (a) represents cfs in Figure 1 and its D-list. (Dimensions that are near-misses for *cfs* have *'s.) Successor nodes contain pro-plaintiff (π) or pro-defendant (δ) trade secrets cases that are on point to cfs. Nodes closest to root that do not have near-miss dimensions contain mopc's; otherwise they may contain potential mopc's. Leaf nodes are least-on-point. Each major branch of lattice that contains mopc's represents one way of arguing the cfs. Mopc's **distinguish** cases in successor nodes. Potential mopc's suggest fruitful hypothetical variants of cfs like that in (b). (b) is lattice for same cfs as (a) *plus* fact that disclosees agreed to treat π's secrets as confidential. Argument for π is stronger in (b) than (a) because *Data General*: (1) has been promoted to being pro-π mopc (*Restricted-Disclose* dimension is no longer near miss in (b)); (2) is more on point than δ's mopc's.

Figure 3: Two Claim Lattices.

General but is only a near-miss for the cfs.)

The *fifth* step in HYPO's reasoning process is to generate hypotheticals that are useful for testing the strengths and weaknesses of a party's position. HYPO uses its knowledge of how a case may be distinguished to suggest hypothetical modifications of the cfs that would strengthen or weaken the plaintiff's position [Rissland and Ashley, 1986]. For example, HYPO uses the relative positions of π's potential mopc *Data General* and δ's mopc *Midland-*

Ross in the claim lattice of Figure 3 (a) to suggest a hypothetical variant of the cfs in which π's disclosures we made on a restricted basis. Then *Data General* can used to distinguish *Midland-Ross* using the third method of distinguishing, significantly improving π's position. Figure 3 (b) shows the claim lattice that would result for the modified cfs. The basic differences between the two claim lattices are that the *Restricted-Disclose* dimension, a near miss in Figure 3 (a) is an applicable dimension in F

[a] ↪ For Side 1: (Δ's point)

Cite: *Midland-Ross, Yokana*
(Δ should win because Δs in cited cases won where Πs disclosed secrets to outsiders.)

[b] ↪ For Side 2: (Π's response to [a])

Distinguish: *Midland-Ross*
(In *Midland-Ross*, Π disclosed to 100 outsiders. Π in cfs disclosed to only 7 outsiders.)

Cite: *Data General*
(Π in *Data General* won eventhough Π disclosed to 6000 outsiders, more than in *Midland-Ross*.)

[c] ↪ For Side 1: (Δ's rebuttal to [b])

Distinguish: *Data General*
(In *Data General* disclosees agreed to keep secrets but not so in cfs.)

Figure 4: Citing & Distinguishing Precedents: 3-Ply Arguments

ure 3 (b) and that *Data General* has become π's real mopc and one that is more on point (i.e., closer to the root) than δ's mopc's.

HYPO illustrates the new strength in the plaintiff's position by replaying the three-ply argument. Given the facts of the modified hypothetical in Figure 3 (b), HYPO can now generate a stronger response to the point in Figure 4 [a]:

[d] ↪ For Side 2: (Π's response to [a])

Cite: *Data General*
(Π should win because in *Data General*, Π won where Π disclosed secrets and disclosees agreed to keep disclosures secret.)

Distinguish: *Midland-Ross, Yokana*
(*Data General* is *more on point* than these cases where disclosees did not agree to keep disclosures secret.)

V. Comparing and Contrasting Cases in HYPO

Using information contained in the case-analysis-records and claim lattice, HYPO expressly compares and contrasts cases at three levels: (1) Facts; (2) Justifications; and (3) Arguments.

At the level of facts, HYPO compares the cfs to relevant cases from the claim lattice by focussing on the important facts they share as indicated by the dimensions they have in common. As we have seen, in making points, HYPO draws the analogy between the cfs and various cases by reciting these facts. HYPO contrasts cases when it responds to points by distinguishing the cited cases. Using the first two methods of distinguishing (i.e., focussing on differing strengths along shared and unshared dimensions), HYPO is able to point out factual differences that justify *not* treating the cfs like a cited case.

At the level of justifications, HYPO compares relevant cases *to each other* using the claim lattice to see which make better precedents for deciding the cfs. Cases are compared in terms of: how on point they are relative to the cfs (mopc's vs. less on point cases); how useful they are in a legal argument about the cfs (e.g., using the third method of distinguishing to contrast a cited case with a more on point opposing case.); and how *potentially* useful they would be in a legal argument about the cfs (e.g., finding pro-opponent cases that can be used to distinguish mopc's).

HYPO makes comparisons at the arguments level by comparing the claim lattices. In moving from the cfs, Figure 3 (a) to the variant in (b), there has been a big shift in the balance of the argument in favor of the plaintiff, a comparative legal conclusion that HYPO can infer from a simple comparison of the claim lattices. One of HYPO's evaluation functions for comparing claim lattices involves simply comparing mopc's. In Figure 3 (a) there are pro-δ mopc's but no pro-π mopc, indicating a strong argument for the defendant. In Figure 3 (b), beside the same pro-δ mopc's, there is a new pro-π mopc, *Data General*, which is more on point (i.e., closer to the root) than *Midland-Ross* or *Yokana*, indicating a strong argument for plaintiff. In other words, claim lattices can be used to evaluate the arguments in favor of a proposition, essentially by comparing the relationships of the pro and con mopc's.

VI. Assessing HYPO's Performance

In its selection of *Midland-Ross* as defendant's best case, HYPO agreed with what the court actually did in its opinion in the case on which the cfs is based, *Crown Industries, Inc. v. Kawneer Co.* The court said,

> Even though the Plaintiff's power packs, exemplified by PX-121, might have had to be rendered inoperative and examined by an engineer in order to discover the alleged trade secrets contained therein, the sale of the power packs nevertheless constituted a public disclosure which defeats a claim founded upon alleged misappropriation of the trade secrets allegedly contained in the power packs. *Midland-Ross Corp. v. Sunbeam Equipment Co.*, 316 F. Supp. 171, 177 (W.D.Pa. 1970), affirmed, 435 F.2d 159 (3d Cir. 1970).

HYPO's analysis of a cfs by comparing and contrasting it with mopc's is similar to that actually performed by courts. Consider the opinion of the court in another case with similar issues to our cfs, *National Rejectors, Inc. v. Trieman* 409 S.W.2d 1, 40–42 (Sup. Ct. Mo., 1966):

[W]e do find some significant parallels between the facts of this case and those of *Midland-Ross Corporation v. Yokana* (D.C. N.J.), 185 F.Supp. 594 [The *Yokana* case involved the same plaintiff as *Midland-Ross Corp. v. Sunbeam Equipment Co.* and the same defense that plaintiff had disclosed its secrets to outsiders].... Thus the claim of trade secrets by National and by plaintiff in Midland-Ross have essentially the same basis. ... What was lacking in *Yokana* as in this case, was any evidence that, prior to defendant's competition, plaintiff considered the information which Yokana sought to use trade secrets. The court pointed out that plaintiff's blueprints in *Midland-Ross* were furnished plaintiff's suppliers and customers and potential customers. The court found an absence of precautions on the part of plaintiff to keep secret information regarding its machines.

Although the following cases do not parallel the present case as closely as *Yokana* our conclusion here is consistent with that reached in: [citing and describing other cases.]

Not only are the facts of *Midland-Ross Corporation v. Yokana* comparable to those in this situation, but we find the relief afforded in that case also appropriate in this....

VII. Conclusion

In this paper, we have presented three key elements of case-based reasoning (CBR): 1. That prior cases select and *assign credit* to factual features and weight conflicting features; 2. That prior cases are *justifications* for deciding a new fact situation (cfs) with similar combinations of features; and 3. That CBR yields *arguments* how to decide the cfs based on these potentially conflicting justifications. We have reviewed our indexing scheme based on "dimensions" that organizes cases in the Case-Knowledge-Base (CKB). HYPO performs indexing and relevancy assessment of past cases dynamically by (1) analyzing how prior cases can be viewed from the point of view of the cfs and (2) determining what aspects of these prior cases apply, and how strongly, to the cfs. This sort of analysis – accomplished through HYPO's dimensions, "case-analysis-record" and "claim lattice" mechanisms – allows HYPO to promote some prior cases over others as precedents for interpreting and arguing the cfs. HYPO compares and contrasts the cfs and prior cases at the levels of facts, justifications and arguments to come up with the best cases pro and con a decision and to pose instructive hypothetical variants of the cfs.

References

[Ashley, 1986] Kevin D. Ashley. *Modelling Legal Argument: Reasoning with Cases and Hypotheticals - A Thesis Proposal*. Project Memo 10, The COUNSELOR Project, Department of Computer and Information Science, University of Massachusetts, 1986.

[Ashley and Rissland, 1987] Kevin D. Ashley and Edwina L. Rissland. But, See, Accord: Generating "Blue Book" Citations in HYPO. In *Proceedings: First International Conference on Artificial Intelligence and Law*, Northeastern University, 1987.

[Carbonell, 1983a] J. G. Carbonell. Derivational Analogy and its Role in Problem Solving. In *Proceedings of the Third National Conference on Artificial Intelligence*, American Association for Artificial Intelligence, Washington, D.C., 1983a.

[Carbonell, 1983b] J. G. Carbonell. Learning by Analogy: Formulating and Generalizing Plans from Past Experience. In Michalski, J.G. Carbonell, and T. Mitchell, editors, *Machine Learning: An Artificial Intelligence Approach*, Tioga Publishing, CA, 1983b.

[Hammond, 1986a] Kristian J. Hammond. CHEF: Model of Case-based Planning. In *Proceedings of the Fifth National Conference on Artificial Intelligence*, American Association for Artificial Intelligence, Philadelphia, PA, 1986a.

[Hammond, 1986b] Kristian J. Hammond. Learning to Anticipate and Avoid Planning Problems through the Explanation of Failures. In *Proceedings of the Fifth National Conference on Artificial Intelligence*, American Association for Artificial Intelligence. Philadelphia, PA, 1986b.

[Kolodner, 1983] Janet L. Kolodner. Maintaining Organization in a Dynamic Long-Term Memory. *Cognitive Science*, 7(4):243-280, 1983.

[Kolodner, Simpson and Sycara-Cyranski, 1985] Janet Kolodner, Robert L. Simpson, and Katia Sycara-Cyranski. A Process Model of Case-Based Reasoning in Problem Solving. In *Proceedings of the Ninth International Joint Conference on Artificial Intelligence*, International Joint Conferences on Artificial Intelligence, Inc., Los Angeles, CA, 1985.

[Levi, 1949] Edward H. Levi. *An Introduction to Legal Reasoning*. University of Chicago Press, 1949.

[Rissland and Ashley, 1987] Edwina L. Rissland and Kevin D. Ashley. A Case-Based System for Trade Secrets Law. In *Proceedings: First International Conference on Artificial Intelligence and Law*, Northeastern University, 1987.

[Rissland and Ashley, 1986] Edwina L. Rissland and Kevin D. Ashley. Hypotheticals as Heuristic Device. *Proceedings of the Fifth National Conference on Artificial Intelligence*, American Association for Artificial Intelligence. Philadelphia, PA, 1986.

[Rissland, Valcarce and Ashley, 1984] Edwina L. Rissland, E.M. Valcarce, and Kevin D. Ashley. Explaining and Arguing with Examples. In *Proceedings of the Fourth National Conference on Artificial Intelligence*, American Association for Artificial Intelligence, 1984.

CONTRIBUTED PAPERS

An Adaptive Planner

Richard Alterman

Computer Science Division
University of California, Berkeley
Berkeley, California 94720

ABSTRACT

This paper is about an approach to the flexible utilization of pre-stored plans called **adaptive planning.** An adaptive planner can take advantage of the details associated with specific plans, while still maintaining the flexibility of a planner that works from general plans. Key elements in the theory of adaptive planning are its treatment of background knowledge and the introduction of a notion of planning by situation matching.

1. Introduction

A planner that has access to general plans (alternately abstract or high-level plans) is flexible because such plans will apply to a large number of situations. A problem for a planner working exclusively with general plans is that many of the details associated with more specific plans (e.g. sequencing information and causal relationships) must be recomputed. For a planner that works from more specific plans the situation is reversed: There is a wealth of detail, but there are problems with flexibility. I will refer to planners with the capacity to use a mix of pre-stored specific plans and general plans as **adaptive planners.** Adaptive planners foreground specific plans, but gain flexibility, in situations where the pre-stored plan and the planner's current circumstances diverge, by having access to more general plans.

The adaptive planning techniques that will be described in this paper are sufficiently robust to handle a wide range of relationships between a pre-stored specific plan and the planner's current circumstances. For example, suppose a planner is about to ride the NYC subway for the first time, and attempts to treat a pre-stored plan for riding BART (Bay Area Rapid Transit) as an example to guide the current planning activity. Consider the steps involved in riding BART. At the BART station the planner buys a ticket from a machine. Next, the ticket

---

This paper was originally published in AAAI-86. A few minor modifications have been made to this paper.

This research was sponsored in part by the Defense Advance Research Projects Agency (DOD), Arpa order No. 4031, Monitored by Naval Electronic System Command under Contract No. N00039-C-0235. This research was also supported by the National Science Foundation (ISI-8514890).

Author's current address: Computer Science Department, Brandeis University, Waltham, MA 02254
Richard Alterman, An Adaptive Planner, (America Association for Artificial Intelligence - 1986). Reprinted with Permission.

is fed into a second machine which returns the ticket and then opens a gate to let the planner into the terminal. Next the planner rides the train. At the exit station the planner feeds the ticket to another machine that keeps the ticket and then opens a gate to allow the planner to leave the station. Compare that to the steps involved in riding the NYC subway: buy a token from a teller, put the token into a turnstile and then enter, ride the train, and exit by pushing thru the exit turnstile. There are a great number of differences between the BART Plan and the plan that the planner must eventually devise for riding the NYC Subway.

- In the BART case a ticket is bought from a machine, in the NYC subway case there is no ticket machine and instead a token is bought from a teller.
- In the BART case the ticket is returned after entering the station, in the NYC subway case the token is not returned after entry.
- In the BART case the ticket is needed to exit, in the NYC subway case the token is not needed to exit.

This paper will describe an adaptive planner called **PLEXUS** that can overcome these differences and in an effective manner use the BART Plan as a basis for constructing a plan for the NYC subway situation. Two versions of PLEXUS have already been constructed. This paper gives an overview of adaptive planning and PLEXUS. It includes a discussion of adaptive planning in relation to the literature, descriptions of four key elements of adaptive planning, and some details of PLEXUS' adaptation mechanism.

2. Adaptive Planning

There are four keystones to the adaptive planning position on the flexible utilization of pre-stored, situated, specific plans.

- An adaptive planner has access to the **background knowledge** associated with a pre-stored plan.
- In adaptive planning the exploitation of the background knowledge is accomplished by a process of **situation matching.**
- An adaptive planner foregrounds **specific plans.**
- Adaptive planners treat the failing steps of a plan as **representative of the category of action** which is to be accomplished.

Adaptive planning makes the **background knowledge** associated with a prestored specific plan explicit. Previous approaches to re-using pre-stored plans have dealt with a pre-stored plan in relative isolation and therefore the task of re-using a pre-stored plan has been considerably more complicated. By making the content and organization of the background knowledge explicit, it becomes possible to re-use a pre-stored plan in a wider variety of situations. Background knowledge includes general plans, categorization knowledge, and causal knowledge.

Exploitation of the background knowledge is accomplished by a process of **situation matching.** Adaptive planning uses the position of the pre-stored plan in a planning network as a starting point for finding a match to the planner's current circumstances. The **interaction** of planning knowledge and the current situation determine a plan which fits the current context and realizes the goal. The interaction works in both directions. In the direction of planning knowledge to situation, the pre-stored plan serves as a basis for interpreting the actions of other agents and the various objects in the new situation. Moreover, it provides the planner with a course of action. In the direction of situation to planning knowledge, it is the situation which provides selection cues that aid the planner in determining an alternate course of action when complications arise.

Adaptive planning foregrounds **specific plans**. It has been previously argued by Carbonell (1981) that the importance of being able to plan from more specific plans is that many times a more general plan is not available. But there are other reasons why the capacity to work from more specific examples is important. Many times a more specific plan is tailor-made for the current planning situation. Furthermore, the more specific plans make available to the planner previously computed causal and ordering relationships between steps. For a more general plan these can not be determined until that steps are instantiated. Consequently, even in the cases where the more specific plan must be re-fit, many times the cost of such changes are much less than the cost of dealing with the subgoal and subplan interactions inherent in a process that works by instantiating more general plans.

Adaptive planning treats the failing steps of the pre-stored plan as **representative of the category of action** which is to be accomplished. In the case of the BART-NYC planning problem, each of the failing steps is representative of the category of action the planner eventually wants to take. An adaptive planner uses the category knowledge, as represented by the failing step, to access more general versions of that step and also to determine its eventual course of action. For example, the first step of the BART Plan, 'buying a BART ticket', is representative of the planner's eventually course of action - adapting a plan to 'buy a theatre ticket'.

3. PLEXUS - An adaptive planner

For PLEXUS the background knowledge associated with a pre-stored plan is determined by the pre-stored plan's position in a knowledge network. The network includes **taxonomic, partonomic, causal,** and **role** knowledge; the network acts as a structural backbone for its contents. PLEXUS uses the taxonomic structure not only for the purposes of property inheritance, but also as a basis for reasoning about categories. The partonomic structure (i.e. step-substep hierarchy) is used to aid in determining the pieces of network which need to be refitted in a given situation. The causal knowledge serves several functions: The **purpose** relation identifies the abstraction which maintains the purpose of a step in a plan. The **precondition, outcome, and goal** relations act as appropriateness conditions. The **reason** relation provides dependency links between a step and its justification (c.f. Stallman & Sussman, 1977). Roughly, in PLEXUS, **purpose** is synonymous with 'intent', **goal** with 'aim', and **reason** with 'justification'. The purpose of 'buying a BART ticket' is to 'gain access', the goal associated with it is to 'have a ticket', and the reason for doing it is that it makes it possible to 'enter the BART station' (see figure 1). Associated with roles are type constraints on the types of objects which can fill them. The **role** relations are used by PLEXUS for both cross indexing purposes and to control inferencing. For further arguments on the importance of background knowledge and more details on the representation of the background knowledge see Alterman (1988).

PLEXUS is modelled to act on the retrieved plan and delay refitting until actual circumstances deem it necessary. It uses the pre-stored plan to interpret its course of action in its current circumstances. It considers the steps, one step at a time, in order. If a step is not an action it adapts substeps in a depth-first fashion before moving onto the next step in the plan. When a given step of the pre-stored plan has been adapted to the current circumstances, PLEXUS is modelled to take action on that step before moving onto the next step in the plan - thus, as did NASL (McDermott, 1978), PLEXUS **interleaves planning and acting.**

Associated with each step (substep) in a plan are **appropriatness conditions.** The appropriatness conditions are intended to be suggestive that a particular course of action is reasonable to pursue. Before a step is applied, PLEXUS treats the preconditions and goals of the pre-stored plan as appropriateness conditions. After a step has been applied, PLEXUS treats the expected outcomes as appropriateness conditions. Appropriateness conditions are checked by testing the type constraints associated with each of the roles attached to the appropriateness condition. The type constraints are interpreted in terms of the network.

A rough outline of the top-level decision procedure is shown below:
1) Are any of the before conditions associated with the pre-stored plan failing?
    a) Is this a case of step-out-of-order?
    b) Is this a case of failing precondition?
2) Has the current circumstances aroused a goal not accounted for by the current step?
    a) This is a case of differing goals.
3) Is the current step an action?
    a) If yes, perform the action.
    b) If no, proceed to adapt substeps.
4) Are any of the outcomes associated with the current step failing?
    a) This is a case of failing outcome?
5) Adapt next step.

If one of the before appropriatness conditions fails, or the current circumstances indicate a goal not accounted for by the pre-stored plan, one of three different types of **situation difference** is occurring: failing precondition, step-out-of-order, or differing goals. There is a fourth kind of situation difference, failing outcome, that occurs when one of the expected outcomes of a given step fails to occur. Associated with each of the types of situation difference are varying strategies that will be briefly described in the fifth section of this paper. PLEXUS does not always consider the steps in order, under certain circumstances it looks ahead to the latter steps of the plan and adjusts them in anticipation of certain changes - thus PLEXUS has an element of **opportunism** (Hayes-Roth & Hayes-Roth,

1979).

The core of PLEXUS are the matching techniques it uses for finding an alternate version of a step once it determines that the step needs to be refit. To find an alternate matching action for a given situation, PLEXUS treats the failing step as **representative of the category** of action it needs to perform, and then it proceeds to exploit the background knowledge in two ways.

- By a process of **abstraction** PLEXUS uses the background knowledge to determine a category of plans in common between the two situations.

- By a process of **specialization** PLEXUS uses the background knowledge to determine an alternate course of action which is appropriate to the current circumstances.

PLEXUS accomplishes abstraction by moving up the categorization hierarchy until it finds a plan where all the before appropriatness conditions are met. PLEXUS accomplishes specialization by moving down the categorization hierarchy until it finds a plan that is sufficiently detailed to be actionable.

4. Core of the Matcher (Managing the Knowledge)

There are at least two important considerations concerning the control of access to knowledge. One consideration is that there is a danger of the planner becoming overwhelmed by the wealth of knowledge (c.f. **saturation,** Davis 1980) that is available. The problem is that there are potentially too many plans that the planner might have to consider, and consequently, the planner could get bogged down in evaluating each candidate plan. Somehow the planner needs to be able to selectively consider the various alternatives available to it.

Another consideration in the control of access to knowledge comes form the cognitive science literature and is referred to as the problem of **enumeration** (e.g. Kolodner, 1983). The problem of enumeration is that humans do not appear to be capable of listing all the instances of a category without some other kind of prompting. When asked to list the states of the union, human subjects do not accomplish this by simply listing all the members of the category of states. For the concerns of adaptive planning the problem of enumeration comes in a slightly different guise. Given an abstract plan it is not reasonable to assume that a human p<lanner could enumerate all of the specializations of that abstract plan.

The first of these considerations dictates that PLEXUS be **selective** in its choice of planning knowledge to use. The second of these considerations acts as a sort of **termination condition:** sometimes the planner knows the right plan but circumstances are such that it cannot find it. As a result of these considerations, PLEXUS' abstraction and specialization processes must be constrained. While moving up the abstraction hierarchy PLEXUS maintains the function of the step in the overall plan. Movement down the abstraction hierarchy, towards more detailed plans, is controlled by the interaction between the planner's knowledge and the current circumstances.

4.1. Abstraction

The way to think about abstraction of a plan is that it removes details from that plan: if a particular plan fails to match the current situation, some of the details of that particular plan must be removed. Moving up the abstraction hierarchy removes the details that do not work in the current situation while maintaining much of what is in common to the two situations. Effectively, the movement of abstraction is discovering the generalization which holds between the pre-stored and new situations given that a difference has occurred.

A given plan step can have any number of abstractions associated with it. Choosing the wrong abstraction can lead to the wrong action. The planner can avoid this problem by applying the following general rule:

- Ascend the abstraction hierarchy that maintains the **purpose** of the step in the plan that is being refitted.

By moving up the abstraction hierarchy that maintains the purpose of the step, PLEXUS attempts to maintain the function of the step in the overall plan and thereby mitigate the propagated effects of changes.

In general PLEXUS uses two techniques for moving up the abstraction hierarchy.

- If a plan is failing due to the existence of a particular feature of a plan, move to the point in the abstraction hierarchy from which that feature was inherited.
- Incrementally perform abstraction on a failing plan.

The first technique applies in situations where there is a specific feature in the pre-stored plan that does not exist in the current situation. The second technique of abstraction applies in situations where there is no identifiable feature which has to be removed. In such cases, PLEXUS incrementally moves up the abstraction hierarchy. In either case, for each abstraction it tries to find a specialization that will work in the current context. If it fails to find a specialization for a given abstraction, it moves to the next abstraction in the abstraction hierarchy.

4.2. Specialization

Via the process of specialization PLEXUS moves from a more abstract plan towards more specific examples. PLEXUS navigation thru the network is dependent on the planner's current circumstances. PLEXUS descends down the classification hierarchy one step at a time. PLEXUS tests the applicability of a specialization by checking the before appropriateness conditions; if one of these conditions fails the movement is rejected. At each point in the hierarchy PLEXUS is faced with one of five options:

1) Is the plan sufficiently detailed to act on?
2) Is there a feature suggested by the type of situation difference which cross indexes some subcategory of the current category of plan?
3) Is there an observable feature which cross indexes some subcategory of the current category of plan?
4) Is there an observable feature with an abstraction that cross indexes a

subcategory of the current category?
5) Is there a salient subcategory?

PLEXUS stops descending the categorization hierarchy when it gets to a leaf node (option 1). If the node is not a leaf it continues to descend (options 2-5). Sometimes the type of situation difference suggests cues for subcategory selections (option 2). Sometimes 'observable features' act as cues for subcategory selection (options 3-4). These 'observable features' can either directly cross index some subcategory of plan (option 3), or have an abstraction which cross indexes a subcategory of plan (option 4). Certain subcategories are salient regardless of context and can always be selected (option 5).

Many of these techniques are employed in the following example: Suppose a planner wants to transfer between planes at the Kennedy Airport in NYC. The planner's normal plan for transferring between planes is to walk from the arrival to the departure gate. But when the planner arrives at Kennedy Airport the arrival and departure gates turn out to be in different terminals. Suppose the planner decides that the walk between terminals is too strenuous, and thus a new goal is aroused: preserve energy. The detection of this goal has no correspondent in the pre-stored plan and it is determined that the plan must be adjusted to account for this goal; this is a case of the **differing goals** type of situation difference. By a process of abstraction, PLEXUS moves up the categorization hierarchy from the plan to 'walk' to the more general plan of 'travelling'. Next PLEXUS must determine an alternate plan, within the category of 'travelling', from which to act. The newly aroused goal acts as a cue for selecting 'vehicular travel' as a potential subcategory of plan from which to act (option 2). Suppose the planner has never used a shuttle before at an airport, but it sees (observable feature) a sign concerning 'airport shuttles'. An abstraction of 'shuttle' acts as a cue for selecting 'mass transit travel' as a subcategory of 'vehicular travel' (option 4). Moreover, 'shuttle' is a cue for selecting 'shuttle travel' as a subcategory of 'mass transit travel' (option 3). 'Shuttle travel' is sufficiently detailed for PLEXUS to attempt to adapt (option 1). See Alterman (1988) for further details and a trace of PLEXUS handling this planning problem.

5. Four Types of Situation Difference

PLEXUS currently recognizes four kinds of situation difference: failing precondition, failing outcome, different goals, step-out-of-order.

A **failing precondition** situation difference occurs when one of the preconditions of a step (plan) fails. For failing preconditions PLEXUS moves up the abstraction hierarchy, according to the **purpose** of the step, to a point at which the failing condition has been abstracted out. In the event that PLEXUS cannot find a specialization of that category of plans, it continues to incrementally move up the abstraction hierarchy indicated by the **purpose** relation. For failing preconditions either of PLEXUS specialization techniques are appropriate.

A **failing outcome** situation difference occurs, if after applying a plan (step) PLEXUS discovers that one of the expected outcomes of that plan was not achieved. There are three courses of action available. The obvious course of action is to try the plan again. A second course of action, is to use the **reason** relation to determine the other steps of the plan which are effected by the failed outcome, and determine, via abstraction and specialization, if the planner can continue on its course action because there is an alternate interpretation of the latter step which does not require the failed outcome. If all else fails, the third option available to the planner is to find and perform an alternate version of the failing step. For failing outcomes, if the current plan step is being re-interpreted, abstraction occurs incrementally. If PLEXUS is trying to re-interpreted a step related to the current step by a **reason** relation, abstraction occurs using the failing outcome as a feature to abstract out of the plan. For the second and third cases PLEXUS uses both of the specialization techniques available to it.

A **differing goal** situation difference occurs if the planner's current circumstances arouse a new **goal** not accounted for by the pre-stored plan. For this kind of situation difference, abstraction occurs incrementally, and specialization requires that the new plan be indexed under both old and new goals.

A **step-out-of-order** situation difference occurs, when PLEXUS encounters a situation where it needs to apply a step out of order. There are two adjustments that are possible when a step-out-of-order situation difference occurs, PLEXUS can either delete the intermediate step(s), or re-order the steps of the pre-stored plan. If a step can be applied out of order, PLEXUS uses abstraction and specialization in an attempt to find an alternate version of the plan with the correct ordering of steps. Under such a situation, PLEXUS can use the new ordering constraint as an index for specialization purposes. In the event an alternate plan with a different ordering of steps can not be found, PLEXUS performs the step-out-of-order, removes it from the sequence of steps, and proceeds with attempting to apply the failing step.

6. An example

The BART-NYC subway planning problem provides examples of three of the types of situation difference (see figure 1).

Adapting buy a BART ticket.
The first step of the BART plan fails in the NYC subway situation because there is no ticket machine. This is a case of **failing precondition,** and therefore PLEXUS abstracts out the failing condition, 'exist ticket machine', and specializes, using the salient subcategory, to 'buy theatre ticket', which it proceeds to adapt to the NYC subway situation. During the process of adapting this step 'ticket' gets bound to 'token'.

Adapting enter BART station.
The second step of the BART plan involves entering the station. The first substep of this step is to insert the token into the entrance machine, which the planner successfully accomplishes. The next step of 'BART enter' is that the ticket is returned by the machine. But in the NYC subway situation the ticket is not accessible, but it is possible to push thru the turnstile (the third step of 'BART enter'). Hence this is a case of **step out of order.** Having accomplished the last step of 'BART enter', PLEXUS must determine whether it should act on

the intermediate step or instead delete it.

Re-interpreting BART exit.
In order to delete intermediate steps PLEXUS must treat the outcomes of each intermediate step as a case of a **failing outcome** and test to see if the latter steps in the plan effected by the failing outcome can be adapted. In this case there is only one intermediate step, 'ticket returned'. The *outcome* associated with this intermediate step is that the planner 'has the ticket' (or in this case 'token'). PLEXUS applies the second strategy associated with the situation difference type **failed outcome:** Find an alternate interpretation of the situation where that outcome is no longer necessary. PLEXUS uses the *reason* relation associated with 'ticket return' to determine which of the latter steps are effected by the failing outcome. In this case, the reason that the ticket is returned is so it can be used when exiting the station. PLEXUS must try to re-interpret 'BART-EXIT' in such a manner that it can exit without a ticket. This leads to a situation of **failed precondition** for the step 'BART-EXIT'. Via abstraction PLEXUS extracts that 'exiting an institution' is what is in common between the pre-stored plan and the new situation. PLEXUS 'observes' the exit turnstile and uses it as a cue for determining 'exit_building' as an alternate plan for 'exiting the station', where 'exit turnstile' plays the role of 'locking door'. Since it can find an alternate interpretation to 'exiting the station' that does not involve using a ticket, PLEXUS treats the **step-out-of-order situation** that occurs during execution of the plan 'BART enter' as a case of deletion. For a more detailed discussion of this problem and a trace see Alterman (1988).

7. Discussion

Like the early general problem solving planners (Ernst & Newell 1969, Fikes & Nilsson 1971) adaptive planning is concerned with the problems of **generality** and **flexibility.** Unlike them it explores these issues in the context of increased amounts, and larger chunks of, knowledge. Where the early general problem solvers accomplished generality and flexibility by working with a small number of atomic operators, adaptive planning works with increased amounts of knowledge and achieves these twin goals by exploiting the **structure** of that knowledge. Like the work on MACROPS (Fikes et. al. 1972), adaptive planning is concerned with larger chunks of actions, but adaptive planning extends their utilization to planning problems like the BART-NYC subway problem. Adaptive planning is concerned with **tasks** (McDermott 1978) and **commonsense planning** (Wilensky 1983) problems. It is **knowledge-based** in that its approach to refitting pre-stored plans is based on the accessibility of the structure and content of the **background knowledge** associated with a pre-stored plan. As in the case of other knowledge-based planning approaches (e.g. Davis 1980, Wilensky 1981, Stefik 1981), adaptive planning is concerned with **control of access to knowledge:** its approach is dependent on the interaction of the planner's knowledge with the planner's current circumstances. Like the work on analogical planning (Carbonell 1981, Carbonell 1983), adaptive planning attempts to re-use pre-stored specific plans, but its strategies take greater advantage of the available knowledge, exploit categorization knowledge, and its processing is novel in that it takes the form of **situation matching.** As opposed to other efforts in case-based reasoning (Kolodner 1984, Kolodner 1985, Hammond 1985) and various related issues concerning meta-planning (Wilensky, 1981) and plan simulation (Hendler 1985), the emphasis of this work is on the problem of adaptation. Although knowledge acquisition is not the focus of the current research, adaptive planning does provide a framework for dealing with these issues. It promises to promote **additivity** because its procedures are largely based on the structure of the knowledge and not its content. Moreover, as a by-product of abstraction and specialization, PLEXUS discovers the generalizations over the steps of the pre-stored plan and the steps of the new plan, and consequently it provides a framework for the planner to do automatic re-organization and generalization (DeJong 1983, Schank 1982, Kolodner 1983a, Lebowitz 1983).

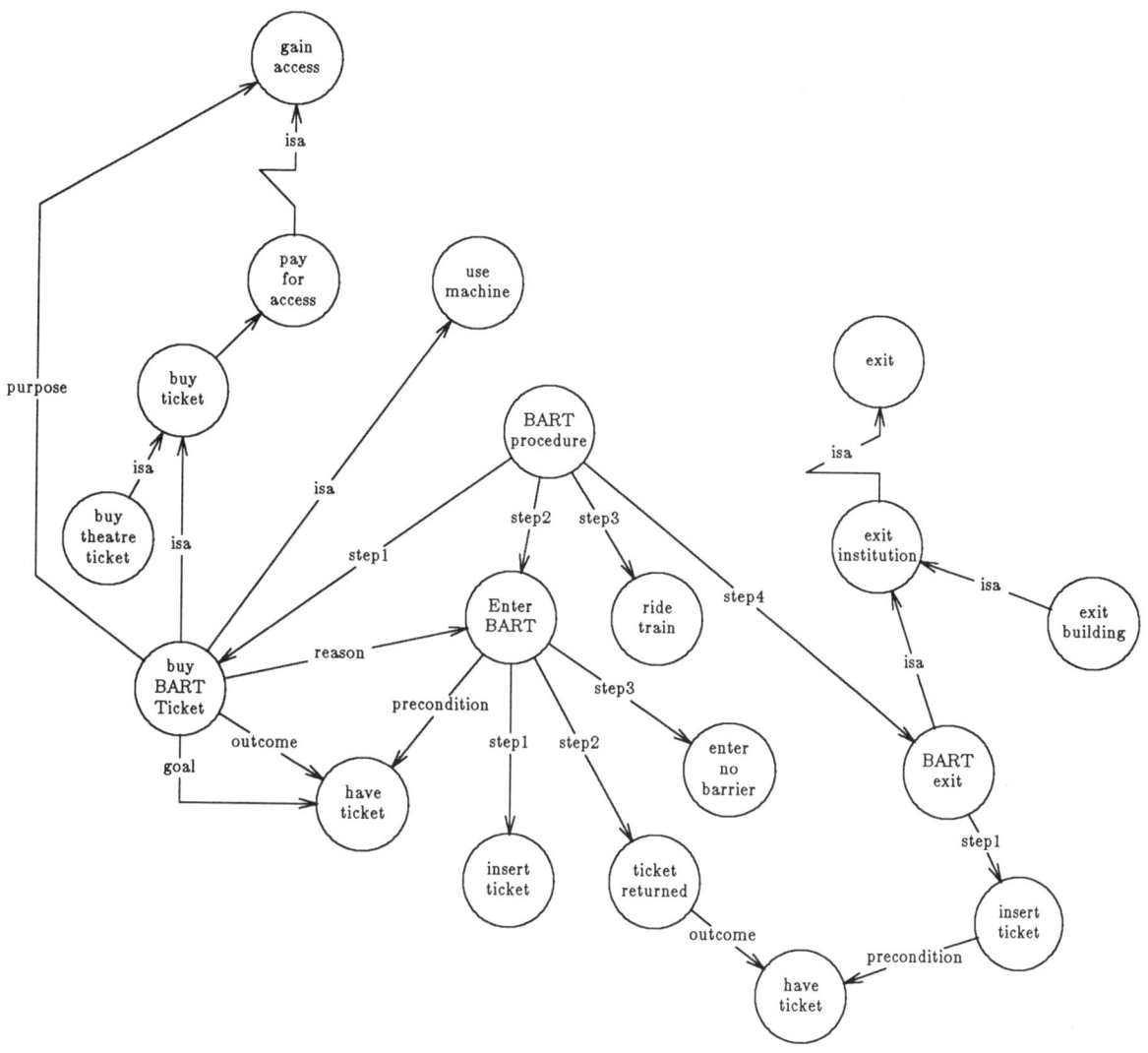

Figure 1a: BART Plan with some background knowledge.

REFERENCES

Alterman, R. (1988) "Adaptive Planning" *Cognitive Science* 12, 3.

Carbonell, J. (1981). "A computational model of analogical problem solving," in IJCAI 7.

Carbonell, J. (1983). "Derivational analogy and its role in problem solving," AAAI-83.

Davis, R. (1980) "Meta-Rules: Reasoning about Control", *Artificial Intelligence* 15, 179-222.

DeJong, G (1983) "Acquiring schemata through understanding and genralizing plans," in IJCAI-1983.

Ernst, G. and Newell, A. (1969). "BPS: A case study in generality in problem solving", Academic Press.

Fikes, R. and Nilsson, N. (1971). "STRIPS: a new approach to application of theorem proving to problem solving", *Artificial Intelligence* 2, 189-208.

Fikes, R., Hart, P. and Nilsson, N. (1972). "Learning and executing generalized robot plans", *Artificial Intelligence* 3, 251-288, North-Holland.

Hammond, K. (1985). "Indexing and Causality: The organization of plans and strategies in memory", Yale Department of Computer Science Technical Report 351. AAAI-86.

Hayes-Roth, B. and Hayes-Roth, F. (1979) "A cognitive model of planning", *Cognitive Science*, 3, 275-310.

Hendler, J. (1985) "Integrating marker-passing and problem solving" in COGSCI-85.

Kolodner, J. L., (1983a). "Maintaining organization in a dynamic long-term memory", *Cognitive Science* 7, 243-280.

Kolodner, J. L. (1983b). "Reconstructive memory a computer", *Cognitive Science* 7, 281-328.

Kolodner, J., and Simpson, R. (1984). "Experience and problem solving: a framework" in COGSCI-84.

Kolodner, J.L., Simpson, R.L., and Sycara-Cyranski, K. (1985) "A process model of case-based reasoning in problem solving" in IJCAI-85.

Lebowitz, M. (1983) "Generalization from Natural Language Text", *Cognitive Science* 7, 1-40.

McDermott, D. (1978). "Planning and acting", *Cognitive Science* 2, 71-109.

Schank, R.C. (1982). *Dynamic Memory*, Cambridge University Press.

Stallman, R. and Sussman, G. (1971) "Forward reasoning and dependency-directed backtracking in a system for computed aided circuit analysis", *Artificial Intelligence*, 9, 2.

Stefik, M. (1981). "Planning and Meta-planning", *Artificial Intelligence* 12, 2, 141-170.

Wilensky, R. (1981). "Meta-Planning: Representting and using knowledge about planning in problem solving and natural language understanding", *Cognitive Science* 5, 197-233.

Wilensky, R. (1983). *Planning and Understanding.* Addison- Wesley.

Explanation-Based Indexing of Cases

Ralph Barletta
William Mark

Lockheed AI Center
2710 Sand Hill Rd.
Menlo Park, CA 94025
(415) 354-5236
Mark@VAXA.ISI.EDU

Abstract

Proper indexing of cases is critically important to the functioning of a case-based reasoner. In real domains such as fault recovery, a body of domain knowledge exists that can be captured and brought to bear on the indexing problem. Explanation based learning techniques provide a means of using a domain theory to justify the actions of a case with respect to the facts known when the case was originally executed. The relevant facts become the primary indices for the case. In some cases the domain knowledge can also be used to determine which facts are known to be irrelevant to the case. The remaining facts are treated as secondary indices, subject to eventual refinement via similarity based inductive techniques.

1 Introduction

Case-based reasoning (CBR) is an approach to problem-solving based on retrieving and applying stored solution examples (cases). This problem-solving methodology brings up a variety of research issues–Given a set of cases, how is the most relevant one selected? How are new cases acquired over time? What happens if the chosen case fails to accomplish the goal? What knowledge is needed to adapt a case to a new problem? How should case memory be organized for efficient retrieval?

Our research focuses on the last of these issues: how to determine the set of storage indices that enable a case to be retrieved "most appropriately" in the future. This is a learning problem: the system must determine a set of index predicates (called simply "indices" from now on) whose values differentially select cases in memory when applied to incoming problem descriptions. The goal is to determine indices that select exactly those cases that are applicable to—i.e., will result in a solution of—the problem. The learning method has available to it: problem-solving experience, including (and especially) the fact that the given case was actually applied successfully in the given circumstances; and theories about how things work in the domain. This paper discusses our current work in combining these sources of information to guide the indexing of cases. The focus is on adapting explanation based learning (EBL) techniques to identify relevant indices, given a set of possibly relevant features. In our test domain of fault recovery in robotic cells, as in any real domain, the number of known features that *could* be relevant is very large, and the available domain theories are incomplete.

2 Indexing Issues

Indexing is a critical issue for CBR because the success of the technique relies so heavily on the selection of the best stored case. Selection of the wrong case can be very expensive; much more so than selecting the wrong rule to fire in a rule based system. It is therefore most important for the system to determine indices that most effectively indicate (or contra-indicate) the applicability of a stored case.

First of all, indices must be truly relevant. Indices are drawn from knowledge about the state of the world when the case occurred. Unfortunately, everything the system knows about the state of the world when the case occurred *might* be relevant to its applicability. Thus, if a fault recovery case occurred when the ambient temperature was 44 degrees F, that temperature might somehow be relevant.

Second, indices must be generalized. Otherwise, only an exact match can be the criterion for case applicability. For example, if ambient temperature really is a relevant indicator for a case, we would want to index the case on a range of temperature values. Without this generalization, the case would only be deemed applicable when it happened to be exactly 44 degrees again.

Finally, indices should not be over-generalized. A case that is a good choice at 44 degrees may be a very poor choice at 34 degrees.

What is needed, then, is a method for indexing that wades through the large quantity of world state knowledge, most of which is irrelevant to the case's applicability, to find the truly relevant facts–and then generalizes the facts just enough but not too much.

Previous approaches have relied upon inductive methods and a restricted description language (to limit the types of world knowledge the system can have) to reduce the index set and generalize the resulting indices. This approach has achieved a rudimentary level of success in early CBR systems. There are, however, some major problems that inductive methods have with respect to the indexing issue. Many cases must be acquired before the relevant indices can be found (i.e., induction is too slow). This method also allows *irrelevant* indices to be put into memory, and remain there, until they are incrementally weeded out by the induction process.

Additionally, coincidental occurrences can cause the generation of erroneous indices. For example, if the system sees 5 fault recovery cases where the same problem occurred and the operator on duty was the same for all 5, then the name of the operator might be chosen as a relevant index. Although this could be an appropriate index, it is more likely just a coincidence.

This leads to the final problem with any inductive method: induction can use only the evidence available to the system. It would be much better if index selection could be based on theories of the domain that are derived from widely held principles of how the world works. This seems like a very reasonable goal to attain given the fact that most real world domains are in fact understood (at least at some level) in terms of physical properties, cause-effect, etc. Of course, this is the fundamental insight of EBL approaches.

3   Approach: Explanation-Based Indexing

For case indexing, we are given a case, and are told that the case was successful with respect to a particular problem description. The EBL objective is to create explanations of what made that particular case relevant to that particular problem description. In the domain of robotic cell fault recovery, the question is: what was it about that state of the world that prompted the given sequence of diagnostic and repair actions? Thus the "goal concept" in EBL terms is the sequence of actions in the case, and the reasoning is aimed at justification, not validation or classification. In other words, we are not attempting to explain the final diagnosis of the case with respect to the initial conditions (validation), but instead are interested in justifying the existence of the actions taken in the case with respect to those conditions. The domain theory available to the EBL reasoner includes knowledge of what diagnostic and repair actions can be performed and *some* knowledge of cause-effect relationships in the robotic cell and its environment.

In our approach, the system reasons with this domain theory in order to divide the potentially relevant indices into the categories "known to be relevant", "known to be irrelevant", and "possibly relevant" (i.e., neither relevant nor irrelevant according to the domain theory). "Known to be relevant" indices may be either indicative or contra-indicative.

To index the case, irrelevant indices are elided; then the remaining indices are used to organize the cases in memory according to a two-tiered scheme. Relevant indices are used to form the main organization of **primary indices**. Possibly relevant indices are used as **secondary indices**. When a new problem comes in, the primary indices are used to determine a set of applicable cases, and the secondary indices are used to choose among those cases. Secondary indices can eventually be promoted to primary indices or dropped as irrelevant through either the addition of domain theory, or through inductive techniques.

The above approach has some interesting differences from much of the previous EBL work. To begin with, the goal of the learner is somewhat different: justification rather than validation or classification. This lessens the demand on the domain theory. We know the series of actions that were actually performed to solve the problem. The system needs only enough knowledge about the purpose of the case and the causal relationships in the domain to explain why this sequence of actions was performed. The domain theory must be much more complete if the goal is to perform validation.

In the fault recovery domain, the answer to the "why" question is clearly going to be some form of "in order to fix the machine", which may include "finding the problem", "making the machine safe for investigation", etc.. Purpose provides focus for the EBL derivation process. For example, in the fault recovery domain, cases are triggered by a "presenting symptom", i.e., observable, behavioral evidence that something is wrong. The system must justify all actions in the case in terms of their role in relating this behavior to a "cause", i.e., correctable problem, and/or their role in correcting that problem. (Actions whose effect is to establish prerequisites for later actions do not require this justification; they are considered to be "covered" if the later actions can be justified.) Thus, if the effect of an action is to provide additional observables, the system will examine its causal model to see how the additional information must have been used to reduce the number of possible causes, increase certainty about a cause, etc. Derivation of what the actual cause turned out to be is not necessary for this justification.

For the domains of interest to CBR, it is extremely unlikely that there will be a domain theory complete enough to allow even this justification reasoning. In a real domain like robotic cell fault recovery, we do not know enough–and we certainly do not know how to represent enough–domain theory to relate each action in each case to what we know about the state of the world when the case was executed. The primary consequence of this incomplete domain theory is that the system cannot assume that a fact is irrelevant simply because it is not shown to be relevant. This means that in addition to deriving explanations for why certain facts are relevant, the system must also derive explanations for why other facts are irrelevant.

In developing our explanation-based indexing (EBI) approach, we made two simplifying assumptions. The first is that the goal of the expert in recovering from the fault is to find *one* cause of the behavior and recover from it (i.e., he doesn't do exhaustive testing to find all possible causes). The second is that the expert determines the cause of the presenting symptom(s) via process of elimination (i.e., process of elimination is his only diagnostic strategy).

Given the simplifying assumptions, the system takes as input: a case, a set of state of the world facts that were true when the case was applied, the set of actions (and their results) that can be performed by the expert and finally, an incomplete domain theory which contains functional and causal information about the behavior of the cell. From this initial information the system then proceeds to justify the individual actions in the case with respect to the state of the world facts via the domain theory. Note that each action is justified with respect to the *current* state of the world when the action actually occurred in the case. The results of prior actions add to the initial conditions in forming the *current* state of the world. In this way, we are able to justify the action not only with respect to the initial state of the world but also with respect to the other actions that were taken in the case.

Forming the justification of an action with respect to the initial state of the world has four basic steps. The first step is to construct a **hypothesis tree** which relates the presenting behavioral symptom to *potential* observables that could have caused such behavior. It is called a hypothesis tree because there are typically many possible scenarios (involving several functional parts) for which the behavioral symptom could have come about. Each of these scenarios is a hypothesis which the expert may support or eliminate through the actions he takes in the case. Each hypothesis can have several sub-hypotheses that will either prove or disprove the hypothesis (forming a tree).

The second step is to apply the actual facts of the case against the hypothesis tree, to determine which potential causes of the fault could actually be supported by the given facts in this case. This step establishes a *diagnostic view* with respect to the model. The diagnostic view shows all of the hypotheses that are still unproven with respect to the model and the given facts. Presumably, performing the actions in the case will resolve these remaining hypotheses, thus being justifiable with respect to the model.

Determining which hypothesis(es) can be resolved by the action to be justified is the third step in the process. The system is able to determine this because it has knowledge of the resulting observables of the actions that can be taken by the expert and how they relate to the domain model. At this point the system has enough information to perform the fourth and final step: determine relevant and irrelevant observables with respect the action. Rules for determining relevance and irrelevance will be described in the "Example" section below.

4 Example

In this section, we will describe our approach in the context of an example case from the fault recovery domain. Part of the case is shown in Figure 1. The operator of a robotic fabrication cell hears a motor "loading up" (i.e., straining) as it is cutting a part. The operator tells this to the engineer. The engineer then performs three actions: checking the air inlet gauge, turning the tool by hand, and re-running the machine's program without the part. The results of this sequence convince the engineer that the problem is in the air supply (the end of the sequence in Figure 1; the actual case continues). As mentioned earlier, the goal is not to explain how the set of symptoms can be used to diagnose "faulty air supply"; we are interested only in determining when this sequence of actions is a reasonable thing to do.

4.1 The Domain Model

Our knowledge of the robotic cell fault recovery domain consists of three parts:

- a set of observables (top of Figure 1);
- a set of actions that the problem solver can perform and their results (bottom of Figure 2);
- a (partial) model of how the parts of the robot function together and causal knowledge about possible malfunction of the various parts.

Observables–both those available initially and those discoverable via actions–are associated with elements in the causal model, if the association is known (e.g., "tool steadily resists turning", "tool catches", etc., are associated with the **abnormal internal friction** node of the model).

Knowledge about problem solver actions is expected to be "complete" in the sense that the system can assume that the operator and engineer are not doing things to affect the cell that are not included in the case (a reasonable assumption in this domain). The rest of the system's knowledge is expected to be incomplete. If the system is unaware of relevant observables (e.g., if the the system is unaware that the engineer makes decisions based on whether or not he can smell insulation burning), indexing will be be incomplete, but it will still be effective with respect to the set of observables that are known. Similarly, if the system is unaware of certain cause-effect relationships, an index that should have been primary may end up as secondary, and certain irrelevancies will go undetected, but the system will still be effective in finding primary indices in the context of its known model.

The model shown in Figure 2 can be read as follows:

> In this cell, there is an air compressor that drives the motor, which turns the tool, which cuts the part. Air pressure delivered from the compressor can be "high", "normal", or "low". The resulting motor speed will in turn be fast, normal, or slow. The motor movement propagates to the tool, which also can turn fast, normal or slow. The tool then cuts the part either normally or abnormally. For every functional part of the cell there are "causes" for functional changes. For example, air feed can change the pressure delivered by the compressor from high to normal to low. Similarly, different values of internal friction in the motor can change the value for motor movement. Likewise, different values for external friction between the tool and the part can affect the turning of the tool. The causal model links the actual behavioral changes in the functional model to observables.

4.2 Creating an Explanation

For simplicity, we will focus on only a single action as the goal concept, and ignore the other actions (which, in the actual process, are considered for their cumulative effect). In the following, then, the goal concept will be the action **Manually Rotate Tool**. So, for our example, the question is: "how does the action Manually Rotate Tool relate to the presenting symptom of 'motor loading up', given the currently known observables and the fact that we have just checked the air gauge and found it to be normal?"

The first step the process takes before justifying any actions is to note the presenting symptom(s) and construct the appropriate hypothesis tree that can explain the actions taken with respect to the symptom(s). The goal is to propagate the presenting symptom (i.e., motor loading) through the functional model (via Motor-movement[slowed]) to determine all the observables that could have caused that behavior in the cell (at least according to this incomplete domain model). In this case, motor-movement[slowed] can be caused by internal friction in the motor, or low air feed in the compressor, or external friction between the tool and the part. We are able to relate changes in other parts of the machine to the motor-movement because the functional model represents the fact that if the compressor drive is low, the motor movement will be slow. The portion of the causal model we have chosen to show in figure 2 turns out to be the the hypothesis tree for this case. The leaf nodes of the tree (shown in boxes) are facts that can be observed through some action or known a priori.

Step three applies the actual observables in the case against the leaf nodes of the hypothesis tree to determine which hypotheses are supported or negated by those facts. This step produces a *view*, with respect to the model, of the diagnostic options available to the expert at the time of the action. It is this view that is used by the system to determine the justification for the action taken in the case.

Once these steps are accomplished, the system can proceed to determine the justifications for the actions in the case. The system infers (based on the results that can be obtained via the action) which hypotheses can be resolved by taking the action. For the manually rotate tool action, the only hypothesis that can be confirmed by its results is the internal friction hypothesis. Given the hypothesis that can be resolved, and the diagnostic view created in a previous step, the system can determine relevant and irrelevant observables with respect to this action.

There are two kinds of relevant observables: indicative and contra-indicative. An observable is relevant and indicative with respect to an action if:

- The presence of the observable removes some of the possible *competing* hypotheses, thereby performing process of elimination which would encourage the action to be taken.

- The observable suggests a conclusion for a hypothesis which can only be verified or strengthened by the action taken.

An observable is relevant and contra-indicative with respect to an action if:

- Some value of the observable (different from what it is) would have eliminated the hypothesis(es) that would have been resolved by taking the action.

- Some other value of the observable would have determined a different hypothesis as the cause of the presenting symptom.

Determining if an observable is irrelevant via the model is a bit tricky. An observable is irrelevant if *all* values of the observable have no bearing on taking or not taking the action. Because of the inherent incompleteness of the model this is not easy to do in general. Additionally, in order for an observable to be irrelevant with respect to the overall case it must be irrelevant with respect to *all* the actions in the case. This is not required of relevant observables. One way in which we can demonstrate the irrelevance of an observable is to show that the observable suggested *not* taking the action, and it was taken anyway. In addition to showing the observable to be irrelevant this approach also pinpoints places in the model that are inconsistent and need to be refined.

For the Manually-rotate-tool action, last-tool-change is relevant and indicative. It is relevant because we know that the tool was last changed two weeks ago and the model tells us that if the tool is changed every three weeks we can conclude that external friction was normal. This situation matches the relevant and indicative rule which says an observable is relevant if it eliminates a competing hypothesis.

The absence of a leak in the motor casing is relevant and contra-indicative. The process is able to conclude this because if the casing *were* leaking, the model would be able to conclude that the quantity of lubricant was low and there was abnormal internal friction due to that. This would confirm the hypothesis of abnormal internal drag that the action was trying to confirm, thus making the action unnecessary. So, knowing there is no leak justifies (in part) taking the action.

Determining irrelevant observables with respect to this action can be done by showing that the observable suggested not doing the action. Ambient temperature is one such observable. The actual temperature was 42 degrees. This fact allows us to infer that the lubricant is too cold, making the lubricant viscosity too high, which causes abnormal internal friction. This inference chain suggests not taking the manually rotate tool action. We know that it was taken anyway. Since we assume that the engineer has a reason for doing every action, we have uncovered an inconsistency in the model relative to ambient temperature and also shown that its actual value was irrelevant to performing the action. Although ambient temperature was shown to be irrelevant to this particular action, it is not irrelevant with respect to the entire case unless it is shown to be irrelevant to all the actions.

5 Discussion

We have tried to show that EBL techniques can be applied to the indexing problem, even in the face of an incomplete domain theory. The existence of the case turns the learning problem into one of justification, which we believe is more tractable when domain knowledge is incomplete. There are many issues that need to be resolved before the work we have outlined can be fully realized. In particular, we need to develop efficient algorithms for deriving the relevance or irrelevance of the known facts; we also need to determine an appropriate inferencing representation that will allow different types of inference links (e.g., implication vs. influence) and determine their impact on the process, additionally we need to improve our generalization techniques for the resulting primary and secondary indices.

Our goal is to explore these issues in the context of a building a working fault recovery system.

6 Acknowledgements

We would like to thank Linda Cook for reviewing and commenting on this paper as well as providing input that helped us understand and solidify our approach.

7 References

Riesbeck C.K., Bain W.M., (1987) "A Methodology For Implementing Case-based Reasoning Systems" A contracted report submitted to Lockheed from Cognitive Systems.

Mitchell T.M., et al, (1986) "Explanation-based Generalization: A Unifying View" Machine Learning Journal, Vol. 1, Number 1, Pg. 47.

DeJong G., Mooney R., (1986) "Explanation-based Learning: An Alternative View", Machine Learning Journal, Vol. 1, Number 2, Pg. 145

Kolodner, J.L., (1983) "Maintaining Organization in a Dynamic Long-term Memory", Cognitive Science, Vol. 7, Pg. 243.

Initial Observables

Operator-name [Austin]
Ambient temperature [42 degrees]
time-of-day [14:30]
tool-type [5/8" cutter]
part-material [metal]
type-of-cut [complex]
time-last-service [34 days]
part-name [Wing Strut - R17]
shift [1]
program-controlled [yes]
humidity [42 %]

time-into-part-run [2:30]
position-of-tool [normal]
machine-name [m82]
model-type [wd1982-a]
number-parts-in-run [6]
end-effector-temp [normal]
hydraulic-pressure [normal]
clamp-position [normal]
Time-to-make-part [4 min.]
Casing-integrity [not leaking]
Tool-last-replaced [2 weeks]

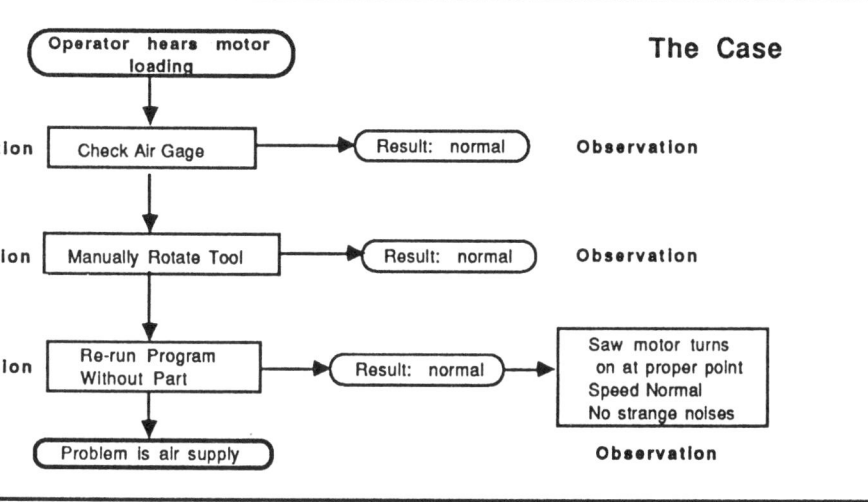

Figure 1

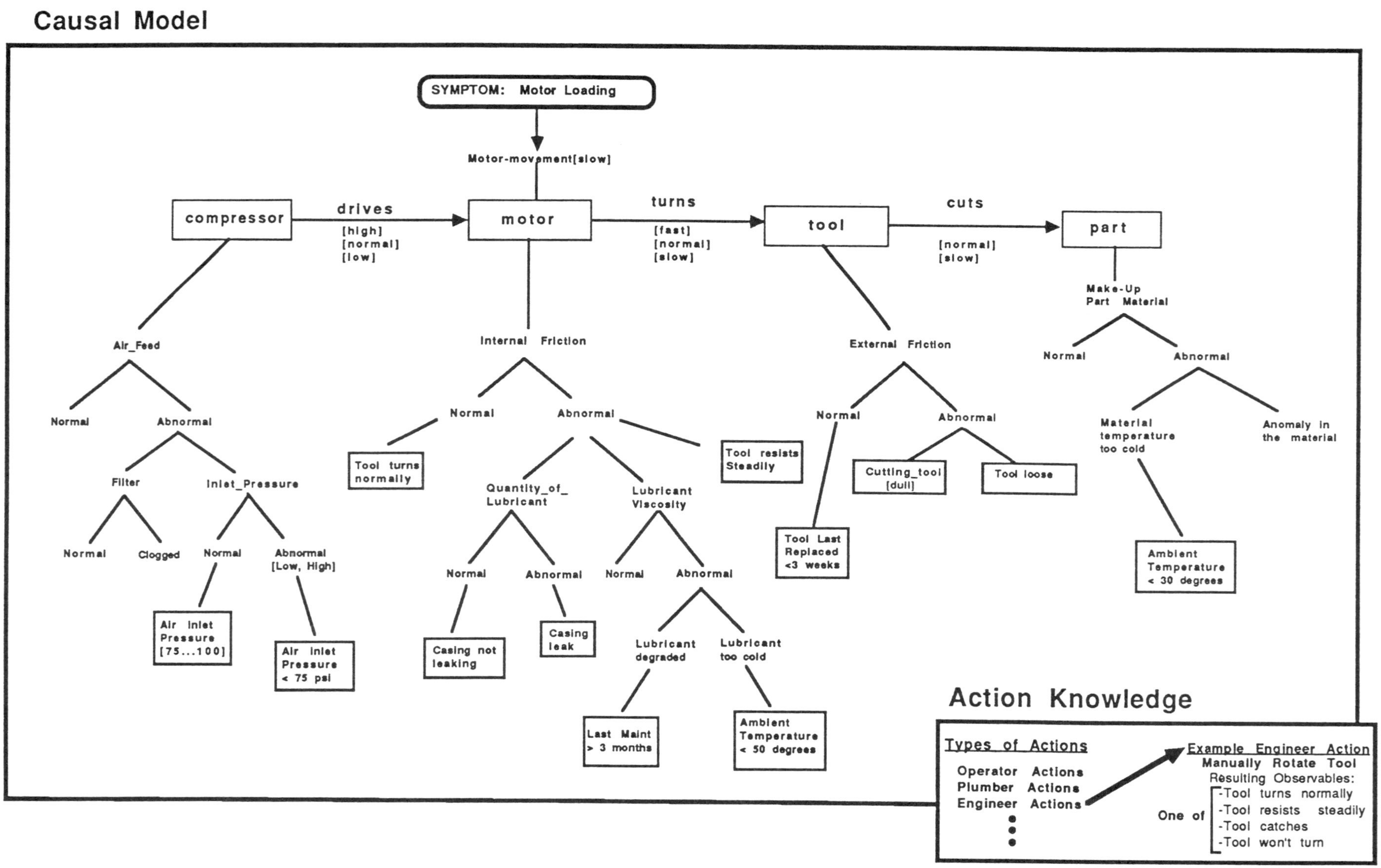

Figure 2: Domain Model

The Transfer of Experience Across Planning Domains Through the Acquisition of Abstract Strategies

Lawrence Birnbaum
Yale University
Dept. of Computer Science
New Haven, Connecticut

Gregg Collins
University of Illinois
Dept. of Computer Science
Urbana, Illinois

Abstract

If case-based systems are to be truly general problem-solvers, they must have the ability to retrieve cases from one domain that are relevant to problems in other domains. The ability of a system to retrieve cases across domain boundaries depends, in part, on its ability to derive indices that reflect the interesting features of a case from a problem-solving perspective. In many areas of problem solving, such as competitive planning, the interesting features of problem situations center around domain-independent strategic concepts that apply in many different domains. The acquisition of such strategic concepts, by improving a system's ability to generate indices, can greatly improve the ability of that system to retrieve relevant cases. Learning a single new strategic concept may therefore lead to better performance in many different domains. In this paper, we consider the problem of deriving concepts for use in indexing through the analysis of specific cases. We suggest a method for acquiring such concepts by analyzing expectation failures by a planner. We present a simple failure explanation algorithm, derived from work in circuit debugging, and show how and why it must be extended in order to enable the acquisition of strategic planning knowledge.

1 Introduction

In case-based reasoning, problem-solving is guided by prior experience. The ability of a case-based system to solve problems is thus dependent upon its ability to retrieve relevant cases. Ideally, a case-base system should be able to retrieve and utilize analogous cases from domains other than the one in which a problem arises (Carbonell, 1983; Burstein, 1986). For example, a system that is playing chess should be able to make use not only of prior chess-playing experience, but also of experience gained in other competitive situations. The ability to transfer knowledge across domain boundaries in this way is of particular importance when the system is a novice in a domain; in such a situation case-based reasoning will be of use *only* if the system can retrieve relevant cases from other domains in which it has more experience.

Cross-domain retrieval is a difficult problem because analogous cases in different domains will in general share few surface features. The ability of a system to index cases by domain-independent features relating to *problem-solving* is therefore of critical importance. In order to carry out such indexing, a system must be capable of analyzing cases in terms of features that underlie problem-solving in general. In many problem solving areas, such as competitive planning, problem solving is based on an underlying level of abstract strategic concepts (Kolodner and Simpson, 1986; Collins, 1987; Collins and Birnbaum, 1987). To facilitate the retrieval of usefully similar cases, the system's indexing vocabulary should be based on these underlying concepts. In such a system, the acquisition of *new* strategic concepts, by expanding the system's indexing vocabulary, will significantly improve its ability to retrieve relevant cases. Learning a single new strategic concept may therefore lead to better performance in many different domains. In this paper, we outline an approach to the development of explanation-based learning methods capable of deriving such domain-independent strategic concepts from the analysis of specific cases. While the work we report on was not specifically case-based, and does not directly address the problem of retrieval, we believe that the process we describe will constitute an important part of any case-based system capable of transferring knowledge across domains.

1.1 Strategic concepts in competitive planning

Planning in competitive situations—whether in games, business, personal life, or even political or military conflict—involves the application of both specific knowledge about the particular domain at hand, and abstract strategic knowledge about competitive planning in general. The domain-specific knowledge includes, of course, the "domain physics"—e.g., how the pieces can move in a board game, or details of the legislative process in politics. It also includes knowledge about the goals that characterize the particular domain, the relative importance of those goals, and most of all, specific plans for achieving those goals. Such domain-specific plans include, for example, *bunting* (in baseball), the *blitz* (in football), the *fork* (in chess), and *cutting a deal* with the opposition (in politics and business). The defining characteristic of domain-specific planning knowledge is that it is represented in terms of a vocabulary that applies only to the particular planning domain at hand.

In contrast, any planning knowledge that is intended to be applicable in many different domains must be represented in terms of a vocabulary that is *not* specific to any one of those domains. That such abstract knowledge exists and plays an important role in both planning and understanding is by now well-established—Sussman's (1975) and Sacerdoti's (1977) "critics," Carbonell's (1981) "counter-planning" rules, Schank's (1982) "thematic organization points," and Wilensky's (1983) "meta-plans" are all examples. Competitive planning is particularly rich in abstract concepts and rules—what we will call *strategic* knowledge. Consider, for example, the concept of a *threat* in a competition—a situation in which an agent gains an opportunity to either win the competition or else significantly boost his chances *vis-à-vis* his opponent. Or, consider the concept of a *sacrifice,* in which the agent allows his opponent to achieve a goal in order to himself achieve a more important goal. Both of these concepts are meaningful in all competitive situations, regardless of the domain in which the competition is carried out. This suggests that they must be represented in terms of an abstract vocabulary applicable to any kind of competitive planning.

1.2 Strategic knowledge and explanation-based learning

Our research is aimed at developing explanation-based learning methods that are capable of acquiring abstract planning knowledge from experience in one domain, and using this knowledge to aid in problem-solving in other domains. (Similar motivations underly current work in learning and problem-solving by analogy—see, e.g., Carbonell, 1983 and 1986; Gentner, 1983; Burstein, 1986.) The development of such methods requires progress on three major research problems: First, a representational vocabulary must be developed in terms of which abstract competitive planning knowledge can be usefully expressed. Second, the role such knowledge plays in the indexing and retrieval of relevant cases must be determined through the detailed analysis of many examples. Third—and most important— explanation-based learning methods must be extended to allow the acquisition of new strategic planning knowledge. This, in turn, will improve a learning system's ability to improve its ability to retrieve and apply relevant cases.

2 Learning by explaining failures

The particular style of explanation-based learning that we think best applies to the acquisition of competitive planning knowledge, both domain-specific and abstract, is *failure-driven* learning (Sussman, 1975; Schank, 1982; Hayes-Roth, 1983; Minton, 1984; Hammond, 1986). On this view, when an expectation or a plan fails, the goal of avoiding a similar failure in the future motivates the attempt to explain the current failure. The explanation of the failure, in turn, suggests ways in which similar failures might be avoided in the future. In this section, we will outline our ideas about how such a process might work within the context of an example.

Suppose that we have a "novice" chess planning program: It possesses a set of domain-specific chess planning rules that—while reasonable as far as they go—admit of a number of qualifications and extensions that a more expert player would know about. One such incomplete rule might be: "*A piece is secure if it is defended by as many pieces as can attack it.*" This rule is basically reasonable, but, as any chess player knows, it entails a number of complications. Our program, however, has yet to learn about these.

Now let's suppose that the program advances its queen to a position where it can be attacked by an opposing knight, believing that it is secure because the position is defended by a pawn. This is a perfectly valid application of the above rule. Nevertheless, the opponent will, sensibly, go ahead and take the queen, giving up his knight in the process. Thus, the program's plan for defending the queen, and its expectations about that plan, will both fail. This failure demands an explanation: Why was the queen taken, despite the applicability of a rule claiming that it would be secure?

To answer this question, the program must first examine why it expected its plan to work in the first place. In this particular case, the explanation for the utility of the rule that was at fault involves the abstract strategic concept of *deterrence*: The opponent is deterred from attacking by the knowledge that if he does so, his attacking piece will be taken in turn. In this case, however, the opponent has attacked despite the deterrent. Therefore he either did not understand the deterrent—did not realize that his piece would be taken in turn—or he went ahead in the full knowledge that it would be taken. Let's leave aside the first possibility. The program must now attempt to explain why its deterrent failed: Why did the opponent attack, knowing full well that doing so would lead to the loss of his knight? The explanation in this case involves the abstract concept of *sacrifice,* as described earlier: The opponent is willing to sacrifice the knight because, by doing so, he gains the greater goal of taking the program's queen. In other words, the program's deterrent was insufficient.

Depending on the state of the program's knowledge, several things might be learned as a result of attempting to explain its failure in this case. First of all, the chess-specific planning rule presented above must be amended to include the condition that the value of the attacking piece (or pieces) must be equal to or greater than the value of the piece under attack. Second, the program might learn that a queen is generally considered more important than a knight, if it did not already know that. Finally—and, from our point of view, most importantly—it is even possible that the program will gain some new strategic knowledge from the analysis of this failure. In particular, suppose that the program's abstract conception of deterrence were incomplete, and it did not know that, *in general,* the threat to its opponent must be equal to or greater than the threat to itself in order to act as an effective deterrent. The program would be unable to explain the failure of its incomplete chess-specific rule on the basis of such an incomplete conception of deterrence in the abstract, because they are in fact completely consistent with each other. Thus, the program would be forced to search harder for an explanation. Ultimately, this effort would lead it to conclude that its abstract conception of deterrence was inadequate, and thereby to learn the general importance of having a sufficient threat. With this new strategic knowledge, the program's ability to apply the concept of deterrence in other competitive domains would be enhanced. At the very least, it would not be forced to repeatedly recapitulate all of the mistakes, and all of the difficult explanatory work, necessary to independently develop an adequate conception of deterrence in each specific competitive domain. Even better, the abstract strategy could be used as a basis for devising new domain-specific deterrent rules in other competitive situations, via some process of *operationalization* (Mostow, 1983).

3 The explanation process

In the last section, we saw that a sophisticated model of explanatory reasoning is necessary in order to implement our approach to the transfer of strategic knowledge across domains. The form of the explanatory reasoning component that is necessary is determined primarily by the fact that what it must attempt to explain are expectation and planning failures. As a result, our approach to the problem of explanation has its roots in the somewhat earlier work on fault diagnosis and debugging in circuit analysis (see, e.g., Stallman and Sussman, 1977). In this approach, when an expectation fails, the program must examine its justification for believing that expectation, and attempt to determine where the fault lies in that justification structure. A justification consists of the inference rule that gave rise to the expectation, together with the facts that served as antecedents for the application of that inference rule. Such justifications, called *data dependencies,* are attached to each fact believed by the program, forming a graph (see, e.g., deKleer *et al.,* 1977; Doyle, 1979).

The basic process of failure explanation, given such justification structures, is a simple recursive procedure. The failure of an expectation is explained by hypothesizing that one of the antecedents of the inference rule that gave rise to the expectation, although mistakenly *believed* to be true at the time the rule was applied, was in fact false. (The failure could also be due to the rule itself being incorrect. This can be handled, in part, by viewing the rule as another antecedent fact, with its own justification structure.) If it is decided that one of the antecedents was mistakenly believed to be true, this is viewed as a prior expectation failure, responsible for the failure that we are attempting to explain. At this point, the explanation process can recur and attempt to explain the prior failure. The recursion stops when some assertion without a supporting justification is faulted. Such an assertion may be a premise, an explicit assumption, or an assertion produced by some method, such as induction, that does not produce an accompanying justification structure.

It would, of course, be unreasonable to expect that this simple process alone will be sufficient to explain expectation failures in any complex domain. Nevertheless, it does provide a framework in terms of which a more adequate model can be constructed, if only by calling attention to those aspects of the explanation problem which cause it to fail. In order to illustrate how these problems arise, and to sketch out how we propose to address them, let's consider another example. Suppose that our program is given the role of a novice coach in some time-limited game such as football, basketball, or soccer. Suppose further that the team being coached by our program has built up a large lead late in a game, by means of a high-risk, fast-paced attack. We might expect that a novice coach, such as our program, would follow the strategy that *"if something has been working, keep doing it."* From such a perspective, it would be sensible for the program to continue with the aggressive game plan that has gained it such a big lead.

In order to apply this strategy, the program must have some measure of whether or not a game plan is working—in other words, whether it seems likely to lead to victory. Thus, as the game proceeds, the program will be making predictions about its outcome, based on the current situation.

In particular, if a team has a sufficient lead over its opponent, we would expect the program to predict that it will win. In the situation described above, therefore, our program will predict victory for its team, and—since it seems to be working well— continue pursuing an aggressive and risky game plan. Suppose now that, as a result of pursuing such a risky plan, the program's team manages to lose the game despite its big lead. We would expect our program to learn from this mistake: As any human planner knows, when you have a big lead in a game that will end at a fixed time, at some point *conservatism* becomes the best strategy. By slowing the game down—pursuing offensive plans that minimize risk and maximize the time used, rather than maximizing the potential gain—you can make it impossible for an opponent to overcome your lead before it ends.

In order to learn this strategy, our program must first be able to explain *why* it lost, in a way that highlights the need to take a less risky approach. The expectation that failed in this case, of course, is the expectation that the program's team would win. This expectation was based on the fact that the team was far ahead late in the game. More precisely, the justification for this expectation must involve something like the following rule: *"If a team's lead over its opponent exceeds the number of points its opponent can be expected to score in the time remaining, then predict victory for that team."* The number of points an opponent could be expected to score in the time remaining depends, in turn, on two other factors: the amount of time remaining, and the maximum number of points the opponent can be expected to score per unit time. Assuming that the program can quickly rule out having made a mistake about either the size of its lead or the time remaining, it should be fairly simple for it to determine that it was its expectation about the maximum number of points that the opponent would score per unit time that was at fault—in other words, the opponent scored at a faster rate than expected. The program must now, in turn, try to explain why *this* expectation failed.

Here, however, we encounter the first of the complications that our basic explanation algorithm cannot be expected to address. It is very unlikely that the particular maximum rate at which the program expects an opponent to be able to score has a complete deductive justification. Most likely, it represents a compilation of the program's experience—in other words, it was derived *inductively*. As a result, this expectation will not have a justification structure with data dependencies pointing to inference rules and antecedent expectations, that our basic explanation algorithm could examine in turn. (The same situation would also arise if an expectation resulted from something that the program had simply been told without further justification.)

How should the program deal with the failure of such an expectation? The most straightforward approach would be to conclude that the expectation simply failed in this case, and that the program will not be able to formulate a deeper explanation because there is no existing justification structure to give any insight into possible reasons for the failure. In effect, this would lead to the answer, *"sometimes your opponent scores faster than would normally be expected, and in this case you may lose when you thought you would win."* This is true, but it is not very helpful. A slightly more sophisticated approach might adjust the failed expectation somewhat to account for the new instance, say by increasing the value of the expected rate of scoring. Such an approach would be consistent with the original inductive derivation of the fact. It would not, however, shed any more light on why the expectation failed *in this case*.

We can do better by taking advantage of our explanatory facility. Inductively derived facts can be given causal explanations—in fact, we would in general be disturbed if we were unable to see any possible causal justification for a fact that we believed as a result of induction. We would thus like our program to attempt to *construct* an explanation for the expectation in question. If a plausible explanation can be generated, it can serve as a hypothetical justification for the failed expectation. Once this justification has been built, the program can continue on as though it had been in place all along. So we must make a major extension to our basic failure explanation algorithm, namely:

- The program must be prepared to construct an explicit justification for an expectation that, while well-founded, lacks one.

In this way, it can transform implicit expectations—which, precisely because they are implicit, cannot adequately be taken into account in planning—into explicit expectations that it can reason about (Collins, 1987).

Constructing a hypothetical justification for a previously unjustified expectation crucially involves determining the major factors relevant to the truth of that expectation. In this case, for example, the major determinants of the rate at which a team can score are, we might expect, the efforts of the two competing actors: One side is trying to maximize its gain per play, while the other side is attempting to minimize its risk per play. Previous work in explanation-based learning (see, e.g., DeJong and Mooney, 1986; Mitchell *et al.*, 1986) has identified the need for an adequate causal model of the domain in order to determine relevant factors of this sort. We are particularly interested in developing heuristics that are capable of guiding such causal reasoning.

For example, we might ask what it is that makes these two factors seem the most relevant in this case. One possible answer lies in the fact that the program knows not only *that* it lost, but also many of the details of *how* it lost. It will have observed, for example, the particular plays on which its opponent scored, and those on which its team made major mistakes. Such knowledge can be expected to provide important clues about what factors might be relevant in explaining the loss. In particular, if the loss really were a result of the program's use of high-risk plays, then there must have been specific instances when the opposing team capitalized on mistakes by the program's team. Such mistakes would have been noticed as expectation failures at the time—since the program of course would not have run the plays in question unless it expected them to succeed—and would have required explanation. In these cases, the explanation constructed at the time would simply be that the plays were risky and the failures were a known possibility. However, since the plays were pursued in accordance with the principle of adhering to previously successful strategies, despite their known risks, the program could conclude that there was no cause for alarm.

Now, if a record of this sort of reasoning were stored in the planner's memory, rather than being discarded, it would provide a good reason for focusing on risk as a likely factor in the explanation for its loss of the game, since it had been a factor in the explanation of less catastrophic expectation failures during the course of the game itself. The record of other "local" expectation failures—such as particularly unusual or spectacular plays made by the opponent—would suggest other causally related factors. The necessary focusing heuristic in this case would be something like the following: *"In trying to construct a hypothetical justification for a failed expectation, consider using factors involved in the explanation of prior, subsidiary expectation failures about which the program took no action."* This sort of heuristic for guiding causal reasoning seems crucial to the development of efficient explanation algorithms.

Assuming that the appropriate justification structure has been constructed, we can now continue applying our basic algorithm to explain the failure of the expectation concerning the rate at which the opponent would score. There are two possibilities: Either the opponent's efforts to increase their expected gain were greater than expected, or else the program's efforts to minimize risk were less than expected. Each of these possibilities is, potentially, very expensive to examine. Moreover, there is no *a priori* reason to decide that one or the other is a more likely explanation—in fact, a sophisticated analysis would probably decide that both were relevant. This raises the second major problem that requires substantially extending our basic explanation algorithm. There will generally be *many* explanations for the failure of an expectation. Depending upon the program's motivation for explaining the problem in the first place, some of these explanations may be much more useful than others. In particular, a planning program is most interested in explanations that depend on factors *under the program's control*, since these are likely to be more productive in averting future violations of desirable expectations. This, then, is the second major extension that must be made to the basic explanation algorithm:

- The goals of the explanation process must play a role in determining which possible avenues of explanation to explore.

In general, the selection of which explanatory path to pursue on the grounds of utility, rather than of likelihood alone, depends on the program's ability to reason about the purposes underlying the invocation of the explanation process in the first place. The main motivation for explaining why you lost when you expected to win is the desire to avoid losing if a similar situation arises in the future. The motivation to correct the expectation is only secondary. We believe that it is of fundamental importance that a model of the explanation process be able to take account of the purposes to which the system intends to put the resulting explanation in determining how the search for that explanation should proceed.

In this particular example, if the problem lies in the risk-taking policy of the program, then the explanation will be likely to suggest a way of avoiding a similar expectation failure in the future. If the problem lies in the opponent's ability to maximize his gain, however, there is little reason to think that an investigation of this will yield any way of changing the outcome. Thus, it makes more sense to pursue an explanation that involves the program's risk-taking strategy.

Following this approach, the program can tentatively decide that its expectation concerning the rate at which its opponent could score failed in this case because it depends on the assumption that the program will minimize risk. To proceed from this point, the program must now examine the justification for such a belief. This particular belief can be justified by an appeal to a general axiom of planning, namely, *"unless other strategic considerations interfere, any planner wants to reduce risk as much as possible."* This, along with the assumption *"no other strategic consideration is interfering,"* implies that the planner is currently minimizing risk. The only way that this expectation can fail, therefore, is if there is, in fact, some strategic consideration that conflicts with the goal to minimize risk.

The program must therefore examine, in turn, the justification for that belief. Notice, however, that the expectation that *"no strategic consideration is interfering"* is universally quantified (i.e., it is equivalent to "for all strategic considerations S, S is not interfering with the goal to minimize risk"). This is problematic, because *its* justification is, in a sense, the arbitrarily long conjunction stating, individually for each strategic consideration known to the program—i.e., one strategy per conjunct—that that strategy is not expected to interfere. Obviously, such a justification structure cannot actually be built. One important method for dealing with this problem—though by no means the only one—is to interpret a decision to fault such a universally quantified claim as an instruction to search for *specific counterexamples* to the claim. If such a counterexample is found, then the corresponding portion of the justification structure can be built to represent the expectation that that particular counterexample would not arise; then *that* expectation can be faulted by the explanation process. This constitutes the third major extension to the basic explanation algorithm:

- The faulting of a universally quantified expectation may be taken as an instruction to search for a specific counterexample.

How can the program go about searching for such a counterexample? In this case, before some other strategy could have interfered with the implicit goal to minimize risk, that strategy must actually have been adopted by the program. Thus, the program can retrieve potentially interfering strategies simply by asking itself, in effect, what strategies it was pursuing. The answer, in this case, is that it was following the strategy of continuing to apply what had worked previously. The program must now ask itself the following question: Did this strategy interfere with the goal to minimize risk? The answer, in this case, is yes: The program knows that the use of this strategy resulted in the selection of high-risk plans, since that was how it explained the failures of those plans as they occurred.

Having found a counterexample, the program must now construct a corresponding justification for its expectation that *"no strategic consideration is interfering"* with the goal to minimize risk—namely, its implicit expectation that *"the strategy of continuing to apply what has been working is not interfering."*— and then fault that expectation. In this way, the program can represent its insight that it was its adherence to the strategy of continuing with what had been working which committed it to high-risk, high-payoff plays, and thereby caused the expectation to fail. Because of this failure, the program could not minimize its risk, and the greater level of risk it was forced to accept made it possible for the opponent to score more points than he normally could. The opponent was able to take advantage of the opportunity in this case, and therefore the program lost when it had expected to win.

Collapsing all of the intermediate steps brings the program to the critical conclusion: The sacrifice of low risk for potential greater gain is the cause of the failure of its expectation that it would win the game. This conclusion forms the basis of what we want the program to ultimately learn, namely the expectation that whenever it has sufficient lead over its opponent, it will win if it stops sacrificing low risk for gain, and simply minimizes risk—i.e., if it plays *conservatively*. It is tempting to see this as a simple reformulation of the previous conclusion, but that is not the case: The program has not yet ruled out the possibility that, should it refrain from sacrificing low risk for potential gain, its expectation to win would fail for some other reason. That is, just because the program has identified a factor that caused an expectation failure, it does not follow that if that factor were eliminated, the expectation would then succeed. If the program *cannot* reach such a conclusion, however, the explanation is of only academic interest.

This, then, constitutes our final major extension to the basic explanation algorithm:

- The program must be able to determine whether the elimination of a factor that caused an expectation failure would in fact have resulted in the success of that expectation—in other words, that it would not cause the expectation to fail in some other way.

To determine this, the program must have the ability to reason hypothetically. In this instance, it must, in effect, ask whether sacrificing potential high gain to reduce risk—rather than the other way around—might in some way still cause the failure of its expectation to win. Although the process of hypothetical reasoning seems very different from the process of explaining failures, it makes use of the same justification structures. That is, the program must determine whether its expectation of high potential gain plays any role in its expectation to win by examining the justification structures in which those expectations are implicated. Despite its difficulty, therefore, there is no reason to believe that the sort of hypothetical reasoning that is necessary will require radically different forms of representation, and in fact there is some reason to think that it will share basic mechanisms with the explanation process discussed above.

This example has necessarily been rather complicated: The main point that we wish to emphasize, therefore, is that the basic failure explanation algorithm must be extended in several crucial ways in order to provide the explanations necessary to learn abstract strategic concepts, and to apply them across different domains. The extensions that are necessary include the following capabilities:

- Constructing hypothetical explanations for beliefs that are not deductively justified, using the problem context to direct causal reasoning in fruitful directions.

- Considering the goals of the explanation process in deciding what avenues of possible explanation to explore.

- Dealing with faulted universally quantified expectations by searching for a specific counterexample.

- Hypothetical reasoning to determine whether the elimination of a factor that caused an expectation failure would in fact prevent that failure.

In this section, we have sketched what we believe to be reasonable approaches to achieving each of these goals. However, it should be clear that a good deal of study is needed before we can provide detailed theories of how each is carried out.

4 Conclusions

Our work to date has had three major results. First, it provides evidence that explanation-based learning can result the acquisition of new concepts at the strategic level. These concepts may constitute a refinement of a known strategic concept, as in the deterrence example of section 2, or they be entirely new concepts, as in the conservatism example of section 3. The purpose of analysis at the strategic level is to suggest appropriate ways of indexing cases so that insights gained in the processing of those cases can be applied in other domains. When this is possible, it represents a dramatic advance for a learning system, because the ability to apply knowledge acquired in one domain to problems encountered in another can reduce—or even eliminate entirely—the need to learn by trial and error in the new domain. For example, a program that has acquired a sophisticated notion of deterrence from playing chess will be able to apply the results of this experience in checkers without being forced to recapitulate the painstaking process of discovery in this new domain. Or, to take another example, a program that has learned about conservatism coaching soccer will be able to recall and utilize this knowledge in coaching football.

Second, it argues that the acquisition of abstract strategic knowledge can best proceed through the explanation of expectation failures. The major advantage of such a *failure-driven* approach, in our view, lies in its answer to the question of *when* learning should occur. As DeJong and Mooney (1986) point out, determining when to learn is one of the biggest challenges facing any learning system. Clearly, an explanation-based learning system cannot attempt to explain every single fact that comes to its attention. Rather, it should have some *motivation* in trying to explain a particular fact. A failure-driven approach to learning is based on the rather natural intuition that an intelligent system is motivated to learn in just those situations in which its current knowledge proves to be inadequate, as signaled by the failure of one of its expectations.

Finally, our work has resulted in the identification of four necessary extensions to the basic failure explanation algorithm, itself due to previous work in problem-solving and debugging. These are, first, the need to construct explanations for beliefs that are not explicitly justified, second, the need to consider the goals of the explanation process in deciding which explanations to pursue, third, dealing with faulted universally quantified expectations by searching for a specific counterexample, and fourth, reasoning hypothetically to determine whether the elimination of a factor that that caused an expectation failure would in fact have prevented that failure. Our analyses also provide some possible approaches to the fulfillment of these requirements.

More broadly, we believe that our theory of cross-domain transfer of learning can be applied to many problem-solving domains, and is not limited to competitive planning alone. In particular, our approach can be applied to the transfer of knowledge across a class of domains whenever an abstract representation theory can be constructed to express important principles that apply to all domains in the class. In addition to competitive planning, there are a number of other domain classes that appear to have this property. These include qualitative physical reasoning (see, e.g., Forbus, 1984), diagnostic problem-solving, and engineering design. And, finally, planning of all kinds—not only in competitive situations—seems ripe for such an approach: None of our arguments have depended, in any essential way, on the decision to focus on competitive planning in particular. We can expect, therefore, that our approach can be applied to planning in general.

Acknowledgments: The authors would like to thank Chris Riesbeck for his helpful comments on an earlier draft of this paper. We also thank Jerry DeJong, Roger Schank, and especially Kris Hammond, for many illuminating discussions on learning. Our work was supported, in part, by the Defense Advanced Research Projects Agency, monitored by the Office of Naval Research under contract N00014-85-K-0108, and by the Office of Naval Research under contract N00014-87-K-0874.

5 References

Burstein, M. 1986. Concept formation by incremental analogical reasoning and debugging. In R. Michalski, J. Carbonell, and T. Mitchell, eds., *Machine Learning: An Artificial Intelligence Approach, Vol. 2,* Morgan Kaufmann, Los Altos, CA, pp. 351-369.

Carbonell, J. 1981. *Subjective Understanding: Computer Models of Belief Systems.* UMI Research Press, Ann Arbor, MI.

Carbonell, J. 1983. Learning by analogy: Formulating and generalizing plans from past experience. In R. Michalski, J. Carbonell, and T. Mitchell, eds., *Machine Learning: An Artificial Intelligence Approach, Vol. 1,* Tioga, Palo Alto, CA, pp. 137-161.

Carbonell, J. 1986. Derivational analogy: A theory of reconstructive problem solving and expertise acquisition. In R. Michalski, J. Carbonell, and T. Mitchell, eds., *Machine Learning: An Artificial Intelligence Approach, Vol. 2,* Morgan Kaufmann, Los Altos, CA, pp. 371-392.

Collins, G. 1987. Plan creation: Using strategies as blueprints. Ph.D. thesis, Yale University, Dept. of Computer Science, New Haven, CT.

Collins, G. and Birnbaum, L. 1988. An explanation-based approach to the transfer of planning knowledge across domains. In Proceedings of the 1988 AAAI Symposium on Explanation-based Learning, Palo Alto, CA, pp. 107-111.

DeJong, G. 1981. Generalizations based on explanations. *Proceedings of the Seventh IJCAI,* Vancouver, B.C., pp. 67-70.

DeJong, G. 1983. Acquiring schemata through understanding and generalizing plans. *Proceeding of the Eighth IJCAI,* Karlsruhe, West Germany, pp. 462-464.

DeJong, G. 1986. An approach to learning from observation. In R. Michalski, J. Carbonell, and T. Mitchell, eds., *Machine Learning: An Artificial Intelligence Approach, Vol. 2,* Morgan Kaufmann, Los Altos, CA, pp. 571-590.

DeJong, G., and Mooney, R. 1986. Explanation-based learning: An alternative view. *Machine Learning,* vol. 1, pp. 145-176.

deKleer, J., Doyle, J., Steele, G., and Sussman, G. 1977. AMORD: Explicit control of reasoning. *Proceedings of the ACM Symposium on Artificial Intelligence and Programming Languages,* Rochester, NY, pp. 116-125.

Doyle, J. 1979. A truth maintenance system. *Artificial Intelligence,* vol. 12, pp. 231-272.

Forbus, K. 1984. Qualitative process theory. *Artificial Intelligence,* vol. 24, pp. 85-168.

Gentner, D. 1983. Structure-mapping: A theoretical framework for analogy. *Cognitive Science,* vol. 7, pp. 155-170.

Hammond, K. 1986. Case-based planning: An integrated theory of planning, learning, and memory. Research report no. 488, Yale University, Dept. of Computer Science, New Haven, CT.

Hayes-Roth, F. 1983. Using proofs and refutations to learn from experience. In R. Michalski, J. Carbonell, and T. Mitchell, eds., *Machine Learning: An Artificial Intelligence Approach, Vol. 1,* Tioga, Palo Alto, CA, pp. 221-240.

Kolodner, J. and Simpson, R. 1986. Problem solving and dynamic memory. In J. Kolodner and C. Riesbeck, eds., *Experience, Memory and Reasoning,* Erlbaum, Hillsdale, NJ, pp. 99-114.

Minton, S. 1984. Constraint-based generalization: Learning game-playing plans from single examples. *Proceedings of the 1984 AAAI Conference,* Austin, TX, pp. 251-254.

Mitchell, T., Keller, R., and Kedar-Cabelli, S. 1986. Explanation-based generalization: A unifying view. *Machine Learning,* vol. 1, pp. 47-80.

Mitchell, T., Utgoff, P., and Banerji, R. 1983. Learning by experimentation: Acquiring and refining problem-solving heuristics. In R. Michalski, J. Carbonell, and T. Mitchell, eds., *Machine Learning: An Artificial Intelligence Approach, Vol. 1,* Tioga, Palo Alto, CA, pp. 163-190.

Mostow, D. 1983. Machine transformation of advice into a heuristic search procedure. In R. Michalski, J. Carbonell, and T. Mitchell, eds., *Machine Learning: An Artificial Intelligence Approach, Vol. 1,* Tioga, Palo Alto, CA, pp. 367-403.

Sacerdoti, E. 1977. *A Structure for Plans and Behavior.* American Elsevier, New York.

Schank, R. 1982. *Dynamic Memory: A Theory of Reminding and Learning in Computers and People.* Cambridge University Press, Cambridge, England.

Schank, R., and Collins, G. 1982. Looking at learning. *Proceedings of the First European Conference on Artificial Intelligence,* Orsay, France, pp. 10-16.

Silver, B. 1986. Precondition analysis: Learning control information. In R. Michalski, J. Carbonell, and T. Mitchell, eds., *Machine Learning: An Artificial Intelligence Approach, Vol. 2,* Morgan Kaufmann, Los Altos, CA, pp. 647-670.

Stallman, R., and Sussman, G. 1977. Forward reasoning and dependency-directed backtracking in a system for computer-aided circuit analysis. *Artificial Intelligence,* vol. 9, pp. 135-196.

Sussman, G. 1975. *A Computer Model of Skill Acquisition.* American Elsevier, New York.

Utgoff, P. 1986. Shift of bias for inductive concept learning. In R. Michalski, J. Carbonell, and T. Mitchell, eds., *Machine Learning: An Artificial Intelligence Approach, Vol. 2,* Morgan Kaufmann, Los Altos, CA, pp. 107-148.

Wilensky, R. 1983. *Planning and Understanding: A Computational Approach to Human Reasoning.* Addison-Wesley, Reading, MA.

Winston, P., Binford, T., Katz, B., and Lowry, M. 1983. Learning physical descriptions from functional definitions, examples, and precedents. *Proceedings of the 1983 AAAI Conference,* Washington, DC, pp. 433-439.

Some Experiments With Case-based Search

Steven Bradtke
Wendy G. Lehnert
Department of Computer and Information Science
University of Massachusetts
Amherst, MA 01003

March 14, 1988

Abstract

Knowedge-based problem solvers traditionally merge knowledge about a domain with more general heuristics in an effort to confront novel problem situations intelligently. While domain knowledge is usually represented in terms of a domain model, the case-based reasoning (CBR) approach to problem solving utilizes domain knowledge in the form of past problem solving experience. In this paper we show how the CBR approach to problem solving forms the basis for a class of heuristic search techniques. Given a search space and operators for moving about the space, we can use a case-base of known problem solutions to guide us through the search. In this way, the case-base operates as a type of evaluation function used to prune the space and facilitate search. We will illustrate these ideas by presenting a CBR search algorithm as applied to the 8-puzzle, along with results from a set of experiments. The experiments evaluate 8-puzzle performance while manipulating different case-bases and case-base encoding techniques as independent variables. Our results indicate that there are general principles operating here which may be of use in a variety of applications where the domain model is weak but experience is strong.[1]

topic: Automated Reasoning
subtopic: Search
length: 3450 words, plus approximately 800 words in figures

---

[1] This research was supported by an NSF Presidential Young Investigators Award NSFIST-8351863, DARPA contract N00014-87-K-0238, and the Office of Naval Research under a University Research Initiative grant, contract N00014-86-K-0764.

1 Introduction

Case-based reasoning (CBR) systems have been designed to address a variety of task orientations including diagnostic reasoning, adaptive planning, hypothesis generation, explanation, adversarial reasoning, analogical reasoning, and hypothetical reasoning [9]. Traditionally, CBR techniques are invoked when a domain is characterized by problems that do not have right or wrong answers as much as answers that are strong or weak along various dimensions. When a novel problem is encountered, a case base of previously encountered problems and solutions is consulted to determine what experiences are relevant to the current situation. Solutions from more than one case may be merged to address the current problem, and multiple solutions are typically generated with an assessment of their respective strengths. If external feedback is provided to the system, newly solved problems can be added to the case base to strengthen it, thereby realizing a form of knowledge acquisition that is qualitatively distinct from the knowledge engineering techniques traditionally associated with rule-based systems.

In an effort to test the boundaries of CBR technology, we have applied CBR to a classic problem in heuristic search: the 8-puzzle. We have demonstrated that a heuristic search for the 8-puzzle can be conducted by accessing nothing more than a case base of previous problem solutions. For this application, the problem solutions consist of board sequences that take us from an arbitrary 8-puzzle problem state to a final goal state using legal 8-puzzle operators. No additional knowledge about subgoals ([4]), chunking ([5], [6]), or any other form of derivational abstraction ([1], [3]) is used.

We further wanted to ask questions about the construction of an effective case base, and the techniques used to index available cases in memory. Is it possible to optimize a case base? Or customize effective indices for a given case base? How can learning curves be influenced by indexing techniques or initial case bases? Although space limitations prohibit us from reporting all of our experimental results, we will describe a few of our experiments, some of which were suggested by a preliminary investigation [7]. We will also describe an index that makes it possible to generate optimal solutions for any solvable 8-puzzle state from a case base containing a single case of 31 moves.

2 The Case-based Search Algorithm

We have implemented a Case-Based Search algorithm (CBS) which attempts to transform a given problem state into a targeted final state by copying past problem solving performance. Each case in the case-base is a list of problem states from a start state to a goal state. Figure 1 shows one (very short) case consisting of four states. Note that if we were to remove the start state from any given case, we would be left with a new case showing the solution from a new start-state to the same goal state. Thus each case implicitly contains many others as sub-cases.

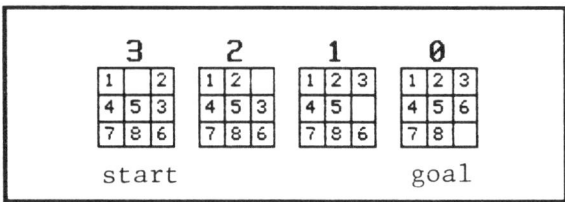

Figure 1: A Solution Case for the 8-puzzle.

CBS has a number of operations for transforming problem states. But it should only choose *good* operations, that is, operations that transform problem states into states closer to the goal state. The case-base is intended to help the system find good operations and operation sequences. However, the case-base cannot be used to store solutions for all possible start states. Even the simple 8-puzzle has 181,440 legal board positions. CBS must be able to generalize from the solutions it finds in its case-base.

Generalization from old solutions to new solutions is done in three steps.

1. CBS uses a *coarse index function* to encode the cases in the case-base. The coarse index function maps problem states onto a set of integers (or symbols), dividing the problem states into equivalence classes. It is possible for different problem states, and thus different cases (sequences of problem states) to be mapped to equivalent coarse-coded representations. In particular, it is possible for the coarse index function to place a number of problem states in the same equivalence class as the goal state. This is not a problem as long as there is a known path from each goal-equivalent state to the goal state. These paths can be pre-computed and automatically appended to any solution found by CBS as needed. The coarse index function acts like a partial pattern matcher,

relaxing similarities between structures (problem states) at the risk of allowing inappropriate matches.

2. Case-base solutions implicit in the coarse-coded case-base must be made explicit. This can be done efficiently by organizing each case in the case-base within a discrimination net. Figure 2 shows a coarse-coded case-base containing five cases, and the discrimination net that results. Every path from the dummy root node to a goal node represents a solution. Every node with no children is a goal node.

3. The final step in generalizing from old solutions to new solutions occurs during the actual search conducted for a given problem. CBS restricts exploration of the problem space by using the discrimination net described above and a masking procedure. The mask works by overlaying the discrimination net of old solutions on top of the search space generated by the given initial state. Any branches not allowed by the discrimination net are then pruned from the tree.

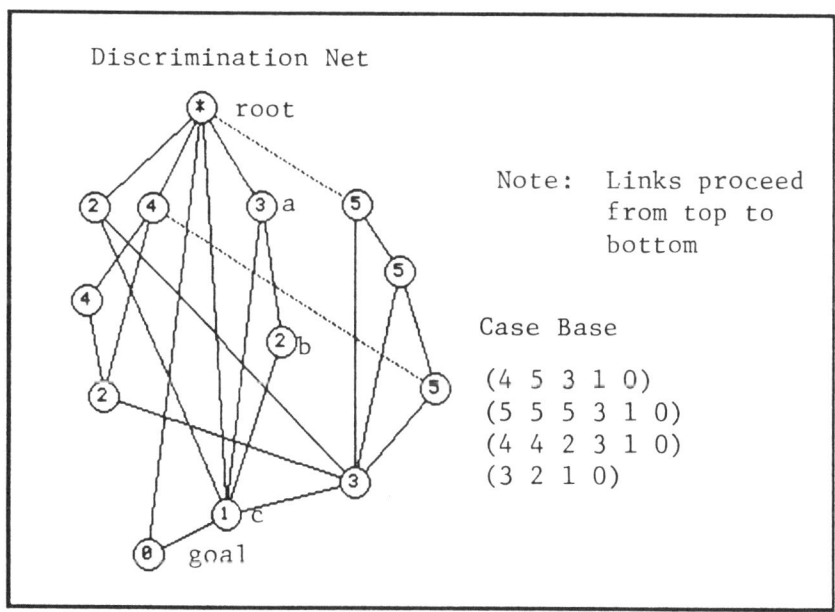

Figure 2: A Case-base and Corresponding Discrimination Net.

This masking process is best described by example. Figure 3 shows a portion of the search space reachable from a designated start state. Each node on the tree has been labelled with its coarse index value. (The actual indexing function used is not important at this time.) The tree has already been pruned so that no node is shown twice. Nodes marked (a), (b), (c), and

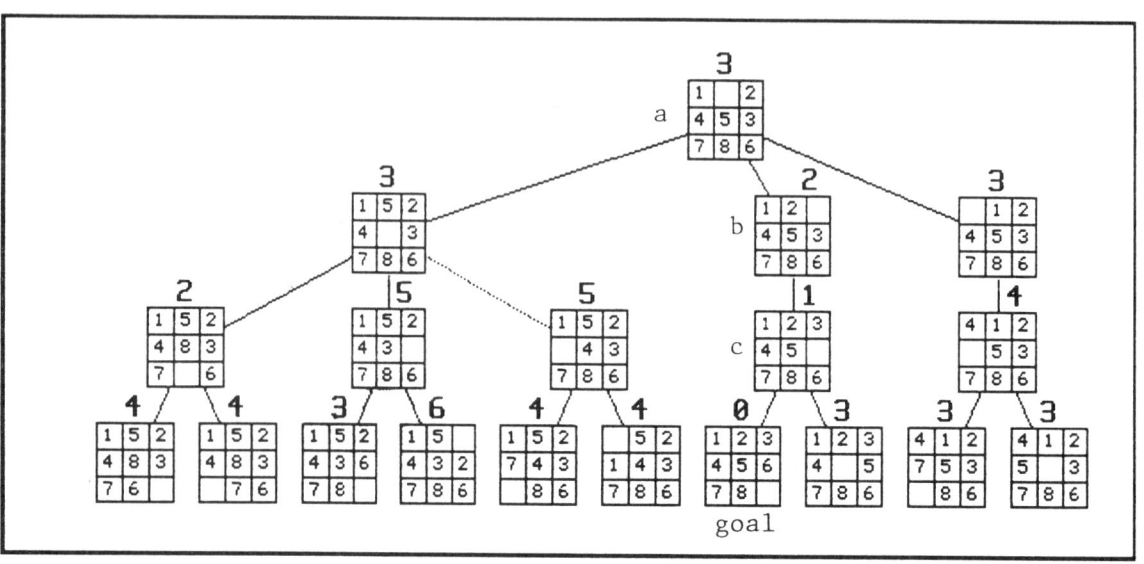

Figure 3: The Search Space Beneath a Given Problem State.

(goal) in figures 2 and 3 correspond to one another as the mask overlays the search space and the discrimination net. Example:

1. Take the index value of the current problem state. The index value of the start state is 3. Since the root node of the discrimination net has a child with index 3, move a marker from the root node to that child, labelled (a).

2. Look at the indices of the states reachable from the start state in the search space. These are 3, 2, and 3. But the only transitions allowed from our current position in the discrimination net are to states with indices 1 or 2. Therefore, the successor states with indices 3 are pruned from the search space. Move the discrimination net marker to node (b), and reset the current search space problem state to the successor with index 2.

3. Continue in this manner, moving down both the discrimination net and the problem search tree until we reach the goal node, or until we reach a point from which we cannot advance. If we reach a stuck state, we backtrack and continue until the entire search space is exhausted.

3 Overcoming an Inadequate Case-base

If we apply the mask to a search space and find a solution, we are done. But it may be possible that the experience captured in the case-base is inadequate to solve the current problem. Then the mask-directed search will fail. In this event, standard heuristic search techniques can be used to move from an unsolvable initial problem state to a new problem state that, we hope, *is* solvable using the current case-base.

In CBS, we have implemented two simple heuristics to assist inadequate casebases. The first is a "near-miss" heuristic based on neighborhoods within the search space. Let us define the N-family of a state to be the set of all states that can be obtained by application of N or fewer operators. If the masked search fails to produce a solution for the initial state, we then execute additional searches for each element of the initial state's N-family until either (1) a solution is found, or (2) the N-family is exhausted without success.

The second, "far-miss", heuristic is applied if the near-miss heuristic fails. Suppose we have conducted a near-miss search on the N-family of a state, and no solution has been located. Rather than extend the near-miss search into the (N+1)-family or (N+2)-family (increasing the size of the near-miss search space exponentially with each expansion), we apply a different modification to the initial state in order to generate a new search space. Given the initial state, we take a random walk of M legal moves. The resulting state will now serve as the basis for continued search. We first apply the case-based search to the new state, and if this search fails, we then apply an N-family near-miss search with the hope that our luck will be better in this region of the state space. We can keep alternating between the near-miss and far-miss heuristics until we have found a solution or we terminate at some predefined cutoff point.

4 Description of the Experiments

We ran a series of experiments to test CBS's performance on the 8-puzzle, given a variety of case-bases and coarse index functions. Each experiment tests system performance on finding solutions to 1000 randomly selected initial boards. The parameters M and N from the near-miss and far-miss heuristics were set to 10 and 4 for all experiments. The (mask, near-miss heuristic, far-miss heuristic) cycle was repeated until a maximum of 200 boards derived from the initial board via the near and far miss heuristics were looked at.

The cases-bases used in all experiments are summarized in table 1. The cases in the Random case-base were generated by randomly walking away from the goal state for an average of fifty moves, and then reversing the sequence of boards visited. The random walk was constrained to never repeat a state. The cases in the Human case-base were generated by presenting random board positions to a human player and recording the board sequences resulting from her solutions. The human player followed the usual strategy of breaking the problem into a sequence of subgoals, each to move the next tile into position while preserving the solutions to the previous subgoals [4]. The cases in the Perfect case-base were generated by choosing a random board and then generating and saving a minimum length solution from that position. The Random-2, Human-2, and Perfect-2 case-bases were generated in the same way, except that we tried to keep the number of *unique* boards equal instead of the *total* number of boards.

Case-base	# of cases	Total # of boards	# of unique boards
Random	21	1002	898
Human	23	1002	662
Perfect	45	1002	731
Random-2	23	1160	1009
Human-2	31	1514	1015
Perfect-2	65	1492	1016

Table 1: The case-bases.

Index function	# of classes	Size of goal class
City-block	13	1
Binary City-block	10	2
Quad City-block	9	4
Adjacency	12	1
Relaxed Adjacency	12	4
Toroidal Adjacency	15	9
Relaxed Toroidal Adjacency	11	36

Table 2: The index functions.

We used seven different index functions[2], summarized in table 2. The city-block index function computes the city-block or "Manhattan" distance from the current board to the goal board. This index has frequently been used in previous studies of heuristic search techniques using the 8-puzzle [8]. The binary city-block index is a generalization. It computes the minimum distance from the current board to the goal board and to the 180° rotation of the goal board. The quad city-block index further generalizes the city-block index by computing the minimum distance from each of the four possible rotations of the goal board.

The four adjacency indices are based on a comparison between the neighbors each tile has in the current board and the neighbors each tile would have in the goal board. Different definitions of "neighbor" give rise to the different indices. The neighborhood of a tile under the adjacency index consists of those tiles to the right and below. The neighborhood under the relaxed adjacency index consists of those tiles to the right, left, above, and below. The neighborhood under the toroidal adjacency index is the same as for the basic adjacency index, but the board is placed on a torus, so that the first row is below the third row and the first column is to the right of the third column. The neighborhood under the relaxed toroidal adjacency index is the same as for the relaxed adjacency index, but also on a torus.

5 Results

Table 3 summarizes CBS's problem solving performance over two sets of 21 experiments, each matching one of the coarse index functions against one of the Random, Human, and Perfect (Random-2, Human-2 and Perfect-2) case-bases. The parenthesized numbers are the results of the second set of experiments. System performance was measured on two criteria: the number of problems solved (out of 1000), and the average number of boards that had to be considered before finding a solution.

Analysis of the first set of experiments reveals two things.

First, as might be expected, CBS's performance depends on the number of goal equivalent states under the current coarse index function, but not all indices with the same number of goal equivalent states yield the same performance. Consider CBS's performance for a given case-base and across the coarse index functions from the city-block group. The number of problems solved rises as we move from the city-block to the binary city-block to the

---

[2] We would like to thank Dennis Kibler for his suggestions on possible index functions.

Index	Case-base	# solved	Avg. # searches
City	Random	598 (628)	87.2 (86.5)
Block	Human	385 (487)	88.1 (87.0)
	Perfect	533 (596)	87.9 (82.7)
Binary	Random	827 (863)	67.3 (65.3)
City	Human	639 (770)	80.6 (76.8)
Block	Perfect	775 (849)	73.3 (68.5)
Quad	Random	939 (943)	55.5 (46.8)
City	Human	846 (914)	66.1 (57.9)
Block	Perfect	906 (932)	62.2 (55.7)
	Random	485 (486)	93.1 (88.3)
Adjacency	Human	305 (375)	91.1 (84.1)
	Perfect	402 (483)	97.1 (90.5)
Relaxed	Random	871 (886)	66.4 (64.4)
Adjacency	Human	689 (841)	72.9 (70.6)
	Perfect	809 (899)	74.8 (63.9)
Toroidal	Random	708 (699)	79.7 (79.2)
Adjacency	Human	581 (668)	88.7 (79.3)
	Perfect	617 (745)	82.3 (79.0)
Relaxed	Random	1000 (1000)	21.9 (21.0)
Toroidal	Human	998 (1000)	31.5 (24.9)
Adjacency	Perfect	1000 (1000)	26.5 (18.3)

Table 3: Experimental Results.

quad city-block index, and the average number of searches falls. Notice that the number of goal states varies from 1 to 2 to 4. The results aren't so clean cut within the adjacency index group. The overall trend matches that within the city-block group, except that the relaxed adjacency index (with 4 goal states) leads to better performance than the toroidal adjacency index (with 9 goal states). This can be explained to some extent by noticing that the relaxed adjacency and the toroidal adjacency indices are different *kinds* of generalizations upon the basic adjacency index, while the binary and quad city-block indices are the same *kinds* of generalizations.

Second, we hypothesize that CBS's performance depends on the number of unique problem states represented in the unencoded case-base. Consider, for example, CBS's performance using the city-block index. CBS does better as we move from the Human (662 unique boards) to the Perfect (731 unique boards) to the Random (898 unique boards) case-base.

We performed the second set of experiments to test this hypothesis. The results are given in parentheses in table 3. CBS's performance for a given index function is now much more equal across the three case-bases. The remaining variations in performance may be ascribed to a combination of two factors. First, it may be that the different case-bases are more or less efficient in encoding problem solving information. The cases in the Human case-bases are constructed following an algorithm that quickly moves into a small area of the search space. It seems, then, that the human case-base would encode less of the problem solving strategy for this domain. Second, our far-miss heuristic introduces a random element which would account for some of the variation.

The striking performance of the relaxed toroidal adjacency appears to correlate with its relatively high number of goal states (36 goal states vs. an average of 3.5 goal states for the other indices). As long as we have a finite-table lookup routine that can direct us home from each of these 36 boards, we are fine. Indeed, one could argue that the overhead required to handle 36 boards is not significantly greater than the overhead associated with 4 boards, especially in view of the dramatic reduction in the number of searches required by this index. Without question, the relaxed toroidal adjacency index is superior to all other indices tested.

6 The "Perfect" Index

The "perfect" index function maps every input problem state onto a number that encodes the minimum number of moves required to transform the problem state into a goal state. Two things are apparent. First, a perfect index function needs considerable knowledge about the problem space and the current goal state. Second, access to a perfect index allows the case-based search algorithm to derive perfect hill-climbing solutions for an arbitrary problem, given an adequate case-base. Surprisingly, the minimal adequate case-base consists of a single case! That case transforms the problem state furthest from the goal into the goal state using the minimum number of operations[3]. A proof is simple. Under the perfect index, no state can have an index that differs from that of any of its neighbors by more than 1. Also, every state but the goal must have a neighboring state with a lesser index (otherwise

---

[3] Assuming that there *is* a maximally difficult problem. CBS will have difficulties performing in domains where there is no bound on the possible distance of a problem from the goal. Some mechanism to allow looping, as Carbonell uses in [2], is needed.

it would have no path to the goal). Note that it is not necessary for each state have a neighbor with a *greater* index. Under the perfect index, there may exist local maxima, but *no* local minima. Thus, any perfect case of maximum length, when abstracted by the perfect index, will contain the abstraction of every other possible minimum length solution, each of which is but a step-by-step downhill march.

Table 4 summarizes the results of an experiment testing the minimum perfect case-base hypothesis, which is shown to be correct. We used the function derived in [10] as the perfect index for the 8-puzzle. CBS displayed perfect performance while using the minimum case-base. It performed nearly as well using the Perfect case-base described in table 1. The difference in the average number of searches can be explained by the fact that it had to resort to the near-miss heuristic several times in order to find a solution. This happened because no case in the Perfect case-base covered several particularly difficult boards. It was initially surprising to see CBS perform nearly as well using the Random and Human case-bases. Again, the average number of searches was somewhat higher. In retrospect, these results are not really surprising, because they, too, follow from the argument for the existance of a minimum perfect case-base. The argument follows. Take an arbitrary solution path and encode it using the perfect index. The index profile for this case may ineffeciently wander up and down hill, but it will eventually reach zero, the index of the goal state. Since the index of every state can vary from those of its neighbors by no more than 1, any state whose index appears somewhere on the arbitrary solution path will be solvable by following a path with exactly the same index profile of the arbitrary solution, though the sequence of operators employed may be quite different.

Case-base	# solved	Avg. # searches
Random	1000	1.01
Human	1000	1.85
Perfect	1000	1.01
Minimum	1000	1.00

Table 4: Performance of the perfect index.

7 Conclusions

Given the results reported here, it appears that the most dramatic factor influencing the effectiveness of a case base is the number of unique problem states underlying the case base encoding. This explains why a case base of humanly-generated 8-puzzle solutions should be weaker than a case base of randomly generated solutions since people tend to solve the 8-puzzle by laying in the first row first, and then dealing with the remaining pieces. Once one border for the 8-puzzle has been solved, we reduce the coverage of the case base by a factor of roughly 6. This reduction is further exacerbated by the fact that the remaining boards are not distributed evenly throughout the potential search space.

In comparing competing indices, it seems that indices can trade-off different kinds of overhead against their masking hit rates. The relaxed toroidal adjacency index illustrates one such successful trade-off. Here we attain superior performance by increasing the postprocessing needed to handle 36 goal states. Since the postprocessing increase is neglible, the trade-off is quite successful.

It may also be possible to incorporate varying degrees of domain knowledge in an index. For example, the perfect index requires an extreme amount of domain knowledge (knowledge of the optimal solution lengths for all possible start states). In return, it guarantees optimal performance as long as it has access to a case base that covers the maximal solution length (31 moves for the 8-puzzle). Once domain knowledge for the perfect index has been compiled, the operation of CBS is trivial, but a substantial preprocessing overhead is required to compute this index.

In closing, we must note that CBS is not a good prototype for CBR system development in general. Because the 8-puzzle has so little domain knowledge associated with it, CBS is strictly limited to a heuristic search algorithm. This makes it impossible to merge multiple solutions from the case base, or generate multiple solutions to the current problem state that can be compared in interesting ways. Unlike most other CBR applications, answers to an 8-puzzle problem *are* either right or wrong. We must also point out that CBS cannot make any claims about psychological plausibility, whereas most CBR systems are inspired by techniques presumed to be useful in human problem solving.

While the results reported here may not provide answers to the most compelling problems of CBR system development in domain-rich applications, we believe we have made a contribution to the CBR research effort by showing how general the CBR approach to problem solving really is. We have successfully applied CBR to a classic problem in heuristic search, and have therefore extended the range the potential CBR applications beyond their previous scope.

References

[1] Jaime G. Carbonell. Derivational analogy: a theory of reconstructive problem solving and expertise acquisition. In R. S. Michalski, J. G. Carbonell, and T. M. Mitchell, editors, *Machine Learning, vol. 2*, chapter 14, Morgan Kaufmann, Los Altos, CA, 1986.

[2] Jaime G. Carbonell. The FERMI system: inducing iterative macro-operators from experience. In *Proceedings of the Fourth National Conference on Artificial Intelligence*, American Association for Artificial Intelligence, August 1985.

[3] Jaime G. Carbonell. Learning by analogy, formulating and generalizing plans from past experience. In R. S. Michalski, J. G. Carbonell, and T. M. Mitchell, editors, *Machine Learning*, chapter 5, Tioga Publishing Company, Palo Alto, CA, 1983.

[4] Richard E. Korf. Macro-operators: A weak method for learning. *Artificial Intelligence*, 26:35–77, 1985.

[5] J. Laird, A. Newell, and P. Rosenbloom. SOAR: An architecture for general intelligence. *Artificial Intelligence*, 33:1–64, 1987.

[6] J. Laird, P. Rosenbloom, and A. Newell. Towards chunking as a general learning mechanism. In *Proceedings of the Fourth National Conference on Artificial Intelligence*, pages 188–192, American Association for Artificial Intelligence, Morgan Kaufmann Publishers, Inc., 95 First Street, Los Altos, CA 94022, 1984.

[7] W. G. Lehnert. *Case-Based Reasoning as a Paradigm for Heuristic Search*. COINS 87-107, Department of Computer and Information Science, University of Massachusetts at Amherst, Amherst, MA, 1987.

[8] Nils J. Nilsson. *Principles of Artificial Intelligence*, page 85. Tioga Publishing Company, Palo Alto, CA, 1980.

[9] Edwina L. Rissland. *Research Initiative in Case-Based Reasoning*. CPTM 17, Department of Computer and Information Science, University of Massachusetts at Amherst, Amherst, MA 01003, 1987.

[10] Paul Utgoff and Sharad Saxena. *A Perfect Lookup Table Evaluation Function for the Eight-Puzzle*. COINS 87-71, Department of Computer and Information Science, University of Massachusetts at Amherst, Amherst, MA 01003, 1987.

The Role of Explanation in Reasoning from Legal Precedents[1]

L. Karl Branting   lkarlb@pheasant.cs.utexas.edu

*Department of Computer Sciences,
University of Texas, Austin, TX 78712*

Abstract

A computational model for the process of reasoning from legal precedents to new cases is outlined in which legal concepts consist of the facts of precedent cases together with explanations for the satisfaction of the concept by each case. Classification of new cases is accomplished by coercing the explanation structure of a precedent classification onto the new case. Techniques for representing and mapping explanation structures are presented.

1 Introduction

Much of legal reasoning can be described as the task of determining whether a given set of facts is an instance of a legal concept. For example, determining whether one party is liable to another for negligence is equivalent to determining whether the facts of the case are an instance of the concept *negligence liability*. Legal reasoning is thus a form of classification. To a greater extent than in more familiar forms of classification, such as taxonomic classification or diagnosis, a significant part of expertise in law consists of creating, anticipating, and weighing the persuasiveness of arguments for and against a given classification. This process is heavily dependent upon reasoning from precedent cases.

In order to describe the role of reasoning from precedent cases in legal problem solving, it is necessary both to outline the general process of legal reasoning and to describe the nature of precedent cases themselves. It will be argued that much of the value of a case in is the chain of reasoning employed in explaining its classification. Techniques for representing and re-using detailed explanations are therefore critical to a computational model of precedential reasoning in law.

2 The Process of Legal Reasoning

Many of the characteristic activities of attorneys, including advocacy, legal planning, adjudication, and answering law school and bar examination questions share a common pattern. The *analytical legal reasoning* model is a proposed information processing model for this ubiquitous form of legal reasoning.

The input to the process typically consists of two basic elements. The first is a set of facts, usually in the form of a *narrative history*: a sequence of related events, together with any contextual or background information necessary to understand the events. The second component of the input is an *analysis goal*, which specifies the analytical task to be

---

[1] Support for this research was provided by the Army Research Office under grant number ARO DAAG29-84-K-0060.

accomplished by the reasoner. An analysis goal consists of a set of relationships, termed *goal* relationships, whose applicability to some subset of the actors in the narrative is to be determined.

The analytical reasoning process itself consists of three steps. The first is *legal situation recognition*, the process of identifying sequences of events from the narrative history that might satisfy a given legal theory, such as negligence or worker's compensation. The matching involves instantiating an abstract story or schema that corresponds to the legal theory [O'Neil 87] [Hastie & Pennington 86]. The potential legal claims recognized by an attorney are those associated with a theory for which the corresponding schema has been instantiated.

The second step, *rule decomposition*, is the process of repeatedly applying statutory or common-law rules until the goal relationship has been completely re-expressed in terms of legal relationships to which no more legal rules are applicable. Legal relationships to which no legal rules are applicable are "open textured." Any open-textured legal relationships that are neither clearly satisfied nor clearly unsatisfied by the instantiated story are *issues* in the analysis.

The final step is *argument construction*, the process of creating and evaluating plausible explanations for the satisfaction or non-satisfaction of legal relationships at issue under the analysis. Plausible arguments are constructed by mapping the explanations associated with relevant exemplars—generally precedent cases, but possibly paradigmatic hypotheticals [Christie 69]—onto the new case. If the instantiated story is incomplete, as it usually will be, the reasoning in precedent cases will indicate what facts must be established if the case is to share relevant similarities with a given precedent.

The primary focus of our research[2] is on the third of these steps. A central research hypothesis is that case-based reasoning about whether a set of facts falls within a legal category requires, in general, determining whether there is an exemplar of the category such that the explanation associated with the exemplar is applicable to the given facts without extensive modification.

3 Category Structure and Classification

Classification with respect to open-textured legal concepts resists formalization because of the absence of any deductive scheme capable of deciding whether an arbitrary factual situation satisfies a given open-textured concept [Moore 81]. How then is it possible to automate problem solving with open-textured concepts?

The approach that we have adopted is to draw directly from the experience of Protos [Bareiss et al.], a learning apprentice for heuristic classification with a demonstrated capacity to perform at expert levels in domains characterized by ill-defined and polymorphic categories.

Protos performs classification in two steps. When a new case is input, Protos heuristically combines *remindings* compiled from past explanations, and uses the strongest reminding to select an exemplar. The similarity of the new case to the exemplar is then evaluated by attempting to construct an explanation of featural equivalence between the cases.

---

[2]Participants in the AI and legal reasoning project at The University of Texas Department of Computer Sciences include Bruce Porter, Rich Mallory, Neil Cohen, and the author. All but Bruce Porter were attorneys in their former lives.

The development of Protos was guided by a body of psychological literature indicating that few natural concepts conform to what is now termed the *classsical* model of a concept as a conjunction of necessary and sufficient attributes [Smith & Medin 81]. Discovery of phenomena inconsistent with the classical model, including the absence of known classical definitions for most objects, the existence of unclear or borderline cases, the common use of non-necessary properties in classification, and typicality effects, led to the proposal of alternative concept models.

In one such alternative model, termed the *exemplar* model, a concept is defined extensionally as consisting of distinct representations of some or all of its exemplars. Under this model, classification is performed by comparing the features of new cases with those of exemplars of relevant categories.

The exemplar and other prototype-based concept models are free from many of the problems observed with the classical model, but they do not in themselves account for the coherence of concepts [Murphy & Medin 85]. An understanding of why some collections of entities seem to form meaningful and useful categories whereas others seem absurd or useless is essential for classifying new instances. Unless it is known why a concept has a given set of instances, neither reliable classification with respect to the concept nor cogent justification for classifications will be possible.

The category model adopted by Protos steers a middle course between a purely intentional concept model, such as the classical model, and a purely extensional exemplar model. Protos retains both a featural representation of each exemplar of a category and an explanation of the relevance of each feature of the exemplar to the category. Categories are structured by a network of domain knowledge derived directly from explanations provided by the teacher, together with embedded exemplars.

Protos has demonstrated expert level performance in the domain of clinical audiology despite the polymorphy of diagnostic categories. Such performance is possible because retained explanations provide a domain theory for evaluating featural similarities between new cases and old. The experience of Protos strongly argues for a model of legal concepts that includes precedent cases, explanations for the resolution of the issues in those cases, and sufficient domain theory to support construction of explanations for new cases.

4 Explanation Generation vs. Explanation Re-use

It has been observed that it is the relevance and significance, not just the quantity, of similarities between a new case and a previous case that determines whether the classification of the previous case is applicable to the new one [Murray 82]. This obervation emphasizes that legal precedents are more than just a collection of facts and a legal categorization. Precedent cases also represent a bundled package of reasoning which may be applicable to future cases.

The central importance of the explanations associated with precedent cases has been recognized in the literature of legal philosophy. For example, [Raz 79] states that reasoning by analogy to past cases is "essentially an argument to the effect that if a certain reason is good enough to justify one rule, then it is equally good to justify another ...." In a similar vein, [Murray 82] observes that if a new case "furthers the same purposes of, or is justified by, the same factors as [a prior case], then the analogy is significant." Somewhat more bluntly, [Golding 80] states that "[I]t is only because explicit reasons are given for ... earlier decisions that they are of any use for later cases."

Although the success of Protos in reasoning with category structures embodying both exemplars and explanations suggests that the Protos paradigm is the logical approach to modeling open-textured concepts and argument construction, in one important respect the design of Protos is inappropriate for legal reasoning. Although Protos retains explanations of past classifications, explanations for new cases are generated dynamically. No problem arose from dynamic explanation generation in the domain of clinical audiology, because the domain theory of audiology is considerably less complicated than that of law. The search space for explanations of category membership is tractable because adequate explanations in audiology are seldom very complicated.

In law, by contrast, the explanation of satisfaction of a legal relationship by a given factual situation can be very complex. As a result, the search space for possible legal arguments is apparently intractable. Moreover, it seems to us that attorneys seldom generate such explanations from whole cloth. Instead, an argument for, or explanation of, a legal classification is generally a modification of a past explanation of category membership.

The challenge presented by legal reasoning is therefore to extend the Protos paradigm by explicitly associating explanation structures with precedent cases and by showing how these explanation structures can be used to reason about new cases. The recognition that explanation structures of legal precedents must be re-used is consistent with the analysis of re-use of everyday explanations in [Schank 86].

Research thus far has focused on investigating the analytical legal reasoning framework described in Section 2, developing a computational model of the explanation structures of legal opinions, and modeling the process of mapping explanations for the resolution of issues in a precedent onto new factual situations. The next step will be to construct a case library spanning a small legal domain. We plan then to construct a system for applying plausible arguments drawn from the library of precedents to new factual situations.

The next section presents an example from the domain of worker's compensation law that illustrates some of the techniques we have used for representing explanation structures in precedent cases and mapping them onto new cases.

5 Explanation Structures in Legal Opinions

The domain of law is unique in having explicit, official explanations of the classification of cases with respect to legal categories. Such official explanations are embodied in judicial opinions, the written justifications for legal judgments. Expressed in terms of the analytical legal reasoning model, the elements of a legal opinion include the following:

- a narrative history

- a rule decomposition of the goal relationships of the case

- explanations for the evaluation of *nondecomposable relationships* (those to which no further statutory or common law rules are applicable) in terms of the facts of the narrative history.

A formal model of the explanation structure of a legal opinions must be capable of representing each of these elements.

A typical worker's compensation case involving transportation with both personal and business purposes which we have studied is *Janak v. Texas Employers Ins. Assoc.*, 381 S.W.2d 176 (1964). The facts of *Janak* can be briefly summarized as follows:

Janak was employed as an oil driller in central Texas. Because the job entailed strenuous work under sunny and hot conditions, it was customary for the oil drillers to bring ice to the job site to chill water for drinking. No ice was available on the direct route from Janak's home to the work site, so on the day of the accident Janak took an indirect route that led by a store that sold ice. After he purchased the ice, but before he rejoined the direct route, Janak was involved in an accident.

Briefly summarized, the court in *Janak* held that Janak's injuries were compensable under worker's compensation because they occurred "in the course of" Janak's employment. Injuries occurring during transportation are ordinarily excluded from compensation, but an exception exists if the employee is "directed in his employment" to travel as he did. The court found that there was sufficient evidence for the jury to have found that Janak was implicitly directed to take the detour to get ice, because ice was "reasonably essential for" the continuance of the drilling activities, given the hot conditions and the strenuous nature of the job.

5.1 Explanation representation

The first element of the explanation structure of *Janak* is the representation of the events of the case, which requires representing habitual and anticipated actions and a network of goals and plans. We have adopted a semantic network representation that includes activities, states, individuals, collections, and "action sequence categories," exemplar-based categories of event sequences graded by typicality, similar to the E-MOP's described in [Schank 82]. Links between nodes include causal, temporal, and intentional links.

The second element of the explanation structure is a representation of the rule decomposition of the goal relationship of *Janak*, that is, the set of statutory and common law rules that the court used to justify its decision. For each step in the decomposition, it is necessary to identify the following items:

- the relationship being decomposed

- the applicable rule

- the authority for the rule

- the instantiation of the rule's antecedents by the facts of the case.

These items, which correspond to the conclusion, warrant, backing, and data, respectively, in Toulmin's [Toulmin] model of argument structure, are linked to a *rule explanation node*.

The third element of the explanation structure of an opinion is the representation of explanations for nondecomposable relationships. Thus far, we have identified two types of explanation nodes in addition to rule explanation nodes useful for representing such relationships. The first, termed an *ordinal* explanation node, provides an explanation for *variable standards* [Gardner 85] such as the concept "reasonably essential for" in *Janak*. Such concepts can be explained by the dimension (*cf.*, [Rissland & Ashley 87]) over which the standard ranges—in this case criticality—together with a partial ordering of examples and some explanation for the values along the dimension of the examples. For example, the court in *Janak* contrasted the facts of the case with two hypotheticals. The court observed

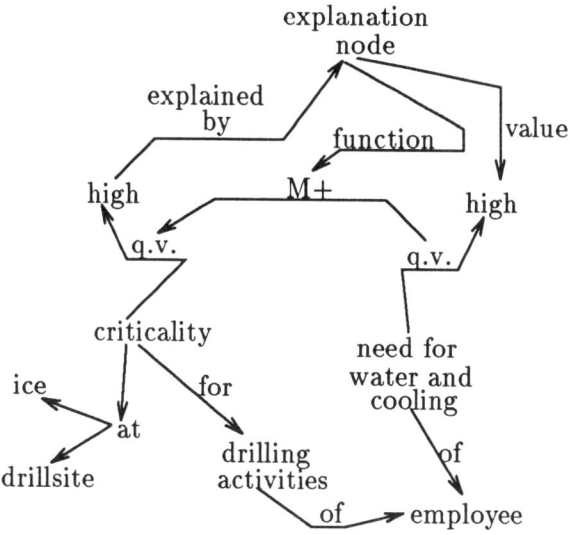

Figure 1: Explanation of the high criticality of ice

that had the deviation been for the purpose of obtaining tools essential to the drilling operation, the travel would "clearly [have been] impliedly directed by the employer", whereas if the deviation had been for the purpose of buying a particular kind of hamburger for lunch, the travel would clearly not have been "impliedly directed" by the employer. *Janak*, 381 P.2d at 182. Ice to chill drinking water falls somewhere in between these extremes.

A second form of explanation node is necessary to represent the explanation of qualitative values ("q.v.'s"), such as the high criticality of ice or the low criticality of a particular kind of hamburgers, upon which the partial ordering of examples depends. Such nodes, termed *qualitative valuation* nodes, explain qualitative values by showing their functional dependency [Kuipers 84] upon other qualitative values. For example, Figure 1 represents an explanation for the qualitative value of the criticality of ice by means of a qualitative valuation node. The criticality of ice for the drilling activities of the employees is explained by the high qualitative value for the employee's water and cooling needs, together with the functional dependency of the criticality of ice upon those needs.

The functional dependency between the criticality of ice and the need for water and cooling in Figure 1 is explained by a common sense rule of amelioration. In terms of the facts of *Janak*, the rule is that the hotter and thirstier an employee performing an employment activity is, the more critical drinking cool water is to the employment activity. The core functional relationships underlying this explanation are shown in Figure 2. The general form of the rule is that if the value of a parameter (e.g., water and cooling need) reduces the effectiveness of activity1 (e.g., drilling) and some activity2 (e.g., drinking cool water) reduces the value of the parameter (e.g., reduces water and cooling need), then the degree of criticality of activity2 is a direct function of the value of the parameter.

A rule of this nature is not likely to be made explicit in a judicial opinion because the importance of reducing states that interfere with desirable activities is both painfully obvious and difficult to articulate at an appropriate level of abstraction: it is "just commonsense". At the same time, applying this rule is the crucial step in justifying the criticality

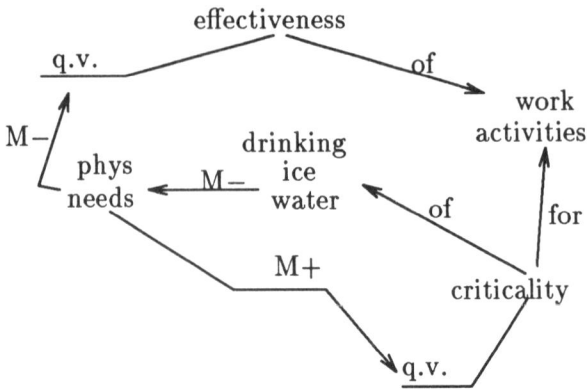

Figure 2: Functional explanation for the dependency between criticality of ice and physiological needs

of ice to Janak's job activities.

The two M− relationships in Figure 2 are explained by naive physiological knowledge, of which a sketch is set forth in Figure 3. The figure indicates that the qualitative value of certain physiological needs (such as thirst) is increased by work activities and increases spontaneously over time. The value of such needs is decreased, however, by need satisfaction activities (such as drinking water). Such needs, in turn, decrease the effectiveness of the work activities of the employee who experiences them. The spectrum of possible values of this diminution of effectiveness ranges from no impairment to death.

5.2 Explanation mapping

How can the explanation structure of a precedent case be applied to a new case? Suppose that our system is presented with a new case:

> M is a maintenance man whose job includes keeping various machinery in good repair. On arriving at work one day, M is told that a certain machine needs work, but he discovers that he has left his socket wrench at home. M has a crescent wrench, but he knows from past experience that he will be able to perform the job much more quickly and efficiently with socket wrench. He therefore decides to drive back home to get it. On the way, M is involved in an accident and injured.

Does M have a worker's compensation claim? The first step in analyzing the new case is the rule decomposition of the goal relationship, worker's compensation liability. Under one possible rule decomposition, the main issue will be whether the socket wrench was reasonably essential for the performance of M's job, an issue for which *Janak* is a precedent. The task of the system will therefore be to coerce *Janak's* explanation for "reasonably esssential for" onto the new case.

The ordinal explanation node of the *Janak* explanation structure represents that "reasonably essential for" is a variable standard ranging over criticality. We are given that the use of a socket wrench increases the effectiveness of M's employment activity by some significant amount. A successful analysis will relate the increase of effectiveness caused by

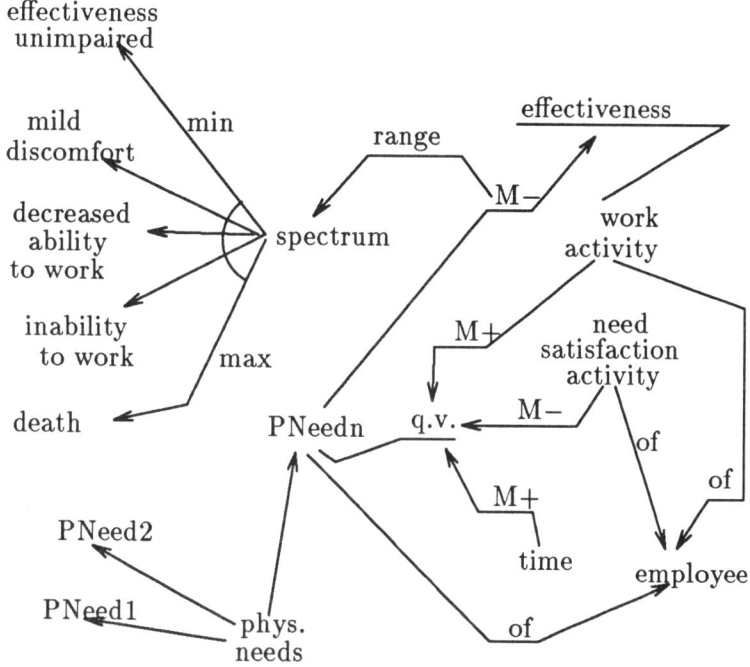

Figure 3: Naive model of the relationships between physiological needs and work

use of the wrench to the wrench's criticality. Under such an analysis, evidence that the wrench would increase of job effectiveness will tend to establish that the socket wrench was therefore reasonably essential to the job activities.

In the *Janak* explanation structure, drinking iced water reduces physiological needs—thirst and excessive warmth—that interfere with job effectiveness. When such physiological needs are high, drinking iced water increases efficiency. Indeed, as represented in Figure 2, the higher the physiological needs, the greater the increase in job effectiveness over what it would have been without the iced water, and the greater the criticality of ice to the employment activities. Ice was reasonably essential to the job activities because the heat and strenuousness of the job made these physiological needs high.

Given that the physiological needs were high in *Janak*, the connection between need satisfaction activities and effectiveness shown in Figure 2 can be simplified to a single M+: drinking iced water increased job performance. Thus, we have a case where a state (having ice) has high criticality because it is a prerequisite for an activity (drinking iced water) that increases job effectiveness. Moreover, there is a direct connection between the increase in job performance and the degree of criticality. Figure 4 shows this simplified explanation applied to the hypothetical case.

The increase in job effectiveness caused by using a socket wrench has been substituted for the effect of drinking water, and Δ, the amount of the increase in efficiency resulting from using the wrench, has been substituted for the qualitative value of physiological needs, which determine how much drinking water can improve drilling performance. The result is a modified explanation structure that can entitle one to say that, under the reasoning of *Janak*, evidence that the socket wrench could greatly improve job efficiency would tend

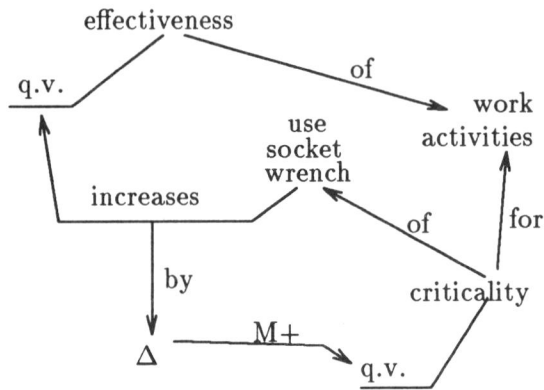

Figure 4: Transformed explanation applied to hypothetical

to establish that the socket wrench was reasonably essential to the performance of M's job duties. This, in turn, would establish that transportation to obtain the wrench was in furtherance of those duties.

6 Conclusion

We have argued that a case is more than just a set of facts. A case is also a bundle of explanations that can be applied to future situations. Recognizing a new case means not just matching its features to those of a former case, but forcing a match between a known explanation and new facts. This requires both retention of explanations and a sufficiently detailed domain theory to support extensive mutations of explanations to accomodate new situations that differ significantly from past experience.

References

[Bareiss et al.]   Bareiss, E.R., Porter, B.W., and Wier, C.C. *Protos: An Exemplar-Based Learning Apprentice.* Proceedings of the Fourth International Workshop on Machine Learning, University of California at Irvine, 1987.

[Christie 69]   Christie, G.C. *Objectivity in Law.* 78 Yale L.J. 1311–1350, 1969.

[Gardner 85]   Gardner, A.L., *An Artificial Intelligence Approach to Legal Reasoning.* Ph.D. dissertation, Stanford University, 1985.

[Golding 80]   Golding, M.P. *Legal Reasoning*, pp. 15–16. Commission on Undergraduate Education in Law and the Humanities of the American Bar Association, 1980.

[Hart 58]   Hart, H.L.A. *Positivism and the Separation of Law and Morals.* 71 Harvard Law Review 593–629, 1958.

[Hastie & Pennington 86]   Hastie, R. and Pennington, N. *Evidence Evaluation in Complex Decision Making.* 51 Journal of Personality and Social Psychology No. 2, 242-258, 1986.

[Kuipers 84]   Kuipers, B.J. *Commonsense reasoning about causality: deriving behavior from structure.* 24 Artificial Intelligence 169–204, 1984.

[McCarty & Sridharan 82]   McCarty, L.T. and Sridharan, N.S. *A Computational Theory of Legal Argument* LRP-TR-13. Laboratory for Computer Science Research, Rutgers University, 1982.

[Moore 81]   Moore, M.S. *The Semantics of Judging.* 54 Southern California Law Review 151-294, 1981.

[Murphy & Medin 85]   Murphy, G. and Medin, D.L. *The Role of Theories in Conceptual Coherence.* 92 Psychological Review 289-316, 1985.

[Murray 82]   Murray, J.L. *The Role of Analogy in Legal Reasoning.* 29 UCLA Law Rev. 833–871, 852, 870, 1983.

[O'Neil 87]   O'Neil, D.P. *A Process Specification of Expert Lawyer Reasoning.* Proceedings of the First International Conference on A.I. and Law, 1987.

[Raz 79]   Raz, J. *The Authority of Law*, p. 204. Oxford: Clarendon Press, 1979.

[Schank 86]   Schank, R.C. *Explanation Patterns.* Hillsdale, N.J.: Lawrence Erlbaum Associates, 1986.

[Schank 82]   Schank, R.C. *Dynamic Memory.* Cambridge University Press, 1982.

[Smith & Medin 81]   Smith, E.E. and Medin, D.L. *Categories and Concepts.* Cambridge, MA: Harvard University Press, 1981.

[Toulmin 58]   Toulmin, S.E. *The Uses of Argument.* Cambridge University Press, 1958.

[Rissland & Ashley 87]   Rissland, E.L. and Ashley, K.D. *HYPO: A Case-Based Reasoning System.* Project Memo 18, The COUNSELOR project, Department of Computer and Information Sciences, University of Massachusetts, 1987.

Integrating derivational analogy into a general problem solving architecture*

Jaime Carbonell
Manuela Veloso
Computer Science Department
Carnegie Mellon University
Pittsburgh, PA 15213

March 1988

Abstract

True expertise requires knowledge-intensive reasoning as a primary mental activity and a fallback to general problem solving in order to bridge gaps in the domain knowledge or to handle otherwise unexpected situations. This paper unites derivational analogy, a form of case-based reconstructive reasoning driven by rich episodic knowledge, with a general problem solving and planning architecture. The primary learning mechanism consists of extracting and organizing derivational traces of search-intensive problem solving episodes augmented with (and indexed by) explicit justification paths of success and failure conditions. This store of new episodic case knowledge drives the derivational analogy machinery in subsequent reasoning about problems that share substantial parts of the justification structure. The method is being implemented in the PRODIGY problem solving system and demonstrated in the domain of linear algebra.

---

*This research was supported in part by ONR grants N00014-79-C-0661 and N0014-82-C-50767, DARPA contract number F33615-84-K-1520, and NASA contract NCC 2-463. The views and conclusions contained in this document are those of the authors alone and should not be interpreted as representing the official policies, expressed or implied, of the U.S. Government, the Defense Advanced Research Projects Agency or NASA.

1. Introduction

The central dream of many AI researchers, present authors included, is the construction of a general purpose learning and reasoning system that given basic axiomatic knowledge of a chosen domain lifts itself up to expert performance through practice solving increasingly complex problems. A small step toward that dream is the development of methods for encapsulating past experience into richly indexed episodic structures that help to avoid past mistakes and enable the reasoner to repeat and generalize past success. In general, we wish to compile past search-intensive behavior into increasingly knowledge-intensive reasoning in the chosen domain, all the while retaining the safety net of the general problem solver.

Whereas classical AI techniques for problem solving and planning require vast amounts of search to produce viable solutions for even moderately complex problems, humans typically require much less search as they accrue experience over time in any given domain. Inspired by this ubiquitous observation, researchers in various subdisciplines of AI sought methods of encapsulating more knowledge to reduce search, ranging from expert systems, where all knowledge is laboriously handcoded at the outset, to machine learning approaches, where incrementally accumulated experience is stored, processed and compiled into generalized reusable "chunks".

The machine learning approaches typically start with a general problem solving engine and accumulate experience in the process of solving problems the hard way (via extensive search), or via demonstrations of viable solutions by an external (human) teacher. The knowledge acquired can take many forms:

- Memorized actual instance solutions annotated with intermediate problem solving states (such as subgoal trees, causes of intermediate planning failure, justifications for each selected planning step, etc.). These are used in analogical reasoning [2,3] and case-based reasoning [7,12,14,31,32] to reduce search by using the solutions of similar past problems to guide the planner in constructing the solution to the new problem.

- Reformulated left-hand-sides of operators and inference rules, where the new left-hand-sides are stated in terms of "operational" or initial-state conditions so as to facilitate their selection and application. This is one typical output of explanation-based learning systems [6,20,25,26].

- Explicit control rules (or meta rules) that guide the selection of domain-level subgoals, operators or inference rules in the planning process. These may also be generated by the explanation-based learning process when the basic architecture of the problem solver itself is axiomatized and available to the learning module, along with the domain theory [20,21].

- Macro-operators composed of sequences of domain-level operators which, if applicable, take "large steps" in the problem space and thereby reduce search [1,5,8,15,19]. In essence, intermediate decisions corresponding to steps internal to each macro-op are bypassed, in the construction of a parameterized fragment of the proven solution path into a macro-op.

- Generalized "chunking" of all decisions taken by the problem solver, including goal selection, operator selection and other impasse-driven decisions that required search. The output of these internal decisions are at once compiled into new chunks by a background reflex process and become immediately available to the problem solver's recognition process [17,28].

All of these methods seek to compile existing domain knowledge into more effective form by combining it with search control knowledge acquired through incremental practice. In essence, the idea is to transform book knowledge into practical knowledge that can be applied much more readily, occasionally compromising generality for efficiency of application, but retaining the initial knowledge as a safety net.

Analogy and case-based reasoning are two sides of the same proverbial coin: both rely on encapsulating episodic knowledge to guide complex problem solving, but the former emphasizes the process of modifying, adapting and verifying past derivations (cases), whereas the latter emphasizes the organization, hierarchy indexing and retrieval of case memory. This paper focuses on the smooth integration of derivational analogy into a general purpose problem solving and planning architecture, the PRODIGY system [22]. Whereas both derivational analogy and generalized operator-based planning have been developed and reported previously, never have the twain been totally integrated into a functional and demonstratable system. The integration requires that the general problem solver be able to introspect into its internal decision cycle, recording the justifications for each decision (what subgoal to pursue next, what operator to apply, and what objects to select as variable bindings for each operator). These justifications augment the solution trace and are used both for indexing and to guide the future reconstruction of the solution for subsequent problem solving situations where equivalent justifications hold true.

We now present the overall structure of a general system and we motivate the need for justifications in case-based learning through derivational analogy.

2. The overall picture

The work reported here integrates case-based analogical reasoning into PRODIGY, a general search-intensive problem solver. Episodic knowledge, when applicable, is used to bypass classical search. The knowledge sources in PRODIGY consist of:

- static domain knowledge - a conceptualization of the underlying predicates and objects in the domain in axiomatic form.

- working domain knowledge - a description of the legal actions in the domain, namely in terms of a set of operators, inference rules, and heuristic control rules.

- solvable classes of problems - a categorization of general problems capable of being solved using the static and working domain knowledge.

- episodic knowledge library - a collection of cases and generalization thereof to draw from in derivational analogy, currently under continued development.

These three basic (and one episodic) knowledge sources provide a consistent store of information to be used by the learning module.

The non-episodic portion of PRODIGY's domain knowledge is specified in terms of a set of operators, inference rules, and control rules. The episodic knowledge is encoded as a set of derivational traces with justifications links among the reasoning steps so that the same reasoning strategy can be reconstructed or modified to solve related problems. Moreover, in order to draw meaningful analogies for problem solving, we believe it is necessary to make explicit the underlying reasons for the presence of certain predicates in the non-episodic knowledge as well. That is, a certain amount of higher level knowledge is required so that the problem solver can explain to itself why a retrieved case was (or was not) successful, and thereby know how to modify it to the requirements of the new problem.

This kind of fundamental knowledge is useful even for well known toy domains, let alone areas of realistic expertise. As an example, consider the well known operator PUT-DOWN from the blocks world [8] (see Figure 1).

```
(PUT-DOWN
 (params (<ob>))
 (preconds
   (and
     (object <ob>)
     (holding <ob>)))
 (effects
   ((del (holding <ob>))
    (add (clear <ob>))
    (add (on-table <ob>)))))
```

Figure 1: The PUT-DOWN operator from the blocks world

We can come up with several justifications at different levels of abstraction on why this operator achieves the effects. These justifications can range from specific properties of the object, e.g. being a solid block, to general assumptions, e.g. the presence of Earth gravity. Testing these assumptions may not be relevant at all in the problems that a system was designed to solve. However this implicit information might be crucial when the system is asked to solve problems from a slightly different analog domain, and these causal links to general knowledge are particularly relevant for learning by analogy between far-apart domains or between far-apart classes of problems. As an example, imagine that the system is asked to learn how to solve problems of manipulating blocks in an orbiting space station. (Without gravity, PUT-DOWN will not achieve its goal, as the block will not drop from the hand, nor stay where placed.) However, stacking wooden blocks or plastic ones, or doing so on Tuesday rather than Thursday are probably immaterial differences. In brief, causal justification links bypass the the old frame problem [24] for analogical reasoning by explicitly encoding the limits of justifiability for the initial solution. Other domains within those limits ought to permit direct transfer, but domains outside those limits will require at least local replanning to establish the same effects by other means.

We are aware that unexpected situations may occur (consider a solid block of ice that melts when you hold it for a while...) and that even an elaborated initial set of justifications could prove incomplete. Here we advocate experimentation [4] as the learning tool to use in case the system runs out of consistent alternatives. Experimentation will be used not only to refine incomplete and incorrect knowledge but also to refine the internal justifications. This approach allows the system to be flexible enough so as not to require an exaggerated initial effort in getting the full justifications at every level of abstraction.

3. The basic analogical replay method

We now present the general method of analogical replay process and case learning mechanism in PRODIGY.

- A teacher introduces a problem and guides the planner through its different alternatives while constructing the solution. This process produces the initial entries into the case library. Subsequence sources for analogy can come from the case library (teacher or system-generated solutions). This initial guidance provided by the teacher is done at three different levels:
    1. choice of the next subgoal to work on from the current set of goals,
    2. choice of the operator or inference rules to apply to achieve a particular goal,
    3. choice of particular bindings for the variables.

  The key fact for this step is that the teacher presents *justifications* for her/his choices. In section 6 we formalize these justifications and in section 7 we present how they are used by the learner. The problem and the solution path are stored together with the related justifications.

- Upon demand to solve a new problem, PRODIGY considers its exiting case library of previously solved problems. The generation of the new solution is guided by the justifications that affect the steps of past solution paths. Conservatism (minimal change of the retrieved solution) is an emergent property of this method, as search for alternative methods of solving a problem is only triggered when an exiting method fails (i.e., no analogy is found, or there is no way to repair a failed justification in the retrieved case).

- The new solution is stored in the episodic case library, along with its complete set of justifications, and used as a candidate analog for future problem solving. Methods for producing packed encoding for solution derivations to related problems that share substantial substructure offer promise to keep memory requirements if not modest, at least tractable.

- Generalization methods apply to collections of derivational traces (i.e. cases) with the same analog parentage, in order to produce a generalized plan for such commonly recurring problems, whereas those problems with few if any analogs continue to retain their full derivational traces as ground-instance cases.

4. An example from elementary linear algebra

Case-based or analogical reasoning works equally well whether one focuses on expert system domains (such as factory scheduling), robotic planning problems, toy domains (such as the blocks world), mundane domains (selection of recepies) or mathematical reasoning. Here we have selected the latter one, in part to be different from other projects. In particular, we focus on the familiar domain of linear algebra, such as Gaussian elimination, Jordan elimination, coping with truncation errors, solving systems of n equations with n unknowns, inversion of matrices, etc. [10].

4.1. The initial state representation

To start the problem solving process, let the initial state be any well defined matrix, and let final (desired) state be a particular configuration of that matrix. As a concrete example, consider the following system of equations shown using matrix representation as $Ax = b$,

$$\underbrace{\begin{bmatrix} 2 & -1 & 3 \\ 1 & 2 & -2 \\ 4 & 1 & 2 \end{bmatrix}}_{A} \underbrace{\begin{bmatrix} x_1 \\ x_2 \\ x_3 \end{bmatrix}}_{x} = \underbrace{\begin{bmatrix} 2 \\ 1 \\ -3 \end{bmatrix}}_{b}$$

The initial state given to PRODIGY that represents this problem has two predicates:

mat with attributes *row*, *column*, and *value*; the predicate (mat 2 3 -2) is true if the matrix element $A(2,3)$ has the value -2.

dimension with attributes the number of *rows* and *columns*.

For the example given above, the initial state is the matrix $[A|b]$ corresponding to the following set of formulas:

        (dimension 3 4)
        (mat 1 1 2)   (mat 1 2 -1)   (mat 1 3 3)   (mat 1 4 2)
        (mat 2 1 1)   (mat 2 2 2)   (mat 2 3 -2)   (mat 2 4 1)
        (mat 3 1 4)   (mat 3 2 1)   (mat 3 3 2)   (mat 3 4 -3).

To perform Gaussian elimination in this matrix the goal is stated in terms of a predicate *(triangular upper)* that must be true in the final state (matrix).

4.2. The original search tree

When there is no previous case for guidance, PRODIGY generates an augmented *and-or* search tree. If there is a previous case its derivation consists of a successful path through the (earlier) search tree, and analogical problem solving consists of modifying that path (expanding small portions of the search tree) when justifications required in the retrieved derivation are not valid for the new problem situation.

We should note an important difference between PRODIGY and previous problem solvers (such as STRIPS [8], NOAH [30], NASL [18], etc.), where all variables were assumed to be existentially quantified. PRODIGY also permits universally quantified variables as well (with the quantifier in the precondition part of an operator [23]). These are exploited to the hilt in large domains containing regular structure. We introduce a new kind of node in the tree, the *forall-node*. This node has three fields: the list of bound variables (V), the generator (G), and the subexpression (E). As an example, consider the operator TRIANGULIZE in Figure 4. Node 5 in Figure 5 is a forall-node. It is expanded into its children nodes 6, 7, 8, and 9. In the process of constructing a solution by analogy with a past solution path, the links from specific steps to the related *macro* forall-node are taken into consideration. These steps are therefore expanded according to the new state.

4.3. Static domain knowledge

The static knowledge consists of a set of axioms or primitives on which the operators are act. Figure 2, for instance, defines the notion of an upper triangular matrix, as a small illustrative example. We assume that the mentioned concepts, such as *table-of, objects, vectors, cprod* (cartesian product), etc., are also present in the system.

```
(FRAME matrix                                   (FRAME upper-triangular
  (is-a data-structure)                           (is-a triangular)
  (definition                                     (definition
    (def1 (table-of objects))                       (def1 (forall (elt (row i) (column j))
    (def2 (ordered-set-of vectors))                       (such-that (greater-than i j))
    (def3 (map (cprod setA setB) objects)))             (elt-value 0)))
  (characteristics                                  (def2 (forall (elt (row i) (column j))
    (dimensions (number 2)                              (such-that (below diagonal i j))
                (name row column))                      (elt-value 0))))
    (diagonal (set (elt (row i column j))
      (such-that (equal i j)))))
```

Figure 2: Static knowledge - a snapshot

4.4. Working domain knowledge

We introduce below a subset of the base-level operators currently used in the linear algebra domain. These operators specify the legal operations to perform on a system of linear equations. The name of each predicate is an abbreviation of its function; for instance the operator UPDATE-ELT-SC-ADD stands for *update an element by scaling and adding*. The goal of updating an element (*clearedelt*) on the working row *wrow* and working column *wcol* to the new value *val* is achieved by applying this operator UPDATE-ELT-SC-ADD. Note that in order to change the value of a coefficient in a system of linear equations we affect the whole equation (row of the matrix), so that whereas the application of an operator may achieve a desired goal, it will also have multiple, possibly undesired, side-effects. Such is true for most operators, and the name of the game in linear algebra is to protect desired portions of the state while achieving necessary changes elsewhere. The result of applying this operator is to scale a pivot row in the matrix (*prow*) with the constant c and substituting the working row *wrow* by the sum of the scaled *prow* and *wrow*.

```
; Updates an element by scaling and adding    ; Scales the pivot row and adds
; the pivot row with the working row           ; it to the working row
(UPDATE-ELT-SC-ADD                             (SCALE-ADD
 (params (<wrow> <wcol> <val>))                 (params (<prow> <wrow> <c>))
 (preconds                                      (preconds
   (and                                           (and
    (rowpivotfor <prow> <wrow> <wcol> <val>)      (dimension <n> <m>)
    (const <wrow> <wcol> <val> <c>)               (forall (<col>) (range-f <col> 1 <m>)
    (scaled&added <prow> <c> <wrow>)))              (and
 (effects                                             (mat <prow> <col> <pval>)
   ((add (clearedelt <wrow> <wcol> <val>)))))        (mat <wrow> <col> <val>)
                                                    (mult-f <pval> <c> <mval>)
                                                    (changed <wrow> <col> <val> <nval>)))))
                                                (effects
                                                  ((add (scaled&added <prow> <c> <wrow>)))))
```

```
; Selects a row for pivoting              ; Substitutes an element by a new one
; different from the working row          (PERFORM-UPDATE
(CHOOSE-ROW-PIVOT                           (params (<row> <col> <old> <new>))
 (params (<prow> <wrow>))                   (preconds
 (preconds                                    (mat <row> <col> <old>))
   (and                                    (effects
   (row <prow>)                              ((add (changed <row> <col> <old> <new>))
   (diff-f <prow> <wrow>)))                  (del (mat <row> <col> <old>))
 (effects                                    (add (mat <row> <col> <new>)))))
   ((add (rowpivotfor <prow> <wrow> <wcol> <val>)))))
```

Additional operators (by name only) consist of:

UPDATE-ELT-SC Updates an element by scaling its row.

UPDATE-ELT-ADD Updates an element by adding two rows.

ADD-ROWS Adds two rows and substitutes one by the obtained sum.

SCALE-ROW Multiplies a row by a constant and substitutes the row by the obtained result.

SELECT-WROW Selects a working row.

CREATE-CONST Creates a multiplicative constant.

4.5. Solvable classes of problems

The problems we have been dealing with lay within the area of elementary linear algebra. We show in Figure 3 a simplified hierarchy of the classes of solvable problems. The current set of operators is directed to solving a system of linear equations. The actions specified are however general enough to be applied to other classes of problems.

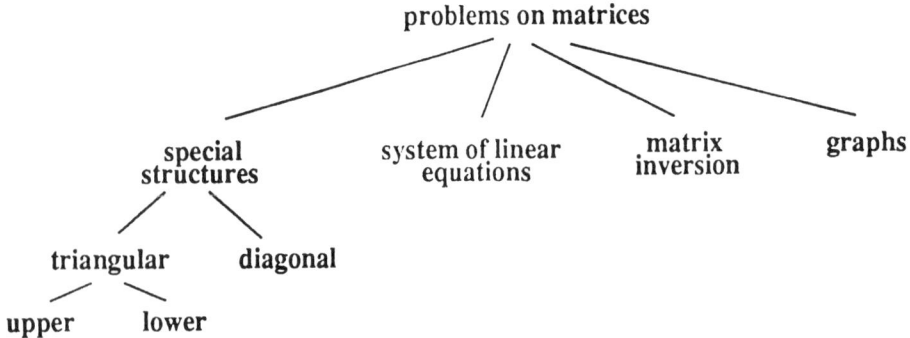

Figure 3: Solvable classes of problems

5. Introducing justifications

Different kinds of justifications are required by the derivational analogy process to insure applicability (or to guide modification) of the retrieved derivational trace. This section introduces and motivates each type of causal justification link.

5.1. Justifications at the operator level

An operator or inference rule in PRODIGY is encoded as a data structure with three primary fields, as we saw in the examples of the previous sections: parameters (params), preconditions (preconds), and effects (effects). We add the additional field for justifications (justifs). Justifications are both links to external domain knowledge and to other operators on which the present operator depends. These links may be viewed as higher-order (immutable) preconditions, and come in three varieties:

assumes expects a list of operators that are assumed to be also valid in this domain. For instance, unlocking a door is useful to exit a room only if opening that door is also a valid operation.

refers-to points to static domain knowledge underlying the meaning of this operator. For instance, robotic manipulation operators refer to the definition gravity (including the value of the gravity constant, and the direction of the gravity vector).

prob-class enumerates the class of problems where this operator is assumed to be applicable. For instance, matrix manipulation operators list mathematical (and perhaps other) domains, but not selection of recipes for low cholesterol intake.

```
(TRIANGULIZE
 (params ())
 (preconds
   (and
   (dimension <n> <m>)
   (pred-f <n1> <n>)
   (forall (<k>) (range-f <k> 1 <n1>)
   (and (workrow <r> <k>)
   (forall (<col>) (range-f <col> <st> <k>)
       (clearedelt <r> <col> 0))))))
 (effects
   ((add (triangular upper))))
 (justifs
   ((assumes INTERCHANGE-ROWS)
     (refers-to ((upper-triangular (definition def1)))
     (probl-class ((system-of-equations))))))
```

Figure 4 : The operator TRIANGULIZE

As an example we show the operator TRIANGULIZE in Figure 4. This operator refers to the definition of an upper triangular matrix named def1 (see Figure 2). The state achieved by this operator can be transformed into the referred definition by applying the operator INTERCHANGE-ROWS. This is the meaning underlying the *assumes* property.

5.2. Justifications at the goal choice

While the planner runs, there is a current (partially ordered) set of active goals, rather than a totally-ordered goal stack typical of more limited linear planners. Since the set can be dynamically (re)ordered, PRODIGY can interleave subgoals and produce non-linear plans. When being instructed by an external teacher (or while blindly searching for a solution under weak heuristic guidance) justifications for each goal choice are recorded. The planner itself is able to come out with some of these justifications by exploring the search space, or by post-facto explanation based learning methods [20]. Five different types of goal justifications are presented:

unique this means that this was the only available alternative.

stack this means that this goal was the latest to be posted, and in the absence of any reason to the contrary, becomes the default selection.

arbitrary this goal was picked up arbitrarily from the goal set.

protect enumerates a list of previously achieved subgoals that the system can assure will not to be destroyed by working on this subgoal. In essence, a goal selection may be dictated by protection criteria, even though in isolation of the problem solving context there may have been a locally superior selection.

necess-before lists subgoals that have to be worked out after the current subgoal in order for these latter to be achievable; in this way we capture the concept of serializable goals [16].

5.3. Justifications at the choice of alternatives among operators

There may be several operators that can be potentially applied when working out a goal. The justification for operator choice, and for its successful application is recorded using the following three predicates:

unique no more operators were available; the system may learn in the future alternative operators; therefore when solving a problem by analogy with this current one, the information that this chosen operator was unique at that time is taken into consideration.

information that this chosen operator was unique at that time is taken into consideration.

arbitrary expects a set of operators as an attribute; its meaning is that it was an arbitrary choice among the specified set of operators.

failure this predicate lists the set of operators known to have failed and the reason why they failed; we store either the related end condition responsible for the failure or the fact that this operator lead the system into a *loop*; in this case we store a reference to the subgoal on which it looped. Thus, an operator may be chosen because alternatives that appeared better are known to fail for recorded (well defined) reasons. In the subsequent analogical reconstruction, if these failure reasons hold, the same selection is made, and if not, the potentially better operators can be reconsidered.

Note that the justifications *arbitrary* and *failure* are not mutually exclusive. In fact the union of the two sets of operators mentioned should generate the total set of alternative operators. We are planning to introduce other justifications for the use of an operator in terms of statistical analysis of its frequency of successful application. Consider the situation where an operator was chosen arbitrarily. Consider further that in the sequence of solving similar problems, we are faced always with the same set of operators and we get a continuous success by choosing the same operator *arbitrarily* without exploring the alternative operators. We claim that the justification for the use of this operator is becoming *stronger* than simply an arbitrary choice. We will therefore introduce a measure of its frequency of success related to a specific class of solvable problems.

5.4. Justifications for the bindings of variables

The planner has the choice of applying an operator with a different set of bindings for its variables. We approach separately the choice of bindings for a particular operator and the choice of an operator among a set of alternative operators (see section 5.3). We consider that any specific constraint that might exist for the choice of bindings is encoded as a precondition of the operator. Therefore the justifications show only the set of bindings that have failed and the set of bindings not explored. The union of these two sets and the chosen binding is the set of all possible bindings for that operator. In order to use these justifications while learning by analogy, the system should be able to reason about the set of failed bindings and generalize from the reasons of failure. We postpone this point for future research.

5.5. An example of a justified solution path

Consider the example of the plan generated to perform Gaussian elimination on a matrix representing a system of equations. In fact we deal with a generalized version of Gaussian elimination where we admit that rows can be interchangeable (see the operator TRIANGULIZE in Figure 4). Furthermore assume that we also want the system matrix to have diagonal unit elements. On Figure 5 we sketched an initial piece of the search tree for a system of three unknowns. We refer to the goals by the corresponding numbered nodes. PRODIGY is given initially goals 1 and 2. Below we introduce the justifications at the goal choice. Note that the legal actions on the matrix affect the elements on an entire row - the element we wish to change, and by side-effect all the other elements as well. This is what is encoded as the justification (necess-bef 2) at node 0, for example, when node 1 is chosen to be worked out before node 2. The predicate (workrow r k) on node 5 is true if row r was chosen to have k many null elements in it. Note that the values of r are different for nodes 8 and 9. In fact the operator SELECT-WROW is responsible for achieving the subgoal (workrow r k) and its preconditions guarantee that r is bound to different values for different k values.

At node	Goal selected	Selected among goals	Justification
0	1	1,2	(necess-bef 2)
1	3	3,4,5,2	(necess-bef 4 binding)
	4	4,5,2	(necess-bef 5 binding)
	5	5,2	(stack)
5	7	6,7,8,9,2	(necess-bef 9 binding)
			(arbitrary 6,8)
	9	6,8,9,2	(arbitrary 6,8)
	11	6,8,11,12,2	(arbitrary 6,8,12)
	6	6,8,12,2	(necess-bef 8 binding)
			(protect 10 11)
	8	8,12,2	(necess-bef 12)
	10	10,12,2	(necess-bef 12)
			(protect 11)

...

The solution path also mentions the operator choices. As an example, note that TRIANGULIZE is chosen because it is the *unique* relevant operator. On the other hand there are three candidate operators to clear an element: UPDATE-ELT-SC, UPDATE-ELT-ADD, and UPDATE-ELT-SC-ADD. This last operator is chosen as the only successful one (the other fail).

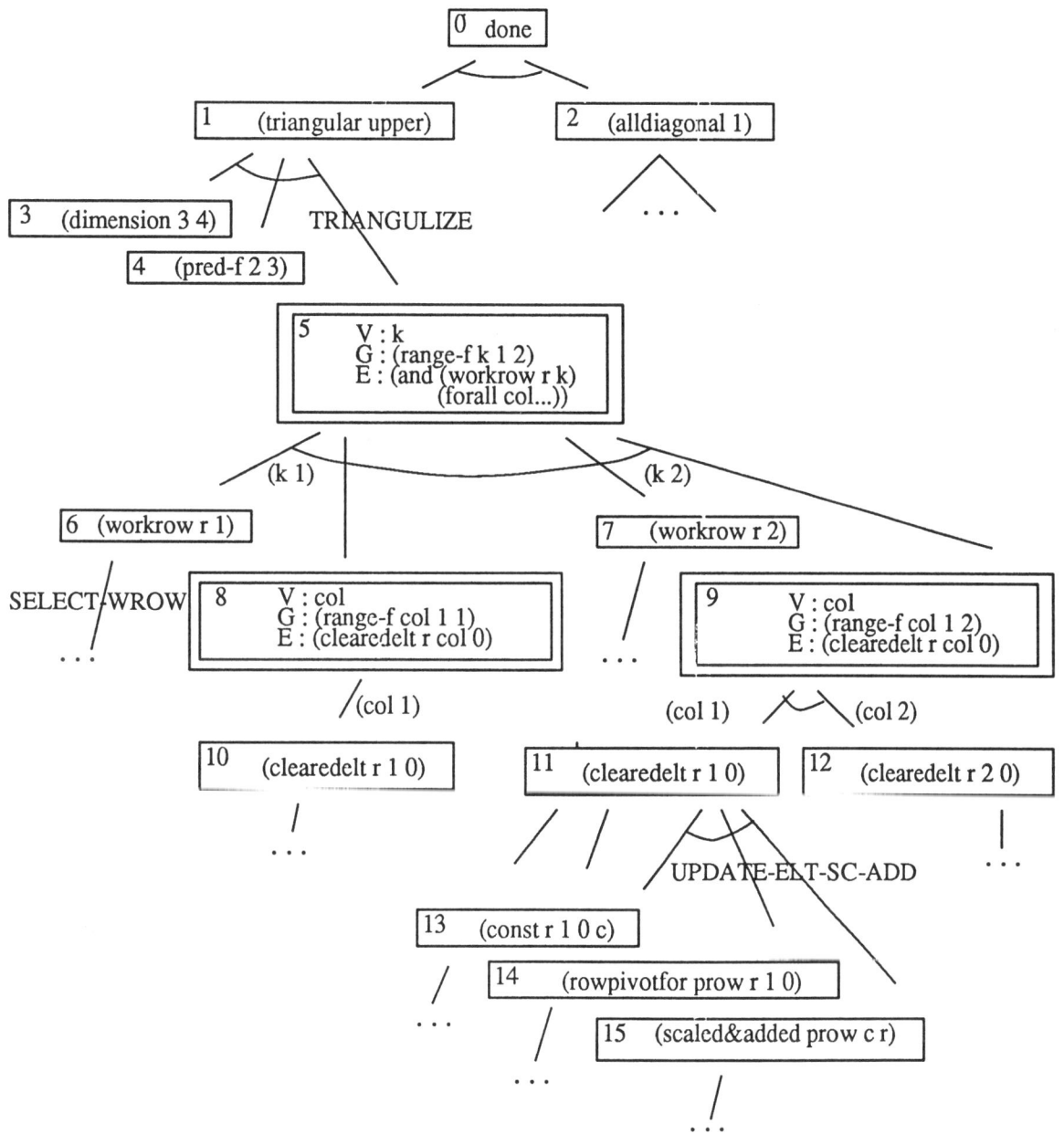

Figure 5: A piece of the search tree for generalized Gaussian elimination

6. Analogical reconstruction and learning: The algorithm

Learning by analogy involves the recognition of a previously solved similar problem, the derivation of the new solution by reconstruction of the old one, and finally the capability of generalizing individual solutions achieved to higher levels of abstraction. As stated in the introduction, our current work in PRODIGY addresses the problem of rational reconstruction of a solution from the derivational trace of an earlier similar case. We do not address here the equally important problem of indexing and retrieving from an extensive case library. The retrieved case re-establishes the earlier problem solving context, and the process of reconstruction, essentially replays the solution path (without regenerating a potentially vast search tree with innumerable unsuccessful side branches).

The stored derivational trace contains the full justifications for all the steps required to derive the old solution. We introduced in the previous section these justifications at the different points in the decision cycle of the reasoner. We now present how the system intelligently uses the past reasoning process to reconstruct a solution for a new problem without going through a painful blind planning process again. One can envision two approaches:

A. *The satisficing approach* - Minimize planning effort by solving the problem as directly as possible, recycling as much of the old solution as permitted by the justifications.

B. *The optimizing approach* - Maximize plan quality by expanding the search when to consider alternatives of arbitrary decisions and to re-explore failed paths if their causes for failure are not present in the new situation.

Presently we are implementing only the satisficing approach in full, although work on establishing workable optimizing criteria may make the optimizing alternative viable (so long as the planner is willing to invest the extra time required). Satisficing also accords with observations of human planning efficiency and human planning errors.

In the satisficing paradigm, the system is fully guided by its past experience. The syntactic applicability of an operator is always checked by simply testing whether its left hand side matches the current state. At goal choice, operator choice, or variable bindings choice, PRODIGY tests the validity of all the justifications. In case the choice remains valid in the current problem state, it is merely copied, and in case it is not valid the system has three alternatives:

1. replan at the particular failed choice to establish the current subgoal by other means (or to find an equivalent operator, or equivalent variable bindings) substituting the new choice for the old one in the solution sequence;

2. re-establish the failed condition by adding it as a prioritized goal in the planning, and if achieved simply insert the extra steps into the solution sequence, or

3. attempt an experiment to perform the partially unjustified action anyway; if success is achieved the system refines its knowledge according to the experiment. For instance, if the justification for stacking blocks into a tower required objects with flat top and bottom surfaces, and there were none about (so the first fix does not work) nor is there a way to make surfaces flat (so the second fix also fails), the robot could attempt to forge ahead. If the objects were spherical it would fail, but if they were interlocking LEGO pieces, it would learn that these were just as good if not better than rectangular blocks for the purpose of stacking tall towers. Thus, the justification would be generalized for future reference.

In the first case (substitution), deviations from the retrieved solution are minimized by returning to the solution path when making the most localized substitution possible.

The second case occurs for example, when the assumptions for the applicability of an operator fail. The system may then try to overcome the failed condition, and if it succeeds, it returns to the exact point in the derivation to proceed as if nothing had gone wrong earlier. Failures, however can be serious. Consider as an example, applying to the context of matrix calculus, some previously solved problems on scalars that rely on commutativity of multiplication. Facing the failure to apply this commutation operator in the matrix context, the system may try to overcome this difficulty by checking whether there is a way of having two matrices commute. In the general this fails, and a totally different approach is required (at least for the subgoal in question).

The experimentation case can be blind attempts to perform the same action with partially unjustified conditions, or can digress from the problem at hand to perform systematic relaxation of justifications, and establish whether a more general (more permissive) set of conditions suffices for the instance domain. Then, returning to the problem at hand, it may find possible substitutions or possible re-establishments of these looser conditions via steps 1 or 2 above.

6.1. Some learning examples

The process of reconstructing a new solution may lead to the learning of new operators. Consider the example in the domain of linear algebra presented above. Further consider the step of the solution path for solving a system of linear equations that involves the selection of a pivot row. Suppose in the previous solution the justification for the choice of a particular pivot row is just *arbitrary*. Repeating the same choice on a different matrix may lead to choosing a zero element for pivot element. The solution fails further down in the selection of a multiplicative constant; division by zero is attempted. At this point, the system takes the failed precondition (divisor different from zero in the division operator) and moves it back up the derivational trace (in an "on-demand" version of weakest precondition propagation) to point where the binding occurred for the variable in question, in this case in the operator for choosing a pivot row. A new, corrected version of the operator is learned by copying the CHOOSE-ROW-PIVOT operator and adding the precondition that failed.

In the learning process the new knowledge acquired is considered *conjectured* until a formal proof for its truth may be constructed. The example just described shows an operator that was learned and whose truth value can be proved to be true immediately for scalar arithmetic.

In a more complex variant of this example, PRODIGY encounters difficulties after selecting a very small pivot element (leading to truncation errors after repeated divisions). This time the added condition that the selected pivot be within several orders of magnitude as the other elements in the column remains a conjecture - and in fact is only valid as a function of the precision with which the scalar calculations are made.

Other learning examples deal with the notion of symmetry and the resultant ability to perform Jordan elimination [10] given the fact that the system knows how to perform Gaussian elimination. We are working on testing the analogical methods to arrive at a plan for generating a lower triangular matrix from the plan to generate an upper triangular one. We are also working on generating a diagonal matrix from the plan to generate a triangular one. And, finally we are investigating matrix inversion, again derived from earlier experience (e.g. the diagonalization trace). In other words, we are investigating the use of derivational analogy to rediscover algorithms in linear algebra, given structurally similar algorithms from this domain. At present it is too early to report on the success (or lack thereof) of our method as applied to this task.

7. Concluding remarks

In this paper, we have reported on the total integration of derivational analogy into the general purpose PRODIGY problem solving architecture, including the operator based domain knowledge encoding in PRODIGY, the causal justification structure encapsulating episodically-required domain expertise, the use of this knowledge to guide problem solving behavior, experimentation to test the validity of conjectured justifications, and the ability to fall back upon the general problem solver either when justifications fail or when episodic expertise is lacking.

The primary research thrusts we envision for the near future include:

- Demonstrate cross-domain generality: In addition to linear algebra, PRODIGY solves problems in domains as diverse as robotics root planning and factory scheduling. We expect that the derivational analogy method can function equally well in any of these domains.

- Unify derivational analogy with explanation based learning (EBL): PRODIGY supports a general EBL implementation [20], and derivational analogy is an alternate method to EBL for compiling episodic acquired knowledge. Therefore, PRODIGY provides a common framework for comparative analysis and possible integration.

- Integrate derivational analogy with abstraction planning and domain-level experimentation: Parallel developments in PRODIGY have produced a multi-level dynamic abstraction planner [13] and a proactive experimentation method to refine empirically a partial domain theory [4]. In principal, the power of both these methods could be augmented significantly by judicious exploitation of derivational analogy, but in practice such integration is yet to be realized.

As Artificial Intelligence systems grow to face increasingly complex task domains, they must acquire and compile domain expertise incrementally through experience. We have provided a first step in this direction via the integration of derivational analogy into a general problem solver, and expect to see many subsequent developments in this promising direction.

References

[1] Anderson, J. R. (1983). *The Architecture of Cognition*, Harvard University Press, Cambridge, Mass.

[2] Carbonell, J. G. (1983). Learning by Analogy: Formulating and Generalizing Plans from Past Experience. In R. S. Michalski, J. G. Carbonell and T. M. Mitchell (Eds.) *Machine Learning, An Artificial Intelligence Approach*, Tioga Press, Palo Alto, CA.

[3] Carbonell, J. G. (1986). Derivational Analogy: A Theory of Reconstructive Problem Solving and Expertise Acquisition. In R. S. Michalski, J. G. Carbonell, and T. M. Mitchell (Eds.). *Machine Learning, An Artificial Intelligence Approach, Volume II*, Morgan Kaufmann.

[4] Carbonell, J. G. and Gil, Y. (1987). Learning Domain Knowledge by Experimentation. *Proceedings of the Fourth International Machine Learning Workshop*, Irvine, CA.

[5] Cheng, P. W. and Carbonell, J. G. (1986). Inducing Iterative Rules from Experience: The FERMI Experiment. *Proceedings of AAAI-86*.

[6] DeJong, G. F. and Mooney, R. (1986). Explanation-Based Learning: An Alternative View. *Machine Learning Journal*, 1, 2.

[7] Doyle, J. (1984). Expert Systems Without Computers. *AI Magazine*, 5, 2, 59-63.

[8] Fikes, R. E. and Nilsson, N. J. (1971). STRIPS: A New Approach to the Application of Theorem Proving to Problem Solving. *Artificial Intelligence*, 2, 189-208.

[9] Gentner, D. (1980). The Structure of Analogical Models in Science. *Bolt Beranek and Newman*, 4451.

[10] Golub, G. H. and Van Loan, C. F. (1985). *Matrix Computations*, The Johns Hopkins University Press, MD.

[11] Greiner, R. (1985). Learning by Understanding Analogies. *Proceedings of the Third International Machine Learning Workshop*, 50-52, Skytop, PA.

[12] Hammond, K. (1986). Case-based Planning: An Integrated Theory of Planning, Learning and Memory. *Ph.D. Thesis*, Yale University.

[13] Knoblock, C. A. (1988). Automatic Generation of Abstractions for Planning. *AAAI-88*, submitted.

[14] Kolodner, J. L. (1980). Retrieval and Organizational Strategies in Conceptual Memory: A Computer Model. *Ph.D. Thesis*, Yale University.

[15] Korf, R. E. (1985). Macro-operators: A Weak Method for Learning. *Artificial Intelligence*, 26, 35-77.

[16] Korf R. E. (1987). Planning as Search: A Quantitative Approach. *Artificial Intelligence*, September, 33, 1, 65-68.

[17] Laird, J. E., Rosenbloom, P. S. and Newell, A. (1986). Chunking in SOAR: The Anatomy of a General Learning Mechanism. *Machine Learning*, 1, 11-46.

[18] McDermott, D. V. (1978). Planning and Acting. *Cognitive Science*, 2, 2, 71-109.

[19] Minton, S. (1985). Selectively Generalizing Plans for Problem Solving. *Proceedings of AAAI-85*, 596-599.

[20] Minton, S. (1988). Learning Effective Search Control Knowledge: An Explanation-Based Approach. *Ph.D. Thesis*, Computer Science Department, Carnegie Mellon University.

[21] Minton, S. and Carbonell, J.G. (1987). Strategies for Learning Search Control Rules: An Explanation-Based Approach. *Proceedings of IJCAI-87*, Milan, Italy.

[22] Minton, S., Carbonell J. G., Knoblock C. A., Kuokka, D. R., Etzioni, O., and Gil, Y. (1988). Explanation-Based Learning: Optimizing Problem Solving Performance through Experience. *Paradigms for Machine Learning*, forthcoming.

[23] Minton, S., Knoblock, C. A., Kuokka, D. R., Gil, Y., and Carbonell, J. G. (1988). PRODIGY 1.0: The Manual and Tutorial. *Technical Report*, Computer Science Department, Carnegie Mellon University, forthcoming.

[24] McCarthy, J. and Hayes, P. J. (1969). Some Philosophical Problems from the Standpoint of Artificial Intelligence. In B. Meltzer and D. Michie (Eds.) *Machine Intelligence 4*, Edinburgh University Press, Edinburgh.

[25] Mitchell, T. M., Utgoff, P. E. and Banerji, R. B. (1983). Learning by Experimentation: Acquiring and Refining Problem-Solving Heuristics. In R. S. Michalski, J. G. Carbonell and T. M. Mitchell (Eds.) *Machine Learning, An Artificial Intelligence Approach*, Tioga Press, Palo Alto, CA.

[26] Mitchell, T. M., Keller, R. M. and Kedar-Cabelli, S. T. (1986). Explanation-Based Learning: A Unifying View. *Machine Learning*, 1, 47-80.

[27] Mostow, J. (1988). Automated Replay of Design Plans: Some Issues in Derivational Analogy. *Artificial Intelligence Journal*, to appear.

[28] Newell, A. (1980). Physical Symbol Systems. *Cognitive Science*, 4, 2, 135-184.

[29] Rosenbloom, P. S. and Newell, A. (1983). The Chunking of Goal Hierarchies: A Generalized Model of Practice. *Proceedings of the 1983 International Machine Learning Workshop*, 183-197, Urbana-Champaign, IL.

[30] Sacerdoti, E. D. (1977). *A Structure for Plans and Behavior*, North-Holland, Amsterdam.

[31] Schank, R. C. (1982). *Dynamic Memory*, Cambridge University Press.

[32] Schank, R. C. (1983). The Current State of AI: One Man's Opinion. *Artificial Intelligence Magazine*, IV, 1, 1-8.

[33] Shell, P. and Carbonell, J. G. (1988). Towards a General Framework for Composing Disjunctive and Iterative Macro-operators. *AAAI-88*, submitted.

MILITARY HISTORY AND CASE-BASED REASONING

A New Approach to the Application of Artificial Intelligence to Battlefield Decision-Making

by

Col. T. N. Dupuy, USA, Ret.

Background

Artificial Intelligence (AI) has existed in the computerized scientific community for more than 20 years. It has been used to deal with a variety of medical and engineering problems, for instance, largely by the application of "expert systems." In essence this has been by means of an "if -- then" approach, in which a computer program has been designed to simulate the problem-solving procedure of one or more experts in the analysis of medical symptoms or details of technical problems by means of an exhaustive, itemized, logically-organized compilation of the relevant knowledge of the expert(s).

Military operations research analysts have long recognized that AI techniques could theoretically be very useful to commanders in coping with the numerous, rapidly-changing problems of battlefield decision-making. Efforts to do this, however, have not been very successful to date, for a number of reasons, of which some are obvious and well-understood (but stubbornly intractable), while others (equally intractable) have been only dimly perceived.

Among the obvious reasons are such things as:

- The sheer complexity of the multifarious, interacting, interrelated problems with which a combat commander must cope.

- The fact that a majority of these problems are related to the individual, idiosyncratic behavioral reactions of a large number of unpredictable human beings.

- Unlike the diagnosis of illnesses, and the treatment of routine engineering problems (both amenable to current AI techniques) neither the inputs to, nor the progress of, any battle are ever exactly the same as previous combat examples, even in instances in which there is at least superficial similarity.

- There are no living "experts" personally familiar with all -- or even with most -- of the varieties of combat circumstances and situations that have been encountered in the past.

- While one human body is relatively identical to all other human bodies, and reactions of bodies to illnesses and treatments will be generally similar, major components of today's battlefield (weapons and equipment) will be markedly different from past battlefields.

- Doctrine for the employment of armed forces in battle must change as weapons and equipment change, and yet the validity of the doctrine cannot be determined until the commander is faced with the necessity for battlefield decisions under circumstances differing in many respects from those of the past.

It would be possible to expand on the reasons why military expert systems are not easily applied to new battlefield situations, but the few listed above should demonstrate why it is so difficult to apply expert systems, or knowledge-based systems, to military problem-solving in combat.

Nevertheless, although history in warfare never repeats itself, it does paraphrase itself, and many military scholars, going back as far as Sun Tze about 500 BC, have noted patterns and similarities in the conduct and results of battles. In more recent times such theorists as Carl von Clausewitz and J.F.C. Fuller have demonstrated that there must be a theory of combat that will apply over all of history and in all regions of the world. This author has written extensively on how large bodies of historical combat data do indeed reveal consistent patterns in battlefield statistics under a wide variety of circumstances.*

Just a few years ago, furthermore, this writer (no specialist in AI) published an article suggesting that military history should be used as the basis for an expert system for combat artificial intelligence, since it will be impossible to produce living experts on all aspects of battlefield decision-making.** But, until recently, AI specialists have paid little attention to that suggestion, since the other complexities of battlefield decision-making have made it difficult to develop a systematic approach to the use of expertise based upon military history.

This seems to have been changed, however, by the relatively recent emergence of the concept of Case-Based Reasoning (CBR) in the AI realm.*** The purpose of this paper is to show how CBR specialists

---

*T.N. Dupuy, <u>Numbers, Predictions, and War</u>, New York, 1984, T.N. Dupuy, <u>Understanding War; History and Theory of Combat</u>, New York, 1987, etc.

**"Artificial Intelligence for the Armed Forces", <u>Army</u>, February, 1984. (Published with Editor's title: "The Computer as a Tool for MI.

***See Simpson, Lt. Col. Robert L., Jr., "DARPA Research Initiative in Case-Based Reasoning."

can be successful only if they utilize military history as the source of information, or the "cases" needed as the basic content, in a new and systematic computerized reasoning process.

An Example of Employing the Methodology.

Let me suggest how a division commander might actually make use of a decision-making methodology developed from the CBR approach, in an actual combat situation. Obviously I can only present this in an abbreviated, impressionistic fashion.

The situation has the commander's mechanized infantry division as an interior formation in a corps which is preparing to attack an enemy occupying prepared or fortified positions in rolling, mixed terrain (a combination of woods, farmland, and towns). The division commander has received orders from the corps commander, informing him that the corps main effort will be made by a reinforced armored division, just to the right of our commander's division. Our division is to undertake a secondary attack against the enemy positions to its front. Because this is a secondary effort, the division has been assigned a relatively broad front of perhaps 20,000 meters, and is opposed to a defending force of comparable size and strength. Our division commander, using his CBR-Methodology, must make an estimate of the situation, make his decision, and issue his orders.

While the data describing the situation is being entered into our hypothetical methodology, the Corp's G-3 presents to the commander a battle concept consistent with the doctrine he had been taught at the Command and General Staff College at Fort Leavenworth:

- The first brigade (reinforced), on the left, to attack on a front of eight kilometers, making the division's main effort.

- The second brigade, on the right, to make a secondary attack on a front of twelve kilometers.

- The third brigade (-), in reserve.

Simultaneously the CBR methodology informs the commander that its files contain twenty more-or-less analogous historical situations, as follows:

1. Soult's corps, Austerlitz, 1815

2. Pickett's division/Longstreet corps, Gettysburg, 1863

3. Longstreet's corps, Chickamauga, 1863

4. Wright's VI Corps at Spottsylvania, 1864

5. Warren's V Corps at Five Forks, April, 1865

6. British Fourth Army, Somme I, 1916

7. German Eighteenth Army (Hutier), Somme II, 1918

8. US II Corps, Meuse-Argonne, Nov., 1918

9. Rundstedt's Army Group "A", Flanders/Ardennes, 1940

10. German 7th Pz Division (Rommel), Amiens, 1940

11. British XXX Corps, Alamein, 1942

12. Canadian II Corps, Operation "Goodwood", Normandy, 1944

13. US VIII Corps, Operation "Cobra", Normandy, 1944

14. German Fifth Pz Army, Ardennes/Bulge, 1944

15. German 18th Vksgr Division, Ardennes/Bulge, 1944

16. Wallach's Division, Abu Agheila, 1956

17. Sharon's Division, Abu Agheila, 1967

18. Syrian 7th Division, Golan, 1973

19. Syrian 5th Division, Golan, 1973

20. Adan Division, Kuneitra-Firdan, 1973

From these twenty examples the methodology narrows its consideration to four that are more similar to his situation than the others: Numbers 5, 12, 15, and 17. The methodology then recommends:

- Concentration of the second brigade on a 5 kilometer front on the division's right flank, to make the division main effort, attempting to exploit favorable terrain and a boundary between two enemy defending divisions, while coordinating its attack with that of the armored division (making the corps main effort) on its right.

- The division's first brigade, on a 15 km front, to make a strong demonstration along its front.

- The division's third brigade (-) located to be able to exploit success of the first brigade.

The division commander notes that this course of action is similar to that which was suggested by the G-3, based on doctrine. But he sees that the CBR concept is designed to exploit certain aspects of the terrain, and of the enemy situation, as well as endeavoring to coordinate the division's main effort with that of the corps.

Based upon the information in its data base, the methodology offers the following cautions:

- An enemy counterattack against the thin second brigade could threaten success.

- Enemy reserves can "mouse-trap" a penetration by the first brigade.

The methodology still has something more to offer. It suggests that the division's commander consider a possible alternative, somewhat risky, course of action, based upon the case of the German 18th Vksgr. Division in very similar circumstances in the Battle of the Bulge:

- Second brigade (not reinforced), to make a main effort on a 5-km front on the right, as in the recommended COA.

- First brigade to make a main effort on a 5-km front on the left. (In other words, two penetrations leading to a double envelopment.)

- One battalion of the third brigade to hold the 10-km front between the two main efforts, demonstrating vigorously.

- Third brigade (-) in reserve, prepared to exploit success of either the first or second brigades.

For this alternative course of action, the methodology offers the following cautions:

- Both of the cautions for the recommended COA apply, particularly the first one.

- An alert and aggressive enemy, exploiting its strong defensive positions, may be able to repulse both of the double-envelopment main efforts.

Concept

How would one go about developing a methodology which could provide a division commander with such advice as suggested above, based upon the use of cases from actual historical experience?

Presented below is an approach to the application of CBR to battlefield decision-making from the non-technical standpoint of a military/military historical domain specialist. It is very similar to the classicial US Army approach to the Estimate of the Situation, and involves the following steps or components:

        Assessement of Current Situation: friendly,
            enemy, environment
        Cases from Historical Combat
        Experts' Distilled Wisdom Review
        Doctrine Review
        Analysis
        Courses of Action Possible
        Evaluation
        Decision

No effort will be made here to suggest how AI/CBR specialists will integrate these eight elements of the approach, or the extent to which they may be able to utilize Memory Based Reasoning (MBR) with CBR. As domain specialists, the author and Data 55mory Systems, Inc. (DMSI), stand ready to assist.

    I. <u>Assessment of Current Situation</u>. This will be a structured summary of the current military situation which faces the commander, and for which he must make the necessary combat command decisions. In essence, it will comprise the data which would appear in the standard military estimate of the Situation, in five major categories currently expressed in terms of the acronym: METT-T:

        1. Mission
        2. Enemy
        3. Terrain
        4. Time, and
        5. Troops available.

Entries will be made in a detailed worksheet, with each item relatable to the Index entries for Cases from Historical Combat, Experts' Distilled Wisdom Test, and Doctrine Test.

    II. <u>Cases From Historical Combat</u>. This is a comprehensive data base of historical battles, which will provide the cases which a the essence of CBR.* As a basis for determining the relationship of historical battle, or of any aspect thereof, to the Current Situation a detailed Battle Index will be prepared, which will include any reasonable basis for categorization or comparison of an existing situation with a historical battle situation. This will permit a listing of all historical battles which are in any way similar to the current situation, and a summarization of all ways in which there are similarities and differences.

---

*The most comprehensive data base currently available is the Land Warfare Data Base (LWDB) of 605 battles in engagements between 1600 and 1973. This was developed by the HERO Division of DMSI.

Where there are similarities in the two situations, the details of the historical situation will be elaborated, and the extent to which the similarity contributed to either victory or failure in the historical case will be stated as briefly, but as comprehensively, as possible. This will perhaps require some kind of sensitivity analysis.

III. *Experts' Distilled Wisdom Review.* This component of the system will be a data base containing the integrated or combined knowledge of past theorists and successful commanders who have written extensively on the art of war. Initially it will include a summation of the Maxims of Napoleon, the Principles of War of Clausewitz, the German Field Service Regulations of 1935, and the 54 "timeless verities" of combat which this writer presents in Chapters 1, 12, and 13 of Understanding War; History and Theory of Combat.* In the future, as time permits, this distilled wisdom data base can be expanded to include concepts from Clausewitz's On War, the works of J.F.C. Fuller, Sun Tze, and others. Entries in this component of the system will be in the form of postulates, rules, axioms, maxims, theories, hypotheses and laws (PRAMTHLs), each related to the Battle Index referred to above. Displayed, or printed out, for the commander will be a listing of those PRAMTHLs relevant to his current situation. (The volume of these may be large; an alternative approach may be to print out or display those PRAMTHLs that appear to conflict.)

IV. *Doctrine Review.* Doctrine is a set of principles, policies, and concepts which are combined into an integrated system for the purpose of governing all elements of a military force in combat, in order to assure the consistent, coordinated employment of those components. Doctrine can be derived from experience or theory; usually both. Doctrine represents the best available thought on the employment of currently available forces that can be defended by reason. Doctrine is methodology, and if it is to work, all military elements must know, understand, and respect it. Doctrine is the binding force which underlies a coherent military force. Doctrine must be one of the essential inputs to the decision-making process of a commander, for it conveys to him what is possible and what, under a given set of circumstances, is most likely to be desirable. Doctrine is found in policy documents, regulations, manuals, lesson plans, and the unwritten traditions of the Service. Currently, the principal expression of doctrine for the US Army is the latest version of Field Manual 100-5, Operations.

It must be remembered, however, that after a long period of peace, current doctrine is relatively untried and untested. It contains obvious or apparent inconsistencies which can be reconciled only in the crucible of battle. Thus its application must be tested against Distilled Wisdom, and if the two appear to be inconsistent, the commander must use his judgment as to the extent to which he must temper, adjust, or ignore doctrine. The experience from Cases from Historical Combat can provide guidance to the commander in this evaluation process.

---

*op cit.

As with Cases from Historical Combat and Distilled Wisdom, each element of Doctrine is identified in terms of the Battle Index. This permits the display, for the consideration of the commander, of all aspects of Doctrine that are relevant to his existing situation.

V. <u>Analysis</u>. In this process the system will examine the relationship of the Current Situation with Cases from Historical Combat, Distilled Wisdom, and Doctrine. It will display for his benefit the extent to which these components of the system agree with each other in their applicability to the Current Situation. With respect to the Cases, it will provide the following summary:

    a. What the winners did (the "do's");
    b. What the losers did (the "don'ts");
    c. What exceptions to "do's" and don'ts" succeeded (the "long-shots"); and
    d. Special considerations to be alert to (the "cautions").

VI. <u>Courses of Action</u>. In terms of a comprehensive list of all possible Courses of Action (COA) conceivably open to a commander, the system will produce from the above Analysis two lists. The first of these will be a list of the various courses of action open to the commander. The second will be a list of courses of action which could conceivably be undertaken by the enemy.

The system will display upon demand how each of the potential Enemy Courses of Action (ECOA) could impinge upon his Own Courses of Action (OCOA), excluding from the display any of the potential ECOAs that are inconsistent with that particular OCOA.*

VII. <u>Evaluation</u>. From the above comparison of OCOAs and ECOAs, the system will produce:

- Listing of Feasibility OCOAs

- Assignment of Success probabilities to each potential OCO

- Recommended OCOA, with reasons for adopting it from the Historical Cases, Distilled Wisdom, and Doctrine.

- (Only under special circumstances) Highlighting of Exceptional OCOA, different from (and usually more risky than) the recommended OCOA, with reasons from one or more of th same sources why it should be considered. (Such an Excep tional OCOA will be presented only if the risks it entail appear to be likely to result in more decisive success.)

- Errors to be avoided.

---

*It may also be worth mentioning that there is some similarity in thi approach to the concepts of game theory. Presumably, however, this i something that should be dealt with by scholars more qualified to discuss game theory and its applicability than is the author of this paper.

VIII. <u>Decision</u>. The Decision will summarize the application of the Recommended OCOA to all major elements of the command. In the event that the Estimate included an Exceptional OCOA, a similar summarization will be provided for that OCOA. In the latter event, the commander must elect between the alternate decisions. (He must base this decision in part upon his assessment of the capabilities of his forces and those of the enemy's, and in part upon his own self-assessment as a MacArthur or a Patton, versus a Montgomery or a Bradley.*)

<u>Testing the Methodology</u>

Obviously there will be a need to test the viability and utility of this ACEDACED approach to battlefield decision-making. Again, it will be necessary to fall back upon military history as a basis for developing test plans and procedures, and to provide the data for the test or tests.

One way would be through an exhaustive survey of military combat decision-making in modern times. This probably should be done from three standpoints.

First, an examination should be made of decision-making by commanders of generally acknowledged brilliance, beginning with Napoleon and continuing through such leaders as Douglas MacArthur, George Patton, Joseph Stilwell, William Slim, Eric von Manstein, and Erwin Rommel in World War II. To do this exhaustively would be a herculean task; however it is possible to develop an appropriate data base as an open-ended project, beginning in each case with information derived from reliable biographies.)

Second, there should be a general review of decision-making in wars since World War II, such as Korea, Vietnam, and the 1967 and 1973 Arab-Israeli wars. (This, too, can be a reference data base that can be started with a relatively small list of entries, to be gradually built up over time.)

Third, an examination should be made of decision-making blunders which led to defeat, beginning with the cordon defense dispositions of Gen. Jean Pierre Beaulieu along the River Po, in 1796, inviting penetration by young General N. Bonaparte. (This can be initiated by looking at the losing side in each of the battles and engagements in the "Cases from Historical Combat" data base.)

---

*Alternatively, the commander may use a simple, rapid force-on-force simulation to assess the likely results of the engagement for each OCOA to be evaluated. One such simulation is the Quantified Judgment Model (QJM) which, since it was devised from historical analysis, is conceptually compatible with the ACEDACED approach. If such a simulation were to be incorporated into the ACEDACED methodology it should be included as an element of Step VII, Estimate of the Situation.

The historical examples used in this test should not include any of those contained in the initial compilation of Cases from Historical Combat. After the test, however, these testing cases could be added to that data base.*

A possible alternative way of using military history for testing would be to prepare detailed scenarios of a number of important and decisive battles or engagements of modern military history. (Again, these should be new examples, not already included in the Historical Cases Data Base.) If possible, there should be 30 such test scenarios, 10 from the 19th Century, 10 from World Wars I and II, and 10 from wars since 1945, such as Korea, Vietnam, and the Arab-Israeli wars.** Test procedures would have to be worked out after the ACEDACED system prototype has been developed.

Remaining Uncertainties

In many, if not most, cases of applying the ACEDACED methodology, there are likely to be uncertainties. It would seem that the most difficult problem in any CBR approach will be the matching of cases to the current situation. There will almost inevitably be some uncertainties that cannot be automatically resolved without some additional, analytical, methodology. As noted above, history never quite repeats itself, even though it paraphrases itself. Thus, it is likely that a commander will find that the ACEDACED approach as described above may not produce an overwhelmingly convincing match of the characteristics of the historical examples to the characteristics of the situation which is facing him.

Thus an additional component is probably required, probably in Step VII, which will analyze the likely outcome of the ensuing battle or engagement when one of the OCOAs is adopted by the commander. This will be particularly important in those instances when the methodology suggests that an Exceptional OCOA should be highlighted for the commander's consideration. This analytical component should be able to demonstrate why -- and possibly how -- the risk entailed in such an OCOA is warranted.

The Quantified Judgment Model (QJM) could provide such a component, and could rapidly, and without need for further inputs, perform the analysis here suggested. Since the QJM was derived from analysis of historical experience, its processes will be fully consistent with the ACEDACED methodology, which in turn is based upon analysis of historical cases.

---

*One way to accomplish this, with a minimum of additional historical research, would be to withhold from the Cases From Historical Combat approximately one-fifth of the entries in the Cases data base.

**It must be recognized that lack of reliable data from the communist forces in the Korean and Vietnam wars will render this task difficult

Conclusion

Only military history can provide the cases for the application of CBR to battlefield decision-making. Only military history can provide the richness of experience necessary as the basis for a comprehensive evaluation of the relevance of the cases to a current situation. And only military history can provide a basis for testing. No possible peacetime testing measure unrelated to military history -- whether field exercise, computer simulation, or other war game -- can provide assurance that the test circumstances are realistic and authentic. Without positive results from such a test, a prudent decision-maker must assume that the answers or predictions from any other -- non-historical -- decision-making methodology are at least as likely to be wrong as to be right.

Facilitating Self-Education by Questioning Assumptive Reasoning using Paradigm Cases

Robert Farrell

Yale University
Department of Computer Science
Box 2158 Yale Station
New Haven, CT 06520-2158

March 14, 1988

Abstract

Making assumptions limits the depth of inference chains and reduces the potential for complex interactions, but assumptions that are made implicitly can blind the reasoner to important inferences and interactions. A self-education aid makes students aware of their assumptions by demonstrating how these assumptions might be violated. DECIDER is a self-education aid for history that tracks student assumptions using political models and illustrates possible violations using dramatic stories and video sequences from real historical cases.

This research was supported in part by the Advanced Research Projects Agency of the Department of Defense and monitored by the Office of Naval Research under contract N00014-85-K-0108.

When people confront novel and complex problems, they make assumptions and simplifications in their reasoning. Making assumptions facilitates efficient reasoning by reducing the depth of inference and the potential for complex interactions. However, when these assumptions are implicit, they blind the reasoner to important inferences and interactions. This blindness hinders learning because the reasoner is unaware of the need to learn.

1 What is a Self-Education Aid?

A self-education aid (SEA) is a program that makes a student aware of their assumptions by demonstrating how these assumptions can be violated. It focuses the student on where they need to do more reasoning without doing that reasoning for them.

Creating a self-education aid for a task domain involves:

- Creating an environment where the student can confront problems in that domain

- Tracking their reasoning in that environment and uncovering key assumptions

- Inferring plausible violations of these assumptions

- Finding lessons that explain why these violations are likely to be repeated in other situations

- Deciding which of these lessons is most important to teach

- Refocusing the student's reasoning by communicating their implicit assumptions, possible violations of these assumptions, and the lessons

An SEA should not be viewed as a simulator [23] because it gives feedback about assumptions, not about the execution of plans. It should not be viewed as a solution debugger [7,5,1,10,22] because there is nothing buggy about student solutions. Student solutions are often quite reasonable given the assumptions the student has made. To facilitate learning, one must find those assumptions and make them explicit so the student can become aware of them.

1.1 DECIDER: A Self-education Aid for History

DECIDER is a self-education aid for history that confronts students with past or present foreign policy problems [9] (e.g. in Nicaragua, Afghanistan, Israel) and tracks students' reasoning as they develop plans for these problems. DECIDER builds and refines an explicit model of student knowledge [8] and uncovers assumptions by examining inferences connecting this model with student

```
What do you want to do about the situation in Nicaragua?

--> send in the marines

IN THE MID 1960s, THE UNITED STATES HAD THE LARGEST MILITARY
FORCE IN THE WORLD. VIETNAM WAS A THIRD-WORLD COUNTRY WITH A
MUCH SMALLER MILITARY. WHEN THE COMMUNIST NORTH VIETNAMESE
THREATENED TO OVERTHROW THE U.S. CLIENT GOVERNMENT IN SOUTH
VIETNAM, PRESIDENT LYNDON JOHNSON DECIDED TO SEND U.S. FORCES.
BUT, AFTER 8 YEARS OF WAR, THE U.S. WAS FORCED TO WITHDRAW THEIR
MILITARY FORCES AND VIETNAM BECAME A COMMUNIST NATION.

DO YOU WANT TO HEAR ABOUT IT? yes

[Audio and Video illustrating problems arising from
 public protests during the Vietnam War]
```

Figure 1: The DECIDER program

solutions. The program makes students aware of their assumptions by illustrating how similar assumptions were made or could be made about past cases in history and how these assumptions were violated in the actual course of events. Historical cases, as communicated by DECIDER, point out the possible invalidity of one or more student assumptions and illustrate an important explanation for the teleology of past events.

DECIDER's expectation-based parser [15,16] uses approximately 300 concept definitions and syntactic patterns to map student inputs to expectations. DECIDER communicates historical cases to the student using a customized videodisc with photographs and footage from actual historical events (e.g. the US war in Vietnam, Castro's guerilla campaign against Batista). These images, along with a text overlay describing the historical events as a story, give the student a situated, attached, and dramatic view of history [6,14] rather than the typical remote, detached, and analytic view offered by books and lectures.

1.2 Comparison with Tutoring System Approach

Intelligent Tutoring Systems [21] typically represent problems as a set of goals for the student to achieve, then interpret student answers as achieving or failing to achieve these goals [7,10]. These systems tacitly assume that students adopt the goals specified in the problem description. However, as any human tutor knows, students often produce solutions for entirely different goals. Rather than giving students feedback on their own goals, "intelligent" tutoring systems misinterpret students as giving buggy answers to the system's own goal descriptions! It is not surprising that many students feel frustrated by the feedback given by these systems. Students spend most of their time learning what the computer "wants" instead of learning the problem domain.

A self-education aid avoids giving this kind of inappropriate feedback because it allows the student to formulate and pursue their own goals. SEAs have no notion of correct and buggy solutions [2,11] because they assume that student solutions are a reasonable attempt at some set of goals. An SEA must identify those goals - or give no feedback at all. If the student is unable to formulate a set of goals, an SEA can provide information to help them decide on a set of goals (e.g. "Nicaragua received a large shipment of attack helicopters from the USSR"), but it will never set goals for the student explicitly (e.g. "Get the Contras into power").

This paper will focus on the representations and processes needed to:

- Infer student assumptions about the causal relationships between plans (e.g. "invasion using ground forces") and policy-level goals (e.g. "maintain influence over governments in security zones")

- Demonstrate that these causal relationships do not always hold by finding a case where they failed for a reason that could plausible apply to the current case

2 Representation of Mental Models

We believe that people approach complex problems by quickly retrieving a set of overlapping mental models (frames [12], scripts [18], or stereotypes [20]) forcing these mental models to fit the problem situation, and drawing inferences from them [3]. These models all have the effect of focusing the reasoner on certain parts of the problem to the exclusion of others, thus making reasoning efficient by ignoring problems and interactions not described by the model. Blindness [24] results from failing to question the assumptions underlying the applicability of these models, the inferences within these models, or the possible interactions between models [13]. This paper will address how to recover and violate assumptions arising from inferences within models.

2.1 Converging on a Useful Set of Models

Because the task of formulating a foreign policy involves complex interactions, we assume that students are making heavy use of their simplified political models. These models vary depending on the age and sophistication of the target age group. We have chosen students in their teenage years because many teens develop an interest in international events when they near voting age. We assume that teenage political models are relatively simple and incomplete compared to the models of our expert historians. Using informal interviews, news reports, and high school history books, we hope to approximate a significant subset of the average teenager's political models.

Our models currently cover group organization, goals, abilities, and resources, and foreign relations, policies, and plans. We have not yet empirically tested our models against the target age group. However, it is not important that we close every gap between the student's mental models and the program's student models because the system can partially understand the student's input and still give useful feedback on their assumptions. Furthermore, the student is permitted to disagree with what they think are the program's assumptions about their goals and beliefs (e.g. "I wasn't trying to get the Contras into power"), thus allowing the system to gradually converge on a more accurate student model.

2.2 Understanding Plans and Goals using POLICYs

POLICYs are an important class of political models because they encode inferences about how plans work collectively to achieve certain conditions that are desirable to political groups. Typically, these conditions exist over long periods of time (e.g. control Jerusalem) and political groups use plans repeatedly in attempting to achieve and maintain them (e.g. terrorist attacks).

If the system believes the student has goals to achieve one or more of the conditions described by a POLICY and the student proposes a set of plans, the policy reduces the search involved in explaining how these plans could achieve the student's goals. This paper will describe how policies are represented and used in explaining student plan choice, recovering assumptions behind that choice, and retrieving paradigm cases to illustrate the possible invalidity of those assumptions.

Policies have 3 parts:

Conditions - What qualitative states exist and when

Inferences - A causal chain that explains how plans can work collectively to achieve the Conditions.

Prototypes - Prototypical examples of the objects, states, and actions that make up the Conditions and the plans to achieve the Conditions.

The Reagan administration's policy in Nicaragua between 1981 and 1984 partially matches a POLICY we call INCREASE-INSURGENCY-POWER (see Figure 2). The essence of this POLICY, stated as an outline for a plan on the part of a SUPPORTER, is that increasing the ability of an insurgency to inflict costs on an incumbent can facilitate the insurgency's ascent to power.

The Conditions of a POLICY can be satisfied in many different ways. The incumbent can be maintaining power through military force, public support, or

```
POLICY: Increase-insurgency-power(SUPPORTER, INSURGENCY,
LOCATION)

    Conditions:
        C1:   exists(INSURGENCY)
        C2:   increase(S2)
        C3:   increase(S12)
        C4:   increase(S9)
        C5:   decrease(S11)

    Inferences:
        PA1:  RESULTS(P1, C1)
        TC1:  ENABLES(C1, P2)
        PA2:  RESULTS(P2, C2)
        TC2:  ENABLES(C2, P3)
        PA3:  RESULTS(P3, C3)
        TC3:  MAINTENANCE-FAILURE(C3, S7)
        TC4:  NECESSARY-SUBGOAL(S7, S8)
        PA4:  GOAL-SACRIFICE(P4, S8)
        TC5:  RESULTS(P4, (C4 C5))

    Prototypes:
        Objects:
          INSURGENCY: Revolutionary-nationalist-group
          RESOURCE:   Guns
          INCUMBENT:  Corrupt-elite-government
          LOCATION:   Third-world
          SUPPORTER:  Rich-superpower-government
        Plans:
          P1: Propaganda(SUPPORTER, LOCATION)
          P2: Aid(SUPPORTER, INSURGENCY, RESOURCE)
          P3: Guerilla-warfare(INSURGENCY, INCUMBENT, S4)
          P4: Surrender(INCUMBENT, INSURGENCY, S6)
        States:
          S1:   POSSESS(RESOURCE)
          S2:   NUMBER(RESOURCE)
          S3:   MILITARY-CONTROL(S4)
          S4:   LOC(S5)
          S5:   OPERATE-ORGANIZATION(INCUMBENT)
          S6:   GOVERNMENT-POWER(LOCATION)
          S7    MAINTAIN(S10)
          S8:   MAINTAIN(S11)
          S9:   IN-STATE(INSURGENCY, S6)
          S10:  IN-STATE(INCUMBENT, S3)
          S11:  IN-STATE(INCUMBENT, S6)
          S12:  IN-STATE(INSURGENCY, S3)
```

Figure 2: The Increase-insurgency-power POLICY

recognition by foreign governments. These methods can be challenged by an insurgency using guerilla warfare, the media, or diplomacy and these challenges could be aided by a greater power providing arms, intelligence information, or a peace plan. Finally, the increase in the insurgency's power could be due to surrender, coup, or coalition. A POLICY is not particular to a given set of plans for the political groups involved, but instead serves to explain how plans collectively achieve various conditions.

It is important that models are represented so that they are neutral with respect to use. In this way they can be used for planning, prediction, understanding, and a range of other tasks. When used as an outline for a global plan of action, a POLICY helps explain how local plans (e.g. have the US marines invade Managua, infiltrate the Sandinista military with CIA agents) can achieve policy-level goals (e.g. decrease the power of the Sandinistas in Nicaragua). When used predictively, a POLICY helps explain how plans (e.g. sending humanitarian aid) can avoid or undo undesirable side effects (e.g. civilian casualties) of a global policy (e.g. war of attrition). When used as an explanation, a POLICY helps explain how plans of other agents (e.g. USSR aiding South Yemen) can achieve their global policy goals (e.g. increase power of communist groups in South Yemen), thereby helping explain how counterplans (e.g. request Saudi Arabia to intercept arms shipments to South Yemen) can block these goals.

2.3 Using Prototypes and Paradigmatic Examples

Because models are abstract and qualitative, they are difficult or impossible to learn, retrieve, and apply without their accompanying prototype information. This is because qualitative conditions (e.g. existence of an object or increase in a state variable) are highly ambiguous, even in context. The prototype information helps the student assemble the model, retrieve the model in situations similar to when it was learned, and apply inferences from the model predictively.

POLICYs include prototypes for each of the Conditions, plans to achieve these Conditions, and any objects or states that are part of these plans and Conditions. Prototypes are not individual examples; they are part of one coherent and connected paradigmatic example of how the POLICY works. The paradigmatic example of supporting an insurgency involves providing the insurgency with guns so that they can perform guerilla warfare to gain military control of the seat of government, which is controlled by an elite and corrupt government using military force. The paradigmatic example need only be partially applicable for the model to be retrieved, but once it is retrieved, the paradigmatic example is used to create coherent and connected expectations for future conditions, and plans to achieve those conditions.

3 Recovering Mental Models

Let's trace how DECIDER uses POLICYs to understand plans for an input situation. First, DECIDER picks an input problem that the student has not tried and asks them for a plan of action:

What do you think the US should do about the situation in Nicaragua?

--> have the US marines invade Managua

DECIDER is initialized with a decision maker (e.g. USA), a set of prototypical goals for that decision maker (e.g. "achieve and maintain influence within security zones"), and a set of qualitative state changes that describe important trends in foreign affairs within a given region (e.g. "stopped elections in Nicaragua", "increase in Nicaraguan military resources", "increasing influence of USSR in the region").

3.1 Qualitative States and Goal Monitoring

The program starts by assuming the student is adopting the prototypical goals of the decision maker. These goals can be retracted if the student later explicitly rejects them ("I don't want to increase US influence in Nicaragua") or if DECIDER cannot find a plausible interpretation of the student plan using them.

DECIDER then retrieves and applies a set of explanatory models (e.g. POLICYs used as explanations for the plans of other agents) to the qualitative state changes to predict future qualitative states. It assess at each step whether a future qualitative state change could possibly threaten any of the assumed goals. The result is a causal graph linking the qualitative state changes with possible threats to the student's goals (see Figure 3).

The program then creates expectations for possible student plans to resolve, alleviate, or dissolve these threats. First, each qualitative state in the graph is transformed into an A-goal [18] that could be pursued to address a threat (e.g. "abandon Central America as a security zone", "increase US influence in Nicaragua", "decrease the power of the Sandinistas", etc.). Then the desired conditions of these A-goals are matched to the Conditions that POLICYs are meant to achieve.

3.2 Retrieving POLICYs Using Prototypes

If an A-GOAL matches a prototypical Condition in a POLICY, DECIDER predicts that the student will try to carry out that POLICY. This means that they will produce plans to achieve and maintain the various Conditions that the

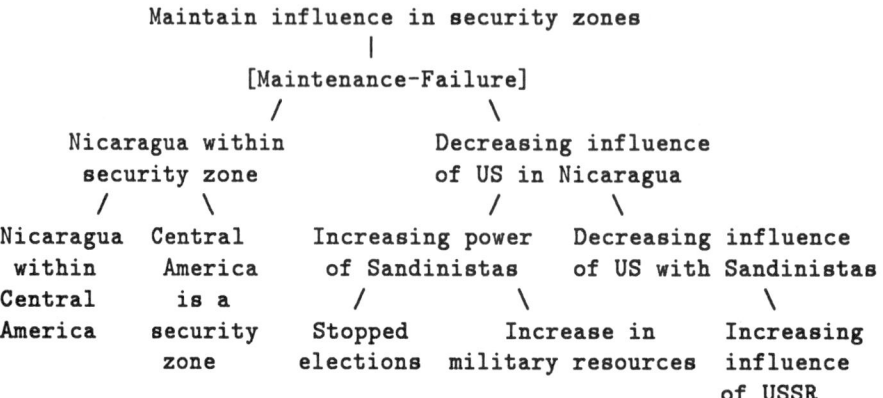

Figure 3: A Qualitative Causal Graph

POLICY describes. For example, the A-goal "decrease power of Sandinista government" matches the GOVERNMENT-POWER prototype of the INCREASE-INSURGENCY-POWER POLICY (see Figure 4).

```
C5: decrease(IN-STATE(INCUMBENT,
                     GOVERNMENT-POWER(LOCATION)))
  = decrease(IN-STATE(Sandinistas,
                     GOVERNMENT-POWER(Nicaragua.loc)))
```

Figure 4: The student's A-GOAL matches a POLICY Condition (C5)

Therefore DECIDER will interpret the student plan ("have the marines invade Managua") as a way of carrying out the predicted policy INCREASE-INSURGENCY-POWER. DECIDER does this by using the POLICY prototypes to guide the application of Inferences. First, DECIDER tries to interpret the student's plan as a prototypical plan for the POLICY. If this fails, it tries to find a causal connection between the student's plan and the prototypical Conditions. This may involve retrieving and applying other models.

The student plan ("have the US marines invade Managua") does not directly match any prototypical plans in the INCREASE-INSURGENCY-POWER policy (e.g. Propoganda, Aid) and does not directly bring about any of the prototypical Conditions (e.g. increasing resources of the insurgency, increasing military power of the insurgency). Therefore, the program searches for another POLICY that will connect the INVADE plan to one of the prototypical POLICY Conditions. Using the results of INVADE and the conditions of INCREASE-

INSURGENCY-POWER, DECIDER finds a POLICY called ACHIEVE-AND-TRANSFER-CONTROL that explains how the INVADE plan could result in military power for the insurgency (see Figure 5). At this point, DECIDER has inferred that the student believes the U.S. should invade Managua so that it can transfer its share of military control to an insurgency, so as to increase the military power of the insurgency in the city of Managua.

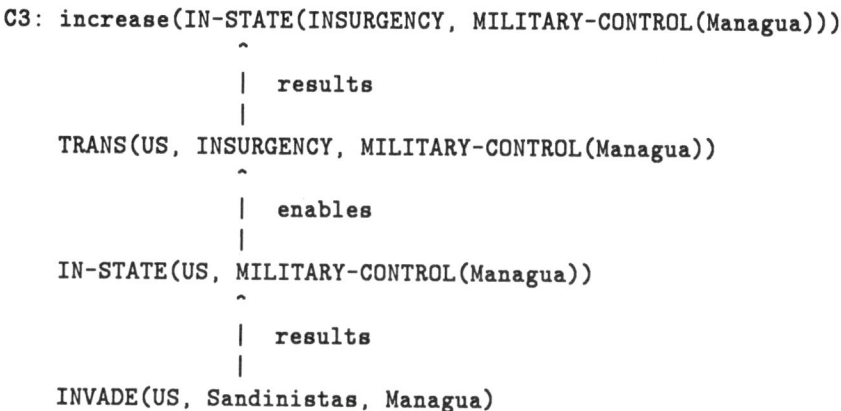

Figure 5: The student's plan (INVADE) achieves a POLICY Condition (C3)

Next, DECIDER uses the Inferences section of INCREASE-INSURGENCY-POWER to connect the desired state of the A-GOAL (C5: Decreasing power of the Sandinistas) to the POLICY Conditions achieved by the student's plan (C3: Increasing military control of the insurgency in Managua) (see Figure 6)

The final output of this model recovery phase is a causal chain (CC) connecting the student's plans ("have the US marines invade Managua") to their policy-level goals ("achieve and maintain influence in security zones"). The explanation for why the plan works is that the marines will take control of Managua, an important stronghold for Sandinista power in Nicaragua. After the marines transfer control of Managua to an insurgency group, the Sandinistas will be forced to surrender governmental power to this insurgency, thus increasing US influence in the region and satisfying the goal of maintaining influence in security zones.

4 Questioning Model-based Assumptions

A self-education aid is not designed to evaluate student solutions or to force students to learn a particular set of concepts or cases. Instead, it is designed to find opportunities to teach when students are most prepared to receive information:

```
C5:  decrease(IN-STATE(Sandinistas,
GOVERNMENT-POWER(Nicaragua.loc)))
                    ^
                    | TC5: RESULTS
                    |
PA4: Surrender(Sandinistas, INSURGENCY,
GOVERNMENT-POWER(Nicaragua.loc))
                    ^
                    | PA4: goal-sacrifice
                    |
S8:  maintain(IN-STATE(INCUMBENT,
GOVERNMENT-POWER(Nicaragua.loc)))
                    ^
                    | TC4: necessary-subgoal
                    |
S7:  maintain(IN-STATE(INCUMBENT, MILITARY-CONTROL(Managua)))
                    ^
                    | TC3: maintenance-failure
                    |
C3:  increase(IN-STATE(INSURGENCY, MILITARY-CONTROL(Managua)))
```

Figure 6: Inferences connect the POLICY Condition C3 with the student's A-GOAL

when they are in the process of pursuing their own goals [19]. Therefore, an SEA must identify when a student's learning is restricted by the use of oversimplified models and must try to derestrict their learning by making them aware of their assumptions. DECIDER does this by finding a set of models that explains how the student's solution is a reasonable attempt at one or more of their goals and then questioning the assumptions in that model. It does this by asking questions that the student didn't ask because they were blinded by the constraints of their models.

DECIDER generates a question from each of the inferences in the final explanation of the student's plan (CC):

- Q: How might a US invasion against the Sandinistas fail to result in US military gaining control of Managua?

- Q: How might the Sandinistas maintain governmental power in Nicaragua despite them not maintaining military control of Managua?

- Q: What plan besides surrendering might the Sandinistas choose despite failing to maintain governmental power in Nicaragua?

- Q: How might the surrendering governmental power to an insurgency fail to result in an increase in the governmental power of the insurgency?

These questions constrain the search for alternate states that can invalidate the inferences in the causal chain.

4.1 Locating Plausible Assumptions Violations

DECIDER finds possible states to invalidate the student model-based inferences by examining a causal network stored with the model that produced the inference. For example, when questioning the inference that INVADE will result in the US gaining mlitary control, DECIDER finds a causal network explaining the state S7: IN-STATE(US, MILITARY-CONTROL(Managua)) by looking in the model for INVADE (see Figure 7). This network explains the detailed conditions that need to hold for the INVADE plan to succeed. DECIDER only looks at the RESULTS part of this network because the type of inference connecting INVADE and MILITARY-CONTROL in the causal chain was a RESULT inference. Under each of the specific states in this network are types of failures and explanations for those failures. Here are the failures for the condition "maintain troops at-loc and attacking" (see Figure 8). Each failure can organize one or more explanatory models. In this network, DIVERT-RESOURCE-FOR-CONFLICT provides an explanation for why an attack might not be able to maintain attacking troops at the location of an invasion.

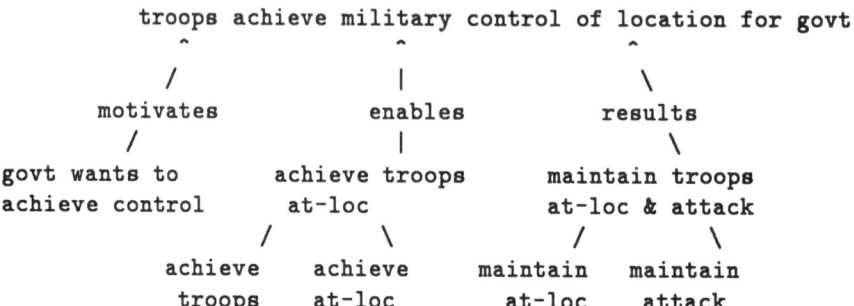

Figure 7: Causal Network for the desired effects of INVADE

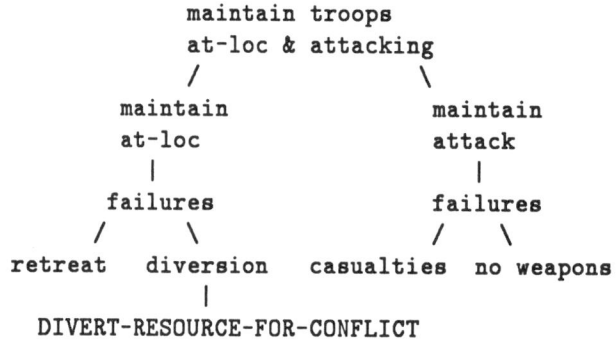

Figure 8: Failures and Explanatory Models for the AT-LOC and ATTACKING Conditions of INVADE

4.2 Explanatory Models

Explanations for failures are often models that encode important interactions that were overlooked when the plan was chosen. In this case, the explanatory model DIVERT-RESOURCES-FOR-CONFLICT, details how an organization can be forced to withdraw resources even when it wants to continue a conflict, because of more pressing needs for those resources elsewhere. Here is an abbreviated version of this model (see Figure 9)

The DIVERT-RESOURCES-FOR-CONFLICT model would be applicable to the student's INVADE plan if, for example, the US was involved in another war that needed marines and the US did not have enough marines to maintain both conflicts at once.

```
POLICY: DIVERT-RESOURCES-FOR-CONFLICT(GOVT, W1, W2, RESOURCE)

Conditions & Inferences:
   GOVT in conflict W1 at L1
   GOVT using RESOURCE for W1
   GOVT in conflict W2 at L2
   Shortage of RESOURCE for W2
   GOVT beliefs W2 more important than W1
   GOVT diverts RESOURCE from W1 to W2
   Failure to maintain RESOURCE for W1 at L1
   Increase in RESOURCE for W2 at L2
```

Figure 9: The DIVERT-RESOURCES-FOR-CONFLICT POLICY

4.3 Communicating Explanatory Models with Paradigmatic Examples

A paradigmatic example of DIVERT-RESOURCES-FOR-CONFLICT causing problems with INVADE was when Spanish troops invaded the Netherlands. Although Spanish Habsburg king Phillip II desperately wanted to put down the revolution in the Netherlands, and probably had enough troops to accomplish that goal, he eventually surrendered. This was partially because he was constantly diverting troops to the war with France, a war of much greater threat to Spain's national security.

Cases are indexed in memory by 4 things:

- Plan - The type of plan (the fact that it was an invasion)

- Reasons for Choice - The conditions that succeeded and would normally be reasons to choose this Plan (the government wanted to achieve military control and had the resources to do so)

- Failures - The conditions that led to the failure of the Plan (did not maintain troops at the location of the invasion)

- Explanatory Models - Model(s) that explain why the Failures happened despite the Reasons for Choice (the government was forced to divert its troops to the more pressing war with France)

DECIDER chooses a paradigm case to display by rating the importance of learning the explanatory models that it retrieves. It does this rating using methods similar to those used in the WHY tutor [4]. For example, explanations for the failure of higher-order factors are more important to learn than explanations for the failure of lower-order factors.

Once DECIDER has chosen a paradigm case to display, it communicates the plan, the success conditions, and the failure using text and video. Then, if the student wants to hear the explanation for the failure, DECIDER collects those parts of the paradigm case that exemplify the explanatory model and displays them using dramatic video sequences and/or story-like text.

4.4 Student Reactions to Explanatory Models

Once DECIDER has displayed a paradigm case, it allows the student to respond to the points that are part of the explanatory model. The student can:

- Disagree with the program's assumptions about their beliefs by stating those beliefs explicitly

    - *But I don't want to get the Contras into power,
    I just want to rescue the Nicaraguan people*

- Disagree with the explanatory model by communicating a competing model using a difference

    - *But Nicaragua is in the Western Hemisphere*

- Accept the explanatory model and change their solution

    - *Hire mercenaries instead*

These responses are not answers to be recorded and scored, but are instead a starting point for furthur self-education using the student's new beliefs, the new explanatory model for the old solution, or the student's new solution using the old model.

We believe that computers have played a relatively minor role in education largely because the communication between student and machine has been a one-way street, either directed toward the student (most CAI and ITS programs) or directed toward the computer (most microworld programs). A self-education aid (SEA) and a student should become a "coupled" learning system. The SEA and student initially have different models and different databases, but by mutual communication of arguments about the applicability of models, they settle on a set of models that are acceptable. The output of this coupled learning system is a set of new models and new database facts for the student to use during future problem-solving.

4.5 Extensibility of the DECIDER model

DECIDER's ability to aid the student's learning process depends on:

- A database about the input situation that includes many facts unknown to the target group of students

- A large database of past cases and the models they exemplify

- A detailed model of causality for evaluating inference chains in student models

Our input situation databases include facts about geography, national resources, internal politics, and diplomatic and economic status that we feel are unknown to most teenagers. We are aiming for several hundred such facts per case.

We have recorded and partially analyzed a large number of reminding episodes [17] with one historian and are extending our data collection and analysis to other historians with different backgrounds and ideologies. We gave these historians a set of current crises (Gaza Strip, Nicaragua, Panama, Haiti, South Africa, and the Persian Gulf) and asked them for alternative policies. We then asked them to argue against these policies by giving a paradigmatic example from history. Historians find this task effortless; they are easily reminded of several cases, many of which they have used in classes or scholarly works.

Expert historians seem to collect and remember a staggering number of paradigmatic cases. Our best experts had at least a passing familiarity with about a million such cases (approximately 2,000 years of expertise * 25 crises initiated per year * 20 simultaneous spheres of activity). Although this is purely speculative, it clarifies the large amount of scaling up to be done before a case-based program could hope to approach human performance.

Indexing a large number of cases of foreign policy failures forces forces us to make important distinctions in the inferences section of our POLICY models. We are currently implementing two sets of POLICY models: "plan" models used to link students plans and goals and "explanatory" models for failures in these "plan" models. We are planning to extend the system to handle 200 paradigm cases, 10 "plan" models, and 50 "explanatory" models.

5 Conclusion

Guided by the intuition that student solutions are often plausible given student-like assumptions and these same assumptions are implicit in a large number of student solutions, we have proposed a new paradigm for computers in education: facilitated self-education. A self-education aid tracks student reasoning and acts on opportunities to communicate possible assumption violations in that reasoning. We have built a system called DECIDER that tracks student reasoning using political models and communicates possible assumption violations in a dramatic, story-like way using text plus actual footage and photographs of paradigmatic cases of foreign policy problems.

Acknowledgments

Special thanks to Dr. Gilles Bloch who single-handedly created the DECIDER videodisc and did a considerable amount of work on the DECIDER parser. His input, advice, and expertise were invaluable to the DECIDER project. Thanks to Drs. Moon, Etheridge, and Westerfield for their detailed knowledge of history. Thanks to Eric Jones for many key ideas on use-independent representation and to Eric Domeshek and Ashwin Ram for useful feedback on this paper. Thanks especially to my advisor, Roger Schank, who provided the theoretical framework and facilities to make this work possible.

Bibliography

References

[1] Farrell R. Anderson J.R., Boyle C. and Reiser B.J. Cognitive principles in the design of computer tutors. In P. Morris, editor, *Modelling Cognition*, John Wiley and Sons Ltd., 1987.

[2] J.S. Brown and R.R. Burton. Diagnostic models for procedural bugs in basic mathematical skills. *Cognitive Science*, 2(2):155–192, 1978.

[3] M. Burstein. *Reasoning Using Multiple Analogies*. PhD thesis, Yale University, January 1985.

[4] A. Collins and A.L. Stevens. *Goals and Strategies of Interactive Teachers*. Technical Report 4345, Bolt, Baranek, and Newman, March 1980.

[5] Sleeman D. and R.J. Hendley. Ace: a system which analyses complex explanations. In *Intelligent Tutoring Systems*, Academic Press, London, 1982.

[6] L.S. Etheridge. *Can Governments Learn?* Pergamon Press, New York, 1985.

[7] J.R. Farrell, R.G. Anderson and B.J. Reiser. An interactive computer-based tutor for lisp. In *Proceedings of the Fourth Annual National Conference on Artificial Intelligence*, AAAI, Austin, TX, August 1984.

[8] R. Farrell. Intelligent case selection and presentation. In *Proceedings of the Eleventh International Joint Conference on Artificial Intelligence*, IJCAI-87, Milan, Italy, August 1987.

[9] R. Farrell and G. Bloch. Design and argumentation in case-based teaching systems. In *Proceedings of the Second International Conference on Intelligent Tutoring Systems*, IJCAI-87, Italy, August June, 1988. Submitted for review.

[10] L. Johnson and E. Soloway. *PROUST: Knowledge based program understanding.* Technical Report 285, Yale University Department of Computer Science, August 1983.

[11] W.L. Johnson, E. Soloway, B. Cutler, and S.W. Draper. *Bug Catalogue: I.* Technical Report, Yale University Department of Computer Science, October 1983.

[12] M. Minsky. A framework for representing knowledge. In P. Winston, editor, *The Psychology of Computer Vision*, chapter 6, pages 211–277, McGraw-Hill, New York, 1975.

[13] R.E. Neustadt and E.R. May. *Thinking in Time: The Uses of History for Decision Makers.* The Free Press, New York, 1986.

[14] S. Papert. *Mindstorms.* Basic Books and Harvester, 1980.

[15] C. Riesbeck and R.C. Schank. *Comprehension by Computer: Expectation-based Analysis of Sentences in Context.* Technical Report 78, Yale University Department of Computer Science, October 1976.

[16] C.K. Riesbeck. From conceptual analyzer to direct memory access parsing: an overview. In N.E. Sharkey, editor, *Advances in Cognitive Science 1*, pages 236–258, Ellis Horwood Limited, Chichester, 1986.

[17] R.C. Schank. *Dynamic memory: A theory of learning in computers and people.* Cambridge University Press, 1982.

[18] R.C. Schank and R. Abelson. *Scripts, Plans, Goals and Understanding.* Lawrence Erlbaum Associates, Hillsdale, New Jersey, 1977.

[19] R.C. Schank and R. Farrell. Creativity in education: a standard for computer-based teaching. In *Machine-Mediated Learning*, Taylor-Francis, New York, NY, 1987.

[20] C.M. Seifert. *Mental Representations of Social Knowledge.* PhD thesis, Yale University, May 1987.

[21] D. Sleeman and J.S. Brown. *Intelligent Tutoring Systems.* Academic Press, London, 1982.

[22] E. Soloway, E. Rubin, B. Woolf, J. Bonar, and L. Johnson. *MENO II: An AI based programming tutor.* Technical Report 258, Yale University Department of Computer Science, December 1982.

[23] A. et al Stevens. *Steamer: Advanced Computer Aided Instruction in Propulsion Engineering.* BBN Technical Report 4702, Bolt Baranek and Newman, Inc., July 1981.

[24] T. Winograd and F. Flores. *Understanding Computers and Cognition.* Ablex Publishing Co., Norwood, NJ, 1987.

Opportunistic Memory: Storing and recalling suspended goals.[1]

Kristian J. Hammond
Department of Computer Science
The University of Chicago
Chicago, IL 60637

Abstract

While the issue of opportunism has always interested the planning community, most models of planning offer little room for opportunism in that they exclude the feature that enables it: plan execution. Fortunately, a recent shift in perspective on planning has added execution to the list of issues considered by planning researchers. In this paper we present a model of opportunistic planning that uses planning-time reasoning about the opportunities that might arise during plan execution. The model is composed of three parts: a planning-time mechanism that places blocked goals into memory for later activation, an understanding system that activates suspended goals as a by-product of parsing the world, and an execution-time process for evaluating opportunities and merging newly activated goals into the planning/execution agenda. We discuss this model in terms of examples from TRUCKER, a route scheduling system, and RUNNER, an errand planner.

1 Planning and Acting

Current research in planning has taken a rather dramatic change in course in the past few years. The notion that a planner can exhaustively preplan for a set of goals prior to execution has been largely abandoned. In part, this change is the result of demonstrations that planning for conjunctive goals is undecidable (Chapman 1987). A more important factor has been the realization that the dual assumptions of traditional planning (a closed world and complete knowledge of operators) are untenable in any but the simplest domains.

The planning theories that have grown out of this shift in paradigm differ from earlier theories in that they attempt to integrate planning and execution into a single process. The most extreme example of this has been the idea of *situated activity* (Agre & Chapman 1987), which argues that plan-like behavior rises out of reflexive responses to external cues rather than from the guidance of a declarative plan. Less extreme theories center around the notion that plans have to be refined and repaired at execution time. These theories include:

---

[1]This work was supported, in part, by an Independent Research Grant from Lockheed Missiles and Space Co.

- Alterman's *Adaptive Planning*, in which execution-time problems are handled by moving between "semantically" similar plan steps.

- Firby's *RAPS*, which allow a hierarchical planner to select between alternative plans on the basis of bottom-up information obtained at execution time.

- Hammond's *Case-based Planning* and Simmon's *Generate Test and Debug*, both of which use causal explanations of execution time failures to choose between a variety of repairs.

Moderate or extreme, each of these theories argues that the world changes and a planner must respond to those changes. They define a class of planner which, for lack of a better name, we will refer to as *active planners*: planners that both produce a plan and then actively pursue that plan in the face of a changing environment.

Thus far, the stress on integrating planning and execution in this work has been on the issue of recovering from plans that unexpectedly fail. Little work has been done on the corollary concern of exploiting unexpected opportunities. In this paper, we will address this concern and suggest a theory of memory organization that addresses this issue. We will also describe two planners that are aimed at implementing the theory: TRUCKER, a planner developed at Chicago in the domain of pick-up and delivery scheduling; and RUNNER, a new planner under development in the more general domain of errand running.

2 Opportunistic Memory

Our approach in both TRUCKER and RUNNER uses episodic memory to organize, recognize and exploit opportunities. Briefly the algorithm includes the following features:

- Goals that cannot be fit into a current ongoing plan are considered blocked and, as such, are suspended.

- Suspended goals are associated with elements of episodic memory that can be related to potential opportunities.

- These same memory structures are then used to "parse" the world so that the planner can make execution-time decisions.

- As elements of memory are activated by conditions in the world, the goals associated with them are also activated and integrated into the current processing queue.

In this way, suspended goals are brought to the planner's attention when conditions change in a way that allows the goals to be satisfied.

Because the planner's recognition of opportunities depends on the nature of its episodic memory structures, we call the overall algorithm presented here *opportunistic memory*.

3 An Example

Before we get into any details, it is important to understand the type of behavior we want to capture. We'll do this by looking at a simple example. Although this example is couched in terms of a story, we are interesting in modeling the planning behavior described, not in understanding the text.

This example is taken from the RUNNER domain of errand running:

> On making breakfast for himself in the morning, John realized that he was out of orange juice. Because he was late for work he had no time to do anything about it.
>
> On his way home from work, John noticed that he was passing a Seven-Eleven and recalled that he needed orange juice. Having time, he stopped and picked up a quart and then continued home.

There are a number of interesting aspects to this example. First of all, the planner is confronted with new goals during execution as well during planning. This makes complete preplanning impossible. Second, the planner is able to stop planning for a goal before deciding exactly how to satisfy it. In effect, he is able to say—"I don't have all the information or the time to completely integrate a plan for this goal into my current agenda." Using Schank's vocabulary, we call this the ability to *suspend* a goal (Schank and Abelson 1977). And third, although the goal is suspended, the planner is able to recognize the conditions that potentially lead to its satisfaction.[2]

There is a final element to this example that does not lie quite so close to the surface: in order to decide to suspend planning for the goal to possess orange juice, John has to do some reasoning about what a plan for that goal entails. That is, he has to see that the goal is blocked by lack of time to go to the store. As a result, he has a clear idea, at planning-time, as to what an execution-time opportunity would look like.

Note that we have used some highly loaded language in this piece of text. John "suspends" his goal to possess the orange juice, he "notices" a Seven-Eleven, and thus "recalls" the suspended goal. We consider it our responsibility to provide computational accounts of these terms. In particular, we will try to define them in the context of planning, acting and opportunism.

---

[2]One could argue that in this example the planner does completely preplan for this goal and that the plan is to get the orange juice on the way home. But this is begging the question, in that we can take any version of a plan designed to satisfy this goal and still argue that opportunities to satisfy it in other ways should be exploited. For example, if John passes by someone giving away free samples of orange juice on the way to work, we would certainly want him to recognize that this is a chance to satisfy a currently suspended goal. The point being that we want a planner to exploit opportunities to satisfy goals, whether or not it has already planned for them.

4 Opportunistic Planning

The idea of *opportunistic memory* builds on two views of opportunism in planning—that of Hayes-Roth and Hayes-Roth (1979) and that of Birnbaum and Collins (1984).

Hayes-Roth and Hayes-Roth presented the view that a planner should be able to shift between planning strategies on the basis of perceived opportunities, even when those opportunities are unanticipated. Their model, which they called *opportunistic planning*, consisted of a Blackboard architecture (Lesser, Fennel, Erman and Reddy 75) and planning *specialists* that captured planning information at many levels of abstraction. These specialists included domain level plan developers (*e.g.* specialists that know about routes, stores, or conditions for specific plans) as well as more strategic operators (*e.g.* specialists that would look for clusters of goals and goals with similar preconditions). The planner could jump between strategies as different specialists "noticed" that their activation conditions were present. For example, in scheduling a set of errands, a specialist with knowledge of clustering of errands by location could be invoked while another specialist was scheduling them by goal priority. In this way, the planner could respond to opportunities noticed at planning time.

Unfortunately, there are some problems with this view of opportunism. Primarily, it includes no model of execution. As with many planners, all planning is done in absence of the ability to execute the plan and thus respond to the effects of that execution. It is a model of opportunism at planning-time rather than execution-time. It fails to capture the behavior we are interested in modeling.

More recently, Birnbaum and Collins (1984) presented a view of opportunism that does include a role for execution. Under their model, goals are viewed as independent processing entities that have their own inferential power. When a goal is suspended because of resource constraints, it continues to examine the ongoing flow of objects and events that pass by the agent. If circumstances that would allow for the satisfaction of the goal arise, the goal itself recognizes them and projects a plan into the current action agenda.

They present a simple yet compelling example of the behavior that interests them in a description of an agent trying to obtain both food and water in the wild. In their example, the agent suspends the goal to find water while trying to satisfy the goal to find food. While searching for food, however, the agent jumps over a stream and is able to recognize that the stream affords an opportunity to satisfy a suspended goal.

Birnbaum and Collins argue that this is managed by giving the suspended goal the ability to examine the current situation and inference directly off of it. They argue that this must be the case, since there can be no way to decide, at the time of suspending a goal, the exact conditions under which it should be activated. Any planner that has to store and then activate suspend goals will miss opportunities that it could not anticipate.

Birnbaum (1986) has argued further that indexing of suspended goals by descriptions of the conditions that allow their satisfaction is an unworkable approach. Not only will the indices will be too complex but the planner will have to constantly compare the current state of the world to the features used to index suspended goals in what amounts to a memory of unsatisfied tasks. As Birnbaum says, this is hardly opportunism.

We share Birnbaum and Collins' philosophical stance of trying to explain complex execution-time opportunistic behavior (even up to the subtle form of opportunism exhibited in Freudian slips). However, we disagree that this behavior results from goals constantly monitoring the world. We believe that indexing suspended goals is a far better explanation.

Birnbaum's arguments against indexing apply to models that separate a memory of goals from the planner's memory and understanding of the world. Under our model, however, there is no such distinction between types of memory. There is only one memory that is used to understand the world and to store suspended goals. Thus the act of recognition is the same as the act of indexing.

A simple example will clarify this. Imagine that our planner from earlier is doing house renovation and during the day realizes that he needs a new hammer, some nails, work gloves, plaster and twenty or so other items. Under Birnbaum and Collins' view, the goals associated with these items would each be examining the ongoing situation in hopes of seeing a hardware store. When one is seen, each goal would then assert itself and all items would be purchased. Throughout the process, however, each of the goals is observing the situation and drawing inferences about it.

Our version of this scenario places each goal in memory, associated with the representation corresponding to the planner being near a hardware store. Once the hardware store is recognized, all goals associated with the structures used in that recognition are asserted. We get the same behavior, but as a straightforward by-product of understanding.

5 The Assumptions

The ideas of opportunistic memory in this paper exist in the context of a more general theory of planning and memory called *case-based planning* (Hammond 1986; Kolodner *et al* 1985). Case-based planning views planning as a memory task. Memories of past successes are used as prototypes for new plans; memories of past failures are used to avoid repeating the failures; and memories of past plan modifications are used to tailor old plans to new situations. This contrasts with the view of planning as a task of composition in which large plans are constructed piece by piece out of primitive actions.

There are certain assumptions that we make in case-based planning:

- First, we do not have a closed world. This limits the usefulness of preplanning and projection.

- Second, we have an incomplete and imperfect model of the world. This is assumed of not just the domain in general but also of the steps in plans that we use on a regular basis. In practice, this means that a planner cannot fully trust either its knowledge of the world's physics or its understanding of the world's current state.

- Third, we cannot do projection. That is, we cannot run simulations of our plans in order to tease out problems due to step interactions. This follows from our first and second assumptions. While we can project on the basis of *what the planner knows*, there is no guarantee that the projection will match what really happens.

We do not make these assumptions because we want to. We make them because we have been forced to. Such is the nature of real world domains. But human planners are able to plan in complex domains, often with little knowledge of the true physics of those domains. This makes us believe that it is possible for a planner to plan and do where it cannot understand.

Strangely enough, the need for opportunistic reasoning and the tools for developing it both grow out of these assumptions. Having assumed, then, that the planner cannot completely model the effects of its own actions or predict those of other agents, we must provide it with some sort of mechanism that will allow it *react* to the world as well as *act* in it.

Likewise, because the planner cannot completely model the world, we must assume a mechanism for parsing or understanding the world that provides the planner with enough information to make execution-time decisions. In effect, the lack of a perfect world model requires that any planner must watch what it is doing as it is doing it. We will use this understanding process as the core of our opportunistic reasoning mechanism.

There are other ramifications to the use of a case-based planner, having to do with what constitutes a planning step and the nature of projection. The most important point we want to make in this section, however, is that a planner must understand and interact with the world in which it executes plans.

6 TRUCKER and RUNNER

Our *opportunistic memory* algorithm is only part of an overall approach to planning. Because of this, we must include some discussion of the two planners TRUCKER and RUNNER. Both planners are case-based in design and *active* in the sense that they test their plans through interaction with complex simulated worlds. As we mentioned before, the crucial difference between the two is that at this point in time TRUCKER is implemented and RUNNER is not.

6.1 TRUCKER

TRUCKER is a University of Chicago planner that interacts with a simulated world in order to test out its plans and learn from both failure and success. Its domain is a UPS-like pick-up and delivery task in which new orders are received during the course of a day's execution. Its task is to schedule the orders and develop the routes for its trucks to follow through town.

TRUCKER creates new plans using two means: a map and a memory. TRUCKER uses its map when it initially builds a route for an area. Once it has built a new route and verified it by running it in the world, it stores the route in a case memory, indexed by its literal endpoints as well as by neighborhood and part-of-town descriptors. When it is able to find a plan for an order in memory, the plan is expanded and placed at the end of TRUCKER's action agenda. TRUCKER never tries to optimize over multiple goals unless it already has a plan in memory that does so.

TRUCKER optimizes its planning for multiple goals only when it notices an opportunity to do so during execution. If TRUCKER notices an opportunity to satisfy a goal that is scheduled later in the queue, it stops and reasons about the utility of merging the later plan with the steps it is currently running. If it is able to construct a plan that is significantly better than one which treats the plans independently, it uses the new plan. It also stores the new plan in memory, indexed by each of the separate goals. When either goal re-occurs, TRUCKER searches its action queue for for the partner goal and uses the plan that it has created for the pair.

Even when a goal is placed on the action queue, TRUCKER treats it as though it is blocked. That is, it establishes the conditions that would allow TRUCKER to satisfy the goal and then associates the goal with the memory structures that would be active during the recognition of those conditions. For example, while planning for a pick-up at the Sears Tower later in the day, TRUCKER associates the goal with its internal representation of the Tower. This allows it to activate and then satisfy the goal if it recognizes the Sears Tower earlier in the day.

6.2 RUNNER

The RUNNER project is the direct descendent of TRUCKER. RUNNER's domain is similar to the errand running domain used by Hayes-Roth and Hayes-Roth to study opportunistic planning (1979). Unlike TRUCKER, RUNNER has only a single agent to control, but RUNNER's agent is capable of a wider range of activity, and its domain allows for a richer set of goal interactions than does TRUCKER's. This change of domain was motivated by our desire to study a wider range of issues in both opportunism and execution-time failure recovery

RUNNER does some planning-time integration. RUNNER's plans are MOP structures (Schank 1982) that organize steps by their function: establishing preconditions, side-conditions, goal satisfaction, or post-condition clean up. For each new goal being planned for, RUNNER checks for prototypical plan interactions that would allow it to merge preconditions, piggy-back plans or subsume them under single plans. For example, RUNNER looks for plans that have similar precondition steps in order to splice them together.[3]

---

[3]Note that this approach does not involve looking at all potential mergings or orderings of plan steps, only those that fall into certain categories of possible interaction. Work on this vocabulary of interactions is part of our overall philosophy that planning is a domain with a knowledge base of its own that must be made explicit. These categories are part of this epistemology.

Like TRUCKER, RUNNER is not designed to fully optimize plans at planning-time, and instead waits for the world to inform it about positive plan interactions. RUNNER ends up suspending many of its goals in much the same way that TRUCKER does. Unfortunately, RUNNER's goals and plans are more than just the simple pick-up and delivery structures used by TRUCKER. As a result, RUNNER must do more of an analysis of what might constitute an opportunity to satisfy a goal than TRUCKER was forced to do.

RUNNER analyzes blocked plans and goals using two knowledge sources: precondition information associated with each plan and knowledge of opportunities with which it should be concerned. For example, in the case of John realizing that he cannot go to the grocery store to get orange juice, RUNNER would examine the preconditions (*e.g.*, the planner has money, is at the store, and has time) and look for specific conditions that might lead to an opportunity (*e.g.* the planner has a missing resource, the planner is at the appropriate location or the planer has a time window). Each potential opportunity is evaluated as to how normative it is—with non-normative features ranking as better opportunities as well as whether or not it is actually blocked in the current situation. In our example, having money, being at a grocery store and having time are all preconditions for buying orange juice. But there is a difference between them in that having money is a normative condition and as such does not constitute an opportunity while being near a store is a non-normative precondition and as such does constitute an opportunity.

7 Opportunism in TRUCKER and RUNNER.

In both TRUCKER and RUNNER, blocked goals are associated with the elements of memory that will be active when opportunities to satisfy those goals arise. The main difference between the two planners is that establishing these conditions is relatively trivial in the TRUCKER domain—goals are of the same basic type. While the details of goal blockage and the analysis of opportunity differs between these planners, the basic approach to dealing with blocked goals is the same.

While these two planners are different, both require the ability to halt planning on a goal, suspend it and then recall it when opportunities for execution present themselves. The approach used by TRUCKER and RUNNER to suspend and recall blocked goals has three basic parts:

First, the planner suspends the blocked goals by associating them with the elements of memory that describe potential opportunities. This requires that the planner have access to a vocabulary that differentiates between the different types of planning problems *e.g.* resource limitations, time constraints, the planner's limitations).

Next, the planner executes the plans for its active goals. During execution, it has to monitor the ongoing effects of its plan as well as the effects of the plans of others in its world. The representational elements used to do this parsing are the same elements with which suspended goal have been associated. As a result, the planner's general recognition of a situation that constitutes an opportunity can immediately activate any goals that have previously been associated with that situation.

Finally, any activated goals are integrated into the current set of scheduled steps, and the plan is executed. This requires reasoning about resources, protections, as well as the effects of actions.

In our example of John and orange juice, these steps translate into:

- John's goal to possess orange juice is blocked by lack of time to run the default plan.

- He decides, on the basis of the preconditions on his plan to possess orange juice, that being at a store would constitute an opportunity to get the orange juice. As a result, he links the suspended goal to the condition of being near a store.

- While coming home, he sees and recognizes a Seven-Eleven. This activates the goal to obtain orange juice that he associated with this condition earlier in the day.

- He then tests the preconditions on the plan and merges it into his current agenda.

7.1 Suspending blocked goals

When either TRUCKER or RUNNER finds a goal blocked, that goal is suspended. In TRUCKER, this requires associating a request with the memory token for the locations it involves. For RUNNER, this requires somewhat deeper reasoning about the various conditions that might provide opportunities to satisfy a blocked goal.

When TRUCKER receives a new request for a pick-up and delivery, it attempts to satisfy the order using a variety of methods. First it checks all active requests on its truck's agendas for one that has a known positive interaction with the new request. If this fails, TRUCKER attempts to find a truck that is currently idle to take up the order. If this also fails, TRUCKER searches its "desk top" for a suspended request that might be usefully combined with the new order. If all else fails, TRUCKER is forced to place the request on a queue of orders waiting for idle trucks.

When this is done, TRUCKER considers the goal blocked, and suspends it. To suspend a goal TRUCKER marks its representation of the goal's pick-up and delivery points with an annotation that there is a goal related to those locations. Because TRUCKER plans for only one type of goal, it doesn't have to do any more reasoning than this to identify good opportunities to satisfy the suspended goals.

RUNNER's domain and the goals it must plan for are more complex than TRUCKER's. As a result, it must reason far more than TRUCKER about the conditions that might constitute opportunities to satisfy a blocked goal.

In general, opportunities to run plans can be derived from the preconditions on each of the steps of a plan. A planner could, given time, move through a plan step by step and collect the preconditions that have to obtain at that point in the plan. But this would require the examination of many conditions that are not particularly useful in the context of opportunism. Some preconditions for obtaining orange juice—having money, having time, and being able to carry the carton—are not useful if we are looking for the features that will allow us to recall the suspended goal at the appropriate time. This is because there are more constraints on "opportunities" than on simple preconditions. These constraint include features such as ease of recognition, likelihood of occurrence and predictiveness.

For example, having money is a strong precondition for buying orange juice, but it is also a normative condition. As a result, it is a bad predictor of an opportunity to satisfy the goal to have orange juice. If the suspended goal is tied to having money, the planner will be reminded of the goal far too often.

Rather than test all preconditions of a plan for these constraints, RUNNER uses a taxonomy of *opportunity types* to derive the conditions that will serve as opportunities to satisfy the plan. This taxonomy guides RUNNER's search through the plan for appropriate preconditions. Once a plan has been analyzed in terms of this taxonomy, it is annotated with pointers to the features associated with opportunities to run it. Features are removed from this list if they cause the goal and plan to be recalled at inappropriate times.

This taxonomy takes the form of a set of tests or questions that RUNNER asks of plan:

- **Is there a non-normative resource that is needed to run the plan?**
  If so, associate the goal with the resource.

- **Is there a special tool that is needed to run the plan?**
  If so, associate the goal with the tool.

- **Is there a special location associated with the plan?**
  If so, associate the goal with the location.

- **Is there a special agent or skill associated with the plan?**
  If so, associate the goal with the agent or skill.

- **Is there a specific time constraint associated with the plan?**
  If so, associate the plan with the time.

There are also special purpose rules for suspending particular goals. Possession goals, for example, are associated with the object of the possession.

Using these rules, RUNNER associates the blocked goal to possess orange juice with the location, GROCERY-STORE, and the object itself, ORANGE-JUICE. This association takes the form of a *SUSPEND* link from the representation of these items to the suspended goal itself. RUNNER associates the goal with the least likely conditions with the hope that most of the other conditions will obtain when the suspended goal is activated. The other conditions are checked when the goal is recalled, but they are not linked to the suspended goal in memory.

7.2 Recalling suspended goals

Both TRUCKER and RUNNER tie execution of actions to locations, landmarks and addresses that they recognize in the world. Thus they must parse and interpret the objects in the world. It during this parse that they both recognize and recall previously suspended goals.

A typical TRUCKER plan, when fully expanded, is a route in the form of a list of the turns that have to be made, described in terms of street names and compass directions. So the plan step (GOTO (920 E-55th)) after a pick-up at (5802 S-WOODLAWN) expands into:

```
(START NORTH (5802 S-WOODLAWN))
(TURN EAST E-57TH)
(TURN NORTH S-CORNELL)
(TURN EAST E-55TH)
(STOP (920 E-55TH))
```

As TRUCKER moves through its world, it parses the objects at its current location and responds to any changes that the tokens it has recognized suggest: turning, for example, when it recognizes the 5700 block of Woodlawn. But TRUCKER does more than this when it recognizes individual tokens. It also checks the token for any annotation of a goal that might be associated with it. If one is found, TRUCKER activates the suspended goal and attempts to integrate it into the current schedule. This allows TRUCKER to easily and effectively activate suspended goals when the opportunities to satisfy them arise. Further, the overhead on this activation is trivial, in that all that TRUCKER has to do is look for a specific type of link on each of the objects it recognizes.

The only problem with this implementation lies in TRUCKER's parser. In this implementation, TRUCKER passively receives tokens that correspond to particular objects and locations in the world instead of doing active object recognition on its own. While this has no real effect on the further activation of suspended goals, we would prefer that the planner be using a more general-purpose recognition system. This does not lead to problems in TRUCKER because the opportunities that TRUCKER can exploit are all associated with particular locations, so there is no value in associating a goal with more general descriptions of opportunities. For example, TRUCKER is never asked to do a pick-up at *any* office building. All pick-ups and delivery requests are for *particular* office buildings. So any suspended requests are also associated with *particular* locations.

For RUNNER, however, this is an issue in that RUNNER has a variety of options for any one goal. RUNNER can pick up orange juice at *any* grocery store, not just a particular one. As a result, we are using a much more general and realistic approach to parsing than we used in TRUCKER.

To deal with this, RUNNER is designed to use the DMAP parser (Riesbeck & Martin 1986) as its recognition system. DMAP uses MOPs (Schank 1982) to represent *concept sequences* to recognize concepts by recognition of their parts. DMAP uses a smart marker-passing algorithm in which two types of markers are used to *activate* and *predict* concepts in an ISA and PART-OF network. *Activation markers* are passed from primitive features up an abstraction hierarchy. In RUNNER, these features include type descriptions such as "road", "wall", "window" and "sign" but no tokens such as "the Seven-Eleven on Cornell and 47th". When any PART-OF a concept is active, *prediction markers* are spread to its other parts. When a predicted concept is handed an activation marker, it becomes active. Likewise, when all parts of a concept are activated, the concept itself is activated.[4]

For our uses, we add a new type of link to DMAP. This link associates suspended goals with concepts that represent opportunities to achieve them. Pointing from concepts to goals, this SUSPEND link is traversed by any activation marker that is placed on the concept. So, the activation of a concept also activates any suspended goals associated with it.

In our example, the suspended goal to get the orange juice is associated with the concept GROCERY-STORE. As the world is parsed, a Seven-Eleven is recognized as a sequence of "parking lot", "building" and "Seven Eleven sign". Because DMAP is passing activation markers up ISA links, the Seven-Eleven is recognized as a particular Seven-Eleven, an instance of Seven-Elevens in general, a CONVENIENCE-STORE, a GROCERY-STORE and a STORE. While the suspended goal is not directly associated with the concept Seven-Eleven, it is associated with GROCERY-STORE. So the recognition of the Seven-Eleven causes the activation of the suspended goal. In general, RUNNER uses this property of DMAP to recall goals associated with general characterizations of opportunities through the recognition of specific situations.

In both planners, the basic approach is the same. In order to execute a plan the low-level features must be disambiguated into tokens representing specific objects in the world. As this is done, each token is checked for an associated goal. And if any goal is found it is considered a candidate for immediate satisfaction.

7.3 Exploiting the opportunities.

Once a suspended goal is reactivated, it has to be evaluated for integration into the current execution agenda.

Here again, the TRUCKER approach uses special purpose techniques tailored to the domain. When a suspended goal is recalled by the planner, it attempts to find the best placement in the current route for the awakened request. Scheduling the pick-up is trivial, in that a truck is at the pick-up location. The difficulty lies in scheduling the delivery. TRUCKER does this by stepping through each location already scheduled and finding the section of the route that will be the least altered by the insertion of the delivery. This can

---

[4]A full description of DMAP is well beyond the bounds of this paper and we point the reader to two excellent descriptions of this work (Riesbeck & Martin 1986, Martin & Riesbeck 1986).

be done even before the exact routes are selected, by using the map and simple rules of geometry.

Because this optimization is fairly time consuming, TRUCKER saves the resulting route, so that it can re-use it when the same conjunct of goals arises again. We see the recognition of execution-time opportunity as a special case of expectation failure (Schank 1982) and treat it as an indication of a gap in TRUCKER's knowledge base.[5]

The solution to this problem in RUNNER is not quite so clean. Because RUNNER deals with a wider variety of goals, the special purpose techniques used in TRUCKER are not applicable. Still RUNNER's plan merging techniques are not as general as those used by most planners. RUNNER falls back on the same techniques for merging plans that it uses for planning construction.

Steps in RUNNER's plans are specifically labeled as to function (PRECONDITION, GOAL-SATISFACTION, POST-CONDITION, CLEAN-UP). RUNNER uses these labels to search for specific ways to merge plans. Although RUNNER goes through the same process during preplanning, the task is somewhat easier when applied to a newly activated goal. Just as TRUCKER knows that it is already at the pick-up location, RUNNER knows that the conditions associated with the activation of the suspended goal are already satisfied. If they weren't, the suspended goal would not have been noticed in the first place.

In our orange juice example, the steps required to get the planner to a store can be ignored, in that the being *at the store* is the condition that activated the goal in the first place. But the planner can also ignore other steps. In particular, the steps that are used to "recover" from the precondition of being at the store once the plan is over can be ignored. Because the planner did not need to run the steps in the GROCERY-STORE plan to get to the store, it will not have to run the steps in that plan that will get it away from the store. In general, precondition/clean-up pairs can be canceled together. The planner knows that the running plan must include the same pair, and need not be concerned with the part of the recalled plan that includes it.

The remaining steps—going into the store, buying the orange juice, and exiting—have to be integrated in a fairly traditional way. The planner checks the preconditions not set by the activation conditions, and it notes the use of resources and their interaction with existing protections. The final product is a small change in the overall plan that takes the planner into the store for a moment before resuming his trip home.

In both TRUCKER and RUNNER, the task of integrating recalled goals is essentially the same as the task of creating an initial plan. The only difference is both planners have added information about the conditions that currently hold and, as a result, are able to avoid consideration of the steps that establish those conditions. RUNNER is able to go beyond this and avoid consideration of steps involving post-condition clean up.

---

[5]For a more detailed discussion of this type of learning, see (Hammond, Converse & Marks [In preparation.]).

8 Conclusions

In this paper, we have argued the need for an execution-time ability to recognize and exploit planning opportunities. Our goal was to present a model of opportunistic planning that provides this ability with little overhead.

We argue that our model of *opportunistic memory* does exactly that. By associating blocked goals with the same structures used to represent the planner's world, we are able to get activation of suspended goals as a by-product of the understanding process.

The process, implemented in TRUCKER and currently being expanded on in RUNNER, requires three basic steps. Suspended goals are associated with the elements of memory that are related to potential opportunities. During execution, these same memory structures are then used to parse the world. As elements of memory are activated by conditions in the world, any the goals associated with then are also activated and integrated into the current planning queue.

This combination of planning-time suspension and execution-time activation gives both TRUCKER and RUNNER the ability to halt consideration of a goal and with the assurance that the goal will be brought back to mind when the conditions change to allow its satisfaction.

9 Acknowledgements

I'd like to thank both Tim Converse and Mitchell Marks for their work on TRUCKER and their helpful comments concerning the issue of opportunism and this paper. I'd also like to thank the other members of the University of Chicago AI group: Jeff Berger, Tom McDougal, Neil Hurwitz and Oleg Voloshin for their help on this paper and numerous conversations.

10 References

Agre, P.E. and Chapman, D., Pengi: An implementation of a theory of activity. In *Proceedings of AAAI-87*, AAAI, Seattle, WA, July 1987, 268-272.

Alterman, R., Adaptive planning: refitting old plans to new situations. In *Proceedings 7th Cognitive Science Society*, 1985.

Birnbaum, L., *Integrated Processing in Planning and Understanding*, Yale Technical Report # 480. (New Haven, CT, 1986).

Birnbaum, L., and Collins, G., Opportunistic Planning and Freudian Slips. in *Proceedings of the Sixth Annual Conference of the Cognitive Science Society*, Boulder, CO, 1984.

Chapman, D., *Planning for Conjunctive Goals*, Technical Report TR 802, MIT Artificial Intelligence Laboratory, 1985.

Firby, R. J., An Investigation into Reactive Planning in Complex Domains. In *Proceedings of the Sixth National Conference on Artificial Intelligence*, AAAI, Seattle, WA, 1987.

Hammond, K., *Case-based Planning: An integrated theory of planning, learning, and memory.* Ph.D Thesis, Yale University, 1986.

Hammond, K., Converse T., and Marks, M., Learning from opportunities: Storing and re-using execution-time optimizations, (in preparation).

Hayes-Roth, B., and Hayes-Roth, F., A cognitive model of planning. In *Cognitive Science*, 2, 1979, 275-310.

Kolodner, J. L., Simpson R. L., and Sycara-Cyranski, L., A process model of case-based reasoning in problem solving. In *The Ninth International Joint Conference on Artificial Intelligence*, 1985.

Lesser, V. R., Fennell, R. D., Erman, L. D., & Reddy, D. R., Organization of the Hearsay-II speech understanding system. In *IEEE Transactions on Acoustics, Speech and Signal Processing.* ASSP-23, 1975, 11-23.

Martin, C., and Riesbeck, C., Uniform parsing and inferencing for learning. In *Proceedings of the Fifth National Conference on Artificial Intelligence*, AAAI, Philadelphia, PA, 1986.

Riesbeck, C., and Martin, C., Toward Completely Integrated Parsing and Learning. In *The Eighth Annual Conference of the Cognitive Science Society*, Amherst, MA, 1986.

Schank, R. *Dynamic Memory: A theory of reminding and learning in computers and people.* Cambridge University Press, 1982.

Schank, R. and Abelson, R., *Scripts, Plans, Goals and Understanding.* Lawrence Erlbaum Associates, Hillsdale, NJ, 1977.

Simmons, R., and Davis, R., Generate, Test, and Debug: Combining Associational Rules and Causal Models. In *Proceedings of the Tenth Internation Joint Conference on Artificial Intelligence*, Milan, 1987.

Extracting Diagnostic Features from Explanations[1]

Kristian J. Hammond and Neil Hurwitz
Department of Computer Science
The University of Chicago
Chicago, IL 60637

Abstract

In this paper we present an approach to explanation and diagnosis that bridges the gap between associational and first-principle diagnostic systems. Associational systems relate predetermined sets of symptoms with pre-existing explanations, but do little or no causal reasoning within the domain. First-principle systems use causal reasoning to build explanations, but must rederive each new diagnosis. As a result, associative systems are inflexible while first-principle systems are slow. Our approach addresses the shortcomings of both types of diagnostic systems by making use of EBL and case-based reasoning techniques. In our approach, a diagnosis consists of a causal explanation of the observed failure in the mechanism. These explanations are used to determine feature relevance. Relevant, predictive features are then associated with derived diagnoses so that previous explanations can be reused. We also introduce causal relatedness heuristics that assist causal reasoning when domain knowledge is imperfect.

1 Diagnosis and Explanation

Machine diagnostic systems fall into two categories: those that use predefined links between observable features and diagnoses (Buchanan, B. G. & Shortliffe, E. H. 1984) and those that construct diagnostic explanations out of first-principle rules describing a domain (Davis, R. 1984). Systems of the first type (henceforth referred to as *associational systems*) tend to be inflexible in that they lack the domain knowledge to deal with problems that lie outside their preset rule bases. Systems of the second type (henceforth referred to as *first-principle systems*) are more flexible, but each new diagnosis has to be rederived from first-principles — even if a similar or identical diagnosis has been seen before.

To deal with these problems, we suggest a hybrid system for diagnosis that makes use of ideas from both EBL (DeJong, G. & Mooney, R., 1986 and Mitchell, T. M., Keller, R. M. & Kedar-Cabelli, S. T., 1987) and case-based reasoning systems (Hammond, K., 1986 and Kolodner, J. L., Simpson, R. L. & Sycara-Cyranski, K., 1985). From EBL we

---

[1]This work was supported, in part, by an Independent Research Grant from Lockheed Missiles and Space Co.

take the idea of using causal explanations to determine feature relevance. From case-based reasoning we take the idea that past efforts (in this instance, explanations) can be reused in later processing.

We also borrow from existing ideas in diagnostic systems. From *associational systems* we take the idea that the best way to store and find diagnoses is through the association of hidden problems with observable surface features. From *first-principle systems* we take the idea that the form of a diagnosis should be a causal explanation of a deviation from an internal model.

The domain that we consider is lawnmower repair. We have chosen a level of knowledge for the program corresponding to a person who has read lawnmower repair manuals, but has had no experience in the field. That is, a fairly sophisticated understanding of how lawnmowers work, but little knowledge of the ways in which lawnmowers tend to break down and the effects these breakdowns have on the lawnmower.

This level of knowledge raises issues not relevant to the extreme knowledge states of complete knowledge or total ignorance; in particular the issue of how to apply domain knowledge and domain independent heuristics to the task of determining which features out of a set of observed features in a given case are possibly related to a mechanical failure and which features are just incidental. Dirt and grass covering a lawnmower may be predictive of a plugged air filter while a bent handlebar probably is not - although in neither case does there exist a direct causal chain from the failure to the feature. A program with little knowledge of the domain would have no basis for deciding whether a feature is predictive of a given breakdown other than through sheer repetition; a program with perfect knowledge could always search through its rule base to determine a feature's predictive value. Both of these knowledge states are unnatural in any realistic diagnostic domain.

Our approach addresses this issue by augmenting its specific causal knowledge with more general knowledge of what types of features *tend* to be causally related. These *causal relatedness* heuristics are similiar to an approach taken by Pazzani (1987), although his heuristics involved characterizing temporal proximity while ours emphasize physical proximity and failure type. Together, specific causal knowledge and the *causal relatedness* heuristics are used to identify features that can be used to index diagnoses for later retrieval and to guide the explanation construction of the current case.

2 Bridging the Gap

The main idea behind case-based diagnosis (CBD) is that causal explanations of problems can be used to determine which observable features are predictive of that problem. In effect, a CBD uses reasoning from *first-principles* to construct *associational* links. As we already mentioned, a diagnosis is a causal description of why a particular behavior differs from a model. As a result, a retrieved diagnosis is treated as a hypothesis that can be altered by a *first-principle* reasoner. Because the diagnosis can be altered, the CBD system retains the flexibility of a *first-principle system*. Furthermore, the *first-principle system* need not do as much work because past diagnostic explanations are retrieved by *associational* links. Finally, because causal links can be suggested by *relatedness* heuristics, CBDs are also freed from the requirement of a complete causal model.

The CBD approach offers the flexibility of *first-principle systems* and the speed of *associational systems*. Deep causal knowledge of a domain is used to avoid using it again. That is, it is used to identify when a constructed explanation can be reused so as to avoid rederiving it. But for those instances where a diagnosis does not account for all anomalous features, the explanation can be altered or "tweaked" (Schank, R., 1987, Kass, A., 1986 and Leake, D. & Owens C., 1986). Finally, the use of *causal relatedness* heuristics means that the construction of explanations does not require a complete causal model.

There are five features that give CBD systems these advantages. We argue that these are necessary features of any diagnostic system:

1. A diagnosis is a causal explanation of why a set of observations deviates from an initial model.

2. New diagnoses are constructed out of existing ones, allowing the reuse of partial explanations.

3. Newly constructed diagnoses are used to indicate which features of a situation will be linked to the diagnosis for future use.

4. Causal construction is guided and then augmented by *relatedness* heuristics that suggest causal connections between features.

5. Diagnostic explanations are reused — retrieved from memory using the features in an initial problem description.

3 Terminology

There is some terminology that we should define before continuing with the discussion.

A **normative model** consists of a description of a mechanism's parts, their connections and network that allows the propagation of effects from a change in one part to another. This model is hierarchical in that it is broken into systems, sub-systems and then actual parts. A **use model** is a description of the actions that are performed on and with the mechanism.

An **anomalous feature** is a feature that is not initially predicted by the normative model of a mechanism. **Observable features** are anomalous features that require no testing to discover. **Testable features** require the application of tests. All testable features have costs associated with them that reflect the difficulty of running the test. Observable features can be thought of as testable features having zero cost. **Symptoms** are observable features that impair the functioning of the mechanism. All symptoms require explanation.

By **case** we mean a structure placed into memory that includes a **diagnostic explanation** as well as links to similar cases, to more specific cases, and to more general cases. Cases are indexed under observable features. Cases are linked to other cases through LATERAL and SPEC links which are indexed by testable features. ISA links are unindexed.

A **physical explanation** is the set of causal chains linking anomalous features to a **base-level cause** or the use model. A **base-level cause** is a discrepancy between a physical part and its description in the normative model such as a clogged air filter. A **use model explanation** is a causal chain that links the base-level cause to events in a use model that give rise to it. A **diagnostic explanation** is the set of chains formed by the physical and use model explanation.

Links in the diagnostic explanation are formed using either **domain-level causal rules** or **causal relatedness heuristics**. **Domain-level causal rules** define connections between actions and effects and are mediated by changes in state. **Causal relatedness heuristics** describe situations in which causal connections can be inferred.

Explained features are those anomalous features that are included in the diagnostic explanation. **Related features** are those anomalous features not linked to the diagnostic explanation by a direct causal chain. **Irrelevant features** are those anomalous features inferred from the normative model. **Unexplained features** are those for which no explanation can be found.

4 Case-based diagnosis

The space of possible breakdowns for most any system is non-homogeneous. A system will break down in some ways more often than in others. For example, a fouled spark plug is more likely the cause of a lawnmower not starting than a snapped fuel line, although either is possible. CBD takes advantage of the non-homogenaeity by forming new explanations out of existing ones for similar situations. This requires that a CBD system store past explanations in memory, indexed by relevant observable features, and use them as bases for future explanations. Features of a new problem "remind" the program of previous explanations via predictive links to past cases in memory. Any "reminding" may or may not need to be modified to suit the present case. Thus, once a pocket of explanations has been discovered, diagnosing problems that lie in this pocket becomes a much simpler task.

An important point to note is that a CBD system must do more than just add new cases to its memory of past diagnostic explanations. It also has to establish the observable features used to get to the explanations, as well as alter the predictive value of any that led the system astray. For example, if a particular diagnosis is indexed in memory by the symptom of smoke coming from a motor, but does not fit the current situation, the system must do more than simply construct the new diagnosis and store it in memory. It must also alter the indexing of the spurious diagnosis by refining the features (*e.g.*, black smoke or white smoke), forcing a conjunction (black smoke *and* a loud rattle) or removing the predictive link between the feature and cases in memory in general. The important point is that as the contents of a CBD system changes, so does its organization .

The CBD algorithm is a variation of that found in case based planning (Hammond, K. (1986)):

- **Selection:** Observable features are used to find existing cases in memory. This involves:
  - Spreading activation from the observable features is used to initially "wake-up" a set of cases in memory.
  - Differential diagnosis between multiple case activations.

- **Matching:** Portions of the candidate explanation are matched against features and states included in initial problem description. Further matches of testable features against the explanation are done by examining the mechanism — with the lower cost tests done first.

- **Modification:** Any deviation from the existing physical explanation is repaired using backward chaining, guided by the CBD's *causal relatedness* heuristics. This mechanism is in transition and will eventually be driven by a set of transformation rules similar to those in CHEF (Hammond, K. (1986b)). Construction stops when a base-level cause is found.

- **Connection:**
  - A use-model explanation connects the base-level cause to the use model.
  - Remaining unexplained anomalous features are connected to the events and states in the explanation or the CBD's use model through causal chains. The CBD may not be able to attach some features.
  - The *causal relatedness* heuristics are used to link unexplained anomalous features to the physical or use model explanations.

- **Extraction:** Explained features are extracted for use in indexing. Any features not included in the diagnostic explanation are ignored.

- **Indexing:** The new case is placed in memory, indexed by the features that predict its applicability. This involves the standard problems of any categorization system including:
  - Case collision — colliding cases are distinguished by testable features. LATERAL links are created between cases.
  - Generalizing cases and refining indexing — colliding cases with shared explanations are generalized and SPECs are created with indexing based on testable features.

5 An example

These ideas can be brought into focus in terms of a simple example from the domain of lawnmower diagnosis.

> The CBD system is presented with a faulty machine. The fault is described as a single symptom - "low power". Along with the symptom of low power is the observable features of "black smoke" billowing from the exhaust and a "rattle" coming from the pistons. Other observable features of the mower include grass jammed in the wheels, a bent handle, twisted throttle and worn paint.

The first step is to use the input features to **select** an explanatory case from memory that can be used as a base of diagnosis. In this example, selection requires activation of the only case in memory associated with the feature of low power. This case involves a crimp in the fuel line causing a reduction in fuel flow. This it turn causes a less powerful combustion leading to lower piston pressure which results in low power. In other, more complex cases, there would have to be some mediation between features and cases, but in this example there is only a single link between input features and cases in memory so there is no choice but to start with this initial case.

Once the case is selected, it is **matched** against the features in the new problem. This matching is driven by the cost of testing for features in the retrieved explanation traded-off against the utility of testing for those features. For example, the cost of testing for the fuel line crimp is low compared to testing for piston pressure and determines if the overall diagnosis is correct, so this test is run first. Unfortunately, in this example, little is gained from the retrieval of the past diagnosis. The causal chain retrieved only matches down to the first few links - the low power being caused by low piston pressure.

Once the match between the old and new is established, the partial chain that remains is **modified** to fit the facts of the current situation. Any deviation from the existing explanation is repaired using causal rules for the domain, guided by the causal relatedness heuristics. The heuristics serve to indicate which of the observed or discovered features may be candidates for connection to the usable portion of the explanation. In effect, they guide the search through the space of possible explanations. In this case, the CBD system chains backward from the low piston pressure to the diagnosis of worn piston rings. The chain constructed leads from the worn piston rings, to pressure leakage to low piston pressure which was already established as causing the existing symptoms. Note that at this point the only interest is in building an explanation of the failure itself. The other features in the input have yet to be connected.

Once the central failure has been explained, the CBD system **connects** other features from the input either to the primary chain or a normative description of a typical lawn-mower. Features such as the grass in the wheels and bent handle can be explained as byproducts of the normal use of the machine. The black smoke, however, is explained in terms of the failure — oil is leaking into the cylinder head through the worn rings and is being burned, thus causing the black smoke.

Other features cannot be directly causally connected. The rattling noise, the bent throttle and the worn paint cannot be fit into either the explanation of the failure or the normal use of the machine. Features in this category are dealt with using a set of heuristics to evaluate the *likelihood* that the features are causally related to the failure. These heuristics consider physical connection of parts, proximity of parts, parts in shared sub-systems and similarity of failure. In this example, the piston noise is connected to the failure because of physical proximity and the worn paint is connected because of similarity of failure (wear). The bent throttle is not connected because no rationale can be found for thinking that there is a causal connection between it and the worn piston rings. It remains unexplained. At the end of the connection phase, then, features fall into one of three categories: those that are explained by the normal use of the machine, those that are explained by the causal chain leading to the failure and those that remain unexplained.

Once the CBD system has explained all that it can, it then tries to **extract** indexing information from the three categories of features.

Features resulting from normal use of the machine are ignored. In fact, once a feature is explained as resulting from normal use, it is added to the normative description of the machine. This allows the system to become less as less "surprised" by features that are actually normal by-products of normal use. In this example, the grass in the wheels and bent handle are simply added to the set of features that are considered by the system to be normal.

Likewise, those features in the third category are also ignored for indexing because there is no reason to believe that they will tend to show up in future instances of similiar failures since no causal connection was found.

Features in the second category, direct- and side-effects of the events in the causal chain leading to the failure and causally related features, form the list of candidates for indexing. This is not to say that each of these features will be useful in discriminating between cases. Some may result from many different causes, but all are candidates. In this example, the problematic feature itself — low power — and the side-effect of the cause of the problem — black smoke — are both candidates for indexing.

Once a list of candidate features is extracted from the case, it is placed in memory, **indexed** by those features. Indexing involves dealing with collisions between cases, construction of generalizations and the choice of features for differential diagnosis. The details are beyond the scope of this abstract. The important issue is that the case is indexed by a combination of those features that *must* be present in any instance of the diagnosed problem and those features that *might* be causally related, as determined by the relatedness heuristics. As with any categorization system, these guesses have to be refined and tested through use (using what have been called "similarity based" methods). The importance of using such techniques is that they constrain the set of features used to index a case in memory by filtering them through relatedness heuristics.

6 Relatedness heuristics

The core of CBD system's ability to go beyond pure deduction in extracting indexing information from explanations of failures is its heuristics concerning causal relatedness. Along with its strict causal rules, the /sc Cbd system has heuristics for evaluating the *likelihood* that two features are causally related. These heuristics assume first and foremost that the features to be evaluated have not already been connected either to the normative model of the machine or to the causal chain explaining the failure.

Is the feature in the same proximity as the mechanical failure?

An unexpected feature near the failure is more likely to be causally related to that failure than one that is more distant since physical interactions are often limited by distance. A high combustion temperature might affect the condition of the spark plug, but is unlikely to affect the condition of the wheels.

Is there a physical connection between the feature and the mechanical failure?

An unexpected feature might not be near the failure, but nonetheless be causally related to the failure because there is a physical connection between it and the failure. The speed lever on the handlebar is not near the throttle in the carburetor, but there is a physical connection between the two that makes it reasonable to assume that a problem with one could be predictive of a problem with the other.

Are the feature and the mechanical failure part of the same system?

Any system can be viewed as a collection of interrelated systems — a fuel system, compression system, electrical system, or oil system. Each of these systems has a flow of fuel (gas and air), vacuum, electricity, or oil running through the parts that it comprises. An unexpected feature in the same system as the failure is more likely to have a causal relation to that failure than one in another system. For example, dirt in the gas tank might be predictive of a clogged fuel line, but is unlikely to be related to a ruptured crankcase.

Is there a connection between the feature and the way in which the part or parts have failed?

Mechanical failures can be viewed as a failure in a part or interaction between parts. These failures can be categorized into about ten different types, maladjustment, improper installation, and broken connection. An unexpected feature might turn out to be the cause of the failure type or it may be an effect of the same underlying cause of the failure. Recent repairs may turn out to be a predictive of improper installation failures, or possibly specific installation failures for parts that are more difficult to install properly. Likewise "wear" of one part may be related to "wear" of another in that they may have the same cause.

7 Conclusions

The CBD approach combines the basic methods of explanation based learning with the problem solving techniques of case based reasoning. This approach yields the speed of the associational approach and the flexibility of the first-principle approach. Causal reasoning is used not only to build explanations, but also to assist in relating easily identifiable features with the failures that they predict. These explanations can then be quickly retrieved for future use in similar cases. Furthermore, we have attempted to move beyond the strict and unrealistic requirements of complete knowledge that the explanation based technology enforces. Using both causal rules and heuristics about causal relatedness, the system can make guesses about the predictive power of certain features that allow it to function while waiting for further experience to verify or deny the validity of the causal relations it has hypothesized.

CBD is an attempt to treat explanation as a domain, in much the same way Sacerdoti treated planning as domain (Sacerdoti, E., 1975). That is, there is knowledge of explanation construction and use that goes beyond both the domain level rules included in explanations and the weak methods that are currently used to create them. The CBD relatedness heuristics are a first pass at a knowledge base for explanations.

8 References

Bareisis, E. R. & Porter, B. W. (1987). Protos: An exemplar-based Learning Apprentice. *Proceedings of the Fourth International Workshop on Machine Learning*, 12-23.

Buchanan, B. G. & Shortliffe, E. H. (1984). *Rule-based expert systems: The MYCIN experiments of the Stanford Heuristics Programming Project*. Reading, MA: Addison Wesley.

Dejong, G. & Mooney, R. (1986) Explanation-based learning: an alternative view. *Machine Learning, 1, 2*, 145-176.

Hammond, K. (1986a). *Case-based Planning: An integrated theory of planning, learning and memory.*, Ph.D. Thesis, Yale University.

Hammond, K. (1986b), CHEF: A model of case-based planning., AAAI-86, 267-271.

Kass, A. (1986). Modifying Explanations to Understand Stories. In *Proceedings of the Eleventh Annual Conference of the Cognitive Science Society*.

Kolodner, J. L., Simpson, R. L. and Sycara-Cyranski, K. (1985). A process model of case-based reasoning in problem solving., In *The Ninth International Joint Conference on Artificial Intelligence*.

Leake, D. and Owens C. (1986). Organizing Memory for Explanations. In *Proceedings of the Eleventh Annual Conference of the Cognitive Science Society*.

Mitchell, T. M., Keller, R. M. & Kedar-Cabelli, S. T. (1987) Explanation-based generalization: A unifying view. *Machine Learning, 1, 1*, 47-80.

Pazzani, Michael J. (1987). Inducing Causal and Social Theories: A Prerequisite for Explanation-based Learning. In *Proceedings of the Fourth International Workshop on Machine Learning*.

Sacerdoti, E. (1975), *A structure for plans and behavior,* Technical Report 109, SRI Artificial Intelligence Center.

Schank, R. (1987). *Explanation Patterns*, Cambridge University Press.

Refitting Plans for Case–Based Reasoning

James A. Hendler[†]
Subbarao Kambampati[‡]
University of Maryland, College Park

The value of enabling a planning system to remember the plans it generates for later use was acknowledged early in planning research [FHN72]. The systems developed, however, were only marginally useful as the reuse was primarily based on simple strategies of generalization via variablization and later unification. More recently, the focus has shifted to more complex adaptation of plans, primarily in case–based systems. This adaptation of plans has been generally been studied as a separate component of planning [Alt86,KSS85], leading to a need for strong domain models. Further, much of the work in case–based planning has concentrated on the indexing and retrieval aspects of the cases, rather than on the internal structures of the plans. This again leads to a need for strong domain models to be used during case transformation [Ham86].

In our current research, we are interested in characterizing the type of information that should be remembered along with the stored plans so that they can be reused flexibly. We are examining an approach to plan reuse that enables a planner to flexibly reuse its own previously generated plans in solving new planning problems efficiently. The planner leaves information relevant to the reuse process in the form of annotations on the generated plans. These annotations provide a validation (justification) of the generated plan in terms of the planner's knowledge, and encapsulate the reasoning traces of the planner. Our annotation process is inexpensive and can be carried out incrementally by the planner. The approach is based on Carbonell's [Car83] proposed methodology for analogous reasoning which includes the storage of derivational histories along with problem solutions.

In our system, we reuse the annotated plans by mapping them on to new problem situations and contrasting with the stored annotations. This process, *annotation verification*, focuses the adaptation of the old plan to the new situation by locating the places where the old plan will fail to be applicable to the new problem. These applicability failures are then classified and refitting strategies for each of them are proposed. These suggestions are then appropriately incorporated into a task network, preserving the applicable portions of the old plan. The planner is then called upon to reduce this task network. This neatly

---

[†]University of Maryland Institute for Advanced Computer Studies, Center for Automation research, Computer Science Dept.
[‡]Center for Automation Research, Computer Science Dept.

separates the adaptation decisions (eg. whether to replace a failing step or establish its preconditions) from the planning decisions (eg. how to find a replacement, how to ensure that the plan steps will not interact), and leaves the planning decisions to a generative planning component.

System Overview

Our current system implements the plan reuse capability for a domain independent, nonlinear, conjunctive planner. The planner in our system, based on Nonlin [Tat77], has the capability of reducing a task network into an executable plan. Unlike normal nonlinear planners, however, it also annotates the plans it generates and stores each annotated plan in its plan library.

The planning cycle proceeds as follows: Given a planning problem to be solved, our system first checks if the planner's library contains a plan for a similar problem. If no such plan is found, the planner is invoked to solve the problem generatively. If the plan for a similar problem is found in the library, it is adapted to the new problem as follows:

(1) The old plan along with its annotations is *interpreted* in the new problem situation. This process maps the old plan along with its annotations into the new problem, taking the differences between old and new situations into account. At the end of this process, we have a partial plan that is consistent with the old and new problem specifications.

(2) The *annotation verification* traces the validations of the interpreted plan and suggests changes to be made to the interpreted plan to fit it to the new problem. In the current system, annotation verification suggests four types of modifications—removing steps that achieve unnecessary goals, adding tasks to achieve any extra goals, adding tasks to establish failing preconditions, and replacing plan steps with failing filter (relevance) conditions.

(3) A task network is constructed, which contains the applicable portions of the interpreted old plan, along with the changes suggested by the annotation verification procedure.

(4) The planner is then called to reduce this task network, generating a plan for the new problem. As inter-step order of the old plan is left undisturbed as much as possible during annotation verification, many interactions do not have to be re-analyzed. For the domain independent non-linear planner that we are using, this approach produces a significant savings in planning effort.

Unlike previous non-case-based approaches to plan-reuse, our system uses an old plan not just as a MACROP [FHN72], but as a plan which can be

---

Ths work was supported in part by DARPA contract DAAB07-86-K-F073.

transformed to work in a similar new situation. This is largely the result of remembering the internal justification structure of the plan in the annotations. More importantly, integration of planning and plan reuse allows us to do adaptation without recourse to any domain knowledge other than that already known to the planner; thus obviating the need for deep domain models. In contrast to PLEX [Alt86] and CHEF [Ham86], our approach couples the information relevant to adaptation along with the individual plans.

References

[Alt86] Alterman, R. An Adaptive Planner *Proceedings of AAAI-86* 65–69.

[Car83] Carbonell, J. Derivational Analogy and its Role in Problem Solving *Proceedings of AAAI-83* 64–69.

[FHN72] Fikes, R., Hart, A., and Nilsson, N. Learning and Executing Generalized Robot Plans *Artificial Intelligence, 3(1)*, 1972. 251–288.

[Ham86] Hammond, K. CHEF: A Model of Case–Based Planning *Proceedings of AAAI-86* 267–271.

[KSS85] Kolodner, J., Simpson, R., and Sycara–Cyranski, K. A Process Model of Case–based Reasoning in Problem Solving *Proceedings of IJCAI-85*, 284–290.

[Tat77] Tate, A. Generating Project Networks *Proceedings of IJCAI-77*, 888–893.

Towards an Architecture for Open World Problem Solving*

Thomas R. Hinrichs
School of Information and Computer Science
Georgia Institute of Technology
Atlanta, Georgia 30332

Abstract

Problem solving in open worlds involves the management of inconsistency, imprecision, and lack of knowledge. In this paper we examine some specific problems that arise in open worlds and describe inferences that are needed to deal with them. We present a problem solving architecture that integrates case-based reasoning and constraint propagation to achieve flexibility in open domains. This architecture is implemented in a computer program called JULIA.

1 Introduction

Problem solvers must often work with incomplete or inconsistent knowledge, either because the domain is unbounded, continually changing, or not well understood. Two general techniques for dealing with such situations are: 1) to postpone commitment until more information is available, and 2) to make an assumption, or educated guess, about the missing information. Individually, these techniques may be insufficiently flexible: If a problem is under-constrained, delayed commitment by itself may never solve it. On the other hand, a problem solver that always leaps to conclusions may fail to exploit information that arrives late. To remedy these problems, we are exploring an approach that integrates both methods in the form of constraint propagation and case-based reasoning.

Case-based reasoning involves recalling previous problem solving episodes, or *cases*, that are similar to the current situation and adapting parts of those cases to fit the new problem. In this paper, we describe a problem solving architecture which integrates case-based reasoning with constraint propagation in order to support reasoning in open worlds. We have implemented this architecture in a program called JULIA [Cullingford et al. 1986], which is an interactive catering advisor that helps users to plan meals.

In the following section, we use the meal planning domain to illustrate some problems that arise in open worlds and techniques that address them. Section 3 describes the problem solving process with an extended example and section 4 presents a layered architecture which implements this process.

2 Open Worlds

An open world is any domain for which a problem solver has incomplete or inconsistent knowledge. Typical situations in which open worlds arise are: 1) interactive problem solving, 2) under-constrained problems, 3) incomplete domain theories, and 4) problems of ill-defined scope. In this section, we will discuss each of these situations and show how they involve reasoning with incomplete knowledge.

---

*This research was funded in part by NSF Grant No. IST-8608362, in part by ARO contract No. DAAG-29-85-K-0023, and in part by Lockheed Grant No. DTD09-25-87

2.1 Interactive Problem Solving

Problem specifications are often incomplete. Many problem solvers cope with this by asking questions and accepting advice from a user. To be effective, such interactive problem solvers must meet two criteria: they must be reactive and they must reason opportunistically. A *reactive* problem solver is one which responds dynamically to changes in its environment [Kaelbling 1986]. An *opportunistic* problem solver exploits serendipitous features of the environment to satisfy multiple goals or constraints [Hayes-Roth et al. 1979]. These criteria are illustrated in the following hypothetical dialog:

Caterer: How much do you want to spend?
Client: Let's have something cheap like Mexican food. I'm on a diet though, so it should be a light meal.
Caterer: How about a taco salad?

In this exchange, the client answers the original question, changes the focus of the conversation, and volunteers additional information. The problem solver, in turn, must react to the shift in focus and assimilate the new information opportunistically to derive a solution which satisfies the goals and constraints.

In addition, the requirements of interactive problem solving prohibit chronological backtracking. First, because the focus shifts dynamically, the search space cannot be explored hierarchically. Second, responsibility for decisions is shared between the system and the user, and the system must not unilaterally revoke the user's decisions. Therefore each decision must be individually justified to permit dependency-directed backtracking, and the problem solving architecture must include truth maintenance.

2.2 Under-Constrained Problems

Sometimes a problem has no single right answer, or even an optimal one. There may be many solutions that satisfy the given constraints; for example, there are usually many possible menus that will be acceptable for a given meal. How can a problem solver generate these potential solutions, and how should it choose among them?

Often, it is not practical to generate the complete search space. For instance, the class of all dishes is both too large and too poorly defined to enumerate. A better strategy is to generate a small subset of possibilities, use constraints to filter out unacceptable values, and choose among the remaining satisficing candidates.

One way to generate candidates is to recall them from previous cases [Kolodner et al. 1985]. If the problem solver is reminded of cases which were similar to the current one, this provides a limited set of candidate values among which to choose. Using case-based reasoning in this way amounts to a kind of early commitment which complements the delayed commitment of constraint propagation.

2.3 Incomplete Domain Theories

When a problem solver does not know all of the relationships that hold in a domain, it may make incorrect inferences or fail to make any inferences at all. Sometimes the only recourse is to make an assumption about what is probably true. For instance, a caterer can usually assume that money is important to a client and should be conserved. This may not be true, however, if the goal of the meal is to impress a guest. Determining when such assumptions apply is difficult when the domain theory is incomplete.

To complicate matters, these assumptions may change over time. In the short term, a problem solver must revise its assumptions as new information becomes available. For example, if a problem solver plans an inexpensive meal and later learns that the boss is coming to dinner, then it must retract the 'conserve money' assumption and its consequences, and make new assumptions about cost, ease of preparation, and formality. In other words, the problem solver must ensure that the plan is consistent with its assumptions. This consistency can be enforced by constraint propagation and truth maintenance.

Assumptions may also change over the long term, as a problem solver learns when an assumption does or does not apply. Such learning is simplified if the problem solver can recall previous cases, and if those cases contain feedback indicating why they succeeded or failed. For instance, a meal may fail because the planner neglected to provide for vegetarian guests. In the future, the planner should be reminded of this failure and try to determine whether or not there will be vegetarians present. Over time, this should be generalized to accomodate any special case eaters. Case-based reasoning of this sort can offset an incomplete domain theory by helping a problem solver to recognize implicit assumptions, thereby allowing it to anticipate and avoid failure [Hammond 1986,Kolodner 1987].

2.4 Ill-defined Problem Scope

Real world problems are seldom stated in terms of an initial state, a goal state and a set of operators. Usually, a problem solver must infer the nature and scope of the problem and the desired specificity of the solution. For instance, if a client says: "I'm having a party for my research group..." a catering advisor must first assume the existence of a meal based on its own role as caterer. Next, it must look at the context of this meal in order to propose relevant constraints, such as cost and formality. As the solution evolves, the problem solver must also decide how specific to be. For example, a dish might be specified as a salad or more particularly as a waldorf salad. The locale of a meal might be sufficiently specified with an address, or it might be necessary to indicate a particular room. The required level of specificity is seldom given explicitly, and must often be inferred from previous cases and constraints.

In addition to determining the specificity of the solution, the problem solver may also have to infer how specific its own operators should be. In particular, a case-based reasoner may be able to adapt and modify previous solutions at different levels of granularity. For example, situations such as Thanksgiving Dinner are sufficiently traditional that menus from previous cases may be adapted almost intact. More often, bits and pieces of cases can be mixed and matched to derive a satisficing solution. Sometimes, however, the repertoire of known dishes isn't quite sufficient. In this situation, it may be possible to modify recipes by substituting one ingredient for another to satisfy a constraint. Thus, the granularity of problem solving operators never really bottoms out. The adaptation of previous cases just becomes progressively more like reasoning 'from-scratch'.

3 Problem Solving in JULIA

JULIA solves open world problems by reasoning from previous cases and propagating constraints to refine a problem statement (see figure 1). We illustrate this process with a portion of an execution trace in which the problem is to plan a party for about 20 guests. First, the problem solver posts a goal to refine the problem and retrieves a plan to achieve it:

```
GOAL = REFINE (PROTOCOL3)
PLAN = REFINE-SOCIAL-OCCASION
```

The scope of this problem is ill-defined because it is not explicitly stated whether JULIA should plan the entire party, the meal by itself, or just the menu. The problem solver hedges initially by assuming that the problem is to plan a meal in the context of the party:

```
Assuming problem is to refine meal.
GOAL = REFINE (MEAL-1)
PLAN = REFINE-MEAL
```

This problem is under-constrained because there are an infinite number of possible solutions. Therefore, rather than immediately working on the menu, JULIA asks for information which could constrain the search:

```
How much do you want to spend?
-> (cheap-meal Mexican-cuisine p-diet)
```

The user's reply is a list of desired features: cheap-meal is a range of costs per person,

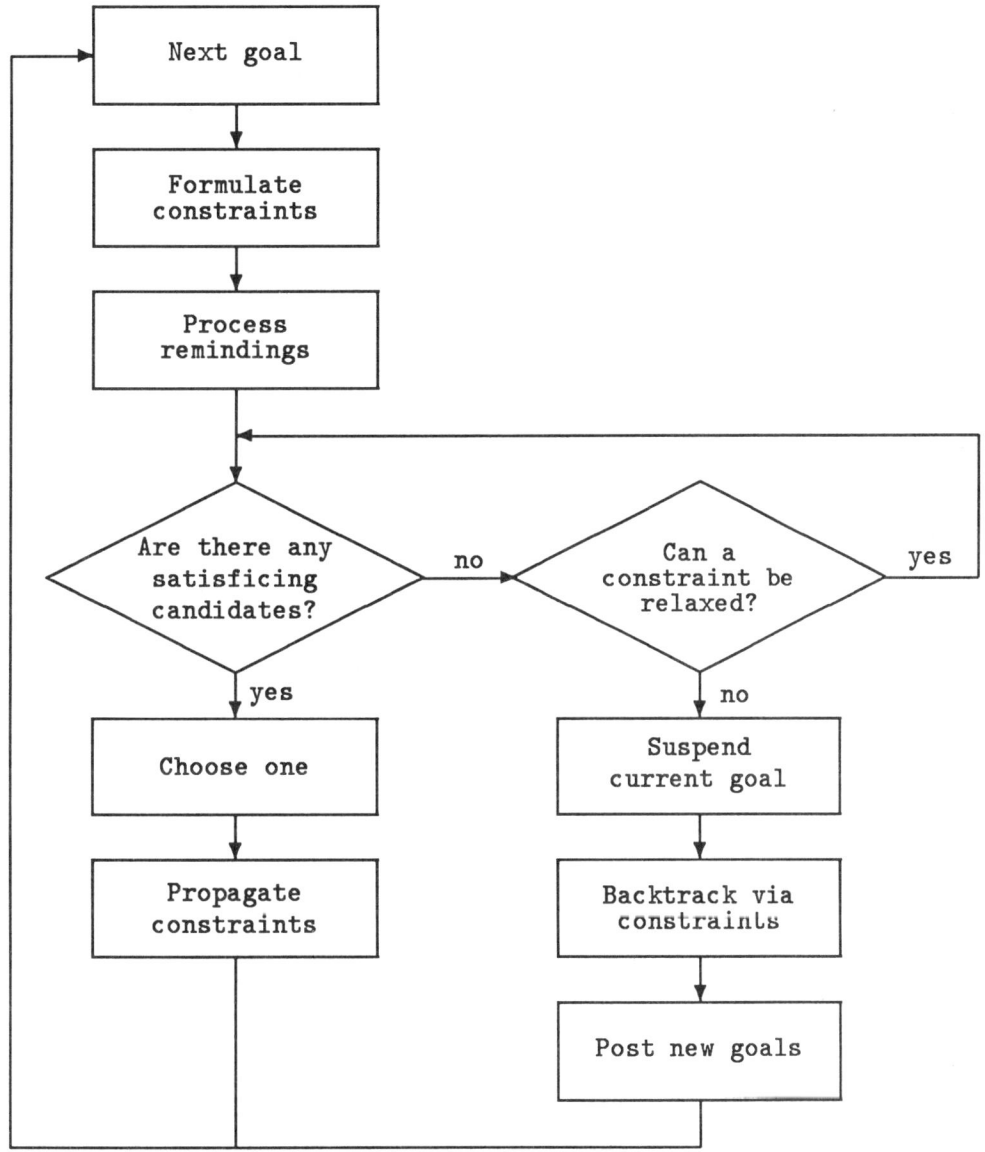

Figure 1: Abbreviated Problem Solving Algorithm

Mexican-cuisine is a description of a typical Mexican meal, and p-diet is a preservation goal. Therefore, the English translation would be "I would like a cheap, Mexican meal which is also low-calorie." Not only has the user answered the question, but he has also volunteered new information. In order to opportunistically use this information, the problem solver formulates and propagates constraints on the new features. When it does, a contradiction is found between the default meal structure (appetizer, salad, main course, and dessert), the structure of a typical Mexican meal (omit salad), and the structure of a typical diet meal (a single main course). JULIA assumes that p-diet, an explicit goal, is more important than Mexican-cuisine, a descriptor, and therefore chooses the single course:

```
Withdrawing plan step ?REFINE-APPETIZER
Withdrawing plan step ?REFINE-SALAD
Withdrawing plan step ?REFINE-DESSERT
```

Thus, JULIA reacts to the user's input by revising its own problem-solving plan as well as the meal plan. At this point the problem solver starts to look for a main dish. Although the problem is still under-constrained, there is enough information available for the case-based reasoner to retrieve similar cases:

```
GOAL = FIND-VALUE (MAIN-DISHES)
Reminded of case:   DECEMBER-MEAL
Reminded of case:   LO-CAL-DINNER
Reminded of case:   DEATH-CHILI-MEAL

I remember the DEATH-CHILI-MEAL which
failed because Tom didn't eat spicy
food.  Will this be a problem in the
current situation?
-> yes
```

To avoid repeating a previous mistake, the problem solver adds a constraint to reject any dish whose taste is spicy:

```
adding constraint:
(DIFFERENT (?DISHES TASTE) SPICY)
```

The case-based reasoner ranks the meals it remembers by similarity and suggests values from the most similar case. When it finds a value that satisfies the constraints, it suggests it to the user:

```
Would you like a taco-salad?
-> yes
```

If a taco-salad were unacceptable, the problem solver would try to relax constraints on other candidates, and failing that it would postpone this goal in the hope that other features would generate new remindings and suggest other candidates. The problem solver continues on from here to fill in other descriptors and dishes until the meal plan is complete.

4 Architecture

The preceeding example suggests some of the functions that are needed to reason with incomplete knowledge. Specifically, there must be some means of: 1) selecting a goal or focus of attention, 2) formulating, propagating, and relaxing constraints, 3) retrieving cases from memory, analyzing failures, and transferring values and constraints, and 4) modifying the problem structure and justifying individual decisions.

Ideally, these functions should be integrated as much as possible in order to minimize redundancy and maximize constructive interaction. At the same time, good software engineering practice dictates information hiding and modularity. These requirements are reconciled in JULIA with a layered architecture which consists of four modules, as shown in Figure 2.

The goal scheduler and TMS are fairly traditional. The goal scheduler is a problem reduction problem solver, and the TMS is a justification-based truth maintenance system based on [Doyle 1979]. In the next sections, we discuss the constraint propagator and the case-based reasoner, which form the core of the problem solving architecture.

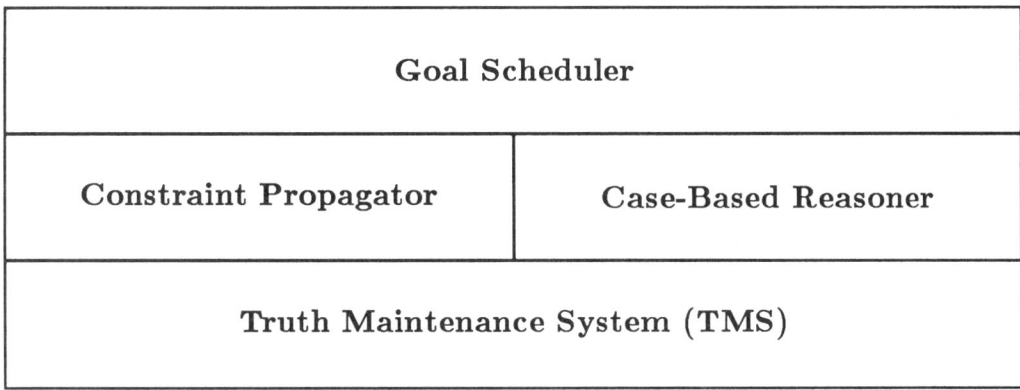

Figure 2: The Problem Solving Architecture

4.1 Constraint Propagator

The constraint propagator has two main functions. First, it evaluates and filters suggested values in a manner similar to Molgen [Stefik 1981]. Second, it propagates values and constraints through a network as in the constraint propagators of [Waltz 1972] and [Steele 1980].

Constraints in JULIA consist of a type, arguments, and an importance. The constraint type is a frame with slots containing a predicate and a generator function, as in ISIS [Fox 1983] and PRIDE [Mittal *et al.* 1986]. An argument may be either a constant or a path to a slot. The importance indicates whether or not the constraint may be relaxed. For example, the constraint to rule out spicy dishes looks like:

(different (?main-dishes taste) spicy required)

where different is the constraint type, the first argument is a path, the second argument is a constant, and the importance is required.

Constraints reside under slots. This permits a constraint to be triggered when its slot receives a value, and it also determines the scope of the constraint. For instance, if the not-spicy constraint is stored under the ACTIVITIES slot of the meal, then all courses inherit it. If, on the other hand, it were stored under a subslot of this such as MAIN-COURSE, then only the main course would be required to be non-spicy.

4.2 Case-Based Reasoner

Two important elements of case-based reasoning are: 1) recalling similar cases in previous situations and 2) adapting parts of those cases to fit the new situation. In JULIA, the case-based reasoner retrieves previous cases from a dynamic memory [Schank 1982, Kolodner 1984]. It then ranks them in order of similarity to the current problem, weighing similar goals more heavily than similar descriptors. The reasoner suggests values from the most similar cases by constructing TMS nodes that package the values along with the reasons for and against them. The Constraint Propagator checks the suggested values and rules out those that violate constraints.

Another function of the case-based reasoner is failure avoidance. Previous cases contain feedback from the user in a slot called Actual-Events. The feedback is a sketchy causal chain which indicates 1) a *goal* which either succeeded or failed, 2) an *event* which resulted in the success or failure of the goal, and 3) a *reason* which is either a theme or a constraint which enabled (or disabled) the event. When the case-based reasoner detects a previous goal failure, it tries to determine whether or not it is relevant by comparing the default function of the object of the event with the current focus of attention. Thus, in the example in section 3 the failure event was that Tom didn't eat chili. The default function of chili is to serve as a main dish, so when the problem solver is looking for a main dish, this failure will be considered potentially relevant.

At this point, the current implementation of JULIA simply asks the user whether the failure is in fact relevant, and if so it transfers the constraint in the *reason* slot. A more sophisticated approach would be to analyze the reason itself to determine how the failure is relevant and how to best avoid it in the current situation.

5 Discussion

Although constraint propagation and case-based reasoning are not new in and of themselves, their integration provides a novel approach to problem solving in open worlds. In particular, it allows a problem solver to deal with incomplete information in five ways:

- The problem solver can react to a user or to a dynamic environment by triggering constraints when new information arrives.

- The problem solver can opportunistically satisfy multiple goals and constraints by combining the bottom-up inferences of constraint propagation with the top-down expectations of case-based reasoning and goal scheduling.

- The case-based reasoner can help reduce the search space when a problem is under-constrained by suggesting values from previous cases.

- The problem solver can deal with an incomplete domain theory by making plausible assumptions based on previous successes and failures.

- The case-based reasoner can help the problem solver to infer the scope of a problem by referring to previous similar cases.

These capabilities suggest several ways in which constraint propagation and case-based reasoning are complementary:

- **Commitment.** Constraint propagation is a form of delayed commitment; inferences are made as information arrives. Alternatively, case-based reasoning can be viewed as a kind of early commitment because it provides a way to make plausible assumptions about missing information.

- **Rate of adaptation.** Constraint propagation permits a problem solver to react immediately to new information. Reacting within a problem-solving session like this can be thought of as short-term adaptation. Case-based reasoning, on the other hand, reacts by altering behavior between sessions, thus adaptation is long-term.

- **Source of information** Information provided by one technique is used by the other: constraints index cases, and in turn, cases suggest additional constraints.

Because constraint propagation and case-based reasoning are complementary, their integration is a first step towards an architecture for open world problem solving.

Acknowledgements

I would like to thank Janet Kolodner for her guidance and encouragement during this research, and Craig Stanfill and Reid Simmons for their comments on an earlier draft of this paper.

References

[Cullingford et al. 1986] R.E. Cullingford and J.L. Kolodner. Interactive advice giving. In *Proceedings of the 1986 IEEE International Conference on Systems, Man, and Cybernetics*, 1986.

[Doyle 1979] J. Doyle. A truth maintenance system. *Artificial Intelligence*, 12(3), 1979.

[Fox 1983] M.S. Fox. *Constraint-Directed Search: A Case Study of Job-Shop Scheduling*. PhD thesis, CMU, 1983. CMU-RI-TR-83-22.

[Hammond 1986] K.J. Hammond. *Case-based Planning: An Integrated Theory of Planning, Learning and Memory.* PhD thesis, Yale, 1986. YALE/CSD/RR-488.

[Hayes-Roth *et al.* 1979] B. Hayes-Roth, and F. Hayes-Roth. A Cognitive Model of Planning. *Cognitive Science*, (3):275–310,1979.

[Kaelbling 1986] L.P. Kaelbling. An architecture for intelligent reactive systems. In M.P. Georgeff and A.L. Lansky, editors, *Proceedings of the Workshop on Reasoning about Actions and Plans*, pages 345–410, Morgan Kaufman, Los Altos, CA, July 1986.

[Kolodner 1984] J.L. Kolodner. *Retrieval and Organization Strategies in Conceptual Memory: A Computer Model.* Lawrence Erlbaum Associates, Hillsdale, NJ, 1984.

[Kolodner *et al.* 1985] J.L. Kolodner, R.L. Simpson, and K. Sycara. A process model of case-based reasoning in problem solving. In *Proceedings of IJCAI-85*, pages 284–290, Los Angeles, 1985.

[Kolodner 1987] J.L. Kolodner. Capitalizing on failure through cased-based inference. In *Proceedings of the Ninth Annual Conference of the Cognitive Science Society*, Seattle, Washington, July 1987.

[Mittal *et al.* 1986] S. Mittal and A. Araya. A knowledge based framework for design. In *Proceedings of AAAI-86*, pages 856–865, Philadelphia, PA, August 1986.

[Schank 1982] R.C. Schank. *Dynamic Memory: A theory of reminding and learning in computers and people.* Cambridge University Press, London, 1982.

[Steele 1980] G.L. Steele Jr. *The Definition and Implementation of a Computer Language based on Constraints.* PhD thesis, MIT, 1980. AI-TR-595.

[Stefik 1981] M.J. Stefik. Planning with constraints (molgen: part 1). *Artificial Intelligence*, 16(2):141–169, 1981.

[Waltz 1972] D. Waltz. *Generating Semantic Descriptions from Drawings of Scenes with Shadows.* Technical Report, MIT Artificial Intelligence Laboratory, 1972. AI-TR-271.

Case-Based Reasoning Applied to Constructing Explanations[1]

Alex M. Kass and David B. Leake
Department of Computer Science, Yale University

Introduction

Case-based reasoning (CBR) is a very general idea with a lot of intuitive appeal. There is a core CBR framework for which there is consensus agreement among researchers in the field, and there are also a number of successful implementations which demonstrate the framework's viability (see, for example [Schank 83], [Kolodner, Simpson and Sycara 85], [Simpson 85], [Hammond 86], [Carbonell 86], and [Sycara 87]). In order for this emerging research paradigm to solidify further it is important that the community establish a group of key questions which researchers in the field are expected to address. It may take some time before there is agreement about the answers, but that doesn't diminish the importance of establishing a common set of questions.

This paper will attempt to explicitly address what we consider to be basic questions for CBR: What exactly is a case? How is the knowledge associated with a particular case represented? How is it made available to help the system process another case?

We propose Explanation Patterns (XPs) [Schank 86], [Kass, Leake and Owens 86] as a simple case representation with important properties for CBR, and present methods for deciding when an XP applies and for adapting XPs to apply old cases to new situations.

A quick overview of CBR

The general idea behind case-based reasoning is to process some input situation using the following steps:

Generic CBR framework

1. **Retrieve** a **case** from **case memory**.

2. Compare the retrieved case to the current situation. **Evaluate** the relevance of the past experience to the current situation.

3. If necessary, **adapt** the current case in order to generate a case description that applies to the current situation.

4. Use the previous case to **generate inferences** that can be transfered to help process the current input.

---

[1]This work is supported in part by the Air Force Office of Scientific Research, under grant 85-0343, and by the Defense Advanced Research Projects Agency, monitored by the Office of Naval Research under contract N00014-82-K-0149.

We gratefully acknowledge the influence that our frequent collaborator Chris Owens has had on our work.

At this level of generality, the paradigm outlined above is not interesting as a solution to anything (because it is too vague), but is interesting for the questions it raises. Each of the words in bold refers to an aspect of case-based reasoning that must be precisely defined in any case-based system, but different kinds of reasoning tasks will require different answers. In work on case-based explanations, the crucial questions to address include the following:

Crucial questions for CBR

1. How are cases retrieved?

2. What is a case? What are the components of cases? How are they structured so that they can be useful processing future cases?

3. How is the applicability of an old case determined?

4. How does case adaptation proceed?

5. How are insights from the old case applied to the new situation?

The SWALE system and its descendants

We started looking at explanations because we wanted to build a computer program that could understand interesting, novel stories — stories containing events that were anomalous, in the sense that none of the program's processing structures predicted the event. We wanted to build a program that, in addition to using MOPs [Schank 82] to understand the routine portions of its input, could construct creative explanations when confronted with unexpected input.

SWALE [Kass, Leake and Owens 86] dealt primarily with a single example, the story of the death of the racehorse Swale. Swale, the star 3-year-old racehorse of 1984, was found dead a few days after winning a major race. Many explanations were suggested for Swale's death, but the actual cause was never found.

We were driven toward a case-based approach to explanation construction by our observations of how people tried to explain the death. When students at the Yale AI lab were asked to explain Swale's death, they were often reminded of other deaths. One student was reminded of the death of Jim Fixx, who also died when he seemed to be in peak physical condition. Fixx died suddenly when his jogging overtaxed a heart defect, and the student suggested that a heart defect might have caused Swale's death. Another had a reminding of the death of another young superstar, Janis Joplin, who died from a drug overdose. The fanciful explanation that resulted was that Swale couldn't take the pressure of his stardom, and also succumbed to an overdose. While this was obviously unreasonable, it led to the idea that someone might have given Swale an overdose of performance-enhancing drugs.

As we worked on case-based explanation, we identified three major areas to address: retrieval of candidate explanations, evaluation of how well the candidate explanations fit the new situation, and adaptation of inapplicable explanations to apply. SWALE processed stories by integrating each fact into memory, detecting anomalies when facts conflicted with expectations. It then attempted to retrieve XPs indexed under the anomalies, and under other indices if direct search failed. Retrieved XPs were then evaluated, and problem XPs were adapted. The best explanation was then generalized and installed in memory for future use. This was implemented in SWALE as three modules: the ACCEPTER (by David Leake) detected anomalies and characterized the problems, did direct XP search, and evaluated candidate XPs. When it accepted an XP, it updated the system's beliefs to include those hypothesized by the explanation, and generalized and installed in memory the accepted XP. The EXPLORATORY SEARCHER (by Chris Owens) retrieved candidate XPs when routine search failed, using two retrieval strategies: indexing by unusual features of the anomalous event, and indexing into a library of folkloric XPs. The TWEAKER (by Alex Kass) generated additional XPs by revising those that failed to apply. These processes are described further in [Kass 86] and [Leake and Owens 86].

SWALE generated a range of explanations for Swale's death, some of which were unusual. More importantly, it identified many issues in the areas of retrieval, evaluation, and revision of explanations, which we were anxious to address in more detail, in the context of more examples. Since the program became large and unwieldy to work on as a single unit, each member of the SWALE team began to address a set of these issues independently. Although both of authors are still working within the SWALE paradigm, the ACCEPTER and the TWEAKER have evolved into separate computer programs.

What follows is a brief description of XPs, and then separate sections by each author on the current version of his program.

Using explanation patterns to represent cases

Case-based explanation depends on having explanations available as memory structures that can be retrieved to deal with new situations. A major part of the SWALE effort was devoted to representing explanations in the system's memory. XPs (as they evolved during development of the SWALE project) are fossilized explanation schemas, much the way scripts are fossilized plan schemas. They capture the reasoning which was done when the situation was originally explained in a variablized pattern. An instantiated explanation is produced by binding the variables of an XP.

XPs are composed of hypothesised facts and belief-support nodes that link the facts together. The facts include premises, intermediate facts which can be inferred from those facts, and conclusions, which include the event to be explained. The XP is thus a network of plausible inference connecting a set of premises to a set of conclusions through belief-support links.

The box below contains a sketch of an XP that explains the death of Janis Joplin by an accidental overdose of recreational drugs. The premises appear at the top, connected by the causal network to the conclusion at the bottom.

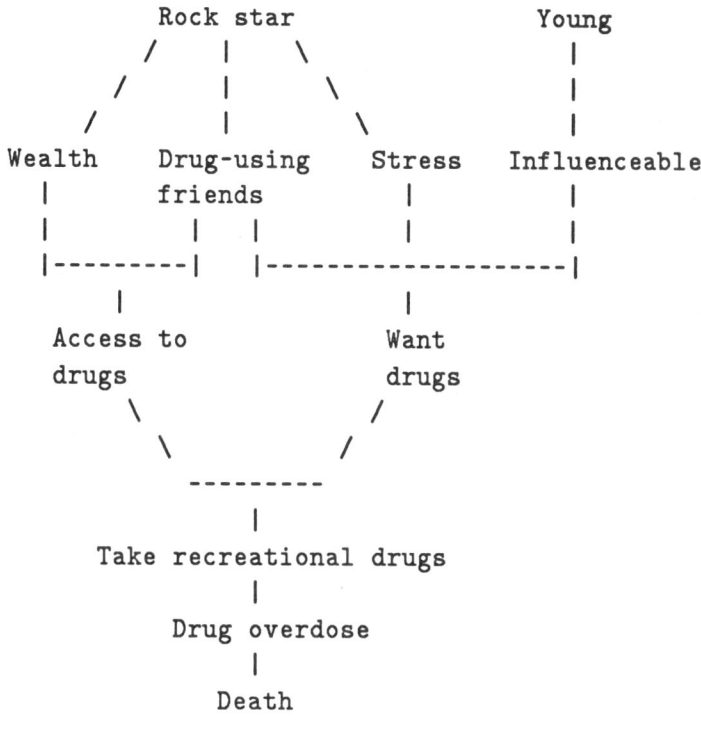

The vocabulary used to represent facts is based on Conceptual Dependency theory [Schank 72]). Belief-support nodes contain pointers to the supporting belief (or beliefs, if it is a conjunctive node), to the supported belief, and to the inference rule that licenses the inference. For example, if an explainer believes that John is taking part in the restaurant MOP, then it will also believe that he will pay the bill. This would be represented in the XP as a MOP-scene support node, where the supporting belief is that John was performing the restaurant MOP and the supported one is that he payed the bill.

Why are XPs a good case representation? There are two main reasons. First, in their belief-support network, they explicitly state the inferences an old case licenses in a new situation. Thus the scope of the old case is precisely delimited by the XP. Second, adaptation of XPs to new situations is facilitated by the explicit causal connections between facts. When an XP's premise does not fit the new situation, the relevant features of a replacement fact are clear, and a causally-equivalent fact can be substituted.

TWEAKER — Alex Kass

The **TWEAKER** program is a decendant of the SWALE system which focuses on the tasks of explanation application and adaptation. TWEAKER is designed to explain deaths and disasters, and to augment its initially sparse library of explanations as it does so, by adding the explanations it constructs to its library.

Because TWEAKER is involved with such tasks as generalizing and elaborating explanations, my research relates to many of the issues addressed the explanation-based learning literature, especially the work going on in Dejong's research group, such as that discussed in [DeJong 83] and [DeJong and Mooney 86]. The focus of our efforts is somewhat different however; EBL researchers tend to be most interested in having their systems arrive at the most general valid concept definition, whereas we are more concerned with having my system develop interesting new hypotheses for inclusion in its case library. For a brief discussion of some of the similarities and differences between our approaches see [Kass and Owens 88].

In order to fully exercise its adaptation functions the system avoids the difficult issues involved in anomaly detection, XP selection, and explanation evaluation by allowing the user to perform these functions interactively.

The current version of the system has represented in it four anomalies which the user can choose to have it try to explain:

- The death of the racehorse Swale
- The death of basketball player, Len Bias
- The explosion of Space Shuttle Challenger
- The Meltdown of the Chernobyl nuclear reactor

Eventually we expect to include several more death and disaster anomalies for the system to work on (such as the sinking of the Titanic, the deaths of other celebrities, etc.)

Knowledge structures in TWEAKER

There are two principal sources of knowledge available to the TWEAKER program: a large semantic network contains the system's general knowledge, and a library of XPs contains the system's case-related knowledge. As the system constructs new explanations in response to a user's request that explain a particular anomaly, it augments both of its knowledge sources; it adds the new explanations that it learns to its XP library, and it adds the hypothesized facts that these explanations entail to its semantic network. This is what the system learns.

Each node in the system's semantic network represents a concept (such as Swale, Len Bias, the jogging script, the concept of marriage, etc.) The nodes are connected to each other by abstraction and sub-part relationships, and by other semantic relationships as well. All the "facts" that system knows are somehow indexed in the semantic memory.

The system requires that a set of XPs be hand-coded into its XP library to get it started. The current version begins with five death and destruction XPs. These are based either on specific episodes or general stereotyped causes of death, but in either case the XPs are initially variablized just enough so that they could be applied to another case that matched exactly except for the names of the actors.

A brief synopsis of the XP's that have been coded into TWEAKER's library are listed below:

- MAFIA-REVENGE-XP

    One mobster wants to weaken another so he kills someone in the first mobster's mob. The first then gets angry and kills the other in retaliation.

- SPOUSE-INSURANCE-XP

    Someone who is greedy and doesn't really love his/her spouse kills the spouse in order to collect the life insurance money.

- TOO-MUCH-SEX-XP

    Too much sex can kill you.

- JIM-FIXX-XP

    A hidden heart defect is exacerbated by the heavy exertion associated with jogging. This causes a person who looks like he's in great condition to suffer a fatal heart attack.

- JANIS-JOPLIN-XP

    A rock star takes drugs and dies of an OD.

    (Described in greater detail in the previous section.)

What TWEAKER does

Top-level control structure

TWEAKER is an interactive program which the user directs (via a series of menus) to explain an anomaly. The program's top-level menu allows the user to choose between either explaining an anomaly or examining the current state of the program's knowledge sources.

The user can peruse the semantic network or can ask the program to display its XP's to see how the knowledge sources are updated by the explanation process.

When the user chooses to have the system explain an anomaly he is presented with the set of anomalies that the system knows about and is allowed to choose one. Once an anomaly is chosen to work on an XP must be chosen to apply to that anomaly.

With regard to selection of an XP, the program offers the user two options: Either the user can select which XP to apply, or the system can attempt to apply each XP in its entire library. The first mode requires more user intervention and is more likely to produce a high percentage of useful explanations. The second mode can cause the system to run for much longer, and will cause the system to consider a lot of silly explanations, but can have the advantage of causing the system to produce a surprising explanation by adapting an XP that seemed only distantly related to the anomaly. Of course, the current version of the program requires a good deal of intervention even in the second, apply everything mode, since it is up to the user to evaluate the explanations that the system produces. A third mode, in which the system selects the XP to apply itself has not yet been implemented because the process of selecting XPs involves many difficult research issues which are beyond the current scope of the project.

XP application

Once an anomaly and an XP have been chosen, the system attempts to produce an explanation by applying the XP to the anomaly. Applying an XP involves finding a belief in the XP which matches the anomaly. When the anomaly is matched to one of the beliefs, the resulting variable bindings are used to instantiate the rest of the beliefs in the XP. Once an explanation has been produced, the program enters an interactive presentation/adaptation cycle.

The presenation/adaptation cycle

During explanation presentation the system displays the explanation it has produced and allows the user to dispose of it in one of three ways: The user can direct the system to abandon the proposed explanation; adopt the proposed explanation; or tweak the proposed explanation. If the explanation is to be abandoned, the system returns to XP selection phase, ready to apply some other XP to the anomaly. If the user directs the system to adopt the explanation, then the XP is installed in the explanation library. In addition, all the beliefs included in the explanation are added to memory. This step, in which the system learns specific new facts (as opposed to the general knowledge structures represented by XP's) represents an ability which is often by AI systems because it is not as glamorous as learning generalizations. But we feel it is an important kind of learning.

The hard part, of course is when the user decides that an explanation needs tweaking. When this occurs the systems provides a series of menus which allow the user to pinpoint his objection to the explanation, isolating both the portion of the explanation that is objectionable (assuming the problem is a localizable kind), and the kind of objection.

Each kind of failure that the system knows about indexes a set of one or more adaptation strategies. Once the system has gotten a diagnosis of the problem from the user it attempts to apply any adaptation strategies that it has indexed to fix the problem. If there is more than tweak that can apply to a given problem (and there often is) the system sorts them (currently this is done according to a static ranking assigned by the programmer) and applies each in turn. The explanations which result from this tweaking are once again presented to the user for evaluation.

Ways that TWEAKER's explanations can go awry

There are a number of ways in which the explanations generated by applying an XP to a new situation can be deemed inadequate. In this section we propose a taxonomy of XP failure types In the next section present a catalogue of XP tweaking strategies which can be used to fix these problems when detected.

The space of explanation failures can be grouped into three high-level categories. To some extent this grouping scheme relates to both the ways that the failures are detected, and to some extent they relate to the way they are repaired. For want of a better set of terms, I call the groups, **syntactic**, **local semantic**, and **global semantic**.

Syntactic explanation failures

One simple type of explanation failure occurs when the XP cannot even be instantiated into an explanation because the pattern matcher is unable to match the anomaly to any of the beliefs that the XP can explain. I call this a syntactic failure because it is mismatch between the syntactic structure of the representation of the anomaly and the representation of the beliefs in the XP, as recognized by the pattern matcher. No reliance on the semantic network representing long term memory need be made in order to detect such problems.

Local semantic explanation failures

A second class of problems involves beliefs which are rather clearly in conflict with knowledge stored in semantic memory. The most common sub-category within this group of problems involves selectional restrictions. For example, when instantiating the FIXX-XP to explain Swale's death, the explanation that results implies that Swale was taking recreational drugs. However, this raises the obvious objection that SWALE is not in the category of actors that perform the action M-RECREATIONAL-DRUGS.

These selectional restrictions vary with regard to two things: which roles they find incompatible; and why they find them incompatible. So, for example, three failures of this type are:

- ACTOR-ACTION-INCOMPATIBLE:STEREOTYPE-VIOLATION

  The actor is not stereotypically associated with the action.

- ACTOR-ACTION-INCOMPATIBLE:PHYSICAL-DISABILITY

  The actor could not perform the action because of some actual disability. For example, an explanation that involved a small woman lifting a large man would be suspect because she probably wouldn't be strong enough.

- ACTION-INSTRUMENT-INCOMPATIBLE:PHYSICAL-DISABILITY

  A pistol probably could not be used to cause the Chernobyl meltdown because it simply wouldn't do the job.

Another kind of local failure applies to explanations that refer to non-existent slots. For example, applying FIXX-XP to Challenger results in an explanation that hypotheses that Challenger's heart was weak. Of course, Challenger doesn't have a heart, so that this would cause a NON-EXISTENT-SLOT problem.

Non-local semantic explanation failures

Some of the problems that occur in explanations produced by TWEAKER are less explicit and less localizable than the ones described above. These are often complaints that parts of the explanation are just too vague or implausible without further evidence. Examples:

- The proposition that some (unspecified) enemy destroyed the Challenger out of revenge could be considered too vague. (VAGUE-DESCRIPTION).

- The proposition that the Libya destroyed the Challenger could be considered too implausible without further support. (IMPLAUSIBLE-PREMISS).

Note that this is a different sort of objection from the INCOMPATIBILTY objections listed in the previous section; it's not that LIBYA *couldn't* have performed the action, its that there's not enough evidence to make it believable.

- The link between someone having too much sex and someone dying might be considered too weak (INADEQUATE-CAUSAL-SUPPORT), requiring further elaboration.

TWEAKER's explanation repairs

Below is a catalogue of the tweaks that TWEAKER might use to repair an explanation that the user has complained about. Not all of these have been fully implemented. Some have been, while others are partially complete and still others have just been designed. Implementing one often suggests some others that might be useful as well, so that the list that describes the final version of TWEAKER will probably be somewhat larger.

I have divided the group into three main taxonomic groups: **Specifiers**, which fix problems associated with vague, incomplete, or unconvincing explanations by adding details; **Generalizers**, which remove details from explanation which are too specific, and **Substituters**, which fix incompatibilities that arise when applying an XP in a new situation, without changing the level of generality at which the XP is represented.

Specifiers

Specifiers add content to an explanation. Explanations can be specified by adding beliefs, strengthening causal links, binding unbound variables, or adding constraints. By making the predictions an explanation makes more elaborate and specific a specifier makes an explanation more useful in the contexts where it is applicable, at the cost of reducing the range of situations in which it can be applied.

TWK-SPECIFY-CATEGORY-DESCRIPTION: Sometimes an explanation may have been over-generalized. Explanations that could apply in too many situations are often unconvincing because they predict that the anomalous situation would occur in too broad a set of circumstances. Such a problem can be alleviated by modifying the explanation to alter some of the components which constrain the set of role-fillers that the XP can be applied to, making them more specific.

This tweak attempts to find a more specific version a category description appearing in an XP, while ensuring, of course that the description still applies to the role-filler suggested by the current anomaly. IF possible, it chooses a level of specificity at which it find additional support for the explanation.

TWK-ADD-LINKS: Sometimes an explanation that the system produces contains beliefs which all seem plausible individually, but the overall explanation is still week because connections between the beliefs is not strong enough. TWK-ADD-LINKS and TWK-SPLICE-CONNECTING-XP both attempt to fix this.

Sometimes additional causal relationships can be found between beliefs that are already aspects of an explanation. When this can be done it can often make an explanation more convincing without introducing additional beliefs.

TWK-SPLICE-CONNECTING-XP: A second way to strengthen the connection between to beliefs in an explanation is to splice another XP (which forms a sub-explanation connecting the two beliefs which were previously not strongly connected) into the XP. Sometimes some amount of forward and backward chaining is necessary in order to connect the sub-XP to the larger XP.

TWK-ADD-SUPPORT:MOTIVATION: A very simple, very common problem with an explanation is that there is not enough evidence for one of the beliefs. In this case the system has a number of ways to search for additional pieces of explanation to elaborate on the original. In general, these tweaks can be very expensive; they are, in effect recursive calls to an explainer with a request for explanation of one of the beliefs in the original explanation. They are not implemented as recursive calls however, since it is hoped that the full power of the explainer can be avoided. The context provided by the rest of the explanation should cut down the search. One possible implementation would be to fall back to a full recursive explanation if no other tweaks work. But the current implimentation operates under the assumption that any explanation that cannot be tweaked with the simpler special-purpose TWK-ADD-SUPPORT tweaks is not worth tweaking.

TWK-ADD-SUPPORT:MOTIVATION: attempts to search the semantic network for motivation that an actor might have had for performing a particular action in the explanation.

TWK-ADD-SUPPORT:OPPORTUNITY: Attempts to support a belief by showing how an actor could have performed an action. Actions have preconditions (for example, buying drugs requires money). One way to make an explanation more specific (and perhaps more convincing) is to show how the action's preconditions preconditions were satisfied (for example, explaining how the actor might have gotten the money to buy the drugs).

TWK-ADD-SUPPORT:PHYSICAL-FAILURE: Tries to explain why a particular physical failure (such as a heart attack, or a mechanical failure in a reactor) might have occurred.

TWK-BIND-VARIABLE: As mentioned above, variables in an XP are initially bound in an explanation by matching the representation of the anomaly against one of the beliefs in the XP. However, this does not always cause all of the variables to be bound. For example, the MAFIA-REVENGE-XP posits that X kills Y in retaliation for Y having killed Z (who was an associate of X). When applying this explanation to some anomaly (say, the death of Len Bias for example), the system produces an explanation in which the variable Y is bound to Bias but in which X and Z are not bound at all. This explanation essentially claims that some unspecified X killed Bias because he killed some unspecified Y. (Actually there is a lot more detail in the XP, but the fact that X and Y are unspecified is the point).

In some contexts explanation with unbound variables might be acceptable, but in others it leaves the explanation too vague. If the user decides that an XP is too vague, then one way to make it less so is to search memory for plausible bindings for any unbound variables.

Generalizers

A generalizer is a tweak that modifies an XP in some way that makes it applicable to a broader class of situations at the cost of producing an explanation with somewhat less specific content.

TWK-GENERALIZE-ANOMALY: This is the only tweak that is designed to work on syntactic failures (as defined in the section on failure types above). Sometimes an XP that might eventually prove relevant, initially cannot even be instantiated to form an explanation because there is no belief in the XP that the pattern matcher can match to the anomaly. This is likely to happen when trying to transfer an XP to a slightly different domain. For example, when trying to apply the FIXX-XP to the Challenger disaster, the system finds that there is nothing in the XP which matches its representation of an explosion. An explosion may seem like a death to analogically-minded humans, but to the TWEAKER's pattern matcher it is not a match.

In this case the XP can only be saved by finding a belief that comes close to matching the anomaly (in the current implementation this means sharing the same main predicate) and attempting to generalize the role-fillers that don't match the anomaly. This is done by moving up the abstraction hierarchy in the system's semantic network, until a generalization is found which matches the corresponding role-filler in the anomaly. With the FIXX-XP — Challenger case, this means altering the XP to make it an explanation of a general malfunction rather than specifically of a death.

This allows the XP to be instantiated. Of course, the instantiated XP has other problems (for example, it posits that Challenger was a jogger), but these are handled by other tweaks.

TWK-GENERALIZE-CATEGORY-DESCRIPTION: Obviously, this is the inverse of TWK-SPECIFY-CATEGORY-DESCRIPTION. It can be used when a category description in the XP is not applicable to the object involved in the current explanation. It operates by finding some more general node in the abstraction hierarchy that does apply to the actor. For example, the JOPLIN-XP demands that the dead person be a rock star, which generates a failure when applied to Len Bias. The system can generalize the constraint to any star performer, producing a reasonable explanation.

Of course this process will often wreck the entire XP by making it too general. But sometimes the TWEAKER will hit on an interesting generalization which is useful to learn. The user decides during the presentation phase of the cycle.

TWK-DELETE-BELIEF: Sometimes it makes sense to simply delete a problematic belief from the XP. This may weaken the explanation by removing some of the support of other beliefs, but if there is enough other, redundant support for these beliefs this may not be a fatal problem. XPs sometimes have spurious beliefs, or beliefs that are at least not strictly necessary.

Substituters

Substituters map one explanation to another which is not necessarily more specific or more general. It does this by replacing some role filler, or some entire beliefs with *causally equivalent* counterparts. Substituters are called for when a proposed XP generates some minor problems when applied to a given anomaly, but is at an appropriate level of generalization.

Substituters are generally specified along two dimensions, what part of the belief they alter (which role-filler they look for a substitute for), and how they search memory to find the substitution. Of course, the memory-search process may have choice points at several levels so that the decision about when to call different branches at a choice point different tweaks, or simply different ways a tweak can accomplish its job is arbitrary. In what follows we've chosen to name only the highest level decision about how te search.

TWK-SUBSTITUTE-ACTION:ACTOR-THEMES: A very common explanation problem involves a mismatch between an actor and action he was supposed to perform. When this happens one way to fix the problem is to find some other action to substitute for the problematic action. The action must play the same role in the explanation that old discarded action played, but must be compatible with the current actor.

There are several ways to search memory for actions that might fit these criteria. One of which is simply to check for ROLE-THEMES indexed under the actor, or under one of the categories to which the actor belongs.

TWK-SUBSTITUTE-ACTION:RELATED-ACTION: Another search method is to start with discarded action and check the brother nodes in the abstraction hierarchy.

TWK-SUBSTITUTE-ACTION:CAUSAL: A third way to search for a suitable action is to check for actions that are indexed as causal antecedents of one of the causal consequents of the discarded action. It is unreasonable to assume that any belief which could conceivably cause a particular event (through some arbitrary intermediate causal chain) can be found efficiently, but is not unreasonable to hope that some potential causes of some event (the common ones) might be directly indexed under the event in memory.

TWK-SUBSTITUTE-ACTOR:MOTIVATION: Sometimes when there is a mismatch between actor and action it is possible to find an alternate actor rather than an alternate action. (Of course, changing the actor may introduce new failures, but these may be solvable by additional tweaks). One obvious way to search memory for an alternate actor is to check the nodes representing the results of the action to see if anyone is indexed as having such results as a goal.

TWK-SUBSTITUTE-ACTOR:THEME: A second way to find an actor to substitute is to see if there is someone who is indexed under the action itself as having the action as a stereotypical ROLE-THEME.

TWK-SUBSTITUTE-INSTRUMENT:ACTOR-STEREOTYPES: When an action involves some instrumental object (such as a gun, or a syringe) the instrument appearing in the XP might be inappropriate for in the new explanation. One way to find another instrument is to check any of the instruments indexed as stereotypically associated with the actor, to see if they might have accomplished the action. For example, if the hypothesised actor of a murder was a baseball player, and the MAFIA-REVENEGE-XP is applied, predicting that a gun was used in the murder, but it is known that a gun was not used, a baseball bat might be a reasonable substitution, since it is indexed off baseball player in memory and could be used to perform the job.

TWK-SUBSTITUTE-INSTRUMENT:ACTION-STEREOTYPES: A second search method for finding alternate instruments is to check for instruments stereotypically associated with the action, and then see whether any of them would have been available to the actor.

ACCEPTER — David Leake

In order to decide whether a case is applicable, a case-based reasoner needs to locate any relevant discrepancies between the old and new situations. ACCEPTER is a program that detects anomalies in stories and determines whether hypothesized explanations are satisfactory to resolve them.

At the start of an ACCEPTER run, the user selects a story to process (the library of stories currently focuses on incidents of premature death). The system integrates facts in the story into its memory, using a MOP-application process modeled on [Cullingford 78]. Input facts are checked to see whether they satisfy the expectations provided by active MOPs. If so, they are stored in memory, organized by the accepting MOPs ([Schank 82], [Lebowitz 80], [Kolodner 80]). Installing a fact in a MOP activates expectations for future scenes of that MOP.

When an input fact conflicts with an expectation, ACCEPTER considers the fact anomalous, and prompts the user for an explanation. The user has two choices: either to select a predefined XP from ACCEPTER's XP library, or to interactively define a new XP in terms of the system's library of causal rules. Nine predefined XPs for death are currently available, including the Jim Fixx and Janis Joplin XPs, and the XP *murder for insurance money*.

When the user has selected the candidate XP, ACCEPTER evaluates how well it explains the anomaly, and whether it would be useful to an actor driven by a user-selected *role theme* [Schank and Abelson 77]. If problems are detected, the user is given a description of the problems. The system provides an interface that allows a user to interactively tweak a problematic XP; this increases the range of candidate explanations for the system to evaluate. As each new version of an XP is generated, the program evaluates its applicability.

User-generated XPs are added to the system's XP library to be available for explaining future anomalies. When an explanation is accepted, the system also updates its beliefs to include the assumptions that follow from the explanation.

Evaluating explanations

In case-based explanation, static criteria are inadequate to decide when an old case is relevant. Evaluation of explanations cannot be done in the abstract: it must be influenced by what the explainer knows and needs to learn [Leake 88]. Any situation includes numerous aspects that might be explained, and context determines which are important: when an *expectation failure* [Schank 82] occurs, the aspects that need to be elucidated are those that conflict with expectations. What constitutes an acceptable explanation also depends on the system's existing beliefs, since the explanation must reconcile the anomalous event with other beliefs in memory. Finally, when a system encounters an expectation failure as it performs a task, the task it is trying to perform determines what information it needs from the explanation.

Thus whether an old case is accepted depends on context, current system knowledge, and active goals. These are reflected in ACCEPTER's criteria for judging explanations: a good explanation must address the factors that made a situation anomalous in the curren context, must be believable in light of the system's other knowledge, and must give the system the information it needs for a goal-based response. ACCEPTER's procedures for judging these are described below.

Relevance of an explanation to an anomaly

The aspects of a new situation that merit explanation are those that contradict expectations, since failed expectations reflect deficiencies in the knowledge structures that were being applied. For example, people hearing for the first time about a recall of cars would explain different things depending on the circumstances. If the recall is mentioned during a conversation about greedy companies' refusal to accept responsibility for problems after sale, the admission of a defect would be surprising. A useful explanation would reconcile it with old beliefs: perhaps the company thought lawsuits would cost more than the repairs. If it's mentioned during a discussion of the excellent quality control of the company, an explanation might address how the defect slipped through the company's checks.

Expectation failures prompt ACCEPTER's requests for explanations, and the system requires that candidate explanations account for the specific features of a new situation that caused the expectation to fail.

Judging believability: Efficient problem detection

In a rich memory, any hypothesis of an explanation might relate to many beliefs. Although the most reliable way of checking a hypothesis would be to compare all its ramifications with the knowledge in memory, the inference involved would be overwhelming— the efficiency gained by re-using prior reasoning would be counterbalanced by the cost of verifying applicability of an old case. Thus efficient tests for problems are needed.

However, rapid tests cannot be guaranteed to detect all problems; the level of of verification used should depend on the importance of the explanation to the system. When important decisions hinge on the explanation's correctness, finer-grained verification may be necessary. For example, a doctor diagnosing a patient in intensive care might be more concerned about coming to the correct diagnosis than an armchair quarterback explaining a lost game. Also, coarse-grained checks may suggest problems that would be ruled out in finer-grained analysis. Consequently, basic-level checks need to be augmented with other tests when they locate potential problems, or when accuracy is especially important.

ACCEPTER's theory of belief evaluation involves three phases:

- **See if hypotheses match expectations or prior beliefs.**

  If so, the hypotheses are confirmed.

- **Do basic believability checks.**

  These checks rely primarily on patterns. For example, ACCEPTER checks to ascertain that a hypothesized action's actor belongs to the standard category for fillers of the actor role. ACCEPTER uses such tests to detect a problem in applying the Jim Fixx XP as an explanation of Swale's death: the XP requires that the victim was jogging immediately before his death, and jogging is normally done only by people.

- **Perform more expensive checks when when basic-level checks detect potential problems, or when accuracy is especially important.**

  When conflicts with patterns are found, ACCEPTER examines the situation with more precise tests. For example, when an actor's choice to participate in an action fits no patterns, ACCEPTER looks for motivations by inferring some of the effects of participation and comparing them to the actor's active goals.

  Another supplementary check uses *basic-action decomposition*. When a role-filler in an action belongs to an unusual category for the role, the the non-normative filler type does not necessarily preclude the action from occurring (*e.g.*, jogging is normally done by people, but there is no reason that a monkey could not be trained to jog). However, it is a sign of possible problems. When a MOP with a non-normative filler is found, ACCEPTER decomposes the MOP into its constituent actions, and checks each one to see whether the role-filler violates causal restrictions.

  ACCEPTER's current implementation does detailed checks when basic-level checks find possible problems, but checks driven by special needs for accuracy have not yet been implemented.

Detecting basic problems

In order to detect problems efficiently, ACCEPTER relies heavily on stereotyped patterns. Just as knowledge structures such as MOPs [Schank 82] can facilitate understanding by providing stereotyped expectations to deal with events in a situation, other kinds of stereotyped patterns can provide normative expectations to facilitate problem detection.

While stereotypes are usually only viewed as ways to characterize routine objects or situations, it is also useful to have stereotypes about classes of events that are usually ruled out in some way. ACCEPTER uses the following patterns to check hypothesized actions:

1. **Information stored under packaging structures**

    - **Event sequence patterns**, such as the stereotyped information in schemas such as MOPs and plans. For example, the knowledge that in restaurants, a customer enters, is seated, orders, etc.

    - **Role-filler patterns**, which supply information on classes of objects likely to fill particular roles in a knowledge structure. These may be expressed in terms normative restrictions on the allowable role-fillers, which rule out fillers of the wrong types. They may also state features that make a role-filler of the normal type more likely to actually fill the role, which can give additional confirmation for the role-filling.

        - **Normative role-filler types** give information on the types of object that usually fill particular roles in a packaging structure, such as the restriction that actors in the jogging MOP are usually human. Checks of hypothesized role-fillers against normative role-filler types can identify potential problems.

- **Predisposing features for filling a role** give partial confirmation of a hypothesized role-filler. For example, a predisposing feature for being a jogger is being health-conscious; we are more likely to believe that someone went jogging if we know he is health-conscious.

2. **Information stored under objects and actors**

    - **Object limitations.** An object may belong to some category despite having features or functional limitations that are unusual for category members. If our stereotyped view of expensive sports cars is that they are fast and handle well, but we find that cars of brand X have bad handling, it might be useful to index information under limitations of that car with respect to its categorization as a sports car. The information could then be retrieved when considering the car in terms of stereotypes for sports cars. (Tests using object limitations checks are not yet implemented in ACCEPTER.)

    - **Decision patterns**

        (a) **Actor participation and avoidance patterns.** For example, fraternity members seek out wild parties; athletes in training are supposed to avoid them.

        (b) **Role-filler choice and avoidance patterns for the director of an action.** When an actor has control over the role-fillers of an action, the choice of fillers can be compared to expectations about how he will select those role-fillers. For example, some bosses try hire the best-qualified candidates, regardless of how long they're likely to stay at the companies; others try to avoid hiring people who are likely to be seeking other jobs.

ACCEPTER tests the reasonableness of hypothesized actions along the dimensions given by each of these patterns. Tests are applied as follows:

Checks associated with packaging structures: Given an action that is hypothesized to fit within a MOP or plan, ACCEPTER matches the action against the packaging structure's expectations in order to identify problems such as premature events, delayed events, or missing events. Restrictions on role-filler types are retrieved from the MOP or its abstractions, and the system compares hypothesized role-fillers to them.

Checks associated with knowledge of objects and actors: Knowledge of normative types for a role-filler can also be used to retrieve those limitations of the role-filler that are significant in the current context. Given the normative type for a role-filler, and the object that fills the role, an evaluator can ask *does the object have an limitations with respect to the normative type?*. If so, it can check those limitations to see if they cause problems.

Retrieving limitations *with respect to a particular category* is important, since any object can be categorized in many ways, only a few of which are relevant to a given event. For example, if a hypothesized car theft is being evaluated, the normative role-filler type for the object of the theft is *valuable object*. With respect to *valuable object*, brand X cars from the above example would have no limitations indexed under them, so the object of the theft would have no basic-level problems. However, if the outcome of a hypothesized automobile race was being considered, and *sports cars* were the normative filler type for vehicles involved, a limitation of cars of brand X with respect to sports cars could be retrieved: their bad handling. The significance of this could then be checked by decomposing the events of the race into specific components, and seeing if handling was important (which it would be on a curved route, but not on a straight one).

Checks for decision patterns are indexed under abstractions of an action's actors, for abstractions of the action and the role involved. ACCEPTER uses them to test each role-filler's participation in an action.

Summary of the basic-level test strategy

By first comparing an input to specific beliefs in memory and active expectations, and then verifying in terms of the patterns described above, ACCEPTER can often detect potential problems without doing extensive inference. Only when potential problems are detected is it necessary to apply more costly checks to the situation.

Evaluating detail

Even if an old case applies to a new situation, it may not provide all the needed information. What information is necessary depends on the explainer's purpose. For example, when a car owner who doesn't do his own repairs has car trouble, all he needs to know is whether the problem is transient (such as getting a bad tank of gas) or needs to be repaired. A mechanic requires a more detailed explanation, since he must trace the problem to a faulty part or a needed adjustment.

ACCEPTER has a library that associates role themes with tests for the detail that theme-driven actors need in different situations. For each theme, the information has two parts:

- **A list of types of anomalies whose resolution is important to the theme.** For example, two types of anomalies important to a veterinarian are animals' physical changes (*e.g.*, weight loss) and behavioral changes (such as loss of appetite), since they might be signs of a health problem. A detective would investigate anomalies such as premature deaths and violent acts.

- **For each relevant anomaly, a test to judge whether the explanation provides enough information for a theme-driven actor to respond.** For example, a detective would need to trace the cause of a premature death until he found whether it was due to natural causes or foul play.

At the start of each ACCEPTER run, a guiding role theme (either that of a vet or a detective) is selected for the program. This theme is used to shape the requirements for detail in an explanation. A future goal is to augment these criteria so that in addition to standard theme-based requirements, requirements for detail could be determined on the basis of other goals and plans of the system.

Summary of ACCEPTER's approach

Rather than having fixed criteria for applicability of an explanation, ACCEPTER's evaluation of the applicability of an old case is dynamic: it depends on context and on specific system needs. By relying on stereotyped patterns do facilitate a preliminary screening for believability, it limits the need to do costly verification.

Once a problem is found, a case-based system has two strategies available for dealing with it. One is to recursively apply the case-based explanation process, attempting to retrieve an XP that accounts for the anomalous hypothesis or link. The other is to try to repair the explanation by replacing or removing the problematic node from the structure of the XP. When ACCEPTER detects a problem, it generates a characterization of the problem. This aids either approach to resolving the difficulty: the problem characterization can be used as an index for retrieving other XPs dealing with similar difficulties, or as an index for retrieving tweaking strategies to fix the problem.

Conclusion

The above sections have described our case-based approach to constructing explanations. In describing our framework and the current versions of our programs, we have attempted to address some of a specific set of questions that we consider important to CBR: what is a case, how is it represented, and how is it applied to a new situation. We have argued for a specific case representation, the explanation pattern, and specific procedures for adapting and deciding the applicability of XPs.

Bibliography

[Carbonell 86] Carbonell, J. G., Derivational Analogy: A Theory of Reconstructive Problem Solving and Expertise Acquisition, Michalski, R.S., Carbonell, J.G., Mitchell, T.M. ed., Volume 2: *Machine Learning: An Artificial Intelligence Approach*, Morgan Kaufman Publishers, Inc., Los Altos, CA, 1986, pages 371–392.

[Cullingford 78] Cullingford, R., *Script Application: Computer Understanding of Newspaper Stories*, Ph.D. Thesis, Yale University, 1978. Technical Report 116.

[DeJong and Mooney 86] DeJong, G., and Mooney, R., *Explanation-Based Learning: An Alternative View*, Machine Learning, 1/1 (1986), pp. 145–176.

[DeJong 83] DeJong, G., An Approach to Learning From Observation, *Proceedings of the International Machine Learning Workshop*, University of Illinois, Monticello, IL, June 1983, pp. 171–176.

[Hammond 86] Hammond, K.J., *Case-based Planning: An Integrated Theory of Planning, Learning and Memory*, Ph.D. Thesis, Yale University, 1986. Technical Report 488.

[Kass and Owens 88] Kass, A. and Owens, C. C., *Learning New Explanations by Incremental Adaptation*, 1988. To appear in proceedings of the 1988 AAAI Spring Symposium on Explanation-based Learning.

[Kass, Leake and Owens 86] Kass, A. M. and Leake, D. B. and Owens, C. C., SWALE: A Program that Explains, *Explanation Patterns: Understanding Mechanically and Creatively*, Lawrence Erlbaum Associates, Hillsdale, NJ, 1986, pp. 232–254.

[Kass 86] Kass, A., Modifying Explanations to Understand Stories, *Proceedings of the Eighth Annual Conference of the Cognitive Science Society*, Cognitive Science Society, Amherst, MA, August 1986.

[Kolodner, Simpson and Sycara 85] Kolodner, J., Simpson, R. and Sycara, K., A Process Model of Case-Based Reasoning in Problem Solving, A. Joshi ed., *Proceedings of the Ninth International Joint Conference on Artificial Intelligence*, IJCAI, Los Angeles, CA, August 1985, pp. 284–290.

[Kolodner 80] Kolodner, J.L., *Retrieval and Organizational Strategies in Conceptual Memory: A Computer Model*, Ph.D. Thesis, Yale University, November 1980. Technical Report 187.

[Leake and Owens 86] Leake, D., and Owens, C., Organizing Memory for Explanation, *Proceedings of the Eighth Annual Conference of the Cognitive Science Society*, Cognitive Science Society, Amherst, MA, August 1986.

[Leake 88] Leake, D. B., *Using Explainer Needs to Judge Operationality*, 1988. To appear in proceedings of the 1988 AAAI Spring Symposium on Explanation-based Learning.

[Lebowitz 80] Lebowitz, M., *Generalization and Memory in an Integrated Understanding System*, Ph.D. Thesis, Yale University, October 1980. Technical Report 186.

[Schank and Abelson 77] Schank, R.C. and Abelson, R., *Scripts, Plans, Goals and Understanding*, Lawrence Erlbaum Associates, Hillsdale, New Jersey, 1977.

[Schank 72] Schank, R.C., *Conceptual Dependency: A Theory of Natural Language Understanding*, Cognitive Psychology, 3/4 (1972), pp. 552–631.

[Schank 82] Schank, R.C., *Dynamic Memory: A Theory of Learning in Computers and People*, Cambridge University Press, 1982.

[Schank 83] Schank, R.C., *The Current State of AI: One Man's Opinion*, The AI Magazine, 4/1 Winter-Spring (1983), pp. 3–8.

[Schank 86] Schank, R.C., *Explanation Patterns: Understanding Mechanically and Creatively*, Lawrence Erlbaum Associates, Hillsdale, NJ, 1986.

[Simpson 85] Simpson, R.L., *A Computer Model of Case-based Reasoning in Problem-solving: An Investigation in the Domain of Dispute Mediation*, Ph.D. Thesis, School of Information and Computer Science, Georgia Institute of Technology, 1985.

[Sycara 87] Sycara, E. P., *Resolving Adversarial Conflicts: An Approach Integrating Case-based and Analytic Methods*, Ph.D. Thesis, School of Information and Computer Science, Georgia Institute of Technology, 1987.

HOW DO PEOPLE USE ANALOGUES TO MAKE DECISIONS?

Gary A. Klein Roberta Calderwood

Klein Associates Inc.
Yellow Springs, Ohio 45387

Acknowledgement

The studies for this paper were conducted under the following research contracts: Contract #MDA903-85-C-0327 from the U.S. Army Research Institute for the Behavioral and Social Sciences, Contract #MDA903-85-C-0099 from the U.S. Army Research Institute for the Behavioral and Social Sciences, and Contract #MDA903-86-C-0170 from the U.S. Army Research Institute Field Unit, Leavenworth, Kansas.

The views, opinions, and findings contained in this paper are those of the authors and should not be construed as an official Department of Defense position, policy, or decision, unless so designated by other official documentation.

Abstract

What functions are served by analogical reasoning during planning and decision making? In order to determine the functionality of analogue use, we reviewed a data base of protocols describing over 400 decisions made by experienced decision makers performing a variety of tasks. Three primary functions were identified: understanding situational dynamics, generating options, and evaluating the probable success or failure of implementing an option. These uses of analogues are discussed in relation to a recognitional model of decision making.

Submitted for presentation at
Defense Advanced Research Projects Agency (DARPA)
Sponsored 1988 Case-Based Reasoning Workshop,
Clearwater Beach, Florida, May 11-13, 1988

Introduction

A design engineer was writing the specifications for a control panel. The panel had to be used under restricted lighting conditions so special switches were needed. The engineer recalled an earlier time when these switches were used. One drawback was that operators left papers and books on the control panel, and the plastic covers of the switches melted. He therefore made sure that the panel sloped enough to shed any books, and he eliminated a lip at the bottom of the panel that might catch books before they fell to the floor.

Another design engineer had to determine if a 60 degree field-of-view display would allow effective training. The requirement was for an aerial refueling trainer, and he was being pressured by the users to go for a more expensive display with a larger field of view. He recalled an earlier refueling training device with a 60 degree field-of-view that worked quite well, and so he opposed the request for a more expensive system.

A fireground commander was coordinating his crews as they combatted a fire at a 4-story apartment building. He looked up and noticed billboards on the roof, and he recalled an earlier incident where the flames had burned through the wooden supports of billboards, sending them crashing to the street below. He ordered that spectators be moved further back.

Another fireground commander noticed some peculiar properties in a cloud of smoke at a fire. He recalled an incident in which toxic smoke had been given off showing the same features of density and color and heaviness as the cloud he saw. He ordered his crews to use breathing support systems.

These examples illustrate some of the ways that analogues are retrieved and used as a basis for decision making. In these examples, prior experiences are recalled and examined for their implications for a current decision problem. In several recent studies of decision making in operational environments (Klein, in press), we have concluded that processes involved in retrieving and comparing prior cases are far more important in naturalistic decision making than are the application of abstract principles, rules, or conscious deliberation between alternatives. Unfortunately, very little is known about such spontaneous use of analogues in judgment and decision tasks. Most of our knowledge about analogue use has come from experimental sessions in which similarity relationships are derived for specified sets of stimuli, not from spontaneously generated analogues. Our knowledge of spontaneously generated analogues comes primarily from anecdotal reports of scientists and mathematicians who claim analogues were responsible for creative insights in their field. It seems obvious that analogue use is not limited to these special cases.

The goal of this paper is to review protocols obtained in several recent studies of decision making for evidence of analogue use and to propose a preliminary taxonomy of the functions that the analogues appeared to be serving in these tasks. The studies obtained retrospective verbal protocols of decision strategies used by urban fire ground commanders (Calderwood, Crandall & Klein, 1987; Klein, Calderwood & Clinton-Cirocco,

1985), wildland fire incident commanders (Taynor, Klein & Thordsen, 1987), tank platoon leaders (Brezovic, Klein, & Thordsen, 1987), and design engineers (Klein & Brezovic, 1987). Over 450 decision points were probed in order to elicit the natural decision strategies employed by these personnel. As part of the elicitation effort, we recorded instances in which analogues were reported to have influenced a decision outcome. For purposes of this study, analogue cases are limited to cases in which a specifically recalled episode was referenced (as opposed to general procedural knowledge or cases that appeared to be merged into a schematic or prototypical memory). Before describing the analogue cases, we will briefly describe the five relevant studies that served as the data base for this effort.

Critical Decision Protocols

In order to study naturalistic decision strategies, we developed a Critical Decision method CDM (Klein, Calderwood, & MacGregor, in progress) that generates a retrospective verbal protocol of decisions made by an individual in a specific case or incident. The method is a variant of Flanagan's (1954) Critical Incident technique and uses a set of probes to obtain detailed information about information use and decision making strategies. One of the probes related to what (if any) prior experiences had been recalled and used in making a decision. The cases in which specific prior experiences were recalled as entering into the decision process form the basis of this investigation.

The domains that we have studied using the Critical Decision method, urban fire ground command (Calderwood et al., 1987; Klein et al., 1985) wildland incident command (Taynor et al., 1987), tank platoon command (Brezovic et al., 1987) and system design engineering (Klein & Brezovic, 1987) were selected to represent varying degrees of time pressure and personal risk. In contrast to most laboratory-based decision tasks, all of the tasks involve problems that may change over the course of the decision. The decision makers ranged in experience from individuals who were still in training or were newly promoted to those with over 30 years of experience in the decision making role. In some of the studies the strategies of the most- and least-experienced decision makers were directly compared.

The decisions probed ranged from routine to highly unusual. In the two studies of urban firefighting, each incident contained at least one decision judged to have been exceptionally challenging by the fire ground commander. But other decisions within the same incident were also probed, and many of these were routine. In the Klein & Brezovic (1987) study of design engineers, only non-routine decisions were probed. In the study of tank platoon exercises, the most difficult decisions within a fairly standard training exercise were probed.

These studies represent interviews with over 100 decision makers and over 400 decision events. Some of the study parameters, along with the number of analogue cases in each study, are summarized in Table 1.

Table 1

Number of Critical Decision Interviews, Decisions,

and Analogues by Study Domain

Domain	Interviews	Decisions	Analogues
Urban firefighting[a]	54	226	8
Wildland firefighting[b]	17	110	4
Tank platoon[c]	21	55	8
Design engineering[d]	50	51	13

[a]Klein, G. A., Calderwood, R., & Clinton-Cirocco, A. (1985). Rapid decision making on the fire ground (KA-TR-84-41-7). Alexandria, VA: U.S. Army Research Institute.

[b]Taynor, J., Klein, G. A., & Thordsen, M. (1987). Distributed decision making in wildland firefighting (KATR-858(A)-04F). Yellow Springs, OH: Klein Associates Inc. Prepared under contract MDA903-85-C-0327 for U.S. Army Research Institute Alexandria, VA.

[c]Brezovic, C. P., Klein, G. A., & Thordsen, M. (1987). Decision making in armored platoon command (KATR-858(B)-87-05F). Yellow Springs, OH: Klein Associates Inc. Prepared under contract MDA903-85-C-0327 for U.S. Army Research Institute, Alexandria, VA.

[d]Klein, G. A., & Brezovic, C. P. (1987). Human performance data needed for training device design decisions. Technical Report AAMRL-TR-87-010. Wright Patterson Air Force Base, OH: Harry G. Armstrong Aerospace Medical Research Laboratory.

Analogue Cases

A total of 33 analogues were identified in the target studies and are described in Appendix A. The major functions of the analogues appear to fall into three categories: situation assessment, generating expectancies, and the suggestion of options and methods.

Situation Assessment. Some analogues appear to contribute to situation assessment by alerting the decision maker to causal factors operating during an incident. For example, in Analogue Case #6, a fireground commander sees a white cloud of smoke and is reminded of a previous incident where toxic smoke showed the same color and density, so he treated the fire as a "hazardous materials" incident following specified procedures.

Expectancies. Frequently, decision makers used analogues to anticipate what might happen if a course of action was implemented. Many of these analogue cases have an affective or evaluative component, sometimes warning about dangers unless the option is modified, and sometimes reassuring the decision maker that the option had been used successfully before. An example of how an analogue can provide a warning is Case #11. Hot tar running off a roof had ignited a secondary fire in an earlier incident. Remembering this, the commander made sure to avoid this problem by putting water on the hot tar. This aspect of analogue use is essentially a "plan repair." Another example is Case #2. The commander recalled administrative problems in an earlier forest fire where two teams were in the same fire camp, so he went through the effort of setting up an additional camp.

Analogues can reassure the decision maker that the option worked before and can be relied on. In these cases the analogue seems to be signalling that there are no major difficulties to watch out for, and plan repair may not be necessary. Case #16 shows how a tank platoon leader simply used the same avenue of attack as in an earlier exercise because it had worked so well.

Option Generation. Analogues were sometimes used to suggest options. An example is Case #1, where an analogue suggested the strategy of directing a fire into a box canyon with poor fuel. Some other examples show this use of analogues: Case #5 involved an analogue that suggested the strategy of letting a fire self-ventilate by burning through the roof; in Case #13 the analogue suggested the tank strategy of forcing the attackers to use a bounding approach that would slow them down; in Case #27 the analogue let the decision maker identify a method for assessing workload in a training device design.

The frequency of the number of analogues fitting each category is summarized in Table 2. The two subcategories of the expectancies category are also indicated, those that served as warning "flags", and those that served to reassure the decision maker of the likelihood of a successful outcome. In all but two of the cases in which analogues suggested options or methods, the analogues also served to generate this kind of expected outcome evaluation, so 12 of the analogue cases are included in both the Options and Expectancies categories.

We also have some data on the value of analogues. These data were collected in the study of design engineers. The interviews covered human factors problems that arose during design tasks, and we tried to find out how they handled such problems. A number of sources were identified, including the use of mock-ups and pilot research, the use of human factors literature, and so on. The highest category was informal use of mode-ups and pilot research, but the second highest category was analogue use. In the 76 decision points we probed for this study, 13 of them referred to analogues. In six cases the analogues were felt to have been the basis for making the decision, and in the other 7 cases they were cited as being helpful. Thus, the analogues were seen as at least helpful in 20% of the decisions. To put this in perspective, looking at all data sources, 35 were cited as the basis for the decision, 30 as being helpful, 18 as being used but not particularly helpful, and 9 as being useless. So, 13 of the 65 data sources that were useful, were analogues.

Discussion

Up to now there have been no clear functions for analogues in formal models of decision making. Multi-Attribute Utility Analysis views decision making as the identification of options, the identification of evaluation dimensions, the assignment of weights to the evaluation dimensions, the rating of each option on each dimension, and the tabulation of the results to select the option with the highest score. Decision Analysis views decision making as the identification of options, the identification of reactions to each options, and counter-reactions (as in a chess game), and the assignment of utilities and probabilities to each node in a decision tree. There is little room for analogical reasoning in these formulations.

Table 2

Frequency of Analogues by Functional Category

Category	Frequency
Situation assessment	5
Expectancies	14
Warnings (10)	
Reassurances (4)*	
Options	14
Total	33

----

*Twelve of the analogue cases coded as primarily functioning to generate an option, there was also an expression of the expectancy of success. So 16 cases could be said to have served as reassurance.

The findings reported in this paper were carried out in the context of a descriptive model of decision making that we have proposed called the Recognition-Primed Decision (RPD) model (Klein, in press). A schematic of this model is presented in Figure 1. Briefly, the distinguishing features of the description are that the framework for a decision is the recognition of typicality; options are generated serially rather than concurrently; the first option generated is usually the most promising one; options are evaluated serially rather than concurrently; the attempt is to satisfice

Figure 1 -- Recognition-Primed Decision (RPD) Model

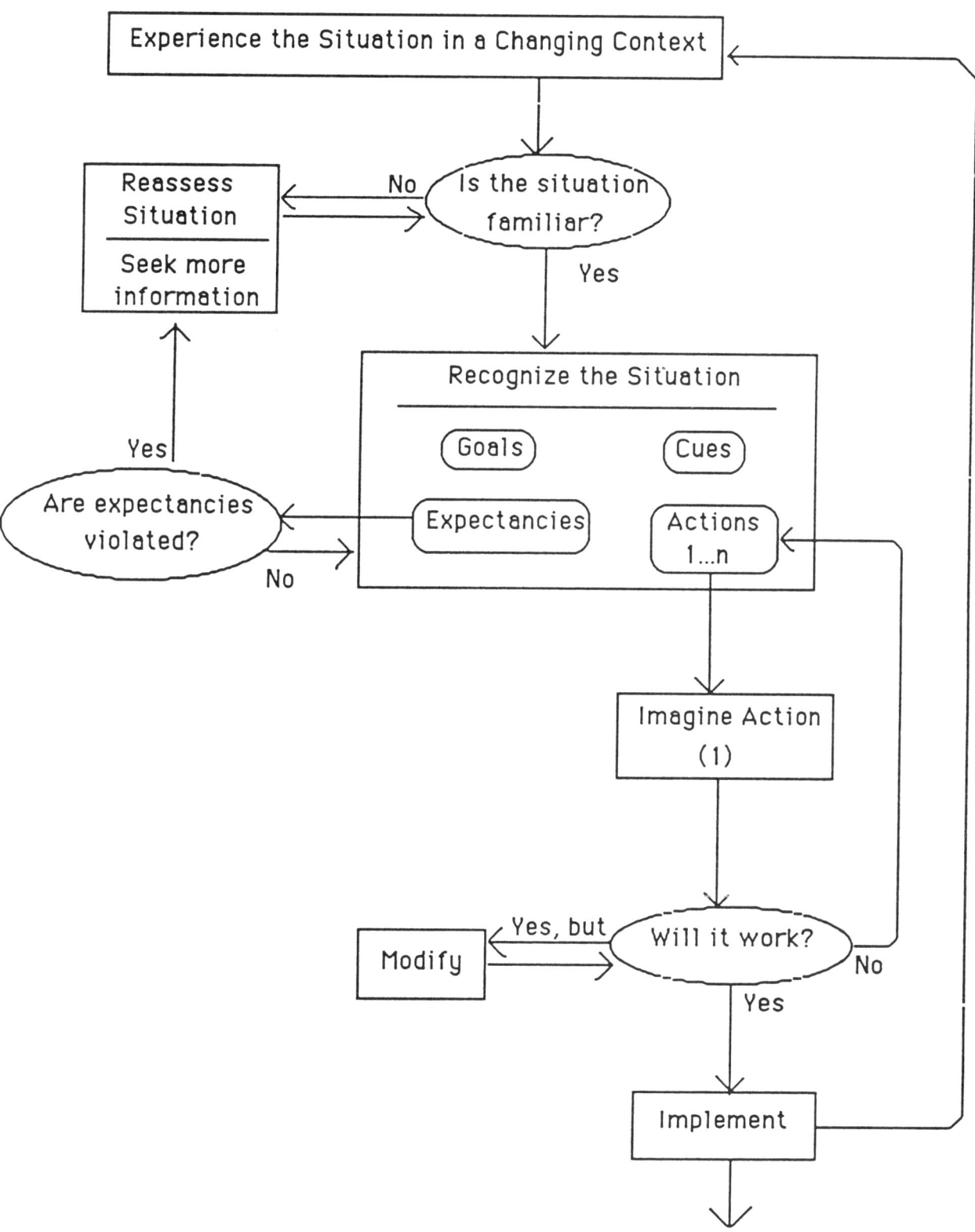

rather than optimize; evaluation is through a simulation process of imagining the option being implemented to see if any problems arise; and the decision maker generally is prepared with an action to take rather than having to wait until the deliberations are completed.

Thus, the RPD model highlights the importance of prior experiences in decision making: in formulating an assessment of situational dynamics, generating expectancies, and evaluating options. In our research, we have found that the great majority of decisions were based on recognition rather than analysis. The decision makers could draw on their experience to judge a situation as typical and thereby recognize feasible goals, critical cues and factors to watch out for, events to expect, and typical options. The process of decision making consisted of reviewing these options, starting with the most typical, to see if there were any barriers to implementing it. If there were, then modifications were considered, and if these were not judged as satisfactory then it was rejected in favor of the next most typical option.

Early in our research based on the RPD model (e.g. Klein et al., 1985), we proposed that analogical reasoning would be the primary mode of evaluating suggested options. The fact that we found relatively little evidence of the direct use of analogues has led us to reconsider this conceptualization. It may be that analogues (cases that retain the episodic nature of the original experience) disappear under the weight of cumulative experiences for experienced personnel. The fireground commanders we interviewed averaged 23 years of service and frequently responded that an incident reminded them of scores of previous incidents rather than any particular one. Individual incidents have blended together in their memory into what may be considered a prototype or schema representation, and these carry important information about typicality that is not represented when people recall a single analogue.

Other reasons for the low rate of analogical use found in these studies is undoubtedly methodological. We collected data by conducting retrospective interviews about actual events. It may simply be quite difficult for people to recall the use of analogues. We noticed a higher rate of analogue recall for studies where we conducted the interviews immediately after the incidents, compared to studies of events that occurred much earlier. The study of tank platoon leaders included interviews immediately after the exercises, while memory was still fresh, and the recall rate for analogues was higher. Also, many of the analogues in that study were of exercises on the same terrain on a previous exercise.

We are currently carrying out a study of urban fire ground decision making using an on-going verbal protocol technique during simulated incidents. Preliminary results suggest that reported analogue use will be substantially higher under these conditions (Calderwood & Crandall, in progress).

In summary, in this review of analogue use from our studies of decision making, the functions of analogues seemed to fall into three categories: the identification of causal factors operating in a situation; the recognition of outcomes if an option is implemented (including both warnings and reassurances); and the generation of options and methods. There are obvious linkages between these categories. Identifying causal factors helps to develop situation assessment, which in turn enables a decision maker to recognize what responses are appropriate in the situation. Identifying an option from a previous case also carries with it the outcome of the previous case, providing reassurance or warnings about the option.

The assessment of analogue use overlaps somewhat with Hammond's (1986) system concept for case-based reasoning. The function of identifying an option is served by Hammond's "Retriever" capability, and the aspect of expectancy that we see as anticipating problems matches with Hammond's "Anticipator." We do not see any correspondence to the function we have described as using analogues for reassurance. The use of analogues for situation assessment is partially covered by the "Assigner" function of Hammond's system, but it is not clear how key features and goals are identified by prior cases. Rather Hammond's domain assumes goals to be understood, and, since it is not a dynamic domain there are no cues to monitor.

References

Brezovic, C. P., Klein, G. A., & Thordsen, M. (1987). Decision making in armored platoon command (KATR-858(B)-87-05F). Yellow Springs, OH: Klein Associates Inc. Prepared under contract MDA903-85-C-0327 for U.S. Army Research Institute, Alexandria, VA.

Calderwood, R., & Crandall, B. (In progress). Verbal protocols of expert and novice command decisions during simulated fire ground incidents. Yellow Springs, OH: Klein Associates Inc.

Calderwood, R., Crandall, B., & Klein, G. A. (1987). Expert and novice fire ground command decisions (KATR-858(D)-87-02F). Yellow Springs, OH: Klein Associates Inc. Prepared under contract MDA903-85-C-0327) for U.S. Army Research Institute, Alexandria, VA.

Flanagan, J. C. (1954). The critical incident technique. Psychological Bulletin, 51, 327-358.

Hammond, K. J. (1986). Case-based planning: An integrated theory of planning, learning and memory. Ph.D. Thesis, Yale University, Department of Computer Science.

Klein, G. A., & Brezovic, C. P. (1987). Human performance data needed for training device design decisions. Technical Report AAMRL-TR-87-010. Wright Patterson Air Force Base, OH: Harry G. Armstrong Aerospace Medical Research Laboratory.

Klein, G. A., Calderwood, R., & Clinton-Cirocco, A. (1985). Rapid decision making on the fire ground (KA-TR-84-41-7). Alexandria, VA: U.S. Army Research Institute.

Klein, G. A., Calderwood, R., & MacGregor, D. (In progress). Critical decision method for eliciting knowledge. Yellow Springs, OH: Klein Associates Inc.

Taynor, J., Klein, G. A., & Thordsen, M. (1987). *Distributed decision making in wildland firefighting* (KATR-858(A)-04F). Yellow Springs, OH: Klein Associates Inc. Prepared under contract MDA903-85-C-0327 for U.S. Army Research Institute Alexandria, VA.

Appendix A

Listing of Analogues for the Four Domains Studied

1. <u>Design Engineers</u> (Klein & Brezovic, 1987).

<u>Case #1</u>

A new administrator needed to write formal specifications for a part of a training device, and relied on a previous set of specifications to organize it, to cover the boilerplate, and to structure the writing.

<u>Case #2</u>

An experienced designer remembered a previous incident where maintenance workers were unable to find critical parts because they were only looking for what they had been trained on in the simulator, so he made sure to include actual photographs in the new training device.

<u>Case #3</u>

A designer feared that the instructor's workload would be too high but found a similar instructor station that had not had excessive workload rates.

<u>Case #4</u>

A previous device suggested to a designer how much physical resistance to build into a switch so that it was neither too hard to operate nor too easy.

<u>Case #5</u>

A designer was fighting users about how large a field-of-view was needed to produce acceptable training for people engaged in aerial refueling and found an earlier training device where 60 degrees had worked well, verifying his own position.

<u>Case #6</u>

A designer needed a method for identifying workload levels and found an earlier project where an appropriate method had been used. He adapted that method for his own needs.

<u>Case #7</u>

A previous device had a flat panel and users left books on it which melted switches, so the designer built in a slope and made sure there was no lip at the end to catch books or papers. In this way he attempted to avoid the problem by preventing misuse.

Case #8

A previous training device was used to suggest how large an entrance was needed into the instructor station.

Case #9

A previous device was used to suggest the types of cues and the clarity of their presentation in order to have acceptable low altitude flight training.

Case #10

A designer wanted to avoid the expense of a motion base for a training device and used a prior training device to confirm that he could use a G suit to impart the necessary motion cues.

Case #11

A previous device was used to suggest a mechanism for a control loader.

Case #12

A designer was worried that a visual system produced too much distortion if the trainee moved his head, and found an earlier case where the system did not adversely affect training.

Case #13

A designer needed to write a specification about how much workload to tolerate for an instruction/operator station of a training device. He borrowed portions from one previous specification for the same aircraft but the wrong mission and from another case where the aircraft and mission were the same but a different format was used.

2. Tank Platoon Leaders (TPLs). (Brezovic, Klein, & Thordsen, 1987).

Case #14

A TPL remembered that in an earlier exercise his group had gone into a bounding approach formation which greatly slowed their rate of advance so he set up his defensive position to force the attackers into a bounding approach.

Case #15

A TPL recalled seeing the opposing force at a certain point in the approach path and realized that since he was going to send 3 tanks by the same route, that is where they would be spotted. However, he just resolved to accept the risk.

Case #16

In a previous exercise a certain avenue of approach worked very well and so the TPL decided to use it again.

Case #17

The TPL remembered that a certain defensive position was overrun from the western side during an earlier training exercise and became alarmed to notice that he had set his position such that only one tank was guarding that approach. He shifted the tanks around to provide more coverage.

Case #18

The opposing force was occupying a ridgeline position that the TPL had used a few days earlier so he used his knowledge of it to identify its vulnerabilities.

Case #19

The TPL decided to use for an avenue of approach a path that had worked several days earlier. However it had rained during the intervening time and the path became impassibly muddy, leading to failure.

(There were a few cases like this where the analogical reasoning led to a poor decision, by the admission of the person interviewed. The major problem seemed to be a lack of understanding of how to factor in situational cues to recognize when to reject an analogue or when to adjust it. This failure was most pronounced in the tank platoon leaders who had the least experience. We estimated that in almost half the cases of analogue use in this group, the reasoning resulted in an inadequate decision. Such problems were much less frequent for the more experienced people we studied in the other domains. Ineffective uses of analogues, based on self-report, are flagged below.)

Case #20

The TPL realized he could use the same battle position that had worked well in the morning exercise that day.

Case #21

During an advance, the TPL was reminded of an earlier exercise over similar terrain, and this alerted him to become more sensitive to ridgelines and places for cover and concealment.

3. <u>Urban Fireground Commanders (FGCs)</u>. (Klein et al., 1985; Calderwood et al., 1987).

Case #22

Recall of a training film suggested the idea of letting a fire burn through the roof and self-ventilate.

Case #23

A white cloud was recalled as similar to one in an earlier fire that had turned out to be toxic smoke. Breathing apparatus was assigned to reduce risk to the firefighters.

Case #24

A FGC examines structures of a certain type by checking whether there is balloon construction, because of an incident early in his career when there was a foul-up in a building with balloon construction. He always remembers that incident in doing his examination.

Case #25

A FGC decided to park a truck in the same place where it had been on an earlier practice run. He noted that it was a poor location for reaching the fire during the actual incident.

Case #26

A FGC recalled an earlier fire where there had been a shortage of water so he decided to avoid the problem by using a larger hose and more crew members on the pumping truck. He regretted this decision because it required too many crew members manning the truck and didn't leave enough to enter the building with the hose.

Case #27

A FGC remembered an earlier fire that appeared to be extinguished but was actually hiding in the duct work, and since the current situation involved a building with many renovations, he was suspicious that the fire was hiding from them. (He was right.)

Case #28

A FGC saw hot tar running off a roof and remembered an earlier fire at this location where the tar started a secondary fire so he ordered water to be sprayed on the roof.

Case #29

A FGC noticed billboards on the top of a building and remembered a fire where the flames burned through the wooden supports of billboards, sending them crashing into the street. He ordered the crowds to be moved back.

4. Forest Fire Incident Commanders. (Taynor et al., 1987).

Case #30

A commander remembered an earlier fire that had been directed into a box canyon where there was a poor fuel supply and he ordered the same strategy since the opportunity was present.

Case #31

A commander wanted to save resources by housing two fire teams in the same base camp but remembered an incident recalled where administrative problems arose when two teams shared a camp, so separate camps were set up.

Case #32

A commander recalled an incident where firefighters were treated poorly and relieved of their assignment by jealous local forces, and so the commander placed some unnecessary telephone calls to smooth the way and avoid political fights.

Case #33

Management problems in one team led a commander to reassign responsibilities in another team to prevent a similar problem.

USING ANALOGUES TO PREDICT AND PLAN

Gary A. Klein   Leslie A. Whitaker

Klein Associates Inc.
Yellow Springs, OH 45387

and

James A. King

J. A. King Associates
Cambridge City, IN 47327

Acknowledgement

The systems described in this paper were supported by Contract F29601-87-C-0216 from the Air Force Systems Command/Air Force Weapons Laboratory at Kirtland AFB, New Mexico, and Contract F33615-87-C-5300 from the Materials Laboratory/Air Force Wright Aeronautical Laboratories at Wright Patterson AFB, Ohio. We would like to thank Aaron Perea and Steve LeClair.

Abstract

Formal procedures have been developed to use analogues for administrative planning. A rationale for analogue use is presented, along with examples of applications and evaluations of analogical prediction. Implications are discussed for developing systems that make use of analogical reasoning.

Submitted for presentation at
Defense Advanced Research Projects Agency (DARPA)
Sponsored 1988 Case-Based Reasoning Workshop,
Clearwater Beach, Florida, May 11-13, 1988.

Introduction

Analogical reasoning can occur in every situation in which people are required to make judgments and predictions. A very simple example of the use of analogical reasoning may be seen when a person is selling a home. The realtor in this transaction sets a price for a property, not by using a formal model and calculating all the variables, but by choosing a comparable sale and adjusting its price on the basis of small differences between the two properties (such as an extra bathroom or a location on a corner lot). Engineers have traditionally made use of analogies in prediction and design. They typically look for structural comparisons. If their task is to predict how reliable a new piece of equipment is going to be, engineers use historical data for a basis of estimate.

Rationale for Analogical Predictions

We can describe the use of analogues as Comparison-Based Prediction (CBP). The CBP model of analogical reasoning emphasizes the role of causal factors (Klein, 1982; Weitzenfeld, 1984). This model states that for Situation Y there is a set of causal factors (a,b,c...) that will determine or influence T_Y, the target characteristic of Y to be estimated. Situation Y could be a new automotive part. Causal factors a, b, and c could be the shape of the part, the materials used, and the number of pieces required. T_Y could be the reliability of the new part.

In determining the target, T_Y, we are saying that we want to quickly obtain a prediction of the reliability of part Y to see if the design will be adequate. We usually cannot identify all of the determining causal factors involved, their effects and interactions. Instead, an analogous situation or comparison case (Situation X, a similar part) is identified which reflects the same determinants as the target case. That is, for the comparison part study, the same causal factors (a,b,c...) determine a corresponding specification, T_X, as a guideline for part X.

The primary power of analogical predictions is that they reflect variables that may be unknown or uncharted. If the causal factor affects the comparison datum T_X, then it is a part of the prediction even if no one has identified it as a factor. Therefore, it might never appear in abstract, analytical models.

Although the same causal factors affect both T_Y and T_X, it is unlikely that the role of the causal factors will be the same in both cases. But, by using T_X as an estimate of T_Y we can note the differences in the roles of the better-defined causal factors and make adjustments in our predictions to take into account their differential impact.

The Subject Matter Experts (SMEs) then are guided through an examination of the effects of the causal factors (either singularly or in combination). This assures that they consider all relevant factors that might affect their judgments, and results in the production of an "applicable adjustment factor." This adjustment factor is then applied to operational data for T_X, to yield a prediction for T_Y.

Consider the following prediction problem prompted by a local mental health facility.

> Are there enough potential clients to warrant an inservice facility in Greene County? When asked, the practitioner had no idea of the number to expect. Even when pressed, she could not offer a prediction. We then used the CBP method to predict the number of clients the facility could expect.
>
> For the specific instance of the mental health facility, we used CBP in the following way. T_Y was the number of clients to be predicted. The subcausal factors were the size of the County's population, the extent of the troubled subpopulation, the level of public transportation, and the number of competing facilities. We then used the practitioner as the SME. We found there was a similary facility in adjacent Montgomery County. The number of clients at that facility (T_X) was 80 per year. We asked about each causal factor and found the following data: The Greene County population was 1/10 the size of Montgomery County. The subpopulation at risk was higher in Montgomery County. The transportation system was better in Montgomery County. However, there were competing facilities within Montgomery County. The proposed Greene County facility would be the only one in the County. The audit trail documented these selected factors and the quantitative and qualitative adjustments that were made: The population is 1/10 (expect 1/10 x 80 = 8). The at-risk subpopulation is lower (adjust down); the transportation is poorer (adjust down); there are no competing facilities (adjust up). T_Y was predicted to be from 7 to 11 clients per year.

The CBP technique relies upon the use of SMEs, knowledgeable about the domain of interest, to select optimal comparison cases and to identify relevant causal factors. The CBP approach elicits judgments in a carefully structured interview. The approach is data-driven since the SMEs are generating adjustments of operational data and giving their reasons for making these adjustments.

Prediction problems may arise for which no operational data are available. The CBP approach may be effective if the SMEs will estimate the operational data. This is not the ideal application of the CBP method and will reduce confidence in the outputs. However, this is often the state of affairs where CBP is used for predictions, since there are usually no other methods that can be applied.

The CBP process is documented to provide an Audit Trail. The Audit Trail allows the assessments to be understood, refined, and communicated to others. It consists of a detailed description of the causal factors considered by the SME, and how each is used, either singly or in combination, to arrive at the assessment. Consequently, the Audit Trail provides the building blocks for an expert system based upon case-based reasoning.

From a methodological standpoint, the Audit Trail serves another function. By having an explicit set of causal factors to consider in determining adjustments, the SME has a set of concepts to use in posing the differences between the target case and the comparison case. This facilitates communication among SMEs and helps to standardize the variables considered in the assessment process. In addition, if the assessment is found to be inaccurate once operational data are obtained for the target case, the Audit Trail provides an opportunity to go back and see which causal factors, and assumptions about causal factors, were responsible for the misjudgment (John, Strobhar, & Klein, 1986). Thus, the Audit Trail provides a means of monitoring the reasoning processes of the experts.

The approach is data driven since the SMEs are generating adjustments of operational data and giving their reasons for making these adjustments. The production of the Audit Trail allows the expertise of SMEs to be scrutinized, compared, evaluated, and adjusted. This expertise can then be built into a case-based reasoning system.

--Formally, CBP is a system of reasoning by analogy, and thus taps the basis of case-based reasoning. For example, by using CBP one can predict to an unknown case by using what is known about a comparable case.

--Operationally, it is a way of structuring the judgments that experts make when they are called upon to estimate unknown properties of a new situation.

--Empirically, it is a means of significantly increasing the validity and reliability of very difficult predictions.

Review of Comparison-Based Prediction Research

We have used CBP as a front-end analysis tool early in the procurement cycle to test the effectiveness of three proposed training devices: maintenance trainers, tank gunnery simulators, and Howitzer trainers (Klein & John, 1985). We also showed that CBP could be used to make predictions about the costs of the Howitzer trainers, and that these predictions could be made very early in the procurement cycle, early in concept development, before there was even a firm definition of the weapons system itself.

In addition, we have used CBP to predict the number of clients who would use a new mental health facility (the prediction was too low to justify the facility, and the plans were dropped) and to predict the sales of a new chemical detection system for testing water contamination.

We have summarized this experience by developing a Guidebook for CBP (Klein, John, Perez, & Mirabella, 1986), giving step-by-step instructions for the use of CBP for predicting cost and effectiveness of new systems.

How Good are Analogical Predictions?

We have conducted a series of validity and reliability studies (Klein, 1986). The CBP method successfully predicted transfer of training in a fault-diagnosis task. A correlation between predicted and actual learning-time of this task was .89. Other evaluations of predictive validity have ranged from correlations of .84 to .36 (the lower correlations were obtained for cases where there were no operational data to adjust, and the SMEs had to estimate these data as well as adjust the estimates). It also has been demonstrated that CBP judgments produced standard deviations that were 25% to 30% lower than those obtained using unstructured predictions. On the basis of these results, the validity of this method is strong and its reliability clear.

Implications for System Development

Comparison-Based Prediction is a viable basis for computerized decision support systems. We have examined two distinct domains for such applications and are in the process of building two software systems based on CBP.

The first domain is in structural engineering. We are developing two related systems to aid in the prediction of the survivability of buried concrete structures. We have named these systems SURVER II and SURVER III. SURVER stands for SURvivability/Vulnerability Analysis through Experiential Reasoning.

The goal of the SURVER II system is to provide training for structural engineers who are new to the specific domain of blast effects on buried structures. The first portion of the system (SURVER I) provides a tutorial introduction to the use of the SURVER system. SURVER II guides the user in the development of predictions about structural survivability. In making these predictions, the engineer can access a data base which contains descriptions of prior cases. A searching algorithm enables the engineer to select one or more prior cases which are similar to the current one. The similarity match and retrieval is accomplished by attributes of the case. In this system, the primary searching algorithm searches for cases with similar stress to strain ratios. The data base includes textual and graphic information, all of which can be displayed for the engineer when the case is retrieved. The expertise to interpret the graphic information has been captured in textual material stored with the graphs. The engineer accesses these expert rules by clicking the portion of the graph to which they apply. For example, the engineer says, "If my predicted peak velocity at the interface is like that pictured in this graph, what does that mean for the structure?" The engineer clicks on the peak of the velocity curve, and a text window appears which states "INTERFACE PEAK VELOCITY: Concrete cylinders buried at 0.67 meters will not survive peak velocities in excess of 300 cm/sec."

SURVER III is designed to provide guidance for the engineer who is predicting structural survival. The objective is not only to provide intelligent access to a data base of prior cases, but also to aid the engineer in making adjustments from a previous case to a similar current prediction problem. These adjustments are based on the causal factors we have obtained from CBP interviews with SMEs. They include burial depth, type of structure, burial soil composition, structure diameter, wall thickness, and blast size. Adjustment rules have also been obtained from these experts and will be used as the basis for making predictions from the prior cases. An Audit Trail is critically important here because the weight assigned to each causal factor and the interactions of these causal factors in determining structural survival are particularly complex in this domain. It is therefore critical to be able to follow the reasoning used to reach the current prediction.

Another domain we have examined for the development of a CBP system is the bidding on contracts for manufactured products. Manufacturing firms must engage in competitive bidding to acquire military or commercial contracts. The bidder must decide what costs will be incurred to purchase existing components, manufacture new components, assemble the product, and ship the completed assembly to the customer. Many of the variables considered in arriving at a quoted bid are complex and ill defined. Determining a quoted price is therefore a problem for which a totally determined solution does not exist. Hence, there is no algorithm which incorporates the bidder's knowledge into a final quote. Many parts, however, can be quoted as variants on previously bid parts. In these cases, the bidder will want to use as much information as possible from the manufacture of the prior part to target a good price as efficiently as possible.

We have developed preliminary specifications for a decision-support system which will provide intelligent access to an existing data base of prior bids for a medium-sized manufacturing firm. The problem is one of intelligently retrieving the best prior cases to support the bidder's current quoting process. We think this will be a particularly appropriate domain for the application of a case-based decision support system because it meets all the criteria listed in the next section.

Criteria for Domain Problem Appropriate for Comparison-Based Predictions

We identified a number of areas where a comparison-based system would not work out. Most notably, if the data base were not already available, the development cost might be prohibitive. If the adjustment variables (causal factors) interacted too severely, the job of tracing rules of thumb became unmanageable. If the data base were missing too much information or had low quality date, there was no sense in proceeding. If the domain was so complex that nothing usable could be produced without modeling everything, we rejected that domain. Moreover, if the domain allowed an algorithmic solution then a CBP approach was undesirable. Other prohibitive constraints were that a requirement existed for an optimal solution, or that the projected system impact was too low to justify the effort.

Applications of Comparison-Based Prediction in a computer decision-support system require that the domain have several characteristics. These characteristics are described below and illustrated with examples from the manufacturing domain described above.

1. <u>Prior cases</u>. The domain must require expertise which works from prior corporate history (cases). We found that using prior cases as the basis for current manufacturing decisions is the most common method of making these decisions. Seldom is the case-match sufficiently good to allow an exact solution-match, but usually there is something that can be used from a previous case (or cases) to give the manufacturer guidance in planning the current case. In contrast, at the opposite extreme, seldom will the design be so radically different that all knowledge from prior cases would be worthless.

2. <u>Rules of thumb</u>. Applying these cases to the current problem must require judgments and adjustments. The domain expert uses a variety of rules of thumb to make adjustments from previous cases. For example, aluminum parts are punched out by dies. The parts are then welded into the final product. Dies wear out with use. A welder knows that the condition of the die determines quality of the parts and hence the amount of scrap that will be produced as a result of poor welds. When a firm makes retooling decisions, it can use this experience to determine the best retooling schedule to trade off scrap vs. retooling costs. This judgment is provided by prior experience with similar parts and dies. Analytical solutions can not make use of much of this expertise because it can not be quantified, but instead requires verbal rules. These verbal rules often allow only qualitative adjustments. In addition, the causal variables should not interact so severely as to make rules of thumb too complex.

3. <u>Non-algorithmic</u>. It must be sufficiently complex and fuzzy that algorithmic solutions are not possible. This criterion eliminated process control and multiline-multiproduct control from our considerations because there are algorithmic solutions provided in these domains. In contrast, manufacturability and bid quoting are domains which have not been reduced to algorithmic solutions because of the number and complexity of their drivers.

4. <u>Non-optimal</u>. It need not require an optimal solution. A satisficing (good enough) solution will do. When there are several possible solutions for a problem, the designer is often satisfied with a good enough solution. This satisficing solution does not have any major pitfalls and meets all the goals of the product at an acceptable cost. Manufacturers often prefer such solutions because the costs to determine the optimal solution exceed the savings that would be obtained. In the extreme, efforts necessary to obtain an optimal solution may be prohibitive in their expense and complexity, without yielding economically better solutions.

5. <u>High-impact</u>. It must be sufficiently important to have an impact on the operating costs of the firm. The cost-benefit constraint means that the problem domain must be a high driver or a bottleneck within the manufacturing system. Regardless of how elegant its solutions, the system will not be implemented if the "problem" is not an important one for the firm.

6. <u>Bounded knowledge base</u>. It must be sufficiently circumscribed that applicable domain knowledge can be obtained in a reasonable period of development. If the amount of knowledge necessary to make decisions is so large and so general that knowledge engineering is an impossible task, the domain is not appropriate for case-based reasoning. Realistic time constraints for

knowledge elicitation impose restrictions on the application domain. There must be a sufficiently rich data base available or planned.

Synthesis: Case-Based Reasoning -- A Near-Term Strategy

There are a number of tough issues which make it difficult to produce an automated system which functions at the level of the experienced expert. One of the most difficult is the modeling of domain rules and general world knowledge which experts and even novices have acquired. Therefore, as a near-term strategy, our goal is to develop a Comparison-Based system which will serve as a decision-support system. This decision aid is intended to enhance rather than replace the expert's role in the prediction process. One crucial component of such a system is the interface which allows the user to retrieve relevant comparison cases and make the necessary adjustments to match the current prediction problem. We argue that the intelligence of this system is in that interface. Well-designed interfaces will save the expert many laborious steps in arriving at predictions.

Consider the prediction task of the structural engineer using our SURVER system described above. When asked to build a mesh and to predict the effect of blast on a buried structure, the engineer will be able to enter the current case's relevant attributes and ask for the best matching case. With our system, there is a retrieval algorithm which computes the stress-over-strain ratio and retrieves one or more similar cases from the data base. This system is case based because it retrieves all of the stored information about the prior cases, not just the value of the stress/strain ratio. The system is knowledge based because it contains rules which will allow the engineer to see whether the current mesh accurately describes the expected blast effects, based on prior comparable cases. The system will provide supplemental analyses (e.g., one-dimensional wave propagation simulator) which will augment the engineer's knowledge of the expected blast characteristics.

We believe that such systems are a very real help to experts who must make these predictions now. Although the present version of SURVER does not provide a prediction -- that is left to the expert -- it does accomplish two important functions: (1) it helps the less-experienced engineer see how the analysis is done (by an Audit Trail which aids learning); (2) it provides relevant data and rules for manipulating those data to support the engineer's decision about the expected survivability of that structure.

References

John, P. G., Strobhar, D. A., & Klein, G. A. (1986). _Structuring expert judgment in survivability/vulnerability analysis_ (AFWL-TN-86-07). Kirtland Air Force Base, NM: Air Force Weapons Laboratory.

Klein, G. A. (1982). The use of comparison cases. _IEEE 1982 Proceedings of the International Conference on Cybernetics and Society_, 88-91.

Klein, G. A. (1986). Validity of analogical predictions. *Technological Forecasting and Social Change*, *30(2)*, 139-148, September.

Klein, G. A., & John, P. G. (1985). *Predicting workload requirement during the predesign stage*. Wright Patterson Air Force Base, OH: Armstrong Aerospace Medical Research Laboratory.

Klein, G. A., John, P. G., Perez, R.S., & Mirabella, A. (1986). *Comparison-based prediction of cost and effectiveness of training: A guide* (TR-85-45-11, August). Yellow Springs, OH: Klein Associates Inc. Technical Report prepared for the Army Research Institute for the Behavioral and Social Sciences, Contract No. MDA903-83-C-0270.

Weitzenfeld, J. (1984). Valid reasoning by analogy. *Philosophy of Science*, *51*, 137-149.

Retrieving Events from a Case Memory: A Parallel Implementation[1]

Janet L. Kolodner
School of Information and Computer Science
Georgia Institute of Technology
Atlanta, GA 30332

Abstract

Perhaps the most important support process a case-based reasoner needs is a memory for cases. In this paper, we describe a parallel retrieval algorithm that can be used to retrieve cases from a hierarchically organized memory for cases given the description of some new case as a retrieval probe. We also describe the structure of the memory it works on. The organization of cases in memory is based on previous work by Schank and Kolodner. The retrieval algorithm is a concept refinement search algorithm and is based on work by Riesbeck and Martin that is implemented in DMAP. It is implemented in a program called PARADYME (Parallel Dynamic Memory) that is designed to work alongside a case-based problem solving program. There are four parts to PARADYME: a hierarchically-organized memory for cases, a concept refinement retrieval process, heuristics for choosing the best out of several retrieved cases, and heuristics for respecifying a retrieval probe when it is over- or under-specified.

1 Introduction

Perhaps the most important support process a case-based reasoner needs is a memory for cases. The memory must make cases accessible when appropriate retrieval cues are provided to it and it must incorporate new cases into its structures as they are experienced, in the process maintaining accessibility of the items already in the memory. It must be able to handle cases in all of their complexity, and it must be able to manage thousands of cases in its memory. In this paper, we discuss a parallel retrieval scheme for a conceptual memory based on previous research into memory organization and retrieval methods (e.g., Kolodner, 1983, Kolodner & Cullingford, 1986, Schank, 1982, Reiser, 1983, Martin & Riesbeck, 1986). While the abstract principles of the previous work remain the same, the details have been modified in several ways. The model to be presented, called PARADYME, has four parts:

1. a hierarchical organization of knowledge and cases

2. a parallel memory retrieval process that uses a concept refinement approach to retrieval

3. a set of transformation rules that transform and elaborate a retrieval probe to get a better "best match" than is possible from the original set of cues

---

[1]This research was supported in part by DARPA under Contract No. N0039-87-C-0026 to Thinking Machines, in part by NSF under grant No. IST-8608362, and in part by Georgia Tech, the Georgia Tech Foundation, and Lockheed AI Center. This work was done while the author was on sabbatical at Thinking Machines, Inc., Cambridge, Mass. Thanks to Thinking Machines for providing machine and programming support for the project. Programming was done by Eyal Yaari. Thanks also to Alex Kass, Phyllis Koton, Chris Owens, Chris Riesbeck, and Robert Thau for enlightening comments made during discussion of my scheme. A shorter version of this paper was submitted to AAAI-88.

4. a set of heuristics that choose the best matching case from those that are activated

PARADYME is implemented on the Connection Machine, a SIMD parallel machine, in a program by the same name. Because we want PARADYME to be able to work along with a problem solving system, we have given it knowledge and cases from a case-based reasoning system that is under development. Thus, PARADYME currently uses JULIA's (Hinrichs, 1988, Kolodner, 1987a, b, Shinn, 1988) knowledge structures and cases. Because the cases are some that JULIA has processed, the cases are full problem solving experiences represented in their entirety. JULIA's, and therefore PARADYME's, domain is meal planning.

2 Background

There are several requirements we put on a memory for cases:

1. Best matching cases must be retrieved using a set of retrieval cues that provide a partial description of the item to be retrieved.

2. Memory should return small numbers of cases rather than large numbers. If large numbers of cases match an underspecified description, then either a prototype, a generalization, or a request for more information should be returned by memory.

3. Retrieval should be fast. It is done in the context of reasoning and we want reasoning to be fast. Therefore, it is preferable to have the hard work done at memory update time rather than at retrieval time. Retrieval processes should be fairly uncomplicated.

4. Retrieval time should not increase as the memory grows.

5. Generalizations and cases should be equally accessible.

Retrieving appropriate cases from a case memory is essentially a massive search problem that requires retrieval of a best match rather than an exact match. Given a partial description of a situation, it is up to the case memory to recall the case from memory that best matches the new situation. In our initial work on this problem, we chose to take our inspiration from people (Kolodner, 1983, 1984, Schank, 1982). The models that came from these studies, Schank's (1982) dynamic memory and Kolodner's (1983, 1984) CYRUS, hypothesized several things:

1. Memory categories are associated with concrete types of situations. Each category holds general information about the contents of such situations, the relationships between characters, props, and actions in such situations, and the causal and temporal consequences and antecedents of the situations. These categories are arranged in abstraction hierarchies and packaging hierarchies (Schank, 1982).

2. These memory categories, called MOPs, also organize indexing structures. Indexes associated with each category differentiate items in the category from each other. When several items share the same set of indexes, a more specialized category (a subMOP) is formed and items are organized in the same way within those categories. Physically, in our implementations, items in categories were organized in multiple redundant discrimination nets (Kolodner, 1984, Lebowitz, 1983).

3. Items are found in memory by first choosing a small set of categories to confine search to and then using the features of the specified event to designate which branches of the organizational structure should be traversed. Traversal happens in parallel among indexes at the same level of memory, and traversal finishes when an appropriate item or set of items with a subset of the specified features is found. (Kolodner, 1984 explains in more detail.)

4. There are several circumstances under which such search does not succeed, and there are retrieval strategies to deal with each of these search problems. One kind of strategy identifies categories for search if none is designated in a retrieval probe. Another elaborates retrieval probes if memory traversal fails before a particular event is found. Another creates context for the retrieval probe and directs traversal functions to search in a different part of memory for items with this created context.

5. Memory update functions choose indexes for events by choosing those features from an event that specialize or violate norms of the category the event is being indexed in and lead to unanticipated consequences within that category. These functions create specialized categories by a similarity-based induction method: When several items are indexed by the same feature or set of features, the similarities of those items is extracted and a new category is formed.

The search method embodied here is a "concept refinement" method, which provides much more control over the portions of memory that get activated than does an intersection search.[2] In concept refinement search, a concept is not "turned on" until its parent in the abstraction hierarchy is accessed and some feature that specializes it with respect to the parent is specified. CYRUS (Kolodner, 1983, 1984), IPP (Lebowitz, 1983), and MOPTRANS (Lytinen, 1986) did this through a "locked network" in which traversal to a lower level of an abstraction hierarchy could not be done unless the higher level had already been accessed and the label associated with the index to the item at the next lower level was specified. DMAP (Riesbeck & Martin, 1986; Martin & Riesbeck, 1986), which our method is based on, implements concept refinement in another way. An item can be accessed if one of its antecedents in the abstraction hierarchy is activated by the probe, if that abstraction predicts another concept, and if some specialization of the predicted concept is specified in the probe. DMAP's method has the advantage of not requiring a redundant indexing scheme. The predictions DMAP makes are linguistic, but we have generalized them for searching a conceptual memory for events.

---

[2] MBR (Stanfill, 1987) is a massively parallel search technique that uses intersection search. It also runs on the Connection Machine. Its representations are both flat and monolithic (homogeneous). MBR broadcasts to each item in its memory in parallel. Its major activity is running a similarity metric to measure how close each of the items in memory is to what it is looking for. MBR has been run on large databases but never on hierarchical, heterogeneousm, or distributed structures.

In the scheme to be presented, we have created a memory system that upholds the principles presented above in a parallel implementation. While memory remains hierarchical, we have decoupled the retrieval procedures themselves from memory's organization. Memory organizes generalizations but does not require that the organization be used to access memory. While in CYRUS' implementation, indexes were used to block passage through memory, insuring that only relevant nodes were accessed, in PARADYME, predictions made by memory's knowledge structures identify which cases are good candidates for retrieval. We have also changed representations significantly. While in CYRUS, events were monolithic structures, PARADYME has a distributed representation.

3 Representing Knowledge and Cases

Representation in PARADYME is similar to that described in Schank's *Dynamic Memory* (1982). That is, the details of any particular event (case) are distributed throughout memory in two ways. First, they are distributed in an abstraction hierarchy associated with the kind of situation the event is an instance of (i.e., its type). Thus, a particular Mexican meal with death chili as its main course will have its description distributed in "meal", which says this kind of event has several eating scenes (only some are shown in Figure 1), that the participants want to satisfy hunger, that the main event is ingesting the main dish of the main course, etc.; "mexican meal", which says this kind of event has food of mexican cuisine, that a particular set of spices can be expected, that the drink of choice is Mexican beer, that food tastes spicy, etc.; and "death-chili-meal", which gives the details of this meal, e.g., who the eaters are, that they are mostly people who like very spicy food, where the meal took place. The center of Figure 1 illustrates this.

Second, details of events (cases) are distributed throughout abstraction hierarchies associated with scenes of the event. Schank (1982) called this a packaging hierarchy. In the case of meals, its scenes include food preparation, eating the appetizer, eating the main course, etc. Thus, details about what was served in the death-chili-meal appear in memory in knowledge structures describing meal scenes. The fact that the main course was death chili is distributed through the abstraction hierarchy of "meal-main-scene', as shown on the right side of Figure 1, while the fact that the appetizer was guacamole is distributed through "meal-appetizer-scene's" hierarchy, on the left side of Figure 1. "Meal's" other scenes are not shown.

We distribute representations in this way to allow the case-based reasoner to use small chunks of cases in its reasoning rather than having to wade through large cases and to allow generalization across scenes common to several kinds of situations (Schank, 1982). A retrieval probe might activate a full event with its scenes or only the representation for a particular scene. With a flat representation (i.e., no abstraction), generalizations must be recreated each time they are needed. With a monolithic structure (i.e., all aspects of the event in one hierarchy), it would be hard to make generalizations across different types of events.

There are several things to notice about this representational scheme that will be significant in judging the retrieval process. First, general knowledge (e.g., about meals and mexican meals) and details of particular cases are organized in the same structures. Thus both are equally accessible and accessible by the same retrieval methods. Second, we provide retrieval algorithms with a

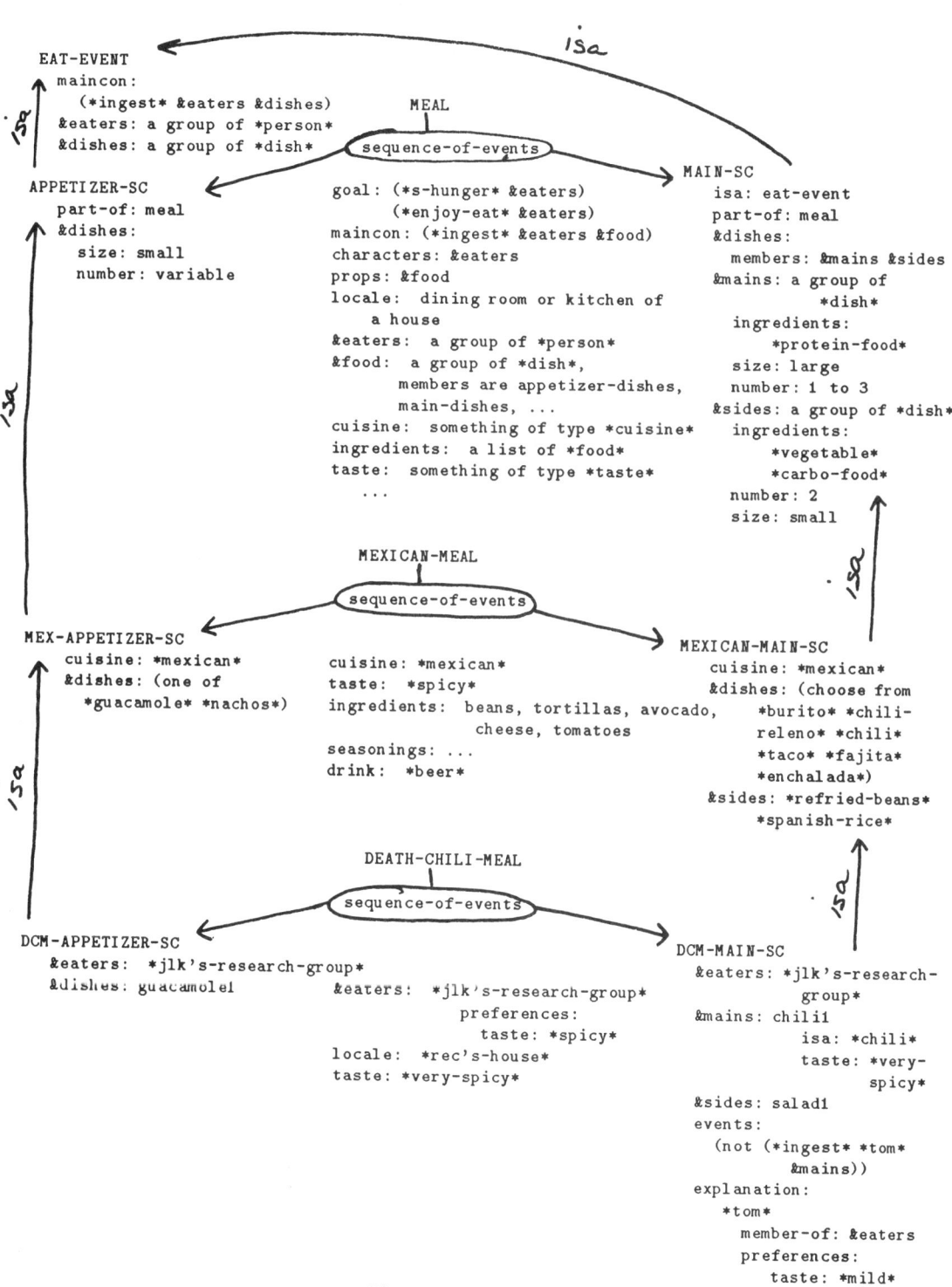

Figure 1

natural way of knowing if there are a large number of cases that partially match its retrieval probe without requiring it to activate all those cases. This is possible because details that appear high in the hierarchy do not get repeated lower in the hierarchy. This will allow memory to either return general knowledge that is activated by a probe or to ask for more specific knowledge to differentiate between the items with a given description. In a memory with many similar cases, this is an advantage.

The memory scheme also imposes a hard problem on the retrieval functions. The problem is that during retrieval, retrieval cues might hit event descriptors in several different structures. There must be a way to put those structures back together again. We shall see that the "concept refinement" step of the retrieval algorithm addresses that issues.

4 Retrieval Probes

Retrieval probes partially describe an event to be retrieved by specifying a subset of the target event's features. Let us consider, for example, some of the ways the "death chili meal" might be partially described. [3]

1. a meal with chili

    (and (? isa meal) (? dishes chili))

2. a mexican meal with very spicy chili

    (and (? isa meal) (? cuisine mexican) (and (? dishes chili) (? dishes (taste very-spicy))))

3. a mexican meal with very spicy food

    (and (? isa meal) (? cuisine mexican) (? dishes (taste very-spicy)))

4. a meal with chili as the main course

    (and (? isa meal) (? appetizer-scene (dishes guacamole)))

5. a mexican meal with avocado

    (and (? isa meal) (? cuisine mexican) (? dishes (ingredients avocado)))

6. a mexican meal with guacamole and very spicy chili

---

[3] We do not discuss here how this translation happens. A phrase-based analyzer such as DMAP (Riesbeck, 1986) or PHRAN (Arens, 1981) could do it easily. Were DMAP used, it could be easily integrated with what we describe here. A very well integrated system, however, would probably do the language and memory retrieval work at the same time without the need to explicitly create these queries. Their equivalent would have to be created internally, however.

```
(and (? isa meal) (? cuisine mexican) (? dishes guacamole) (and (?
    dishes chili) (? dishes (taste very-spicy))))
```

The important thing to notice in these representations is that they do not distinguish which scene of the specified meal holds the specified descriptors unless that fact is given explicitly in a query. While it is easy to determine that prepared dishes (e.g., chili and guacamole) referred to in a query about a meal refer to its dishes, it requires a lot more knowledge to determine in which scene those dishes were served. In fact, it requires the full extent of knowledge represented about meals in the memory. It would be inefficient to first disambiguate and then find matches since both use the same knowledge. And some of the ambiguity is useful. Instead, disambiguation happens at retrieval time as a byproduct of the retrieval process.

One might ask whether such ambiguous probes will be made by a problem solver that is in control of what gets asked of memory. Sometimes probes to memory made by a problem solver will specifically mention a scene and sometimes they will not. If the problem solver is trying to plan a particular scene, it will be specified. But if the problem solver is trying to deal with a vague statement by a user, the probes may be as above. Suppose, for example, that a user asking JULIA to plan a meal said "Let's serve something with avocado". The problem solver might send a probe to memory that looks like (5) above in order to get ideas about how to use avocado in the meal.

5 The Retrieval Process

During retrieval, each of the features of the memory probe is broadcast into memory. Each item in memory with a broadcast feature is activated. As in DMAP's (Martin & Riesbeck, 1986) memory access process, each time an item is activated, it sends activation to each item above it in the abstraction hierarchy and it sends predictions to items that are normally seen in the context of the activated item. When those messages meet at a node, the concept that sent the prediction gets refined (specialized) to the level of detail of the concept that sent the activation. The algorithm has the following steps:

1. Each item (cue) in the memory probe is transmitted to memory (a serial process) and each is broadcast through the whole memory in parallel. Memory is activated as follows:

    (a) If the probe names a memory concept, (e.g., is of the form (? is-a x)), then the named concept (x) is activated.

    (b) If the probe is descriptive (e.g., is of the form (? property-name property-value)), any item that holds that description is activated.

2. As in DMAP, each node that is activated sends prediction messages to the things it predicts. At present, events predict their sequence of events. This is in keeping with observations of people that show that more concrete descriptions are better for reminding (Kolodner & Cullingford, 1986). By predicting the parts of an event, we are predicting its concrete features. A prediction message in PARADYME has three parts: [4] its source, its target, and the relationship between them.

---

[4] In DMAP, it has four.

3. Also as in DMAP, each activated node sends an activation message to each of its antecedents in the abstraction hierarchy. The activation message contains the source of the activation and instructs the nodes it is sent to to activate themselves.

4. When predictions and activations meet each other, "concept refinement" happens. During concept refinement in PARADYME,[5] the concept that sent the prediction gets specialized to the level of detail of the concept that sent the activation. This is done by finding the node that has the same relationship to the concept that sent the activation that the predicting concept has to the predicted one. "Meal-main-sc", for example, is related to "meal" through "meal"'s "sequence of events". If "meal" is activated and predicts "meal-main-sc" and "dcm-main-sc" is activated and activates "meal-main-sc", then "meal" is refined by finding the item whose "sequence of events" "dcm-main-sc" is in ("death chili meal"). Extra activation is then given to those nodes taking part in the concept refinement to distinguish them from other activated nodes in memory.

An example will illustrate. Consider, for example, a probe of the memory shown in Figure 1, using the probe "a meal with chili", represented as follows:

$$(\text{and } (? \text{ isa meal}) (? \text{ dishes chili}))^6$$

Step 1 will activate the "meal" node and each node with chili specified as a dish. The "death-chili-main-scene" will be activated by the chili probe, as will mexican-main-sc and any other eating scene where chili was a dish. In step 2, "meal" will predict its scenes and "death-chili-main-scene" and other activated scenes will predict their sequence of events. In step 3, "death-chili-main-scene" and other activated scenes will activate "meal-main-scene", which will activate anything above it. "Meal will also activate anything above it. In step 4, the connection between "meal" and "death-chili-main-scene" will be made (as well as connections between "meal" and any other eating scenes with chili). Because "meal" predicts "meal-main-scene" and "death-chili-main-scene" activates it, and because the relationship of "meal" and "meal-main-scene" is through sequence of events, memory activates the item that has "death-chili-main-scene" in its sequence of events, specifically "death-chili-meal". "Death-chili-meal" and the constellation of nodes that contributed to its activation receive extra activation.

Let us go back to the algorithm and examine what it does in each step. At the end of step 1, every item in memory that partially matches the retrieval probe is activated. This step is linear in the size of the retrieval probe. After step 1, all possible candidates are activated, but we do not yet know the connections between them. Some are descriptions of situations (MOPs) and some are descriptions of scenes. We want to retrieve those situations that have had concrete features of their scenes described in the retrieval probe. The next three steps make those connections.

In step 2, situations predict their scenes while scenes predict their events. Each is predicting its more concrete parts. We do not currently do this recursively, so this is a one-step process.

---

[5] This is somewhat more limited than in DMAP, where an arbitrary function can be executed to refine the concept. We will add additional capabilities of this type as we find we need them.

[6] We ignore the fact that chili is embedded in the representation for now. The program can take care of that, and in terms of complexity, it adds a number of cycles equal to the depth of the embedding.

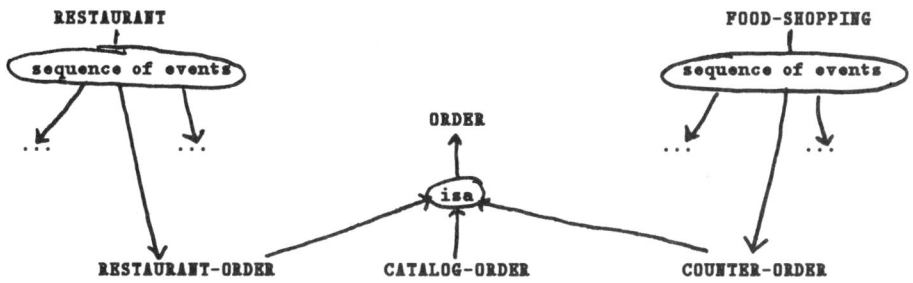

Figure 2

In step 3, each activated item sends activation up its abstraction hierarchy, in essense notifying more abstract nodes that it was described in a probe. This step is linear in the depth of the longest hierarchy being traversed.

Step 4 collects up those predictions that were fulfilled, usually scenes that were described. For each fulfilled prediction, the abstract concept that made the prediction is specialized to the level at which it meshes with the scene that was activated. The full event (case) that is retrieved (given high activation) is the specialized concept that is both of the right type (e.g., meal) and at a level of specificity consistent with the scene descriptions specified in the retrieval probe. This number of cycles required here is the depth of the abstraction hierarchy between the abstract node and the refined one.

While we can see from this small example how connections between different parts of the memory get made, it is hard to appreciate the full power of this algorithm from the examples given. We give one more example from a different domain to show how the concept refinement step narrows down the set of candidate matches to only those that are in the right ballpark. Consider a memory that knows about restaurant visits and buying. The structure of the memory is shown in Figure 2. We can see that the "ordering" scene is shared by both "restaurant visit" and "buying", and that the "ordering scene" holds instances of ordering bluefish in a restaurant and ordering bluefish over the counter in a supermarket. Suppose the query is "remember when we ordered bluefish in that restaurant in Boston". Step one of the query would activate "restaurant visit" and each of the instances of ordering bluefish, among other things. Because "restaurant visit" predicts a particular type of "ordering", namely "restaurant ordering", that ordering scene and the restaurant visit will be hooked up during concept refinement, and the supermarket ordering scene will not get further activated. In a memory with a lot of instances of ordering bluefish at a supermarket and only a small number of instances ordering bluefish in a restaurant, concept refinement will narrow the set of retrieved cases to only the relevant ones. In other words, it confines search to the specified context.

6 What Gets Returned

The result of running this retrieval algorithm on the memory is that several constellations of memory nodes are highly activated. Each constellation represents a case or set of related cases that partially match the retrieval probe. A case in memory is represented by a constellation of nodes spread over several abstraction hierarchies. The cases that are accessed by this method can be found by finding the most specific nodes in the hierarchy whose top is of the type requested in the retrieval probe. Sometimes the most specific active node in a hierarchy will be a generalized description of several cases (e.g., "mexican meal"). If so, memory returns the generalization in lieu of the myriad of cases it organizes. Sometimes there will be several most specific nodes highlighted in a hierarchy. If there are a small number (1 - 3), memory returns them all. If there is a large number, memory has a choice of returning some generalized description that subsumes them all (if one exists), creating and retruning a generalized description that subsumes them (if none exists), returning the entire set, or returning a message saying that more information is needed. Based on our experiences with case-based reasoners, the generalized description that subsumes them all plus the message saying that more information is needed would be most helpful.

7 Choosing the Best Case

While "concept refinement" insures that recalled events are in the right ballpark, it does not by itself choose which is the best match. A fully automated case-based problem solver needs to know which of the many events made available to it is the best to use for problem solving. This could be done by some sort of counting scheme or weighted counting scheme in which the match between the retrieval probe and each activated item gets points for each match to the retrieval probe and loses points for each mismatch. Such a method is problematic, however, for two reasons. First, if the evaluation function is static, it doesn't allow for dealing with the changing importance of features in context. Second, such a method requires a principled way of determining how to weight the features. Although we do not present the choice of a best match as a weighting scheme, one could think of our approach as addressing the problem of how to choose weightings for the features.

There are two major ways people are addressing this problem in the case-based reasoning community. Some people are addressing it by trying to determine how to best choose indices (e.g., Hammond, 1986, Hunter, 1988, Kolodner, 1983) so that only the best cases will be retrieved from the memory. Addressing the problem this way, the work happens at memory update time and retrieval remains a fast process. Others have filtering methods that are used after retrieval (e.g., Koton, 1988, Owens, 1988, Riesbeck, 1988, Stanfill, 1987). Others combine those two methods (e.g., Simpson, 1985, Barletta, 1988).

Our approach to choosing the best case borrows from both methods. In PARADYME, cases are analyzed for their most important features at memory update time, and conjunctions of predictive features are marked as important. At retrieval time, selection processes working after concept refinement prefer those events with full matches in those conjunctions of features. In this way, best events are chosen not merely by counting the number of features that match or even by ranking features with respect to each other, but rather by taking into account which features or combinations of features have been found to be most important in the past. In principle, this allows the importance of features to be judged in context, where context is provided by the retrieval probe and the items that are retrieved by applying a concept refinement retrieval algorithm to it.

Conjunctions of features that are marked as important in PARADYME are those that predict solutions or solution methods. The reason for this is that PARADYME is designed to work along with a problem solver, and these are the kinds of predictions a problem solver needs. There are two kinds of conjunctive feature sets PARADYME uses.

1. Goals, constraints on these goals, and environmental features that went into choosing the method or solution for achieving the goal or goal set are marked.

   A set of features may include one goal or several goals. It includes one if the solution that was chosen for that goal did not involve other goals. It includes several if their solution was integrated. Constraints and descriptors on these goals are also included, as are features of the world or features of the problem that determined which of several possible solutions or solution methods was chosen. If all of the features in one of these conjunctive feature sets is designated in a retrieval probe, the solution or solution method used in the previous case can be predicted.

2. Outcomes that arose using some solution or applying some solution method are marked.

   When outcomes of previous cases match desired outcomes of a current case, the solution or solution method from the previous case can be predicted.

For any particular case, there may be several conjunctive feature sets associated with it. If memory is aware of the goal(s) the problem solver is attempting to achieve, it can choose from among the cases that are retrieved by preferring those where goals and constraints match and full conjunctive feature sets are specified.

While we do not yet have a complete implementation of the choice process, and we do not yet know the priorities of the preference rules we've proposed, PARADYME has several preference heuristics for choosing a best-matching case. Some of the preference heuristics are implemented as part of the retrieval process presented above (e.g., 1 and 2). The others are used to choose between those items retrieved using that algorithm.

1. Prefer predicted pieces of memory over those that are not predicted.

2. Prefer the most specific of those in the same hierarchy.

3. Prefer items that match a retrieval probe completely.

4. If a probe describes specific details, prefer items that have those details.

5. Prefer items that share a major goal or set of goals and constraints on those goal.

6. Prefer those items whose full set of salient features are specified in the retrieval probe.

7. Prefer those items where the goals and constraints of a fully matched conjunctive feature set match current goals and constraints of the problem being solved.

8. Prefer those items with more full sets of salient features specified in the retrieval probe.

9. Prefer those items that match on dimensions that are known to be difficult to fix.

8 Cue Elaboration

The process we have presented is appropriate when the retrieval probe accurately describes an item or several items in the memory. Some retrieval probes, however, are unsuitable for finding matches, either because of the complexities of representational embeddings in memory's structures or because they are too vague or overly-specific. We have identified four circumstances under which a retrieval probe or part of a retrieval probe is unsuitable for retrieval:

1. The retrieval probe might not directly specify a type of situation. A retrieval probe might describe features of a situation without naming the type of situation. We have no examples of this in JULIA's domain. In CYRUS' domain, questions such as "Has Vance ever talked to Woodward or Bernstein?" and "Has Vance's wife ever met Mrs. Begin?" are examples of this. A probe that does not include an "isa" clause, or whose "isa" clause points to a kind of event that happens in many different contexts falls into this category. We will introduce a *condensation heuristic* to deal with this problem.

2. The retrieval probe may describe a situation that is not stored in memory but that is a "near miss" to something stored in memory. Memory, for example, might have a description of a "meal in a particular small Italian restaurant in which eggplant-filled manicotti was served". A probe of "remember the time we had eggplant-filled stuffed-shells for dinner in a little Italian restaurant" would be a near miss to this event. If enough of the rest of the event is describe to make it unique among the other events in memory, the near miss event can be retrieved anyway (e.g., if this was the only visit to a small Italian restaurant where something with eggplant filling was served), but if not, the probe will not retrieve it (e.g., if in may restaurant visit eggplant was eaten as the filling for something). This situation exists when a retrieval probe provides concrete features but memory retrieves only a generalized node that does not mention the concrete features or when memory retrieves many cases that match the retrieval probe, but none match exactly and none are better matches than the rest. A *cue transformation heuristic* that expands a cue into a set of cues conjunctively describing it will solve this problem.

3. The retrieval probe might describe a character or a prop without naming it or its type. The embedding of memory's frame-like structures makes it hard to directly activate events whose features are vaguely described. Memory recognizes this if an event is requested, nodes describing particular characters or props are highly activated, and no such features are highlighted in the events that have been activated. *Condensation heuristics* will deal with this problem too by recognizing a particular character or prop that has been described and then probing memory using the particular character or prop as a replacement for its description.

4. The retrieval probe might describe a relation that is specified more finely in memory's representations than in the retrieval probe. "A meal with a dish with spinach in it" is one example of such a probe. In memory's representations, ingredients of dishes are divided into "mains", "secondaries", and "seasonings", a useful distinction for the problem solver. This fine distinction may not be made in a probe, however. While it is easy to distinguish spices as "seasonings" and sometimes an ingredient is specified or implied to be the "main" one or a "secondary" one, more often this information is not known at the beginning of problem solving and it is memory that must provide this information to the problem solver. Memory knows which of its descriptors are represented this way and recognizes specific situations in which this happens. A *cue transformation heuristic* that expands a cue into its set of disjunctive descriptors will solve this problem.

In each of these cases, heuristics are used to redescribe the retrieval probe and retrieval is attempted again with the set of newly-defined cues. We describe these heuristics below.

1. *Cue Transformation*

   Cue transformation expands a cue to create a larger set of reasonable cues. These new cues might describe the original one conjunctively, provide a disjunction of descriptions equivalent to the original cue, or provide additional information associated with the original cue but not part of it.

   (a) *Replace cue by a conjunct of descriptors*

   As stated above, this type of cue transformation is used when a retrieval probe specifies something quite concrete but the best that can be found in memory is a generalized node that does not mention the concrete feature (e.g., if a search for a meal with stuffed shells returns "Italian meals"). In that case, the specific feature that was not accounted for in the set of retrieved nodes is replaced by its description. "Stuffed shells" in the example would be replaced by a set of cues stating that the food had pasta, ricotta cheese, and tomato sauce in its ingredients, that the structure of it was (shell-shaped) pasta filled with ricotta mixture, topped with tomato sauce and cheese, etc. As a result of replacing an item by its description, "near-miss" matches can be found. For example, replacing stuffed shells by its description might result in retrieval of a meal with manicotti, a close match to stuffed shells.

   (b) *Replace cue by a disjunct of descriptors*

   This type of cue transformation is used when a particular cue is known to have several ways of being described. For example, ingredients can be found as main ingredients, secondary ingredients, and seasonings. If "dishes with tomatoes" are requested in a probe, there is no way to know a priori whether the tomatos are to be main ingredient, a secondary ingredient, or a seasoning of the dish. "Dishes with tomatoes" will be transformed to a disjunct of cues: "dishes with main ingredients tomatoes", "dishes with secondary ingredients tomatoes", "dishes with tomatoes as seasoning". Expanding cues in this way will allow each of these descriptors of a dish to combine with other cues in the retrieval probe so that the best match that takes all of the descriptors into account can be found.

(c) *Add a closely associated feature to the set of cues*

This type of cue elaboration is equivalent to CYRUS' component-to-component instantiation strategies, and their usefulness is discussed in Kolodner (1983, 1984). In short, a feature that is not yet part of the retrieval probe but that is closely associated with some cue in the retrieval probe is added. An example of this is adding a place associated with an identified person or organization to the retrieval probe. This can help to distinguish between several events that have been equally activated, where each partially matches the retrieval probe, and there is no clear way to distinguish which is the best.

2. *Cue Condensation*

Cue condensation heuristics condense a set of cues to a single one that describes a larger unit. This process looks for concepts whose marked features are all, or almost all, mentioned in the retrieval probe. It is useful if a type of event has not been specified but has been described, or if features of an event being specified have not been directly named but have been abstractly described. A set of cues describing a dish with shell-shaped pasta filled with ricotta would be replaced by one cue stating that the dish is stuffed shells using cue condensation. An event described as one where people swim in a contest and later get awards would be replaced by one cue stating that the event is a swim-meet using cue condensation.

Cue elaboration is an automatic process done by memory after retrieval. After elaboration, retrieval is attempted again using the newly-defined set of cues. We are still working on probe elaboration methods. While we know many of the heuristics for elaborating a probe, we have not yet experimented with them enough to know exactly how to control their application, nor do we know yet how to fully control their interaction with retrieval processes.

Cue elaboration is similar in spirit to CYRUS' instantiation strategies. CYRUS (Kolodner, 1983, 1984) had two types of elaboration strategies to take care of these problems, each used at a different point in the retrieval process: component-to-context instantiation rules were used prior to memory traversal to infer a context for search, and component-to-component instantiation rules were used after traversal was attempted to elaborate a retrieval probe that did not retrieve a particular event. PARADYME also has two kinds of cue elaboration heuristics, but they are both used after retrieval is attempted and their functions are not exactly the same. PARADYME's *cue transformation* heuristics perform the function of CYRUS' component-to-component instantiation rules in a more expansive way than was done in CYRUS, and PARADYME's *cue condensation* heuristics perform the function of CYRUS' component-to-context instantiation rules and also help with cue transformation rules define a better set of descriptive cues.

9 Discussion

The parallel algorithm presented runs in linear time on a SIMD parallel machine, and its runtime does not vary significantly with the size of the memory as long as memory does not exceed the size of the machine. [7] It works on a hierarchically organized memory where events are stored across several

---

[7]Specifically, its run-time is AN+2B+1. A is a number designating the overhead of dealing with embedded representations and is 1 plus the depth of an embedding. For the examples we have run, it ranges between 1 and

hierarchies. The concept refinement search method limits retrieval to only reasonable parts of the memory and allows memory probes to describe events by describing features of their substructures. The basic algorithm forms the core of a case retrieval process, but it is not complete. While it finds many fewer events than an intersection search would, it does not address the choice of a best case(s) from those that are retrieved; nor does it include a capability for automatically elaborating a retrieval probe that is poorly specified. To take care of these problems, we have introduced preference heuristics for choosing the best set of cases from those retrieved and we have introduced probe elaboration heuristics for redefining a poorly-specified or near-miss probe.

As an added advantage, we have been able to do away with CYRUS' redundant indexing structure. This means the memory takes up considerably less space in the machine. Were we to run CYRUS (Kolodner, 1983, 1984) or the memory parts of any of our case-based reasoners (e.g., MEDIATOR (Kolodner, et al., 1985, Simpson, 1985), JULIA (Hinrichs, 1988, Kolodner, 1987a,b, Shinn, 1988)) using the new algorithm and memory structures, we would get significant speedup, would use much less memory space, and would retrieve exactly the same items as under the serial scheme.

Problems remain to consider, however. First, due to the architecture of the Connection Machine, we have not done an exact translation from our old retrieval scheme to the new one. CYRUS' retrieval scheme (the old one) was linear in the depth of memory's hierarchies, a much smaller number than the length of a retrieval probe. It would be interesting, from an algorithmic point of view, to attempt implementation of CYRUS' algorithms on a MIMD machine. It would also be interesting from a psychological point of view to have a parallel algorithm whose speed is independent of the length of the retrieval probe.

Second, the algorithm we have implemented requires full connectivity between nodes in the hierarchies of MOPs and scenes. Because generalizations must be made independently in each abstraction hierarchy, however, that connectivity may need to be recomputed during retrieval. The "instruction" portion of the prediction messages in DMAP provide one way that is not very elegant. Some other way to overcome this problem must be found. And, of course, it will add to the complexity of the algorithm.

Third, we have hardly considered memory update procedures. They, of course, must be integrated into the memory scheme so that we can insure that memory's structure and the accessibility of events is maintained as the memory gets large.

10 Bibliography

1. Arens, Y. (1981). Using language and context in analysis of text. *Proceedings of IJCAI-81*.

2. Barletta, R. (1988). Explanation-Based Indexing of Cases. *Proceedings of the DARPA Workshop on Case-Based Reasoning*.

---

5. N is the length of the retrieval probe. B is the depth of the hierarchy that needs to be traversed in step 3 of the algorithm. We assume a hierarchy of similar size gets traversed in step 4, thus we must add in B two times. B ranges between 1 and 3 in the examples we have looked at, but the memory we have implemented is small. We expect it to remain a small number and to be significantly smaller than N. The constant is the number of cycles necessary for step 2 of the algorithm. We expect N to dominate the expression.

3. Hammond, K. J. (1984). *Indexing and Causality: The organization of plans and strategies in memory*. Report No. 351. Dept. of Computer Science. Yale University. New Haven, CT.

4. Hammond, K. J. (1986). *Case-Based Planning: An integrated theory of planning, learning, and memory*. Ph.D. Thesis. Dept. of Computer Science. Yale University.

5. Hinrichs, T. (1988). Towards an architecture for open world problem solving. *Proceedings of the DARPA Workshop on Case-Based Reasoning*.

6. Hunter, L. (1988). *The Use and Discovery of Paradigm Cases*. Ph.D. Thesis. Yale University. Forthcoming.

7. Kolodner, J. L. (1983). Reconstructive Memory: A Computer Model. *Cognitive Science*, vol. 7.

8. Kolodner, J. L. (1984). *Retrieval and Organizational Strategies in Conceptual Memory: A Computer Model*. Hillsdale, NJ: Lawrence Erlbaum Assoc.

9. Kolodner, J. L. (1985). *Experiential Processes in Natural Problem Solving*. Technical Report No. GIT-ICS/85/23. School of Information and Computer Science. Georgia Inst. of Technology. Atlanta, GA.

10. Kolodner, J. L. & Cullingford, R. E. (1986). Towards a Memory Architecture that Supports Reminding. *Proceedings of the 1986 Conference of the Cognitive Science Society*.

11. Kolodner, J. L. (1987a). Extending problem solver capabilities through case-based inference. *Proceedings of the 1987 International Machine Learning Workshop*.

12. Kolodner, J. L. (1987b). Capitalizing on failure through case-based inference. *Proceedings of the 1987 Conference of the Cognitive Science Society*.

13. Kolodner, J. L., Simpson, R. L., & Sycara, E. (1985). A Process Model of Case-Based Reasoning in Problem Solving. *Proceedings of IJCAI-85*.

14. Koton, P. (1988). Reasoning about evidence in causal explanations. *Proceedings of the DARPA Workshop on Case-Based Reasoning*.

15. Lebowitz, M. (1983). Generalization from natural language text. *Cognitive Science*, vol. 7.

16. Lytinen, S. (1984). Frame selection in parsing. *Proceedings of AAAI-84*.

17. Martin, C. & Riesbeck, C. (1986). Uniform parsing and inference for learning. *Proceedings of AAAI-86*.

18. Owens, C. (1988). Domain-Independent Prototype Cases for Planning. *Proceedings of the DARPA Workshop on Case-Based Reasoning*.

19. Reiser, B. & Black, J. (1983). The roles of interference and inference in the retrieval of autobiographical memories. *Proceedings of the 1983 Conference of the Cognitive Science Society*.

20. Riesbeck, C. & Martin, C. (1986). Toward Completely Integrated Parsing and Inference. *Proceedings of the 1986 Conference of the Cognitive Science Society.*

21. Riesbeck, C. (1988). An Interface for Case-Based Knowledge Acquisition. *Proceedings of the DARPA Workshop on Case-Based Reasoning*

22. Rissland, E. & Ashley, K. (1987). *HYPO: A Case-Based Reasoning System.* CPTM #18. Department of Computer and Information Science. University of Massachusetts. Amherst, MA.

23. Schank, R. C. (1982) *Dynamic Memory.* Cambridge: Cambridge University Press.

24. Shinn, H. (1988). Abstractional Analogy: A Model of Analogical Reasoning. *Proceedings of the DARPA Workshop on Case-Based Reasoning.*

25. Simpson, R. L. (1985). *A Computer Model of Case-Based Reasoning in Problem Solving.* Ph.D. Thesis. Technical Report No. GIT-ICS/85/18. School of Information and Computer Science. Georgia Inst. of Technology. Atlanta, GA.

26. Stanfill, C. (1987). Memory-Based Reasoning Applied to English Pronunciation. *Proceedings of AAAI-87.*

27. Sycara, E. (1987). *Resolving Adversarial Conflicts: An approach integrating case-based and analytic methods.* Ph.D. Thesis. Technical Report No. GIT-ICS/87/26. School of Information and Computer Science. Georgia Inst. of Technology. Atlanta, GA.

CASE BASED REASONING FOR CONTINUOUS CONTROL

Ludmila Kopeikina, Richard Brandau and Alan Lemmon
GTE Laboratories, Inc.
Waltham, MA 02254

ABSTRACT

Case Based Reasoning (CBR) offers special advantages for continuous control applications, but these applications also have special requirements that demand extensions to the CBR paradigm. We describe a CBR system that is under development at GTE Laboratories for control of telephone traffic, and examine issues it raises, including the need for cases that represent how a situation develops over time, expertise that evolves with the domain, and a dynamic environment that demands time-constrained performance. We examine unique aspects of the system design and trace their motivation to the requirements of a continuous control application.

INTRODUCTION

Case based reasoning techniques have been demonstrated with a number of diverse applications. With few exceptions, however, these have been artificial domains, devoid of many problems that are commonly encountered in practical systems. The research described in this paper explores the applicability of CBR to a specific, real problem, and examines complications that are common to many continuous control applications. We are interested in the ability to retain the unique advantages of the CBR approach (Kolodner [1984], Rissland and Ashley [1986]), while extending CBR techniques to support this class of applications.

The specific problem to which we are applying CBR is the management of traffic flow in the standard, public switched telephone network. Controlling such traffic is a problem of allocating a changing set of network resources to satisfy demands from a fluctuating pattern of calls. This control is exercised by a small group of experienced traffic management personnel, located at a centralized site, who modify the network's call processing in response to a continuous stream of network performance data.

The sources of network data, and the machines that execute the traffic controls, are the automatic telephone switching systems (or, just "switches") that are the distributed nodes of the telephone network, each capable of handling thousands of connections simultaneously. These switches, and the trunk groups which interconnect them, are the finite-capacity network resources being managed. When a switch fails, either partially or completely, or a trunk group is severed, the network's total call processing capacity is diminished, and traffic managers search for the best available ways to complete calls despite the lost capacity. Even when the entire network capacity is available, it may be exceeded by demand, especially during holidays such as Mother's Day when many calls are generated, during radio call-ins, or just on a particularly busy Monday morning. These exceptional demands are usually localized, and traffic managers can often find idle capacity in the rest of the network to satisfy the local demand.

This traffic management application is an instance of a class of *continuous control* problems, in which a stream of data is analyzed to diagnose the situation in the controlled system, an appropriate plan of action is devised for treating the situation, and the effects of control actions are continuously monitored and adjusted. Such a system, then, includes aspects of diagnosis and planning -- classic artificial intelligence domains; indeed, planning is one well-known application of CBR (cf., Hammond [1986], Carbonell [1986], Alterman [1986]). As discussed below, other aspects of the CBR approach are of value for this class of application, but extensions to CBR are necessary to satisfy special requirements of these applications, and are proposed as part of this project.

Advantages of CBR for Traffic Management

Episodic Knowledge. From interviews with a traffic management expert, we have found that a large part of his knowledge of this domain is *episodic*. That is, the expert solves a new problem by relating the current network situation to his previous experiences. These experiences are sometimes specific incidents, with real dates and places, and sometimes general classes of similar occasions. This body of traffic management experience is transferred from expert to apprentice as "war stories" of illustrious and (sometimes) ignominious traffic controls of the past. This "case based" approach to the teaching of traffic management recommends cases to represent knowledge in this domain. Certainly, knowledge acquisition naturally results in traffic management cases.

The appropriateness of cases is justified by more than this anecdotal evidence. From our understanding of the domain, it appears that past experience is the best available guide for decision making. Although there is some knowledge of general causal relationships between control actions and network responses, no complete model of the domain exists; traffic managers often act in accordance with previous success, with an incomplete understanding of why that success occurred. (This is understandable, given the intractable scale of the network dynamics and the time constraints on responses.) Case based reasoning offers the best available means for taking advantage of this shallow, episodic knowledge.

Evolving Expertise. Traffic management, as well as many other applications -- especially control of high technology hardware -- are in a state of continuous, gradual change. In the traffic management domain, these changes occur because the telephone companies increase the number of switches under traffic management, add new types of switches to the operation, or add new hardware/software components that gradually change the behavior of the network. Human experts are often unaware of such changes, adapting gradually and applying a modified version of their previous experience to the new situations. In contrast, conventional, non-CBR-based expert systems, would exhibit a continuous and mysterious degradation in performance in the face of such change.

The CBR approach is a natural fit for such evolving domains: previous experiences (cases) are applied to new situations, and new cases are created to address situations for which the existing cases are inadequate.

Extensions to CBR Required by Traffic Management

Time-Constrained Processing. Any system that performs real time processing must be responsive to deadlines imposed by the environment; it is often better to provide a *just satisfactory* but *timely* answer than to wait for an optimal answer. In such an environment, it must also be able to be interrupted by new, high priority events.

Although these issues are certainly not unique to CBR systems, they do have an effect on the design of our system. To improve the quality of time-constrained responses, this system is particularly dependent on various "best-first" search mechanisms as will be further discussed in the paper. In addition, standard real-time software engineering solutions apply here: the CBR software must be interruptible and reentrant. Also, a "Controller" software layer will have to run concurrently with the CBR system to establish and enforce time budgets and processing priorities, and to manage the system's response to external events.

Cases to Represent How a Situation Develops. In addition to the need for real-time response, traffic management must monitor changing situations over time, where these changes are only partially the result of the system's own actions. This poses a problem for the representation of cases in this domain: a traffic management case must describe the expected course of events, including both system actions and expected network responses. The system must use these temporally extended cases to detect deviations from expectations and to revise its plans to correct unfavorable network responses.

In overview, such a case is viewed as a "string" of temporally disjoint **beads**, where each bead represents a state in the development of a situation. The beads shown in Figure 1 represent a prototypical traffic management case. The first bead, then, corresponds to the situation when a problem was first detected in the network. Subsequent beads represent courses of action that were taken by the system, and the anticipated network responses. Thus, the second bead lists the actions that should be taken to correct that problem, and the third bead describes the expected effect of those actions. The fourth bead describes the situation when the problem has diminished and the actions should be undone, which is followed by a bead describing the plan for undoing the actions, and a final bead that describes the situation that is expected after all actions are undone.

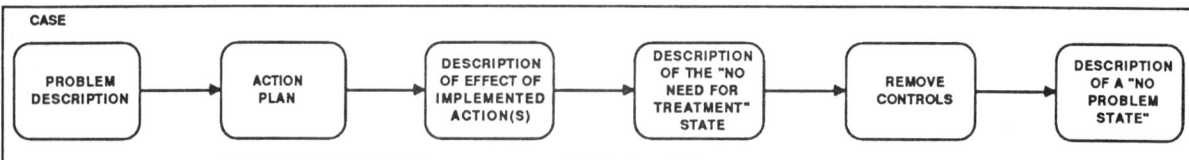

Figure 1: Case Representation of a Developing Situation.

Using these beads, the system monitors the development of the network situation being treated, as described in the "Monitoring" section, below. This determines when control adjustments (new beads in the sequence) are appropriate, and when a case is developing along unexpected lines (matching beads from other case strings). This approach to case representation is a necessary extension to existing CBR implementations, through which continuous control can be exercised by this system.

DESIGN

The design of the system has been influenced by the requirements of the domain that were discussed above: time-constrained processing and the need to represent and maintain cases evolving through time. The following sections present an overview of the system design with detailed descriptions of the major components of the system, and discuss how the above considerations influenced the design.

An overview of the system design is shown in Figure 2.

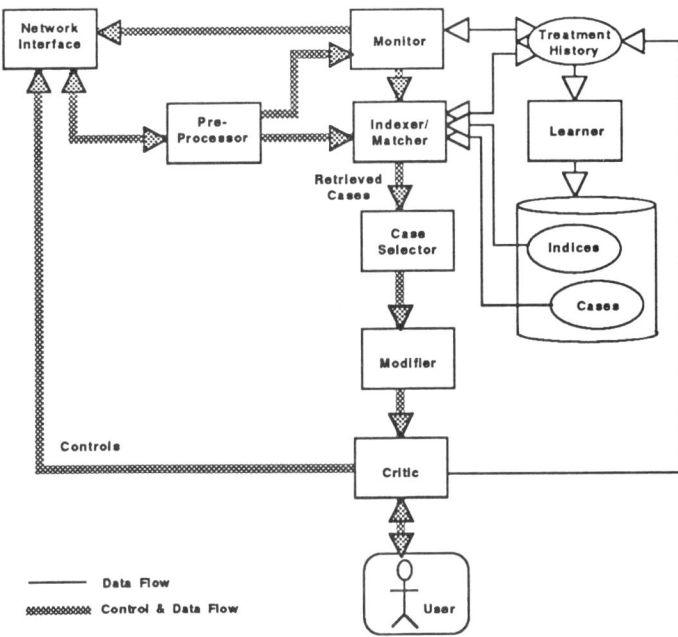

Figure 2: CBR System Architecture for Traffic Management.

The processing starts with the Preprocessor, which parses the input data and forms problem representations, each of which is called a Problem Statement (PS). The Preprocessor has PS skeletons which correspond to different problem types. If a problem is recognized to be an old problem that has already been treated by the system, this Problem Statement with the current data about this problem is passed to the Monitor. The Monitor is responsible for matching the current data with expectations that are based on the model case. If the expected desirable effect is not reached, the Monitor proposes an adjustment or a change of treatment.

If a problem is new, its Problem Statement is passed to the Indexer/Matcher, which is responsible for retrieving those stored cases from the Case Based Memory that are most relevant to the current Problem Statement. As it searches through CBM, it elaborates the current PS. The Selector's function is to choose the "most on point" successful case out of the set of cases retrieved by the Indexer/Matcher. The Modifier must then apply the experience recorded in the selected case to the current situation, modifying it if necessary. These three modules (Indexer/Matcher, Selector and Modifier) compose the core of the system and are discussed in detail in the sections below.

If modification is successful, the modified case is passed to the Critic as a proposed treatment. The Critic employs domain-specific procedures to determine if the proposed treatment is likely to lead to any known ill-effects. Thus, before submitting the case as a proposal to the human user, the Critic makes a "sanity check" of the result, and vetoes any courses of action that it can determine may have disastrous consequences. If a plan is thus vetoed, the Modifier may attempt a different modification of the stored case, the Selector may choose a different case from its candidates, or the Indexer/Matcher may search further in the index network to retrieve other candidate cases.

Once the Critic and the user have approved application of a case's treatment plan, it is implemented by the Network Interface in the form of controls that are placed on switch call processing. The plan is also recorded in the Treatment History, and noted by the Preprocessor, in order to associate new input with the relevant installed treatment.

The Learner acquires new cases on the basis of "surprises" which result from unanticipated responses from the network, vetoes by the user or Critic, or especially time-consuming and "creative" modifications of stored plans. The details of the learning mechanism are not yet known, but the problem of "learnability" is nonetheless an omnipresent consideration in the design and implementation of the other system components, and has resulted in several observations about the nature of case based learning in this system. First, to maintain real-time performance, the majority of learning activity must take place in "batch" mode, outside the peak hours of network operations. Second, the choice of whether or not to acquire a new case for the sake of expediency (to save Modifier work) is a tradeoff between the accessibility of that case and the increment in the search space added by the new case. Third, there is a continuum of complexity in possible Learner capabilities, from the storage of a new case at the same index location where it was first found to apply, to the restructuring of the index network to accommodate new cases and generalize over old cases, to -- most challenging -- changing the behavior of the Selector and Modifier.

Indexer/Matcher

The Indexer/Matcher is the part of the system that retrieves cases that are similar to the current problem statement. Given a situation and a starting point, the Indexer/Matcher produces a list of stored cases sorted according to a preliminary indication of relevance.

There are a number of characteristics of the domain which constrain the choice of indexing structure and technique. The most important of these characteristics is that the domain does not support a single set of attributes which are always significant in discriminating among situations. Rather the relevance of an attribute is locally defined. This means that we cannot use a hierarchical discrimination tree. Instead we use a structure which we call the indexing fabric, which represents a conceptual map of the situations which the system may face. This differs from conventional discrimination nets in two ways:

- The structure is not a tree, but will be a general graph. It contains lateral links, making it re-entrant.

- The discrimination decisions need not be unique.

The result is an indexing structure somewhat like that described by Kolodner [1983] or Carbonell [1987]. This indexing fabric is a network made up of three kinds of nodes, which are connected together in certain ways to form the fabric.

1. The *index-station*, which represents a characterization of a situation. Similar characterizations are represented by *index-station*s which are located close to each other within the fabric.

2. The *dispatcher* node, which connects *index-station*s. Each *dispatcher* is similar to a **case** statement in a programming language; it interprets domain criteria to discriminate among the characterizations represented by the *index-station*s it connects.

3. The *dispatch-port*, which labels the links between *dispatcher*s and *index-station*s. It corresponds roughly to the label on each branch of a **case** statement.

Given the time-constrained nature of the domain, retrieval should be fast; we have chosen a retrieval technique which we expect will run in time proportional to the log of the number of situation classifications currently in use. According to this technique, the Indexer/Matcher searches for a good characterization of the current situation by a best-first spreading activation process. During this process, "weight" is moved from one *index-station* to another. This weight represents confidence that the *index-station* characterizes the current situation. This search starts at one of a set of designated "root" *index-station*s. The search is guided by the *dispatcher*s, which move the weight among *index-station*s. The weight may be divided up among several *index-station*s and later recombined.

The search may be suspended at any point, either for lack of resources or time or because some information is not yet ready. In this case the Indexer/Matcher has an assignment of weight to *index-station*s which represents the best characterization which it has so far developed.

Selector

As candidate cases are retrieved by the Indexer/Matcher, they are presented to the Selector for further consideration. In the current design, candidate cases must match completely on the crucial, "index" features in order to be retrieved by the Indexer/Matcher. More subtle distinctions, for which partial matches are permitted, are made by the Selector. The task of the Selector, then, is to perform a fine-grained match between the current problem statement and the candidate cases and to determine the most relevant of the candidate cases.

A principal issue in the design of a case selector is the level to which the system is committed to the selected case: a simple selector would choose quickly and imprecisely, and rely on subsequent processing to reject poor selections; a more sophisticated selector would devote more resources in an attempt to choose the best available case (although *final* commitment to the case will still await success of subsequent processing). This more sophisticated approach, which is used in this system, is necessary because any rejections of the model case, initially or during the problem's evolution result in incorrect actions and wasted processing time that a time-constrained system cannot afford. This approach improves the probability that subsequent processing of the selected case will succeed, reducing the likelihood that a different selection must eventually be made, or that a sub-optimal result will be produced.

The selection process involves two steps: (1) evaluation of the "closeness of fit" between the selected case and the Problem Statement and (2) success/failure estimation.

Closeness of Fit Evaluation. The selection of a candidate case involves identifying matches and mismatches between the problem statement and the current situation, and assessing the importance of these matches and mismatches. There can be different levels of matching. Features can match at the *logical variable* level, which means that the case being matched is talking about the same concepts as the problem statement. This match will mostly occur when the problem statement is matched against a generic case. Features can also match at the *value* level. In our domain there is a lot of noise in the data and it is very rare that values match exactly. **Sensitivity ranges** are used to define a match for a feature and to filter for stochastic variations in data. The results of both levels of matching are important to the system. For example, the *logical variable* level match is important for the Learner to identify the features outside of the match that might have caused a later problem.

The importance attributed to a match or mismatch, its **weight**, is case-specific: a given feature may be crucial to one case but insignificant to another. Weights will be based, initially, on pre-determined weighting factors. (The run-time acquisition or modification of these weights is an instance of the well-known "credit assignment" problem.) The current design of the Selector organizes features into three categories of importance for each case. An **unimportant** category contains entries for which an inability to match does not affect the selection of this case. For example, names of trunk groups fit into the **unimportant** category because a case describing a problem in one part of the network can be used to treat a similar problem in a different part of the network. The **important** category consists of entries that should match in order for this case to be useful in solving the current problem. If a mismatch in this category is identified, the modifier has the knowledge to be able to modify the case to fit the current problem. Entries that fit into the **very important** category are the ones that define the applicability of this case. If there is a mismatch in this category the case is rejected. Many of the features of this category are used as indices of the indexing fabric.

The process of assigning a feature to an importance category is based on a number of considerations, including the amount of work required to modify the stored case to fit the new situation.

Success/Failure Estimation. In addition to this match-quality ranking, the Selector also considers the desirability of the outcome that was experienced with the stored case. This approach favors those cases which are likely to lead to the best results, and identifies relevant cases with unfavorable results for which the system must be vigilant. A success-evaluation function is driven by the information contained in the string of beads in the case. This outcome-desirability information will be maintained by the Monitor.

Modifier

The Modifier is responsible for transferring the experience of a selected stored case to the current problem situation. This task of resolving differences between the stored case and the current situation is an exercise in reasoning by analogy.

A powerful analogical transfer process can expand the neighborhood of stored cases, and thereby enhance the ability to respond to unforeseen situations and reduce the number of cases that must be stored. This is an important consideration for time-constrained applications (such as continuous control), because fewer cases results in reduced search time. This advantage of a powerful Modifier, however, must be balanced against the extra processing required to supply that power.

The current Modifier design is intermediate in complexity and power, between Carbonell's Transformational [1983] and Derivational [1986] analogies. Unlike Transformational analogy, the Modifier does not employ global transformation operators, because it is difficult to specify when such operators are applicable. To make them apply only when relevant, the operators must include explicit goal preconditions, which must also be present in the case and the problem statement. The Modifier does not employ such explicit goals.

This lack of explicit goals also precludes direct use of the Derivational approach, since it relies on goals for the derivation. More significantly, however, the current approach does not store a complete derivation with each case (and, indeed, could not, since no such derivation is performed).

The Modifier *does*, however, maintain a "justification linkage" between treatment actions and those features of the case which determine the validity of the actions. These linkages serve to guide the modification process in a manner similar to Derivational reasoning traces.

The "justification linkages" are referred to as **roles**. Roles link features of a case with those treatments in the case that were in some way dependent on those features. Each feature in a case may participate in one or more roles, as may each treatment. By knowing which roles a feature supports, the Modifier knows which treatments may need to change when the case is applied to a situation with a different value for that feature. In order to know for sure whether or not a different-valued feature actually invalidates a treatment, roles specify **constraints** on their features. In order to know what alternatives are available when a role is invalidated, roles are themselves linked in a **role-hierarchy**.

The basic approach of the Modifier is to do as little modification as possible, both to save time and to limit the opportunity for error. Thus, Modifier processing is terminated at the earliest successful stage, of the following three processing levels.

1. For each feature that isn't matched between the selected case and the problem statement, role **constraints** (if any) which that feature satisfied in the selected case are identified. If every constraint of each mismatched feature continues to be satisfied with the problem statement values, no modification is necessary.

2. For each unsatisfied constraint, the Modifier tries to find another way to satisfy the same constraint. This amounts to an attempt to find another binding between situational variables and role features that will satisfy the failing constraint. If a new combination of bindings can be found that will satisfy all constraints, "serious" modification is again unnecessary, and the new bindings are the only change.

3. For those roles that cannot be satisfied by rebinding, the Modifier traverses a **role hierarchy** in search of a role that can be substituted for the unsatisfiable role. If any substitutable role is found that can itself satisfy its constraints with some feature binding, the search is complete and that role and its

features are substituted for the unsatisfiable role. If no successful substitutable role can be found, the Modifier abandons the case, and requests an alternative from the Selector.

Monitor

One of the major features of continuous control applications is the fact that corrective actions once installed have to be monitored until the need them disappears. The initial treatment might need to be adjusted or the course of action changed completely because of unforeseen problems in the environment. This task is performed by the Monitor. The design of the Monitor has not been finalized; this section presents a possible approach that is currently being considered.

The Monitor uses the selected case to know what to expect after a treatment is installed. The Monitor is responsible for determining whether the treatment had the desired effect. If the effect was achieved, the Monitor is responsible for creating an expectation for the future development of this problem treatment based on the selected case. If the effect was not reached, the Monitor must propose an adjustment or change of treatment.

To follow the progress of a problem treatment, the Monitor matches the current data with the expected effect of the treatment. The expected effect is created by the Monitor each time a treatment is installed, based on the effect produced by the similar treatment that is described in the case. In matching this expectation with the current data, the Monitor must disregard stochastic variations in data. When a mismatch is identified the Monitor must determine whether this mismatch is a positive or a negative experience -- whether the treatment did better than expected or produced a worse than expected effect.

When the system is "unpleasantly surprised" because the treatment does not produce the desired effect, the Monitor needs to either change the treatment or adjust it to perform better. One possible approach that is Being considered is the use of the Case-Based Memory (CBM) for proposing adjustments and changes. In this approach, the indexing fabric will be extended with the monitoring information: cases will connect to other cases through "degrade" links which index the space of possible adjustments and changes to treatments. The Monitor can utilize these links to find similar cases that know how to handle the current problem with the current treatment. The Monitor will have to rely on the Indexer to retrieve such cases from memory, and on the Selector to choose the best applicable case. The Modifier will also be involved, to transfer the solution from the selected case to the current problem.

This approach presents several technical problems. One of them is the difficulty of solution modification. Solution modification is more difficult for monitoring than for a new problem. In monitoring, the new model case might have used a treatment that was similar to -- but subtly different from -- the treatment in the current case, and might have gone through many stages in its development. The difference between the assumptions of the current context and those of the new model context will have to be resolved before transfer can succeed. In other words, the Modifier can easily get into the situation of "apples and oranges" in an attempt to modify a subtly different solution to fit the current problem description.

CONCLUSION

The CBR system design that has been described above specifically addresses problems of continuous control applications such as traffic management. These problems include a need for time-constrained performance, and for cases that represent the development of a situation over time.

Although the functions of the major components of this system are common to many case based reasoning systems, the criteria imposed by a continuous control application are responsible for unique aspects of their design in this system. For example, as we discussed in this paper, to limit the spread of a network problem, this application demands that the system respond within time constraints; thus, to provide a satisfactory response to meet a deadline, the Indexer/Matcher performs a best-first spreading-activation search. The Selector in this system is relatively sophisticated, devoting resources to increase its chance of choosing the most relevant case on its first attempt; this reduces the likelihood that the Modifier will waste time trying to transfer from a poorly matched case or that the Monitor will have to reject the case during the problem's evolution which would result in retrieving the current treatment and installing a new one. The Modifier itself is of intermediate complexity: less powerful than a full-scale planner -- sacrificing this power for reduced need for processing and storage, but more flexible than a set of transformational operators.

The design approach of this CBR system, then, is motivated by the requirements of continuous control applications; the system thereby extends the applicability of CBR into a wide range of practical problems. As the system is implemented and evaluated, it will demonstrate the benefits of CBR for such applications, suggest requirements for further extensions to the CBR paradigm, and test the generality of the approach for other, related applications.

REFERENCES

Alterman, R., "An adaptive planner." *Proceedings AAAI-86*, Philadelphia, PA, August 1986, pp 65-69.

Carbonell, J., "Derivational analogy: A theory of reconstructive problem solving and expertise acquisition." In R.S.Michalski, J.G.Carbonell, & T.M.Mitchell, *Machine Learning: An Artificial Intelligence Approach* (Vol.2). Los Altos, CA: Morgan Kaufmann, 1986, pp 371-392.

Carbonell, J., "Learning by analogy: Formulating and generalizing plans from past experience." In R.S.Michalski, J.G.Carbonell, & T.M.Mitchell, *Machine Learning: An Artificial Intelligence Approach*. Palo Alto, CA: Morgan Kaufmann, 1983, pp 137-161.

Carbonell, J., Personal Communication, 1987

Hammond, K., *Case-based Planning: An integrated theory of planning, learning and memory*. Ph.D. Thesis, Yale University, 1986.

Kolodner, J., "Reconstructive memory: A computer model." *Cognitive Science*, 7(4), 1983, pp 281-328.

Kolodner, J.L., *Retrieval and Organizational Strategies in Conceptual Memory: A Cognitive Model*, Lawrence Erlbaum Publishers, London, 1984

Rissland, E. and K. Ashley, "Hypotheticals as heuristic device." *Proceedings AAAI-86*, Philadelphia, PA, August 1986, pp 289-297.

Reasoning about Evidence in Causal Explanations

Phyllis Koton*
MIT Laboratory for Computer Science
Clinical Decision Making Group
545 Technology Square, Room 371
Cambridge, MA 02139

March 14, 1988

Abstract

Causal models can provide richly-detailed knowledge bases for producing explanations about behaviors in many domains, a task often termed interpretation or diagnosis. However, producing a causal explanation from the model can be time-consuming. This paper describes a system that solves a new problem by recalling a previous, similar problem and modifying that problem's solution to fit the current problem. Because it is unlikely that any new problem will exactly match a previous one, the system evaluates differences between the problems using a set of principles for reasoning about evidence in causal explanations. These *evidence principles* allow the system to reason about such concepts as alternate lines of evidence, additional supporting evidence, and inconsistent evidence. If all differences between the new situation and the remembered situation are found to be insignificant, *causal repair strategies* are used to adapt the previous situation's causal explanation to the new case. Although the evidence principles and repair strategies have thus far been tested only for the domain of managing patients with heart disease, their reasoning is domain-independent and should be generally applicable.

1 Explanation transfer

Causal models are frequently proposed for knowledge-based systems because they have a wide range of applicability, they are robust, and they contain detailed information for providing explanations of their reasoning. In practice they are not widely used because they are inefficient compared to associational rules or other types of "compiled" knowledge. This inefficiency could be reduced by using a paradigm such as Case-Based Reasoning [3] or Memory-Based Reasoning [11]. These methods use a memory of previously-solved problems to avoid complex reasoning when presented with a new problem. They recall a similar problem and adapt its solution to the new case. However, the match between a new problem and a previously solved problem usually is only partial. This presents a difficulty when producing a causal explanation. Some feature of the previously-solved problem that was

---

*The work reported here has been supported (in part) by National Institutes of Health grants R01 LM 04493 from the National Library of Medicine and R01 HL 33041 from the National Heart, Lung, and Blood Institute.

```
(defpatient "Newman"                    VITAL-SIGNS
HISTORY                                 (blood-pressure 138 80)
(age . 65)                              (heart-rate . 90)
(sex male)                              (arrhythmia-monitoring normal)
(dyspnea on-exertion)                   (resp . 20)
(orthopnea absent)                      (temp . 98.4)
(chest-pain anginal)                    PHYSICAL-EXAM
(anginal within-hours unstable)         (appearance nad)
(syncope/near-syncope on-exertion)      (mental-status conscious)
(palpitations none)                     (jugular-pulse normal)
(nausea/vomiting absent)                (pulse slow-rise)
(cough absent)                          (apex-impulse normal)
(diaphoresis absent)                    (parasternal-impulse normal)
(hemoptysis absent)                     (chest clear-to-auscultation-and-percussion)
(fatigue absent)                        (abdomen normal-exam)
(therapies none)                        (extremities normal-exam)
LABORATORY-FINDINGS
(ekg lvh normal-sinus)
(cxr calcification)
(calcification mitral aortic-valve))
```

Figure 1: Patient description for Newman

used as evidence in the causal explanation may be absent from the new problem. Similarly, the new problem may exhibit features that are absent from the previously-solved problem and which must be explained. This requires that the program have a set of principles for reasoning about dependencies between pieces of evidence and the states that they support in the causal explanation, and about the relationships (such as equivalence or incompatibility) between different pieces of evidence. The program can then determine whether a new problem with a somewhat different set of features can still be explained by a previous causal explanation. I have developed and implemented such a set of principles in a new system, CASEY.

2 Overview of CASEY

CASEY integrates case-based and causal reasoning techniques with a model-based expert system for managing patients with cardiac disease, the Heart Failure program [7]. CASEY contains a self-organizing memory system [4] for storing previously-seen problems (called *cases*). The memory contains descriptions of patients the program has seen and generalizations derived from similarities between the patients. The patient description is comprised of *features*. These include both input data, such as signs and symptoms, test results, history and current therapy information, and solution data, such as the causal explanation for the patient, the diagnosis, therapy recommendation and outcome information. A typical patient description in CASEY contains about 40 input features. For example, Figure 1 shows the patient description for Newman, a new patient presented to the system.

CASEY produces a causal explanation and therapy suggestions for a new patient using a three-step process. First, CASEY searches for a similar case in its memory; second, it

Feature name	Value for David	Value for Newman
age	72	65
pulse-rate	96	90
temperature	98.7	98.4
orthostatic-change	absent	unknown
angina	unstable	within-hours & unstable
mean-arterial-pressure	107	99.3
syncope	none	on exertion
auscultation	murmur of AS	unknown
pulse	normal	slow-rise
ekg	normal sinus & lv strain	normal sinus & lvh
calcification	none	mitral & aortic

Figure 2: Differences between patients David and Newman.

evaluates the significance of any differences between the new case and the retrieved case; and finally, if none of the differences rule out the match, it adapts the solution from the retrieved case to fit the particulars of the new case. If no acceptable previous case is found, CASEY uses the Heart Failure program to produce a solution for the case *de novo*. This paper focuses on evaluating and adapting a retrieved solution.

The *new case* is the case that CASEY is currently trying to solve. A *retrieved case* is a case that has been retrieved from memory as a result of matching against features of the new case. CASEY will often retrieve more than one case that matches the new case. CASEY's method of choosing among retrieved cases is described in [6]. The *precedent case* is a retrieved case in which all differences from the current case have been judged insignificant and from which solution transfer will occur. The *precedent solution* is the solution associated with the precedent case. The *transferred solution* is a copy of the precedent solution that is repaired to fit the new case.

A retrieved case for the patient Newman is a patient named David. The cases of David and Newman have many similarities. They also have some differences, which are shown in Figure 2. CASEY must decide if these differences are serious enough to rule out the match. In this example, the first four differences are insignificant. The remaining differences are important but the precedent solution can be adapted to explain them. This will be demonstrated in section 4.

3 The causal model and causal explanation

CASEY reasons about the model of the cardiovascular system contained in the Heart Failure system. The building blocks of the Heart Failure model are *measures*, *measure values*, *parameters*, and *states*. Measures correspond to observable features. Measure values are the allowed values of the measures, for example the patient's heart rate, and are entered by the user. Parameters are physiological parameters of the patient, such as "left atrial pressure." States represent specific qualitative values of parameters, for example "high left atrial pressure." The model also has information about the relationships between the entities: for example, the probability of one state causing another, and the probability of observing a particular measure given a particular state. There are just over 100 measures and about 140 states defined in the model. Some states are distinguished as "diagnosis"

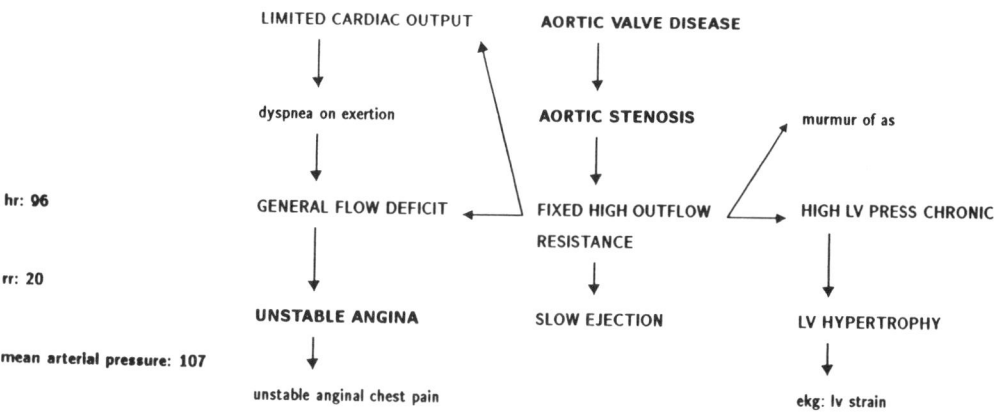

Figure 3: Causal explanation produced by Heart Failure program for David.

states. If a diagnosis state established, the name of the state is added to the patient's diagnosis. Others are defined as "goal states". These are states that can be treated. If a goal state is established, the therapy associated with the state is added to the list of therapy suggestions for the patient.

The Heart Failure program produces a causal explanation consisting of a set of measures, states, and directed links. The causal explanation describes the relationship between physiological states and observable features. A link between two states, or a state and a measure, indicates that one causes the other. Only abnormal findings are explained, but the program may not be able to explain all the abnormal findings.

A graphical representation of the Heart Failure program's causal explanation for David's symptoms is shown in Figure 3. David was diagnosed as having aortic valve disease, specifically aortic stenosis, and unstable angina. Abnormal features in his patient description accounted for by the causal explanation are: unstable anginal chest pain, evidence of LV strain on EKG, a heart murmur, and dyspnea on exertion. David's high heart rate, high respiration rate, and high blood pressure were not explained.

CASEY translates its input into the Heart Failure program's representation before it begins to use the causal model. The causal explanation produced by CASEY is in the same form as one produced by the Heart Failure program. CASEY translates the solution into its own representation before storing it for future use.

4 Principles for reasoning about evidence

Most new cases will not exactly match any previous case in the memory. To allow partial matches, differences between cases must be evaluated. Two cases might have many similar features yet have one critical difference that invalidates the match. Alternatively, many differences may not affect the validity of a match. The feature involved may have no relation to the solution of the case (the patient's name, for example) or the difference may be explainable. The module in CASEY that performs this evaluation is called the *justifier* because it must justify using a retrieved case as a precedent for the new case. The justifier relies on a set of principles for reasoning about evidence, termed *evidence principles*, that are presented below. The first evidence principle is used to determine whether a state in the retrieved casual explanation is ruled out by evidence in the new case. The next four attempt to show that the difference in question is insignificant or repairable, and the last three handle features which have special values that are easy to reason about. Other principles for determining significance are being explored.

1. *Rule out.* A state is ruled out from the transferred solution if there is some feature in the new case which is incompatible with that state. This is detected when the feature has zero probability for some state in the retrieved solution. For example, a heart rate of 40 beats per minute is incompatible with the state HIGH HEART RATE.

2. *Other evidence.* This is used when a feature present in the retrieved case is missing in the new case. It tries to find a piece of evidence in the new case which supports the state that the missing feature supported.

3. *Unrelated oldcase feature.* This is used when a feature is present only in the retrieved case. If the feature was not used in the causal explanation, its absence has no effect on any states in the explanation, so it can be ignored.

4. *Supports existing state.* This principle is used when a feature is present in the new case but not in the retrieved case. It tries to attribute this feature to a state in the retrieved causal explanation.

5. *Unrelated newcase feature.* This is also used when a feature is present only in the new case. If the feature is abnormal, but is not evidence for any existing state and does not strongly suggest a new state, then add it to the explanation as an unexplained feature.

6. *Normal.* Normal values are not explained by the Heart Failure program, so a normal value in the new case does not need to be explained. (Note that if a model did reason using normal values, this rule would be eliminated).

7. *No information.* If there is no information given about a feature in one of the cases and it is known to be absent in the other case, then assume that it is also absent in the former case.

8. *Same qualitative region.* CASEY evaluates differences between features with numerical values by translating them into qualitative value regions. For example, a blood pressure of 180/100 becomes "high blood pressure." Features whose values fall into the same qualitative region are judged not to be significantly different. The regions are determined using range information for the corresponding measure in the Heart Failure model.

CASEY can reject a match on either of two grounds: a significant difference could not be explained, or all the diagnosis states in the retrieved solution were ruled out. If all differences between the new case and the retrieved case are insignificant or repairable, then the transfer of solutions from the precedent to the current case proceeds.

CASEY makes the following inferences about the differences between patients David and Newman:

- David's age is judged to be insignificant by the rule *unrelated oldcase feature.* Newman's age is judged to be insignificant by the rule *unrelated newcase feature.*

- Both patients' heart-rates are in the same qualitative region (moderately high heart rate) so the difference is considered insignificant.

- Both temperatures are in the "normal" qualitative region so the difference is considered insignificant.

- David's mean arterial pressure is high, but Newman's is not. However, this feature was not accounted for by the causal explanation, so it is judged insignificant by the rule *unrelated oldcase feature*. Newman's mean arterial pressure is normal, so it does not have to be explained.

- Orthostatic change is absent in David, but not specified for Newman, so the rule *no-info* concludes that it is also absent in Newman.

- Newman's finding of angina within hours is additional evidence for the state UNSTABLE ANGINA.

- Syncope on exertion is additional evidence for the state LIMITED CARDIAC OUTPUT.

- Murmur of AS, which is absent in Newman, is evidence for the state FIXED HIGH OUTFLOW RESISTANCE in the precedent solution, but this state has other evidence supporting it in the new case.

- Newman's pulse has slow rise. This is evidence for the existing state SLOW EJECTION.

- LV strain on David's EKG is evidence for the state LV HYPERTROPHY. Newman's EKG shows LVH, which is evidence for the same state.

- Newman's finding of aortic calcification is evidence for the existing state AORTIC VALVE DISEASE.

- Newman's finding of mitral calcification has only one cause, MITRAL VALVE DISEASE, so this state is added to the causal explanation. MITRAL VALVE DISEASE has no causes in the model, so it remains unlinked, forming a separate causal chain.

All the differences between David and Newman are insignificant or repairable, so the match is justified.

5 The repair strategies

CASEY uses *repair strategies* to adapt a previous solution (consisting of causal explanation, diagnosis, and therapy) to a new case. Causal explanation repair strategies add or remove nodes and links to the transferred causal explanation.[1] CASEY can make the following repairs:

1. *Remove state.* When all evidence for a state has been removed, or if the only cause of a state has been removed from the transferred causal explanation, CASEY removes that state from the explanation. This also checks to see if states that this state caused have to be removed. This strategy is invoked by the *rule out* principle.

---

[1] Diagnosis repairs add and remove diseases from the transferred diagnosis. Therapy repairs add and remove therapy suggestions. They are describe in [6].

2. *Remove evidence.* When a piece of evidence that was used in the retrieved case is absent in the new case, this removes the feature and any links to it. It is invoked by the principles *other evidence* and *unrelated oldcase feature*.

3. *Add evidence.* This repair adds a piece of evidence to the causal explanation, and links it to the states for which it is evidence. This is invoked by *other evidence* and *supports existing state*.

4. *Substitute evidence.* When two numerical values have the same qualitative value, this repair replaces the old value with the new as evidence for some state. It is invoked by the *same qualitative value* principle.

5. *Add state.* In one instance, it is very easy for CASEY to add a state to the causal explanation. This is when the evidence has only one possible cause. This is invoked by the principle *supports existing state*.[2] The state is added to the causal explanation, and CASEY tries to link it to existing states and features in the causal explanation (using *add link*).

6. *Add link.* This adds a causal link between two states.

7. *Add measure.* This adds a feature which CASEY cannot link to the causal explanation. It is invoked by *unrelated newcase feature*.

In order to adapt the explanation transferred from David to fit the data for Newman, the following repair strategies are invoked by the justifier:

```
(substitute-evidence hr:90 hr:96)
(remove-evidence mean-arterial-pressure:107)
(add-evidence within-hours unstable-angina)
(add-evidence syncope-on-exertion limited-cardiac-output)
(remove-evidence murmur-of-as)
(add-evidence slow-rise slow-ejection)
(remove-evidence lv-strain)
(add-evidence lvh lv-hypertrophy)
(add-evidence aortic-calcification aortic-valve-disease)
(add-state mitral-valve-disease)
(add-evidence mitral-calcification mitral-valve-disease)
```

CASEY's causal explanation for Newman is shown in Figure 4. It states Newman's diagnosis as aortic valve disease, aortic stenosis, mitral valve disease, and unstable angina. It does not explain his high heart rate or his high respiration rate. The causal explanation for Newman produced by the Heart Failure program is identical.

The user has the option of rejecting CASEY's solution and running the Heart Failure program on the data. In either case, the patient description and solution are saved to be used for future problem-solving.

---

[2] The fact that a feature has only one cause is discovered while we are searching for existing states that cause this feature.

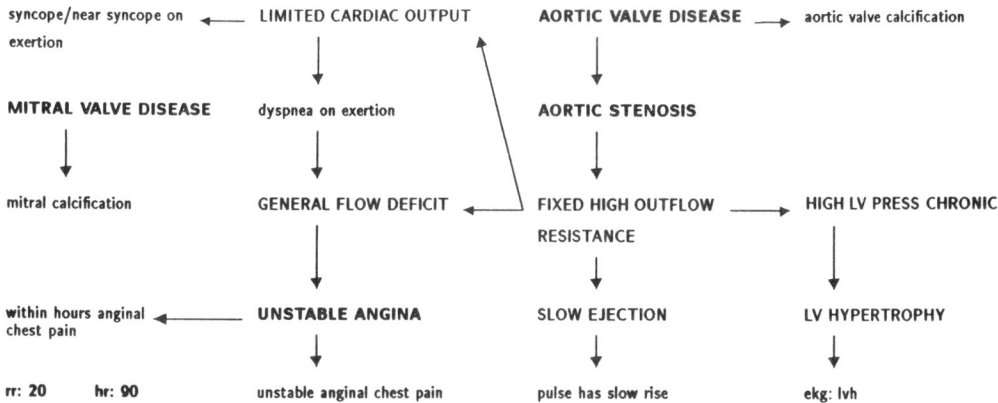

Figure 4: CASEY's causal explanation for Newman.

6 Discussion

6.1 Related work

SWALE [2] uses a memory of previously-solved problems to create explanations. It remembers prototype explanations, which it attempts to modify to fit a new situation. SWALE's process model is very similar to CASEY's. However, SWALE's explanations are very abstract, and require a large amount of real-world knowledge to evaluate and repair differences. CASEY's explanations are very concrete. In order to evaluate or repair a difference, it needs only examine local information about states and evidence. CHEF [1] also combines case-based reasoning with a causal model. It uses causal knowledge to explain plan failures, so its causal reasoning consists of chaining rules backward from an observed failure to the cause. Also, the program does not save the explanations and repair them to fit a new situation as CASEY and SWALE do. Recent work by Resnick and Davis [8] uses a memory of previously-solved problems and a causal model to explain hardware faults. It differs from CASEY in that it requires an exact match between the descriptions of a new fault and a previous fault.

6.2 Generalizing the results

CASEY requires the following information for its reasoning:

- a set of features that can be used to describe some problem,
- a set of states that can explain these observations,
- specific information about features:
  - the set of possible values for this feature,
  - the set of states that use this feature as evidence,
  - the advisability of ignoring a particular feature. This information is used to determine if a match is invalid because it can't explain an important feature.[3]

---

[3] The Heart Failure program represents this information numerically, as the percentage of time a feature is explained by the model. CASEY determines this information experientially by examining the role the feature played in similar past cases. The same information could be represented and reasoned about qualitatively.

- specific information about states:
    - the set of features that are evidence for this state,
    - features that rule this state out,
    - a list of states that cause this state,
    - a list of states that this state causes.

CASEY's reasoning does not depend on any knowledge specific to the domain. However, it accommodates certain assumptions of the Heart Failure program, the most important being the assumption that there is only limited interaction between states (for example, the Heart Failure program has no concept of two states jointly causing a third state). CASEY's evidence principles currently are being extended to handle more complex interactions.

The criteria by which a match is ruled out can be made more or less stringent. For example, a match could be ruled out if any state in a retrieved case was ruled out. CASEY is very accommodating of differences between new and retrieved cases because the system currently does not have enough cases to allow very stringent similarity requirements. A more conservative criterion might be implemented if the systems acquires a great many more cases. This would mean that CASEY would do less modification to a retrieved causal explanation, but might also increase the number of times that it failed to find an acceptable match.

The ability of the technique to produce a meaningful solution depends on selecting a good precedent case. Much research has been done in this area (for example [5], [10], [11], [2]). CASEY uses a novel matching algorithm specifically designed for reasoning about causal explanations. This algorithm gives extra importance to features that played a role in the causal explanation of previous similar cases [6].

6.3 Limitations of the method

CASEY's current implementation has limitations. Some problems presented to the system have a large number of "reasonable" explanations. CASEY does not use all the quantitative information available in the Heart Failure model that would allow it to distinguish between statistically more- and less-likely solutions.

For example, the program is parsimonious about adding additional states to the causal explanation. If a new feature could be attributed to two different physiological states, one of which is already included in the transferred explanation, CASEY will use the state that is already there rather than add a new state. It is possible that a feature has a higher probability of being caused by the state not already in the explanation. The model contains information that CASEY could use to discover this circumstance.

CASEY works by modifying one particular solution, rather than by generating a solution. This makes it difficult to evaluate the likelihood of its solution being correct compared to other possible explanations for the same data. The Heart Failure program, on the other hand, calculates the probabilities of all possible causal explanations that fit the data, and chooses the one with the highest probability. Again, the model contains information that could be used to roughly determine whether or not CASEY is pursuing the most likely explanation for the data.

For certain applications (e.g. [9]), any explanation for the input features is acceptable. In the Heart Failure domain, the users require the most likely explanation. CASEY's justifier will soon be extended to recognize when the solution it is creating is not the most likely one, in which case it can reject the match.

7 Conclusions

CASEY demonstrates that combining a memory of past cases with causal reasoning can have significant advantages over either method used alone. CASEY's causal reasoning ability lets it produce a complete causal analysis of the new case, not simply a reference to a previous solution. CASEY can produce a causal explanation even for problems that the Heart Failure program cannot solve. This is because a problem could lack sufficient information for the Heart Failure program to calculate a solution, but still have enough information for CASEY to find a matching case. This also suggests an interesting area for future work: using CASEY to integrate several causal models developed for different domains, where no one model could account for all the features in the problem. CASEY can produce causal explanations for common problems by recalling a similar problem and adapting its solution through simple modifications. It resorts to detailed causal analysis when it lacks experience, then remembers its solution for future use.

Acknowledgments

Robert Jayes, MD kindly provided the example cases. William Long's Heart Failure program provided an excellent testbed for this work. Thanks to Peter Szolovits, Ramesh Patil, and William Long for their supervision of this research, and to Janet Kolodner, Michael Wellman, and Paul Resnick for their helpful comments on this paper.

References

[1] Kristian Hammond. *Case-based Planning: An Integrated Theory of Planning, Learning and Memory*. PhD thesis, Yale University, 1986.

[2] A. M. Kass, D. B. Leake, and C. C. Owens. Swale: a program that explains. In *Explanation Patterns: Understanding Mechanically and Creatively*, Lawrence Erlbaum Associates, Hillside, NJ, 1986.

[3] Janet L. Kolodner. *Experiential Processes in Natural Problem Solving*. Technical Report GIT-ICS-85/22, School of Information and Computer Science, Georgia Institute of Technology, 1985.

[4] Janet L. Kolodner. Maintaining organization in a dymanic long-term memory. *Cognitive Science*, 7:243–280, 1983.

[5] Janet L. Kolodner. Reconstructive memory: a computer model. *Cognitive Science*, 7:281–328, 1983.

[6] Phyllis A. Koton. *Using Experience in Learning and Problem Solving*. PhD thesis, Massachussetts Institute of Technology, 1988 (in preparation).

[7] William J. Long, Shapur Naimi, M. G. Criscitiello, and Robert Jayes. The development and use of a causal model for reasoning about heart failure. In *Symposium on Computer Applications in Medical Care*, pages 30–36, IEEE, November 1987.

[8] Paul Resnick and Randall Davis. Improving performance of model-based reasoning by learning from experience. March 1988. Submitted to AAAI-88.

[9] Reid Simmons and Randall Davis. Generate, test, and debug: Combining associational rules and causal models. In *Proceedings of the Tenth International Joint Conference on Artificial Intelligence*, pages 1071–1078, 1987.

[10] Robert L. Simpson. *A Computer Model of Case-Based Reasoning in Problem Solving: An Investigation in the Domain of Dispute Mediation*. Technical Report GIT-ICS-85/18, Georgia Institute of Technology, 1985.

[11] Craig Stanfill and David Waltz. Towards memory-based reasoning. *Communications of the ACM*, 29(12):1213–1228, 1986.

Planning in an Open World: A Pluralistic Approach.[1]

Mitchell Marks, Kristian J. Hammond and Tim Converse
Department of Computer Science
The University of Chicago
Chicago, IL 60637

Abstract

Recent work in planning has rejected the assumption of a closed, stable world, and the associated paradigm of exhaustive preplanning, which encounters serious problems trying to plan in a world where that assumption does not hold. Several alternative strategies have been proposed, responding to these new problems in a variety of ways. We review this spectrum, finding the various approaches in part incompatible but not bereft of some common themes and complementary strengths. We suggest factors in the application domain which should influence the appropriate mix, and describe the TRUCKER project to illustrate some of the problems and benefits in implementing such a mix.

1 Problems with Traditional Planning

The classical development of the theory of planning and problem-solving emphasized exhaustive preplanning, with the goal of being able to guarantee that an optimal or near-optimal plan would be found if one existed. Planners in this paradigm required certain assumptions to hold:

- The world will be stable; it will behave as projected.

- Time consumed in planning is independent of the time that can be devoted to execution, so that the efficiency of the planner has no side-effects on the feasibility of the constructed plan.

- The information available to the planner is complete, and execution will be flawless.

- Any initially correct plan will remain correct and can in fact be carried out.

---

[1] This work was supported, in part, by an Independent Research Grant from Lockheed Missiles and Space Co.

In the real world, however, these assumptions simply do not hold. The world is not stable; agents must trade off planning time against execution time; and planners generally have to function under conditions of spotty rather than complete information. The simplifying assumptions were made in order to initiate progress in the serious investigation of planning. The harsh realities were consciously abstracted out of the theories initially, not merely overlooked. But with advancing theory, researchers have recently begun finding it feasible to explore the problem of planning in more realistic situations where these assumptions do not hold.

1.1 New problems in planning

In this paper we will attempt to classify the different kinds of issues that any planner must confront as we relax these traditional assumptions. We will discuss the different theories of planning that have arisen in response to these issues. And we will present TRUCKER, a planner that combines features of many of these theories in an attempt to deal with the complexities of combining planning and acting in one system.

We now give a rough classification of the major sorts of problems a traditional planning system can encounter when required to deal with a more realistic domain. These problems, in turn, provide a basis for understanding what motivates the departures taken by theorists in recent work.

The Immediate Complexity Problem. This concerns the computational effort required in constructing one plan. If the planner searches for a correct and safe plan by projecting forward the effects of early steps to compare with preconditions of later steps, goals, and preservation conditions, the computational complexity can rise to a high order. In fact Chapman (1987) has shown the problem to be NP-hard, and undecidable in the worst case. This behavior is unacceptable simply from an external point of view, even without considering the internal effect of the Planning/Execution Crowding Problem (below).

The Asymptotic Complexity Problem. As a planner interacts with the world, it is confronted with a stream of goals, or sets of conjunctive goals, rather than independent problems. If these are all treated singly, independently, the total planning and execution effort would be at least the sum of the separate costs (possibly worse, due to unfavorable interactions). But if the planner can somehow convert the interdependence from a problem to an advantage, then the average cost per goal can be reduced in the long run, offsetting the Immediate Complexity Problem. That is, if the planner can learn specific plans that are tailored to a domain of recurring sets of goals, it can avoid the Immediate Complexity problem inherent in weak methods.

The Execution-time Failure Problem. A plan which looked correct when it was constructed may turn out to be incorrect during execution. This may be because conditions in the world have changed in the meantime, invalidating the preconditions of a plan step, or because the plan was incorrect in the first place, based on incorrect assumptions in the planner's limited world-knowledge. To cope with this, a planner must have some facility for replanning, recovery, and repair.

If the recovery does not take advantage of the work which went into the original plan construction, and of the new information implicit in the circumstances of the failure, replanning can be as difficult as planning was in the first instance (or more so), exacerbating the Complexity Problems.

The Planning/Execution Crowding Problem. If planning and execution are to be carried out by the same agent, essentially without parallelism, then time consumed in planning can deplete the time available for execution. This can create a situation where some series of actions would be a correct response to the goals and the world state, and could be feasibly executed within the total time available, but become infeasible within the time left after planning.

The Costly Information Problem. The planner cannot count on having complete information about a domain, either its underlying causal "physics" or its current state. To minimize the effects of this information shortage (namely inefficient plan construction and inaccurate plans), the planner should have information-gathering as a background goal. But understanding the world correctly, and storing new information in a usable form, can be expensive operations. They must be carried out in the normal course of execution if they are to be a help and not a hindrance.

The Missed Opportunities Problem. A corollary to the Execution–time Failure problem is the Missed Opportunities problem. Because the world does not necessarily match the planner's understanding of it, it is often the case that opportunities to satisfy goals are missed at planning time and must be noticed and exploited at execution time.

2 New Approaches to Planning

Several new directions in planning have arisen in response to problems like those enumerated in Section 1. All of them address the Immediate Complexity problem in one way or another, but differ in the additional emphasis they give to the various other problems. The outlook we propose here is that in most realistic environments, all of the problems will have to be addressed; so an ideal planner would combine the strengths of these different approaches, marshalled against the respective problems they most directly ameliorate.

One such new approach has come to be known as *reactive planning* (Agre & Chapman 1987a, Agre & Chapman 1987b) or *situated activity* in the preferred terminology of Agre and Chapman, following Suchman (1986). The major assumption of the traditional paradigm challenged by these authors is that adequate planning time is always available; along with the Immediate Complexity problem they are most directly concerned with the Planning/Execution Crowding problem. To function in a fast-changing world, a planner may have to pay more attention to execution or interpretation of plans and less to construction of plans. In the purest realizations of this idea, the planner will end up working from reflex-like stored responses for each immediate situation rather than true goal-directed plans. These are useful ideas, even when complexity or sensitivity of the problem domain dictates that they cannot be applied in pristine, radical form.

A key point from this line of thought is that planning and execution cannot be as neatly separated as traditionally supposed. This is not just because planning and execution share the same pool of available time (though that is an important aspect); rather, this represents a change in the very fundamentals of how to think and talk about planning. There isn't planning plus execution, there is one combined activity.

An interesting compromise version of the situated-activity paradigm informs one component of the system described by Firby (1987). This planner works with units of action called reactive action packages or RAPs. A RAP "is essentially an autonomous process that pursues a planning goal until that goal has been achieved." The system fits the reactive-planning concept inasmuch as it eschews the overall action-consequence projection of hierarchical planning and the costs associated therewith; yet it differs significantly from PENGI (Agre & Chapman 1987a) in that a RAP is not restricted to primitive actions or even sequences of primitive actions, but rather may invoke sequences of other RAPs. Information about the resulting parent-child relations link activated instances of RAPs waiting in a linear queue, thereby providing an inplicit hierarchy and some of the benefits of hierarchical expansion. But the queue is always linear, and new RAPs are placed in it in an order stored in the parent RAP; this avoids the costs usually incurred in full-scale hierarchical planning where effects of actions are projected across a search through a space of alternate linearizations. This structure, and the provision of the queue in itself, gives the system a capability of "planning for the future," forming complex intentions and attempting to carry them out piece by piece, of a sort infeasible in, or not required for, the purest kind of situated-activity domain.

An approach generally called case-based reasoning has become an emergent paradigm in several areas of AI, including planning, natural language understanding, diagnosis/repair systems, and problem-solving (Hammond 1986a, Kolodner *et al.* 1985, Hammond & Hurwitz in press, McDougal 1988). As an approach to planning (Hammond 1986b), *case-based planning* departs from traditional methods via an emphasis on the rôle of memory; more specifically, an episodic memory of past goals and the plans that succeded or failed in satisfying them. This emphasis is directed at taming the Immediate Complexity problem and especially the Asymptotic Complexity problem.

In the purest form of case-based planning, new plans are *always* derived from plans in old cases, and are *never* computed purely from scratch (world knowledge and inference rules). A pristine case-based planning approach is best suited to a domain where execution failures or at least suboptimal execution can be tolerated. When a less fault-tolerant domain or task requires giving up this purity of approach, the correct response, we argue, is not to retreat to a full-scale projection of the plan's effects in the world. In the first place, that would mean giving up the efficiency advantages which form part of the motivation for case-based planning. Second, such a course is not in general possible; it depends on several of the assumptions we are trying to do without—assumptions of a stable world and complete knowledge. What is needed, instead, is a capability for *plan repair*.

The *adaptive planning* approach of Alterman (1985), and the *generate-test-debug* approach of Simmons and Davis (1987) are directed especially against the Execution-time Failure problem, as is (Hammond 1987). In adaptive planning, failure leads to replanning using semantically linked features; in generate-test-debug, replanning is guided by a causal description of the failure. Case-based planning also uses a causal description of plan failure, both to repair the current plan and to discover the features that will predict the problem in the future.

We have so far been treating the issue of failure as though it exclusively meant failure of a single plan to work correctly in execution, either through simple bad planning or through confrontation with unexpected conditions in the world. A planner dealing with multiple goals must also deal with possible failures deriving from the interactions of the plans for two or more goals. Interactions where plans may interfere with each other have long been a focus in planning research. Here we will place some emphasis on another sort of interaction between plans, interactions in which some benefit could be derived from combining plans. If a useful interaction could be obtained, but the planner does not take advantage of this possibility, it has fallen into another sort of interactive failure. This failure to take advantage of potentially beneficial plan interactions constitutes the Missed Opportunities problem.

Clearly, the necessity for making use of opportunities—avoiding the Missed Opportunities problem—springs ultimately from considerations of efficiency; that is, from the concerns we have labeled the Immediate Complexity and Asymptotic Complexity problems. Indeed, our whole taxonomy of problems has been revealed as a tangled network of mutual dependencies. The moral is obvious: they cannot be solved singly and piecemeal. Active planning in a realistic domain requires combined work on all these fronts simultaneously.

3 Strategy mix depends on domain

In the previous sections we listed several fundamental problems encountered in the traditional approach of full preplanning under a closed-world assumption; examined several recent directions in planning, each one aimed at ameliorating selected items from that list of problems; and called for efforts to develop an integrated approach. But we will not get very far by arguing about these issues at the level of generality in the previous sections. There is no best (and of course this could only mean "currently-best") integrated approach to planning in general, for the simple reason that there is no such thing as planning-in-general. Rather, the best approach will depend on the domain and the problem, and perhaps other constraints, such as requirements for efficiency or for accuracy (these are in competition).

As happens almost anywhere in AI or computer science, we have reached the point of confrontation with trade-offs. A planner trying to operate in an unstable world, of which it has incomplete knowledge, is forced to trade correctness for efficiency, first-time success for long-run success, planning time for execution time. If the planner is trying to solve an NP-hard problem in the real world, the dilemma can only become sharper.

The best—or let us only say the least unsatisfactory—resolution of these trade-offs is not given by general considerations but instead depends on the domain, the task, and perhaps an externally-decided performance-level criterion. To make our discussion more concrete, we will focus on the choices stemming from the domain and task used in the TRUCKER project, whose implementation is described in the latter sections of this paper.

TRUCKER is a planner operating in the domain of messenger-service scheduling. A dispatcher controls a fleet of trucks which roam a city or a neighborhood, picking up and dropping off parcels at designated addresses. (Our implementation uses Chicago and its Hyde Park neighborhood.) Transport orders are "phoned in" by customers at various times during the simulated business day, and the parcel delivery sequence and truck routing are adjusted to efficiently accommodate the new orders. The relevant sense of efficiency here includes both the cost of the planner's own efforts and the evolving delivery sequence and routing.

TRUCKER's task involves receiving requests from customers, making decisions about which truck to assign a given request to, deciding in what order given parcels should be picked up and dropped off, figuring out routes for the trucks to follow, and monitoring the execution of the plans it constructs. A number of limited resources must be managed, including the trucks themselves, their gas and cargo space, and the planner's own planning time. TRUCKER starts off with very little information about the world that its trucks will be negotiating; all it has is the equivalent of a street map, an incomplete and potentially inaccurate schematic of its simulated world.

Thus, this is the sort of domain and task where the problems contemplated in our earlier list all naturally arise. Traditional approaches to planning, with emphasis on exhaustive preplanning, would therefore be inadequate to this task for a number of reasons:

- TRUCKER lacks perfect information about its world.

- TRUCKER does not know all of its goals in advance – new calls come in that must be integrated with currently running plans.

- Planning time is limited. TRUCKER's world does not wait for it to complete plans before new events occur.

- Even given perfect advance information, an optimal solution to the problem TRUCKER faces is computationally intractable. Even scheduling the pickup and dropoff points for a single truck to minimize travel time is a variant of the traveling salesman problem, which is known to be NP-complete.

To stave off the effects of the Planning/Execution Crowding problem, we might try a situated-activity approach. But the complexity of the domain rules out a pristine situated-activity/reactive-planning approach to this task. Very few pickups and deliveries would get done if the trucks were commanded by a frenetic dispatcher constantly issuing new instructions based only on the current locations of the trucks and the last transport-request received.

However, an appropriate modification within the reactive-planning school of thought, we believe, can be derived along the lines taken in (Firby 1987). We separate out classes of actions which require temporally-extended control (routing) from those which can be but the matter of a moment (navigation), and assign execution of the latter to semi-autonomous agents.

To deal with Asymptotic Complexity, we might want to cast our planner in a case-based mold, storing and re-using plans. The relevant plans here are the routes for driving from one given block to another. That's fine, as far as it goes, and indeed TRUCKER has a route-memory. But by itself this technique doesn't go nearly far enough. A delivery truck cannot afford to work sequentially through its list of orders, driving directly from the pickup point of each request to the corresponding dropoff point before dealing with the next request, even if the list has been put in some rational order. There will be a clear case of interaction failure, contributing to the Missed Opportunities problem, if the planner is not able to combine nearby stops. On the other hand, the planner will be swamped in the Immediate Complexity problem if it checks for all route-combination possibilities every time a new request is phoned in. Clearly, it needs something beyond the situated-activity and case-based components demanded so far, something to help it select reasonable occasions for making the computational effort to detect advantageous combinations.

To deal with these combinations, then, we would want to give the planner an opportunistic component, whose job it is to detect apparent opportunities for route-combination. But if hammered together in isolation, such a facility would introduce its own new computational costs. It would be at least problematic, and perhaps no net gain at all, if this component were introduced as a new planning expense on top of everything else—say, as a collection of daemons attached to each pending delivery request.

This consideration takes us from *opportunism* in general to the more specific model of *opportunistic memory*.[2]

A pending delivery goal gets attached to memory structures which will be used or activated anyway when an appropriate opportunity for dealing with that goal arises in the normal course of other activity. In the TRUCKER domain, the relevant normal activity is simply that of (simulated) driving. With that step, we have asked for another component, an observing/understanding component which "parses the world" from the raw stream of incoming information. In the course of interpreting the presence of a certain recognizable

---

[2] The idea of *opportunistic memory* builds on two views of opportunism in planning—that of Hayes-Roth and Hayes-Roth (1979) and that of Birnbaum and Collins (1984).

building or other landmark as meaning that the truck has reached a now-identifiable location, it must find and access a memory structure corresponding to that location. Waiting in that memory structure is a notation about other delivery goals associated with that place—but waiting quietly, as a notation, not waiting busily, as a daemon. Thus our response to the Missed Opportunities problem has demanded that we deal with the Costly Information problem at the same time.

When an opportunity for route-combination arises, the planner must be able to take advantage of it by reorganizing the delivery plans. (And of course it should store the combination for later re-use.) Besides the potential interaction failures represented by missed opportunities, TRUCKER must also be prepared to deal with direct execution failures. For both these reasons, it requires a replanning component.

4 Structure of the TRUCKER Program

The TRUCKER planner is embedded in a demonstration program consisting of three modules: the world simulation, the map, and the planner itself. Trucks move through the world, along routes constructed by the planner, assuming that the directions are valid, that there is gas in the tank, and so on (they may find out otherwise). The map is a schematic of the simulated world, but with considerably less information, lacking buildings, "visual" cues, one-way streets and other features. The simulated world, on the other hand, does contain cues of those sorts, which play an essential role in navigation. Though the program has to know where all the trucks are at any given moment, this information is not directly available to the planner; instead, it must construct and maintain this information as it goes along, "parsing the world." This intimate connection with locality provides the basis for having places remind the planner of possible opportunities. See (Hammond, in preparation) for an account of opportunistic memory in theory and in TRUCKER.

Input to the planner consists of delivery requests (which may arrive at any time during the day), data from the map (when explicitly accessed by the planner), and feedback from the trucks themselves as they move through the world. Most of the communication from the planner to the trucks is expressed in the form of plans at two levels of description.

The high-level agenda for a truck is a sequence of instructions about where to travel and what to do there. Typically it consists at any one time of alternating instructions for travel-steps and parcel transactions:

```
(GOTO (5802 S-WOODLAWN))
(PICKUP PARCEL-3)
(GOTO (920 E-55TH))
(DROPOFF PARCEL-5)
```

Plans of this sort are created as needed, and consumed piecemeal as each portion is executed. Each truck has such a plan. Portions not yet executed are available for reordering, cancellation, addition of new steps along the way, or transfer to another truck.

The planner also provides specific plans for the routes that trucks follow when executing a GOTO step. A route is represented as a series of turns, using street names and compass directions (with a start and stop instruction at the beginning and end). In particular, it is *not* a series of step-by-step or block-by-block instructions; a truck driving under the guidance of a route can travel several blocks without using a new portion of the route, until it must turn or make a stop. The route expanding the travel step (GOTO (920 E-55TH)) in the delivery plan given above would be the following:

```
(START NORTH (5802 S-WOODLAWN))
(TURN EAST E-57TH)
(TURN NORTH S-CORNELL)
(TURN EAST E-55TH)
(STOP (920 E-55TH))
```

The planner's memory stores and retrieves active goals, route plans, records of goals that have been satisfied in the past, facts about the world that the trucks observe, and previously noted opportunities for merging plans. These pieces of knowledge are indexed by the place in the world with which they are associated.

Together, these provide the material on which the several active components demanded in the previous section do their work.

4.1 Reactive-planning component: central planning agenda

At the center of the TRUCKER implementation lies a "main loop" planning and execution supervisor, corresponding to the dispatcher in the domain model. The implementation is intended to connect with the ideas of (Firby 1987). The basic task of this component is to answer the phone, examine each new delivery order, and either assign it to a truck immediately or else decide to temporarily lay it aside.

The planner controls its own agenda by means of a request-based action queue, ordered by predefined priorities for various types of tasks. The central planning component is treated as time-bound. That is, almost all of the actions it can take, both those involving its own state and those involving the domain more directly, have costs in the simulated time-stream. As a consequence, it is designed to act in units of atomic actions that require little time singly; the atomic components of a complex action are placed in a priority queue, to be carried out when time allows. The contents of this queue at any given moment constitutes a tentative plan for the planner's actions in the near term. To achieve this atomization, most of the action-types built into the planner are molecular.

The central planner is essentially an interpreter for the "language" of its own action-packets as they reach the front of the queue. When interpreted, a molecular action packet has the effect merely of inserting several other actions into the priority queue. The lower-level actions may be linked as sequences or as alternatives, meaning that the molecular action containing them can be thought of as an "and" packet or an "or" packet, respectively. The relations of which actions cause which others to be enqueued amounts to an implicit planning hierarchy, but without explicit projection of effects and checking of preconditions; instead, if one way of accomplishing a task fails, another way is already somewhere behind it in the queue, and ultimately some default method will apply if nothing else does. When an action succeeds, it triggers the deletion of actions further down in the queue to which it is linked as an alternative.

The most important molecular action is to try assigning a delivery request to a truck which will be able to handle it well. These are "or" packets. When a new order is received, the planner's only immediate response is to place such an assign-delivery-to-truck action somewhere in its queue. At some point that action is interpreted, and the result of that interpretation is to place four new packets into the queue.

```
handle-new-req-expansion:

    try-assign-to-truck-going-near    ; only if reminded
    try-assign-to-idle-truck
    try-combine-with-unassigned-reqs  ; only if reminded
    dump-in-unassigned-reqs
```

The order in which the new packets will be tried is given by priority values associated with them, [3] which influence where they will be placed in the queue; the resulting order is shown here. First it will try to assign the request to a truck whose current route takes it through the pickup or dropoff point of the new request—but only if it knows that some request already assigned to the truck has been successfully combined with the new request on some other occasion. If no truck with such a request is found, the planner will assign the new request to any truck which is sitting without work. Failing that, if it knows (from prior successful combination) that the new request can be combined with some other request that was phoned in earlier today but has not yet been assigned to a truck, then it will leave the two requests unassigned, but will "clip them together." If none of these three possibilities succeeds, the dispatcher will simply "toss it on the desk" for later reconsideration. (There are action packets not discussed above which will lead to later reconsideration of these suspended requests—these ultimately come from a "look for something constructive to do" action which always sits at the back of the queue, and gets executed whenever the queue has been otherwise cleared.)

By keeping the atomic actions generally inexpensive individually, even at the cost of multiplying their number, we prevent the planner from being tied up and uninterruptible when it should be noticing events in the world, a particular version of the Planning/Execution Crowding problem. But the main contribution of this architecture is against the Immediate Complexity problem, by avoiding projection of effects and enforcing an early (indeed, immediate) linearization of implicitly hierarchical structures.

---

[3] In our implementation, these are preselected and in effect constant. In principle, the planner could adjust these values as it learned which order gave it more successful strategies.

4.2 Case-based component: route and combination memory

When a truck, working through its delivery agenda, completes one pickup or dropoff and prepares to drive on to the next, it requires a driving route from the dispatcher. If necessary, the dispatcher will consult the map and its memory of road conditions and typical speeds (a memory quite distinct from the map) in order to compute, by two-way best-first search, a near-optimal route from the truck's current location to its next stop. This computation is one of the two inherently expensive operations in TRUCKER, and the planner will avoid undertaking it if possible. The computation can be skipped if the planner already knows the desired route, having previously computed it and stored it. This, of course, is the core idea of case-based planning and we employ it very directly here: the planner cannot entirely avoid this expensive search, but it can avoid repeating it for the same locations. [4]

When two delivery requests are opportunistically combined and their routes are merged, the merged route is stored, along with the fact that these two pickup-dropoff location pairs proved combinable. This provides some interesting challenges in memory indexing, but otherwise the basic idea is still the same, and addresses especially the Asymptotic Complexity problem.

4.3 Opportunistic memory and replanning components: detecting and constructing plan combinations

TRUCKER merges requests in an effort to optimize over travel time. But it does so only when it encounters an opportunity to satisfy one request while it is actually running the route for a previous one, or if it has learned from a previous such opportunity that two requests are combinable. Initially, the effect of the queued action packets in the dispatcher is that TRUCKER runs requests in order of "call-in," assigning them singly to idle trucks until all trucks are occupied. It also links each new request with the memory nodes in its representation associated with the locations that would serve as opportunities for satisfying the request, *i.e.*, the pickup and delivery location. As the planner executes each stage of its plan, recognizing locations, it sometimes finds requests associated with locations that it is passing. When this happens, TRUCKER considers the possibility that the new request could be merged with the current plan—as well as the possibility that the resulting route should be stored and re-used.

The basic example of this behavior requires just one truck and two delivery requests. We consider four places A, B, C, and D, with C located close to the path between A and B, and with B located close to the path between C and D. (Their linear order then is A-C-B-D.) The first request is for transport of a parcel from A to B. This request gets

---

[4] This aspect was not our main theoretical emphasis in TRUCKER, so we did not implement certain interesting variations which suggest themselves as additional time-saving measures. New routes, for example, could be constructed by extending old ones; or the planner could model the city in terms of neighborhood centers, major intersections, and local "feeder" streets, and try to adapt any route found in memory which has the same start and end neighborhoods as the desired new route, or the same nearby major intersection.

assigned to the idle truck. While the truck is still driving from A to B (and has not yet gone beyond C), a request is phoned in for a C-to-D delivery. There is no available truck, and the planner does not yet know of any promising combination possibilities for C-D, so it places the C-D request on the desk for later reconsideration. But there is one more crucial factor: because the planner has at least considered the C-D request, the memory nodes for locations C and D have been activated, with a notation in each one to the effect that there is a currently blocked goal involving that location.

As the truck navigates from A to B, it keeps track of where it is and what it should be doing next by watching the passing view and "parsing" sequences of familiar landmarks. As it does so, it checks its memory node for each location that it passes through (obtaining there the association sequences that help establish the location). When it reaches point C, it is reminded of the blocked C-D delivery request.

This is enough to trigger the planner into checking whether the two requests can be combined to produce an improvement in overall driving time. If it finds that such a combination would be useful, the truck should stop and pick up the parcel at C, continuing then with dropoffs at B and D. The successful combination is saved as part of the long-term memory records of the A-B and C-D travel routes.

On another occasion, if the same pattern of requests comes in, the planner is able to make use of the optimization more easily. Again the A-B request has come in first, and the delivery is under way. When the C-D request comes in, and the planner retrieves the travel route from memory, it also finds there the notation of the past successful combination. Checking the nodes involved in that combination, it finds that A-B are involved in a currently active delivery request. If the truck has not yet passed C, the planner can make use of the optimization immediately, assigning delivery C-D to the truck now and replacing its travel route with the stored combination route.

If, on the other hand, the locations were not so well placed, and the attempted combination proved unfruitful, the planner would still store a notation to that effect. Otherwise, it would have to try the unsuccessful combination once again the next time the same requests came in (in fact every time), with significant wasted effort.

This combination process involves the other significantly expensive operation in TRUCKER (especially in the general case with more than two routes to be checked and perhaps combined), and as with route-construction we must constrain when it will be done, and save the results. Sometimes TRUCKER checks for potential combinations when nothing useful can be obtained (otherwise it wouldn't really be checking); but we think the procedure suggested above gives a good balance of taking advantage of opportunities without spending excessive effort in detecting them.

4.4 Situated-activity and Understanding components: driving and navigating

As we write this, a major stretch of Chicago's busiest expressway has been closed down for repairs, and distressed commuters are using the surface streets in unfamiliar neighborhoods. Residents of those neighborhoods, who previously had a good idea of the traffic conditions on their local roads, find that they have to adjust those ideas and take into account the extra rush-hour congestion stemming from the closed expressway. The particular adjustments that must be made to their daily routines change from day to day and hence cannot be planned in advance.

Like these real drivers, TRUCKER cannot preplan all the driving steps involved in carrying out a sequence of deliveries. It first supplies the trucks with highest-level plans, a sequence of the locations where they are to stop for pickups and dropoffs. Only when such a step is ready for execution is it expanded into a plan at the next lower level, a sequence of major travel legs punctuated by turns or change of street name. This gives the planner the flexibility to rearrange the higher-level plans as needed for repair or opportunity, without wasting the effort of repeatedly changing the expansions at the lower level when the major steps get interleaved differently.

The same considerations apply at the next lower planning level. To drive from one intersection to another, five blocks down on the same street, a plan that merely says "Continue south for 0.4 miles" will not suffice. The driver must stop at stop signs, change lanes to be ready for the next turn, perhaps even make a detour. Sufficient flexibility for adjustments like these must be left in the hands of at least semi-autonomous agents during execution.

This also means that the progress of the execution must be monitored. The fact that the odometer has turned a given number of times does not mean that the truck is really where calculations would place it. How does a real driver know whether the vehicle has actually reached a certain corner? By looking, and gathering information from the surroundings.

So in TRUCKER we do not assume that every primitive step carried out by the trucks has the expected effect. Progress is constantly monitored, and environmental cues are compared to memories regarding the expected locations.

The continual use of place-memories also provides the basis for opportunistic route-combination as described previously.

5 Summary

Recent developments in planning have separately addressed various of the major problems that arose when traditional planning ideas were presented with domains and tasks for which the assumptions of a closed world and complete knowledge do not hold. The new theories have shown considerable success in taming some of those problems, by regarding plan construction and execution as intimately tied together, and thus monitoring and guiding the execution of their plans. But even with this measure of success, no one of these theories can claim complete success, and none can be taken as the unique best direction in which planning research should go. We call for a pluralistic spirit and close attention to the dictates of the particular domains and tasks as a way of developing suitable planning systems.

We have described our work on the TRUCKER project as an example of a planner conceived within the pluralistic approach that the above argument contemplates. We stress in particular the way in which considerations of the domain and task led us to adopt, in different parts of the system, techniques drawn from several of the new planning theories.

6 Acknowledgements

We would like to thank Gregg Collins for discussion of the ideas in this paper and David Miller for advice on the TRUCKER project. We also thank Alex Beels and Oleg Voloshin for their help in the initial TRUCKER implementation, and other students at Chicago for useful discussion and commentary: Jeffrey Berger, Matthew Brand, Neil Hurwitz, and Thomas McDougal.

7 References

Agre, P. E. and D. Chapman (1987a). Pengi: An implementation of a theory of activity. In *Proceedings of AAAI-87*, AAAI, Seattle, WA, July 1987, 268-272.

Agre, P .E. and D. Chapman (1987b). What are plans for? Panel on representing plans and goals, DARPA Planning Workshop, Santa Cruz, CA, October 21-23, 1987.

Alterman, R. (1985). Adaptive planning: refitting old plans to new situations. In *Proceedings 7th Cognitive Science Society*.

Birnbaum, L., and G. Collins (1984). Opportunistic Planning and Freudian Slips. In *Proceedings of the Sixth Annual Conference of the Cognitive Science Society*, Boulder, CO, 1984.

Chapman, D. (1985). *Planning for Conjunctive Goals*, Technical Report TR 802, MIT Artificial Intelligence Laboratory.

Firby, R. J. (1987). An investigation into reactive planning in complex domains. In *Proceedings of AAAI-87*, AAAI, Seattle, WA, July 1987, 202-206.

Hammond, K. (1986a). Learning to anticipate and avoid planning problems through the explanation of failures. In *Proceedings of the 1986 National Conference on Artificial Intelligence*, Philadelphia, PA, August 1986.

Hammond, K. (1986b). *Case-based Planning: An integrated theory of planning, learning and memory.*, Ph.D. Thesis, Yale University.

Hammond, K. (1987). Explaining and Repairing Plans that Fail. In *Proceedings of the Tenth International Joint Conference on Artificial Intelligence*, Milan, Italy, August 1987.

Hammond, K. (in preparation). Opportunistic Memory: Storing and recalling suspended goals.

Hammond, K. and N. Hurwitz (in press). Extracting diagnostic features from explanations. AAAI Symposium on explanation-based learning, Palo Alto, CA, March 1988.

Hayes-Roth, B., and F. Hayes-Roth (1979). A cognitive model of planning. In *Cognitive Science*, 2, 1979, 275-310.

Kolodner, J. L., R. L. Simpson, and K. Sycara-Cyranski (1985). A process model of case-based reasoning in problem solving. In *The Ninth International Joint Conference on Artificial Intelligence*.

McDougal, T. (1988). POLYA: A computational model of problem-solving in geometry. M.A.T. Thesis, University of Chicago.

Simmons, R. F., and R. Davis (1987). Generate, test, and debug: combining associational rules and causal models.

Suchman, L. (1987). *Plans and Situated Actions*. Cambridge University Press, 1987.

Case Based Reasoning in CYCLOPS, a Design Problem Solver

D. Navinchandra
Robotics Institute
Carnegie Mellon University
Pittsburgh, PA 15213
dchandra@isl1.ir.cmu.edu

ABSTRACT

Case-based problem solving is based on the idea that a machine problem-solver should make use of its own past experiences in solving new problems, relying on its memories instead of only on a base of rules. In this paper we present a design problem solver which uses previous cases to recognize potential problems and to repair design problems. The problem solving process involves: (1) finding the problem, (2) setting up corresponding goals and sub-goals, (3) finding appropriate cases which either directly or analogically match the target problem, (4) using an explanation of the current problem to extract relevant knowledge from the case, (5) continuing the process till all sub-goals are satisfied. CYCLOPS works in the domain of Landscape Design and uses CBR as one of its strategies for solving design problems.

1. Introduction

Design Engineers, while working on a design, use analytic techniques, heuristics and previous cases to guide the design process. Over the past two decades, computer-aided design (CAD) tools have been developed to help designers in various ways. A typical CAD tool includes a geometric modeling system and a standard set of analytic tools for tasks such as finite-element and boundary-element analysis. Over the last five years, CAD tools are being extended to include design heuristics. These heuristics come in several forms: as rules, as constraints and as recommendations. It is only very recently that a third aspect of the design process, namely reasoning from past cases, is beginning to be addressed in the Design Automation literature [Mostow 85, Ullman & Dietterich 87, Huhns 87, Carbonell 86, Mostow & Barley 87, Navinchandra et.al. 87]. Cases provide memories of past failures and solutions which can be used to warn the problem solver of impending problems and to repair failures without having to work from scratch [Hammond 86, Kolodner 87]. It is our aim to develop an understanding of how case-based reasoning (CBR) can be integrated into current design automation systems.

2. CBR in Design

A common paradigm used in design automation is that of state-space search. At the core of such systems are two modules: a *synthesis* module and an *evaluation* module. The synthesis module, works within a specified design representation and generates partial designs. The evaluator applies heuristics to select promising alternatives. The selected partial designs are returned to the synthesis module for further detailing. The process continues till a satisficing design is obtained. As the process is inherently combinatoric, clever techniques are used to prune the search early and decisively. Such techniques include constraint propagation, constraint posting [Baykan & Fox 87], failure-handling heuristics [Brown & Chandrasekaran 86], recommendation mechanisms [Mittal 85], and the use of abstraction and refinement techniques. We believe that CBR is yet another technique which can helps prune the search by finding problems early. In addition, CBR reduces the tree size by solving problems directly, that is, without searching from scratch. We have developed a design tool, CYCLOPS which uses CBR in this way. CYCLOPS operates in the domain of Landscape Planning and Design. The program works on problems involving the layout of new neighborhoods. It generates alternatives and solves problems as it goes. CYCLOPS' basic search mechanism produces alternatives which are examined by a case-based reasoning module. The characteristics of the design alternatives cause the reminding of cases. The retrieval of cases is based on matching the characteristics of the case (base) and the current design (target) in three ways:

1. **Direct Match.** If the attributes of base and target are the same, the base is immediately retrieved for consideration.

2. **Relaxed Match.** The attributes of base and target are matched by moving up and/or down an object hierarchy (pre-defined). For example, a base about dogs might match a target about cats because they are both domestic pets.

3. **Systematicity-based Match.** The systematicity-principle states that, in order to find an analogical match, between base and target, it is more important ot find common causal relationships among attributes in base and target rather than just common attributes [Gentner & Toupin 86]. Analogical matching is achieved in CYCLOPS by storing, with each case, a causal explanation of the goals and sub-goals of the case.

Using the above matching techniques, the program is able to find potential failures in target designs. This is done by finding a matching base involving some past design failure. In addition, the matching techniques are used to find cases which solve design problems. This is done in a goal-directed fashion. The problem solving process is composed of the following steps: finding the problem, setting up corresponding goals and sub-goals, finding appropriate cases and applying relevant sub-parts of the case to achieve the goals and sub-goals. The process is recursively applied till all sub-goals are addressed. As a result, a final solution may include ideas drawn from several cases. These cases can be from a variety of sources: from the domain of the current design problem (direct match), from a similar domain (relaxed match), or from a completely different domain (analogical match). In this paper, we present a problem-solving technique which incorporates the ideas presented above. The technique is called ***Demand Posting***. Examples of how the Demand Posting technique is used in CYCLOPS are shown below:

<u>House on a steep hillside - 1</u>

A problem solver is attempting to locate a house on a steep hillside. It decides to place the house directly on the ground. As soon as it does this, it is reminded of a situation in which it had placed a green-block on an incline and the block had become tilted. It's explanation of the situation was that the block is tilted because it is on a tilted surface. Using this explanation it infers that the house will also be tilted (this is done by a relaxed match between the house and the block which happen to be rectangular-paralellepipeds).

The problem solver has recognized that the house will be tilted. It then uses a domain rule to infer that tilted houses are problematic and that the problem needs to be solved:

<u>House on a steep hillside - 2</u>

The problem solver now has the goal of answering the question: "Is there any way of getting rid of the house's tilt?" Using the goal as an index, it looks for an appropriate case, but fails to find one. It then tries to find reasons for the problem. Going back to the explanation of the green-block case it used earlier, it explains the house's tilt as being due to two facts: (a) the house is on the ground and, (b) the ground is steep.

When the CYCLOPS used the block case to recognize that the house will be tilted, it keeps track of the explanation provided in the case. The explanation is used to find the reasons for design problems. Having found two reasons, the program treats them as disjunct sub-goals for solving the problem:

<u>House on a steep hillside - 3</u>

> Using the two reasons for tilt, the program sets up two disjunctive sub-goals to answer the following two questions: (a) "Is there any way of not having the house on the ground?", and, (b) " Is there any way of making the ground not so steep?". While examining the first sub-goal, the problem solver remembers seeing pictures of village homes in Thailand. The pictures showed huts on stilts. The corresponding explanation is that the villagers, who were having problems with flooding and ground dampness, found a way of getting their homes off the ground. They put their huts on stilts. Drawing from this explanation, the problem solver decides to put its house on stilts. It then verifies the action by looking for a case which might detect a new problem. If no such case is found, and if all conjunctive sub-goals are satisfied, it claims success and stops.

When CYCLOPS finds an applicable case it extracts the appropriate action (e.g. use of stilts) and applies the action. When the action is taken, the system appropriately updates all other inferences made. For example, when it decides to put the house on stilts, the original fact that the house is on the ground is not true anymore. Consequently, the green-block case and the rule used to infer tilt, lose support and are retracted. This truth-maintenance facility is built into the Demand Posting technique. In addition to retracting decisions as new cases are brought to bear, the system keeps track of all disjunctive sub-goals. If it fails to find solutions along one path, it is able to backtrack in order to examine other paths.

The examples above, provide an intuitive introduction to the Demand Posting technique. In the rest of the paper we will present representation and implementation details of the algorithm.

3. Demand Posting: Some Background

The *demand posting* technique: (a) performs goal-directed reasoning; (b) manages goals and dependencies among them, using a Truth-Maintenance like framework; (c) builds explanations of solutions to cases as it solves them (this allows reusing the solution as a new case). The main idea behind this technique is that CBR in a design system can be controlled through a process of asking relevant questions and modifying them appropriately. For example, imagine yourself trying to open a screw in your terminal but you don't have a screwdriver. You pose a question to yourself: "Can I think of some other item that will serve as a screwdriver[1]?" Another example: You have just built a tree-house on the branch of a large tree. However, the branch is sagging too much, you ask yourself the question: "Can I think of some way of making the branch stronger[2]?" Such questions are actually demands that are posted to your long term memory. Posting demands on oneself, also called self-interrogation, has been studied by researchers interested in the psychology of creativity. Osborn's work on Brainstorming [Osborn 53] is particularly interesting. He suggests that self-interrogation can lead to creative ideas. In this book *Applied Imagination*, he suggests that one of the ways of brainstorming is to redefine the

---

[1] You end up using your thumb nail.

[2] You end up putting an angle brace under the branch.

problem question by finding and addressing the causes and effects of the problem[3]. In other words, if you cannot think of a way to solve the given problem directly, try addressing its causes. CYCLOPS uses this technique to solve design problems.

The demand posting technique helps CYCLOPS solve design problems by drawing analogies. Whenever CYCLOPS encounters a design problem which does not directly match any past experience, it tries to reason by analogy. Drawing an analogy requires the ability to match a precedent and the target problem even though they have very different characteristics. In our example we saw how a landscape designer, faced with the problem of locating a house on a steep slope, solves the problem by placing the house on stilts. In the example, he got this idea by reasoning analogically from a precedent about how villagers in Thailand put their huts on stilts in order to avoid flooding. Notice that the purpose for using stilts in the base precedent is different from the purpose of the target problem. The matching is not based on surface features of base and target but on a deeper understanding of <u>why</u> the huts are put on stilts. CYCLOPS performs this kind of reasoning by matching against the subgoals in the explanation of the precedent case. This part of the Demand Posting technique is called *subgoal matching*.

The subgoal matching technique can successfully solve design problems only if it is provided with a good set of precedents to draw analogies from. The cases, however, have to be identified from a large case knowledge base (CKB). Techniques for achieving this have been suggested by researchers working on the psychological aspects of human creativity and problem solving. The developers of techniques such as Brainstorming [Osborn 53] and Synectics [Gordon 61] suggest that questions serve as cues into memory and help retrieve appropriate precedents. CYCLOPS performs this kind of reasoning by redefining the problem question given to it. For example, given a problem X the program first asks: "Is there a known way of eliminating X?" If it cannot find an appropriate case, it then asks: "What are the causes of X?", "If it is not known how to eliminate X, can its causes be eliminated?", "Can its effects be reduced or eliminated?". This questioning process is recursively applied until a solution is found. The implemented version of this technique is called *dependency tracking*. The demand posting technique combines dependency tracking and subgoal matching into one problem solving algorithm. Dependency tracking helps identify relevant cases and subgoal matching extracts relevant knowledge from the cases.

4. Demand Posting: Intuitive Ideas
In this section we will see how precedent cases can be used to recognize a problem in a design and how the problem can be solved by CBR. The following section re-views the same example providing implementation details.

Let us start by examining the representation used. In the CYCLOPS system a case is any observation made by the problem solver. An observation has two parts: first, the conditions which existed at the time the observation was made; second, the consequences (effects) of the observed conditions. For example, while playing with wooden blocks, a child might make the observation that: "placing the green-block on a tilted surface causes the block to be tilted." After gaining some experience with blocks, the child might develop an explanation for the observation.

---

[3]The book introduces several other self-interrogation techniques: (1) Can it be put to **other uses**? Are there new ways to use? (2) Can I **adapt**? What else is like this? (3) **Modify**? New twist? (4) **Magnify**? **Minify**? Longer? Larger? Condensed? (5) **Substitute**? Other ingredients? Other power source? (6) **Redefine**? What are the causes and effects? Can rearrange? (7) Can I **reverse**? Turn upside down? (8) **Combine**? Blend? Alloy?

The explanation would capture the fact that the color of the block is irrelevant to the observation. This gives us two types of cases: *unexplained-observations* and *explained-observations*. A third type of observation is an *explained-solution* case. A solution case is composed of two parts, each of which is an explained-observation case. The first case describes a problem situation and the second case describes the solution. These three types of cases make up CYCLOPS' case knowledge base (CKB).

Let us now return to the problem solving examples we examined earlier. In the first example we saw how the problem solver recognizes that the house will be tilted and that a tilted house is unfavorable. The problem is recognized using the following explained-observation case and If-Then rule:

Precedent#123

conditions:	a green block-1 placed on sloped ground
effects:	the block-1 becomes tilted
explanation:	the block-1 is tilted because it is on the ground and the ground is sloped

---

Rule#668

IF:	house is tilted
THEN:	unfavorable: "tilted-house"

The program matches the conditions of the problem to the precedent and infers that the house will be tilted if it is placed directly on the steep slope. This is done by matching against the explanation of the precedent. The explanation represents the real cause for tilt, and helps eliminate detractors such as color of the block. Further, the matching of "house" and "block-1" is based on the fact that they are both rectangular parallelipipeds.

Following the use of Precedent#123, the Rule#668 fires and the program infers the clause: *(unfavorable "tilted-house")*. Whenever CYCLOPS infers an "unfavorable" clause, it treats the clause as a problem that needs to be fixed. The problem is solved using the demand posting technique. As discussed in the previous section, the demand posting process is comprised of two parts Dependency Tracking and Sub-goal Matching. Let us see how the program solves the "tilted-house" problem, the first step is dependency tracking:

Dependency Tracking:
The process starts by asking the following question:

Q1: Is there some precedent that can achieve: *(not (unfavorable "tilted-house"))* ?

If no precedent case is found, the question is transformed by replacing the current problem by its cause. According to Rule#668, the cause of *(unfavorable "tilted-house")* is the clause *(house is tilted)*. The new question reads:

Q2: Is there some precedent that can achieve: *(not (house is tilted))* ?

Assume no case is found. Once again, the cause of the current problem is retrieved. According to the explanation of Precedent#123, the house is tilted because it is placed on the ground and because the ground is sloped. There are two causes, negating either of the causes will solve the problem. Two new questions are posted:

Q3a: Is there some precedent that can achieve: *(not (house on the ground))* ?

OR

Q3b: Is there some precedent that can achieve: *(not (ground is sloped))* ?

Using Q3a, the program finds a case about how huts in Thailand are put on stilts to protect them from floods. Based on this precedent, the program decides to use stilts for achieving: *(not (house on ground))*. By using stilts, the program solves the original problem of putting a house on a steep slope. The program is able to match Q3a with the precedent by examining the subgoals in the explanation of the precedent. We will now see how precedents are represented to facilitate this kind of reasoning.

Subgoal Matching:
The precedent about how villagers in Thailand put their homes on stilts to prevent them from floods is shown below. The precedent is a explained-solution case.

Precedent#1002

Initial Situation:

conditions:	the hut is on the ground and the ground is flooded and the hut is in Thailand
effects:	the hut is water-logged and is unfavorable
explanation:	(B1) the hut is unfavorable <u>because</u> it is water-logged
	(B2) the hut is water-logged <u>because</u> it is on the ground <u>and</u> ground is flooded

Solution:

action:	put the hut on stilts
effects:	the hut is not unfavorable
explanation:	(B3) the hut is not unfavorable <u>because</u> the hut is made not water-logged <u>and</u> (B1) is true
	(B4) the hut is not water-logged <u>because</u> the hut is not on the ground <u>and</u> (B2) is true[4]
	(B5) the hut is not on the ground <u>because</u> it was originally on the ground <u>and</u> the following action was taken: "put the hut on stilts".

The precedent has two parts: a situation and a solution. The first part describes the problem and provides an explanation of the problem. The second part describes how the problem was solved. The explanation consists of causal relations among conditions, effects and actions. The relations in the solution part of the precedent represent how subgoals are achieved. The main goal of the precedent it to achieve: "the hut is not unfavorable" and the subgoals are: "hut is not water-logged" and "hut is not on ground". As the second subgoal (B5) matches the demand Q3a (shown in the previous section), the causal relation B5 is transferred from base to target. Hence, the problem is solved by placing the house on stilts.

Having taken an intuitive look at demand posting, let us now examine how precedents are represented in the computer and what steps are taken by the program when it reasons from precedent cases.

---

[4] In english, this relation would read as follows: "The hut is not water logged because it is not on the ground anymore, which is true because, the original reason for the hut being water logged was that it was on flooded ground."

5. Demand Posting: Details

In this section we will re-trace the tilted house example while providing implementation details. The example started with the use of Precedent#123 (Page 4) to recognize that the house will be tilted. In a semantic network form, the precedent may be represented as shown below:

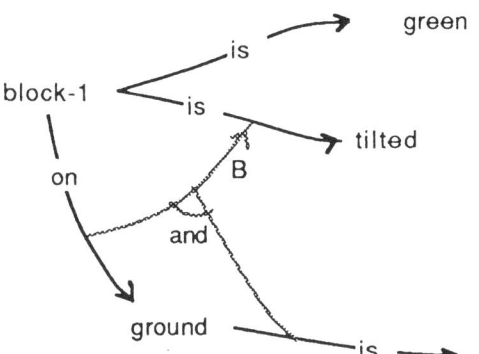

Figure 5-1: Block on a slope: semantic network representation

The figure shows three types of links: attribute links ("is"), an inter-object link ("on") and a causal relation ("B"[5]). The purpose of the causal relation is to specify the structure of the precedent [Gentner 83]. The causal relation in the precedent reads as follows: "The block is tilted because the block is on the ground and the ground is sloped." Attributes (e.g. color) which are not part of the causal structure are not as important [Gentner & Toupin 86]. Although we will continue to keep the fact that the block is green, we will ignore that property while using the precedent to infer causes for tilt. Let us now redraw the precedent, highlighting its causal structure.

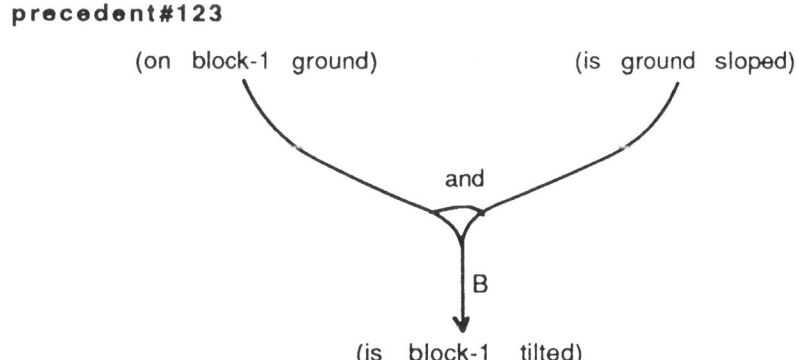

Figure 5-2: Block-1 is tilted **Because** block-1 is on the ground and the ground is sloped

Assume that the design at hand has the following clauses in its description: *(on house ground)* and *(is ground sloped)*. The program matches these clauses with Precedent#123 to infer that the house will be tilted. It matches "block-1" and "house" by walking up and down an object hierarchy. The program uses a hierarchy like the one shown below.

---

[5]The letter "B" denotes the word "Because"

293

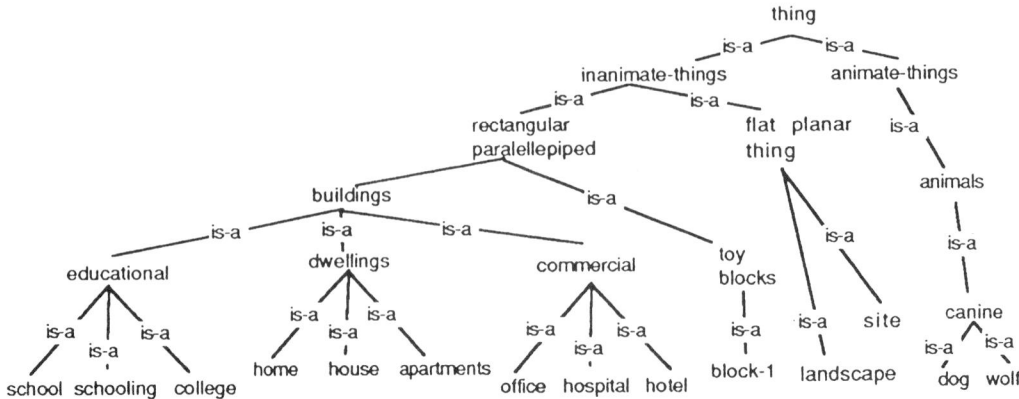

Figure 5-3: Object Hierarchy: used for relaxed matching only

The only purpose of this hierarchy is to match clauses indirectly. CYCLOPS will match any two objects (at the leaves) which are separated by up to six links[6]. This kind of matching is called ***relaxed matching***. After performing the match and inferring from the Rule#668, the design's problem is represented as:

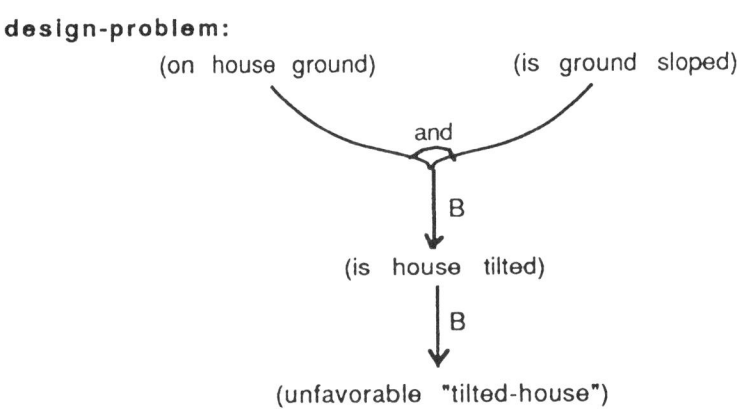

Figure 5-4: The design problem's causal structure

Whenever CYCLOPS infers an "unfavorable" clause, it reports the clause as a design problem that needs fixing. CYCLOPS then enters the demand posting process:

Let us assume, that the first precedent to be examined is the one about huts in Thailand. Using a causal structure representation similar to that of Figure 5-2, the Precedent#1002 is represented as shown in Figure 5-5. The figure has two parts: a situation and a solution. These parts correspond to those shown in the text of the precedent (page 6).

---

[6]There is no theoretical justification for the amount of relaxation allowed. All one can do is to prefer matches which require less number of links to be traversed. CYCLOPS leaves it up to the user to reject matches which seem outrageous.

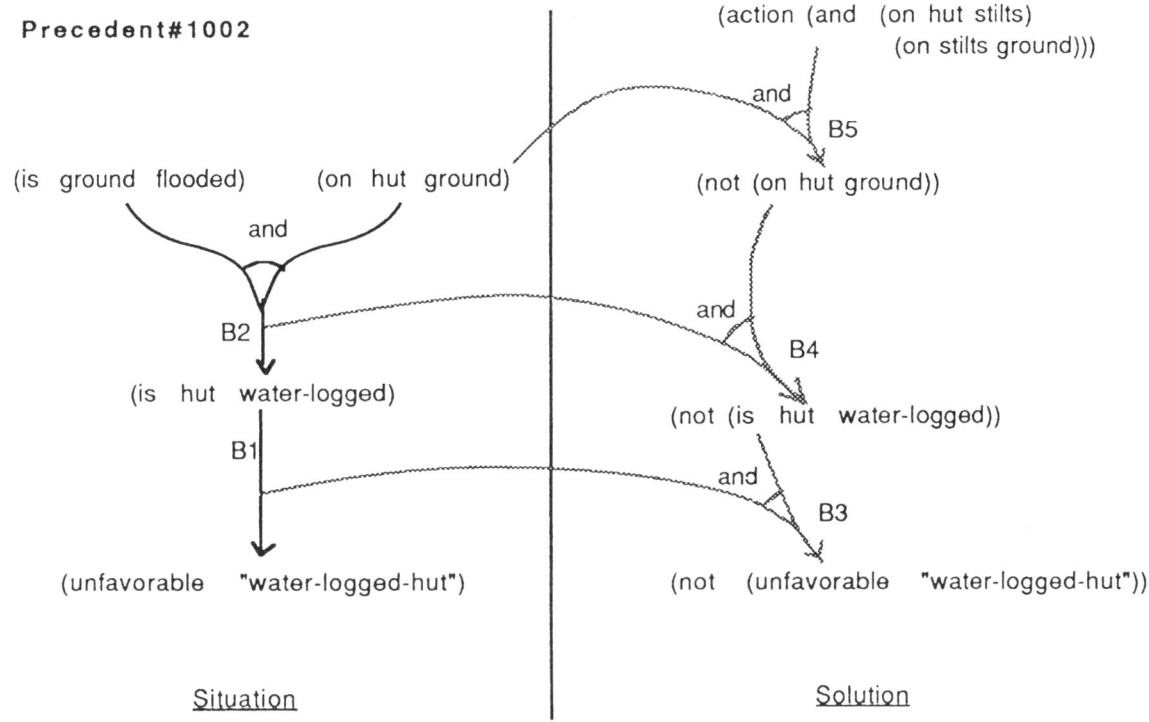

Figure 5-5: Thailand precedent's causal structure

The precedent above has five causal relations:

B1: (unfavorable "water-logged-hut") because (is hut water-logged)

B2: (is hut water-logged) because (and (is ground flooded) (on hut ground))

B3: (not (unfavorable "water-logged-hut")) because (and (B1 is true) (not (is hut water-logged))

B4: (not (is hut water-logged)) because (and (B2 is true) (not (on hut ground)))

B5: (not (on hut ground)) because (and (on hut ground)
(action (and (on hut stilts) (on stilts ground))))

The aim of the demand posting process is to derive a solution to the problem situation of Figure 5-4. The final situation-solution pair will look like the one for the Thailand case (Figure 5-5). The derivation process starts by posting the following question as the first demand:

Q1: *(not (unfavorable "tilted-house"))* ?

The program then tries to match the question against the causal relations of the precedents in the CKB. As no match is found, the cause of the problem is retrieved and posted as a new demand (Q2).

Posting of the first question is shown in Figure 5-6 Part **A**. As the program cannot find an answer

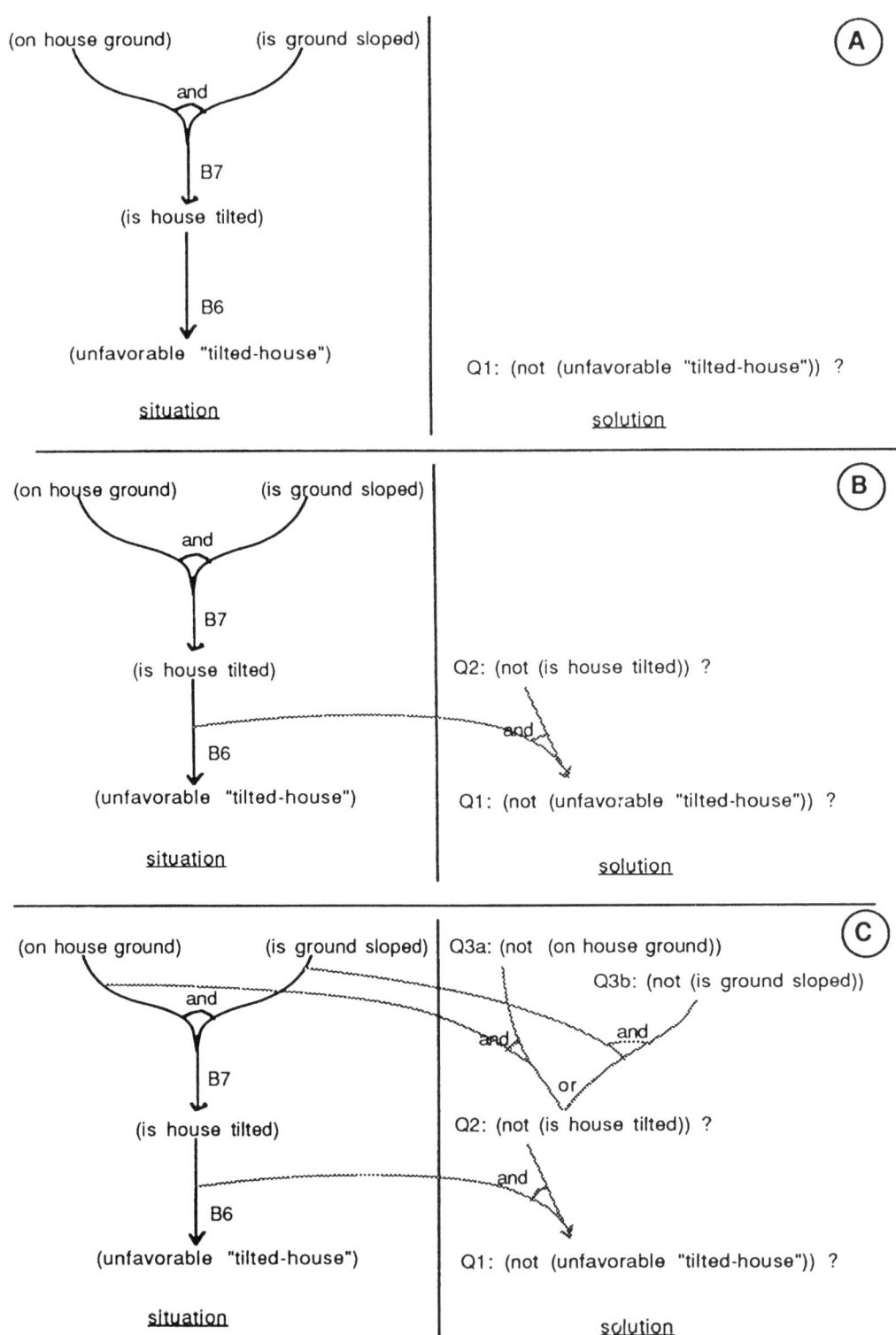

Figure 5-6: Posting Questions Q1, Q2 and Q3

to Q1, it then posts Q2 which corresponds to the cause of Q1. The posting of the second question (Q2) is shown in Figure 5-6 Part **B**. The program justifies Q2 by a causal relation (gray line) which represents the following reasoning: "Q2 can substitute for Q1 because B6 is true." The demand in Q2 is tried against the causal relations of the precedents in the CKB. As no match is found, the question is transformed by retrieving the causes of the latest demand. This is shown in Figure 5-6. The figure shows that the demand in Q2 can be solved by answering either Q3a or Q3b. Once again, the demands are tried against the relations in the CKB. This time, the causal relation: B5 of Figure 5-5 is found to have a subgoal that matches the given demand. The matching is shown in the Figure 5-7.

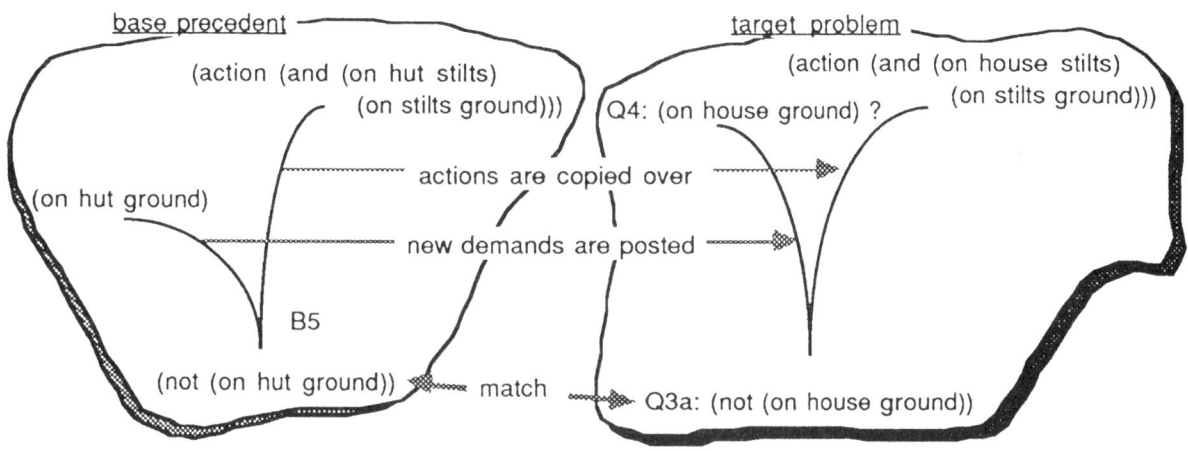

Figure 5-7: The matching of causal structure between base and target

As the clause in Q3a and the clause on the left hand side of B5 match, the causal structure of B5 is transferred to the target problem[7]. The action is copied over directly and a new demand is posted: *(on hut ground)*. If it turns out that the clause *(on house ground)* is already true in the target problem's description, the original goal of achieving *(not (on house ground))* is deemed solved.

Next the Problem solver tries to verify the solution by going back to the CKB to find any case which can detect a problem with the solution. Let's assume that a case is found which requires that the ground be firm for putting stilts. A new demand *(is ground firm ?)* is posted to the CKB. The rest of the problem solving process proceeds like this:

<u>House on Steep Hillside - 4</u>

In order to achieve the sub-goal *(is ground firm)* the problem solver looks for precedent cases which contain the sub-goal in their descriptions or explanations. It then finds a case about the use of piles to make landfills strong enough to support buildings. One of the subgoals of using piles is to make the landfill's soil firm. Using this precedent, the problem solver decides to drive piles into the ground. After solving the problem in this way, it re-invokes the CBR process to find whether any new problems are generated. If no problems are found, the solution is deemed correct.

---

[7]This idea of matching and transferring of causal structure is borrowed from Winston [Winston et.al. 83].

In this way, the demand posting process uses cases to find problems, uses the problems to retrieve new cases, keep track of dependencies among goals and sub-goals and solves problems analogically.

6. Conclusions

6.1. Some Observations about Demand Posting

Multiple support for a problem. What happens if there are two or more independent causes for a problem? When the demand posting algorithm finds a way of eliminating a problem, it unasserts the corresponding clause. If there are other independent causes for the clause, the program is fooled into believing that the problem is solved. This situation, however, is only temporary. When CYCLOPS enters the next inference cycle, the problem clause will be re-asserted if there is independent support for it.

Learning. When the demand posting process is used to solve a problem, the resulting situation-solution structure can be used as a precedent in future problems.

Completeness assumption for causal relations. The causal relations in a precedent are treated independently. For example, the relation B2 (page 9) which reads: "the hut is water-logged because the hut is on the ground and the ground is flooded" is a statement that stands alone[8]. However, some relations are dependent on others, for example B4 is dependent on B2. We assume that a causal relation is complete and that it carries the complete context in its body.

Closed world assumption. CYCLOPS does not actively verify analogies. When an analogy is drawn, the modified design is posted to the CKB. If none of the precedent cases find a new problem, the analogy is deemed correct. We are making the assumption that if a clause cannot be inferred from the knowledge possessed, then it is false. This is a closed world assumption on the knowledge base.

Indexing many precedents. Based on the completeness assumption, all the causal relations of all the precedents are indexed independently. The index is based on the clauses that the relations they assert. We currently use a hash-based indexing mechanism, only because it serves our immediate needs. For very large databases, a discrimination-network based technique could be used for indexing [Kolodner 80].

6.2. Future work

The use of explanation-based methods for CBR has been found to be useful. Particularly for reasoning from cases which do not apply directly to the problem at hand. A problem with our current approach, however, is that the explanations stored in the cases are pre-determined and are static. When a case-based inference is made, the knowledge transferred from base to target is limited to the structure of the explanations in the base. Pre-determining an explanation of a base, pre-determines the ways in which the case can be reused, it fixes the view of the case. In the future, however, we would like to derive explanations on demand, that is, in response to the purpose for which the case is being used. We believe, that work on purpose-directed analogy [Kedar-Cabelli 85] will lead the way for future research in this area. Another related challenge is

---

[8]This is similar to the explanations used in XPs [Schank 86]

to develop a case knowledge base organization scheme which indexes cases not only on their attributes but also on the explanations of the relations among attributes. This is particularly difficult, because the explanations are not fixed, but change in response to the purpose for which the cases are being retrieved.

References

[Baykan & Fox 87]
Baykan, C.A., M.S. Fox.
An Investigation of Opportunistic Constraint Satisfaction In Space Planning.
In *Proceedings of the Tenth International Joint Conference on Artificial Intelligence*, pages 1035-1038. August 23-28, 1987.

[Brown & Chandrasekaran 86]
Brown D.C., B. Chandrasekaran.
Expert Systems for a class of Mechanical Design Activity.
In Sriram D., Adey B. (editor), *Proceedings of the First International Conference on AI applications in Engineering*. Computational Mechanics, U.K., 1986.

[Carbonell 86]
Carbonell, J. G.
Derivational Analogy: A Theory of Reconstructive Problem Solving and Expertise Acquisition.
In Michalski, R. S., J. G. Carbonell, T. M. Mitchell (editor), *Machine Learning: An Artificial Intelligence Approach Vol 2*. Morgan Kaufman, 1986.

[Gentner 83]
Gentner, D.
Structure Mapping: A Theoretical Framework for Analogy.
Cognitive Science 7, 1983.

[Gentner & Toupin 86]
Gentner, D., C. Toupin.
Systematicity and Surface Similarity in the Development of Analogy.
Cognitive Science 10:277-300, 1986.

[Gordon 61]
Gordon W.J.
Synectics: The development of Creative Capacity.
Harper & Row, Publishers, NY, 1961.

[Hammond 86]
Hammond, K.J.
CHEF: A Model of Case-based Planning.
In *Proceedings of AAAI-86*, pages 267-271. 1986.

[Huhns 87]
Huhns M.H., R.D. Acosta.
Argo: An Analogical Reasoning System for Solving Design Problems.
Technical Report AI/CAD-092-87, Microelectronic and Computer Technology Corporation, March, 1987.

[Kedar-Cabelli 85]
Kedar-Cabelli S. T.
Purpose-Directed Analogy.
In *Proceedings of the Cognitive Science Society Conference*. August, 1985.

[Kolodner 80]
Kolodner, J.L.
Retrieval and organizational strategies in conceptual memory: A computer model.
PhD thesis, Yale University, 1980.

[Kolodner 87]   Kolodner, J.L.
Extending Problem Solver Capabilities Through Case-Based Inference.
In *Proceedings of the Machine Learning Workshop*. June, 1987.

[Mittal 85]   Mittal, S., Dym, C. and Morjaria, M.
PRIDE: An Expert System for the Design of Paper Handling Systems.
In Dym, C. (editor), *Applications of Knowledge-Based Systems to Engineering Analysis and Design*, pages 99-116. American Society of Mechanical Engineers, 1985.

[Mostow 85]   Mostow, J.
Toward Better Models Of The Design Process.
The AI Magazine, Spring, 1985.

[Mostow & Barley 87]
Mostow, J., M. Barley.
Automated Reuse of Design Plans.
In *Proceedings of the International Conference on Engineering Design*. February, 1987.

[Navinchandra et.al. 87]
Navinchandra D., D. Sriram, S.T. Kedar-Cabelli.
On the Role of Analogy in Engineering Design: An Overview.
In D. Sriram, B. Adey (editor), *AI in Engineering, Proceedings of the 2nd Intl. Conference, Boston*. Computational Mechanics Publishing, U.K., 1987.

[Osborn 53]   Osborn, A. F.
Applied Imagination.
Charles Scribner's Sons, New York, 1953.

[Schank 86]   Schank, R.C.
Explanation Patterns: Understanding Mechanically and Creatively.
Lawrence Erlbaum Associates, Hillsdale, NJ, 1986.

[Ullman & Dietterich 87]
Ullman, D.G., T.A. Dietterich.
Mechanical Design Methodology: Implications on Future Developments of Computer-Aided Design and Knowledge-Based Systems.
Engineering with Computers 2:21-29, 1987.

[Winston et.al. 83]
Winston, P. H., T.O. Binford, B. Katz, M. Lowry.
Learning Physical Descriptions from Functional Definitions, Examples and Precedents.
In *Proceedings of AAAI-83*. August, 1983.

Domain-Independent Prototype Cases for Planning *

Christopher Owens
Yale University

March 15, 1988

1 Introduction

The motivating idea behind case-based reasoning is compelling and direct: since people obviously learn from experience and reuse old solutions to solve new problems, why not have intelligent computers do the same thing? Rather than expect system builders, domain experts and knowledge engineers to figure out, code and enter into memory all the abstract rules that a system would ever need in order to function, why not just give the machine a large library of experiences and some mechanism for applying those experiences to the task of solving new problems? Furthermore, once this mechanism for recalling specific experiences and applying them to solving new problems is in place, why not allow the system to expand its own library of experiences as it encounters new problems and solves them?

The idea is compelling because it attempts to address two difficult problems that must be solved in order for intelligent systems to exist. Case-based reasoning (henceforth CBR) addresses the questions of how a system can learn from experience, and how a system can represent and store the huge library of individually trivial, seemingly unconnected facts that it must have at its disposal in order to reason.

Knowledge, of course, consists of more than just a big library of undigested experiences. Although in some sense all knowledge ultimately derives from experience (other than the low-level knowledge that can be said to be "wired in"), it does not necessarily follow that all knowledge is represented in memory as a trace of the experience from which it was derived. People can access, apply and reason about commonly-used abstractions like

Don't do something if it has an unacceptable side effect

without having to dredge up a memory of a specific experience in which this generalization held, and without each time having to form from scratch the analogy between that prior experience and the current situation. The abstract knowledge exists as more than just an emergent property of a large number of cases; it has a distinct existence of its own. Although it may have been learned from a number of specific experiences, it exists as a knowledge

---

*This work was supported in part by the Defense Advanced Research Projects Agency and the Office of Naval Research under contract N00014-85-K-0108 and by the Air Force Office of Scientific Research under contract AFOSR-85-0343

structure independent of any of those experiences. The specific experiences underlying this generalization have been abstracted away or compiled away.

On the other hand, viewing this abstract knowledge as totally distinct from cases is probably a mistake. Can anything we learn from building case-based reasoning systems help us with the task of representing and using abstract, domain-independent knowledge? In this paper I examine CBR from the point of view of processing, briefly discussing the kinds of knowledge structures and memory mechanisms necessary to reason from cases. I explore the potential for these knowledge representations and processing mechanisms to help a system deal with abstract knowledge. I present a scheme for representing and indexing domain-independent planning knowledge using prototypical cases, a scheme that has as its basis the idea of common advice-giving proverbs and the abstract knowledge they represent.

2 A view of case-based reasoning

The CBR approach can be characterized as relying upon memories of specific experiences rather than upon rules or abstract generalizations. A case-based system does not explicitly know or manipulate a lot of rules and generalizations, but it is able to create generalizations as needed. The generalizations are implicit in the way experience is represented in memory, and in the way the memory selects which cases to supply in support of a particular reasoning task.

2.1 The goals of CBR

Reasons for taking a case-based approach to building an intelligent system are both practical and theoretical. On the practical side, case-based systems do not require that knowledge about the system's domain be expressed as rules or formal abstractions, thereby obviating the need for a massive knowledge engineering effort. Since domain knowledge is expressed instead as a set of representations of individual experiences, decisions about what to abstract and how far to generalize would ideally be made as needed by the system. Second, again speaking ideally, knowledge about how to deal with rule interactions would not have to be expressed as complex and specialized exceptions to individual rules, but would instead be handled dynamically by the process that selects relevant cases and adapts them to new situations. Third, since the mechanism for adapting old experiences to novel situations must exist at the fundamental core of a case-based system, case-based systems should be more flexible in dealing with unforeseen input.

On the theoretical side, case-based reasoning systems promise a good deal of psychological realism. Whereas expressing knowledge as rules has typically been unnatural and viewed as a problem by domain experts, anecdotal evidence has suggested that domain experts are more easily able to express their knowledge as a set of relevant cases. More formal experiments to test this have been suggested and would be worthwhile. Furthermore, while domain experts have found it difficult to justify their conclusions by citing specific rules, anecdotal evidence in [Bain 86] has tended to suggest that domain experts can find precedents for their conclusions in specific cases.

2.2 The mechanisms of CBR

So what components must a case-based reasoning system embody? The fundamental approach to building a CBR system is that relevant old experiences must be recalled at the time that new problems are being solved, and that, once retrieved, they contain information that will be useful to the current problem-solving task. A "generic" CBR problem-solving algorithm, stated at an extremely abstract level, looks something like:

1. Do a preliminary analysis of the current situation to identify indices.
2. Retrieve old cases that share the same indices.
3. Pick the most similar old case to the current situation
4. Analyze the differences between the old case and the current situation.
5. Use the differences to modify the solution in the old case.
6. Apply the modified solution to the current problem.

For this skeleton algorithm to be made more specific, and for case-based reasoners to be useful, several problems must be solved. Among them are two that are relevant here: what a case should look like in memory and how similarity between the current case and cases in memory should be defined.

2.2.1 The structure of cases

Deciding what a case should look like in memory is important because it is the content of retrieved cases that provides the knowledge that the system needs to solve new problems. It is not really true that a case contains an undigested record of a prior experience: a case must contain a trace of some reasoning as well. For a case-based planner like that in [Hammond 86], a case contains a record of a prior plan, possibly including a record of failures that have been encountered while using that plan and solutions to those failures. For case-based problem solvers like those in [Bain 86], [Simpson 85] and [Sycara 87], cases contain descriptions of problems and annotations as to what solution was chosen for each problem. For a case-based explainer like the one in [Kass et. al. 86] each case is a compound causal structure linking together the subcomponents of an explanation, with each component annotated as to how it fits into the explanation. Far from being undigested records of experiences, these cases contain a lot of causal or other structuring information, and it is this information that is used when the case is applied to novel situations.

Since cases must in fact be at least partly analyzed in order to store this causal information with the case, what is the point of preserving any episodic content at all with the case? Why not just do a complete analysis and store the result? The answer lies in the area of learning and case modification. If all the system's analyses were guaranteed to be correct and guaranteed to be indexed at exactly the right level of generality; if the system's only job were to retrieve the right old case and apply it to new situations, then there would be no reason to store any episodic content with cases. But if in fact the system's job is also to learn by modifying its cases and their indexing, then the concrete content of the cases is what guides this case adaptation and re-indexing process. For example, the believability assessments described in [Leake 88] and the modification strategies suggested in [Kass 86] depend upon concrete cases. When a case is deemed to be inapplicable to a new situation, the episodic contents of the case provide a starting point to suggest substitutions and modifications that can be made in the case; the causal content of the case constrains these modifications.

2.2.2 Choosing the indices

A memory allowing retrieval based on similarity is an important component in a case-based system, as pointed out in [Schank 82], [Kolodner and Cullingford 86] and elsewhere. Cases that bear some similarity to the current situation are obviously the ones to retrieve if one wants to use prior experience as the basis of reasoning. The natural way to implement this is to index cases in memory such that similar cases share common indices, and can consequently be retrieved together. But what kind of similarity should this process use?

Much of the conceptual work of CBR gets done when we define what constitutes similarity. It is clearly not enough for two cases to share a number of low-level perceptual features; the features that the cases share must be abstract enough that the solution indexed with a particular case is applicable to other cases that share those abstract features. Similarity has to be loose enough that cases from one domain can be applied to problems in another, assuming some abstract thematic content is shared. In other words, if a case is to have any broad applicability, the features under which it is indexed in memory must reflect some thematic abstraction. The analysis necessary to derive this thematic abstraction must be done at the time the case is acquired.

But thematic abstraction poses a problem for retrieval. The same kind of abstract indices that give good cross-domain remindings are likely to be the ones that are most difficult to notice in input cases, making the first step of the CBR algorithm, or pre-analysis, more difficult. The better an index is at triggering cross- contextual remindings, the more difficult it is going to be to identify in input.

CBR systems have been able to avoid this problem so far because domains have been fairly restricted, and the features under which cases are indexed have been correspondingly concrete. The memory-based system in [Stanfill and Waltz 86], for example, depends upon input cases being presented and described already translated into the same vocabulary under which old cases are indexed. Work on case retrieval has focused on how cases can organize domain knowledge, not so much on how cases can organize thematic abstraction. Often when systems have required thematic abstractions they have been distinctly separate from case memory, like the planning TOPs in CHEF. But if any of the mechanisms and data structures of case retrieval are to be applicable to retrieving abstract knowledge structures, or if case-based reasoners are to be set up for wide-ranging cross-contextual use of cases, the indexing vocabulary for cases must represent this.

3 CBR meets domain-independent planning

Choosing a case representation scheme and choosing an indexing vocabulary are of obvious importance to the kind of case-based reasoning systems outlined above, in which the primary role of cases is to organize specific knowledge. Can the solutions to these problems also be applied to the task of managing abstract knowledge? Can domain-independent knowledge be made to look like cases so that the same processes can be used with both? Is this a practical or realistic thing to do?

Although domain-independent knowledge enters into every kind of reasoning, the kind of domain-independent knowledge I focus on here is that relevant to the planning process. The use of abstract planning knowledge has been identified by [Sussman 75], [Sacerdoti 75], [Wilensky 83] and others. Plans are often made, evaluated and modified in light of abstract principles like:

- More of a good thing is better

- More of a good thing is worse

- An action has an undesirable side effect

- The cost or side effect of a plan must be endured

- The cost or side effect of a plan is not worth it.

- Time is of the essence; opportunity must be seized

- It pays to wait for favorable circumstances

As stated here, these structures are too abstract to be useful. Furthermore, pairs of them tend to offer contradictory conclusions without offering any means for differentiating between them. In short, they suffer from the faults one would associate with abstract rules. But these abstract structures often correspond to structures that people seem to possess, as witnessed by proverbs whose function it appears to be to capture this kind of planning knowledge:

Many hands make light work

Too many cooks spoil the broth

Make hay while the sun shines

If you chase after two rabbits you will catch neither

There is a general correspondence between proverbs and a class of abstract thematic knowledge, as has been noted by [Dyer 82], [Dyer and Lehnert 80], [Schank 86] and others. What does expressing an abstraction as a proverb add to its utility? Although the primary point of each of these proverbs seems to be to convey a particular abstraction, each proverb also conveys a prototype story. In its primary meaning, *Too many cooks* is not about cooks and broth. It is an abstraction about the bad consequences of putting multiple agents to work on a task. But packaged with the abstraction is a prototypical case involving cooks and broth.

Why should this be? Why should proverbs exist when the abstractions underlying them could be used instead? Why do people like and remember proverbs better than abstract rules? Again like real cases, the prototypical case contained in a proverb would never be needed if all the system did was retrieve abstractions and apply them. But if it becomes necessary to adapt, modify or re-index abstractions, the contents of the prototypical case become useful. For example, most of the time that one uses the proverb *Too many cooks spoil the broth* one would be just as well off using an abstraction like *Multiple agents cause a bad outcome*. But if it becomes necessary to discriminate between situations to which *Too many cooks* apply and those to which *Many hands make light work* apply, knowledge about cooks and cooking can be brought into play to formulate a more detailed representation of the proverb — for example,

> *Multiple agents performing a complex task involving multiple interacting steps yield a bad outcome.*

It is having the knowledge about the prototypical case of cooks spoiling broth that makes this refinement of the abstraction possible.

3.1 Issues for representation

If, as suggested above, a case representation includes some abstract information about the case, then the same basic kind of structure that is used for cases can be used for proverb-like representations of abstract knowledge. For both, the representation must concisely represent an abstraction for routine use, and it must also carry something that looks like a specific experience to back up the abstraction. For a conventional case, the underlying story is likely to be personal experience; for a proverb the underlying story is likely to be somebody else's experience, or more likely a made-up stereotypical story in which the particular abstraction applied.

So a proverbial knowledge structure must contain a representation of the abstraction, like *Multiple agents cause a bad outcome* and a representation of an underlying story such as a story about some broth being spoiled because, due to the large number of cooks involved, some recipe steps got executed twice and others not at all. [1]

3.1.1 A descriptive vocabulary

An important task in representing proverbs is developing a descriptive vocabulary that can also serve as a set of indices. If the proverbial knowledge is viewed as a set of concepts connected by relationships like causation, enablement, and prevention, then the goal of a vocabulary is to capture these connected subconcepts at an appropriate level of abstraction. Decomposing a large list of proverbs and finding the recurring subcomponents is a means of developing this vocabulary.

Work in this area is underway, with the goal to develop a set of core concepts for building representations of abstract planning proverbs, and a program to index and retrieve abstract

---

[1] Beneath the most abstract level (i.e. *Multiple agents cause a bad outcome*) people seem to have differing prototypical cases for this proverb. Some people say it is because the cooks got confused, others say it is because they were following different plans (someone trying to make tomato soup while somebody else thought they were making cream of spinach in the same pot), and others say it is because the cooks fought about who was going to be in charge. The idiosyncratic nature of these prototype cases in no way contradicts the theory that proverbs allow abstractions to be treated as cases.

planning knowledge structures. As an example of this level of abstraction, several of these concepts are:

- The passage of time
- Resources
- Opportunity
- Making choices
- Scaling (i.e. increasing the availability of a resource)
- Good outcome
- Bad outcome
- Side effect

The point is that these features are thematically abstract, yet they are not as causally complex or as extensively overarching as a complete proverb. They, together with causal connectors, are the primitives out of which representations of proverb-type knowledge are built. They are also the index elements under which the representations are stored in memory.

3.2 Issues for retrieval

The straightforward, first-pass approach to retrieving these abstract knowledge structures would be to express the input case in terms of the indexing vocabulary described above, and then to find the abstract cases that share the largest number of indexing features with the input case. The problem with this approach is that selecting the indexing vocabulary involves a tradeoff between indexing power and ease of index calculation. The indices that give the best cross-contextual or domain-independent retrieval are going to be difficult and expensive to extract from input descriptions. If, for example, an index were something like **bad side effect**, then the system would have to analyze the situation well enough to extract **bad side effect** from the input. But **bad side effect** is not there for the asking in the input description of the case, it takes inferential work to find it. If the system had already done enough inferential work to extract this abstraction from the input, then that represents a fairly deep level of understanding the input. If the input is already understood this deeply just to extract some indices, then what is the point of retrieving an abstract knowledge structure part of whose function it is to help identify bad side effect situations?

The world does not present episodes neatly represented in terms of a list of abstract features present in that episode. Nor does any plausible front-end to the understanding process. These abstract indices are not impossible to infer, they are just expensive to infer. If the number of possible indices is large, the front end to the planning process cannot be expected to determine which of them are present in a given situation. But given a list of only a few possibilities, however, the front end might reasonably be expected to verify which if any of them are present in the current situation. The front end, in other words, cannot be expected to suggest **Bad side effect** and the other abstract features that characterize a given situation, but it might be expected to answer the question of whether or not **Bad side effect** applies. There are indices that can be plausibly verified if requested by the memory retrieval process but that cannot be plausibly noticed out of the blue by the input process.

3.2.1 Incremental retrieval

Can anything be done to turn the task of abstract feature recognition into abstract feature verification? Since the system cannot be expected to check all of the possible abstract features against a given piece of input, can it be biased towards checking a few that are likely to be useful for this particular retrieval task?

If the cases in memory were static, and if the system were able to commit in advance to examining features in a particular order, then a discrimination tree would be extremely simple and would work well for this memory. The game program that plays "guess the animal in 20 questions" uses such a strategy. It can discriminate among N animals by worrying about at most log(N) features. This is clearly better than asking about all features in advance and then searching memory for animals that matched the supplied list, which is what the first-pass indexing approach above would suggest doing.

But case memory is not static, nor can the memory of a case-based reasoner commit in advance to worrying about features in a particular order. In order to try nevertheless to capture some of the advantages of the "20-questions" and discrimination tree approach, I have experimented with a retrieval scheme that incrementally develops a list of abstract features believed to be present in the input case, focusing on features that are believed to be likely to be good discriminators for the current search. The algorithm, based loosely on the data-level parallelism approach discussed in [Stanfill and Kahle 86], uses the case library itself to continually update its idea of which features have a high information content, with high information content features being those that tend to split the candidate pool nearly in half. In effect, the approach searches memory by dynamically reorganizing a tree of the remaining candidates at each step during an incremental retrieval process. Each time the system infers that a given abstract feature is either present or absent in the input, the pool of remaining candidates changes. The features that are examined next are those that are present in approximately half of the candidates, since verifying their presence or absence offers the most reward for inferencing effort.

The purpose of this discussion is not to suggest that incremental retrieval using a parallel architecture is a reasonable model of case retrieval, it is only to suggest that there exist methods of dealing with abstract features short of either on the one hand exhaustively checking each feature against the input situation or, on the other hand presupposing that either the world or a magic front-end presents the system with each new situation pre-represented in terms of the same features under which cases are indexed.

4 Conclusions

Case-based reasoning is a powerful approach to the problem of organizing large amounts of information and to the problem of learning from experience. But CBR is not itself a solution or an algorithm; it is a methodological approach whose success depends upon the solution of several problems in the area of memory. Two noteworthy problems are what the representation of a case should contain and how similarity between cases should be defined. Although CBR is typically viewed as a way to organize a large body of domain knowledge, work on these problems applies beyond domain-specific knowledge.

Expressing abstract planning knowledge in the form of proverb-like prototypical cases makes abstract knowledge structures look and act like cases, thereby taking advantage of the memory structures and retrieval and processing mechanisms that must be in place to do CBR. The abstract planning knowledge represented by a proverb can exist in memory, but the prototypical episode exists as well. The prototypical episode carries the role of a case in terms of being a handle by which memory can get hold of the abstraction if it needs to be modified or re-indexed.

Making domain-independent planning knowledge look like cases not only exploits these mechanisms, but also has psychological appeal, as witnessed by people's willingness to express and communicate abstract knowledge via proverbs.

Implementing this approach requires a stable vocabulary of simpler conceptual elements from which representations of abstract planning knowledge can be built, and a retrieval scheme to take advantage of this vocabulary.

References

[Bain 86] W.M. Bain. *Case-based Reasoning: A Computer Model of Subjective Assessment.* PhD thesis, Yale University, 1986. Technical Report 470.

[Dyer 82] M. Dyer. *IN-DEPTH UNDERSTANDING: A Computer Model of Integrated Processing For Narrative Comprehension.* Technical Report 219, Yale University Department of Computer Science, May 1982.

[Dyer and Lehnert 80] M.G. Dyer and W.G. Lehnert. *Memory Organization and Search Processes for Narratives.* Technical Report 175, Yale University Department of Computer Science, April 1980.

[Hammond 86] K.J. Hammond. *Case-based Planning: An Integrated Theory of Planning, Learning and Memory.* PhD thesis, Yale University, 1986. Technical Report 488.

[Kass 86] A. Kass. Modifying explanations to understand stories. In *Proceedings of the Eighth Annual Conference of the Cognitive Science Society*, Cognitive Science Society, Amherst, MA, August 1986.

[Kass et. al. 86] A. M. Kass, D. B. Leake, and C. C. Owens. Swale: a program that explains. 1986. In [Schank 86].

[Kolodner and Cullingford 86] J. Kolodner and R. Cullingford. Towards a memory architecture that supports reminding. In *Proceedings of the Eighth Annual Conference of the Cognitive Science Society*, Cognitive Science Society, Amherst, MA, August 1986.

[Leake 88] D. B. Leake. Using explainer needs to judge operationality. 1988. To appear in proceedings of the 1988 AAAI Spring Symposium on Explanation-based Learning.

[Sacerdoti 75] E.D. Sacerdoti. *A structure for plans and behavior.* Technical Report 109, SRI Artificial Intelligence Center, 1975.

[Schank 82] R.C. Schank. *Dynamic Memory: A Theory of Learning in Computers and People.* Cambridge University Press, 1982.

[Schank 86] R.C. Schank. *Explanation Patterns: Understanding Mechanically and Creatively.* Lawrence Erlbaum Associates, Hillsdale, NJ, 1986.

[Simpson 85] R.L. Simpson. *A Computer Model of Case-based Reasoning in Problem-solving: An Investigation in the Domain of Dispute Mediation.* PhD thesis, School of Information and Computer Science, Georgia Institute of Technology, 1985.

[Stanfill and Kahle 86] C. Stanfill and B. Kahle. Parallel free-text search on the connection machine system. *Communications of the ACM*, 29(12):1213–1228, December 1986.

[Stanfill and Waltz 86] C. Stanfill and D. Waltz. Toward memory-based reasoning. *Communications of the ACM*, 29(12):1213–1228, December 1986.

[Sussman 75] G.J. Sussman. *A computer model of skill acquisition.* Volume 1 of *Artificial Intelligence Series*, American Elsevier, New York, 1975.

[Sycara 87] E. P. Sycara. *Resolving Adversarial Conflicts: An Approach Integrating Case-based and Analytic Methods.* PhD thesis, School of Information and Computer Science, Georgia Institute of Technology, 1987.

[Wilensky 83] R. Wilensky. *Planning and Understanding.* Addison-Wesley, Reading, Mass, 1983.

An Interface for Case-Based Knowledge Acquisition

Christopher K. Riesbeck
Cognitive Systems, Inc.
Dept. of Computer Science, Yale University

March 14, 1988

Introduction

We believe that there are two major reasons why case-based reasoning (CBR) is an appropriate technology for building real-world expert systems. One is that the case-based approach is more practical for many domains where rules are very difficult to formalize or too large in number. The other is that the case-based approach better matches the thought processes of domain experts and end users, and hence, among other things, supports a simpler, non-programming interface for domain experts.

In this paper, we will attempt to support the latter claim by giving an example of a case library acquisition interface being developed at Cognitive Systems as part of its Case-based Reasoning Shell. As shown in Figure 1, the Interface is the key to building the *case library*. A case library is a set of cases plus a set of analysis and matching rules that determine how cases match each other.

The interface is designed to make it simple for the domain expert to input new cases, find old cases, modify how field values match, and what fields are most important in ranking the similarity of cases. At the end, we will touch briefly on the more difficult task of how the domain expert might specify the more complex rules that are needed to adapt cases to new situations.

Knowledge Acquisition in Rule-Based Systems

The success of any knowledge-based system depends critically on how easy it is to get knowledge into that system. When AI systems were primarily university projects, the

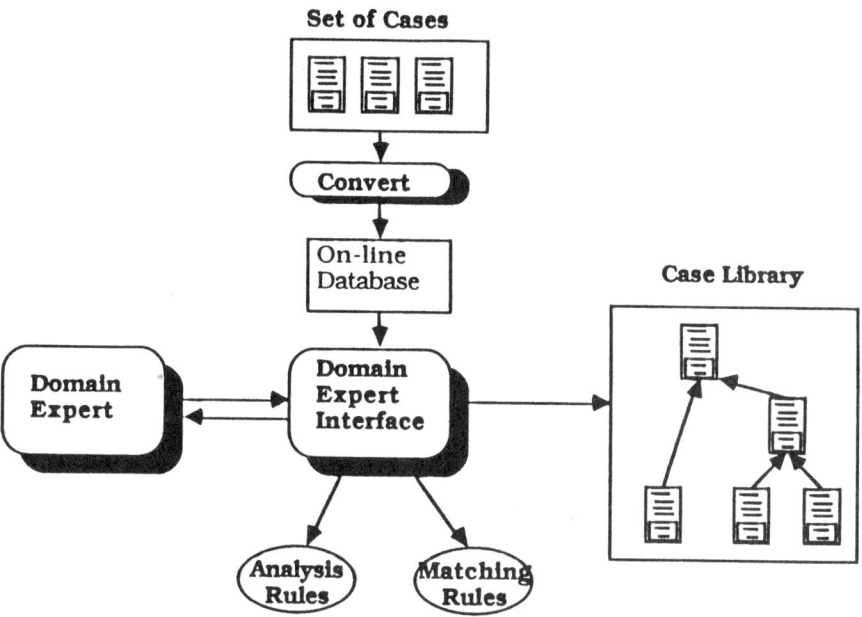

Figure 1: Domain Expert Interface

domain expert and system programmer were the same person, usually a graduate student, and the standard way to get knowledge into a system was to program it in.

As time went on, rule-based programming became the technique of choice because of the ease with which rule-based systems could be prototyped, extended, and experimented with. Within the academic community, rule-based programming is still probably the best choice for exploring poorly understood domains.

Rule-based programming is not a particularly good technique in the real world, however, because most domain experts are not experts in programming. They're experts in solving problems. Hence, the need for "knowledge engineers," who are programmer intermediaries in the dialogue between the domain expert and some rule-based expert systems shell.

As usual, the addition of middlemen increases costs and reduces efficiency. The knowledge engineer not only has to convert what the domain expert knows into a suitable set of rules, he or she also has to be able to describe to the domain expert what the rules are doing. Although the expert may be able to verify that the right answers are being generated for certain examples, he or she may be unable to tell if those answers are being derived in a reasonable way. Hence, the expert has low confidence in the system's future reliability.

One solution that is sometimes proposed is to have the expert present examples directly to the system, and have it induce a set of rules. This is sometimes called example-based programming.

Unfortunately, there are a number of difficulties with this technique:

- the general task of rule induction is computationally intractable; any practical system has to be significantly limited in the kinds of examples it can handle or the kinds of rules it can generate;

- for this reason, the choice of good examples is as important and as tricky as the design of good rules;

- the domain expert still has no way of telling if reasonable rules are being generated;

- in fact, because of the example selection problem and the difficulty of rule induction, the rules generated usually are not very good; they tend to be limited to exactly the variations covered by the given examples.

A variation on rule induction that has also been developed is to have the expert systems shell take examples and derive a number of patterns, usually statistical in nature, characterizing the examples These patterns can sometimes handle a wider range of variation in inputs, but they have one serious problem for knowledge acquisition: the patterns can not be used to explain solutions. At best the statistical inducers can say something like "89% of the time in previous cases the answer was ...." Crucially, they can not say what those cases were. To do so, they would have to store those cases, i.e., become case-based reasoners.

Rule-based systems, whether programmed or induced, explain (justify) their answers by giving a trace of the rules used to derive those answers. Of course, this trace is useful only if the rules are understandable to the expert, and that takes us back to square one.

Case-based reasoning offers a very different solution to the problem of knowledge acquisition and explanation. As in example-based programming, the domain expert presents examples directly to the case-based reasoning shell. Under normal circumstances, there is no middleman. Unlike example-based programming, however, the cases are not converted into rules or merged into statistical patterns. They are kept in their original form, just as the expert presented them.

The benefit of maintaining this library of cases is that a solution to a new problem can be explained simply by presenting the case that was adapted to create the solution. If the adaptation process is fairly limited, as we have argued that it can be, then the differences between the old and new solutions should be fairly small, and the expert should find it much easier to see where the solution came from, and judge its validity.

In other words, the case library allows the case-based reasoning system and the domain expert to "talk in the expert's own terms." All other approaches convert what the expert does into some other form, leading to the difficulties just described.

Organizing the Case Library

The expertise that must be given to a case-based reasoner is more than just a collection of cases. As discussed before, the domain-dependent knowledge that a case-based reasoner must have are:

- the cases themselves,
- rules for analyzing the cases, prior to retrieval,
- rules for matching cases, and
- rules for adapting cases to new situations.

The domain expert gathers together a representative set of cases. The set should contain enough examples to provide a good testbed for structuring the case library. Hence, the set should include:

- classic prototypes of the domain. By definition, most new input cases will be seen as variations of the prototypes.
- important exceptions to the prototypes, i.e., cases that are very similar to one or more prototypes, but which need to be treated very differently because of some particular attribute.

It is not only permissible, but desirable for there to be several examples of each prototype and example. This will help the domain expert clarify what the important attributes are.

Before actually sitting down to use the domain expert Interface, the domain expert should have already pre-sorted the cases into piles of similar cases and exceptional cases. That is, each set of cases that the domain expert would treat very similarly should be grouped into one pile, and beside that pile the domain expert should put those cases that seem like they belong to the pile, but in fact are different in some important, but perhaps subtle way. There might even be exceptions to the exceptions, i.e., cases that look like they belong in an exception pile, but in fact belong in the standard pile, or perhaps yet another exception pile.

It is not necessary for the domain expert to be exact or accurate about this, since one of the functions of the interface is to help the domain expert build a more accurate depiction of the domain than the domain expert would have been able to do on his or her own. The main purpose of the pre-sorting phase is to prevent the domain expert from adding cases on a case-by-case basis, with no feeling for the overall relationships. Without an overall perspective, a domain expert may waste a lot of effort, making a particular pair of of cases match, only to discover that some other pair is more appropriate.

Next, the cases are converted into machine-readable form. In form-based domains, such as loan application handling in a bank, the obvious interface is to present the forms on the screen to be filled in, looking as much as possible like the real paper forms. In a domain that doesn't have standardized forms, it is a good idea to first invent one. Designing forms is a good warm-up exercise for understanding a domain. It forces the domain expert to categorize and organize aspects of the domain in a manner that is consistent across examples. Any such forms of course have to be flexible enough so that the domain expert is comfortable using them to describe the domain's problems and solutions. Quite useful in this regard are domain-based natural language analyzers. They convert the expert's descriptions into the knowledge representation forms. The current technology in domain-based language analysis is especially appropriate for understanding short texts in highly-constrained contexts, e.g., short answers in a large form.

We'll assume here that a standardized well-structured form does exist, or can be invented. Once the cases have been entered using this form, the domain expert now uses the domain expert Interface to begin organizing the cases into a case library. The Interface is designed to help the expert enter, without programming:

- analysis information, i.e., rules about what to look for in input cases,

- matching information, i.e,. rules about how to match cases, and

- adaptation information, i.e., rules about how to make old solutions fit new problems.

The Interface is designed so that the expert is always dealing with whole cases, usually with two or three cases at once, rather than isolated rules or facts. In this way, the expert always has a particular problem in mind when making modifications to the case library, and, hence, the expert should have a better grasp of what to do.

There are many different ways an expert can build the library. One methodology is the following. The expert sorts cases into piles as described above, and they are entered into machine-readable form. Now the expert takes a prototypical example from each pile and tells the interface to add that case to the case library. The expert does this until he or she feels that a reasonably diverse set of prototypes has been entered.

Now, the expert starts testing the system. The expert enters a case from a pile whose prototype has already been entered. The desired behavior is that the prototype will be retrieved. That is, the expert has an input case, call it **I**, and a target case, call it **T**, already in the library, that the expert thinks should be retrieved if some end user enters a case like **I**. If **T** is indeed retrieved by **I**, then the expert tries another test case. But suppose that the Interface says that a different case, call it **C**, is currently retrieved by **I**. Now the expert has to modify the rules until **I** retrieves **T**, not **C**.

There are 3 basic kinds of changes the domain expert can make that will affect case retrieval. The expert can:

- make certain field values match better than others,

- change the importance of some fields, so that matching on these fields has more or less effect on the total match,

- add new calculated fields to the basic case form, so that the number of matching fields is increased in certain situations.

Changing How Field Values Match

Initially, when the expert first enters cases into the library, a field value in one case matches a value in another case only if the two values are equal. Therefore, most cases will match on only a few fields at best. Part of the domain expert's knowledge is how field values fall into classes of values. For example, in the loan application domain, a request for $5000 is really not very different from a request for $5200, and being a carpenter is very much like being a plumber, as far as bank loans are concerned.

In general, in a given domain, numerical field values will fall into ranges, while discrete concepts, such as occupation or purpose of loan, fall into classes. We call ranges and classes abstraction hierarchies, for reasons to be explained shortly.

Different fields may have different abstraction hierarchies, even if the fields take the same kind of value. For example, both the loan request amount and the applicant's monthly salary are dollar amounts, but the ranges a domain expert would set up would probably be quite different. In general, one numeric field value might be divided into a number of small ranges, while another might be divided into a few broad classes, while yet another might be divided into "under a thousand" versus "over a thousand."[1]

By defining ranges and classes, an expert can make two values match, even though they are not equal. For example, by defining the ranges "under a $1000," "$1000 to

---

[1] We also allow number matching by means other than range hierarchies, e.g., two numbers might be considered matching if they're "within 10 percent" of each other.

"$3000," and "$3000 to $10,000" for loan request amounts, an expert would make the two values $5000 and $5200 match (in the loan request amount field), because they both fall into the same range. By defining the class of blue-collar workers for the occupation field, the expert can make the values plumber and carpenter match.

In fact, the expert can give several layers to the ranges and classes for a field. For example, the purpose of loan field might have a set of classes for types of loans, e.g., vehicle purchase, home improvement, luxury item, and so on. Vehicle purchases could be further subdivided into types of vehicles, e.g., cars versus vans versus trucks. Cars could in turn be subdivided according to cost. Note that there are many ways vehicles can be classified, but these particular choices are most relevant for loan decisions. These layers of divisions within division form an abstraction or ISA hierarchy

A particular abstraction hierarchy for a field can be used to determine not just whether two field values match, but how well they match. The best match is equality. The next best match is if both values belong to the same class. The next best match after that is if the classes they belong to belong to the same class.

For example, a Ford Pinto matches a Ford Pinto exactly. A Ford Pinto matches a Plymouth Horizon fairly well, because they are both cars. It matches a boat very poorly, because the best that can be said is that they are both items that could be purchased with a loan. And buying a Ford Pinto matches home improvement worst of all, because the only thing they have in common is that they both are possible purposes of loans.

In other words, how well two field values match is determined by how abstract is their nearest common ancestor. The least abstract match is the best match; this happens when a value matches itself. The most abstract match is the worst match; this happens when the only thing in common between the two values is that they are both permissible values of the given field. When the case library is first built, matches are either best or worst, all or none. By creating ranges and classes, the expert starts introducing partial matches.

The expert creates new ranges and classes in order to make input case **I** match target case **T** better than case **C**. The Interface makes this task easier by showing the three cases in question and, for each field, highlighting that value in **T** or **C** that matches the corresponding value in **I** best. If neither value matches better, then neither is highlighted. An example of this display is shown in Figure 2.

Thus, the expert can see how many "winners" there are in **T** and how many in **C**. If all fields are equally important, then **C** must have more winning matches than **I**. By adding ranges and classes, the expert can add winners to **T**.

Note in the above display that there are no winners for the purpose of loan field. This is because the current abstraction hierarchy puts all cars directly under the abstraction AUTOMOBILE, without any subclassification. By editing the hierarchy, the expert can create a class of low-cost cars, which includes Horizons and Pintos, and a class of high-

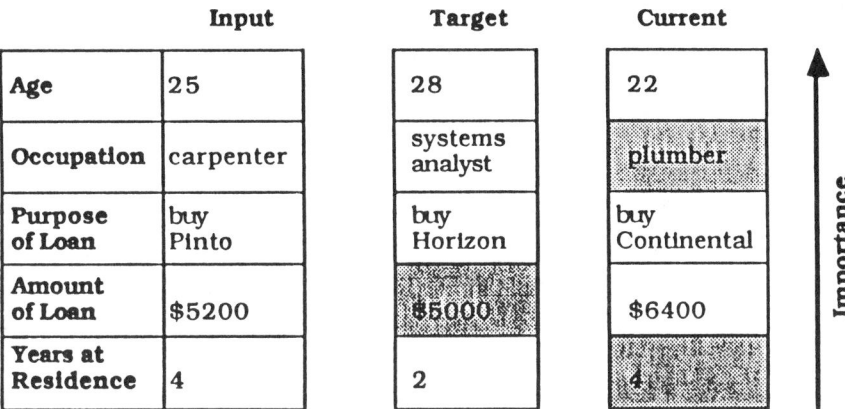

Figure 2: Field Match Display

cost cars, which includes Continentals. Now a Pinto matches a Horizon better than a Continental and Case **T** now has a winner where it didn't before. As more winners are added to **T**, eventually **T** becomes the case retrieved rather than **C**.

Changing the Importance of a Field

It may be that case **C** is retrieved not because it has more matching fields than **T**, but because those fields that it matches on are more important than the fields that **T** matches on. Therefore, another way to make the system retrieve **T** rather than **C** is to change the importance of different fields.

It is important to make this operation and its effects clear to the domain expert. We use a display that presents the most important fields first. When combined with the highlighting of winners, the display shows that case **C** has more highlighted items at the beginning of the display than **T**. This also gives a clear indication to the domain expert which fields needs to be moved up or down to get more of **T**'s winners into more important groups. (It also suggests, when editing the abstraction hierarchies, which fields are worth working on.)

Furthermore, this kind of display supports a very direct manipulation technique for changing the importance of fields. To make a field more or less important, the expert can point to it with a mouse and drag the field into a higher or lower group. Fields that show a winner in case **C** would be dragged lower and fields with a winner in case **T** would be dragged higher. The expert does not have to assign explicit "importance numbers" to fields, and it is always clear in what direction the changes in importance will affect this particular match.

In our loan example, the expert can tell the interface that occupation is more important than purpose of the loan. Now case **T** has a higher winner than **C**. This, along with other changes, would eventually make **T** the better match.

There is an important caveat to this operation, however, that must be made clear to the domain expert. Changes to the importance of fields should be made very sparingly and for good reasons. Fields should not be pushed around just to make a particular match work, because this can undo work on prior matches.

Adding New Fields

It will often be the case that an important feature that makes two cases match will not be found in the value of any one field. Instead, what may be important is some value calculated from other field values, the relationship between several field values, or even the absence of some field value. We call these *derived* or *calculated* fields. They are like calculated fields in database records or calculated cells in spreadsheets.

For example, in the loan application domain, the absence of a significant credit history may indicate an applicant who is hiding something. The age of the applicant may be a salient feature, but may have to be calculated from a birthdate. It may be important to know if the applicant is still living at home, but this can only be guessed by seeing if the applicant's age is equal to the number of years the applicant has lived at his or her current residence.

Calculated fields are almost always going to be important fields; otherwise, why calculate them? The only calculated fields that would not be important are those used as intermediate values for deriving yet other values.

Adding calculated fields will always be more complex than the two other match-changing mechanisms given above, but it need not be any worse than the similar operations that are done in databases, spreadsheets and programmable calculators. Furthermore, there has been a fair amount of work on the human interface in this kind of limited programming to make the operation relatively painless.

The Interface being developed at Cognitive Systems uses mostly point and click. The expert adds a new field to a "second page" of the basic case form, a "for office use only" page, if you like. The expert then builds a formula for this field by connecting this field to other fields in the form via calculating functions selected from a palette of available functions, as shown in Figure 3. Many of these functions are generic, such as standard database functions (e.g., SUM and DIFFERENCE), relationals (e.g., GREATER THAN), and logical connectives (e.g., AND, NOT and IF-THEN-ELSE). Other choices, specific to the domain, would be added by on-site programmers.

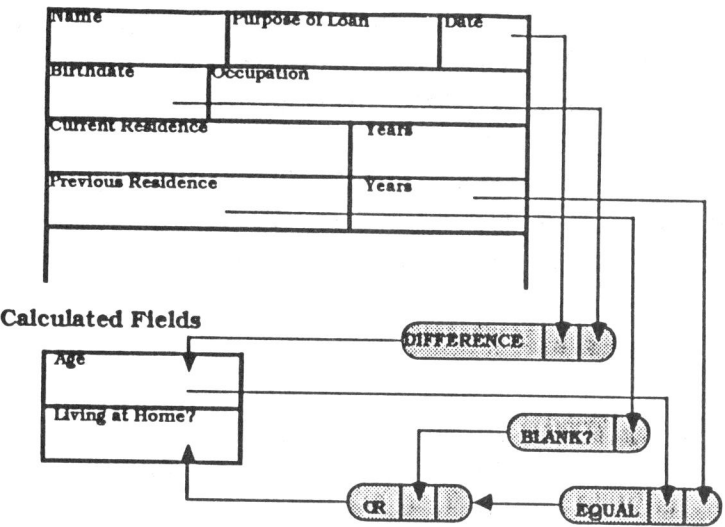

Figure 3: Calculated Field Formulas

Calculated fields are also a way in which the domain expert can make different fields "conditionally important," that is, important in some contexts and not important in others. This way of doing conditional importance is not as general as being able specify the importance of a field as some function of field values (analogous to the way calculated field values can be made a function of field values), but it makes for a much simpler interface.

For example, suppose the domain expert wants to make the age field of a loan application form important only when the amount requested exceeded $1000. To do this, the domain expert would create a calculated field, say AGE-IF-LARGE-LOAN, whose value would be "IGNORE" when for requests under $1000, and equal to the age field for requests over $1000. This new field would be given a high importance, while the original age field would be given a very low importance. Hence, age would be important for matching only when the loan request was more than $1000.

Acquiring Adaptation Rules

The preceding sections have argued that, with the right interface, it can be fairly easy for the domain expert to add cases to a case library, and to create the analysis and retrieval rules that take an input and find a relevant case.

In the simplest case-based reasoners, this is all there is. Cases are stored for later retrieval and application where appropriate. This works fine if:

- There are only a finite number of solutions, e.g., the localization of a fault to one of N modules; no adaptation to current circumstances is needed.

- It is obvious how to adapt relevant old solutions.

- The retrieved cases are intended only to suggest possibilities to the end user, rather than final solutions.

Often, however we want the case-based reasoning system to adapt cases automatically. Having adaptation rules reduces the number of cases that have to be in the database. Minor variants of solutions need not be stored if they can be derived by adaptation rules. Adaptation also supports learning. Successful adapted cases are added to the case library, and can be used with little or no adaptation in future similar situations. Unsuccessful adapted cases guide failure-driven learning processes.

If we want our reasoner to have adaptation rules, the domain expert will have to put them in. Can this process be made as transparent as the creation of the analysis and retrieval rules? The answer is a qualified yes.

In order to write adaptation rules, there has to be a well-defined formatted structure to the solution portion of a case, just as the analysis and retrieval rules required a well-defined structure to the problem part of the case.

In a fault diagnosis task domain, fault descriptions might be formatted as problem report forms. In a planning domain, plans would be lists of formatted actions. In the loan application domain, the decision would be a "yes" or "no", plus a list of formatted reasons for the decision. As can be seen, domains and tasks differ in how structured the solution normally is. A sequence of actions is less structured (i.e., more open-ended) than a problem report form, and a list of reasons for accepting or rejecting a loan is even less structured. The less structure there is, the more complicated the adaptation rules become. The more complicated the rules become, the harder it will be for the domain expert to write them.

Parameterized Solutions

Consider first a domain with a well-structured solution, such as the sentencing domain in JUDGE [Bain 1986]. In this case, the problem is a description of some criminal charges, and the solution is a sentence. A sentence consists of a number of parts, e.g., minimum and maximum years of imprisonment for each charge, to be served concurrently or sequentially, fines, and so on.

We can represent well-structured solutions as forms to be filled out, i.e., with a fixed set of labelled fields to be filled in. Each of these fields is a calculated field. The domain expert can specify how these fields are filled in by building a formula for calculating the values. We say that the domain expert has parameterized his solution.

If the domain expert could write a formula that would calculate a solution given any input field values, then there would be no need for case-based reasoning at all. That is not what is happening here. The formulas for the calculated fields in the solution are valid only for cases similar to this particular case.

Consider, for example, the task of generating a criminal sentence in the JUDGE domain. (The real JUDGE, by the way, used critic adaptation rules.) The formula for calculating punishment in a prototypical case of a heinous murder, with no apparent hope for rehabilitation, might derive its values from the high end of the maximum allowable punishment, while the formula for a prototypical case of manslaughter, with remorse clearly evident, would derive its values from the low end.

The formula deriving the values for the solution may be either absolute or relative. Absolute formulas simply calculate values from the input case field values alone. In the JUDGE domain, an absolute formula for a heinous murder might calculate punishment based on the legal maximum plus an absolute rating of how serious the crime was.

Often, though, it is very hard to come up with any kind of absolute rating, especially for something as subjective as heinousness of a crime. In such domains, relative formulas would be used. A relative formula compares the input field values against the corresponding values in the retrieved case to get a relative value. Thus, in JUDGE, the sentencing formula would calculate the new sentence by increasing or decreasing the sentence from the retrieved case in proportion to the relative heinousness of the new versus old crime.

Critic-based Adaptation Rules

Parameterization works when the solution can be put into a form with a fixed set of fields. It does not work so well for planning tasks, because the output of a planner is an arbitrarily long list of steps, perhaps grouped together by goals and annotated with intermediate checks for success. Although there is a structure to plans, it does not fit into a fixed set of fields, and hence we can't create solutions by attaching formulas to fields.

Critic rules scan the output and make local modifications. This is the technique used in CHEF[Hammond 1986], which adapted old recipes to new ingredients. The main body of a recipe is a list of actions to perform, which can't be put into a fixed field format. CHEF generates new recipes by applying adaptation rules to each step of the retrieved recipe.

The job of the Interface is to make the acquisition of these kinds of rules as simple as possible. The key is to find useful limits to how powerful the rules can be. We need to make sure that the rules are not so powerful that they are as complex as a full programming language.

Note that limiting the power of the rules that the domain expert can create, does not limit the power of the case-based reasoner. If the domain expert cannot create rules that will adapt some retrieved case to a new situation, the expert can just simply do the case "by hand," that is, construct the proper solution and store the case. In case-based reasoning, adaptation rules are primarily a labor and space-saving device. They allow minor variants of stored cases to be generated dynamically as needed. The core of case-based reasoning however depends on the case library, not on the adaptation rules.

Using the Interface, the domain expert builds the adaptation rules in much the same way he or she builds formulas for calculated fields. First, the Interface copies the solution stored in the old case into the new input case. Both cases are shown to the expert. The expert edits the new solutions, by applying rules to various parts of it. The expert can either select existing rules from a menu, or construct new rules as needed. Rules are constructed by piecing together primitive operations stored in an on-screen pallette. (There are several existing "visual programming" languages on the Apple Macintosh that support the kind of interface we're talking about here.) The expert continues until the edited solution is correct for the input case.

When the editing is done, the expert stores the case. The system actually stores the solution the expert created, plus the editing sequence used to generate it. These adaptation rules can then be reapplied to the old case to generate new solutions whenever it is retrieved by an input case.

Here are some examples of the kinds of primitive editing operations that would be useful in creating adaptation rules:

(**SUBSTITUTE** *field*) To build, the expert selects SUBSTITUTE plus a case field. When applied, all occurrences of the value of *field* in the old case in the selected portion of the new solution are replaced with the corresponding value of *field* in the new case.

(**REPLACE** *formula*) To build, the expert selects REPLACE and then builds a formula from case fields, using the same methods for building formulas for calculated fields. When applied, the selected portion is replaced with the value of *formula*.

(**INSERT** *formula*) To build, the expert selects INSERT and then builds *formula*. When applied, the value of *formula* is inserted before the selected portion of the new solution.

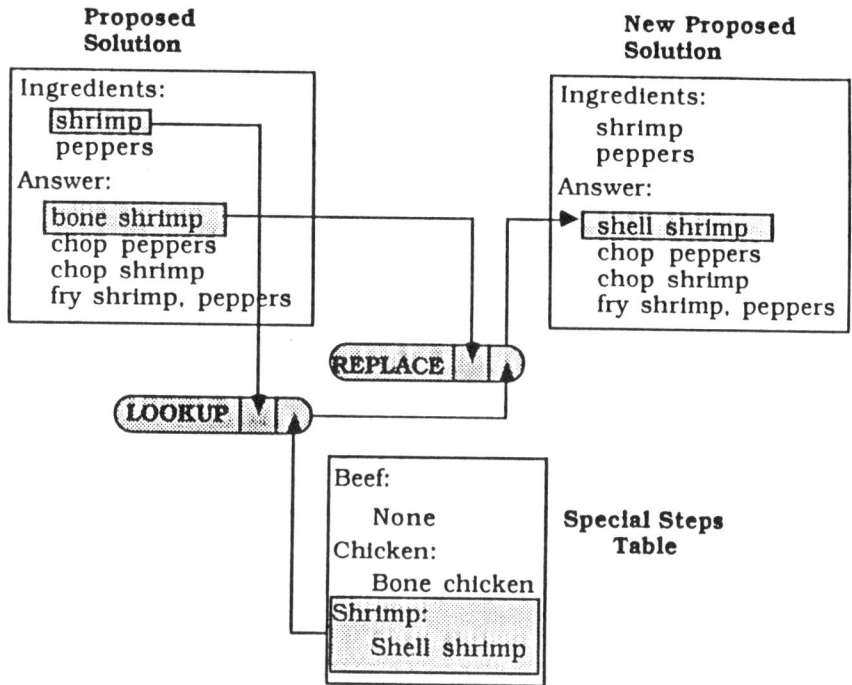

Figure 4: An Adaptation Rule

A very useful function for building formulas for REPLACE and INSERT is table lookup. (A similar function is found in most spreadsheet systems.) A table is simply a list of pairs of keys and values. The formula (LOOKUP *key table*) returns whatever value, if any, is associated with *key* in *table*. If no entry was available for *key*, the expert is asked to add one. If no *table* by that name is known, the expert is asked if he wants to create one.

Figure 4 shows an example of an editing adaptation rule from the CHEF domain. In cooking, certain steps are required only by certain ingredients. For example, chicken requires a boning step and shrimp requires a shelling step. The expert would build a table, calling it say SPECIAL-STEPS, with (BONE CHICKEN) stored for CHICKEN and (SHELL SHRIMP) stored for SHRIMP. To modify an existing recipe to include special steps, the expert would build a rule that inserted the result of looking up the special steps for each ingredient, as shown in Figure 4.

We have only touched on the kinds of solution adaptation primitives that might be useful. However, we hope we have demonstrated that the use of the editing metaphor, along with the techniques described for formula and rule construction, are a feasible solution to the difficult task of creating adaptation rules.

Summary

To summarize, we have shown how a domain expert can add knowledge to a case-based reasoning without having to write rules. The main operations that the expert performs are:

- grouping field values into ranges and classes,
- assigning levels of importance to fields,
- adding new fields, with values calculated from existing fields, and
- adding adaptation rules.

All of these operations can be done using simple point-and-click actions on a well-designed graphical interface. Similar interfaces already exist for database and spreadsheet systems.

We have covered here some of the issues involved in the acquisition of analysis, retrieval, and adaptation rules. For case-based reasoners that learn from failure, there must also be rules for explaining and repairing failures, but this area needs further research before it can be incorporated into a case-based reasoning shell.

The key thing to note here is that all of the domain expert's actions occur in the context of two or three concrete examples. More than anything else, case-based reasoning is highly supportive of the critical task of knowledge acquisition because the domain expert always works in the context of real examples.

Bibliography

Bain, W.M. (1986). *Case-Based Reasoning: A Computer Model of Subjective Assessment*. Ph.D. Thesis, Yale University.

Hammond, K.J. (1986). *Case-based Planning: An integrated theory of planning, learning and memory*. Ph.D. Thesis, Yale University.

Credit Assignment and the Problem of Competing Factors in Case-Based Reasoning [1]

Edwina L. Rissland and Kevin D. Ashley [2]
Department of Computer and Information Science
University of Massachusetts
Amherst, Massachusetts 01003

Abstract

In this paper we describe an approach to the problem of weighting and credit assignment for various factors that contribute to an analysis or outcome of a problem situation and discuss issues about weighting as they touch upon our case-based reasoner HYPO. In HYPO, we take the approach of delaying for as long as possible any assignment of weights and of symbolically comparing the competing factors. We call this approach a *least commitment weighting* scheme.

1. Introduction

Problem analysis and solution can depend on many factors, some of which are more important than others and some of which may compete with and contradict each other. Further, the importance and contribution of a factor can be highly dependent upon the context defined by the problem situation and also the other factors present in it. Rarely are all factors of equal weight or is a problem decomposable in a linear factor-by-factor manner. Experts in domains like the law and tactical planning know this. Nonetheless, they often approach the problem in a manner that at first glance might lead one to believe they are neglecting such complexities. Upon closer inspection, however, one can see that they are pursuing an approach that postpones for as long as feasible any commitment to

---

[1] This work was supported (in part) by: the Advanced Research Projects Agency of the Department of Defense, monitored by the Office of Naval Research under contract no. N00014-84-K-0017; the University Research Initiative, award no. N00014-86-K-0764; and an IBM Graduate Student Fellowship.

[2] Copyright ©1988. Edwina L. Rissland & Kevin D. Ashley All rights reserved.

assign weights or to select a combining function for factors. Experts do this for several reasons:

1. Such a commitment might cut off certain possibly fruitful lines of reasoning and thereby limit their problem solving performance;

2. Reduction to numerical weights, in particular, makes it difficult to recover symbolic information needed for certain reasoning methods like case-based justification and contrast-and-compare discussion of alternatives.

3. Assigning actual "weights" and predicting interactions among the factors is highly problematic and dependent on individual problem situations.

4. Experts in domains like the law simply do not reason in terms of weighting schemes. In fact in the legal domain, any reasoner that based an opinion or course of action upon a purely numerical scheme would be highly suspect.

Nonetheless, reasoning in case-based domains like the law does present the need to deal with factors which both interact and contribute to an overall analysis of a case and which may not be of equal importance. Thus, at some point in the reasoning, the reasoner must resort to some sort of balancing and trading off between the factors. That is, one could say that there must be some sort of consideration of credit assessment and some attempt at a method – symbolic or numerical – to weight the competing factors

In this paper we describe an approach to the problem of weighting various factors that contribute to an analysis or outcome and discuss issues about weighting as they touch upon our case-based reasoner HYPO. In HYPO, we take the approach of delaying for as long as possible any assignment of weights and of symbolically comparing the "weights" of competing factors. We call this approach a *symbolic least commitment weighting* scheme.

2. Background on Weighting

2.1 The Weighting Game in Law

In the legal domain, attorneys do know what factors are important in a particular legal claim. Although they may be willing to say in the abstract that a certain factor is more important than other factors, they almost never will venture numerical weights to distinguish the factors' importance. They are keenly aware that there might be some combinations of facts in which a particular factor, though normally more important than a competing factor, may not be so. Lawyers must also be prepared to justify an assertion that in a particular fact situation one factor is more important than a competing factor and such justification cannot be made in terms of numbers or statistics. It must be a symbolic justification using precedent-based methods such as comparing and contrasting cases [Ashley and Rissland, 1987].

What the lawyer is grappling with is essentially a problem of credit assignment [Samuel, 1963]. While he knows that it is most likely not the case that all factors contribute equally, it is exceedingly difficult to come up with an overall "score" for the case or to assign credit ("weights") to the individual factors. The doctrine of precedent – that similar cases should be decided similarly – is some help in this regard.

For instance, one can try to find a similar past case and through analogical reasoning "map over" the analysis to the new case using the doctrine of precedent by arguing that it should be evaluated similarly. Of course there can be many things which can go wrong in such an approach. For instance, when there exist two precedents with the same cluster of factors but they point to opposite conclusions (e.g., in one case the plaintiff won and in the other, the defendant), one is not sure what "score" to use. In fact, this situation may indicate that one is dealing with a "hard" case [Gardner, 1987], that is, a case about which there is substantial disagreement among the courts.

To assign credit to an individual factor is even more difficult. For one thing, courts seldom make this assignment explicit even though they might provide some indication of importance. One way to clinch the issue of which factors are more important is to find another precedent with exactly the same combinations of factors and to argue that the same cluster of factors should be important in the new case. To assess the contribution of a particular factor, one tries to find cases that have exactly the same factors except for the one of interest and to infer how the absence/presence of the factor affected the outcomes of the cases. This is akin to the componentwise credit assignment strategy discussed by [Subramanian and Feigenbaum, 1986]. See also [Rissland, 1988]. It also is similar to the dropping of an antecedent condition to test its necessity as is done in mathematics and the use of the near miss in machine learning [Winston, 1975].

2.2 Relation to Other Work

The problem of assigning weights to factors and defining functions to combine their contributions and produce an overall evaluation of a problem situation appears in many different areas of AI, particularly machine learning.

In machine learning, the first, and perhaps still the best, discussion of the credit assignment problem was by Samuel in his two landmark papers [Samuel, 1963; Samuel, 1967]. In the experiments reported in the first paper, Samuel approached the problem by using a linear polynomial evaluation function to assess a checkers board position (in conjunction with alpha-beta pruning). From a basic set of terms (e.g., piece advantage, king center control, total mobility) he constructed evaluation polynomials. These factors captured key features of checkers, for instance, that "it is usually to one's advantage to trade pieces when one is ahead and to avoid trades when behind....kings are more valuable than pieces" [p.75]. In experiments on "rote-learning", he used a linear combination of four terms; in a second set of experiments on "learning-by-generalization", where his program, itself, selected the terms included to be included in the polynomial and the weights given them, there were 16 terms, including cross terms to model interactions between factors. In the early experiments, the weights varied over a wide range, (from -2^{18} to 2^{18}); in later experiments they were of more equal magnitude. Gross differences in magnitudes of the weights, in effect, allowed his program control through what might be likened to a big switch that selected which terms to use. For instance, king center control (KCENT) and a cross term (MOC2) involving "total mobility" and "denial of occupancy" had weights of approximately 2^{16} and -2^{18}, respectively, and KCENT ranged between 0 and 8 while MOC2 was binary. Thus, in the appropriate circumstances one could completely dominate the decision or they could cancel each other out and force evaluation of a board in terms of lower order terms. Such cancelling out is in fact an example of a situation where one factor argues strongly towards one conclusion and the other equally strongly to the opposite. In such a situation Samuel's program defers to an analysis of the factors with lesser weights. Conversely, when there is no cancelling out, the evaluation essentially depends on one factor.

It is interesting to note that in learning terms and weights for the evaluation polynomial in one early version of the program, "at least 20 different terms were assigned the largest coefficient at some time or other" [p. 89]. Thus, too frequently a new term (factor) was assigned inordinate credit, so that the program was changing its model of what factor was important in a "fickle" manner. Later versions of the program remedied such instabilities by delaying the rate at which new terms could be selected, that is, by increasing the integration time with respect to moves (and cases) considered.

Also, the program could be fooled by bad play on the part of its opponent and overly dazzled by spectacular moves which "resulted in the misassignment of credit to those board positions which permitted spectacular moves when credit rightfully belonged to earlier board positions which had permitted the necessary ground-laying moves." Again, Samuel corrected this by increasing the span of moves over which the evaluation was computed.

Such problems are not confined to game playing. Although Samuel was able to remedy them to some extent, they still suggest to us deep difficulties in assessing the contributions of competing factors and coming up with weightings. If there are such problems even in a clean domain like checkers, the problem is daunting in blatantly scruffy domains like law and tactical planning.

It is interesting to note that the rote-learning version of the program was better than the learning version in certain contexts, like opening games, when much expertise is "book knowledge"; that is, for some phases of the game, a case-based approach is reasonable. The early program had a case memory containing "something over 53,000 board positions" [p.82], an admirably large case base by any standard. His later program used a case-base approximately five times that large.

In later experiments, Samuel introduced his notion of "signature", a vector whose component entries were restricted to a small range of 3-7 discrete values. These were combined in a hierarchical way to come up with a composite signature and ultimately a score for the board position which could be manipulated and "backed up" in the same way as scores from the polynomial evaluation functions. HYPO's dimensions bear some resemblance to his signatures since both cluster features into a larger structure and both can measure whether a situation is strong, weak or indifferent with respect to it. He used the signatures to index a library of master play (containing approximately 250,000 board situations) and thereby assigned to the current situation the move from the indexed known one. Samuel's experiments showed that his program performed better (by about a factor of two) with signatures than with learning-by-generalization. One major difference between Samuel's program and HYPO is that Samuel's signatures are used to *evaluate* a current board position whereas HYPO's dimensions are used as a retrieval and comparison mechanism only.

In summary, lessons to be learned from Samuel include: (1) one needs to have a rich language for factors to assess strengths and weaknesses and to be able to handle combinations of them; (2) one needs to be able to accomodate situations in which one factor can completely overwhelm another or two competing factors can cancel each other out; (3) one needs to be able to change evaluation functions to suit the requirements of different problem solving contexts (4) a case-based approach can enhance performance, even in domains like game-playing traditionally handled by heuristic search techniques.

In work on expert systems, particularly, on mechanisms affecting control through the use of mechanisms to assess belief and certainty, there is much discussion of how to reason with weights and to combine them [Howe and Cohen, 1987; Cohen *et al.*, 1987; Mostow and Swartout, 1986]. For instance, Cohen *et al.* discuss the trade offs between using tabular or "modifiable" functions for specifying and combining the contributions of factors. The tabular approach in effect defines a multi-variable function by listing its values domain vector by domain vector; Mostow calls this the "compiling out" approach; Samuel's signatures were of this type. The other approach is to build a combining function by specifying a procedure (e.g., certainty factor calculus or probability calculus). Both approaches greatly affect the control of reasoning and its explicitness. At the heart of both is the problem of what to do with weights.

In case-based reasoning research, other projects have had to face the problems of weights, particularly, when they assess factors in a problem situation to assess similarity and index memory. For instance, the CBR systems CYRUS [Kolodner, 1983a; Kolodner, 1983b] and MEDIATOR [Simpson, 1985; Kolodner et al., 1985]. use a "reminding" process that assesses closeness of fit by considering a set of selected features assigned an *a priori* ranking. Their more contextual, dynamic indexing is done with the "E-mop" mechanism, which organizes memory according to the aspects of an event that differ from norms of the conceptual category of the event (e.g., by violating expectations). These systems do not allow for changing assessment of similarity – that is, weighting factors – based on the case at hand. However, by keeping track of successes and failures they are able to generate new factors to consider.

2.3 Overview of Weighting in HYPO

What perhaps makes the situation in our work in case-based reasoning different from past approaches to the problem, such as by Samuel or Kolodner *et al.*, is that the choice of weights and methods for combining them is influenced by the context of the case, specifically:

1. The side or position one is advocating, for instance, whether one represents the plaintiff or defendant, and what legal doctrine one is considering the problem situation to fall under. [3]

2. What cases are relevant or on-point and which side they support. This of course is highly dependent upon the state of the Case Base.

3. The specific path through the space of possible arguments one actually chooses.

Each of these choices "cascades": the choice at 2. depends upon 1. and that at 3. upon 2. There is no single evaluation function that will serve across all cases or all stages of the problem solving or states of the case knowledge base. [4] In fact the same case taken in the context of a different case base very likely would be treated differently. In short,

---

[3] A given case can usually be approached with claims from diverse doctrines. For instance, a misappropriation case might also be approached from tort, contract or criminal law perspectives.

[4] This need for different evaluation functions at different stages of the problem solving was also recognized by Samuel who settled on six different types of signatures and evaluation polynomials to span the game playing from opening to end game.

at the same time, one contemplates problem solutions, one must also contemplate ways to evaluate them.

In the game-playing metaphor, problem solving for a legal situation depends on a knowledge base of past book moves (cases), the stage of the game, as well as projections gained from look ahead (argument paths). As in game playing, each adversary wishes to retain the ability to choose another approach, for instance, in order to respond to a potentially damaging response by one's opponent.

In this paper, we describe a flexible, least commitment approach to weighting which we have used in the context of a case-based reasoning system. In the same spirit in which least committment planning [Sacerdoti, 1975] postpones for as long as possible any commitment to a particular sequence of operator actions, our method postpones for as long as possible any commitment to a particular set of factors, supporting cases or argument steps. In that the method relies on a self-critical phase, it is a generate-and-test method and philosophically, is in the spirit of "proofs and refutations" [Lakatos, 1976]. The approach has three phases:

1. **Clustering** applicable factors according to how they appear in prior cases most-on-point to the problem situation.

2. **Interpreting** the effect of the clustered factors by examining the outcomes of the most-on-point prior cases.

3. **Criticizing and Testing** interpretations in light of salient differences among the most-on-point cases and the problem situation and by heuristically, hypothetically changing magnitudes and combinations of factors.

In HYPO's three-phase model, the determinations of weights among competing factors is deferred. The program waits on weighting competing factors until the preferences can be determined in light of the context of the particular facts of the problem situation and the possible justifications that can be offered for the different outcomes. At the conclusion of phase 3, HYPO would be in a position to assign weights if we felt that were appropriate. However, since we are concerned with case-based advocacy and *not* adjudication, we do not take that step. However, for a case-based reasoner in another domain (e.g., tactical planning), such a decision-making step might be appropriate and we would advocate waiting for the completion of phase 3 before making the commitment to a weighting of factors and the ultimate combination of them into a final, decision-making "score".

3. HYPO's Approach to Weighting

HYPO is a computer program that analyzes legal problem situations in domains like trade secrets and tax law. Inputs to the program are a description of the problem situation. Outputs are arguments in favor of either side to a legal dispute, plaintiff or defendant, concerning various legal claims to which the facts give rise. HYPO justifies those arguments as an attorney would by citing and distinguishing legal case precedents from its own **Case Knowledge Base** (CKB) of cases. For a complete description of HYPO, see [Ashley, 1987; Rissland and Ashley, 1986; Ashley and Rissland, 1987].

The factors that matter in HYPO's legal domain are represented with dimensions. A **dimension** is a knowledge structure that identifies a factual feature that links operative facts to known legal approaches to those facts, specifies which are the most important for the approach, and specifies how a legal position's strength or weakness can be compared to that of other cases. For each dimension, there is at least one real legal case where the court decided the case because, or in spite, of the features associated with the dimension. That case can be cited in a legal argument to justify that a similar fact situation should be decided in the same way.

In any given case, some factors may favor one side while other factors favor the opponent. In addition, a factor may favor a side more or less strongly. The magnitude or strength of a factor in a case is represented by its position along the range of the dimension. The ranges may be numeric intervals, or ordered sets, including binary and partially ordered sets.

HYPO's task in analyzing a problem situation is to combine the competing factors to develop as robust an argument as possible. HYPO manipulates relevantly similar, different and most-on-point cases in proceeding through its three phases of clustering, interpreting, and criticizing/testing. A case is **relevantly similar** if it shares a factor in common with the problem situation. The most relevantly similar cases, called **most-on-point** cases (or "mop-cases"), have the maximal overlap of factors in common with the problem situation. A case is **relevantly different** from a problem situation if it differs with respect to the magnitudes of a shared factor or it differs because there are additional, unshared factors.

3.1 Phase 1. Clustering the Factors

HYPO clusters factors that apply to a problem situation in the process of generating a lattice – called a claim-lattice – of all the cases in its Case Knowledge Base that are relevantly similar. A claim-lattice defines equivalence classes of cases having the same subset of factors in common with the problem situation. Cases having a maximal subset of factors in common with the problem situation are the most-on-point cases; these are immediate children of the root node which represents the problem situation.

For the purposes of illustrating HYPO's least commitment approach to weighting, consider the fact situation and its derived claim-lattice shown in Figures 1 and 2. For details on how HYPO produces such an analysis, see [Ashley and Rissland, 1987] which uses a similar example fact situation.

To produce initial clusters of factors, HYPO employs three simplifying heuristics:

C-1 Consider only those combinations of factors for which there is at least one most-on-point, real precedent case that has that combination.

C-2 Temporarily ignore the fact that the most-on-point cases, associated with a particular combination of factors, may differ among themselves as to other factors that they do not share with the problem situation.

C-3 Temporarily ignore differences in magnitudes of the shared factors among the most-on-point cases and the problem situation.

The first heuristic, **C-1**, means that HYPO only considers cases from the immediate children nodes of the problem situation root node in the claim-lattice. **C-2** means that relevantly similar cases are projected onto the space spanned by the dimensions applicable to the problem situation. **C-3** means that each dimensional factor is "normalized" to be of equal strength. In Figure 2, for example, HYPO uses **C-1** to cluster the factors into three groups corresponding to each group of equivalent most-on-point cases: Node [1] has (a, e), Node [2] has (a, b, c), and Node [3] has (d). Using **C-2** and **C-3**, HYPO temporarily ignores the fact that in Node [3] the *Crown Industries*, *Midland Ross* and *Data General* cases each involve other factors not shared with the problem situation and that, since they each involved different numbers of disclosures to outsiders, they all differ from the problem situation in terms of the magnitude of factor (d).

3.2 Phase 2. Interpreting the Combined Effect of a Cluster

For each cluster of factors associated with most-on-point cases, HYPO interprets their combined effect according to the outcomes of those cases. If all of the mop-cases in the claim-lattice node were won by the same side, then the cluster of factors is treated as warranting a decision of the problem situation for that side. The justification is that every past decision that presented that particular combination of factors has favored that side. Unfortunately, things frequently are not that simple.

If the equivalence class of most-on-point cases is split between those favoring the plaintiff and defendant, then there are two as yet equally justified competing interpretations of the effect of the cluster of factors. Further steps are taken in an attempt to resolve the tie between the competing interpretations.

In Figure 2, the *Analogic* case of Node [1] supports interpreting clustered factors (a, e) for the plaintiff. Likewise, the *Amoco* case of Node [2] favors interpreting clustered factors (a, b, c) for the defendant. Things are a bit more complicated for Node [3]. While the *Crown* and *Midland Ross* cases support interpreting clustered factor (d) for defendant, *Data General* supports interpreting it for plaintiff.[5]

HYPO has three heuristic methods for showing how to resolve ties among two competing interpretations of a particular cluster of factors. These methods discredit an interpretation through discrediting the most-on-point cases justifying the interpretation. HYPO uses them to attempt to show that the clustered factors do not warrant a given result by pointing out salient distinctions between the problem situation and the most-on-point cases. The three interpretation heuristics are:

I-1 Show that alternative clusterings of factors in the problem situation justify a result inconsistent with one of two competing interpretations of a cluster.

I-2 Show that alternative clusterings of factors in the most-on-point cases favoring one of the interpretations can be used to explain away the result in those cases, and that these alternatives do not apply to the problem situation.

I-3 Show that certain of the clustered factors were not as strong in the problem situation as they were in the most-on-point cases and thus that the mop-cases do not support the interpretation.

These interpretation strategies focus on the previously ignored effects of the other clustered factors and of the relevant differences between the most-on-point cases and the problem situation, differences represented by unshared factors that favor different outcomes and differences in the magnitudes of shared dimensions. **I-1** points out distinguishing factors, not shared by a most-on-point case supporting the interpretation, which favor coming to an opposite outcome. In other words, **I-1** causes HYPO to consider sibling nodes (equivalence classes) in the claim-lattice to counter the effect of the clustering strategy of **C-1**. For each most-on-point case favoring the interpretation, **I-2** points out distinguishing

---

[5] Note that one possible way of resolving the tie is to count the number of cases favoring each interpretation. Although one does see this sort of numerical tie-breaking in legal argument from time to time (e.g., attorneys and judges sometimes speak of the majority and minority rules comparing not the number of cases but the number of states that would hold one way or the other on an issue) it is not generally accepted as an appropriate rationale for decision. Another way of breaking the tie is to compare the pedigrees of the courts on either side of the issue and award the decision to the highest court.

factors, not shared with the problem situation, that can be used to explain why the problem situation should have a contrary outcome. In other words, **I-2** is a "lifting" strategy to counter the "projection" strategy of **C-2**. **I-3** is an "unnormalizing" strategy to counter the effects of **C-3**.

The goal of phase 2 is to determine if one of the two "tied" sets of otherwise equivalent most-on-point cases is "less distinguishable" than the other. If so, then the clustered factors are interpreted consistently with the outcomes of that set since they are closer to the problem situation. Otherwise, as is usually the case, HYPO cannot resolve the tie but can only make case-citing arguments favoring each interpretation. In Figure 2, for example, the heuristics do not allow HYPO to resolve the tie in interpreting the effect of the cluster in Node [3]. **I-1** does not avail because the other clustered factors from Nodes [1] and [2], (a, e) and (a, b, c), seem to pull equally in favor of plaintiff and defendant. Although **I-2** allows HYPO to distinguish *Data General*, it also allows HYPO to distinguish *Crown*: Unlike the problem situation, *Data General* involves factor (f) favoring the plaintiff because all of the disclosures were subject to confidentiality agreements and *Crown* has a factor favoring the defendant that the problem situation does not have (it involved disclosures in negotiations with the defendant). **I-3** allows HYPO to distinguish *Midland-Ross*, also, because it involved more disclosures to outsiders than the problem situation (i.e., 100 disclosures as opposed to 50 in the problem situation.)

3.3 Phase 3. Criticizing and Testing

The methods of the final phase are used to criticize and test the results of the first two phases. They are based upon the use of counter-example cases, both real and hypothetical. With them, HYPO attempts to produce counter-examples to the interpretations from phase 2. The types of counter-examples used in phase 3 are:

Boundary – a case in which one of the clustered factors was far more extreme than in either the problem situation or the most-on-point case and yet the factor did not lead to the same outcome as in the mop-case.

More-on-point (or Trumping) – a case won by the opposing side whose cluster of factors shared with the problem situation overlaps, and strictly contains as a subset, the cluster of factors in the most-on-point case.

Overlapping – a case won by the opponent whose cluster of factors overlaps, but does not strictly contain, the cluster of factors in the most-on-point case.

Potentially more-on-point – a case won by the opposing side that would be a most-on-point case if certain factors, currently "near-misses" in the problem situation, were actually present. A factor is a near-miss if the problem situation contains all the information needed to tell if the factor (i.e., dimension) applies except the information about magnitude that determines where the situation should lie on the dimension.

The three phase 3 methods are:

C&T-1 Use "boundary" counter-examples to show that certain of the clustered factors favoring the outcome are not important as justifications.

C&T-2 Use trumping counter-examples to show that the cluster of factors as a whole is not important as a justification.

C&T-3 Use hypotheticals based on potentially more-on-point counter-examples to show that certain of the clustered factors or the cluster taken as a whole are not important as justifications.

The point of **C&T-1** is to show that even extreme examples of particular factors do not warrant the result in the most-on-point case. For example, Figure 3 shows that the *Data General* case is an extreme example of factor (d) in which the plaintiff still won even though it had disclosed to 6000 outsiders. HYPO uses **C&T-1** to attack the assertion that clustered factor (d) of Node [3] necessarily favors defendant by citing *Data General* as a boundary counter-example.

Given a most-on-point case that supports an interpretation of a cluster of factors, the goal of **C&T-2** is to find a more-on-point counter-example that strictly contains the cluster but had the contrary outcome. If all the factors that apply to the problem situation are taken as given, by definition there can be no such trumping counter-example. But there may be other factors that apply to the problem situation that the user has not told HYPO about because he does not know they are relevant. HYPO uses **C&T-2** to probe the user about additional factors in the problem situation that may be relevant. HYPO is guided heuristically by those cases in the claim-lattice that are potentially more-on-point counter-examples. For example, factor (f), which applies to the *Data General* case where all disclosures were restricted by confidentiality agreements, is a near-miss with respect to the problem situation. By hypothetically modifying the problem situation so that all 50 disclosures became restricted, *Data General* would become more-on-point than either of the other cases in Node [3] of Figure 2. The newly applicable factor would be incorporated into a "super" cluster (d, f) which would be interpreted as favoring the plaintiff.

C&T-3 also involves posing hypotheticals, but posing hypothetical variations of most-on-point cases, rather than of the problem situation. Where the program cannot find real boundary or trumping counter-examples, it makes them up. That is, using the most-on-point cases as seeds, it creates extreme cases by exaggerating magnitudes of factors and combinations of factors to create hypothetical cases that are extremely strong for a side, thus overwhelming any contravening factors. These hypotheticals, though cited rhetorically, are useful in obtaining concessions from a side that even though a particular factor may favor an outcome in some contexts, it does not always favor that outcome.

One can view these three criticizing and testing strategies as performing a sensitivity analysis or heuristic search through the space of cases and the space of clusters of factors. **C&T-1** varies magnitudes of factors found in both the problem situation and the most-on-point cases. **C&T-2** varies the problem situation while holding the most-on-point cases constant. **C&T-3** varies the most-on-point cases while holding the problem situation constant.

4. Discussion and Conclusion

Having performed its criticize and test phase, HYPO does not assign weights to competing factors. It does not need to. The outputs of the 3-phase process are ideal for assisting attorneys to make or anticipate reasonable legal arguments about the significance of the factors in the problem situation. HYPO's competing interpretations and concomitant critiques, complete with most-on-point cases, distinctions and counter-examples, map out possible reasonable argument paths for attorneys to follow in arguing about the problem situation.

Since HYPO does not play judge, it does not actually have to decide the problem situation and thus does not actually have to venture assignment of weights. Furthermore as was pointed out by legal realists like Holmes and Llewellyn, a judge's decision is seldom determined solely by the precedents but also upon social and psychological factors and this is outside the ken of HYPO.

Since the comparisons among the cases are not *ceteris parabus* – that is, all other things are not equal – there almost always are grounds for criticizing a case-based interpretation of clustered factors. Inevitably, more than one reasonable interpretation can be assigned for each of the various clusters of factors in the problem situation. HYPO generates such competing interpretations but does not resolve the argument.

HYPO's method illustrates one way of dealing with the central dilemma of weighting: delay and wait for as long as possible. If weights were to be assigned to competing factors, it could be done meaningfully only at the end of this 3-phase process. Only after the criticize and test phase could the a weighting scheme take into account the specific context of the adversarial position one is defending, the combinations of factors and magnitudes presented in the problem situation and the precedent cases that can be used as justifications in arguments, and the possible paths through the space of arguments. But then the weights are so contextual that they might lack utility. Furthermore, collapsing all of this into a number would handicap HYPO's, or any case-based reasoner's, ability to reason about how the weight should be changed as the context changes.

In conclusion, we have discussed how HYPO determines important clusters of factors and evidence pro and con various interpretations of them and how HYPO defers determination of their relative importance. Through the last phase of the 3-phase process, HYPO has not committed to any weighting scheme. HYPO does not venture an assignment of weights in which the relative importance of factors are set down for all future contexts since a normally unimportant factor may yet make a rhetorical difference if it allows an advocate in the context of a particular problem situation to distinguish between otherwise equally most-on-point precedents. Since the determination of the relative importance of factors is not carried across problem solving episodes, HYPO can change it over time as new case decisions are made and added to the CKB.

Although HYPO searches through the space of possible combinations of factors and magnitudes unassisted by an *a priori* weighting scheme, the search is heuristically guided by the combinations that actually have appeared in real precedent cases. This provides some important advantages in terms of search efficiency and justification. By focusing initially on only the combinations of factors that have historical precedent, a potentially enormous search space is enormously reduced. Actual legal cases tend to involve only small collections of factors. Moreover, the pruning of the search space is performed in a justifiable way. Howsoever HYPO combines factors, there is always an actual case to cite in support of the cluster of factors. HYPO interprets the importance of factors only to the extent that its interpreations are justified by the precedents, and since the interpretations are justified, they can also be explained in terms of the precedents.

In April, 1974, the plaintiff SDRC Corp. ("SDRC") began marketing NIESA, a computer program to perform structural analysis, that SDRC had been developing for some time. The employee-defendant named Smith worked for SDRC until January, 1973 as a computer projects leader. Smith generated the idea of the NIESA program and was completely responsible for its development. On beginning his employment, Smith entered into an Employee Confidential Information Agreement in which he agreed not to divulge or use any confidential information developed by him at SDRC. Immediately upon leaving SDRC, Smith was employed by the corporate-defendant EMRC Corp. ("EMRC") as a vice-president of engineering. In February, 1974, EMRC began marketing a structural analysis program called NISA that it had taken eleven months to develop. Smith had used his development notes for SDRC's NIESA program in building EMRC's NISA program. In connection with sales of the NIESA program, SDRC had disclosed parts of the NIESA source code to some fifty customers.

Figure 1: Problem Situation

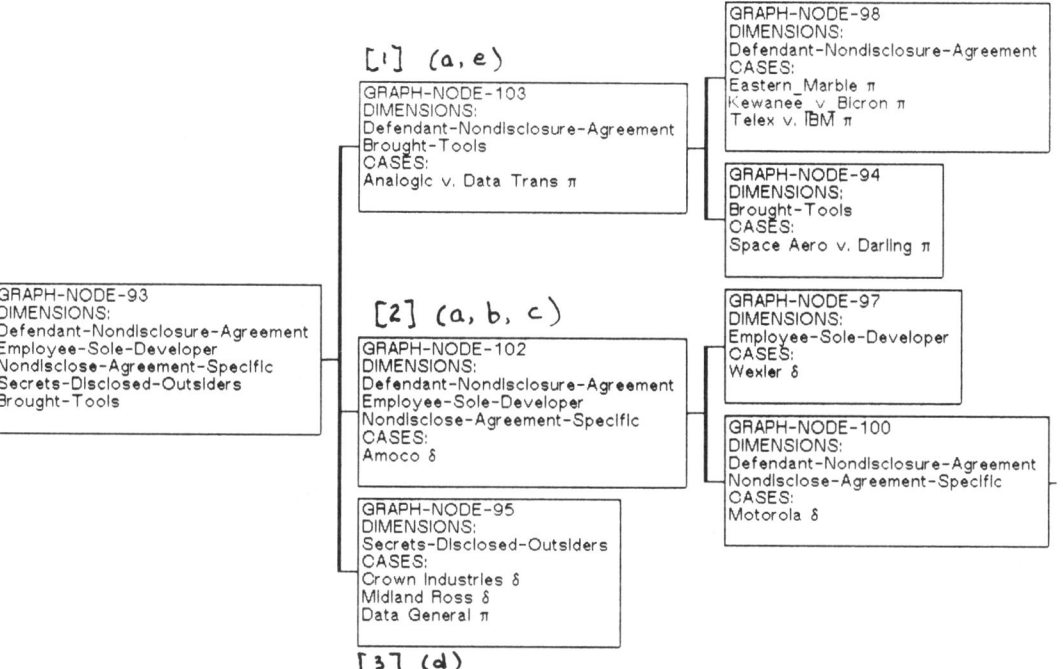

HYPO determines that five factors apply to the problem situation represented by the root node of the claim-lattice and one is a near-miss:

(a) the employee-defendant entered into a nondisclosure agreement
(b) the employee-defendant was the sole-developer of plaintiff's product
(c) whether or not the nondisclosure agreement specifically applied to the product
(d) plaintiff disclosed its product secrets to outsiders
(e) the employee-defendant brought plaintiff's product development tools to his new employer, the corporate-defendant
(f) NEAR-MISS: outside disclosees agreed to maintain confidentiality of plaintiff's product secrets.

Of those factors, (a), (c), and (e) favor the plaintiff; (b) and (d) favor the defendants. If (f) applied, it would favor the plaintiff. The claim-lattice organizes cases from the CKB in terms of overlap of factors shared with problem situation. Each case indicates whether it was won by plaintiff (π) or defendant (δ). There are three groups of equivalent most-on-point cases located in Nodes [1], [2] and [3].

Figure 2: Claim-lattice for Problem Situation

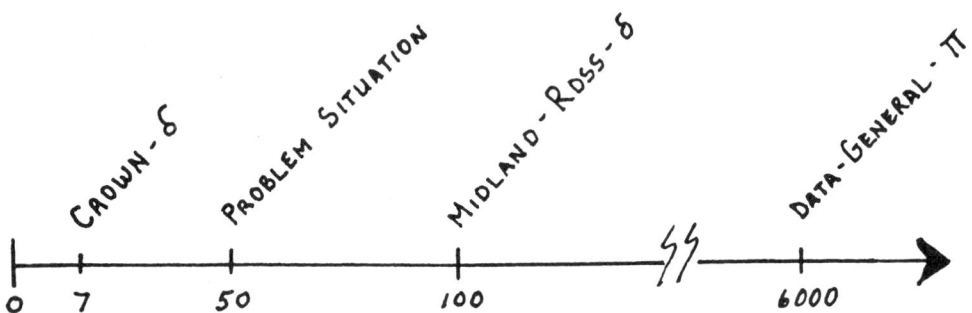

Cases are shown in order of number of plaintiff's disclosures of secrets to outsiders. Case indicates if plaintiff (π) or defendant (δ) won. Plaintiffs in cases toward the right disclosed secrets to more outsiders and are weaker for plaintiff. *Data General* is the weakest case in terms of numbers of disclosures but was still won by a plaintiff.

Figure 3: Cases in Order of Magnitude of Factor (d): Plaintiff's Disclosure of Products Secrets to Outsiders

REFERENCES

[Ashley, 1987] Kevin D. Ashley. *Modelling Legal Argument: Reasoning with Cases and Hypotheticals*. PhD thesis, Department of Computer and Information Science, University of Massachusetts, 1987.

[Ashley and Rissland, 1987] Kevin D. Ashley and Edwina L. Rissland. Compare and Contrast, A Test of Expertise. In *Proceedings of the Sixth National Conference on Artificial Intelligence*, American Association for Artificial Intelligence, August 1987. Seattle.

[Cohen et al., 1987] Paul R. Cohen, Glenn Shafer, and Prakash P. Shenoy. Modifiable Combining Functions. *AI EDAM*, 1(1):47–57, 1987.

[Gardner, 1987] A. vdL. Gardner. *An Artificial Intelligence Approach to Legal Reasoning*. MIT Press, Cambridge, MA, 1987.

[Howe and Cohen, 1987] Adele E. Howe and Paul R. Cohen. *Steps Toward Automating Decision Making*. COINS Technical Report 87-82, Department of Computer and Information Science, University of Massachusetts, 1987.

[Kolodner, 1983a] Janet L. Kolodner. Maintaining Organization in a Dynamic Long-Term Memory. *Cognitive Science*, 7(4):243–280, 1983.

[Kolodner, 1983b] Janet L. Kolodner. Reconstructive Memory: A Computer Model. *Cognitive Science*, 7(4):281–328, 1983.

[Kolodner et al., 1985] Janet L. Kolodner, Robert L. Simpson, and Katia Sycara-Cyranski. A Process Model of Case-Based Reasoning in Problem Solving. In *Proceedings of the Ninth International Joint Conference on Artificial Intelligence*, International Joint Conferences on Artificial Intelligence, Inc., Los Angeles, CA, August 1985.

[Lakatos, 1976] I. Lakatos. *Proofs and Refutations*. Cambridge University Press, London, 1976.

[Mostow and Swartout, 1986] John Mostow and William Swartout. Towards Explicit Integration of Knowledge in Expert Systems: An Analysis of MYCIN's Therapy Selection Algorithm. In *Proceedings of the Fifth National Conference on Artificial Intelligence*, American Association for Artificial Intelligence, August 1986. Philadelphia, PA.

[Rissland, 1988] Edwina L. Rissland. Example Selection: The Underlying Issues. To appear in International Journal of Man-Machine Studies, 1988.

[Rissland and Ashley, 1986] Edwina L. Rissland and Kevin D. Ashley. Hypotheticals as Heuristic Device. In *Proceedings of the Fifth National Conference on Artificial Intelligence*, American Association for Artificial Intelligence, August 1986. Philadelphia, PA.

[Sacerdoti, 1975] E.D. Sacerdoti. *A Structure for Plans and Behavior*. Technical Report Tech. Note 109, SRI International, Inc., 1975.

[Samuel, 1963] A. Samuel. Some Studies in Machine Learning Using the Game of Checkers. In Feigenbaum and Feldman, editors, *Computers and Thought*, pages 71–105, McGraw-Hill, 1963.

[Samuel, 1967] A. Samuel. Some Studies in Machine Learning Using the Game of Checkers. II – Recent Progress. *IBM Journal*, November 1967.

[Simpson, 1985] Robert L. Simpson. *A Computer Model of Case-Based Reasoning in Problem Solving: An Investigation in the Domain of Dispute Mediation*. Technical Report GIT–ICS–85/18, School of Information and Computer Science, Georgia Institute of Technology, 1985.

[Subramanian and Feigenbaum, 1986] Devika Subramanian and Joan Feigenbaum. Factorization in Experiment Generation. In *Proceedings of the Fifth National Conference on Artificial Intelligence*, American Association for Artificial Intelligence, August 1986. Philadelphia, PA.

[Winston, 1975] Patrick H. Winston. Learning Structural Descriptions from Examples. In Patrick H. Winston, editor, *The Psychology of Computer Vision*, McGraw-Hill, New York, 1975.

Exploration of Case-Based Problem Solving

David Ruby   Dennis Kibler

Department of Information & Computer Science
University of California, Irvine
Irvine, CA 92717 U.S.A.
(714) 856-8779

Topic: Machine Learning: Problem Solving

Number of Words: 3400

Abstract

This paper examines an approach to problem solving that guides search by using a memory of past solutions. The approach allows us to illustrate several issues not yet addressed in current case-based reasoning systems. The first issue concerns the abstraction mechanism used to store the cases in memory. The second issue addresses the relationship between performance and memory size. The third issue concerns the computational cost associated with increasing the size of memory. These issues are examined by systematic experimentation with a simple case-based problem solver.

1 Introduction

Practical problem solvers must be able to learn from previous problem solving sessions. Re-solving each and every problem each time it is presented is an impractical approach to problem solving, as well as not being cognitively viable. A number of different approaches to using previous problem solving experiences have been developed. Most research has focused on forming summaries in the form of rules [MUB83, Lan83, PK86] or macro operators [FHN72, Kor85, Iba85, Min85].

Another approach to utilizing previous problem solving or planning sessions is to incorporate them into a global knowledge structure along with any other knowledge about the world and planning [Ham86, Alt86, Kol87, Car86]. Plans in the knowledge base can be indexed by their goals, their failures or impasses encountered, or by their similarity with previous problems. The key issue in these systems is the reasoning required to apply the knowledge about a previous case (or its generalization) to the current situation. Another issue that has been addressed in this context is the type of knowledge that should be maintained about previous solutions:

Work on approaches to using previous problem solving sessions has provided a great deal of information about the types of reasoning that can be done with a memory of previous cases, as well as the type of knowledge that should be kept for each case. Still, a number of important issues have not been addressed. For example, how are the cases in memory abstracted to make them more general? Most recent case-based systems have used *ad hoc* and unprincipled approaches for generalizing cases.

Performance is a key issue in any system, yet most case-based systems have been unable to provide any characterization of the type of problems that they can solve. It is not clear if increased memory size can lead to a decrease in problem solving performance in terms of the problems solvable. It is important to understand the tradeoff between memory size and system performance.

Another issue not yet addressed is whether the computational cost of the problem solver remains tractable as memory grows. Indiscriminate addition of macro operators leads to intractable search problems. This led to the development of filters on the introduction of macro operators [Iba85, Min85]. Without a measure of the cost of using memory it is difficult to measure its true utility.

We will examine a less knowledge intensive case-based problem solver in terms of these issues. Empirical data will be provided from a series of systematic experiments.

2 Lehnert's Case-Based Problem Solver

Lehnert [Leh87] introduced a less knowledge intensive case-based problem solver. The framework is the standard state-space representation where one is given a start-state, operators, and goal-state. The addition is a case-memory which constrains problem solving.

We can regard the case memory as a set of solution traces. A coarse index (number) is associated with each state. We say two states *index-match* if they have identical indices. A *path* P for a state S is the sequence of states from the start-state to S. The path P *index-matches* a memory case C if the corresponding index sequence is identical to a contiguous subsequence of C. The coarse index maps multiple states in the problem domain to the same index, thereby providing a level of abstraction and generalization over the solution sequences in memory.

Given these definitions we can describe the case-based problem solver fairly simply:

Memory-Constrained Search

Do ordinary Depth First Search but terminate any path P that does not *index-match* with some case in memory.

This kind of case-based problem solver can be combined with any search technique such as Breadth First Search, A*, or Best-first Search. Still, there is no guarantee that this case-based problem solver will solve any problem other than the ones already in memory.

Lehnert introduced a "near-miss" solution as a means of solving problems for which there was currently no solution in memory. A problem has a "near-miss" solution if it can be solved with a N-family search. We say a path P is an *i-index-match* with a case C if all but the first i states of P *index-match* with the case C. In a N-family search we iteratively use i-index matching, with i varying from 0 to N. The N-family of a state is defined as those states reachable within N moves or less. Also note that i-index-matching corresponds to standard index matching after the case memory has been expanded by adding the i-family to each node in memory. In this way N-family search uses local search to augment memory.

3 Experiments with the Eight Puzzle

We implemented the above version of Lehnert's Problem Solver for the Eight Puzzle domain. Two experiments were conducted. The first experiment examined the behavior of the system with different indices while memory was varied. Cases added to memory were chosen at random. In the second experiment a case was added to memory only if it could not be solved with the cases currently in memory.

3.1 Experiment One: Index Characteristics

Experiment one evaluated the relative importance of index characteristics. The type of abstraction provided by the indices requires a particular set of properties to be effective. An effective means for generating indices with these properties is to treat the states as structured objects, letting the index be the structured dissimilarity measure between the current state and the final state. One approach to comparing structured objects is to decompose the object into subparts and compare the subparts. By comparing subparts, sequences of indices will implicitly store how much of the object is changing. This restricts the potential number of moves that must be tried, and consequently shrinks the search space.

In experiment one, four indices were tested. Two of the indices were derived based upon the structured object representations of the states. The 'I' index [Leh87] is computed by breaking the Eight's Puzzle Board into 12 pairs of values where each pair consists of the values of adjacent tiles. These sets are generated for the final state and the current state. The index value is the number of sets that are present in the final state that are not in the current state. A second index, the 'L' index, was derived in a similar way but instead of taking adjacent pairs of blocks, three blocks in the shape of an 'L' are used. There are 16 such L's for each Eight Puzzle state.

The third index was a simple 'out-of-place' measure. This is the number

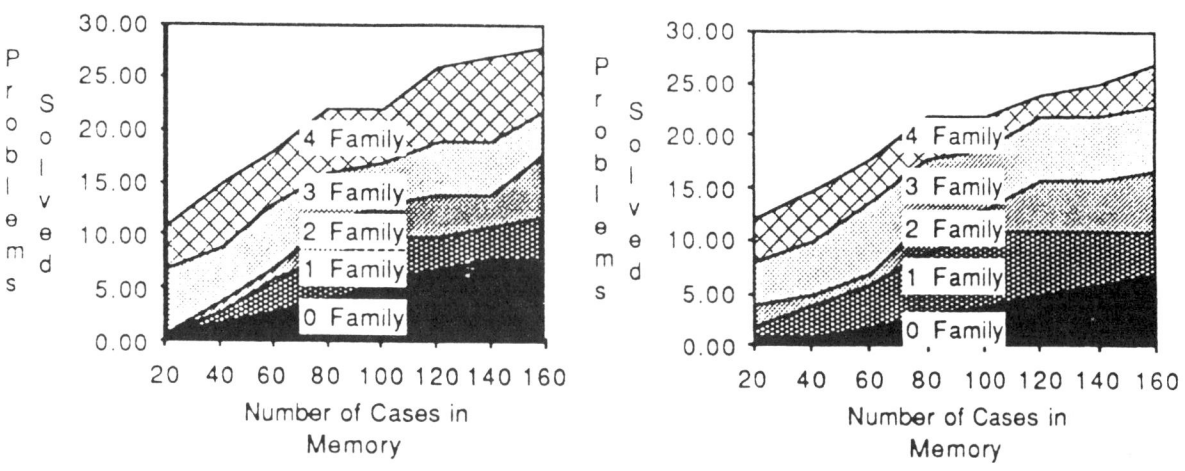

Figure 1: Performance for 'I' index and 'L' index

of squares in the current state that are not in the positions they will have in the final state, a common heuristic for solving this puzzle. The fourth index was a slightly randomized version of the 'out-of-place' index, found by multiplying the 'out-of-place' measure by a hash function derived from the state representation.

For each index, memory size was varied from 20 cases to 160 cases and the system was given 30 problems. Cases and problems were created by taking random walks of length 50 from the final state. For each memory size, the size of N-family search used was varied from 0 to 4 and performance data kept. The only constraint used in generating the cases and the family of states was that the inverse of the previous move was never taken when generating the next state.

3.1.1 Performance

Figure 1 shows the learning curves resulting from tests of the two structured indices during experiment one. It is clear that the relative behavior was the same for these two indices. The 'I' index had slightly better overall performance. The system solved 93 percent of the problems with a memory size of 160 cases using the 'I' index, while only solving 90 percent when using the 'L' index. For both indices, the growth in the number of problems solved roughly tapered off as the size of memory grew.

Because each case in memory covers a small region (defined by the N-family

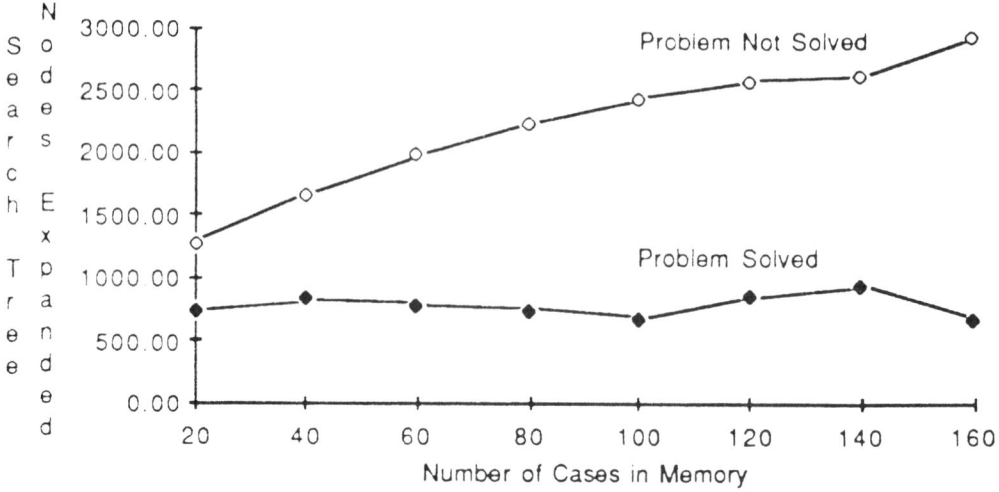

Figure 2: Average Number of Search Tree Nodes Expanded for 'I' index

search) of the solution space, the random cases fragment this space leaving more and more smaller uncovered regions. Since at least a single case is required to cover each of these regions, the amount of coverage provided by new cases will decrease. In this way the learning behavior of the system approximately agrees with the standard power law of learning. This fact is roughly brought out in the data, as shown in figure 1.

In experiment one we are also interested in determining the relationship between the size of memory and the performance of different sizes of "near miss" searches. We expected the "near miss" solutions to operate by effectively enlarging memory by approximately a factor equal to the number of states in the N-family used. For example, the 4-family consisted of approximately twice as many states as the 3-family. Therefore we expected to find the 4-family of near-miss solutions with memory size M to have the same relative performance as the 3-family with memory size $2M$. This relationship was borne out by the data.

For example, the number of problems with a 3-family solution using the 'I' index with memory size of 40, 80, 120, and 160 cases was within 6 percent of the number with 4-family solutions with memory sizes of 20, 40, 60, and 80 respectively. This is an important relationship because it permits an explicit tradeoff between the size of memory and the amount of local search. Performance can be increased by either adding cases to memory or increasing the amount of local search used to access that memory.

Since performance, in terms of problems solved, increased as memory was enlarged, the key question became the computational cost of using additional cases in memory. The results for both structured indices were again similar, though the 'L' index generally required slightly more search than the 'I' index. The results for the 'I' index are presented in Figure 2.

The expected relationship was that the amount of search required to find a solution or determine there wasn't one in memory would increase with memory size. As predicted, this occurred when the problem was not solved, as illustrated in Figure 2. Surprisingly, this was not the case when the problem was solved. The lower curve in Figure 2 shows that the amount of search required when a solution is found remained approximately constant as memory size was increased. Because the number of problems solved approaches 100 percent, the search required when a solution is found dominates the average amount of search. Since it remains constant, memory size can be increased and the computational cost of using it will not outweigh its benefit.

Search remained constant as memory grew because the average size of the N-search required to find a solution decreased. This reduction in the amount of local search offset the additional search required because of additional cases in memory. The net effect makes the approach viable computationally. These search results are comparable with work on the Eight's Puzzle using heuristic search. Nilsson [Nil71] reports a heuristic with an effective branching factor of 1.08. The more natural number of tiles out-of-place plus the length of the search path metric yields an effective branching factor of 1.34. The effective branching factor for the case-based problem solver using the 'I' index when the problem was solved was approximately 1.17 regardless of memory size. This gives a good measure of the effectiveness of case-based problem solving.

Heuristic search is guaranteed to yield a solution, while this case-based method is not. As noted the amount of search required to determine that a problem cannot be solved grows as the case-base grows. The effective branching factor for the search tree generated to determine that a problem could not be solved when the case-base memory size was 160 cases was 1.23. As memory grows, however, the case-based problem solver fails on fewer problems. In addition, the computational cost of finding a solution remains constant. So we are able to bound the amount of search required to either find a solution or determine that one cannot be found. In addition, the expected value for the amount of search required will decrease as memory is increased, approaching the constant amount required when a problem is solved.

3.1.2 'Out-of-Place' and Randomized 'Out-of-Place' Indices

There is no immediate reason to expect case-based problem solving to work. It depends strongly on the character of the indices. This was borne out by our experience with the 'out-of-place' and randomized 'out-of-place' indices. They did not provide the proper abstraction mechanism for the case-based problem solver. The 'out-of-place' metric more easily matched board indices farther from the start-state, but failed to effectively filter the search for a solution. The sequences of states in the solutions led to very regular subsequences of indices. These index subsequences could be generated by a large number of state sequences that did not lead to a solution. For this reason search paths were not pruned quickly, and large search trees were generated. The computational costs associated with these very large search trees made the approach impractical.

The randomized index was also ineffective as an index but for a different reason. The index was not able to generalize the cases in memory enough for them to cover much of the solution space. Its behavior was similar to that of storing only exact traces. Even with 160 cases in memory using the 4-family of "near misses" the system was only able to solve 8 of the 30 problems using the randomized index. The difference between the performance of the randomized index and the structured indices is the degree to which these structured indices encode additional information.

In conclusion, the indices generated by fracturing the structured object provide the right level of abstraction. They were not so specific as to be irrelevant, like the hashed index, nor were they too general to constrain search, like the 'out-of-place' metric.

3.2 Experiment Two

Experiment two was conducted to determine if performance could be improved by selectively rather than randomly adding cases to memory. We were interested in determining if performance could be improved by employing an instance-based learning algorithm to acquire the cases for memory.

Kibler and Aha [KA87] conducted an empirical evaluation of a number of instance based classification learning algorithms. They developed the *Growth algorithm* which was both storage efficient and predictively accurate. The Growth algorithm works by accepting an instance only when it cannot be

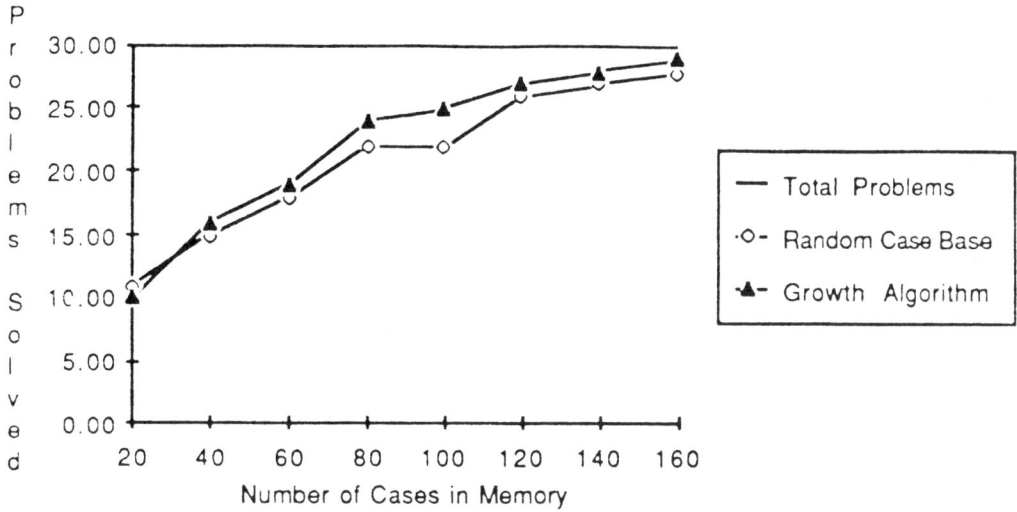

Figure 3: Relative performance of Random Case-Base and Growth Case-Base

correctly classified by the instances currently in memory. A similar algorithm can be used to select cases to place in memory for problem solving. A case is added to memory only if the problem could not be solved with the current memory.

In experiment two, the case-base of the system was assembled using this version of the Growth algorithm. Figure 3 shows the comparative performance for the Growth derived case-base and the random case-base for the 'I' index. The performance when using the case-base derived by the Growth algorithm was slightly better, at first increasing faster as memory grew and achieving a slightly higher level. Still, its performance followed the power curve of learning, and the improvement tapered off quickly after about 80 cases. The Growth algorithm was not able to alter the fact that the rate at which performance increases slows as memory size grows.

4 Summary and Future Work

In this paper we have explored some important yet unaddressed issues in case-based reasoning. These issues involve the index used to access memory, performance effects of increased memory, and the computational cost of increasing memory size. We addressed these issues for a simplified case-based problem solver.

The problem solver operated by using memory as a filter on search. Memory stored abstractions of previous solutions, abstracted through the use of an index. The index would map multiple states in the problem space into the same value in the index space.

Our experiments showed that indices created from heuristic measures were too general and indices from hash functions too specific to guide search. Instead, best performance was found with indices derived by treating the states in the problem space as structured objects and fragmenting them.

Learning behavior exhibited by the system described the standard power law of learning. The degree to which performance increased with an increase in memory size was inversely proportional to the current size of memory. This effect was not countered by adding to memory only solutions to problems not yet solved by the system.

Finally, we found that the amount of search required by our system when finding a solution remained constant as the size of memory increased, providing an effective branching factor of 1.17. The search required did increase when the system was unable to find a solution but remained tractable, yielding an effective branching factor of 1.23 for a memory size of 160. In addition, the number of problems that could not be solved with a memory of 160 cases was only 3%. These results proved comparable to those from heuristic search.

In our future work we plan to explore case-based problem solving in more complex domains. We plan to examine the issue of automatically deriving case-base indices. One possible approach is to apply clustering to solution traces or episodes of solution traces.

References

[Alt86] Richard Alterman. An Adaptive Planner. In *Proceedings of the Fifth National Conference on Artificial Intelligence*, pages 65–69, 1986.

[Car86] Jaime G. Carbonell. Derivational Analogy: a Theory of Reconstructive Problem Solving and Expertise Acquisition. In *Machine Learning: An Artificial Intelligence Approach* (Vol 2), Morgan Kaufmann Publishers, Inc., Los Altos, California, 1986.

[FHN72] Richard E. Fikes, Peter E. Hart, and Nils J. Nilsson. Learning and executing generalized robot plans. *Artificial Intelligence*, 3:251–288, 1972.

[Ham86] Kristian J. Hammond. Chef: a model of case-based planning. In *Proceedings of the Fifth National Conference on Artificial Intelligence*, pages 267–271, 1986.

[Iba85] Glen A. Iba. Learning by discovering macros in puzzle solving. In *Proceedings of the Ninth International Joint Conference on Artificial Intelligence*, pages 640–642, Morgan Kaufmann, Los Angeles, California, 1985.

[KA87] Dennis Kibler and David Aha. Learning representative exemplars of concepts: an initial case study. In *Proceedings of the Fourth International Workshop on Machine Learning*, pages 24–30, Morgan Kaufmann, Irvine, California, 1987.

[Kol87] Janet L. Kolodner. Extending problem solver capabilities through case-based inference. In *Proceedings of the Fourth International Workshop on Machine Learning*, pages 167–178, Morgan Kaufmann, Irvine, California, 1987.

[Kor85] Richard E. Korf. *Learning to Solve Problems by searching for Macro-Operators*. Pitman Advanced Publishing Program, 1985.

[Lan83] Pat Langley. Learning effective search heuristics. In *Proceedings of the Eighth International Joint Conference on Artificial Intelligence*, pages 419–421, William Kaufmann, Karlsruhe, West Germany, 1983.

[Leh87] Wendy G. Lehnert. *Case-Based Reasoning as a Paradigm for Heuristic Search*. COINS Technical Report 87-107, University of Massachusetts, October 1987.

[Min85] Steve Minton. Selectively generalizing plans for problem-solving. In *Proceedings of the Ninth International Joint Conference on Artificial Intelligence*, pages 596–599, William Kaufmann, Los Angeles, California, 1985.

[MUB83] T. M. Mitchell, P. E. Utgoff, and R. B. Banerji. Learning by experimentation: acquiring and refining problem-solving heuristics. In *Machine Learning: An Artificial Intelligence Approach*, pages 163–190, Morgan Kaufmann Publishers, Inc., 1983.

[Nil71] Nils J. Nilsson. *Problem-Solving Methods in Artificial Intelligence*. McGraw-Hill Book Company, 1971.

[PK86] Bruce W. Porter and Dennis Kibler. Experimental goal regression: a technique for learning problem solving heuristics. *Machine Learning*, 1(3):249–285, 1986.

Goals in Reminding

Colleen M. Seifert
UCSD and NPRDC

Abstract

In this paper, I argue that goals affect the process of retrieving cases from memory. The same information, in the presence of different processing goals such as explanation or planning, will result in retrieval of different prior cases from memory. The evidence for this claim consists of a series of experiments demonstrating that activation of cases does not occur automatically, but is dependent on strategic processing goals. Experiments on both thematic knowledge structures (TOPs) and more contentful structures (MOPs) are presented, along with a paradigm for experimental reminding that is successful in generating spontaneous retrieval when the reminding is useful in processing. Prior protocols of remindings are then examined to determine if similar processing goals might be involved in spontaneous retrieval. Finally, a role for processing goals in retrieval is proposed in terms of selection of relevant features. These results argue for attention to the context of a reminding, particularly for computer models of tasks where the nature of the task processing is assumed, and thereby affects the organization and retrieval of cases. Failure to identify contextual goals affecting retrieval of cases will limit the generality of models.

When do remindings occur?

A central problem for models of cased-based reasoning is the retrieval of appropriate cases from memory. Retrieval is assumed to be an automatic process that is dependent solely on matching an input to the contents of memory. Certainly, if an input case has a great deal in common with a particular case in memory, and both cases share little with other cases in memory, then similarity alone may be enough to account for the spontaneous retrieval of the case. However, when there are many instances that overlap in similarity, or when the similarities are abstract in nature, it appears that the predictability of retrieval based on similarity measures alone is less certain.

Consider this example of cross-contextual reminding from Schank (1982):

> X described how his wife would never make his steak as rare as he liked it. When this was told to Y, it reminded Y of a time, 30 years earlier, when he tried to get his hair cut in a short style in England, and the barber would not cut it as short as he wanted it.

Why was Y reminded? There are few similarities in content between the two cases, and a long time lag between them. It appears to be a reminding unique to Y (you may have been reminded about demanding spouses, but probably not barbers), and the basis for resemblence between the two was not consciously available to Y. Schank provides a sketch of the process that may account for why Y was reminded: In order to understand the steak episode, Y uses a schema based on past experiences to encode the new episode. What kind of schema would be appropriate? A schema about cooking steaks would fit, but is not general enough to account for the barber episode; instead, a schema like "provide service" seems to capture what is common to the two episodes. Additionally, both cases involve an unusual request (raw steak, very short hair) that is met with more usual service, probably because the server cannot believe the extremity of the request. (A cultural anthropologist pointed out that both raw meat and shaved heads related to the emasculation theme common across cultures.) Schank argues that the reminding reveals the way in which the event was understood -- that the process of reminding is *mediated* by an abstract knowledge structure used to understand the original event. The claim is that you can't help but pass through old memories when understanding new ones, because cases are activated as a consequence of activating organizing schemas. In the next sections, I will present evidence from my investigations about the conditions under which such remindings occur.

Our colloquial use of "reminding" typically refers to cases in which we are conscious of the result of the retrieval process, but unaware of the features evident in the match. It may also be that we are not always consciously aware of the retrieval of cases, but may partially retrieve concepts in the form of *activation*. Experimental results have shown that concepts connected in memory may activate eachother short of conscious retrieval prior to stimulus presentation but so as to affect responses to the concepts (Meyer and Schvaneveldt, 1971). That is, judging "doctor" to be a word increases speed of response to judge whether "nurse" is a word (as opposed to "nurde"), though when presented with "doctor" no conscious expectation is formed for the presence of "nurse". In the semantic memory results, connection in memory alone is enough to result in the spread of activation from one concept to another. Perhaps cases, like concepts, are activated by accessing their organizing schemas in a manner similar to secondary activation in semantic priming. Schank argues that in cross-contextual reminding, characteristic memory organizations are set up such that attempting to encode a new case with a knowledge structure will call to mind a prior case encoded with that structure. Leaving aside the question of conscious awareness of the result of the retrieval, we can investigate whether the memory organization formed at encoding provides connections between cases such that activating one case in memory will result in the activation of other cases encoded with the same organizing structures. This activation may be the result of an automatic retrieval process, that is uncontrolled and non-optional, as in semantic priming, or it may occur only under some conditions, under strategic control.

Experimental evidence for activation of cases

The question of whether memory organization alone will predict the automatic activation of cases can be investigated experimentally. In this section, several experiments on this issue are summarized, including both thematic organization patterns (Schank, 1982; Lehnert, 1982; Dyer, 1983) and more concrete memory organization packets for action sequences (Schank, 1982). Finally, some experiments on conscious reminding are presented that confirm the utility of experimental methodology for studying the activation of cases. The difficulty in laboratory examination of reminding is that subjects' experiences cannot be used as cases to be retrieved due to variability in rehearsal and frequency; instead, we need to provide cases for subjects to learn as reference instances, equalizing the probability of recall. The story understanding paradigm was adapted to suit this purpose. Stories presented to subjects could share particular similarities, and the experimental context provides a closed set, bounded memory for the comparison of cases overall; that is, subjects are not likely to utilize memories from outside the experimental context when considering the relative similarity of the stories. The basic paradigm involved presenting in sequence pairs of stories that either share or do not share the organizing knowledge structure, and then testing whether the memory organization that results causes differing activation properties. Semantic priming has been shown in a variety of tasks to provide a sensitive measure of differences in accessibility of information (e.g., Gibbs, 1984). In the current studies, time to answer a question about a previously read story is used to measure the accessibility of the story in memory. Priming occurs when answering a question about a related story immediately prior to the test item. If the two stories are connected by the organizing structure in memory, then answering a question from one story should activate the other story in memory, resulting in faster responses to a question from that story.

Experiments with abstract thematic structures

We expected that subjects would find it easier to utilize similarities to encode stories if they have an external validity in the world. The materials chosen for the experiments (Seifert, McKoon, Abelson, and Ratcliff, 1985), therefore, included similarities based on the types of structures evident in protocols of natural remindings; namely, the goal and plan interaction that occur as goals are pursued. Adages were selected as thematic patterns (Schank, 1982; Lehnert, 1982; Dyer, 1983) that would be familiar to subjects and culturally shared, minimizing variability in the structures used for encoding by subjects. For example, the adage "closing the barn door before the horse is gone" can be characterized as a planning failure where X knows a plan to prevent goal failure, but delays execution to avoid the cost until the goal is failing; then, the plan is executed, but fails because it is not a recovery plan but a prevention plan (Dyer, 1983). Here are two stories used in the experiments that represent this thematic pattern:

Story 1: Academia

```
Dr. Popoff knew that his graduate student Mike was unhappy with the
research facilities available in his department. Mike had requested
new equipment on several occasions, but Dr. Popoff always denied Mike's
requests. One day, Dr. Popoff found out that Mike had been accepted to
study at a rival university. Not wanting to lose a good student, Dr.
Popoff hurriedly offered Mike lots of new research equipment. But
by then, Mike had already decided to transfer.
```

Story 2: Wedding Bells

```
Phil was in love with his secretary and was well aware that she wanted
to marry him. However, Phil was afraid of responsibility, so he kept
dating others and made up excuses to postpone the wedding. Finally,
his secretary got fed up, began dating, and fell in love with an
accountant. When Phil found out, he went to her and proposed marriage,
showing her the ring he had bought. But by that time, his secretary
was already planning her honeymoon with the accountant.
```

Two stories were presented in sequence, that either shared the same theme or did not, followed by a test list of items to respond to. Since both stories are encoded with the same theme (Thematic Abstract Unit, from Dyer, 1983), understanding the same-theme stories is predicted to result in this memory representation:

FROM DYER, 1983:

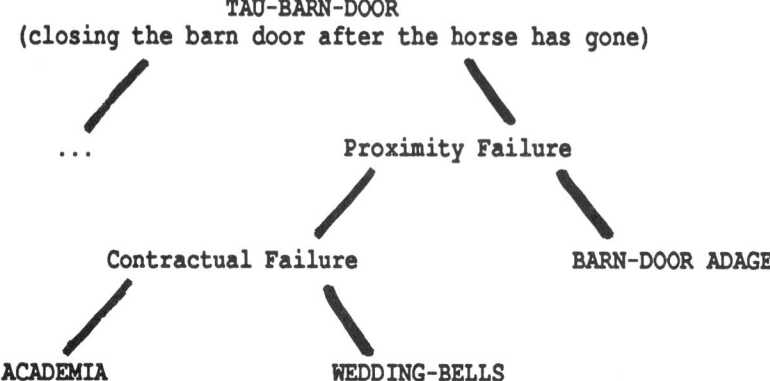

If such a characteristic reminding structure is set up during the understanding process, will reference to the academia story result in activation of the wedding-bells story? To measure activation, subjects respond to a series of test sentences about the two stories, including negatives ("Mike decided to buy his own research equipment") and the two items of interest:

by then, Mike had already decided to transfer

his secretary fell in love with an accountant

If the two stories are connected in memory, responding to an item from one should speed the time to respond to an item from the other. This same-theme response time is to be compared to one where the preceding item refers to a story that does not share the same theme, and therefore should have no connection in memory between the two stories. For example, if one story was based on the "pot calling the kettle black" theme, and the other on the barn door theme, no priming of the response would be expected.

Subjects saw 48 pairs of stories and test lists in the experiment. The results show that the expected same theme result did not affect response time to the test items, 1538 msec when the stories shared the theme, compared to 1516 msec when they did not. The shared knowledge structure did not affect the ease of access of the episodes in memory, so the strong hypothesis that connection alone would result in automatic activation of related episodes was not supported. However, if the process is not automatic, it may still occur under strategic conditions, when subjects attempt to utilize effort or take cues from the task specifications. So, the question is, if we ask subjects to be reminded, will the activation differences result?

In a second experiment, we instructed the subject to think about the theme as they read, and to rate the similarity of the story pair after the test list. Otherwise, this experiment was identical to the first. However, the results were different: this time, there was a significant effect of thematic similarity on response times. The mean response time for stories sharing the same theme was 1567 msec, compared to 1649 for different themes, indicating that responses were faster for test items when the story pair shared the same thematic organizing structure.

The only difference between the two experiments was the instruction to attend to similarity. We conclude, then, that accessing the same schema does not automatically connect two episodes in memory; instead, some strategic purpose is necessary to promote activation of prior episodes. The response times of less than two seconds are still fast enough to make it difficult to utilize conscious expectation about what the target item will be. It seems more likely that the effect is due to the strategic processing at the time of encoding that makes the connection between the stories more "usuable." Note that the comparison alone is not the cause of the effect, since both conditions required comparing story similarity. The strategic basis for the ability to utilize connections between episodes has been replicated in other experiments (Seifert, McKoon, Abelson, and Ratcliff, 1985).

Experiments with contentful structures

One question was whether the strategic result was specific to abstract structures, or would hold true of more content based structures. To test this, we examined the effect of memory organization packets (MOPs) (Schank, 1982) on connections between cases (for a complete description, see McKoon, Ratcliff, and Seifert, 1988). Here's an example of two stories written to instantiate the same MOP but without overlapping lexical items in the description of MOP actions:

> Linda decided to skip work on Thursday and go to the beach. At the beach, Linda found the parking lot ot be surprisingly full for a weekday, but she eventually found a spot. The beach, too, was overcrowded, but Linda was still abel to spread her towel in a dry place close to the water. Not wanting to get a sunburn, Linda put on some suntan lotion. After laying on her towel for some time, Linda was getting hot so she decided to take a dip, and dove into the refreshing water. Although she usually enjoyed the power of her executive secretary position, today she was happy not to be at work. After a short swim, Linda towelled off and packed up her things for the long walk to the car.

> Because the sun was shining so brightly, Nancy decided to spend the day by the sea. When she had gotten to her favorite seaside spot, Nancy parked her car under a tree. Nancy walked quickly over the hot sand until whe found an empthy space where she could lay her blanket. Hoping to add some color to her pale skin, Nancy splashed on some baby oil. The sun was very strong, so Nancy decided to get up and go for a swim. Nancy slowly strolled out into the cool ocean. Her hobby was bird-watching, so she watched the cliffs above her for nesting swallows. When she finally felt water-logged, she headed back to her blanket. She dried off for a while in the warm sun and then dressed for the trip home.

In the experimental procedure, subjects read a long list of stories, and then, after reading all the stories, connections from one story to another were measured by priming in old/new recognition judgments of phrases from the stories. In these experiments, the manipulations involved testing for activation between test items from two stories when the stories shared the same MOP compared to when they did not. Examples of the test items employed are:

MOP-related prime: spread her towel in a dry place

target test phrase: watched the cliffs above for nesting swallows

Unrelated prime: looked over the wine list and ordered chablis

Any priming effect in this experiment may be due to the possibility that understanding the prime results in activation of the MOP representation for the action, which is not specific to either story. As a consequence, activation effects may be due to connections in semantic memory, and not reflect any activation from one case to another case. The somewhat analogous situation in the thematic experiments would be to use a prime from the wedding bells story like "plan executed to late to save goal" and then test an item like "by then, Mike had already decided to transfer." The concern, then, is that the test items used as primes should contain only information that activates the story-specific representation, and through it the MOP and other related story. In a second experiment, the priming items were changed so as not to refer to the generic MOP information. For example, in the first story above, a phrase ("Linda enjoyed the power of her executive secretary position") was added to the story that did not involve MOP information. This phrase was then used as the priming item for the test phrase ("watched the cliffs above for nesting swallows") from the second story. Responding to the priming item requires activating story-specific information, but does not refer to the MOP represented actions.

Results showed priming from one story to another story of the same MOP when test phrases were related to the MOP (1283 msec for same MOP stories, 1417 for different MOP stories). However, when the test phrases were story-specific but not related to the MOP, there was no evidence of priming, 1351 msec for same MOP story pairs, 1360 for different MOP story pairs. This supports the notion that stories are encoded by tagging the generic representation of the MOP in memory, but no evidence for encoding story specifics was found (though subjects were able to recognize story-specific information. So, while MOP information in test items facilitated response times, story-specific information did not activate other story-specific information encoded by the same MOP.

One way to describe the results of these experiments is to say that subjects cannot discriminate whether two MOP-related phrases were from the same or different stories; for example, "spreading out her towel in a dry place" from one story and "found an empty space for her blanket" from another story are equally good primes for "slowly strolled into the cool ocean". This result is consistent with the model of memory proposed by Schank (1982), where information corresponding to MOP actions activated the generic MOP and scene representations, and only novel deviations were encoded distinctly. These experiments are the first to demonstrate the role of such generic knowledge structures in encoding information for later retrieval. Nevertheless, the results as a whole demonstrate that case to case activation is not an automatic phenomenon resulting from connections in memory.

An experimental paradigm for reminding

Since a strategic process appears to be involved in the activation of cases, a next step is to look at reminding within a strategy-based task. Up to this point, in order to keep the subject unaware of the intent of the experiment, we examined activation rather than conscious reminding. Now that the activation appears to be dependent upon a strategic process, we can examine reminding in a paradigm more similar to natural remindings. In these two experiments (Seifert, McKoon, Abelson, and Ratcliff, 1985), subjects were asked to study a set of stories, answering questions and summarizing them. These studied stories serve as the reference cases in memory prior to the reminding. Next, a new set of stories, the test stories, were presented on-line to subjects. Following each test story, a phrase was presented on the screen. This target item was always from one of the studied stories, and subjects were told that this would be the case. However, they were also told to remember the new test stories as well. The test stories had either the same theme (as described in the earlier experiments) or a different theme than the story that the target item was from. In one experiment, the subjects had to answer each target item according to whether it was true in the story it was from; in the second, they pressed a key as soon as they remembered which story it was from, and then wrote a short description to insure they were accurate.

The results for the verification task showed a 185 msec facilitation effect for same theme pairs, and an even bigger difference for the simple identification task. When the test story shared the same theme as the target item's reference story, response times to the item were faster than when the test story had a different theme from the reference story. A story appeared to activate a previous story based on its thematic similarity, resulting in response facilitation. Subjects reported that as they read the test stories, studied stories occasionally "came to mind"; if they did, they were a good predictor of the target item, and so the reminding was useful information to the task. The question is, were subjects systematically searching through the set of stories in order to find the reference story that matched? Two factors argue against this: first, the stories were presented a word at a time until the story was complete, and this average reading rate requires following the presentation closely in order not to miss words (as found in other studies); and second, the subjects were only able to free recall 75% of the studied stories at the end of the test session, despite having plenty of time to do so. Instead, it seems the strategic aspect of this task was that the purpose of the reminding was built into it -- usefulness in predicting the test item provided a functional purpose for the reminding. Also, subjects were conscious of the remindings and their utility, and this may have encouraged attention to themes and the resulting remindings.

This methodology was the first to examine reminding in the laboratory. Other methodologies have since been developed; for example, Gentner and X (1986) had subjects study stories and return a week later for testing. When given a test story, they were told to write down the study story that it reminded them of. The methodology presented in this paper has several advantages over the free recall method. The dependent variable is the ease of access of the reference case. This substantially reduces the variability introduced by the subjects' freedom to choose among responses in untimed free recall methods. The required response is still of short duration (less than two sec), allowing activation and expectation to drive a response to a stimuli rather than a more open ended free recall response, and this gives more of a picture of what subjects are doing in processing. In addition, the use of a target requires the reminding to have been of a particular story; the problem of subjects selecting which one of a set of remindings to report is removed. Most importantly, since presentation time of the test story is controlled (word by word average reading rate), there is less time for retrieval based on searching through the set of reference stories to find a match. Subjects may have notions of which reminding is "appropriate" to report, that interfere with the natural processes that are being modelled in the experimental situation. Because the reading rate keeps the subject engaged in comprehension, the reminding is more likely to be a result of comprehension and inference rather than a deliberate attempt to match among the reference set.

I have described a methodology that provides a functional purpose for the reminding, and consequently appears to generate robust reminding phenomena. Now we can utilize this intentional reminding paradigm to examine aspects of reminding such as the bases of similarity and the adequacy of indexing. In pilot work, I repeated the thematic reminding experiment using single word cues instead of phrases for target items; for example, in the academia story, using "transfer" instead of "by then, Mike had already decided to transfer." The results showed a robust facilitation effect. The next step is to intrude the single word cue into the text at different points; for example, to present only a portion of the barn door theme in the story and interrupt comprehension with the presentation of the test item. By comparing points in the story where there is no facilitation effect to those where there is, the information necessary to access the reminding can be examined. This is important in order to examine the use of cases in planning and problem solving. In these tasks, one is presented with a problem description, and attempts to recall cases that include outcome information. The mapping problem is to take a partial description and retrieve a case with a similar description plus additional information on the solution. This perspective requires models that do not depend on "true analogy" (Gentner, 1982) in order to produce a reminding. For example, if one problem situation ends in death, and a similar one in life, they are not analogous as wholes, but being reminded of both could be quite useful if in that problem situation in the future. In order to take full advantage of past cases, they must be encoded, retrieved, mapped, and generalized in such a way as to take full advantage of relevant information. Models of analogical mapping (Gentner; Holyoak and Thagard, 1988) that examine how to map a complete retrieved description to a complete novel situation may solve a different problem than the one of case retrieval based on problem descriptions. The fact that only the problem description is available as a retrieval cue indicates that the "true analogy" definition will not hold for problem solving in reminding; it may, however, be useful in tasks like instructional learning.

A final caveat is that experimental examination of reminding depends on the experimental context to serve as the whole of memory from which cases are retrieved. The diversity of that feature space will be crucial to claims about the importance of particular content features in perceiving the world. For example, if the only stories presented for study include thematic stories, then we can't be surprised that themes are important in recalling stories within the experiment; we have not demonstrated that this is the case for understanding in the world. This confound is basic to sorting methods of research, where judgments of similarity are always relative to the set as a whole. Particularly when pitting one type of similarity against another, the validity and predictiveness of the features involved may be very different than when present with particular frequencies in the world. For example, a feature that is very distinctive within the story set may be not at all distinctive in similar situations experienced in the world. We may assume that overall featural similarity is the basis for reminding in that two cases which are very similar and very dissimilar to other cases in memory will be more likely to evoke eachother. Given that this is true, it is important to experiments and models of reminding that the memory set reflect realistic proportions of events if claims are to be made about the usefulness of particular features in reminding.

Processing goals in reminding

From the experiments presented above, I conclude that encoding a story does not always activate a thematically similar story *unless* there is also present a functional or strategic purpose for the reminding. These results are reminiscent of analogical transfer studies (Gick and Holyoak, 83; 80), where transfer of a story solution to a new problem was infrequent unless either instructions or multiple example stories were provided. The similarities in the experiments reported here are more obvious than those in the transfer literature, and yet subjects were not reminded unless encouraged by the strategic nature of the task. Intention appears to play a bigger role in retrieval than may have been assumed, because without it the retrieval does not occur. This strategic aspect of retrieval points out the importance of cognitive processing goals; apparently, such goals may act as a level of processing in that activation occurs that would not under other circumstances. In this sense, cognitive goals appear to form a context within which retrieval operates, and the nature of this context determines what remindings occur. The results suggest that, at the least, *intentional reminding* (Schank, 1982) plays a much bigger role than previously indicated. I define intentional very broadly, as not always consciously intended, but as a bias in processing.

With this in mind, we can return to the Steak and the Haircut example. The claim is that retrieval occurs within the context of goals. But what was the context that may have mediated retrieval of the barber case? In that protocol, Y may well have the goal of *explaining* why the steak was underdone to X. He may have been motivated to help X understand why his wife performed such bizarre service behavior, so that X could do more than just complain about it. Y is saying to X, "Sometimes the server can't *believe* the extreme request as you state it, and do the more normal thing." Y's reminding addresses the intention of the server, and utlimately redirects X's attention away from his wife's purposely thwarting the request to a problem in communicating its extremity in the face of a server's strong default notions. What if Y had a goal other than explanation of the steak? If Y was instead motivated to plan to recover from the bad state in the steak story, he might, from the same story but a different processing goal, have been reminded of a recipe for steak tartare. The recipe would provide a way to salvage X's state without explaining it, but with relevance to Y's goal of *planning for recovery*.

A general lesson is evident for the use of protocols to model human thought -- don't ignore context! The irony is that it is usually psychologists who are attacked by AI researchers for failing to consider context not embodied in the current sentence. When collecting natural remindings to use as evidence for a computational model, it is important to attempt to characterize the functionality of the cognition observed. The reminding alone is not enough, but the goal the person was attempting to accomplish at the time of the reminding may also be very relevant to modelling its occurrence. A result that supports this conclusion is that the low transfer rates in the story scenario to new problem solving studies (Gick and Holyoak, 1983) were increased when the context was made congruent in the two cases (Holyoak and Novik, 1988). That is, presenting the first case *as a problem* rather than as a "story understanding task" improved the spontaneous application of the prior solution to the new problem. Because the context of retrieval may play a role in affecting whether or what type of reminding occurs, care must be taken to identify such factors in protocols.

Situations that appear to foster remindings in humans are functions like explanation, planning, argumentation, decision making, and conversation. The kinds of processing goals that may be involved can be described at a general level, but certainly we can discover more about what subtasks of cognition may be involved (Chandrasekharan, 1987). For example, the understander seeks, in his processing of new input in conversation, to be reminded of a memory that relates to what he heard and provides evidence for the point of view he wishes to defend. Remindings can serve to verify your analysis of episode, illustrate why your reasoning is valid, justify or support a claim, give specific solution information, and perhaps provide an analogy. Thus, finding a reminding can be a much more active process than what we refer to as "understanding."

The need to identify these subtasks is pointed out by the fact that particular AI models incorporating cases may use them within only one processing task. Then, since the role of the process is implicit in the model, the memory base for cases, and representational adequacy, will only be capable of handling that process, and will not generalize for use in others. Some tasks being modeled in computer programs may assume reminding occurs with every input. For example, in the *CYRUS* program (Kolodner, 1984), the goal was to retrieve a particular episode in memory given a set of features. Reconstructive strategies were applied to the memory network of episodes and structures to retrieve an episode whenever enough features distinguished an episode from its organizing structure. While activating structures in memory will not be likely to frequently cause a reminding, some types of processing goals may be more likely to produce remindings. Implicit goals in reasoning processes that make use of remindings may foster the retrieval of experiences from memory.

AI models of case-based reasoning tend to select tasks that incorporate a functionality for reminding, and are therefore more likely to produce them. The kinds of tasks which utilize case-based information have implicit goals to guide processing. For example, the *JUDGE* program (Bain, 1984) attempts to determine a fair sentence for an offender by evaluating all possible information. In this task, previous experiences are very useful in evaluating possible outcomes of a sentencing. In addition, remembering cases is important in trying to maintain some consistency in sentencing across individuals. In the *WOK* program (Hammond, 1983), the goal of creating a new recipe guides the search in memory for useful information. Comparing past recipes based on a new feature is an important part of being creative, and therefore the need to examine past cases is an important part of the process. In this type of task, where the creation of new plans occurs by comparing past successes and failures, reminding as a strategy is very important.

What types of tasks will include processing goals that promote remindings? Clearly, any type of problem solving task will tend to require these kinds of processing demands. In situations where complex situations are represented by prototypes, recall of episodes will be important. For example, in the legal domain, cases often stand as prototypes for decisions, and lawyers need to recall cases as exemplars to formulate arguments. Reminding is the basis for analogical thinking, and in situations where there is a lack of domain knowledge, drawing upon past experiences that share some similarities will be necessary. In complex problem solving tasks, where detailed reasoning is required, remindings can aid in thinking through the factors involved in the problem. For example, in the domain of psychiatric diagnosis, where complex information is available to be considered, recall of previous cases may suggest correlations not previously noted (Kolodner & Simpson, 1984). Finally, in examining alternative conceptualizations or scenarios, possible solutions can be used as memory indices to find past instances where the solutions were tried, and the resulting episodes can be compared to the current instance.

Modelling goals in retrieval processes

I have argued from experimental results that strategic purpose is important because automatic processes like retrieval are mediated by processing goals. How might functionality direct the reminding process? I propose that goals play a role in retrieval by affecting what features are attended to most in a similarity match process. Particular features of the case will be attended to based upon the cognitive goals operating at the time.

Here's an example of how goals may act to select features to attend to:

```
Input:  Teletrack has a "no smoking" policy which means, in effect,
that every section is a smoking section.  The rule is disregarded
often enough, by people seated in various sections, that no section can
be guaranteed to be smoke-free.  You argue that the management should
allow smoking in some sections, if only to be sure that some
sections can actually be non-smoking.
```

Suppose that you are engaged in an argument about your comment. Your goal is to buttress your claim that, basically, control is better than abolishment when disobedience is common. Supporting your claim involves retrieving another instance with this pattern; based on the abstract characterization of the claim, an analogous situation is recalled. You may be reminded, on this basis, of the legalization of heroin in England. That case supports the claim by identifying a circumstance where control of heroin use had fewer bad effects on non-participants than the outright banning of the substance.

Suppose instead that your goal is to plan a way to get your assertion implemented. In order to get your solution effected, you have to figure out a way to get the authority involved, Teletrack, to recognize that their control problem is worse now than it would be under the smoking section plan. Planning for implementing your solution selects problem features that are relevant to the management of the policy. You may be reminded, on this basis, of the pet policy in student housing. Pets were banned, but then many students got pets and broke the rules more and more brazenly, causing quite a bit of disturbance. In an attempt to manage the effects of the pets, the management made several buildings "no pets" and let the pet owners congregate in the others. This suggest a plan for the smoking policy: at Teletrack, smoke as much as possible, and encourage others to, in a way that exacerbates the problem for the management. They will be more likely then to see the benefit of control rather than prohibition.

Even if the plan does not seem a like good one, the point here is that the processing that goes on prior to a reminding may be much more involved than simply encoding input facts into a single representation. Instead, the features that play a larger role in retrieval may be ones that are tied to particular processing goals active at the moment. From this, we could expect that retrieval of the new episodes later would depend on a congruency of cognitive purpose. For models where only one processing goal is ever present, the goals may be implicitly encoded in the process model and memory representation, compromising the ability to make claims about how cases are utilized in general.

Cognitive goals may affect other processes besides retrieval, operating to provide a context for saliency of features. The tendency to treat all features as equal, without regard to how particular features may be attended to in certain cognitive contexts, is a major problem in models of learning. For example, parallel distributed models of learning as a class consider all features present as potentially equally important to the rule being learned. Consequently, it takes many trials to determine which features are actually predictive rather than occurring occasionally. This approach hurts learning rates in two ways; first, it may hurt mathematically in the learning algorithms to include so many features that take many trials to be ruled out; and second, it ignores information available in utilizing a priori notions of what features are likely to be related to the rule.

In a learning system, treating all features equally will mean a lot of effort spent on features that have no importance to the rule learned. With the addition of a mechanism to select the features most likely to be relevant to the rule, one can save time by focusing on features that will pay off more quickly. For example, the current state of the network can provide a focus on particular input features based on what features have been given higher weights in previous learning. Consequently, by utilizing prior knowledge, one can shut off features that aren't a priori relevant to learning. Of course, as I have been arguing in this paper, this is not enough when the same network serves other tasks. Which features are relevant in a domain can't be set in an a priori way that will be true across all learning contexts. One needs a mechanism to affect the attention at the nodes *depending upon* the processing context. The goals can affect which features are attended to by interacting in a multiplicative fashion with activation on the input nodes. This method can incorporate changes in relevance due to the particular goals being pursued.

It seems that people often have notions of what features *may* be important to learning in a particular domain. For example, in learning a new video game, the actions effective in killing enemies tend to be predictable from common-sense notions of physical causality (e.g., you have to be in a linear position with the target for a shot to hit it). To the extent that the actual game mechanics violate these notions, they may be increasingly hard for people to learn. In fact, the less face validity to the rule, the more often people may fail to perceive its presence among the possible factors. This is a drawback to the process of using default expectations for the relevancy of features; however, it may be more than compensated for by the ability to quickly detect the operation of more obvious factors. By attending to the seemingly related features, the learning process may be "smartened up" and sped up, at the cost of discovering nonintuitive or novel connections in the data. Within human systems at least, the gain from attention in speed of learning may more than make up for missing counterintuitive or unusual patterns. Utilizing cognitive goals to affect the attention paid to features based upon their inferable connections seems a promising approach for models of learning as well as retrieval.

Conclusion

Abstract reminding is not all that frequent, and yet some models treat such interesting case retrieval as common. This is because tasks selected for computational modelling are ones where reminding depends not so much on similarity-based memory as on the task context. Results from experiments on the automaticity of reminding point to the importance of a processing context for retrieval of cases. In models of case retrieval, the role of task-based goals in affecting whether and what type of reminding occurs must be examined. In models of tasks utilizing cases, there is a need for awareness of the implicit goals within task processes. Accessing a previous episode is fostered by implicit goals in processing. Therefore, in computational models utilizing cases, we must explicitly identify the processing goal context in order to make claims about the generality of the use of cases. Interest in case-based reasoning is now turning to tasks that are more likely to result in remindings, such as decision-making. Modeling these types of tasks will likely give us better evidence about the reminding process, as they are likely to provide more instances of reminding across contexts. However, in order to make claims about access to cases, we must examine and make explicit the role of processing goals in the retrieval of cases.

Reference Notes

Holyoak, K. & Novik, L. (1988). Personal communication.

References

Bain, W. M. (1984). Toward a model of subjective understanding. *Technical Report No. 324*. Computer Science Program, Yale Univ.

Chandrasekaran, B. (1987). Towards a functional architecture for intelligence based on generic information processing tasks. *Proceedings fo teh Tenth International Joint Conference on Artificial Intelligence*, Milan, Italy.

Dyer, M. G. (1983). *In-depth understanding: A computer model of integrated processing for narrative comprehension*. Cambridge, MA: MIT Press.

Gentner, D. (1982). Structure mapping: A theoretical framework for analogy. *Research Report No. 5192*, Bolt Beranek and Newman Inc.

Gentner, D., & Landers, R. (1985). Analogical reminding: A good match is hard to find. *Proceedings of the International Conference on Systems, Man, and Cybernetics*, Tucson, AZ.

Gibbs, R. W. (1984). Literal meaning and psychological theory. *Cognitive Science, 8,* 275-304.

Gick, M., & Holyoak, K. (1980). Analogical problem solving. *Cognitive Psychology*, 12, 306-355.

Gick, M., & Holyoak, K. (1983). Schema induction and analogical transfer. *Cognitive Psychology*, 15, 1-38.

Hammond, K. J. (1983). Planning and goal interaction: The use of past solutions in present situations. *Proceedings of the National Conference on Artificial Intelligence, AAAI*, Washington, D. C.

Holyoak, K. J., & Thagard, P. (1988). Analogical mapping by constraint satisfaction: A computational theory. Unpublished manuscript.

Kolodner, J. L. (1984). *Retrieval and organizational strategies in conceptual memory: A computer model*. Hillsdale, NJ: Lawrence Erlbaum Associates.

Kolodner, J. L., & Simpson, R. L. (1984). Experience and problem solving: A framework. *Proceedings of the Sixth Annual Conference of the Cognitive Science Society*, Boulder, CO.

Lehnert, W. G. (1981). Plot units and narrative summarization. *Cognitive Science*, 5, 293-331.

McKoon, G., Ratcliff, R., & Seifert, C. M. (1988). Making the connection: Generalized knowledge structures in story understanding. Unpublished Manuscript.

Meyer, D. E., & Schvaneveldt, R. W. (1971). Facilitation in recognizing pairs of words: Evidence of a dependence between retrieval operations. *Journal of Experimental Psychology, 10*, 227-234.

Schank, R. C. (1982). Dynamic memory: A theory of reminding and learning in computers and people. New York:Cambridge University Press.

Seifert, C. M., McKoon, G., Abelson, R. P., & Ratcliff, R. (1985). Memory connections between thematically similar episodes. *Journal of Experimental Psychology: Human Learning and Memory*, 12 (2), 220-231.

Abstractional Analogy: A Model of Analogical Reasoning[1]

HONG S. SHINN (shinn@gatech.edu)

School of Information and Computer Science, Georgia Institute of Technology
Atlanta, GA 30332, U.S.A.

Abstract

Our model of analogical reasoning is based on the view that it is necessary to grasp the abstraction common to two analogous problems in order to know exactly what can be transferred from one problem to another. The model consists of two major steps. First, create an abstract schema that represents what source and target cases have in common. The abstract schema consists of a problem schema and its solution schema. The problem schema is created by analogically mapping the source problem to the target problem, then its solution schema is created using the source case. Second, apply the solution schema to the target problem. We call such a model of analogical reasoning *abstractional analogy*.

Abstractional analogy provides a way of extracting all knowledge from a source that can be transferred to a target. Transfer can be of reasoning methods and/or of generalized results. Both types of knowledge are learned in the form of solution schemas as a natural byproduct of abstractional analogy. Abstract schemas together with cases can be organized into abstraction hierarchies. Thus, abstractional analogy is a unifying model of three different aspects of cognition: problem solving by analogy, learning of both declarative (generalized results) and procedural (reasoning methods) knowledge, and memory organization.

1 Introduction

Experiential reasoning plays a major role in human problem solving and learning. Jardine [Jar74] quotes Francis Bacon:

New knowledge is discovered by ingenious adaptation of existing knowledge, rather than by formal inference from fundamental principles.

---

[1]This research has been supported in part by the Army Research Institute under Contract No. MDA-903-86-C-173, is currently supported in part by NSF under Grant No. IST-8608362, and in part by Lockheed AI Center under Grant No. DTD 09-25-87.

Analogical reasoning is one way of adapting existing knowledge to solve a new problem.

Although a number of models of analogical reasoning have been attempted, two contradicting views currently coexist on the process of analogical transfer [Dar83,Ros86]:

1. **Direct transfer of knowledge from source to target**
   Analogy is identified by establishing correspondences between source and target and then interpreting knowledge about the source in the target domain.

2. **Indirect transfer via common abstraction**
   Analogy is identified as a common abstraction and then knowledge transfer is done via the abstraction.

Traditionally, researchers have viewed analogy as direct transfer, and most AI programs that do analogical reasoning employ that method (e.g., [Win80] [Car86]). However, the view of indirect transfer recently has received more attention (e.g., [Pol54,Gen80,GH83,CM85,Der85,And86]). Genesereth [Gen80] states that "the problem of understanding an analogy becomes one of recognizing the shared abstraction."

This is a problem which leads to completely different models of problem solving and learning. That is, does learning by generalization occur during problem solving (i.e., as part of making the analogy) or does it occur afterwards? The direct transfer view implies that generalization occurs after problem solving, while the indirect view suggests that it occurs during problem solving. Ross [Ros86] points out that, while some researchers have seen that generalization is forced by analogical mapping, no one has clearly stated their temporal relationship. We suspect this confusion is caused by failure to understand in detail the process involved in making an analogy. This paper presents a model called *abstractional analogy* based on the indirect transfer approach and also provides some computational accounts of this method.

Another important issue on analogical reasoning is that of what knowledge is transferred and how. Polya [Pol45] identifies two types of knowledge transferred during analogical problem solving. These are the method used and the result. Transfer of a previous result — possibly with some minor modification — shortcuts the reasoning involved for a similar problem by reducing its search for a solution. When result transfer is not appropriate, reasoning can be transferred. These two transfer methods are applied in different stages of problem solving. Abstractional analogy integrates these two types of analogy transfer.

The process of abstractional analogy is implemented as the case-based reasoning (CBR) part of the JULIA system [CK86,Kol87b,Kol87a], designed to be a caterer's assistant. JULIA's task is to interactively plan a meal with a client user who provides constraints for the meal. Some constraints are given early on. The need for specification of others is determined during problem solving. JULIA's problem solver includes constraint propagation and satisfaction, a goal-based reduction planner, and CBR modules. The reasoning described in this paper is JULIA's CBR method. JULIA uses CBR [2] whenever a previous similar case is made available to it by its memory. Examples from JULIA will be used throughout this paper.

2 The Process of Abstractional Analogy

Our model of analogical reasoning, abstractional analogy, consists of two major steps, analogy abstraction and then abstraction application. Analogy abstraction is achieved in two substeps. First, an abstract problem schema is created by analogically mapping the source problem to the target problem. Then, a solution schema is created for the problem schema using the source case. The two abstract schemas formed this way uniquely represent the analogy existing between the analogues. In the next step, the solution schema is applied to the target problem. An additional step refines the solution obtained by analogy to fit constraints of the new problem that were not covered.

In later problem solving with a new problem, whenever an existing schema fits the new problem, the schema is applied to the problem: if the generalized result of the schema is available, it is transferred; otherwise the reasoning method is applied. This process will be discussed here in detail.

2.1 Representing Problems and Cases

JULIA uses frame representations [Min75,Wil86] for describing problem and solution structures. In JULIA, a natural language processing (NLP) system [TC88] interprets a problem description into a frame. Suppose a target problem is

> Find a Thanksgiving main dish for 16 vegetarians. The dining room can accommodate only 10 people. What and how should it be served?

---

[2] Although the JULIA system uses the general term "case-based reasoning" to indicate a method of reasoning with previous cases, in this paper the term "analogical reasoning" will be used instead to emphasize the role of analogy in knowledge transfer.

The NLP would first identify goals of a problem, and then take everything else, which constrains the goals, and make it into a constraint. Figure 1 shows the result.

Problem:
    goals: [g-know(MAIN-DISH) g-know(MEAL-PRESENTATION)]
    constraints: [c-season(THANKSGIVING) c-diet(VEGETARIAN)
        c-number-of-guests(16) c-dining-space(10)]

(Note: Information such as host, guests, location, and time are omitted.)

Figure 1: Problem C50

Each case in JULIA has problem and solution parts. The problem part describes its problem functionally in terms of goals and constraints while the solution part contains a solution plan and the reasoning history. The representation of a case supports hierarchical structure: a case may be decomposed into subcases which may be again decomposed and so on; thus, cases at all levels have the same structure so that they can be viewed as independent cases. This recursive representation facilitates knowledge transfer at any level.

2.2 Analogical Mapping

Our analogical mapping algorithm accommodates Gentner's systematicity principle ([Gen83]) in that it transfers "a system of connected knowledge, not a mere assortment of independent facts". In other words, during mapping between structures, even the highest order predicates may not be mapped separately from their lower level entities. However, in dealing with similarity, we do not accept Gentner's entire theory of structure mapping. In our mapping scheme, two relations which are functionally similar (i.e., their current partonomic roles in both structures are the same) will not be thrown out.

For example, according to Gentner, two relations *equals[add(a,b),add(b,a)]* and *equals[multiply(a,b),multiply(b,a)]*[3] are not mappable to each other because the highest level predicates are identical, but not the lower level predicates (i.e., add and multiply). On the other hand, in our scheme, these are mappable because their high order predicates are the same while the low level predicates "add" and "multiply" are functionally similar due to their same functional roles in the whole structures. Burstein [Bur86] demonstrates with his system CARL the necessity of

---
[3]Polya's analogy example [Pol54]

mapping between nonidentical relations, criticizing Gentner's structure mapping [Gen83] which fails on this kind of similarity.

Another characteristic of our mapping scheme is hierarchical mapping. This is frequently used when problems are represented in hierarchical structure. In fact, analogy between problems usually exists at an abstract level. Thus, mapping starts at the highest level first and proceeds to the next lower level and so on until analogy breaks down. Holyoak [Hol85] also identified hierarchical mapping as a practical necessity.

Thus, in our scheme, the entire mapping process is a recursive application of two-step hierarchical mapping: first identify the next lower level structures, and then map them systematically under functional similarity.

Let's apply our general mapping scheme to a problem from JULIA's domain. As an example, given the target problem C50 (Figure 1), JULIA[4] is reminded of case C38 (Figure 2): "a vegetarian Thanksgiving main dish for 4 people, all seated and served." Case C38, which had two goals, g-know(menu) and g-know(presentation), was decomposed into two subcases C381 and C382, one for each goal. Since cases are represented in hierarchical structure, JULIA begins mapping with the top level problem structures. Then, it identifies functional similarity. In a frame-based representation, a problem is already analyzed into a problem structure [Wil86]. Thus, it is straightforward to identify the same functional components (e.g., goals and constraints). Next, it starts mapping with goals: if goals fully match, the mapping proceeds to constraints; in case of a partial match, which means some goals match but others do not, only the matched goals will be considered for possible transfer; otherwise, the mapping fails. Mapping then proceeds to constraints on only the matched goals to establish correspondences between them. For example, JULIA identifies correspondence between c-number-of-guests(16) and c-number-of-guests(4) because their functional roles in the problems are the same.

2.3 Problem Abstraction

Problem abstraction is the process of building a problem schema as a common abstraction of two analogous problems. A similarity is a commonality at a higher level of abstraction and an identity is a commonality at the same level. Thus, the commonalities abstracted from similarities together with identities form a problem schema.

Similarities can be identified by using an abstraction hierarchy. One hierarchy,

---

[4]'JULIA' usually refers to the entire problem solving system but often is used to refer to only the analogical reasoner, as in this case.

C38:
  Problem:
    goals: [g-know(MAIN-DISH) g-know(MEAL-PRESENTATION)]
    constraints: [c-season(THANKSGIVING) c-diet(VEGETARIAN)
        c-number-of-guests(4) c-dining-space(>4)]
  Solution: [C381 C382]
  Reasoning:
    1. OP: plan for each subcase

C381:
  Problem:
    goal: [g-know(MAIN-DISH)]
    constraints: [c-season(THANKSGIVING) c-diet(VEGETARIAN) c-number-of-guests(4)]
  Solution: STUFFED-SQUASH
    ingredients:
      2 squashes with filling:
      1/2 cup chopped onion, 1 clove garlic, 1 stalk celery,
      1/4 cup walnuts, 1/4 cup sunflower seeds, 1/4 cup raisins,
      1/2 tsp. sage, 1/2 tsp. thyme, 1/2 lemon juice,
      3 tbs. butter, 1 cup wheat bread, 1/2 cup cheddar cheese
Recipe Source: *Moosewood Cookbook* (by Mollie Katzen, 1977, Ten Speed Press)

C382:
  Problem:
    goals: [g-know(MEAL-PRESENTATION)]
    constraints: [c-number-of-guests(4) c-dining-space(>4)]
  Solution: SERVICE
  Reasoning:
    1. OP: "Since the number of guests was less than the dining space,
        the eating configuration was SEATED."
      Input: [c-number-of-guests(4) c-dining-space(>4)]
      Output:[c-eating-configuration(SEATED)]
    2. OP: "Since the eating configuration was SEATED,
        the meal presentation was SERVICE."
      Input: [c-eating-configuration(SEATED)]
      Output:[c-meal-presentation(SERVICE)]

Figure 2: Case C38

which frame-based representations (as in JULIA) support, is an ISA hierarchy. In this hierarchy, given a pair of objects, a common abstraction is found by simply identifying their immediate common ancestor (e.g., "fruit" for "apple" and "orange"). In JULIA, if the existing hierarchy does not contain a common ancestor for the pair of objects, then an abstract object is created by introducing a new symbol. The new object will be given as its property: the set of common properties (i.e., the union of the set of identical properties and the set of abstractions of pairs of similar properties). Note that the existence of an entity does not require its lexicalization in language. This method of commonality abstraction is also applicable to mathematical objects such as variables [Der85,Der86]. For example, the pair [c-number-of-guests(16) c-number-of-guests(4)] creates a common constraint c-number-of-guests(?X) and ?X will be given as its property "number".

A75:
   Problem:
      goals: [g-know(MAIN-DISH) g-know(MEAL-PRESENTATION)]
      constraints: [c-season(THANKSGIVING) c-diet(VEGETARIAN)
         c-number-of-guests(?X) c-dining-space(?Y)]
   Solution: [A751 A752]

A751:
   Problem:
      goal: [g-know(MAIN-DISH)]
      constraints: [c-season(THANKSGIVING) c-diet(VEGETARIAN) c-number-of-guests(?X)]

A752:
   Problem:
      goals: [g-know(MEAL-PRESENTATION)]
      constraints: [c-number-of-guests(?X) c-dining-space(?Y)]

Figure 3: Problem schema A75

Now, consider creation of a problem schema for problems C38 (Figure 2) and C50 (Figure 1). JULIA first creates an abstract problem A75 (Figure 3) at the top-level with the commonalities found between C38 and C50. Next, JULIA checks the next lower level of the source schema to see if it was divided into subproblems; if so, it creates subproblems in the same manner recursively. Here, it creates two subproblems A751 and A752 at the lower level, one for each common goal.

2.4 Solution Abstraction

A solution schema is an abstraction of the source solution that is at the same level of abstraction as the problem schema. Figure 4 outlines our solution abstraction algorithm.

Consider, first, transfer of reasoning. JULIA assumes a reasoning history is well maintained in the form of an operator with its preconditions and justifications, input, and output for each step. For each step, JULIA checks to see if the current state of the schema meets the preconditions of the operator of this step. If the preconditions are not met, the schema needs to be transformed. In general, however, there is no domain-independent method for transformation. The transformation problem can be viewed as another separate problem to which analogical reasoning can be applied. If the preconditions are met, the operator is generalized to fit the schema. The generalized operator also needs to be justified using the previous justifications.

However, since the schema includes variables, there may exist more than one reasoning path depending on the value of input data at that step. This could happen, for example, when the operator is "**compare** two values ?X and ?Y".

If application of the generalized operator to the input of this step always leads to the same reasoning path as that of source case, the applied result will be kept in the schema for the output of that step. If it has more than one alternative reasoning path on this input, JULIA needs to generalize the operator as follows: for the same alternative as that of the source case, JULIA generalizes the operation as in the above case; for the other alternatives, JULIA generalizes the operation in one of the following ways: if an existing schema was retrieved and it has a reasoning path for this alternative, then use it; if the previous justifications similarly fit these other alternatives, then generalize the operator along the similar line; otherwise use domain theory.

Next, consider transfer of result[5]. The source result is generalized to fit the problem schema by considering the generalized requirements in the problem schema and the requirements in the source problem but not in the problem schema. Space does not permit more discussion of this method [Car83,Tur87]; it will be briefly discussed with a simple example below.

Let's now apply the abstraction algorithm to case C38 (Figure 2) for the problem schema (Figure 3). This is split into two subproblems. Consider, first, subschema A751 with subcase C381. Since subcase C381 does not have a reasoning history, JULIA uses the transfer of result. Using the analogy map, JULIA knows the source

---

[5]There are some applications where, even when a reasoning history is available, transfer of result is desirable [Kol87b].

Input: Problem schema, source case, and analogy map
Output: Solution schema
Method:
(The analogy map provides the correspondence information between the problem schema and the source case.)

if a reasoning history is not available for the source case
then do transfer of result:
    generalize the result to fit the problem schema;
    store the generalized result in the schema
else do transfer of reasoning:
    for each step of the reasoning history of source case **do**:
    if the current state of the schema meets the preconditions of the operator
    then
      if there is only one alternative on the input of the schema
      then
        generalize the operator up to the abstract level of the schema;
        store the operator in the schema for this step;
        apply the operator to the current state of the schema
        and keep the result in the schema for this step;
      else if there exist more than one alternative
      then
        generalize the operator for each alternative similarly;
        store the generalized operator in the schema for this step;
    else
      transform the schema to make it meet the preconditions of this operator
        if transformation is successful
        then apply the above method
        else abandon this case for another

Figure 4: Solution Abstraction Algorithm

result needs to be generalized to fit constraint c-number-of-guests(?X). In this case, generalization is done by using the domain knowledge: "The quantity of food is proportional to the number of guests (say, DK22)." JULIA applies this knowledge to the source result and multiples the quantity of each ingredient of the dish by ?X/4. The generalized result[6] is shown in Figure 5.

Next, apply the abstraction algorithm to subschema A752 and subcase C382. Since the reasoning history is available for subcase C382, JULIA uses it to generalize the subschema. For each step of the reasoning history, JULIA checks if it is applicable to the current state of the schema. JULIA finds that the first step requires the constraints [c-number-of-guests(?X) c-dining-space(?Y)] as input. Next, JULIA checks if the reasoning step is general enough to fit into the problem schema. In the source case, since the number of guests was less than or equal to the dining capacity, the eating-configuration was SEATED. But, in the schema, since the number of guests may or may not be greater than the dining capacity, this step of operation in the source case should be generalized, considering both alternatives for the schema. For the case in which the number of guests is less than or equal to the dining capacity, the schema will use the same reasoning as that of the source case (i.e., **if** ?NO-GUESTS $\leq$?DINING-CAPACITY, **then** ?EATING-CONFIGURATION is SEATED). But, for the other alternative (i.e., ?NO-GUESTS > ?DINING-CAPACITY), the operation needs to be generalized using one of the above mentioned generalization techniques. One method is to use the domain knowledge: "The eating-configuration is either SEATED or STANDING." After a simple computation, we get "**If** ?NO-GUESTS > ?DINING-CAPACITY, **then** ?EATING-CONFIGURATION is STANDING." Similarly, the next step will also be generalized using the domain knowledge: "The meal-presentation is either SERVICE or BUFFET." Figure 5 shows the schema so obtained.

2.5 Abstraction Application

After an abstract schema is created, it is applied to the target problem. The basic idea for schema application is to apply the generalized result if one exists, otherwise apply the reasoning method.

Application of schema A75 (Figure 5) to problem C50 (Figure 1) generates two subproblems. The subproblem for goal g-know(MAIN-DISH) is solved by applying the generalized result of subschema A751 which requires instantiating the

---

[6]The generalized result in this case only mediates transfer between source and target cases and may not be interpreted by any means as a solution formula for every case that has the same set of requirements as this case, because it is only one of many possible solutions. There may, however, be times when the generalized result will indeed be a solution formula.

A75:
  Problem:
    goals: [g-know(MAIN-DISH) g-know(MEAL-PRESENTATION)]
    constraints: [c-season(THANKSGIVING) c-diet(VEGETARIAN)
        c-number-of-guests(?X) c-dining-space(?Y)]
  Solution: [A751 A752]
  Reasoning:
    1. OP: plan for each subcase

A751:
  Problem:
    goal: [g-know(MAIN-DISH)]
    constraints: [c-season(THANKSGIVING) c-diet(VEGETARIAN) c-number-of-guests(?X)]
  Solution: STUFFED-SQUASH
    ingredients:
      1/2 ?X squashes with the filling:
      1/8 ?X cup chopped onion, 1/4 ?X clove garlic, 1/4 ?X stalk celery,
      1/16 ?X cup walnuts, 1/16 ?X cup sunflower seeds, 1/16 ?X cup raisins,
      1/8 ?X tsp. sage, 1/8 ?X tsp. thyme, juice from 1/8 ?X lemon,
      3/4 ?X tbs. butter, 1/4 ?X cup wheat bread, 1/8 ?X cup cheddar cheese
  Reasoning: (justifications: case C381 and domain knowledge DK22)

A752:
  Problem:
    goals: [g-know(MEAL-PRESENTATION)]
    constraints: [c-number-of-guests(?X) c-dining-space(?Y)]
  Solution:
  Reasoning:
    1. OP: **If** ?NO-GUESTS $\leq$?DINING-CAPACITY
        then ?EATING-CONFIGURATION is SEATED
        else ?EATING-CONFIGURATION is STANDING
    2. OP: **If** ?EATING-CONFIGURATION is SEATED
        then ?MEAL-PRESENTATION is SERVICE
        else ?MEAL-PRESENTATION is BUFFET

Figure 5: Abstract schema **A75**

C50:
  Problem:
    goals: [g-know(MAIN-DISH) g-know(MEAL-PRESENTATION)]
    constraints: [c-season(THANKSGIVING) c-diet(VEGETARIAN)
        c-number-of-guests(16) c-dining-space(10)]
  Solution: [C501 C502]
  Reasoning: (justification: Schema A75)
    1. OP: plan for each subcase

C501:
  Problem:
    goal: [g-know(MAIN-DISH)]
    constraints: [c-season(THANKSGIVING) c-diet(VEGETARIAN) c-number-of-guests(16)]
  Solution: STUFFED-SQUASH
    ingredients:
      8 squashes with the filling:
      2 cup chopped onion, 4 clove garlic, 4 stalk celery,
      1 cup walnuts, 1 cup sunflower seeds, 1 cup raisins,
      2 tsp. sage, 2 tsp. thyme, juice from 2 lemon,
      12 tbs. butter, 4 cup wheat bread, 2 cup cheddar cheese
  Reasoning: (justification: Schema A751)

C502:
  Problem:
    goals: [g-know(MEAL-PRESENTATION)]
    constraints: [c-number-of-guests(16) c-dining-space(10)]
  Solution: BUFFET
  Reasoning: (justification: Schema A752)

Figure 6: Case C50

variable ?X to 16. On the other hand, the subproblem for goal g-know(MEAL-PRESENTATION) is solved by applying the reasoning method, step by step. The variables ?X and ?Y are bound to 16 and 10, respectively, and each step is applied; the eating configuration is STANDING after the first step; the meal presentation is BUFFET after the second step. The resultant target case is shown in Figure 6.

2.6 Solution Refinement

Application of a schema to the target problem may not lead to a final solution because the instantiated result does not always meet all the requirements. If it is the case, the result of schema application must be refined. In general, the problem of refinement can be viewed as an independent problem where its goal is transforming the current result to make it satisfy the remaining requirements. This means that either an analogical problem solver or other problem solvers can be applied here. In JULIA, refinement with extra constraints is done by using the same reasoning method used for the other constraints.

3 Analogy-Based Learning

Analogical problem solving per se is one form of learning because it learns from previous experience how to solve similar problems. Another form of learning occurs as a byproduct of problem solving in the form of schemas. A schema contains two types of general knowledge: procedural (reasoning method) and declarative (generalized result). This section will discuss the latter form of general learning and the related issues: where and how the acquired knowledge is stored and how it is used later.

3.1 Learning During Solution Abstraction

As shown in the previous section, solution abstraction can be viewed as the process of extracting an embedded algorithm out of the reasoning part of a previous case and/or a generalized result out of the solution part. As a result, a solution schema contains a reasoning method and/or a generalized result for a given problem schema. From the learning point of view, a solution schema represents exactly what is learned from a particular analogy.

We should note, however, that the generalized result of a solution schema may not always be interpreted as a solution formula. If the result is proven to be unique it can be used as a solution formula for any case that is an instance of the problem schema. On the other hand, if the result is just one among many possible solutions (e.g., A751), it should be interpreted solely as a mediator of transferring the source solution to the target problem. If this gets used frequently, it may become a prototypical solution, but not a solution formula. Thus, the generalized result is a potential source of either a solution formula or a prototypical solution.

Analogy-based generalization vs Explanation-based generalization

Schema abstraction (i.e., problem abstraction plus solution abstraction) is a kind of analogy-based generalization (ABG). ABG and explanation-based generalization (EBG) (see [DM86,MKK86]) are as different as they are similar.

If a reasoning history is not available for a solved case and needs to be built, it can be done either by using EBG (because a reasoning history for a case in ABG corresponds to an explanation for an example in EBG) or by applying ABG recursively to another analogous case with a reasoning history (see [KL87] for case-based explanation). The problem of constructing an explanation using the domain theory is similar to a state space search problem if we view a problem as an initial state and its solution as a final state. EBG, in this case, has no strategy of controlling the search space. ABG, on the other hand, can significantly constrain the search space using the reasoning history of another similar case.

In addition, since EBG generalizes on a single case, the generalized explanation accommodates only the one possible alternative that the particular case followed. As a result, EBG fails to consider other potential alternatives so that EBG by itself is not capable of learning general reasoning methods. On the other hand, two cases give ABG a chance to explore more than one alternative in problem solving (as we have seen in Section 2.4). This leads ABG to incrementally learn a general method.

3.2 Organizing Memory with Cases

When a target problem is solved, both the target and source cases are stored in memory as specializations of the abstract schema created by abstractional analogy. The schema itself is stored, replacing the previous source case, and both cases will be made children of this schema. In this way, abstractional analogy forms memory into abstraction hierarchies, where each node represents a specific or generalized case.

A retrieval algorithm similar to that described in Kolodner [Kol84] can be used to find the most specific partially matching schema or case, when a new problem is being solved. If a schema has already been created and is recalled from memory, the analogical reasoner uses it to solve the problem directly. If a case more similar than available schemas is recalled, abstractional analogy is applied to it to solve the problem.

4 Summary

Our goal has been to develop a computational model of analogical reasoning based on abstractional analogy. The process of abstractional analogy proceeds as follows. First, given a new problem, an analogous case is retrieved from memory. Second, analogy abstraction creates an abstract schema that represents what source and target cases have in common. An abstract schema consists of a problem schema and its solution schema. In order to do this, a problem schema is created by analogically mapping the source problem to the target problem, then a solution schema is created, generalizing the source case. The solution schema consists of a reasoning method and/or a generalized result. Third, the obtained schema is applied to the target problem. Fourth, in case the result so obtained does not cover all the target requirements, it should be refined. Finally, the memory is updated. If a new schema is acquired, the target and source cases together with that schema will replace the source node in memory. If the target problem is solved by using an existing schema, the target case will be made as a child of that schema. Note that if analogy transfer fails during the cycle, another analogue should be tried. During the learning stage, this trial and error continues until analogy transfer succeeds.

Abstractional analogy guarantees a natural form of learning as a byproduct of problem solving. Abstraction determines the exact amount of knowledge to be transferred and also, as the product, correctly represents the learning involved therein in terms of both reasoning methods and results. It also organizes knowledge into abstraction hierarchies. Thus, abstractional analogy is a unifying model of three different aspects of human cognition: problem solving by analogy, learning of both declarative and procedural knowledge, and memory organization.

Acknowledgments

I am indebted to Janet L. Kolodner for her guidance and support. I thank Lawrence W. Barsalou, Roy M. Turner, Elise H. Turner, Patsy L. Holmes, Tom Hinrichs, Mark A. Graves, Joel Martin, Mike Redmond, and David Wood for valuable comments and discussion on this paper.

References

[And86] J.R. Anderson. Knowledge compilation: the general learning mechanism.

In R.S. Michalski, J.G. Carbonell, and T.M. Mitchell, editors, *Machine Learning: An Artificial Intelligence Approach*, Kaufmann, Los Altos, CA, 1986.

[Bur86] M.H. Burstein. Concept formation by incremental analogical reasoning and debugging. In R.S. Michalski, J.G. Carbonell, and T.M. Mitchell, editors, *Machine Learning: An Artificial Intelligence Approach*, Kaufmann, Los Altos, CA, 1986.

[Car83] J.G. Carbonell. Learning by analogy: formulating and generalizing plans from past experience. In R.S. Michalski, J.G. Carbonell, and T.M. Mitchell, editors, *Machine Learning: An Artificial Intelligence Approach*, Tioga, Palo Alto, CA, 1983.

[Car86] J.G. Carbonell. Derivational analogy: a theory of reconstructive problem solving and expertise acquisition. In R.S. Michalski, J.G. Carbonell, and T.M. Mitchell, editors, *Machine Learning: An Artificial Intelligence Approach*, Kaufmann, Los Altos, CA, 1986.

[CK86] R.E. Cullingford and J.L. Kolodner. Interactive advice giving. In *Proceedings of the 1986 IEEE International Conference on Systems, Man, and Cybernetics*, 1986.

[CM85] J.G. Carbonell and S. Minton. Metaphor and commonsense reasoning. In J.R. Hobbs and R.C. Moore, editors, *Formal Theories of the Commonsense World*, Ablex, Norwood, NJ, 1985.

[Dar83] L. Darden. Reasoning by analogy in scientific theory construction. In *Proc. of Int'l Workshop on Machine Learning*, Monticello, IL, 1983.

[Der85] N. Dershowitz. Program abstraction and instantiation. *ACM Transactions on Programming Languages and Systems*, 7(3), July 1985.

[Der86] N. Dershowitz. Programming by analogy. In R.S. Michalski, J.G. Carbonell, and T.M. Mitchell, editors, *Machine Learning: An Artificial Intelligence Approach*, Kaufmann, Los Altos, CA, 1986.

[DM86] G. DeJong and R. Mooney. Explanation-based learning: an alternative view. In R.S. Michalski, J.G. Carbonell, and T.M. Mitchell, editors, *Machine Learning: An Artificial Intelligence Approach*, pages 145–176, Kaufmann, Los Altos, CA, 1986.

[Gen80]   M.R. Genesereth. Metaphors and models. In *Proc. AAAI-80*, Menlo Park, CA, 1980.

[Gen83]   D. Gentner. Structure-mapping: a theoretical framework for analogy. *Cognitive Science*, 7:155–170, 1983.

[GH83]   M.L. Gick and K.J. Holyoak. Schema induction and analogical transfer. *Cognitive Psychology*, 15:1–38, 1983.

[Hol85]   K.J. Holyoak. The pragmatics of analogical transfer. *Psychology of Learning and Motivation*, 19:59–87, 1985.

[Jar74]   L. Jardine. *FRANCIS BACON: Discovery and the Art of Discourse*. Cambridge University Press, Bentley House, 200 Euston Road, London, 1974.

[KL87]   A.M. Kass and D.B. Leake. A case-based approach to building explanations for explanation-based learning. 1987. Working paper.

[Kol84]   J.L. Kolodner. *Retrieval and Organizational Strategies in Conceptual Memory: A Computer Model*. Lawrence Erlbaum Associates, Hillsdale, NJ, 1984.

[Kol87a] J.L. Kolodner. Capitalizing on failure through cased-based inference. In *Proceedings of the Ninth Annual Conference of the Cognitive Science Society*, Seattle, Washington, July 1987.

[Kol87b] J.L. Kolodner. Extending problem solver capabilities through case-based inference. In *Proc. of the Fourth Int'l Workshop on Machine Learning*, pages 167–178, Irvine, CA, June 1987.

[Min75]   M. Minsky. A framework for representing knowledge. In P.H. Winston, editor, *The Psychology of Computer Vision*, McGraw Hill, New York, 1975.

[MKK86]   T.M. Mitchell, R. Keller, and S.T. Kedar-Cabelli. Explanation-based generalization: a unifying view. *Machine Learning*, 1:47–80, 1986.

[Pol45]   G. Polya. *How to Solve It: A New Aspect of Mathematical Method*. Princeton University Press, Princeton, NJ, 1945.

[Pol54]   G. Polya. *Mathematics and Plausible Reasoning: Induction and Analogy in Mathematics.* Volume 1, Princeton University Press, Princeton, NJ, 1954.

[Ros86]   B.H. Ross. Remindings in learning and instruction. In *Workshop in Similarity and Analogy*, 1986.

[TC88]   E. Turner and R.E. Cullingford. Conversation planning using conversational mops. 1988. In Preparation.

[Tur87]   R.M. Turner. Modifying previously-used plans to fit new situations. In *Proceedings of the Ninth Annual Conference of the Cognitive Science Society*, Seattle, Washington, July 1987.

[Wil86]   R. Wilensky. *Some Problems and Proposals for Knowledge Representation.* Technical Report UCB/CSD 86/294, University of California, Berkeley, Berkeley, CA, 1986.

[Win80]   P.H. Winston. Learning and reasoning by analogy. *Comm. ACM*, 23(12):689–703, 1980.

A Theory of Debugging

Reid G. Simmons
MIT Artificial Intelligence Laboratory
545 Technology Square
Cambridge, MA 02139

ABSTRACT

We present a theory of debugging applicable for planning and interpretation problems. The debugger repairs bugs by locating and replacing faulty assumptions underlying the bugs. Repairs are proposed using domain-independent strategies that reason about causal explanations underlying the bugs and domain models that encode the effects of events. The relative completeness of our debugging strategies is analyzed with respect to the general assumptions, relevant to planning and interpretation tasks, which are incorporated into models of causality, the problem solving task, and hypothesis construction. Our analysis indicates that only a small set of assumptions and associated repair strategies are needed to handle a wide range of bugs over a large class of domains.

1. Introduction

The case-based reasoning paradigm involves solving new problems by applying solutions to previously solved problems. Often, however, the solutions to previous cases do not fit the new problems exactly, and the solutions must be modified, or debugged, to fit the new situations. Thus, the efficacy of the case-based reasoning paradigm depends, to a large extent, on the ability to do debugging over a wide range of problems.

We present a theory of debugging applicable for planning and interpretation problems. The debugger analyzes causal explanations of bugs to determine the underlying assumptions upon which the bug depends. A bug is repaired by replacing the assumptions, using a small set of domain-independent debugging strategies.

Our theory of debugging is robust, handling a wide range of bugs that arise from unexpected interactions between events. The theory is fairly domain-independent, depending only on rather general assumptions, such as the closed-world assumption that the debugger knows about all occurring events. We characterize the strengths and weaknesses of our current implementation of the debugging theory by analyzing its models of causality, the problem solving task and hypothesis construction.

We are exploring these ideas within the Generate, Test and Debug problem solving paradigm [Simmons]. The GTD paradigm was developed for interpretation and planning tasks, both of which are of the form "given an initial state and a goal state, find a sequence of events which could transform the initial state into the goal state." GORDIUS, our implementation of GTD, has been used to solve problems in several domains, including our primary domain of geologic interpretation, blocks-world planning and the Tower of Hanoi problem.

In geologic interpretation, the task is to find a sequence of events that plausibly explains how a vertical cross section of a geologic region (the goal state) was formed starting from the initial state of bedrock under sea-level (see Figure 1). The goal state describes the compositional, topological and geometric aspects of the cross section. For example, in Figure 1a the goals are that formations **SH1** and **SS1** are composed of shale and sandstone, respectively; that **SH1** is over **SS1**; that **SH1** and boundary **B1** are oriented at 5°; and that **SS1** and **B2** are oriented at 12°.

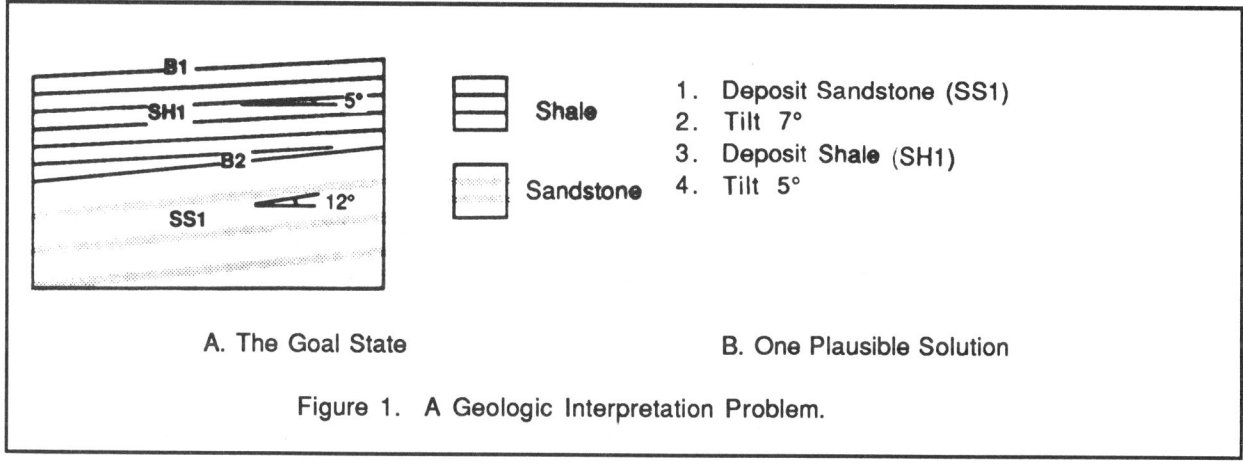

A. The Goal State B. One Plausible Solution

Figure 1. A Geologic Interpretation Problem.

In the GTD paradigm, the generator constructs an initial hypothesis by matching a library of associational rules against the initial and goal states and composing the partial sequences of events suggested by each rule. The rules, which associate patterns in the initial and goal states with sequences of events that could achieve the goal state pattern, in essence form the "cases" of the GTD paradigm. The initial hypothesis is then tested. If the test succeeds, the hypothesis is accepted as a solution. If it fails, the tester passes to the debugger causal explanations for the bugs detected.

The debugger uses the causal explanations to locate the assumptions underlying the bug and then applies domain-independent strategies that know how to repair bugs by replacing assumptions. When the debugger is satisfied that all the bugs have been repaired, the modified hypothesis is submitted to the tester for verification. This debug/test loop continues until the test succeeds. Alternatively, if the debugger appears to be moving far from a solution, the generator may be invoked to produce a new hypothesis.

For the problem in Figure 1a, the generator interprets that the deposition of **SH1** occurs after the deposition of **SS1**, using the heuristic that an overlying sedimentary formation is younger since deposition occurs from above. To interpret the orientation of **SS1** and **B2**, the generator uses the heuristic rule that a sedimentary formation oriented at an angle $\emptyset$ was formed by deposition followed by a tilt of $\emptyset$. This rule derives from the fact that, in our model of geology, deposition occurs horizontally and tilt acts to change orientations. Another application of this rule is used to interpret the orientations of **SH1** and **B1**. Combining all the constraints (and linearizing the sequence), the generator produces the initial hypothesis in Figure 2.

---

1. Deposit1 of Sandstone (SS1) during interval I1
2. Tilt1 of 12° during interval I2
3. Deposit2 of Shale (SH1) during interval I3
4. Tilt2 of 5° during interval I4

Figure 2. Initial, Buggy Interpretation of Figure 1a.

In testing this hypothesis, bugs are detected. A bug, for our purposes, is a difference between the *intended*, or hypothesized, value of some expression and its *actual* value, as predicted by the tester. The bugs in the hypothesis of Figure 2 are that the intended orientation of both **SS1** and **B2** is 12°, while their actual orientation is 17°.

Causal explanations for why the bugs occur are passed to the debugger. For example, the orientation of **SS1** is not 12° because it was zero when deposited, **Tilt1** incremented it by 12° and then **Tilt2** incremented it by an additional 5°. The debugger analyzes whether replacing any of the assumptions underlying the bug will repair it. Several modifications to the hypothesis are proposed, including replacing the assumption that the parameter value of **Tilt1** is 12° with the assumption that the value is 7°, producing the solution of Figure 1b.

Our theory of debugging and general debugging algorithms are presented in Section 2, while Section 3 illustrates in more detail the debugging of the hypothesis in Figure 2. In Section 4, we analyze the problem solving characteristics of our theory of debugging, in particular its completeness and efficiency. Section 5 presents a comparison with other debuggers.

2. A Theory of Debugging

Our theory of debugging is based on the simple observation that the manifestation of a bug is only a surface indication of some deeper failure. In particular, bugs ultimately depend on the assumptions made during the construction and testing of hypotheses. If the actual (predicted) state of the world does not match the intended state needed to solve the problem, then it must be that one of the underlying assumptions is faulty and needs to be changed.

Bugs are repaired by locating and replacing some of their underlying assumptions. Domain-independent debugging strategies propose repairs by reasoning about the type of assumption, the causal explanation underlying the bug, and causal domain models that explicitly detail the preconditions and effects of events. For example, if a bug depends on an assumption about the value of an event's parameter, the strategy is to change the parameter value in such a way as to repair the bug. Each proposed repair is then evaluated to determine its effect on the overall problem — whether it introduces new bugs or serendipitously repairs other existing bugs.

Given that the tester has detected the manifestation of a bug, the debugger first locates the assumptions underlying the bug. This is accomplished by analyzing a causal dependency structure, an acyclic graph that represents justifications for the predicted state of the world. The dependency structures capture an intuitive notion of causality in which time, persistence and the effects of events are represented explicitly. In GORDIUS, they are produced as a by-product of the tester's simulation algorithm and the dependencies are represented and maintained using a TMS [Doyle].

For example, Figure 3 illustrates the causal dependency structure for why the orientation of **SS1** is predicted to be 17°. In the figure, **SS1.orientation@Plan-end** refers to the orientation of the **SS1** formation at **Plan-end**, the time associated with the goal diagram in Figure 1a. **Persistence(SS1.orientation, I4.end, Plan-end)** means that the orientation of **SS1** did not change from the end of time interval

I4 (the interval associated with the **Tilt2** event) through **Plan-end**. The statement **Change(+, SS1.orientation, 5°, I4)** means that over interval **I4** the orientation of **SS1** increased by 5°. The dependecy structure indicates that this change happens because the **Tilt2** event occurs, the parameter value of **Tilt2** is **5°** and the **SS1** formation exists at the time **Tilt2** occurs.

The assumptions underlying a bug are located by tracing back through the causal dependency structure to its leaves (the boxed statements in Figure 3). Each bug actually has two dependency structures — one an explanation for the actual value and one for the intended value, although the latter usually consists of a single assumption. To indicate the direction in which to change underlying assumptions, the debugger regresses the intended value back through the causal dependency structure for the actual value (and *vice versa*). For example, regressing 12°, the intended value of **SS1.orientation@Plan-end**, through the structure of Figure 3 indicates that **SS1.orientation@I2.end** should be 7° rather than 12°.

We have identified five types of assumptions which account for most of the bugs that appear in the domains we have explored. Algorithms associated with each type of assumption know how to replace the assumption with others to achieve the regressed value of the bug. We can repair faulty assumptions about 1) which events occur, 2) temporal relationships between events and 3) parameter bindings of events. In addition, we handle two types of closed world assumptions regarding 4) the persistence of attributes (an attribute of an object persists in value unless some known event affects it) and 5) the persistence of objects (an object continues to exist unless some event explicitly destroys it).

1. **Occurs(process, event, interval)** is the assumption that an **event** of type **process** occurs during **interval**. One debugging strategy associated with this type of assumption is to delete the event altogether if removing the event will achieve the intended value of the bug. Another strategy is to replace the event with a similar event. If the actual value of the assumption is false, implying that the event currently does not occur because not all of its preconditions hold, the strategy is to find an event that achieves all the goals of the event but does not have the offending preconditions. If the actual value is true, implying that some effect of the event helps to cause the bug, the strategy is to find an event without the offending effect that still achieves all the goals of the event. For example, the bug in Figure 3 could be repaired if there were an event that creates a sandstone formation oriented at -5°, rather than horizontally.

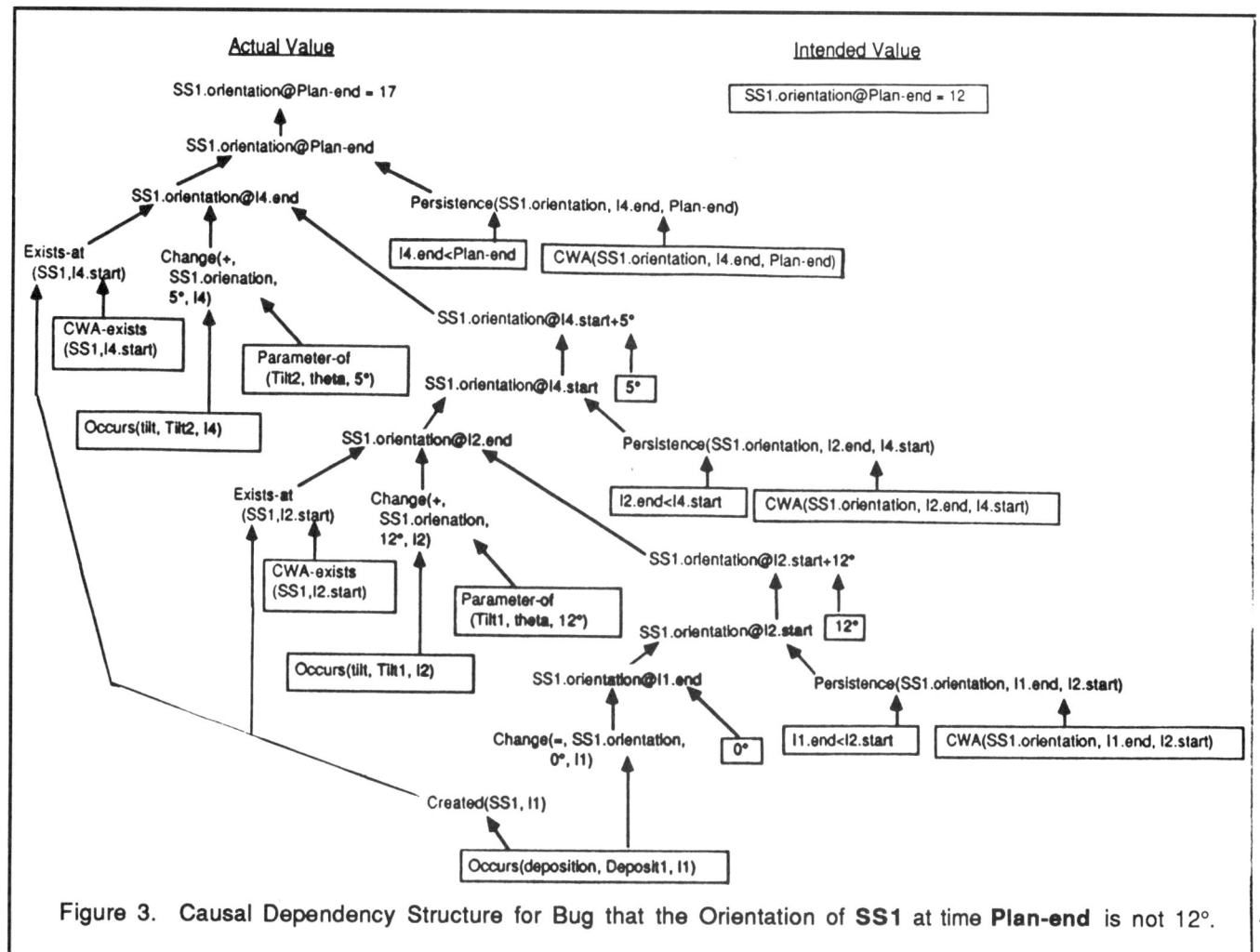

Figure 3. Causal Dependency Structure for Bug that the Orientation of **SS1** at time **Plan-end** is not 12°.

2. **Parameter-of(event, formal, actual)** is the assumption that the **formal** parameter of **event** is bound to the **actual** value. The debugging strategy is to change the value of the parameter, where the new parameter value is derived through the regression. For example, the regression indicates that the intended value of **SS1.orientation@I2.end** is 7°. Our domain models indicate that tilt acts to increase the orientation of objects by some non-zero amount **theta**. From this description, the debugger derives that **SS1.orientation@I2.end** equals **SS1.orientation@I2.start + theta**. Symbolically solving the equations yields **theta = 7° - SS1.orientation@I2.start**. Since the actual value of **SS1.orientation@I2.start** is zero, the debugger determines that changing the parameter value to 7° will repair the bug.

3. **Ix.end < Iy.start** is the assumption that time interval **Ix** precedes interval **Iy**. In our models, temporal ordering assumptions are usually used to support assertions that the attribute of some object persists in value from **Ix.end** to **Iy.start**. The debugging strategy for this assumption is applicable if the regressed value of the attribute is achieved during some interval **Iz** which precedes **Ix**. If applicable, the debugger reorders the events associated with the two intervals by replacing the temporal ordering with the assumption that **Iy** precedes **Iz**. For example, in Figure 3 **I2.end < I4.start** cannot be reordered to repair the bug since there is no interval before **I2** during which the orientation of **SS1** is 7°, its intended value at **I4.start**.

4. **CWA(attribute.object, t1, t2)** is a closed-world assumption that no known event affects the attribute between times **t1** and **t2**. The strategy is to insert an event occurring between **t1** and **t2** that can affect the **attribute** in such a way as to achieve the intended value of the **attribute** at time **t2**. For example, the debugger proposes replacing the assumption **CWA(SS1.orientation, I4.end, Plan-end)** with assumptions that a new tilt event with tilt parameter -5° occurs during interval **I5**, where **I5** is constrained to be between **I4.end** and **Plan-end**. The tilt parameter value of -5° is determined analogously to that in #2 above.

5. **CWA-exists(object, t1)** is another closed-world assumption that the **object** continues to exist at time **t1** since no event is known to have destroyed it. The repair strategy is to insert an event before time **t1** that can destroy the object. For example, one way to repair the bug of Figure 3 is to prevent **Tilt2** from affecting **SS1**. Since tilting applies only to formations that exist at the time of the tilt, we can accomplish this by assuming some erosion event totally erodes away **SS1** before **I4.start**. Overall, however, this is a rather poor repair since it ends up destroying the complete geologic region.

Typically, bugs depend on a large number of assumptions, so many repairs are suggested for each bug. To help control the debugger, best-first search is used. The debugger evaluates the global effects of each repair to focus on the most promising hypothesis. The primary component of the evaluation heuristic is the number of remaining bugs, which includes unachieved top-level goals. This is a reasonable metric since our planning/interpretation task involves finding one plausible solution and the number of remaining bugs is often a good measure of the closeness to solving the problem. The secondary component of the evaluation heuristic is the cost of the hypothesis. This component is used only to differentiate hypotheses that have the same number of remaining bugs, the idea being to prefer simpler hypotheses all else being equal. In our current implementation, each event has unit cost, so the total cost is simply the number of events in the sequence.

3. Debugging a Geologic Interpretation

This section describes the complete behavior of our debugging algorithm for the buggy hypothesis of Figure 2. The hypothesis has two bugs — the orientations of **SS1** and **B2** are both 17°, not 12°. Starting first with the bug that the orientation of **SS1** is 17°, the debugger locates the 17 assumptions in the causal dependency structure of Figure 3 which underlie the bug and regresses the intended value of 12° back through the structure. Of these assumptions, the debugger does not consider the following six because they are declared to be unchangeable premises of the problem — the goal **SS1.orientation@Plan-end=12°**, the values of the constants 12°, 5° and 0, and the temporal ordering **I4.end<Plan-end**, which reflects the premise that the hypothesized events must occur before **Plan-end**.

For the three **CWA** assumptions, the debugger proposes the same basic repair of adding a new tilt event of -5° between the start and end of the persistence. The repairs, however, are rated differently. The evaluation heuristic determines that adding the new tilt between **I4.end** and **Plan-end** repairs both bugs in the initial hypothesis but also introduces two new bugs — the orientation of **SH1** and **B1** are now zero, not 5°. Adding the tilt between **I1.end** and **I2.start** is considered a solution since it repairs both bugs without introducing new bugs. Adding the tilt between **I2.end** and **I4.start** produces a non-linear hypothesis where the new tilt and **Deposit2** are unordered. This repair is also regarded as a solution since one of the possible linearizations (where the new tilt precedes **Deposit2**) achieves all the goals of the problem.

For the **Occurs(tilt, Tilt2, I4)** assumption, deleting the tilt event fixes the bug, since without **Tilt2** the orientation of **SS1** is 12°. This repair does not solve the whole problem, however, since it introduces the same two new bugs as above. For the other two **Occurs** assumptions, deleting the events does not fix the bug. For all three assumptions, replacing events is not an applicable strategy, since our geologic models do not contain events that are similar enough to tilting or deposition.

The two **CWA-Exists** assumptions yield the same basic repair — an erosion event is proposed to destroy the **SS1** formation. The evaluation heuristic rates these repairs poorly, however, since they unachieve all the goals of the problem by destroying all existing formations and boundaries. The reordering strategy does not succeed for the temporal ordering assumption **I2.end < I4.start** because there is no time before **I2.end** in which the actual value of **SS1.orientation** equals its intended value at **I4.start** (12°); similarly for the assumption **I1.end < I2.start**.

The debugger proposes replacing **Parameter-of(Tilt1, theta, 12°)** by the assumption that **theta** is equal to 7°, the difference between the intended value of **SS1.orientation** at the end of **I2** (the interval associated with **Tilt2**) and its actual value of zero at **I2.start**. The evaluation heuristic determines that this repair is a solution. Similarly, for the assumption **Parameter-of(Tilt2, theta, 12°)**, the debugger considers changing the parameter value to the difference between the intended value of **SS1.orientation** at **I2.end** (12°) and its actual orientation at **I2.start** (also 12°). This repair is rejected, however, since the debugger determines that it is inconsistent with a constraint in the **tilt** process model that **theta** must be non-zero.

Thus, for this problem the debugger suggests seven potential repairs, of which three are considered solutions. The evaluation heuristic prefers the repair in which the parameter of **Tilt1** is altered, since this produces an hypothesis with fewer events than the other two solutions, which add tilt events. The preferred solution is the same as in Figure 1b.

4. Completeness and Efficiency of the Debugger

The relative completeness of our debugging algorithms can be characterized by reference to three different models upon which the problem solver is built — a model of the problem solving task, a model of hypothesis construction, and a model of causality. In this context, "model" refers to an understanding of how something works, providing in essence a representational framework. Each model contains assumptions that help define its scope and expressive power. The models described below are sufficient for doing planning and interpretation problems in a number of domains. The completeness of our debugging algorithms depend on the extent to which they can handle the different assumptions underlying the models.

Our problem solving task model defines what are planning and interpretation problems and solutions. A problem is represented by assumptions about the initial and goal states. The model indicates that these assumptions are fixed and cannot be changed by the debugger. A solution is a sequence of events that occurs between times **Plan-start** and **Plan-end** which achieves all the goals of the goal state. Thus, temporal orderings that contain the time points **Plan-start** and **Plan-end** also cannot be changed by the debugger.

Our hypothesis construction model defines the actions available to the problem solver in forming an hypothesis. The model describes how events are specified and how sequences are created. The assumptions licensed by our hypothesis construction model are the events that occur, parameter bindings of events and temporal orderings between events.

Our model of causality explicitly represents time and the effects of events. The model assumes that objects and their attributes continue to persist in value unless some known event changes them. The causality model forms a predictive model for the world, that is, using the causal model one can determine future states of the world given only assumptions about the initial state, the sequence of events and the correctness of the domain models. This predictive attribute forms the basis of our theory of debugging that all bugs can be traced to underlying assumptions of the form given above.

The causal model also contains implicit simplifying assumptions, such as the assumption that the domain models are correct and complete. Although these simplifying assumptions suffice for the problems we have explored, the debugger can be easily extended to handle them by making the assumptions explicit in our causal dependency structures and providing repair strategies to handle them.[1] Handling the assumption that the domain models are correct is somewhat tricky because any bug can be fixed by changing the domain models in an appropriate way. For example, we could repair the buggy hypothesis in Figure 2 by assuming that tilt has a differential effect on sandstone and shale. Clearly any reasonable repair strategy that changes the domain models must constrain the problem, for instance, by reference to a meta-theory of the domain or by induction

---

[1] We have, in fact, recently done just that — adding a bug repair strategy for the closed-world assumption that the system knows about all the objects of a given type. Quantified goal statements, such as "all blocks on the table are red," can now be handled by representing them as a conjunction of propositions plus the assumption that the universe of objects is known.

using multiple examples, subjects well beyond the current scope of our research.

Our debugger currently handles all the assumptions licensed by our hypothesis construction model and the persistence assumptions underlying our model of causality (the assumptions of the problems solving task model are not handled because they are all declared to be unchangeable premises). In practice, our experiments indicate that the debugger is fairly robust, handling a wide range of bugs in several different domains, arising from a number of different combinations of assumptions.

Much of our debugger's strength lies in its ability to decompose bug manifestations into their underlying assumptions and to handle each assumption individually. The local nature of the debugging algorithms, however, is also a source of incompleteness. Although the debugger can handle many problems in which multiple assumptions must be changed, the debugger may fail to find a correct solution in cases where no *single* assumption can be altered in such a way as to bring the hypothesis closer to repairing the bug. This problem stems from the fact that, to keep the number of suggested repair manageable, the debugger avoids proposing modifications gratuitously in the hope that they will combine with subsequent modifications to repair the bug.

One downside of our debugging algorithm is its high computational cost. Although each individual debugging strategy is fairly efficient, the number of assumptions underlying bugs tends to grow exponentially in domains, such as geology, with many potential interactions among events. In addition, the evaluation heuristic is very expensive since determining the number of remaining bugs is, in general, exponential for the types of non-linear hypotheses produced by our debugger (see [Chapman]). It is these computational reasons that led us to develop the GTD paradigm of using heuristic rules to generate an initial hypothesis and relying on the robust, but slow, debugger to focus on the problems handled incorrectly by the generator.

5. Relations to Other Debuggers

The approach of tracing faults to underlying assumptions has roots in work on dependency-directed search [Stallman], model-based diagnosis [DeKleer] and algorithmic debugging [Shapiro]. Our contribution to the dependency tracing approach is in providing principled strategies that determine how to replace the underlying assumptions once they have been located.

Our *assumption-oriented* debugging approach stands in contrast to other approaches in which bug repair heuristics are associated either with bug manifestations or with certain stereotypical patterns of causal explanations (e.g., [Alterman], [Hammond], [Sussman]). Our assumption-oriented approach handles the large number of possible ways bugs can arise by decomposing them into combinations of a small set of underlying assumptions. This approach tends to give greater coverage and also tends to suggest more alternative repairs than other approaches since we do not have to anticipate all possible patterns of assumptions that can lead to bug manifestations.

For example, for the goal protection violation bug manifestion, [Sussman] recognizes only a few explanation patterns, one of which is "Prerequisite Clobbers Brother Goal" (PCBG). This pattern matches situations in which an event **X** achieves the precondition of an event **Y** and also clobbers a brother goal which had been achieved by event **Z**. The only repair actually suggested in [Sussman] is to reorder the events **X** and **Z**. While additional repair strategies could of course be added, our debugging algorithm, by analyzing the assumptions and causal structure underlying the PCBG bug, proposes several additional repairs, such as replacing event **X** with one that does not clobber the goal.

On the other hand, an advantage of using high-level repair strategies is that they essentially encapsulate the assumptions and repairs which are *a priori* likely to be relevant for a particular domain. In the geology domain, for instance, precondition violations can usually be repaired by adding events or changing parameters — reordering events is less likely to work. By encapsulating combinations of assumptions, high-level repair strategies may be beneficial in cases where multiple assumptions need to be changed. We are currently considering how to integrate such domain-dependent debugging heuristics into the overall GTD paradigm.

6. Summary

Our theory of debugging involves tracing each bug manifestation back to the underlying assumptions, made during hypothesis construction and testing, upon which the bug depends. The bug is repaired by replacing the assumptions using a small set of domain-independent debugging algorithms that reason about the type of assumption, the causal explanation underlying the bug, and domain models that encode the effects of events. Our approach subsumes earlier work in debugging by using principled assumption-oriented repair strategies to cover more buggy situations and to suggest more potential repairs for each bug manifestation.

We characterize the relative completeness of the debugger with respect to models of causality, the problem solving task and hypothesis construction. Each model incorporates a set of assumptions and the completeness of the debugger is measured by the range of those assumptions it handles. In practice, we have found that most bugs in planning and interpretation problems can be traced to only five different types of assumptions. Algorithms to handle new types of assumptions, however, can be easily added to our basic debugging framework. One of our research goals is to augment our debugging algorithms to handle problems, such as design, that depend on different underlying models.

The assumption-oriented debugging approach is still quite computationally expensive, due to the large number of assumptions underlying each bug and the expense of evaluating each suggested repair. We achieve overall efficiency using the Generate, Test and Debug paradigm in which domain-dependent associational rules are used to generate an initial hypothesis that is debugged if it turns out to be incorrect.

Acknowledgments

Helpful contributions to this paper were made by Randy Davis, Walter Hamscher, Drew McDermott, Howie Shrobe and Reid Smith. This work was supported by Schlumberger and the Advanced Research Projects Agency of the Department of Defense under Office of Naval Research contract N00014-85-K-0124.

References

[Alterman] R. Alterman, An Adaptive Planner, AAAI-86, Philadephia, PA.

[Chapman] D. Chapman, Planning for Conjunctive Goals, *Artificial Intelligence*, vol. 32, pp 333-377, 1987.

[DeKleer] J. deKleer, B. Williams, Diagnosing Multiple Faults, *Artificial Intelligence*, vol. 32, pp 97-130, 1987.

[Doyle] J. Doyle, A Truth Maintenance System, *Artificial Intelligence*, vol. 12(2), pp 231-272, 1979.

[Hammond] K. Hammond, Explaining and Repairing Plans That Fail, IJCAI-87, Milan, Italy.

[Shapiro] E. Shapiro, *Algorithmic Program Debugging*, MIT Press, 1982.

[Simmons] R. G. Simmons, Generate, Test and Debug: Combining Associational Rules and Causal Models, IJCAI-87, Milan, Italy.

[Stallman] R. Stallman, G. Sussman, Forward Reasoning and Dependency-Directed Backtracking in a System for Computer-Aided Circuit Analysis, *Artificial Intelligence*, vol. 9, 1977.

[Sussman] G. Sussman, *A Computer Model of Skill Acquisition*, American Elsevier, 1977.

Learning to Read: A Memory-Based Model

Craig Stanfill
Thinking Machines Corporation
245 First Street
Cambridge MA 02142

March 14, 1988

ABSTRACT

JOHNNY, a model of the process of learning to read, is presented. The model begins with a set of pronunciation rules and a phonetic vocabulary, but no knowledge of the correspondence between written and spoken words. It then begins reading a short piece of text *without supervision*. In the process of doing so, it learns to read: it acquires a mapping from text-strings to words previously known only by sound. JOHNNY uses Memory Based Reasoning (MBR) to solve three key problems. First, it uses MBR to implement *rules*, in this case rules of pronunciation. Second, it uses MBR to implement *recognition*, in this case recognizing a possibly incorrect pronunciation produced by the rules as corresponding to a known word in the phonetic vocabulary. Finally, it uses MBR to implement *induction*, going beyond the principles of pronunciation contained in the initial set of rules. Two modes of supervised learning are also studied.

1. Introduction

This paper presents JOHNNY, a memory-based model of the process of learning to read: in particular, it learns the associations between written words and a previously acquired spoken vocabulary. JOHNNY starts with some knowledge of phonetic rules plus a phonetic vocabulary. It uses these phonetic rules to predict how a word might sound, then searches its phonetic vocabulary to guess the word. This process would be trivial, except for the fact that these phonetic rules are far short of 100% accurate. If they were, a simple exact-match search of the phonetic memory would suffice. However, because the rules frequently predict incorrect phonemes, a best-match search of the phonetic memory is required. This process suffices to achieve fairly good accuracy in reading. However, more can be done: if the matching process is sufficiently accurate, then additional learning becomes possible. The match between the word being read and the word which has been recognized allows JOHNNY to infer new relations between letters and phonemes, and its reading skills can improve. The result is unsupervised learning. JOHNNY can also operate in two supervised modes.

2. Background

The Memory-Based Reasoning (MBR) paradigm [1] [2] places fast recall from memory at the foundation of Artificial Intelligence: the basis of intelligent action is remembering similar situations from the past. Memory is implemented as a best-match search of memory. In work completed to date, memory is flat, consisting of a set of records. Each record has the same structure, but pointers between records are not allowed at this time. Searching this memory is based on taking a *target record*, computing a numerical measure of similarity between that target record and every record in memory, and retrieving the best matches from memory. This sort of memory operation is computationally expensive on serial computers, but is easily and efficiently implemented on parallel computers such as the Connection Machine® System.

Initial work on Memory-Based Reasoning has been on the word-pronunciation task [3]. In this task, a system (called MBRtalk) is given examples of words and how they are pronounced, and endeavors to infer pronunciations for novel words. This is done by storing the set of examples in memory then, when faced with a novel word, recalling the example forming the best match. For example, faced with the task of pronouncing the word "knight," it might infer that the 'k' was silent by locating other word-initial KN's, such as "knife" and "know", and noting that the 'k' was silent in each of them. Given a memory of several thousand examples, this technique predicts the correct phoneme over 90% of the time.

The pronunciation task has also been used to test an alternative formulation of MBR [4] and to test Connectionist networks which learn via back-propagation learning [5].

This model follows the precepts of *case-based reasoning* [6][7][8], a method of learning from experience. A case-based reasoner has access to an incomplete domain model and knowledge base, plus a set of previously solved problems in that domain. It solves novel problems by adapting previous solutions, using the domain model and knowledge base where possible. When a case-based reasoner solves a problem (either successfully or unsuccessfully), it will remember what it did (creating a *case*) and, when it comes across a similar situation later on, attempt to adapt the case to the current problem. Thus, JOHNNY may be viewed as a sort of case-based reasoner constructed along the precepts of MBR.

3. The Model

JOHNNY simulates the process of learning to read. It starts with some of the same knowledge a child learning to read begins with: it can recognize spoken words, and it has been taught rules for sounding out words, but it has not yet learned the correspondence between the written and spoken forms. It is acquiring such a correspondence, in a way less burdensome than memorizing every possible word, that is the essence of learning to read.*
JOHNNY accomplishes this by sounding out written words and matching them against known spoken words. Later, as it builds a up a large number of such matchings, it can use inductive methods to improve its performance in the sounding-out process.

JOHNNY starts with a set of *pronunciation rules* and a *phonetic vocabulary*, but no written vocabulary. It looks at written words, uses the rules to generate *plausible pronunciations*, then searches the phonetic vocabulary for the most plausible actual word. The pronunciation for that word is then paired with the original written word, and *memorized* (added to the written vocabulary). When a sufficient number of written words are added to the written

---

* No acoustic processing takes place here: the phonetic vocabulary is represented as a phonetic transcription. Also, the system has no notion of what the words mean, and does not exploit any sort of contextual or semantic constraints.

vocabulary, it acts as an inductive engine, so that the process of guessing plausible pronunciations for new words is more accurate.

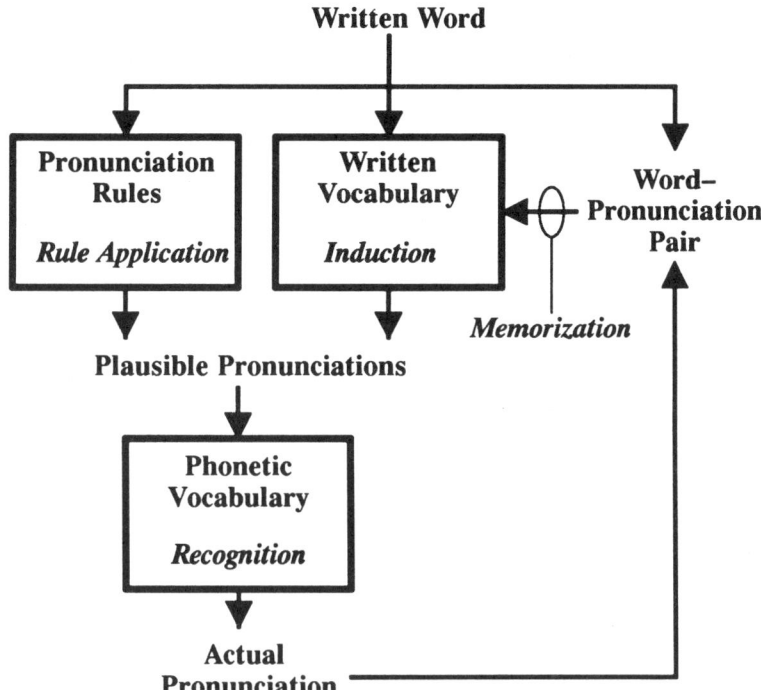

There are four basic operations involved in this model of learning: rule application, recognition, memorization, and induction. All operations in this model are implemented within the Memory-Based Reasoning paradigm. Some of these operations (recognition and memorization) are necessarily memory functions. Induction might be done by other methods, such as inducing a decision tree [9]. Rule application is generally *not* thought of as an associative memory operation, but such an implementation is quite natural within the paradigm.

The successful use of MBR in all aspects of the system demonstrate that MBR is not limited to simple inductive reasoning (as might have been assumed from the initial work on MBRtalk); that memory is a foundation on which complex AI systems may be built.

3.1. Rule Application

The starting point of the model is a set of pronunciation rules, that is, a set of rules for transforming strings of letters to strings of phonemes. A partial list of the phonemic alphabet used in this work is shown in the appendix. Each rule specifies the phoneme corresponding to a letter, optionally taking into account the context of the letters immediately before and after. The character '?' stands for "don't-care." As an example of the rule, the letter 'b' usually gets the phoneme 'b', yielding the rule <?b? = b>. However, for a double-b (as in babble), the second occurrence is silent, yielding the rule <bb? = ->. Compound consonants, such as 'th', often require two rules: one specifying the sound for the compound, which is usually attached to the first letter, and one specifying that the second letter of the compound is silent. Thus one gets the rules <?th = T> and <th? = ->. There are a total of 104 rules, broken down as follows:

Category	Number	Example
Long and Short Vowels	12	<?a? = @>
Terminal E is silent	1	<?e- = ->
Vowels + w	6	<?aw = c>
Second vowel of pair is silent	25	<ea? = ->
Simple consonant rules	26	<?c? = s>
Consonant Clusters	13	<?th = T>
Doubled consonants are silent	21	<bb? = ->

As a note, there is some inefficiency in this encoding of the rules. For example, 25 rules are needed to encode the rule that the second vowel of a pair is silent. At some point, the incorporation of a type hierarchy into our memory software will obviate this problem. Second, these rules are ambiguous. For example, the letter 'c' may give the sound 's' or 'k'. The rules are (of necessity) inadequate to make such distinctions. Thus, the result of rule application is not a single answer, but a set of plausible answers.

It is certainly possible to come up with more complete, less ambiguous rule sets than the above. However, the difficulty of coming up with complete, unambiguous rule sets is a central problem in AI, and one which, it has always been assumed, can best be solved by some form of learning.

To apply these rules, a word is broken into a series of 3-letter windows. For example, the word 'the' yields three target records: '-th', 'the', and 'he-'. Next a best-match associative memory is invoked, one invocation for each target record. Rules are penalized for each position in which they do not match the target. "Don't-cares" are assessed a smaller penalty than regular letters. The best-matches will be the most specific rules which match the target. Take the example of the target '-th'. The rule <?ch = C>

mismatches on a letter, and will receive a large penalty. The rule <?t? = t> mismatches on two don't-cares, and will receive a smaller penalty. The rules <?th = T>, and <?th = D> mismatch on a single don't-care, and will be retrieved from memory as being the best matches.

The ultimate result of this computation is a set of plausible phonemes for each letter of the word. The letter 't' has two possible pronunciations: the voiced and unvoiced TH sounds. The letter 'h' will be silent in either case. The rule <?e- = -> (word-terminal e's are silent) incorrectly deduces that the final 'e' will be silent. Thus, we will get [TD][-][-]. Rules have correctly deduced 2/3 of the letters. This error will be corrected in the recognition phase of the process.

There are, of course, well known algorithms for this sort of rule application which do not require associative memory operations. This implementation was chosen to point out the fact that MBR is a foundation, and a variety of constructs including rules can easily be built upon it.

3.2. Recognition

The recognizer starts with a phonetic vocabulary: a set of words encoded as phonemes. This vocabulary is stored as an associative memory. It is then given a plausible pronunciation for a word which, it assumes, is part of that phonetic vocabulary. In this case, the word is 'the' and the plausible pronunciation is [TD][-][-]. It then rates each word in its phonetic memory according to how well it matches the proposed pronunciation. A large penalty (1000) is assessed for each phoneme of the memory-word which is not part of the plausible pronunciation. In this example, the word 'k@t' (cat) gets a penalty of 3000, as it is a complete mis-match of the plausible pronunciation. The word 'S-i' (she) gets a penalty of 2000, as it matches in the middle position, but not in the first or third. The correct word, 'D-i', gets a penalty of 1000, and will in fact be the best match.

Taken by itself, this process comes up with the wrong word between 12% and 7% of the time (depending on the body of text). Additional mechanisms described below will show how this error rate can be reduced through learning.

3.3. Memorization

So far, JOHNNY has taken a written word, used rules to produce a plausible pronunciation, and recognized a word in its phonetic memory as having a similar pronunciation. At this point, JOHNNY assumes that the word is correct, and commits it to memory. It has now learned a word. The next time it sees that word, it does not need to go through the rule application/ prediction cycle to recognize it. This form of learning is, in essence, a compilation of domain knowledge; no new knowledge is added to the system, but old knowledge is made more quickly accessible

The words are stored in an associative memory as a set of 9-letter windows, each consisting of a letter, the preceding 4 letters, and the succeeding 4 letters (this is the same representation as was used in MBRtalk). One such record is produced for each letter in the word. Each record also includes the phoneme produced by the central letter. Thus, once we know that the word 'the' is pronounced 'D-i', it produces 3 entries in memory:

```
<----the- = D>
<---the-- = ->
<--the--- = i>
```

3.4. Induction

As was noted above, Memory-Based Reasoning has been applied to the pronunciation problem [1][3]. An associative memory composed of known words and their pronunciations, organized into (9-letter) windows as shown above, allows MBR to act as an inductive reasoning algorithm: given a novel word, it will predict the correct pronunciation for that word a high percentage of the time.

At initialization time, this model has known pronunciations, but does not have the word-pronunciation pairings required by the inductive algorithm. However, as it recognizes and memorizes words, it acquires these pairings. Once a sufficient number of words have been recognized and memorized, it is possible to use MBR to supplement the initial set of rules. The result is improved pronunciation performance, and the system now exhibits the phenomenon of unsupervised learning. This phase of learning is more than a compilation of existing knowledge: the inductive process adds new knowledge to the system.

4. Experimental Results

4.1. Basic results for three texts

Three sets of text were used for the first experiment. The first text (called 'first-grade') is a phonetic transcription of 1024 words spontaneously uttered by a child in the first grade. Because the child's pronunciations are often indistinct (for example 'would' is often pronounced as a single neutral vowel '-x---'), a second text ('fixed first grade') was constructed by replacing the child's pronunciations with pronunciations taken from a dictionary, keeping the vocabulary the same. These texts contain many duplicate words. The third text consists of 8192 words randomly selected from a dictionary.

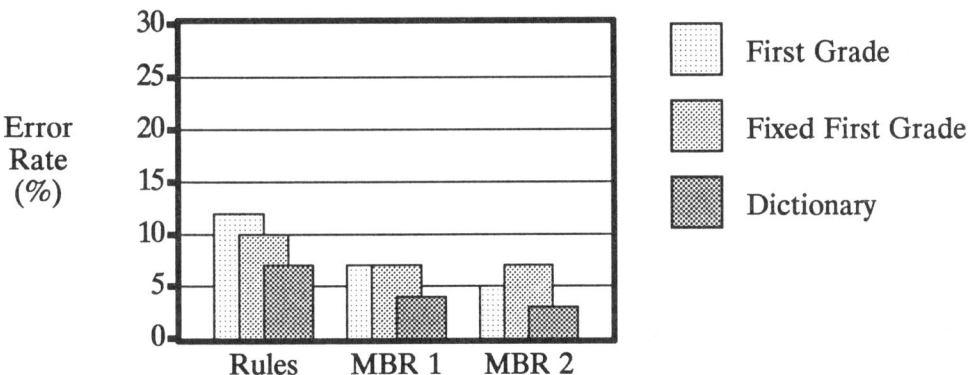

Each experiment consists of three passes. In the first pass, 1024 words from the text are processed using rule-application plus recognition (for the two first grade texts, this amounts to reading the full text; for the dictionary this amounts to reading only 1/8 of the text). This establishes the accuracy of the base algorithm. As is shown above, the error rate (the proportion of words incorrectly recognized) varies between 12% for 'first-grade' and 7% for 'dictionary'. In the second pass, the word-pronunciation pairs produced in the first pass are memorized, and rules + MBR + recognition are employed on the same text. In all cases the error rate is cut by nearly a factor of 2. For the third pass, the results of pass 2 are fed back into the system, and rules + MBR + recognition are again employed. In two out of the three texts, this results in further improvements in accuracy. This improvement is due to the fact that the data being used by MBR in the third pass has a lower error rate.

4.2. Varying the Rule Base

For the remainder of this paper, only results from 'fixed–first–grade' will be shown; results for the other texts are available but space limits preclude their inclusion in this paper.

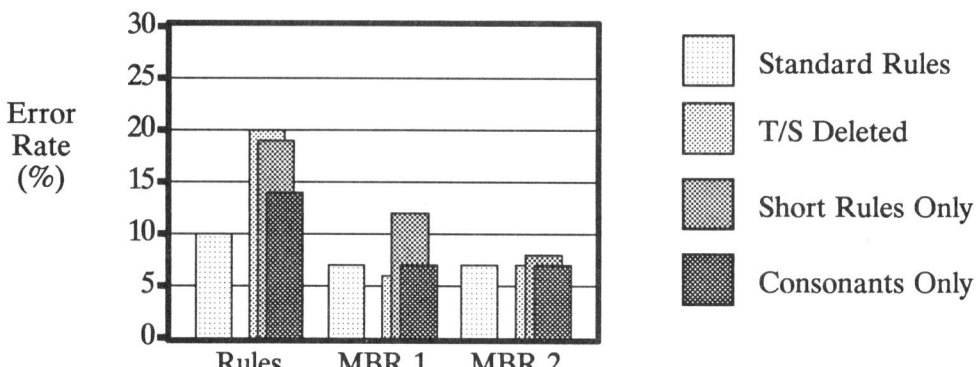

There is possible question as to the sensitivity of this system to the initial set of rules. To answer this question, various subsets of the initial rule set were tested. The first subset was obtained by dropping the rules for 't' and 's' from the rule set. Naturally, this produced a high initial error rate (20%). However, after one pass of MBR the 'damage' had been completely repaired (In fact, after the first pass there is an anomalous 1% improvement over the standard rule set). For the second run, all multi-letter rules (e.g. the rules for SH and TH) were deleted. For the third run, all rules for vowels were deleted. For this text, the damage was essentially repaired by the conclusion of the third pass. For other texts, the repair is less complete, but substantial improvement always takes place.

This basic insensitivity to the starting rule base demonstrates the sort of robustness desired for knowledge-based systems: the omission of important domain knowledge can be overcome by learning.

4.3. Supervised Learning

Supervised learning can also be studied in this model. Two forms of supervision are evaluated in the experiment shown above. The form of this experiment differs from that of the experiments shown above. In the first two experiments, memorization of words was inhibited until the completion of each pass of the algorithm, in order to assess the contributions made by rule application and MBR/induction. When evaluating supervised learning, it is more sensible to observe how the introduction of supervision affects the course of a single pass through the text. Therefore, rather than waiting until the end of a run to memorize words and apply memory-based induction, words were memorized immediately, and the error rate tabulated for every 100-word segment of the text. This is closer to the sort of situation a child learning to read encounters. For this test, the reduced rule set (single-letter rules only) was used.

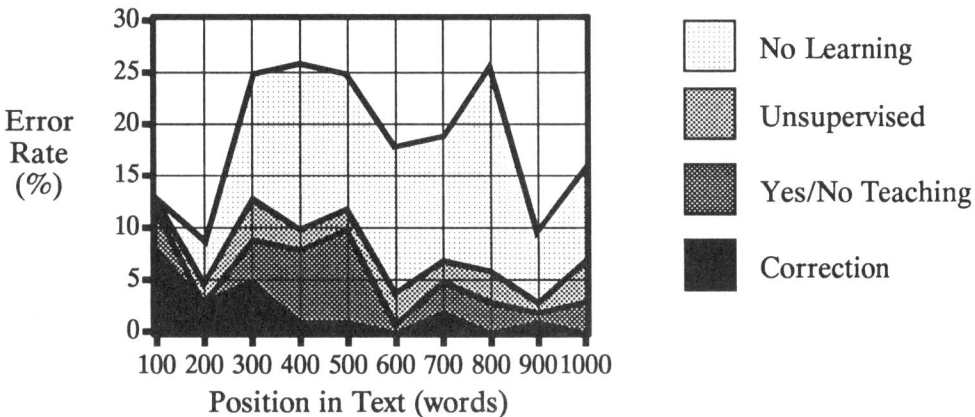

First, for comparison sake, the full body of text was processed with memorization turned off. Second, memorization was turned on, and the unsupervised learning algorithm applied. A substantial improvement results. For the third run, a supervisor is added which tells JOHNNY whether it got the right answer. When this is done, JOHNNY can avoid making the same mistake twice. Results are improved, partly because MBR/induction is operating on completely accurate data, and partly because JOHNNY can use the process of elimination in cases where it is uncertain as to which of several words is correct. Finally, the experiment was run with a correcting supervisor, which gives JOHNNY the correct answer whenever it makes a mistake. Results are further improved. This represents more work for the supervisor than the other methods but, it must be noted, less than 1/10 the work that would be required to teach JOHNNY every word in the text.

5. Discussion

There is value to this work beyond what it contributes to the development of Memory-Based Reasoning. The basic cycle of prediction, recognition, and learning doubtless occurs in domains other than learning to read.

Also, this model turns the usual conceptions of rules and induction up-side down. Ordinarily, it is assumed that the purpose of an inductive algorithm is to take a set of raw data and characterize it by a set of rules (e.g. ID3 [9]). This model suggest that rules are better viewed as a means of communication: a teacher instructs a student in a set of rules; the student then uses the rules to get started in an activity, and proceeds to learn as it solves an increasing number of problems.

APPENDIX

The following summarizes the phonetic encoding used in this work.

@	abAck	E	bEd	J	Jet	Q	QUaint	u	tOO
A	fIle	e	mAke	k	Cat	R	bIRd	v	aboVe
a	cAr	f	Fight	L	abLE	r	Red	w	Wet
b	Bat	G	aloNG	l	Lead	S	daSH	X	boX
C	CHurch	g	Great	m	Meat	s	Sleep	x	Allow
c	OUght	h	Hot	n	Neat	T	THink	Y	cUte
D	baTHe	I	bIt	o	cOld	t	Tin	y	Yet
d	Dull	i	bEAt	p	Pet	U	wOOl	z	siZe

In addition, a dash '-' stands for silent letters, and a tilda '~' stands for the start or end of a word.

REFERENCES

[1] Stanfill, C. and Waltz, D., "Toward Memory-Based Reasoning," *Communications of the ACM*, 12(12), December 1986, pp 1213-1228.

[2] Stanfill, C., and Waltz, D., "The Memory-Based Reasoning Paradigm," Thinking Machines Corporation Technical Report RL87-2, 1987.

[3] Stanfill, C., "Memory-Based Reasoning Applied to English Pronunciation," *Proceedings of AAAI-87*, pp 577-581, 1987.

[4] Lehnert, W. G., "Case-Based Problem Solving with a Large Knowledge Base of Learned Cases," *Proceedings of AAAI-87*, pp. 301-306, 1987.

[5] Sejnowski, T., and Rosenberg, C., "NETtalk: A Parallel Network that Learns to Read Aloud," Technical Report JHU/EECS-86, The Johns Hopkins University Electrical Engineering and Computer Science Department, 1986.

[6] Kolodner, J.L., *Experiential Processes in Natural Problem Solving*, Technical Report No. GIT-ICS/85/32. School of Information and Computer Science. Georgia Institute of Technology, GA, 1985.

[7] Kolodner, J.L., Simpson, R., and Sycara-Cyranski, K., "A Process Model of Case-Based Reasoning in Problem Solving," in *Proceedings IJCAI-85*, pp 284-290, 1985.

[8] Kolodner, J.L., "Extending problem solver capabilities through case-based inference," *Proceedings of the 1987 International Machine Learning Workshop*, 1987.

[9] Quinlain, R., "Discovering Rules from Large Collections of Examples: A Case Study," in *Expert Systems in the Micro Electronic Age*, Donald Michie, editor, Edinburgh University Press, Edinburgh, 1979.

The Memory-Based Reasoning Paradigm

Craig Stanfill and David L. Waltz
Thinking Machines Corporation
245 First Street
Cambridge, MA 02142

ABSTRACT

Memory-Based Reasoning is a new paradigm for AI in which an associative memory using a best-match algorithm is the foundation of reasoning. It is particularly well suited to massively parallel computers such as the Connection Machine System.® In this paper we discuss the memory-based reasoning paradigm and its relationship to artificial intelligence and cognitive science. We first give a brief synopsis of work to date on memory-based reasoning. We also discuss the relationship of this work to Society of Mind models, logic, and knowledge representation.

1. Introduction

Memory-Based Reasoning (MBR) places memory at the foundation of intelligence, rather than at the peripheracy. Memories of specific events are used directly to make decisions, rather than indirectly (as in systems which use experience to infer rules). In its simplest form, MBR uses the global nearest match computation to find the items in memory most similar to a current situation and then uses the actions associated with these items to deal with the current situation. In essence, reasoning is reduced to perception: the current situation is observed, it reminds the system of something it has seen before, and an immediate reaction is forthcoming without further analysis.

The advantages of memory-based reasoning are: 1) It is much easier to generate examples than to generate rules, so the knowledge acquisition for

---

Connection Machine is a registered trademark of Thinking Machines Corporation a memory-based reasoning system is much simpler; 2) Memory-based reasoning systems inherently have a mechanism for judging confidence in an answer -- if there is a very close match in memory to the current situation, one can be quite confident of the outcome. 3) Memory can model a wider variety of phenomena — including both decision making and perception — than can rules.

Significantly, parallel hardware reverses the relative efficiency of memory-based reasoning and rule-based reasoning. On serial hardware, the best-match operation is very expensive because every data item must be considered in turn, while rule-triggering is relatively cheap due to the existence of algorithms (e.g. Rete networks) which allow a database of rules to be efficiently searched. On parallel hardware, the best-match algorithm takes constant time, while rule-invocation takes time proportional to the number of rules which must be chained to obtain an answer. MBR has been implemented on the Connection Machine System [3], where it achieves high performance.

In this paper we first discuss work to date on memory-based reasoning. We then present our plans for further development of the paradigm.

2. Summary of Work To Date

In this section we discuss MBR applied to some problems in word pronunciation. The first of these is an inductive problem: given a set of words with known pronunciations, infer the pronunciation of novel words. The second is an unsupervised learning problem: learning to read. In this problem, the starting point is a phonetic vocabulary plus a set of pronunciation rules; the result is a correspondence between written words and the phonetic vocabulary.

2.1. The MBR Shell

As reported in [9], we implemented an MBR "shell" on the Connection Machine System. This shell computes the nearest match to an input pattern (which may be incomplete) using a set of weighting and distance measures, the net effect of which is to find the distance from every individual example in memory to the current example to be classified.

The shell assumes a relational database-like format for examples. More formally, a *database* is a set of *records*. Each record has a fixed set of *fields*. The field containing the "answer" to a problem is called the *goal field*, and the other fields are *predictor fields*. Novel records which are to be classified are *target records*. *Field Weights* are computed by judging how tightly individual predictor fields constrain values of the goal field. The *distance* between two records is then computed by summing the weights for all predictor fields for which they have different values.

2.2. MBRtalk

The model has been extensively tested on the problem of pronouncing English words given the ASCII characters of the word, reasoning on the basis of a portion of an English pronunciation dictionary [9] [10]. The formulation of the task is deliberately similar to Sejnowski and Rosenberg's NETtalk system [8]. Lehnert has also studied the pronunciation task [5].

This problem is an example of the classification task: given a set of objects which have been classified, classify some new objects in "the same manner". It is also an example of both supervised learning and similarity-based induction (induction in the absence of a pre-existing domain model).

In this case, the database is a dictionary [12] and the classes are phonemes. Each record in the database consists of a nine letter window in a word (a letter, the four previous letters, and the next four letters); the phoneme corresponding to the central letter of the window; and the stress of the letter (primary stress, secondary stress, etc.). For example, the word "file", which has pronunciation "fAl-" and stress pattern "+1- -", would yield the following four records:

```
* * * * f i l e *    f  +
* * * f i l e * *    A  1
* * f i l e * * *    l  -
* f i l e * * * *    -  -
```

The 20,000 words in the dictionary thus yield 146,951 records.

It must be noted that perfect performance on the pronunciation task is fundamentally impossible. First, many English words are borrowed from other languages, often retaining their original pronunciations. Thus, any system which pronounced "fillet" correctly would almost certainly mispronounce "billet." Second, the stress patterns of English words often depends on their part of speech. In some cases, a word will even have two acceptable pronunciations, depending on whether it is used as a noun or a verb ("to object" versus "an object").

In spite of the difficulty of the pronunciation task, Memory Based Reasoning does quite well: MBR produces the correct phoneme 92% of the time. With a database of 128K records running on a 32K processor Connection Machine System, each classification is accomplished in 30 milliseconds.

The MBR algorithm described above was evaluated according to sensitivity to database size, distraction, and noise.

Database Size. The algorithm exhibits graceful degradation as the size of the database shrinks from 128K down to 4K. With 4K records (approximately 700 words), 78% of the phonemes were correct.

Distraction. In an effort to distract the algorithm, between 1 and 7 fields containing random values were added to each record in the database. These caused at most a 1% loss in performance.

Noise. Two types of noise were considered. First, between 10% and 100% noise was added to the predictor fields*. The algorithm was not significantly affected until noise exceeded 90%, at which point performance collapsed. Second, between 10% and 100% noise was added to the goal fields. Performance fell about linearly with added noise.

2.3. JOHNNY

Once MBRtalk had demonstrated the ability of MBR to perform the classification task, it was thought important to extend MBR to handle other forms of reasoning. To this end, a second program called *JOHNNY* was written [11]. JOHNNY uses MBR rule-application, MBR recognition, and MBR induction to teach itself how to read. The result is a very simple system which exhibits unsupervised learning.

---

* For 10% noise, 10% of the predictor-fields in the database would receive a uniformly distributed random value.

JOHNNY simulates the process of learning to read. It starts with some of the same knowledge a child learning to read begins with: it can recognize spoken words, and it has been taught rules for sounding out words, but it has not yet learned the correspondence between the written and spoken forms. It is acquiring such a correspondence, in a way less burdensome than memorizing every possible word, that is the essence of learning to read.* JOHNNY accomplishes this by sounding out written words and matching them against known spoken words. Later, as it builds a up a large number of such matchings, it can use inductive methods to improve its performance in the sounding-out process.

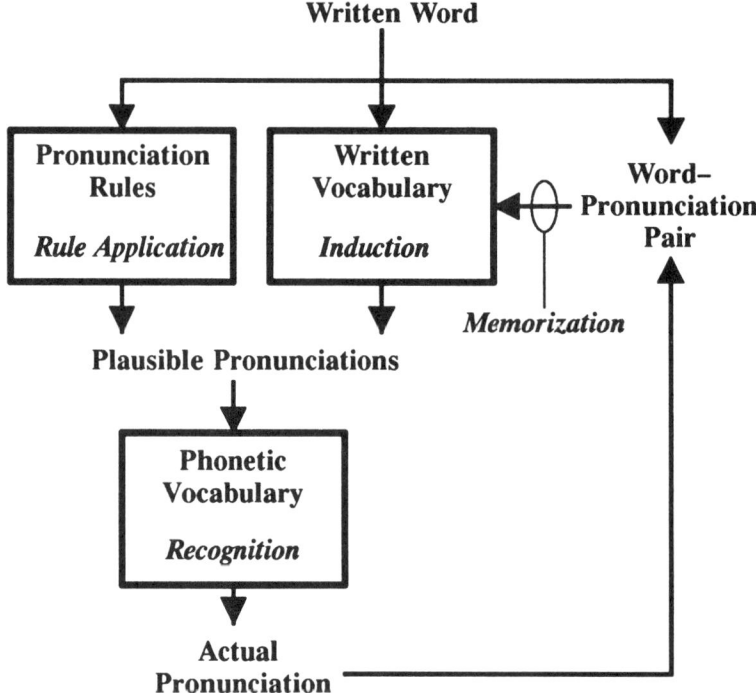

JOHNNY starts with a set of *pronunciation rules* and a *phonetic vocabulary*, but no written vocabulary. It looks at written words, uses the rules to generate *plausible pronunciations*, then searches the phonetic vocabulary for the most plausible actual word. The pronunciation for that word is then paired

---

* No acoustic processing takes place here: the phonetic vocabulary is represented as a phonetic transcription. Also, the system has no notion of what the words mean, and does not exploit any sort of contextual or semantic constraints.

with the original written word, and *memorized* (added to the written vocabulary). When a sufficient number of written words are added to the written vocabulary, it acts as an inductive engine, so that the process of guessing plausible pronunciations for new words is more accurate.

After reading through a 1024 word text 3 times, JOHNNY correctly learns over 90% of the words. The amount of learning is relatively insensitive to the initial set of rules. It is also possible to run this system with supervision, where the supervision either consists of informing JOHNNY whether it got the correct answer or not, or giving it the correct answer whenever it makes a mistake. In either case, JOHNNY learns more quickly and with fewer errors than in the unsupervised case.

All aspects of this system — rule application, recognition, memorization, and induction — are implemented via MBR.

Rule Application. Rules are stored in memory. When a word is seen, a best-match search of this memory is conducted. A large penalty is assessed for each mis-match between the word and a rule, and a smaller penalty is assessed for each place where the rule has a "don't care". The result is that the most specific rule matching the word under consideration is retrieved first. The output of this step is a set of plausible phonemes corresponding to each letter in the word.

Recognition. As noted above, the rule application step of JOHNNY produces a set of plausible phonemes for each letter in the initial word. The recognition step rates each word in the phonetic vocabulary according to how well it matches this set of phonemes, assigning a penalty for each phoneme in the target word which is not represented in the set of plausible phonemes for that position of the word.

Memorization. As noted above, the rule application phase plus the recognition phase produce a pairing of a written word with a pronunciation. The word is broken into records as discussed above in the section on MBRtalk, and they are added to memory.

Induction. The final step in the system is the use of a variant on the MBRtalk algorithm to augment the initial set of rules as predictors of plausible pronunciations for the words. This memory is then used to infer plausible pronunciations for words not yet learned. A similarity measure is applied to the memory, the 20 best matches are retrieved, and the frequency with which each phoneme shows up is tabulated. This produces a set of plausible phonemes, rather than simply the most likely single phoneme for a given position (as was done in MBRtalk).

3. Relationship to AI

We have already suggested that memory-based reasoning systems provide an alternative to expert systems which have certain advantages in terms of knowledge acquisition (though they also require more powerful computers). However, we would like in the following sections to concentrate on advantages that the memory-based reasoning system may have as an overall model for cognition.

Traditional models of artificial intelligence have generally ignored some significant problems that are particularly important for modeling common sense: goal selection, situation assessment and action selection. Most AI planning systems built to date have been based on the heuristic search model [6] and have not had to deal with the problem of deciding what overall goals are achievable in a current situation. Goals have either been formulated for the system by the programmer or there have been a sufficiently small set of goals so that the system could enumerate them all. Similarly, there have generally been only a relatively small set of rules or operators so that the tree generated by trying all operators or rules is reasonably tractable. The role of heuristic search has been to make the tree more tractable by pruning unnecessary branches.

There is a substantial problem, however, when we want to apply heuristic search beyond a single narrow problem domain. If a system may have thousands of goals that it may achieve in any given situation, and tens of thousands of operators, how is it to decide which of these goals and which of these operators are appropriate in any given situation? We believe that memory-based reasoning provides a way of supporting traditional AI models in such a fashion that it may be possible to work on much larger problems than have been attempted to date. Memory-based reasoning can be used to propose a small number of goals that are feasible in any given situation. Once a particular goal is selected for exploration, a memory-based reasoning system can suggest which operators apply to the current situation. Current experiments on the Connection Machine system [3] can easily be extended into the tens of thousands of memory examples, and still operate at a very rapid speed.

In MBR, logic plays a somewhat different role than has traditionally been assigned to it in AI. We believe that there has been a confusion between inference rules used as *searching* mechanisms and inference rules used as *verification* mechanisms. In the memory-based reasoning paradigm it is quite easy to propose or hypothesize a particular goal or operator as applicable in a given situation. However, in general, no operator or goal will match the current situation exactly. The role of logic in the memory-based reasoning paradigm is to account for the differences between the current situation and previous situations in memory, and to verify that the differences will not preclude the pursuit of a goal or the application of an operator. In contrast, traditionally in AI, logic and rules have been used to decide what moves may be made at any given time. Backtracking is used when such moves fail to achieve goals. As argued by Feldman [1] it is clear that in human reasoning there is simply not enough time available for backtracking search within the hundred milliseconds or so required for most human decisions. Memory-based reasoning can account for rapid decision-making, because it does not generally require backtracking, but retrieves previous solutions whole in a single step.

Backtracking search is used when there is sufficient time available to consider the consequences of an action. Thus, the memory-based reasoning model is capable of matching observed human performance: when decisions must be made rapidly or when matches to previous situations are quite close, situations may be retrieved and used whole; when current situations do not match any memories well, or when the decision is of extreme importance and sufficient time is available, the memory-based reasoning system still proposes goals and operators, and a logic system verifies that the goal can really be obtained, and that the differences between the current situation and previously known situations are not important.

This work can be viewed as a generalization of the STRIPS/MACROPS work [2], in that it does not require exact matches in order for operators to be applied.

Another consequence for artificial intelligence may be that less attention needs to be paid to memory organization than has traditionally been assumed. For example, Kolodner [4] correctly observes that there are serious problems in retrieving appropriate episodic memories when the number of memories becomes large. She spends a good deal of effort in explaining how memory might be organized so that the right items could be found in a reasonable time. The memory-based reasoning idea suggests that, given appropriate hardware, the retrieval of nearest match items is a cheap operation and does not necessarily require any great attention to memory organization.

4. Strengths and Weakness of MBR

In its current state of development, MBR has a number of strengths, but some weaknesses remain. Among the strengths:

- MBR works from existing databases, not interviews from experts. This strength is shared by a number of other learning-based approaches.

- MBR can explain its decisions by citing precedents.

- MBR can tell a good match from a poor match, and so it "knows whether it knows."

- MBR is in incremental learning algorithm: learning takes place as soon as a new example is available, without excessive computational costs.

- MBR is a very general mechanism, allowing for the implementation of rules, recognition, and induction within a single framework.

There are, however, a number of weaknesses in the current realization of MBR which require correction.

- MBR is sensitive to representations (though probably no more so than other AI methods). MBR does not yet have any means of modifying its representations.

- MBR has no method for handling such non-flat conceptual structures as causality and histories.

- MBR's dependency on metrics is not fully understood. While it does not appear at this time that MBR is very sensitive to the exact metric which is used, more work is required to study the relationship between metrics and MBR's performance.

With more work, the second and third problems can probably be solved fairly quickly. The first problem — representational sensitivity — has been with AI for many years, and new fundamental insights will be required to solve it.

5. Summary

Initial work concentrated on the application of pure memory-based reasoning to "flat" relational databases, with the representation fixed by the system builder. For the pronunciation task, MBR performs quite well, producing the correct phoneme up to 92% of the time. The algorithms are not sensitive to distraction, are only slightly sensitive to predictor-noise, and degrade gradually as goal-noise is added. More recent work has been concentrated on combining MBR modules into more complex cognitive models.

In the long run, we believe that memory-based reasoning can provide a unifying paradigm for Artificial Intelligence. Most aspects of intelligence, we believe, can be expressed as operations on memory. This includes perception, attention, generalization, learning, and deduction. Indeed, aspects of some of these phenomena appear as emergent behavior of the simple MBR model presented above.

REFERENCES

[1] Feldman, J.A., "Introduction to the Special Issue on Connectionism," *Cognitive Science* 9(1), 1985.

[2] Fikes, R.E., Hart, P.E., and Nilsson, N.J., "Learning and Executing Generalized Robot Plans," *Artificial Intelligence* 3(4), pp. 251-258, 1972.

[3] Hillis, D., *The Connection Machine*, MIT Press, Cambridge Massachusetts, 1985.

[4] Kolodner, J., *Retrieval and Organizational Strategies in Conceptual Memory: A Computer Model*, Lawrence Erlbaum Associates, Hillsdale, NJ.

[5] Lehnert, W. G., "Case-Based Problem Solving with a Large Knowledge Base of Learned Cases," *Proceedings of AAAI-87*, pp. 301-306, 1987.

[6] Newell, A. and Simon, H.A., "GPS, a Program that Simulates Human Thought," in *Computers and Thought*, E.A. Feigenbaum and J. Feldman (eds), pp. 279-293, 1963.

[7] Quinlan, J.R., "Discovering Rules from Large Collections of Examples: A Case Study," in *Expert Systems in the Microelectronic Age*, D. Michie (ed), Edinburgh University Press, Edinburgh, 1979.

[8] Sejnowski, T.J. and Rosenberg, C.R., "NETtalk: A Parallel Network that Learns to Read Aloud," The Johns Hopkins University Electrical Engineering and Computer Science Technical Report JHU/EECS-86.

[9] Stanfill, C., and Waltz, D., "Toward Memory-Based Reasoning," *Communications of the ACM* 29(12), 1986.

[10] Stanfill, C., "Memory-Based Reasoning Applied to English Pronunciation," *Proceedings of AAAI-87*, pp 577-581, 1987.

[11] Stanfill, C., "Learning to Read: A Memory-Based Model," *Proceedings 1988 DARPA Workshop on Case-Based Reasoning, 1988.*

[12] *Merriam Webster's Pocket Dictionary*, 1974.

Using Case-Based Reasoning for Plan Adaptation and Repair

Katia Sycara

The Robotics Institute
Carnegie Mellon University
Pittsburgh, PA 15213

1. Abstract

This paper deals with two important problems in CBR: adapting a retrieved plan to the current situation, and repairing a failed plan. While previous planners have used mostly modification heuristics for adaptation, and critics and meta-planning strategies for repair, we propose a method based on a combination of heuristics and use of previous cases. Constructing an initial solution is an incremental process of adjusting a precedent plan using CBR and heuristics, and anticipating possible failures by accessing similar past failures and using them to get suitable fixes. Plan repair uses the failure explanation provided by environmental feedback to search memory for previous similar failures. The retrieved repair is then adapted to the current situation. The approach is demonstrated using examples from the PERSUADER, a case-based planner that creates and repairs plans to resolve labor conflicts.

2. Introduction

If a planner wants to re-use plans effectively it must have ways of adapting a previous plan to fit the current situation. The problem of plan adaptation is particularly important for Case-Based planners. For these planners, the creation of an initial solution is an *adaptation* problem since it is very seldom that two problem situations will be exactly alike. CBR is especially useful in domains that are ill-defined and have no strong causal theories or well-understood empirical regularities. One consequence of these characteristics is that solutions may fail and may need *repair*. This paper addresses the issues of plan adaptation and repair. The proposed approach involves the integration of CBR and heuristics.

Adaptation in the past has been done using only heuristics (e.g., [Hammond 86]). We are using CBR in a novel way: to suggest means of adaptation. The proposed process of coming up with an initial solution is an incremental process of adjusting the previous plan using CBR and heuristics, and anticipating possible failures by examining the case memory for failures that have the same features as the features in the current problem. Using CBR for adaptation adds flexibility since, as more experiences are acquired, the planner has an increasingly larger repertoire of adaptations that it can choose from. In planning for the satisfaction of multiple goals, the precedent plan selected might not make provisions for all input goals. CBR provides te means of adapting the plan that satisfies some of the goals to satisfy the rest. In addition, since cases incorporate accumulated expertise and changing circumstances, the proposed adaptations are more closely suited to a current problem.

After a plan has been created, it is tried out in the world. If the plan fails, it needs to be repaired.

---

[1]This research was funded in part by the Army Research Office under contract No. DAAG 29-85-K-00230.

Our approach to repair uses an explanation for the failure provided by environmental feedback. This explanation is used to index into the case memory to retrieve and adapt the repair of previous similar failures to the repair needs of the current situation. In other words, Case-Based Reasoning in the space of failures is employed.

The spectrum of situations where plans will fail cannot be anticipated. Thus, use of heuristics or hardwired TOPs alone [Hammond 87, Turner 87] do not provide a flexible enough methodology for dealing with failed plans. CBR is more flexible, since, as memory is enriched with new experiences, new ways that plans can fail and new repairs become available. Simpson [Simpson 85] also has used CBR for failure recovery and repair. His approach differs from ours in that he uses similarity-based retrieval of failed cases. Hammond [Hammond 87] finds an explanation of a plan failure via a set of causal rules that describe effects of actions under different circumstances. The explanation is then used to find a planning TOP with repair strategies. In our model, the explanation is provided via environmental feedback. This is realistic for problem domains with incomplete and changing knowledge and no strong domain model. For such problems, automatic failure explanation methods are not applicable. The features of the explanation are used as indices to retrieve previous failures and access the associated repairs.

Our approach is embedded in the computer program PERSUADER, which, acting as a labor mediator, resolves conjunctive conflicting goals of a union and company by finding compromises acceptable to them. Although the program operates in the domain of labor relations, the techniques it uses are domain independent.

3. Overview of the PERSUADER

The PERSUADER is a planner that integrates Case-Based Reasoning with preference analysis (a planning method based on multi-attribute decision theory [Sycara 87, Sycara 88]) to create acceptable compromises in labor management contract negotiations. The PERSUADER acts as a labor mediator. Its task is to help the disputants arrive at a mutually acceptable settlement (contract). To reach its goal, the PERSUADER must plan actions to achieve instrumental reductions in the difference between the parties' positions. Planning must be iterative and reactive because knowledge is incomplete (e.g., models of the agents' intentions must be inferred), and dynamically changing (success is met by shifts in positions which necessitates further planning).

The PERSUADER's input is the set of conflicting goals (e.g., wages, pensions, holidays, seniority language, management rights) of the company and its local union, and the context of the dispute (e.g., economic conditions in the industry, general economic conditions, information about the disputants). Its final output is either a single plan in the form of an agreed upon compromise, or an indication of failure if the parties to the dispute did not reach agreement within a particular number of proposals (to simulate the inability of the parties in the real world to reach agreement before a strike deadline). To perform its tasks, the PERSUADER brings to bear knowledge of past negotiations and settlements (cases), knowledge of the labor domain, and commonsense knowledge of human goals and behavior. The information present in a case includes the parties to the dispute, the conflicting goals of the parties, the industry to which the company belongs, the international union to which the local belongs, the geographical location of the company, the union members' job classification, the negotiation process, the arguments presented during negotiation, the proposals and counterproposals, and the final contract. Each one of the above components can be accessed either through the case to which it belongs, or through a separate set of indices. The concept of a negotiation failure is an *impasse*, a situation where the planner has proposed a compromise that has been rejected by at least one agent. A list of impasses represent the negotiation process. Each impasse records the PERSUADER's proposal, the parties' feedback (acceptance or rejection), the rejection reason (if known) and the PERSUADER's repair(s) to improve a rejected proposal. Planning is predominantly case-based and proceeds from a retrieved plan (or from scratch if none is available) through an iterative process of transformation and repair leading to the proposal of a contract or generation of an argument. Responses of the negotiating parties lead to further transformations and repairs.

As shown in Figure 3-1, the PERSUADER's algorithm consists in generating an initial compromise that it thinks will be acceptable to the parties and propose it. If at least one party disagrees, the PERSUADER iteratively performs the following tasks: it generate persuasive arguments to change the evaluation of the objecting party with respect to the proposed compromise, or incrementally repairs the rejected compromise to increase its acceptability. As will be described in later sections of the paper, at each stage salient features of past cases are used for case retrieval. Three foci, contracts, impasses and arguments are used as basis for performing CBR at the various stages of problem solving. Because the features that are used for retrieval are different in each task that the PERSUADER performs, the previous experiences that it reasons from are potentially different.

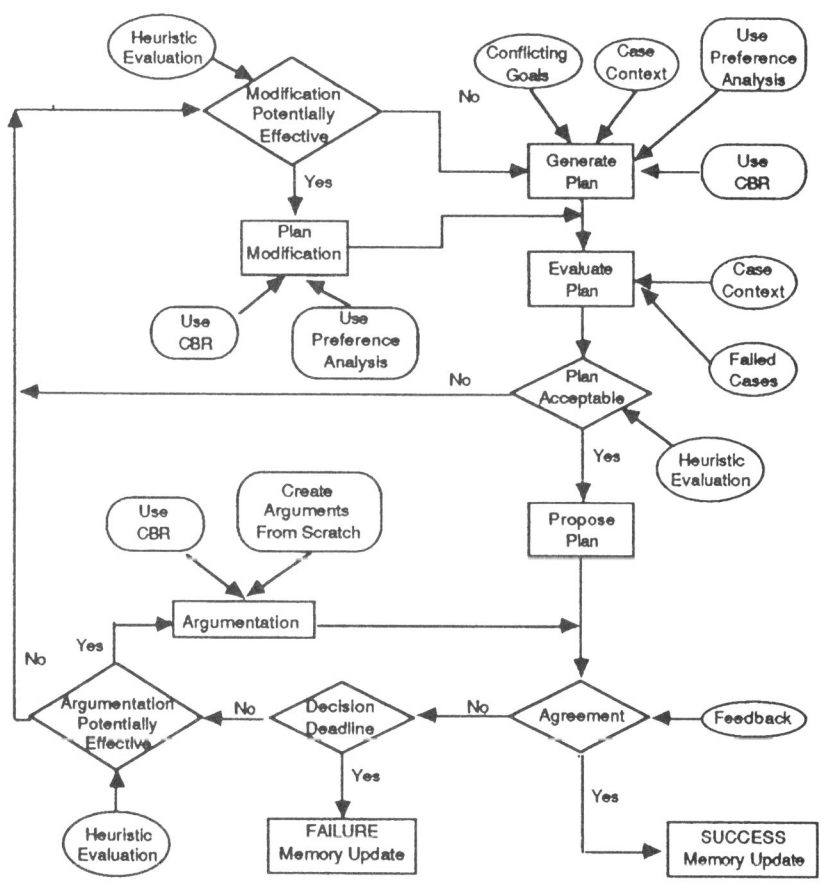

Figure 3-1: The PERSUADER's Planning Process

The PERSUADER keeps track of compromises that have worked in the past in similar circumstances. The most suitable is retrieved from memory and adapted to fit the current situation. The compromise is then proposed to the parties. If the parties agree, the case memory is updated with a successful episode. If one of the parties disagrees, the PERSUADER either repairs the compromise to better accommodate the rejecting party's utilities, or generates arguments to change the utilities of the disagreeing party with respect to the rejected compromise.

Successful plans that satisfy conjunctive goals totally or partially along with their justifications are stored in memory so that they can be reused in similar situations. The PERSUADER also stores failures along with the reason for failure (if one can be found) as well as dependencies among decisions taken at different times of the negotiation. Failures are stored so that they can be recalled in situations with similar features to the one where the failure occurred, thus warning the problem solver about potential problems, as well as providing appropriate repairs. Unlike other case-based planners (e.g. [Hammond 86]) that only avoid problems that they can anticipate at the beginning of planning, in the PERSUADER, warning/avoidance of problems occurs at each decision point.

4. Constructing an Initial Compromise

To construct an initial compromise, the PERSUADER (a) retrieves appropriate precedent cases from memory, (b) selects the most appropriate case(s) from those retrieved, (c) accesses the plan used in the selected case, and (d) adapts the precedent plan to fit the current situation.

To retrieve a set of cases similar to the current one, the PERSUADER uses a set of salient features of the domain as memory probes.[2] Cases are indexed by a multiplicity of features including the industry to which the company belongs, the geographical location, the economic context of the dispute, and the job classification of the union members. The features express the most important dimensions of the problem. Impasses are indexed by the contract issue/goal to which they pertain, and by the cause of rejecting the plan/proposal concerning the issue.

Using the set of features as memory probes, the PERSUADER retrieves an initial set of cases similar to the current case. An evaluation function based on a prioritization of the features is used to select the best (most similar case) out of those retrieved. In labor mediation, the most important feature is the industry to which the company belongs. Hence, if a current case involving a competitor is in the set of retrieved cases, it is the one used as a basis for reasoning. The plan used in the selected case (the contract) is accessed. The PERSUADER enters a phase of incremental adaptation of the precedent plan to fit the current problem circumstances. The plan adaptation process consists of the following steps:

- Adjust the accessed precedent plan to compensate for its dissimilarities from the "ideal" precedent for the current problem

- Modify the adjusted plan to take into account detailed information about the current problem

- Anticipate failures of the modified plan and fix it appropriately

Although we present the steps involved in finding a case-based plan as sequential, a reasoner may go through many iterations of the loop in order to construct a suitable plan. This happens because a contemplated modification may interact with the already existing part of the plan. If this interaction cannot be fixed, another case may need to be retrieved to suggest a more suitable modification.

---

[2] The PERSUADER's case memory is based on *generalized episodes* [Kolodner 84, Schank 82].

4.1. Precedent Adjustment

The ideal precedent plan is one that was used in a case whose indices have the same values as in the current case. In labor mediation, for construction of an initial proposal, the ideal precedent is a case where the disputant company is a competitor of the current disputant company, the geographical location of the companies is the same, th local unions belong to the same international union, the job classification of the union members is the same, and the two companies have the same size and organizational structure. Since a retrieved precedent case usually differs from the ideal, it has to be adjusted. For example, if a precedent case from a similar industry (not a competitor) is available, then an adjustment of the values of wages has to be made to compensate for dissimilarities along the industry dimension. In labor mediation, this adjustment is called the industry differential. If the company in the precedent case is in a different geographical location than the company involved in the current dispute, then the proposed wages have to be adjusted by the difference in the cost of living in the two locations. This is called the area differential.

Precedent adjustment is done using a library of heuristics. The difference between the current precedent and the ideal along the important problem dimensions is used to index into the library of heuristics to find the one to apply.

Consider, for example, the PERSUADER trying to find a compromise for Jung Products, a company producing elastic Health products (e.g., ankle and knee braces, posture aids, hernia aids) and its union. The union wants 15% increase in piece-rates,[3] 7% increase in pensions, no subcontracting, and strict seniority governing promotions and layoffs. The company wants no increase in piece-rates, no pension increase, unlimited subcontracting, and no seniority (i.e., promotions and layoffs to be determined by criteria chosen by the company). The PERSUADER searches memory for similar past contracts. It cannot find contracts of competitors but finds contracts of similar industries. Out of those, it selects the contract of Rampon company since its product (elastic support stockings) is most similar to the products of Jung Products, and since its location (Alabama, a southeastern state) is similar to Jung's (Georgia). The Rampon contract provided 10% increase in piece rates, 4% pension increase and subcontracting for limited time periods. Since the Rampon contract makes no provisions for promotions and layoffs, another contract making such provisions is sought. The contract of Peters Inc., a company that makes nurses' uniforms is selected out of those retrieved. It stipulates that in layoffs and promotions the company should observe the principle of seniority in conjunction with the worker's ability to perform the work.

The information from the Rampon and Peters contracts is combined to form a candidate contract for Jung Products. This contract is adjusted by applying to it industry and area differentials between Alabama and Georgia. These adjustments result in 12% increase in piece rates, 5% pension increase, subcontracting for limited time periods, and seniority and ability as co-determinants for promotions and layoffs.

The result of precedent adjustment is a base-line plan, called the "ballpark" plan. A ballpark plan is the best that can be constructed without taking details into account. Others (e.g. [Bain 86, Elkouri 72]) also have observed that once a judge or an arbitrator has worked out a ballpark figure for a given case, they will adjust it according to more detailed pertinent information.

---

[3] Piece-rate refers to remuneration that a worker receives for processing a product unit.

4.2. Modification of the Ballpark Plan

After constructing a ballpark plan, it has to be evaluated for appropriateness to the current case. There are three categories of knowledge that the PERSUADER takes into consideration when criticizing a ballpark plan:

- Knowledge of unacceptability conditions
- More detailed knowledge of the situation of the disputants
- Knowledge of the dispute context and its effects on the situation

These knowledge sources are used as basis for doing more detailed inference to adapt the ballpark plan to the specifics of the current situation. During evaluation, critics associated with these knowledge sources are activated. These critics are prioritized and considered in order of importance. A critic is most important if failure to apply it would result with greater probability in plan unacceptability. For example, a check is always made to see whether the company will be able to afford the ballpark economic package. This check is important since, if a company cannot afford the economic package, it most probably will reject the proposed settlement. If it is found that the company can afford the economic package, then critics associated with possible states of the company finances are applied. Such possible financial considerations include whether the company has suffered losses in the recent past, and whether the company has traditionally paid above, below, or industry average to further adjust the wages. A set of critics associated with the context of the dispute is then applied. In labor mediation context knowledge is almost entirely economic. Such knowledge includes considerations for the whole economy (recession, inflation etc), economic conditions of the industry to which the disputant company belongs, economic conditions of the geographical location of the company, and labor supply in the area.

If the application of a critic suggests that the plan needs further modification, salient features associated with the critics are used to search memory. The evaluation function is used to select the best out of the retrieved cases. The plan used in that case is checked for applicability. If the considered plan's preconditions match the current situation, then the plan is applied. If not, either the plan is modified using heuristics, or the next best case from those retrieved is considered.

Case-based reasoning is the preferred modification method in the PERSUADER. The rationale is that a previous case best reflects the interactions present in the situation. Moreover, the fact that the suggested modification has worked in a similar situation can be used as justification more convincing to the agents than invocation of a rule. If previous cases are not available, then rules associated with the critics are used for modification.

In trying to modify the ballpark plan for Jung Products, the PERSUADER finds out that the company cannot afford the contemplated economic package. The case memory is now searched for cases where the same situation (inability of the company to afford the economic package) had occurred for similar companies. The case of Futuro Inc., a company making Patients' Aids (e.g., canes, crutches, waterproof sheeting) is selected out of the set of retrieved cases as most similar because of similarity of the product, same geographical area, and similarity of the issues involved in the negotiation. In that case, the plan "pass the extra cost to the consumer" had been applied. A precondition of this plan is that the market for the product is not sensitive to price increases. Since the precondition is satisfied in the case of elastic health products, the plan is applied (i.e. the contemplated contract is not changed).

Company1 cannot afford the contemplated economic package
Searching memory with index INABILITY-TO-PAY and ECON-PKGE
3 cases found

```
Select case2
since it is similar product, same area, same issues in economic package
Looking at the plan "pass the extra cost to the consumer"
from case2
Check preconditions of plan used in this case

Since the market is insensitive to product price change
for elastic health products
plan applicable   .

Apply plan used in case2 to economic package
Pass the extra cost to the consumer
```

The PERSUADER now finds that the company has had losses of 3% in recent years. The case memory is now searched for similar situations. Since no pertinent cases are found, the PERSUADER uses a heuristic associated with the condition of recent losses that supplies the advice to reduce the contemplated increases for pensions and piece rates by half of the percentage losses. This results in 10.5% increase in piece rates and 3.5% increase in pensions.

4.3. Failure Anticipation

Once the modification phase is finished, the PERSUADER is ready to propose the resulting settlement. Before doing so, however, it makes a final check to see whether the solution might engender some unforeseen problems. The knowledge that a plan has failed in the past can suggest to the planner the potential for failure if the plan is adopted in the current situation. In contrast to other case-based systems (e.g., [Hammond 86]) that anticipate problems *before* constructing a plan, the PERSUADER anticipates failures as the *final step* in plan construction. This is appropriate in domains where the sought after plan is a compromise plan and thus, it is not apparent at the beginning of planning what exact form this compromise will take.

Failure anticipation is done through *intentional reminding* [Schank 82] of failures. This is necessary since the PERSUADER does not assume the existence of a strong domain model (which is the case in any domain where there are plethora of variables, time-varying data and inexact and incomplete knowledge). To ascertain whether a contemplated plan has failed in the past, the planner uses the conjunction of the plan's features and the index "FAILURE" as a memory probe. This probe returns cases where the contemplated plan has failed. The most similar case is selected and the adaptation plan used in that case (if present) is accessed. The process (knowledge extraction, evaluation) is applied to the selected modification plan to yield an appropriate adaptation to avoid the potential problem.

Having the repair stored in memory is the best outcome. This is not always possible. Often, it may be known that a plan was inadequate but no explanation or repair was found. In this case, the knowledge of a past failure can still warn the planner of the presence of a potential failure.

Before proposing the updated compromise to the Jung Products labor dispute, the PERSUADER searches memory to discover potential problems. It finds problems with the contemplated subcontracting language. It retrieves a case where the union had filed a grievance protesting that the company resorted to subcontracting instead of recalling laid off workers. The arbitrator in that case did not vindicate the union since the subcontracting clause restricted the company only as to the duration of subcontracting. The arbitrator, however, mentioned in the award the language needed to safeguard the union against such practice. The language was "The company has the right to subcontract for limited periods of time, and when it is clear that no work will be lost to union members".

Searching memory with index FAILURE, SUBCONT-LANG, LIMITED-TIME
1 case found
Looking at the modification "when no work will be lost to union members"
from case1

No precondition to check
Apply modification used in case1 to subcontract language
When no work will be lost to union members

5. Repairing Failed Plans

Even after all this care has been taken to customize a proposed plan to the current problem, feedback from the environment may inform the planner that his plan is unacceptable. Planners need to have the capability to react to environmental feedback. In labor mediation, failure of a proposed compromise means that an agent has rejected it. Repair is needed to improve the acceptability of the rejected plan. The PERSUADER has two ways of reacting to negative feedback (rejection of the solution/plan): changing the rejecting agent's evaluation of the plan through persuasive argumentation, and modifying/repairing the plan so that it will be more acceptable. Persuasive argumentation is tried first, since, if the objecting agents can be convinced to change their utilities and accept the compromise, then a successful resolution has been found. If, on the other hand, a rejected compromise is modified/repaired, the repair may make it objectionable to agents that had agreed before. Thus, only after persuasive argumentation is no longer judged effective by the planner (i.e. all applicable arguments that the planner could generate have been tried and rejected), is repair tried. For details of generating persuasive arguments see [Sycara 87, Sycara 85a, Sycara 85b].

When a failed compromise plan needs to be improved, the PERSUADER ascertains from the rejecting agent's feedback the most objectionable goal, the reason for the rejection and the importance the agent attaches to the goal. The rejected goal and reason are used as probes to select impasses with the same stated impasse goal and impasse cause as in the present failure. In other words, CBR is employed in the space of impasses. The selected impasse supplies repairs that will hopefully improve the rejected solution. If no appropriate impasses can be found, the PERSUADER uses standard heuristics that it knows about.

The PERSUADER's strategy for repair is explanation-based where the explanation (reason for rejection) is supplied by the rejecting agent. This is realistic for complex domains where there is no strong domain model, and plan failure depends in part on idiosyncratic behavior of the agents. Hence automatic failure explanation methods are not applicable. The PERSUADER uses a combination of similarity-based retrieval (during initial compromise generation) and an explanation-based retrieval (during repair of a failed compromise).

For example, confronted with the objection of Jung Products regarding the seniority language, the PERSUADER ascertains the rejection reason. Jung Products says that, since many of its key employees are junior, they will be the first to be laid off. Having this new knowledge, the PERSUADER retrieves a case where the same objection was raised. The seniority language in that case was amended to read: Key employees will be excepted from the seniority rule for layoffs; the company will designate whom it considers key employees.

Searching memory with index FAILURE, SENIORITY, KEY-EMPLOYEES
2 impasses found
Select impasse1
since it is same industry, same area, same job classification
Looking at the repair "except key employees"
from impasse1

No precondition to check
Apply repair used in impasse1 to seniority language
Except key employees

In multivariate planning there are many ways a plan could be modified/repaired. A planner seeks not only a plausible repair but one that with some confidence *improves* the rejected plan. After a repair is applied, the resulting compromise is evaluated using the parties' satisfaction with the compromise.[4] The criterion of plan improvement that the PERSUADER uses is whether the contemplated repair increases the rejecting agents' satisfaction more than it might decrease the satisfaction of the agents who have agreed to the compromise. Without an ability to predict which repair has a chance of being accepted, the planner could propose repairs that do not converge to a mutually acceptable compromise.

6. Summary and Conclusions

We have advocated the integration of CBR and heuristics for plan adaptation and repair. Such integration gives a planner the flexibility to consider a broad range of adaptation and repair strategies that planners that use either of the two methods in isolation cannot have access to. The use of CBR allows the planner to check and select strategies that do not introduce additional problems. Repairing plans using CBR is particularly suitable to domains with incomplete and changing knowledge and no strong domain model. Such characteristics typify many domains of interest to AI, such as medicine, law, economics, manufacturing, or design. In addition, a planner has the flexibility to try multiple strategies suggested by cases and choose the most appropriate. Integration of CBR and heuristics for adaptation and repair gives a planner the advantage of using knowledge in both forms: generalized (inferential rules) or specific (cases).

---

[4] An agent's satisfaction with a compromise, called his payoff, is calculated using a method based on multi-attribute utility theory. For details of this, see [Sycara 87, Sycara 88].

References

[Bain 86] Bain, W.M.
Case-based Reasoning: A Computer Model of Subjective Assessment.
PhD thesis, Yale University, 1986.

[Elkouri 72] Elkouri, F. and Elkouri, E.
How Arbitration Works.
The Bureau of National Affairs, Washington, DC, 1972.

[Hammond 86] Hammond, K.J.
CHEF: A model of case-based planning.
In *AAAI-86*, pages 267-271. AAAI, Philadelphia, PA, 1986.

[Hammond 87] Hammond, K.
Explaining and Repairing Plans that Fail.
In *IJCAI-87*, pages 109-114. IJCAI, Milan, Italy, 1987.

[Kolodner 84] Kolodner, J.L.
Retrieval and Organizational Strategies in Conceptual Memory: A Computer Model.
Lawrence Erlbaum Associates, Hillsdale, NJ, 1984.

[Schank 82] Schank, R.C.
Dynamic Memory.
Cambridge University Press, Cambridge, 1982.

[Simpson 85] Simpson, R.L.
A Computer Model of Case-Based Reasoning in Problem Solving: An Investigation in the Domain of Dispute Mediation.
PhD thesis, School of Information and Computer Science Georgia Institute of Technology, 1985.

[Sycara 85a] Sycara-Cyranski, K.
Arguments of persuasion in labor mediation.
In *IJCAI-85*, pages 294-296. IJCAI, Los Angeles, CA, 1985.

[Sycara 85b] Sycara-Cyranski, K.
Persuasive argumentation in resolution of collective bargaining impasses.
In *Seventh Annual Conference of the Cognitive Science Society*, pages 356-360. Cognitive Science Society, Irvine, CA, 1985.

[Sycara 87] Sycara, K.
Resolving Adversarial Conflicts: An Approach Integrating Case-Based and Analytic Methods.
PhD thesis, School of Information and Computer Science Georgia Institute of Technology, 1987.

[Sycara 88] Sycara, K.
Utility Theory in Conflict Resolution.
Annals of Operations Research, 1988.
(to appear).

[Turner 87] Turner, R.
Modifying Previously-Used Plans to Fit New Situations.
In *The Ninth Annual Conference of the Cognitive Science Society*. Cognitive Science Society, Seattle, WA., 1987.

Organizing and Using Schematic Knowledge for Medical Diagnosis*

Roy M. Turner
School of ICS
Georgia Institute of Technology

Abstract

A major problem for both human and computer diagnosticians is representing and organizing problem-solving knowledge in such a manner that the knowledge can be quickly accessed and easily used. Some researchers (e.g., [Lesgold et al., 1981] and [Feltovich et al., 1984] feel that expert medical diagnosticians have at least some of their problem-solving knowledge in a schematic form—procedures, or plans and scripts—that can efficiently be brought to bear on diagnostic problems.

In this research, we present an approach to diagnostic reasoning, called *schema-based reasoning*, that allows a reasoner to access and use the most specific *procedural* information available for the problem at hand. Our approach represents the problem solver's knowedge as *schemata*: packets of procedural knowledge about how to achieve a goal or set of goals. Schemata are organized in memory by the category of diagnostic problem they are useful for and along hierarchies defined by features of the schemata. When presented with a new problem, the reasoner retrieves schemata based on features of and goals present in the problem; the schemata are then applied by the reasoner to achieve its goals.

The process of schema-based reasoning was designed with an eye towards learning from experience; we discuss some initial ideas along these lines in this paper, specifically comparing our approach to *case-based reasoning* [e.g., Ashley, 1986; Kolodner, 1987; Kolodner et al., 1985; Simpson, 1985].

Our approach is implemented in the MEDIC program, a schema-based diagnostic reasoner whose domain is pulmonology.

1 Introduction

One of the major differences between a novice and an expert is that the expert has his or her knowledge in a readily accessible and usable form. The novice at medical diagnosis—a medical student—does not necessarily suffer from a lack of facts; rather, the novice does not have the facts organized in a fashion that allows them to be brought to bear quickly and efficiently on a problem. In addition, the novice does not have available the procedural knowledge necessary to allow him or her to quickly and easily solve diagnostic problems. The novice's knowledge, in other words, is not operational.

In order to operationalize a diagnostician's knowledge, he or she is given cases to solve, either practice or real. As cases are solved, the student learns what is important in the problem-solving environment, and learns what knowledge to use to solve which kinds of problems. Part of the learning process consists of converting "book knowledge" of signs, symptoms, and diseases into procedural knowledge: schemata for solving diagnosis problems (cf. [Lesgold et al., 1981]). Another part of the learning process is organizing the information learned—new facts as well as new schemata—in a form that allows it to be brought to bear efficiently on future problems.

The problem of how to represent and organize diagnostic knowledge has been studied in several artificial intelligence projects. In CENTAUR [Aikins, 1980], for instance, problem-solving knowledge is represented in the form of *prototypes* (frames) with associated rules; this has the effect of clustering the rules used around the contexts in which they are useful. MDX [Gomez and Chandrasekaran, 1982] is similar, in that its

---

*This research has been funded in part by NSF Grants IST-831771 and IST-8608362 and a grant DTD 09-25-87 from the Lockheed AI Center.

knowledge is represented as rules stored in *specialists* in a specialization (or taxonomic) hierarchy. Kolodner and Kolodner [1987] proposed a scheme in which knowledge used in diagnosis is stored in episodes and *generalized episodes* in a *dynamic memory* [Schank, 1982]. This approach has several benefits: (1) due to the properties of the dynamic memory, the most specific knowledge possible for a particular problem can be retrieved; (2) previous cases of problem solving are available for use in similar situations; and (3) the general knowledge, and the organization of the memory, is changed as new cases are added to the memory.

Though all these approaches organize the reasoner's knowledge in a form that is readily accessible, they tend to ignore the procedural knowledge necessary to perform diagnosis. That is left in the program itself and does not reside in the reasoner's knowledge structures. This assumes that one general method of performing diagnosis, using many specialized pieces of knowledge, can allow the reasoner to effectively diagnose problems. However, many researchers (e.g., [Lesgold et al., 1981] and [Feltovich et al., 1984]) believe that as diagnosticians become more expert, they increasingly use schema-like information—procedures, or plans and scripts—to perform diagnosis, and that this procedural knowledge is gained from experience. By using schema-like information, the reasoner can bring specialized problem-solving procedures to bear on diagnostic problems.

In this paper, we discuss a means of memory organization and retrieval that allows a reasoner to find the most specific problem-solving procedures available for a particular problem, then to use that information to solve the problem. Our work is based, to some extent, on preliminary work which was done on the SHRINK project some years ago [Kolodner, 1983]. In our approach, we represent the problem solver's knowledge as *schemata*, which are packets of procedural knowledge much like SHRINK's "process MOPs". Schemata are organized in memory by many different hierarchies of features present in the schemata, and are retrieved by indexes composed from features present in the problem being solved. When retrieved, a schema guides the reasoner in selecting actions to perform to solve a problem. Our approach, which we call *schema-based reasoning*, is implemented in the MEDIC program, a diagnostic reasoner whose domain is pulmonology.

Our research was begun with the idea that the results should lend themselves to making use of problem-solving experience. We will also discuss in this paper some initial ideas along these lines, as well as the relationship of our work to a form of reasoning from experience called *case-based reasoning* [e.g., Ashley, 1986; Kolodner, 1987; Kolodner et al., 1985; Simpson, 1985].

2 Schemata

According to Bartlett, a schema is:

> ...an active organization of past reactions, or of past experiences, which must always be supposed to be operating in any well-adapted organic response [Bartlett, 1932].

This is very similar to how we view schemata: a schema is knowledge that tells a reasoner how to respond to a particular situation.[1] A schema is basically a packet of procedural knowledge, represented in a declarative form, that can achieve a goal or set of goals; it is somewhat like a program with procedures. A diagnostic reasoner should have many schemata, for the many different situations and goals it will encounter. When the reasoner is confronted with a problem, it retrieves a schema for some portion of the problem, then interprets, or *applies*, the schema by taking the actions it describes.

Figure 1 shows a simplified picture of what one of MEDIC's schemata looks like, in this case a schema that can be used to interpret a finding of dyspnea. In addition to the actions to be taken in following the schema (the schema's *steps*), the schema contains information about goals it can be used to achieve, features of situations in which it is useful, preconditions or restrictions on its use, and the expected results of using it.

Each of the steps of a schema is composed of three parts: an action, a goal, and information used to choose the next step. The action is either a primitive action the reasoner can perform or another schema. The goal is a goal that the step is meant to achieve. The "next step" information consists of tests to perform against the state of the world and steps to be selected if the tests are true. This information is used to order the steps of a schema; there can be several different orderings, depending on the state of the world at the time the schema is used, including optional

---

[1] Though this research does not address how schemata come to exist, they can be thought of as being the result of past experiences, whether of the program or of the human expert who gave them to the program.

```
Goal: interpret a finding of dyspnea
Patient: any patient
Findings: dyspnea
Preconditions: there is a finding of dyspnea
Actions:
    A1: action: ask how many stairs patient can climb
        goal: determine severity of dyspnea
        next:
            if pt. can climb flight of stairs ⟹ A3
            else ⟹ A2
    A2: action: ask how far patient can walk
        goal: determine severity of dyspnea
        next: A3
    A3: action: estimate the severity of the dyspnea
        goal: determine severity of dyspnea
            ⋮
    A10: action: postulate hypotheses of pulmonary disease,
            cardiac disease
        goal: explain dyspnea
        next: done
Indices:
    patient/PATIENT1 → SCENE2
        ⋮
```

Figure 1: sc-dyspnea—a schema for interpreting a finding of dyspnea.

steps. If the action portion of a step is omitted, then the step suggests a goal that should be satisfied at that particular point in schema application.

In many ways, a schema is similar to traditional reasoning knowledge structures. For example, if each step in the schema has an action that is a primitive action, then the schema is equivalent to a *script* [Schank and Abelson, 1977] with *tracks* [Cullingford, 1981]. If, on the other hand, all of the steps of a schema have actions that are either schemata or primitive actions, the schema can be viewed as a abstract plan or as equivalent to one of NASL's [McDermott, 1978] tasks. Finally, we can view a schema as a packet of rules, perhaps similar to MDX's *concepts* or *specialists*. In this view, the rules' "antecedents" would consist of the information in the schema—findings, characteristics of the patient, etc.—(excluding the schema's steps); the "consequents" would be the actions that are specified by the schema.

There are several differences between schemata and these other knowledge structures, however. First, schemata are more general, in effect subsuming the functionality of the others. Second, new schemata can, in principle, be created by applying old schemata to new situations, then generalizing the result. This would allow schemata to be created for situations not anticipated when the reasoner was given its knowledge; the reasoner could adapt to its environment by operationalizing its problem-solving knowledge. And third, schemata are active participants in memory

organization, as will be discussed below. This organization allows the most specialized schemata for a portion of a problem to be retrieved and applied to that problem.[2]

3 Retrieving Schemata

Since a reasoner will encounter many different goals in many different situations, it should have a wealth of schemata at its disposal. The reasoner's memory must organize these schemata in such a way that the most specific schema available to achieve a particular goal can be found when the reasoner needs it. In order to do this, the schemata must be linked to one another in memory so that retrieval is facilitated.

MEDIC's memory organizes its schemata in two general ways: by the category of diagnostic situation in which they are useful, and by the use of specialization hierarchies of schemata. Figure 2 shows a portion of MEDIC's memory. There are four types of memory structure present in the figure (and in MEDIC's memory):

1. *diagnostic memory organization packets* (dx-MOPs) (cf. the memory organization packets (MOPs) of [Schank, 1982])—representing generalized sessions of diagnosis;

2. *cases*—representing individual (presumably unusual) cases of diagnosis that the reasoner knows about;

3. schemata; and

4. *scenes*—representing portions of diagnostic sessions in which a schema was used; in other words, a scene represents an instantiation of a schema in a particular case.

The dxMOPs and cases provide contexts against which a current problem can be matched (cf. the diagnostic categories of [Kolodner and Kolodner, 1987])—i.e., they allow the reasoner to categorize the current problem. These memory structures contain information about the findings which occur in particular types of problems, the hypotheses that are usually considered, patient characteristics, and, most importantly, schemata that can be used to achieve goals arising in consultations of this type. For example, the dxMOP "dx-consult" in Figure 2 represents a generalized consultation. It contains the information that consultations involve a patient, a doctor,

---
[2]MDX's specialists also participate in its memory organization; however, schemata are different from specialists both in the type of information they contain and in the way they are used by the reasoner.

and the program; findings will generally be discovered; and hypotheses will be considered. A dxMOP also contains pointers to schemata that can be used to achieve goals expected in the type of consultation the dxMOP represents: e.g., "sc-finding" to handle goals to interpret findings, "sc-hypothesis" to handle hypotheses, and so forth. A case, though much more specific than a dxMOP, contains basically the same type of information; instead of representing a category or prototype of a diagnostic situation, however, it represents an exemplar of a particular kind of diagnostic session. Its scenes represent instances of schemata having been applied in the past to solve particular goals in the situation represented by the case.

MEDIC's memory is organized in a manner similar to that described by [Kolodner, 1984] for episodic memory structures. The memory is basically an interconnected set of discrimination nets, or hierarchies, in which the leaf nodes are cases and scenes, and the interior nodes are dxMOPs or schemata. Memory nodes are linked by *indices*, each of which is a feature/value pair, where the "feature" is drawn from the more abstract memory structure of the two, and the "value" is the value, in the more specific structure, of the feature. Features are selected based on their predictiveness, or ability to point to useful specializations. For instance, one of the indices between "dx-consult" and "dx-cc-dyspnea" (representing consultations in which the chief complaint is dyspnea) is "chief complaint/dyspnea."

DxMOPs and schemata both serve to organize portions of memory. A dxMOP organizes other (less abstract) dxMOPs and cases along dimensions defined by the features of the consultation described by the dxMOP. Schemata organize more specific schemata and instances of schemata having been applied; this organization is along features of the schemata: goals it achieves, characteristics of the situations in which it is useful, etc. The two types of organization hierarchies—by dxMOP and by schemata—are connected by links between dxMOPs and the schemata useful in the situations they describe, and between cases and the scenes (instances of schema application) that occurred in them.

Retrieval consists of using features present in the current problem (characteristics of the patient, findings present, and problem-solving goals) to *traverse* [Kolodner, 1984] the indexing structure of the memory to find the most specific schemata available that fit the current situation. The actual process of retrieval is beyond the scope of this paper; it is basically the same as that described in [Kolodner, 1984].

As an example of retrieval, suppose the reasoner is working on a problem in which there is a finding of dyspnea on exertion. One of the reasoner's goals would be to interpret the finding: to flesh it out and to explain its occurrence. The schema that contains the information necessary to do this is labeled "sc-DOE" in Figure 2. The reasoner can find this schema by two paths. It can traverse the indices of "dx-consult", using information about the finding present in the problem, to first find "dx-cc-dyspnea", then "dx-cc-DOE". From here, "sc-DOE" can be found by using information about how to satisfy the goal of interpreting DOE. Or the reasoner can begin by looking in "sc-consult" for a schema which achieves the general goal: in this case, "interpret a finding." The indices of this schema can then be traversed, through "sc-dyspnea" to "sc-DOE".

Multiple paths to the same schema serve the purpose of helping ensure that a good schema can be found for specific situations. Since there are redundant paths to each schema, the reasoner can still find a schema even if there is not enough information present in the current problem to allow it to traverse some paths.

4 Applying Schemata

Schema application is somewhat analogous to program interpretation. First, a step is selected. If the step's action is a primitive action, the reasoner executes it directly; if the action is a schema, then the reasoner recursively applies it. If the action fails, or if no action is specified, the reasoner attempts to find and apply another schema to achieve the goal of the step. A new step is then selected by using information contained in the "next step" portion of the step, and the process continues.

There are several control problems that are beyond the scope of this paper. For instance, the reasoner should react to new information as it is discovered by retrieving schemata to handle it: e.g., when a finding is discovered, the reasoner should find a schema that can interpret the finding, and when a hypothesis is proposed, the a schema to evaluate the hypothesis should be found. At any particular time, there may be several active schemata. The problem of selecting the schema to apply at a particular time is one of focusing the reasoner's attention; it depends on (among other things) the reasoner's current goal and the importance of the findings and hypotheses under consideration.

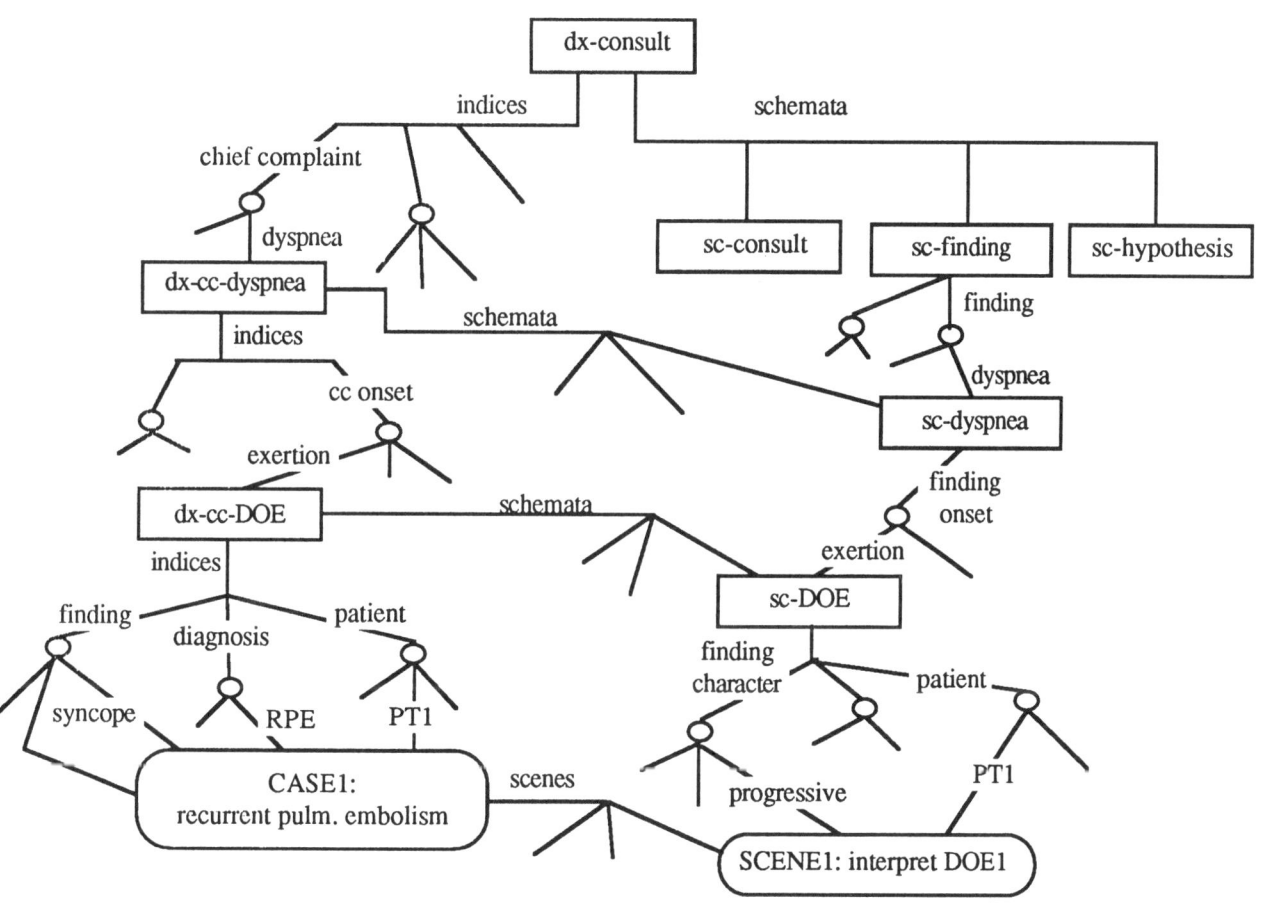

Figure 2: A portion of MEDIC's memory.

5 Medic

Our approach to diagnostic reasoning is implemented in the MEDIC program, a schema-based reasoner working in the domain of pulmonology. MEDIC consists of a memory, a reasoner, and a short-term memory (STM). The memory is organized as we have described in this paper. The reasoner is a bit more complex, in that it is able to respond (to a limited extent) to new information as it occurs. The reasoner operates at all times under the direction of a schema.

Conceptually, MEDIC has two types of schemata in its memory: global schemata and local schemata. A *global schema* is one that can direct the reasoner in performing large segments of a consultation. Examples are: "sc-consult", which directs the entire course of a consultation; "sc-getInfo", which gathers information from the user; and "sc-formDx", which forms a diagnosis from the hypotheses present in STM. A *local schema* is one that can direct the reasoner to achieve very specific goals, such as interpreting a finding or evaluating a hypothesis. Examples are: "sc-finding", an abstract schema which interprets any finding; "sc-dyspnea", which interprets a finding of dyspnea; "sc-dzHypothesis", which can evaluate any disease hypothesis; "sc-pulmDz", a specialization of sc-dzHypohthesis for pulmonary disease; and "sc-RPE", a further specialization for evaluating recurrent pulmonary embolism.

Having very specialized schemata allows the reasoner to act in a more focused manner than if it had only more abstract schemata. For example, a schema for interpreting dyspnea can be used to directly ask the user questions aimed at eliciting specific information to evaluate the severity: "How far can the patient walk?" or "How many stairs can the patient climb?" If a more abstract schema were used, a way would have to be found to gather the information and fill in the severity. Further specializations can be used to make even finer interpretations, or interpretations in rare but important contexts: e.g., a schema for interpreting dyspnea in someone who is restricted to a wheelchair should cause the reasoner to ask different questions than a schema for interpreting dyspnea in someone who is ambulatory.

Currently, MEDIC can diagnose very simple cases of pulmonary disease. Its basic algorithm is described in Figure 3. When the user asks for a consultation with MEDIC, the program attempts to find a dxMOP which describes the situation. This dxMOP is then the source of schemata to achieve goals arising during the consultation. In addition, the reasoner re-

```
begin
    loop forever:
        Wait until user requests a consultation;
        Add goal of diagnosing patient to short-term
            memory;
        Retrieve dxMOP using goal;
        Use strategy from dxMOP, if possible;
        Select a schema from the dxMOP to satisfy
            goal, add it to agenda;
        loop until done:
            Select a schema from agenda using strategies,
                local information in the dxMOP;
            Apply one action of the schema;
            if there was an interruption then:
                Handle interruption;
            fi;
            Specialize current dxMOP;
            if specialization succeeded then:
                Set current dxMOP to be the
                    specialization;
            fi;
        end loop;
        Accept and process feedback;
        Update memory;
    end loop;
end.
```

Figure 3: Basic schema-based reasoning algorithm.

trieves a *strategy* from the dxMOP; the strategy is used by the reasoner to select from among its active schemata. An example of a strategy can be seen in Figure 4; this strategy provides a goal ordering to the reasoner which causes the reasoner to perform a crude form of hypothetico-deductive reasoning: select goals (schemata) related to hypotheses first, then select those that relate to findings (with the hope of generating hypotheses), etc.

```
Situation: any
Goal ordering:
    select goals related to hypotheses
    select goals related to findings
    select goals for gathering information
    select goal for forming diagnosis
```

Figure 4: Strategy "st-HD-Reas" for hypothetico-deductive reasoning style.

Let's look at an example of a consultation with MEDIC, a portion of which is shown in Figure 5. Suppose a user requests a consultation. The reasoner looks in memory for a way of satisfying the goal of diagnosing a patient and finds a dxMOP, "dx-consult", representing how consultations are generally done. This is made the current dxMOP, and it is used as a source both of a strategy and of schemata to satisfy active goals. The strategy it contains is "st-HD-reasoning", the strategic schema mentioned above which provides a goal ordering to induce hypothetico-

```
Please describe the patient.
: (patient (sex female) (weight (value 204)) (height
    (value 64)) (race white))
Adding information about patient to STM.
What is the chief complaint?
: (finding (entity (dyspnea (duration (years 2))
    (character progressive))))
Adding chief complaint to STM...adding finding of
    <DYSPNEA0> to STM.
How many flights of stairs can the patient climb?
: (less-than 1)
How far can the patient walk on level ground?
: (yards 20)
I judge the qualitative value of SEVERITY of <DYSPNEA0>
    to be SEVERE.
        ...(same for cardiac disease)...
...explaining dyspnea...
Processing <HYPOTHESIS0> [pulmonary disease];
        relating to other hypotheses...
...generating expectations given <HYPOTHESIS0>...
...I'm scoring hypothesis <HYPOTHESIS0> (<PULM-DZ0>)
..hypothesis explains: (<FINDING0>) [dyspnea]...
...failed predictions for hypothesis: —
...hypothesis doesn't explain: —
...trying to specialize the hypothesis of
    <HYPOTHESIS0> (<PULM-DZ0>)...
...specialized <HYPOTHESIS0> to <HYPOTHESIS1>
    (<RPE>) [recurrent pulmonary embolism]
...generating expectations given <HYPOTHESIS1>...
    ...
Is there a finding of <SYNCOPE>?
: Yes
    ...
Enter information (<return> if no more).
:
    ...
My diagnosis is: Recurrent pulmonary embolism.
```

Figure 5: Part of a consultation with MEDIC.

deductive reasoning. The only goal active is one to diagnose the patient; the schema to achieve this in dx-consult is "sc-consult". This is added to the reasoner's agenda.

The reasoner now selects a schema from its agenda, using the goal ordering provided by the current strategy; the use of specific information from the dxMOP is not currently implemented. The only schema to select is sc-consult, so the reasoner selects that and begins to apply it. The user is asked for some initial information about the patient, including a description of the patient (a white female who is overweight)[3] and the chief complaint (progressive dyspnea). The information is added to STM. Adding the chief complaint causes the reasoner to be interrupted, and it searches memory for a schema to interpret the finding. Schema "sc-dyspnea" is found and activated.

Since the strategy in use dictates that goals related to findings have precedence over goals for gathering information or forming a diagnosis, sc-dyspnea is selected and used. This schema is a specialized version of a general schema to interpret findings; instead of asking general questions, however, the schema can ask very specific things related to dyspnea (e.g., asking how many stairs the patient can climb as a measure of the severity). The last step of this schema is to explain the finding by postulating diseases that could cause it; using this step, the reasoner postulates hypotheses of pulmonary disease and cardiac disease. Adding these hypotheses to STM again interrupts the reasoner, which finds and adds to the agenda schemata to evaluate the hypotheses: "sc-pulmDz" and "sc-cardiacDz".

The strategy orders goals related to hypotheses before any others; hence, one of the two schemata just added is selected, in this case, sc-pulmDz. The reasoner uses this schema to score the hypothesis of pulmonary disease,[4] and then tries to specialize the hypothesis using information that is in STM. One possible specialization, based on the fact that the patient is overweight, is recurrent pulmonary embolism (RPE); this is hypothesized, resulting in a schema ("sc-RPE") being activated to evaluate it.

The reasoner then selects sc-RPE and begins to evaluate the hypothesis of pulmonary embolism. Eventually, it will have evaluated all the hypotheses it can and will have exhausted the information the use can give it. The main schema, sc-consult, will then suggest the step of forming a diagnosis, which will be attempted.[5] In this case, the best hypothesis is recurrent pulmonary embolism, and that will be proposed to the user.

The current implementation of MEDIC is incomplete in several ways. For example, MEDIC does not have a principled way of choosing from among several active schemata the one to follow at any particular point in diagnosis; i.e., there is currently no theory addressing the control of the reasoner's attention. In addition, there is currently neither the domain knowledge nor the variety and number of schemata present in memory to allow very sophisticated diagnoses to be made; gathering this knowledge from our domain expert is one of the next steps in this project.

Learning is currently not addressed, either. We cannot expect to give a diagnostic reasoner operating in a sophisticated domain all of the knowledge that it will need to solve all of the problems presented it [Kolodner and Kolodner, 1987]; instead, if the program's knowledge is to be made as operational as possible for the domain, the program will need to be able

---

[3]Input to MEDIC is in a version of Conceptual Dependency [Schank & Abelson, 1977]; there is currently no natural language interface.

[4]Using a scoring scheme very similar to that of INTERNIST-1 [Miller et al., 1982].

[5]Again, using a method similar to that of INTERNIST-1.

to adapt its own knowledge, both factual and procedural, to its problem-solving environment. Though learning is not a focus of our work, we have tried to formulate the schema-based reasoning approach (and design MEDIC) in such a way that learning could be added at a later time. We discuss this in the next section.

6 Relationship to Case-based Reasoning

Though we do not explicitly address learning in our work, this research was begun with the idea that the style of reasoning which would evolve from it would be amenable to learning from past problem-solving experience. In this section, we discuss one approach to this type of learning, called *case-based reasoning*.

Case-based reasoning [e.g., Kolodner, 1987; Kolodner et al., 1985; Simpson, 1985] involves reusing information from past problem-solving episodes to help solve a new problem. Case-based reasoning (CBR) basically provides reasoning short-cuts: problem-solving that went on in similar previous cases is retrieved and reused in a new problem. CBR has been successfully applied to several different planning tasks [Simpson, 1985; Sycara, 1987; Hammond, 1986], to advice-giving [Kolodner, 1986; Turner, 1987a, 1987b; Cullingford and Kolodner, 1986], and, in one instance (and in a somewhat limited way), to diagnosis [Kolodner, 1983; Kolodner and Kolodner, 1987].

In our approach, "cases" correspond to consultations that have been performed by the reasoner.[6] When a consultation is finished, the reasoner would represent the result as a case and store it in memory. It would be indexed from the dxMOP or dxMOPs that were used in the consultation it represents, since it is a specialization of those dxMOPs. For example, a consultation involving a young alcoholic man with lung cancer might be solved using information from a dxMOP representing consultations involving alcoholic patients and from a dxMOP representing consultations involving patients with lung cancer. The new case representing the consultation would then be indexed by both of these dxMOPs, using features that differentiate it from them.

A case has information about the patient involved in the consultation, findings that occurred, hypotheses that were considered, the diagnosis, and any feedback about the consultation that was obtained from the user. Most importantly, however, a case contains the actions that were performed to diagnose the patient in that consultation; these actions, as mentioned, comprise the *scenes* of the case.

There are four ways that case-based reasoning can be used in our approach:

1. the results of reasoning done in the past can be reused;

2. a case can suggest schemata to use in a similar situation;

3. a case can provide information to allow the creation of new schemata; and

4. the process of storing cases in memory can produce useful changes in the reasoner's general knowledge structures, including the specialization of existing schemata.

When a reasoner is faced with a new problem, it may be *reminded* [Schank, 1982; Kolodner, 1984] of a previous consultation—i.e., a case representing the previous consultation may be retrieved from memory using the features of the new problem. In this situation, the old case can be used as a source of reasoning short-cuts in the new problem; this is how case-based reasoners usually use cases.[7] For example, considerable reasoning effort may have been expended in the old consultation to interpret a particular finding; if the same finding occurs in the new problem, the reasoner can reuse the interpretation from the old consultation instead of repeating the reasoning that was done. One advantage of this was mentioned in [Kolodner & Kolodner, 1987]: an old case can be used as a source of hypotheses about a new problem.

Similarly, a previous case may suggest actions the reasoner can use to achieve goals in a new problem. In our approach, the scenes of a case generally represent instantiatiations of schemata; thus, the scenes of an old case can suggest schemata to use in a new problem. In addition, the reasoner may choose to instantiate a schema in a particular way, based on how it was instantiated in the old consultation.

The reasoner may choose to create new schemata from the scenes of a case, rather than using the schemata that were instantiated in the case. One reason for this to occur would be if the old case and the new problem are quite similar, but not identical,

---

[6]The cases we mentioned earlier in the paper are given to the program by a human. However, they can be used in the same way as the cases described in this section.

[7]We have not addressed in any detail how these short-cuts are transferred to the new problem. However, a reasonable approach, given the nature of schema-based reasoning, would be to give the reasoner schemata which it can use to perform case-based reasoning.

with respect to features related to a schema that was used in the prior case to achieve some goal. For example, suppose a scene of the old case was concerned with interpreting dyspnea, and the patient was in a wheelchair. In this scene, the usual dyspnea schema would have been modified to take into account that the patient could not walk: i.e., questions such as "How far can the patient walk on level ground?", that would normally be asked, may have been changed to questions that are more useful for that patient. If the new problem involves a patient who walks with crutches, then it is likely that the goal of interpreting dyspnea can be achieved in the new problem using a slight generalization of the actions performed in the old scene. One method of performing this type of generalization is *abstractional analogy*, described in [Shinn & Kolodner, 1988]; alternatively, some sort of explanation-based learning [DeJong, 1983; DeJong & Mooney, 1986] could be used. Once a new schema is formed, it would be indexed from the schema it is a specialization of. It could then be used to solve similar problems in future.

An old case may have scenes that are not instantiations of schemata, but represent instead the end result of some sort of "from-scratch" problem-solving that was carried out in lieu of an appropriate schema to achieve a goal. When the reasoner recalls such a case and has a similar goal, it may choose to create a new schema by generalizing the actions that were performed in the previous scene. Abstractional analogy or explanation-based learning could be used here, too, and the new schema would be stored in memory for future use.

New generalized knowledge, including new schemata, would also be created during the process of storing cases in memory. It is a relatively short jump from the memory described in this paper to a full-fledged *dynamic memory* [Schank, 1982] of the kind implemented in CYRUS [Kolodner, 1984] and used in several case-based reasoning approaches [e.g., Hammond, 1986; Kolodner, 1983; Simpson, 1985; Sycara, 1987]. The differences are that in a dynamic memory: (1) new information can be added; and (2) as information is added, both the existing memory structures as well as the organization changes to facilitate future retrieval.

As mentioned, a new case would be indexed from those dxMOPs it represents a specialization of, using features that differentiate it from those dxMOPs. One of three things can happen for each index in each dxMOP. The index may not currently be used in that dxMOP; in this situation, the case will simply be stored using that index. The index might, however, already point to another dxMOP; in this situation, the new case will be indexed from the dxMOP residing at that index. Finally, there may already be a case at index: in this situation, a *collision* is said to have occurred. Following [Kolodner, 1984], the procedure in this situation would be first to create a new dxMOP by generalizing both cases, then to store the new dxMOP using the index. The two cases—the one that was stored at the index and the new one being added—are then indexed from the new dxMOP by their differences from *it*.[8] The new dxMOP represents a generalization of the two cases and a specialization of the parent dxMOP from which the old case was indexed.

The process of storing cases in memory effectively causes a reasoner to learn new specializations of existing diagnostic categories, based on consultations it has seen. As cases are being added to memory, causing new specialized dxMOPs to be created, we would like for the reasoner to learn specializations of its problem-solving knowledge, too. Each case, recall, represents a consultation the program has had with a user; as such, it contains scenes that represents the actions taken to achieve one goal or set of goals—i.e., instantiations of schemata for the situation faced in that consultation. It would make sense to store the scenes of a consultation in memory by indexing them beneath the schemata they are instantiations of. In this way, new schemata would be created in the same way dxMOPs are created during memory update. These new schemata would represent specializations of existing schemata which were created based on experience using those schemata to solve problems.

The results of creating new dxMOPs and schemata are twofold. First, by creating new dxMOPs, the reasoner learns about new categories of consultations. This allows it to know how to apply its schemata in different situations, since each dxMOP has useful schemata associated with it. By doing this, the reasoner would learn in which types of consultation specific schemata are useful: in other words, the reasoner would be learning the conditions under which its procedural knowledge is applicable. Second, new schemata are produced, allowing the reasoner to solve problems which are similar to the new schemata more quickly, better, or both. In effect, the reasoner is adapting its problem-solving knowledge to better

---

[8] In [Kolodner, 1984], similarity-based learning was used; for a medical domain such as this, however, SBL should probably be augmented with some sort of explanation-based techniques.

fit its domain: it is operationalizing its procedural knowledge.

In summary, then, case-based reasoning techniques would add much to a schema-based reasoner. Cases provide a way of finding schemata for goals present in new situations that are similar to previously-seen consultations. A case can also suggest new a schema, which can be formed by generalizing the instantiation of a schema or a sequence of actions used to achieve a goal in that case. Finally, storing cases in memory affects the schemata the reasoner has available to it: as a case is stored, new schemata and dxMOPs are formed. The new schemata can be used to solve new problems; information from the new dxMOPs can be used to decide when schemata are applicable.

7 Related Work

As we mentioned, our work is based on preliminary research along the same lines done on the SHRINK program some years ago [Kolodner, 1983; Kolodner & Kolodner, 1987]. In its most specific and mature form, the approach taken by that research was to perform diagnosis using information from an experientially-modified memory consisting of two kinds of structures: DIAGNOSTIC MOPs and PROCESS MOPs.

The DIAGNOSTIC MOPs in SHRINK are similar to our dxMOPs, in that they are memory structures that represent generalized information used during diagnosis. However, there are some major differences. Although DIAGNOSTIC MOPs are meant to be derived from experience, using a process similar to that outlined above for dxMOPs, they are not truly episodic structures: that is, they contain no references to actions. Instead, they represent disease categories, in much the same way as do MDX's [Gomez & Chandrasekaran, 1982] specialists; the difference is that DIAGNOSTIC MOPs are dynamic structures that are updated from experience, whereas specialists are static. In contrast, dxMOPs represent categories of *consultations* rather than of diseases; though a dxMOP may refer to diseases as hypotheses, it contains other information relating to the consultation as a whole. An example of this would be a dxMOP representing consultations involving alcoholic patients. Though not representing a disease, this dxMOP holds information which helps the reasoner to diagnose this type of patient. For example, anemia is generally a fairly important finding; however, the dxMOP for alcoholic patients would contain information which would allow the reasoner to ascribe the finding of anemia in such a patient to alcoholism rather than searching for some other cause. In addition, dxMOPs *do* refer to procedural knowledge: a dxMOP refers to a set of schemata that are useful for achieving goals that are likely to arise during consultations of the type described by the dxMOP.

PROCESS MOPs are similar in some ways to our schemata, though more closely related to scripts. As new cases use a PROCESS MOP, "compiled paths" [Kolodner, 1983] are added to it, analogous to the tracks in a script. Schemata, on the other hand, are more general than scripts, as we have mentioned. A schema allows *some* "compiled paths" to be represented as variations in the ordering of the steps due to its steps' "next" information. However, the degree of freedom here is limited by the constraint that the schema, no matter what path is taken, should satisfy a particular goal or set of goals; which path is taken depends on the environment. We allow specialized versions of schemata to exist to handle related or specialized goals, and these are organized in a manner that facilitates their retrieval in particular situations. PROCESS MOPs were meant to be specializable and to participate in memory organization [Kolodner, personal communication]; however, they were not a major focus of the research on SHRINK, and this aspect of their use was not fully implemented.

The manner in which the reasoner uses each kind of procedural information also differs. PROCESS MOPs are recalled and followed by the reasoner from start to finish; only one is active at once. Many schemata, each being used to satisfy a goal, can be active at once, and the reasoner need not completely apply any schema before switching to another. This allows a degree of flexibility that SHRINK does not have to respond to changes in the task during diagnosis.

Our approach also differs from work relying on a strict interpretation of the term "case-based reasoning:" that the reasoner uses information *only* from cases and not from any generalized structures. The MEDIATOR [Simpson, 1985] is an example of such a case-based reasoner. Though it has Generalized Episodes (GEs) present in its memory as a result of storing cases of problem-solving, it uses this information only for the organization and retrieval of cases. In contrast, the use of generalized knowledge structures is central to our approach: schemata and dxMOPs are used preferentially to cases, representing as they do compiled problem-solving information.

Our knowledge structures and memory organization superficially resemble those of MDX. However, our schemata are more general than MDX's specialists in being able to represent scripts and plans as well as rules. This allows MEDIC to represent procedural knowledge of how to perform diagnosis, in addition to domain knowledge, directly and declaratively.

8 Conclusion

The schema-based reasoning process outlined in this paper is one approach towards providing a diagnostic reasoner with information that is operational for its problem-solving environment. Schemata are retrieved by the reasoner and used to achieve goals present in diagnostic problems: interpret a finding, evaluate a hypothesis, etc. Schemata are stored in a memory that organizes them in two ways: by the situations for which they are appropriate, and along hierarchies defined by their features. The reasoner retrieves schemata by using goals in and feature of the current problem to traverse memory, then applies the schemata to achieve its goals.

Our approach was developed keeping in mind the eventual need for learning in a problem solver for real-world problems. If we were to allow cases of problem solving to be added to our memory in the manner described above, several benefits would accrue: (1) the reasoner's knowledge of consultations would increase; (2) it would learn about situations in which its procedural knowledge is applicable; and (3) its store of schemata would increase, with the overall effect that the program's procedural knowledge would adapt to the task environment as problem solving is done.

Our ideas are being tested in MEDIC, a schema-based diagnostic reasoner whose domain is pulmonology. There is no reason to believe, however, that diagnosis is the only domain in which schema-based reasoning is worthwhile. The basic idea is quite general, and should be applicable to other domains and other types of problem-solving tasks.

9 Acknowledgments

Many thanks to our domain expert, Eric Honig of Emory University and Grady Memorial Hospital, and to Janet Kolodner, Elise Turner, Joel Martin, Mike Redmond, and Phyllis Koton for their comments on drafts leading to this paper.

10 References

Aikins, J.S. (1980). *Prototypes and Production Rules: A Knowledge Representation for Computer Consultations.* Doctoral dissertation, Stanford University.

Ashley, K. (1986). Knowing what to ask next and why: Asking pertinent questions using cases and hypotheticals. In *Proceedings of the Eighth Annual Conference of the Cognitive Science Society.*

Bartlett, F.C. (1932). *Remebering, a Study in Experimental and Social Psychology*, Cambridge University Press, Cambridge. Quoted in E. Rich, *Artificial Intelligence*, New York: McGraw–Hill Book Company, 1983.

Cullingford, R.E. (1981). SAM. In *Inside Computer Understanding*, R.C. Schank and C.K. Riesbeck (Eds.), Hillsdale, NJ: Lawrence Erlbaum Associates.

Cullingford, R.E., and Kolodner, J.L. (1986). Interactive advice giving. In *Proceedings of the 1986 IEEE International Conference on Systems, Man, and Cybernetics.*

DeJong, G. (1983) Acquiring schemata through understanding and generalizing plans. In *Proceedings of the Eighth International Joint Conference on Artificial Intelligence.*

DeJong, G.F., and Mooney, R.J. (1986). Explanation-based learning: An alternative view, *Machine Learning* 1:2, (April, 1986).

Feltovich, P.J., Johnson, P.E., Moller, J.A., and Swanson, D.B. (1984). LCS: The role and development of medical knowledge in diagnostic expertise. In W.J. Clancey and E.H. Shortliffe (Eds.), *Readings in Medical Artificial Intelligence*, Reading, Massachusetts: Addison-Wesley Publishing Company, pp.l 275–319.

Gomez, F., and Chandrasekaran, B. (1982). Knowledge organization and distribution for medical diagnosis. In W.J. Clancey and E.H. Shortliffe (Eds.), *Readings in Medical Artificial Intelligence*, pp. 320–338. Reading, Massachusetts: Addison-Wesley Publishing Company, 1984. (Originally published in *IEEE Transactions on Systems, Man, and Cybernetics*, Vol. SMC-11, No. 1, pp. 34–42 (1981).)

Hammond, K.J. (1986c). Case-based planning: An integrated theory of planning, learning, and memory. (PhD dissertation) Yale University Department of Computer Science technical report YALE/CSD/ RR#448.

Kolodner, J.L. (1982). The role of experience in development of expertise. In *Proceedings of the National Conference on Artificial Intelligence*, Pittsburgh, PA, pp. 273–277.

Kolodner, J.L. (1983). Towards an understanding of the role of experience in the evolution from novice to expert, *International Journal of Man–Machine Studies*, vol. 19, pp. 497–518.

Kolodner, J.L. (1984). *Retrieval and Organizational Strategies in Conceptual Memory: A Computer Model*, Lawrence Erlbaum Associates, Publishers, Hillsdale, New Jersey.

Kolodner, J.L. (1985). Experiential processes in natural problem solving. Technical Report #GIT-ICS-85/123, School of Information and Computer Science, Georgia Institute of Technology, Atlanta, Georgia.

Kolodner, J.L. (1987). Capitalizing on failure through case-based inference. In *Proceedings of the Ninth Annual Conference of the Cognitive Science Society*, pp. 715–726.

Kolodner, J.L., and Kolodner, R.M. (1987). Using experience in clinical problem solving: Introduction and framework. In *Proceedings of the 1987 IEEE International Conference on Systems, Man, and Cybernetics*.

Kolodner, J.L., Simpson, R.L., and Sycara, K. (1985). A process model of case-based reasoning in problem solving. In *Proceedings of IJCAI-85*.

Lesgold, A.M., Feltovich, P.J., Glaser, R., and Wang, Y. (1981). The acquisition of perceptual diagnostic skill in radiology. Technical report No. PDS-1, University of Pittsburgh Learning Research and Development Center.

McDermott, D. (1978). Planning and acting, *Cognitive Science*, vol. 2, pp. 71–109.

Schank, R.C. (1982). *Dynamic Memory*, Cambridge University Press, New York.

Miller, R.A., Pople, H.E., Jr., and Myers, J.D. (1982). INTERNIST-1, an experimental computer-based diagnostic consultant for general internal medicine, *New England Journal of Medicine*, vol. 307, pp. 468–476.

Schank, R.C., and Abelson, R. (1977). *Scripts, Plans, Goals and Understanding*, Lawrence Erlbaum Associates, Hillsdale, NJ.

Shinn, H., and Kolodner, J.L. (1988). Abstractional analogy: A general paradigm of analogical transfer, submitted to the Seventh National Conference on Artificial Intelligence.

Simpson, R.L Jr. (1985). *A Computer Model of Case-Based Reasoning in Problem Solving: An Investigation in the Domain of Dispute Mediation*. Doctoral dissertation, Technical Report #GIT-ICS-85/23, School of Information and Computer Science, Georgia Institute of Technology, Atlanta, GA 30332.

Sycara K., (1987). "Adversarial Reasoning in Conflict Resolution", Ph.D. dissertation, Georgia Institute of Technology, Atlanta, Georgia, 30332.

Turner, R.M. (1987a). *Issues in the Design of Advisory Systems: the Consumer-Advisor System*, Technical Report #GIT-ICS-87/19, School of Information and Computer Science, Georgia Institute of Technology, Atlanta, GA 30332.

Turner, R.M. (1987b). Modifying previously-used plans to fit new situations. *Proceedings of the Ninth Annual Conference of the Cognitive Science Society*, Seattle, Washington.

The Use of Domain Semantics
for Retrieval and Explanation in
Case-Based Reasoning

Rajendra S. Wall
Dan Donahue
Stan Hill
Texas Instruments Inc.
P. O. Box 655474 M/S 238
Dallas, TX 75265
wall@csc.ti.com
Topic: Cognitive Modeling
Length: 3989 Words

ABSTRACT

Reasoning from previous experience, or case-based reasoning, has been used in numerous domains. Various techniques have been used to retrieve appropriate cases for use at appropriate times. Two important techniques have been the use of *dimensions* to index the cases and a *goal-directed* retrieval process. Our approach is to use a semantic representation structure that embodies the notion of dimensions while providing for goal-directed retrieval. Previous work has also shown that one of the key needs in making effective use of previous experience is how the cases are presented to the user. The semantic representation approach aids the explanation process. Our domain is that of tactical planning in a military command and control environment where case-based reasoning has previously been shown helpful.

The Use of Domain Semantics for Retrieval and Explanation in Case-Based Reasoning

ABSTRACT

Reasoning from previous experience, or case-based reasoning, has been used in numerous domains. Various techniques have been used to retrieve appropriate cases for use at appropriate times. Two important techniques have been the use of *dimensions* to index the cases and a *goal-directed* retrieval process. Our approach is to use a semantic representation structure that embodies the notion of dimensions while providing for goal-directed retrieval. Previous work has also shown that one of the key needs in making effective use of previous experience is how the cases are presented to the user. The semantic representation approach aids the explanation process. Our domain is that of tactical planning in a military command and control environment where case-based reasoning has previously been shown helpful.

1 INTRODUCTION

Reasoning from previous experience, or case-based reasoning has been of interest to numerous researchers (e.g., [Carbonell83], [Kolodner85], [Rissland86], [Ashley87], [Hammond86b]). Case-based reasoning has been used in planning domains [Wall83]. Three questions in the use of case-based reasoning for planning domains are: (1) how should the case library be organized, (2) how should retrieval be performed so that all arguably relevant cases are retrieved, and (3) how should the cases be presented so that a correct decision can be made?

1.1 Related Work

An important development to answer these questions has been the notion of *dimensions* [Rissland84], [Rissland86]. Dimensions are indicies used to identify cases and aid in the analysis and exposition of arguments. Each dimension has prerequisites that provide an initial filter to cases, and focal slots that identify what can be changed in a case to make the case stronger or weaker along that dimension [Ashley86]. Dimensions provide a lattice of relevance that allows similarity between cases to be determined yet emphasizes the key differences between the cases [Ashley87].

In answer to question (2), using the goals of the planner to guide retrieval has been shown to be effective in planning domains [Hammond86b]. Goal-directed retrieval focuses on those cases most relevant to the success or failure of the plan [Hammond86c]. This is especially important in the domain of military tactical planning. In this domain the cases are plans that either succeeded or failed in previous similar situations [Wall82].

Question (3) has been addressed by the idea of explaining and arguing through a series of cases in order to make the purpose of presenting the cases understood [Rissland83], [Rissland84]. The use of dimensions provides a mechanism for examining the strengths and weaknesses of an argument [Ashley87].

1.2 Our Approach

Our approach is to use a representation of domain semantics to capture the notion of dimensions, provide for goal directed retrieval, and support the explanation and argumentation of cases. We use NIKL [Kaczmarek86], a member of the family of KL-ONE languages [Brachman78] to express the semantics of the domain, and the NIKL classifier [Schmolze83] to perform retrieval.

Dimensions are expressed using *roles*. Roles are used in NIKL to define a relationship between concepts [Robins86]. Using NIKL roles as dimensions, a given dimension is specified by the concepts that it is connected to. The definition of the dimension is a function of how deep in the taxonomy one goes. While the overall nature of the dimension doesn't change (it will still be attached to the same types of concepts), its applicability to a given situation will. Use of NIKL provides a semantic "ordinal scale" for the dimension.

Retrieval of cases uses the NIKL classifier. Cases are attached to concepts in the taxonomy which represent previous situations. The current situation is described using the same taxonomic concepts. Roles are specified to the extent that information is certain. The classifier finds the most accurate match (as defined by *subsumption* see [Schmolze83]) between the current situation concept and the previous situation concepts. The cases attached to concepts that are semantically similar to the current situation concept are then retrieved. Including a semantic description of the goal in the situation concept being classified implicitly provides goal-directed retrieval.

Our studies have shown that in the military decisionmaking environment, explanation — arguing for or against a particular tactic and the examples used to illustrate the argument — is crucial in selecting a plan [Wall87]. Using NIKL allows the explanation process to describe the relevance of the cases in terms of the semantic representation of the domain. In particular, explanation can show the relationship between aspects of the current situation and those of the remembered experience in terms of the connections those facets have in the NIKL taxonomy.

2 CURRENT WORK

Our current work centers around command decisionmaking in a simulation of modern military command and control. Our domain model is represented in NIKL. Previous experiences, or cases, are attached at conceptual levels and reflect the attached roles. Retrieval is performed by a multistep use of the NIKL classifier to select a range of relevant experiences. Explanation is done by mapping key roles of the experience to the roles in the current situation.

2.1 The Tactical Decisionmaking Domain

"... tactical decisionmaking is a skill which falls in the category of an art, not a science. ... The 'best' solution is the one which works and it is developed on the basis of the application of sound tactical principles; experience gained over years of trial and error in countless situations; knowledge of soldiers, units and commanders; and, often, 'gut-feel.'"
— Col. D. R. Collins[Collins86]

The command and control process[1] requires a commander to formulate a course of action (or, tactical plan) for the friendly forces to perform in order to accomplish their goal given their current situation. Often there is uncertainty about the exact details of the situation. Furthermore, there is an opponent whose goals conflict with the commander's. The complexity of this domain precludes standard search techniques. The exact details and mechanics of command decisionmaking have been investigated by computer scientists and military researchers [Collins86], [Seymour82], [Farrell86], [Andriole86], [Fineberg84]. Case-based reasoning has been used as an aid to decision-making in tactical conflict domains; it is embedded in our model of command and control planning, called *scenario generation* [Wall83].

The Scenario Generation Model

The scenario generation model breaks the command decisionmaking process into two major parts. The first is building a *scenario* [Wall82], a collection of examples of possible future events, and the second is using the information from the scenario to select a course of action to pursue.

Each example in a scenario depicts a course of events that might happen if: a given course of action was selected; the opponent followed an assumed response; and

---
[1] The examples presented in this paper are in no way meant to reflect the tactics or doctrine of any real military organization.

the random processes acted in assumed ways. A different example might show a different course of action or the same course of action but with a different opponent response.

The future is thus divided up into classes or categories. From each class one or more experiences are chosen from a case library to illustrate the characteristic events that could occur in that class of worlds. A better choice of course of action can be made based on the knowledge gained from seeing the spectrum of example futures.

The steps of scenario generation are:

1. The situation analysis routine generates a description of the current engagement and identifies key situational factors. Part of the situation description is the goal of the unit, either given by a higher level unit or derived from the situation and the previous goal.

2. Examples of potential futures, given various choices of course of action, are retrieved from the case library of tactical experiences.

3. The examples are used to explain the advantages or disadvantages of a given course of action. This explanation may involve the modification of an example to illustrate a hypothetical future development. The goal of the explanation process is to present the "full range" of potential futures.

4. The commander then selects a course of action based on such issues as surprise or indirection.

5. The unit carries out the plan to the best of its abilities.

6. When the engagement is over, the actual course of events is analyzed by the historian process to determine what went right; what went wrong; whether the experiences, their modifications and explanations, were appropriate; and whether the commander made the correct (or at least a legitimate) choice. This analysis could then lead to the addition to or modification of the experiences in the case base or the alteration of the organization of the case base.

Conceptually, step 3 is similar to [Rissland86], in that we attempt to "stretch" the cases retrieved. Although we have populated our case base with historical and simulation-based entries it will have sparse areas. We use our domain model to suggest "what if" situations, good or bad [Rissland84]. Step 6 is similar to [Hammond86a]. The historian must record the successes and failures and relate

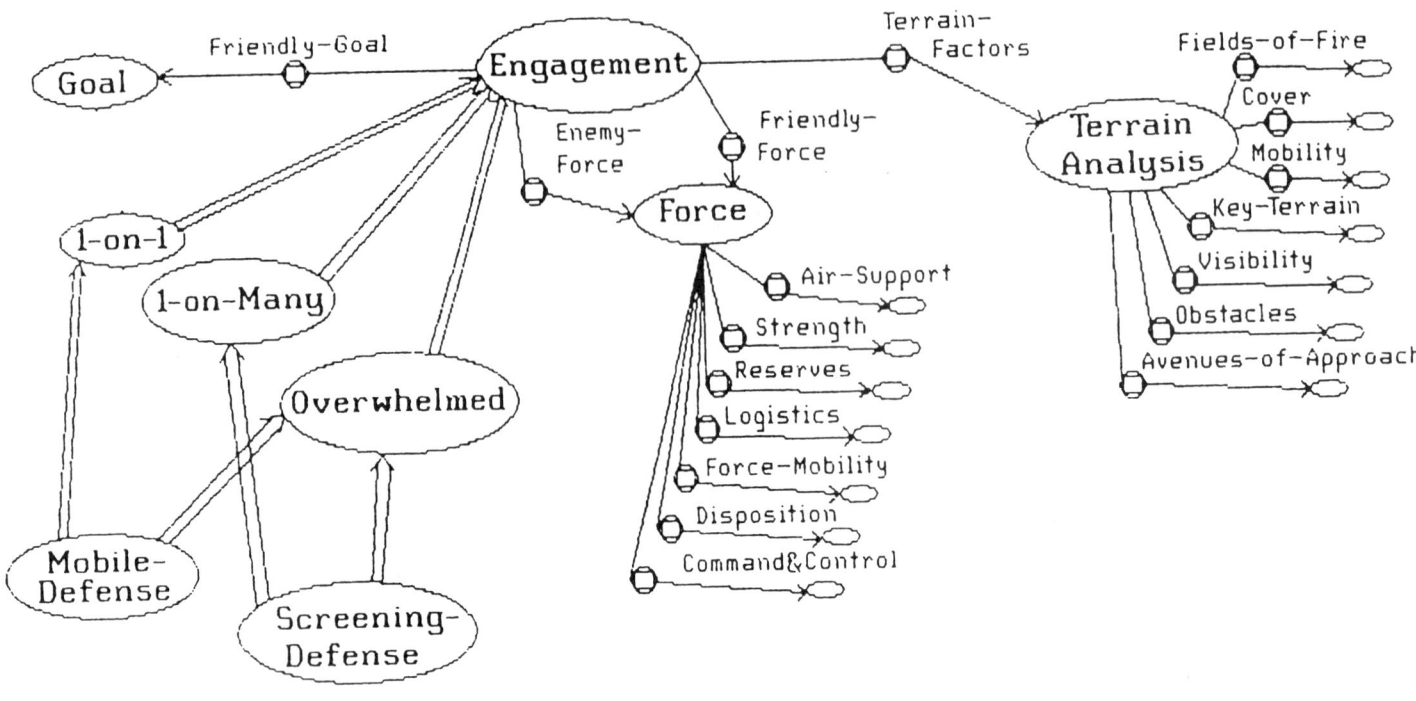

Figure 1: Top Level of the Case Taxonomy

them back to situational features for later retrieval. We have not yet formed separate case libraries for success and failure [Hammond86c].

2.2 The Case Library

An *engagement* represents a situation analysis — a case. It conceptually summarizes the details and points to potential tactical responses. Cases are attached as data to engagement concepts in the NIKL taxonomy. Figure 1 shows the top level of the taxonomy. Deeper into the taxonomy, roles are specified in greater detail, defining the type of engagement they are attached to.

Each Case in the Library

In the command and control domain each case contains:

- The conditions at the start of the experience were—what was the situation analysis;

- The sequence of events actually took place—the sequence of activities performed by all units and the results of those activities,

- The planner's intentions—the goals of the system;

- The intended actions—the course of action selected by the planner as well as anticipated responses from the opponent;

- The dispositions of the opponent forces—what were the perceptions of opponent's goals;

- The assumptions about other domain unknowns or random processes (e.g., weather)—would they aid or prevent completion of the goals;

- The post-engagement analysis—how things actually turned out with respect to the desired goals; what turned out to be the key situation or tactical feature or features that led to success or failure.

2.3 Retrieval of Experiences

As seen in figure 1, each engagement has the following roles: FRIENDLY-FORCE-FACTORS, ENEMY-FORCE-FACTORS, FRIENDLY-GOAL, and TERRAIN-FACTORS, restricted to FRIENDLY-FORCE-FACTOR-CONCEPT, ENEMY-FORCE-FACTOR-CONCEPT, FRIENDLY-GOAL-CONCEPT, and TERRAIN-ANALYSIS respectively. These roles are *situational factors* — the dimensions of the case. Each of the dimensional concepts has a classification taxonomy.

Retrieval proceeds as follows:

1. A NIKL concept is built for each situational factor. The information available determines the level of detail. This includes information about the terrain on which the engagement takes place, the friendly goal and the friendly and enemy forces that will be engaged. A role may be specified as unknown.

2. Each situational concept is classified separately: the terrain analysis, the friendly forces, and the enemy forces.

3. Due to the nature of NIKL, each of these classifications may identify more than one possible matching situational concept. In addition, "nearby" concepts can be identified by their network proximity. These nearby concepts are used to generate hypothetical, "what-if" alternative classifications.

4. A series of current engagement concepts are created, one for each combination of situational concepts.

5. Each current engagement concept is classified.

6. This classification may indicate more than one possible match with previous engagement concepts in the taxonomy.

7. The cases attached to each matched engagement concept are extracted and made available for presentation.

An Example

Figure 2 shows an example situation from the testbed. Seven Red T-80 tank platoons are advancing en echelon with heavily protected flanks (hexes 1409, 1509, 1608, and 1708), with the headquarters (HQ) unit in the rear. A Blue M-1 tank platoon has just established contact with the left flank of the advancing Red force. Four Blue M-1 tank platoons (including the company headquarters) are located almost due south of the engagement, to the Red far left (hex 1213).

The key situational factors are: both forces have *MODERATE* to *HIGH* MOBILITY due to the presence of roads. Command and control facilities are *GOOD* for Blue because company HQ is present. Command and control is *BELOW-AVERAGE* for Red both because of the strict command hierarchy of Red forces and because the Red HQ is out of visual range of the units that have established contact with Blue. (The woods in hex 1509 block the Red HQ's view of hex 1409.)

The intermediate retrieval steps resulted in classifying FRIENDLY-FORCE-FACTORS as either *MOBILE-FORCE*, *MODERATE-FORCE*, or *HIGHLY-MOBILE-FORCE*; ENEMY-FORCE-FACTORS as either *MODERATE-OFFENSIVE-FORCE* or *LARGE OFFENSIVE-FORCE*; FRIENDLY-GOAL as *DEFEND* (specified by orders from higher command) and TERRAIN-FACTORS as *MOBILE-TERRAIN*.

Constructing complete situation concepts for each combination of these situational factors led to the retrieval of cases attached to the previous engagement concepts: MOBILE-DEFENSE, SCREENING-DEFENSE, MOBILE-OR-SCREENING-DEFENSE, COUNTER-ATACK, and ASSUME-OFFENSIVE.

Figure 3 shows some of the cases retrieved from the concept MOBILE-DEFENSE.

Domain Semantics vs. Explicit Links

The use of NIKL to describe the domain with explicit specification of the roles and relationships is an attempt to create a retrieval mechanism that does not de-

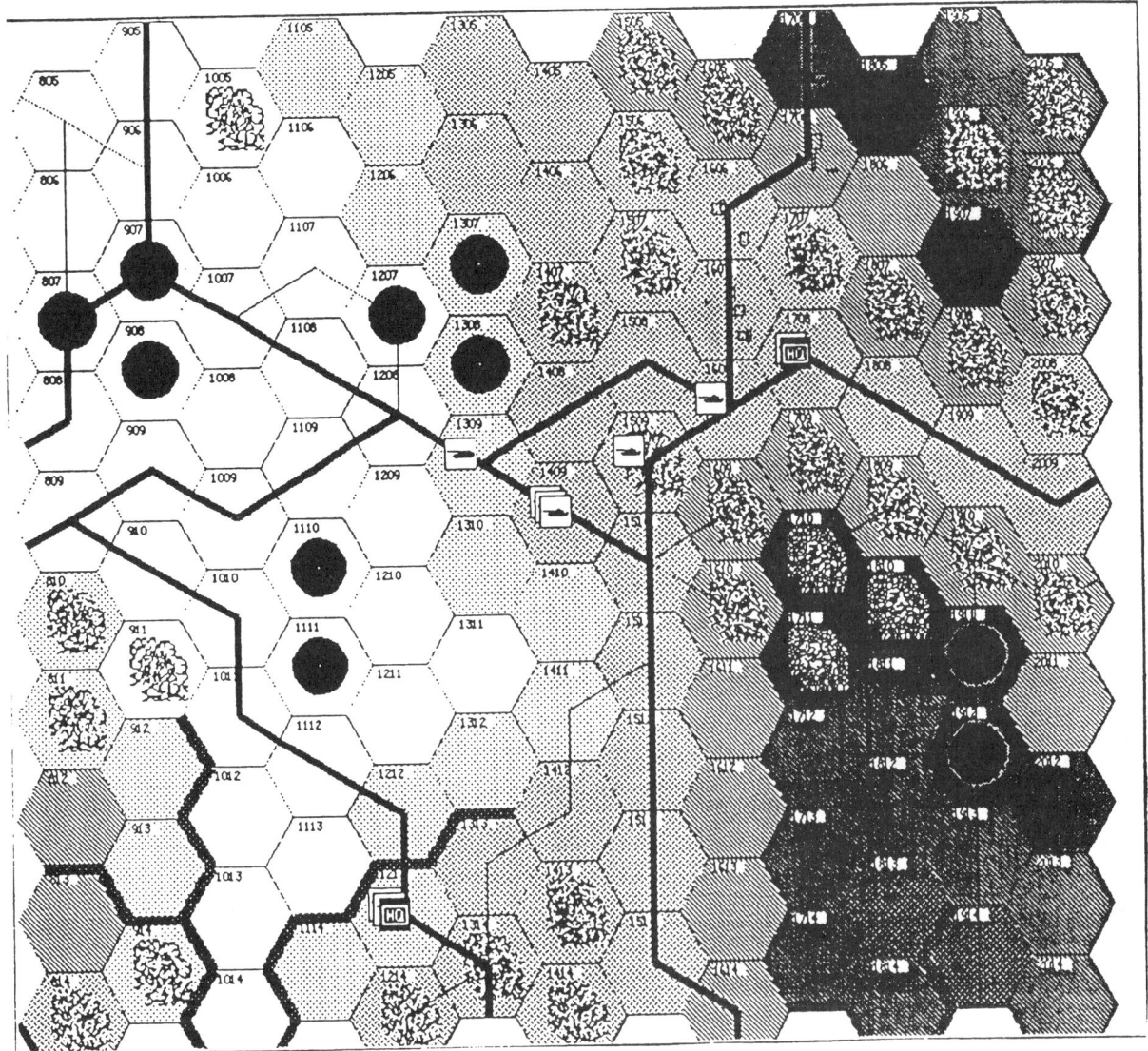

Figure 2: An example situation

pend on specific links or indicies. Previously, situational features were connected to experiences via token matching or explicit links of one sort or another.

Using the NIKL Classifier brings independence to the matching process. The concepts in the domain must be explicitly specified, and the relationships between domain concepts must also be explicitly specified. This forces the case base knowledge engineer to have taxonomic justification of retrieval matches. While there is still the process of adjusting the structure of the case library until the correct experiences are retrieved at the correct time, this adjustment must be made in the context of the overall domain model expressed by the NIKL network.

To some extent, instead of matching a list of tokens, retrieval now demands matching a graph structure. However, the graph structure represents the underlying semantics of the token match [Brachman79]. Thus a match using the NIKL classifier implies a semantic similarity.

2.4 Explaining Tactical Relevance

All relevant cases are retrieved before explanation begins. A separate explanation is made for each tactic that has been found relevant in the case library. This is done by dividing the cases into those supporting the tactic, which are given to an advocate process, and those opposing it, which are given to a critic process. Explanation of why the system retrieved the case is done by the use of key factors. First the advocate, and then the critic show cases to the user.

2.4.1 Use of Key Factors

A *key factor* is a NIKL role attached to a dimensional concept that has been identified by the historian as having played an important part in the outcome of the engagement. Associated with each key factor is a short description of why it was important. Key factors are similar to focal slots [Ashley86]. According to Ashley's notion of dimensions as a "mechanism to judge the strength of a line of reasoning"[Ashley87], in the command and control domain we treat dimensions as a means to explain the rationale for or against a particular tactic.

During explanation, these key factors are highlighted. Each correspondence between a situational factor and key case factor implies a stronger rationale that the case should be heeded.

Key factors are based in the semantics of the descriptions of the situation and the experience. They allow the user to focus on the most important parts of the case being shown.

2.4.2 Example

From the situation of figure 2, some additional cases were retrieved as relevant. Figure 4 shows three additional cases related to a hypothetical "stretch" of the situation to that of a SCREENING-DEFENSE engagement. The cases PETERSBURG and SUCCESSFUL-DEFENSE-IN-DEPTH are presented by the tactic advocate. The case UNSUCCESSFUL-DEFENSE-IN-DEPTH is presented by the tactic critic.

The key factors of the current situation are MOBILITY and COMMAND-AND-CONTROL. Most of the arguments relating to SCREENING-DEFENSE had COVER as a key factor, and COVER is not a key factor of the situation. The SCREENING-DEFENSE cases have COMMAND-AND-CONTROL as a key factor which is a key factor

---

CASE

This is a case representative of a(n) MOBILE-DEFENSE engagement.
Case ID: MEETING-ENGAGEMENT
The details of the case were: Red units of unknown strength are exploiting a breach in the front. The Blue has one armored battalion of M-1's with two infantry companies mounted on M-2's with which to delay, and if possible seal off and eliminate the penetration.
The friendly course of action was: MOBILE DEFENSE
And the results were: Heavy attrition on both sides. Initial Red overextension presented an effective counterattack opportunity for Blue, which was successfully exploited by splitting the Blue forces into wings.
Key Factors:
MOBILITY: Mobile Blue units reconnoitered enemy force quickly.
DEPLOYMENT: Splitting forces opportunistically.

CASE

This is a case representative of a(n) MOBILE-DEFENSE engagement.
Case ID: CANNAE
The details of the case were: The Cartheginians, and their allies faced the Romans on the plains of Cannae. Outnumbered, the Spaniards and Gauls formed a convex line facing the Romans with the Cartheginian and African infantry. Cavalry formed wings on both flanks. The Romans assaulted the weak center forces using infantry in the center and cavalry on both flanks.
The friendly course of action was: MOBILE DEFENSE, DOUBLE ENVELOPMENT
And the results were: The convex line gave way, drawing the Romans into a trap as the strong Cartheginian wings repulsed the Roman cavalry and surrounded the infantry on both sides and rear. The Romans were completely annihilated.
Key Factors:
MOBILITY: Using the mobile cavalry wings for envelopment.
DEPLOYMENT: Placing weak troops in main line, designed to fall back.

CASE

This is a case representative of a(n) MOBILE-DEFENSE engagement.
Case ID: BLUE-VS-RED-CASE-1
The details of the case were: A Blue battalion of mechanized infantry (3 companies of mounted infantry, an anti-tank platoon, a scout platoon, and a mortar platoon), was defending a broad, deep front (5 km by 3 km) against an advancing Red Force consisting of a motorized rifle battalion and recon elements of the 91st regiment. The Blue force is to deny passage to the Red force.
The friendly course of action was: FORWARD DEFENSE: COVERING FORCE, DEFENSE IN SECTOR, COUNTERATTACK
And the results were: Initial Red forces penetrated deep into the sector. Heavy attrition ratios, due to DEFENSE IN SECTOR, slowed the Red advance sufficiently to prevent further penetration.
Key Factors:
COMMAND-AND-CONTROL: Blue had high Command and Control abilities that enabled coordination.
MOBILITY: Blue had high mobility.

Figure 3: Some retrieved cases for the concept MOBILE-DEFENSE

> ### CASE
> This is a case representative of a(n) SCREENING-DEFENSE engagement.
> Case ID: UNSUCCESSFUL-DEFENSE-IN-DEPTH
> The details of the case were: A platoon of Blue M-1 tanks was facing 2 companies of Red tanks (T-80's and T-64's) approaching on a broad front (500 meters). The M-1's were in cover but restricted in movement by dense woods to the rear. Communication with company HQ was limited. The Blue forces were to delay, if not stop, the approaching Red force.
> The friendly course of action was: DEFENSE IN DEPTH
> And the results were: The Red approach was delayed for a short time, but company HQ could not be reached for support. A breach in the FLOT resulted.
> Key Factors:
> COVER: Blue made use of terrain for cover.
> COMMAND-AND-CONTROL: Poor communications responsible for breach.

> ### CASE
> This is a case representative of a(n) SCREENING-DEFENSE engagement.
> Case ID: PETERSBURG
> The details of the case were: Beauregard's small army at Petersburg was to defend the southern approaches to Richmond while Lee's Army of N.Virginia battled Grant's Army of the Potomac to the north. Grant secretly disengaged and unexpectedly approached Bearegard's force southeast of Petersburg. Grant outnumbered Beauregard by as much as 10 to 1. Beauregard was to keep Grant from capturing Petersburg until Lee's army arrived.
> The friendly course of action was: DEFENSE IN DEPTH
> And the results were: By defending in the trenches of the Dimmock Line, then retreating under the cover of darkness to Petersburg's defenses, Beauregard delayed Grant's advance long enough for Lee to arrive.
> Key Factors:
> COMMAND-AND-CONTROL: Bearegard had interior lines of communication to Lee.
> PLANNING: The Dimmock and Petersburg lines were built earlier.

> ### CASE
> This is a case representative of a(n) SCREENING-DEFENSE engagement.
> Case ID: SUCCESSFUL-DEFENSE-IN-DEPTH
> The details of the case were: A platoon of Blue M-1 tanks was facing a company of Red T-80 tanks approaching on a broad front (500 meters). The M-1's were in cover. The Blue forces were to delay, if not stop, the approaching Reds.
> The friendly course of action was: DEFENSE IN DEPTH
> And the results were: The Red approach was delayed long enough for friendly air forces to strike.
> Key Factors:
> COMMAND-AND-CONTROL: Blue able to call in a friendly airstrike.
> COVER: Blue made use of terrain for cover.

Figure 4: Some retrieved cases for SCREENING-DEFENSE.

of the situation. Most of the MOBILE-DEFENSE cases have MOBILITY as a key factor.

The case BLUE-VS-RED-CASE-1 has both COMMAND-AND-CONTROL and MOBILITY as key factors and thus gives the strongest argument for MOBILE-DEFENSE.

3 Conclusion

Use of a semantic representation of the domain to capture the notion of dimensions, provide for goal directed retrieval, and support the explanation and argumentation of cases is an effective way to support these crucial steps of case-based reasoning.

Dimensions can be represented in a NIKL taxonomy as roles. Dimensions are defined semantically by the role connections in the taxonomy, and the retrieval step of case-based reasoning relies on classifying NIKL concept structures rather than matching tokens or following links. Expressing goals in a similar semantic fashion implicitly provides for goal-directed retrieval.

The explanation of experiences is aided by using key factors from the experience. These factors are roles from the engagement concept that played an important part in the resolution of the experience. They are highlighted during explanation. They focus attention on similar aspects of the current situation. The degree of similarity influences the strength with which the experience should be considered an argument for selecting the course of action depicted.

Future Work

The use of previous experience, or case-based reasoning, to aid a human decision-maker in the selection of course of action has already been demonstrated. The current approach still keeps a "man in the loop", in that the final decision of which tactic to pursue is left to the user.

Future work is intended to examine this decisionmaking ability. A problem is the need to judge which is the "correct" argument that can be said to "win". Although with the described approach an estimation of the strength of an argument can be made, a commander able to use surprise and indirection might not choose the plan with the strongest case.

References

[Andriole86] Andriole, S. "The Design and Development of an Intelligent Planning Aid", Army Research Institute Note 86-101, July 1986.

[Ashley86]   Ashley, K, "Modelling Legal Argument: Reasoning with Cases and Hypotheticals: A Thesis Proposal", University of Massachusetts Computer and Information Science technical memo CPTM 10 (the Counselor Project), June, 1986.

[Ashley87]   Ashley, K., and Rissland, E., "Compare and Contrast, A Test of Expertise" in *Proceedings of the National Conference on Artificial Intelligence 1987 (AAAI-87)*, Seattle, Washington, pp 273–278.

[Brachman78]   Brachman, R., "A Structural Paradigm for Representing Knowledge", Bolt, Beranek, and Newman, Inc., Technical Report 3605, May 1978.

[Brachman79]   Brachman, R. "On the Epistemological Status of Semantic Networks." In *Associative Networks*, Edited by N. V. Findler. New York: Academic Press, 1979, pp. 3–50.

[Carbonell83]   Carbonell, J. "Learning by Analogy: Formulating and Generalizing Plans from Past Experiences", in *Machine Learning, An Artificial Intelligence Approach*, Michalski, Carbonell and Mitchell, editors, Tioga Publishing Company, Palo Alto, CA, 1983, pp 137–161.

[Collins86]   Collins, D. & Baucum, T., "Knowledge-Based Planning Model for Courses of Action Generation", Army War College Technical Report AD-A170608, April, 1986.

[Farrell86]   Farrell, R., et al, "Capturing Expertise: Some Approaches to Modeling Command Decisionmaking in Combat Analysis", *IEEE Transactions on Systems, Man, and Cybernetics (16,6)*, (1986), pp 766–773.

[Fineberg84]   Fineberg, M., *An Integrated Plan for Human Performance Enhancement in Command and Control Operations*, ARI Technical Report 84-135, (1984)

[Hammond86a]   Hammond, K., "Learning to Anticipate and Avoid Planning Problems through the Explanation of Failures" in *Proceedings of the National Conference on Artificial Intelligence 1986 (AAAI-86)*, Philadelphia, Pennsylvania, 1986, pp 556–560.

[Hammond86b]   Hammond, K., "CHEF: A Model of Case-based Planning" in *Proceedings of the National Conference on Artificial Intelligence 1986 (AAAI-86)*, Philidelphia, Pennsylvania, 1986, pp 267–271.

[Hammond86c] Hammond, K., "Case-Based Planning: An Integrated Theory of Planning, Learning and Memory", Yale University Computer Science technical report YALEU/CSD/RR #488, October 1986 (Ph.D. dissertation).

[Kaczmarek86] Kaczmarek, T., Bates, R., and Robins, G., "Recent Developments in NIKL", in *Proceedings of the National Conference on Artificial Intelligence 1986 (AAAI-86)*, Philadelphia, Pennsylvania, 1986, pp 978–985.

[Kolodner85] Kolodner, J., Simpson, R., Sycara-Cyranski, K., "A Process Model of Cased-Based Reasoning in Problem Solving", *Proceedings of the International Joint Conference on Artificial Intelligence*, (IJCAI-85), Los Angeles, California, (1985), pp 284–290.

[Rissland83] Rissland, E., "Examples in Leagal Reasoning: Legal Hypotheticals", *Proceedings of the Eighth International Joint Conference on Artificial Intelligence (IJCAI-83)* Karlsruhe, West Germany, August, 1983, pp 288–294.

[Rissland84] Rissland, E., Valcarce, E., and Ashley, K., "Explaining and Arguing with Examples", *Proceedings of the National Conference on Artificial Intelligence 1984 (AAAI-84)*, Austin, Texas, 1984, pp 288-294.

[Rissland86] Rissland, E. & Ashley, K., "Hypotheticals as Heuristic Device" *Proceedings of the National Conference on Artificial Intelligence 1986 (AAAI-86)*, Philidelphia, Pennsylvania, 1986, pp 289–297.

[Robins86] Robins, G. "The NIKL Manual", Information Sciences Institute technical report, 1986.

[Schmolze83] Schmolze, J., and Lipkis, T. "Classification in the KL-ONE Knowledge Representation System", *Proceedings of the Eighth International Joint Conference on Artificial Intelligence (IJCAI-83)* Karlsruhe, West Germany, August, 1983, pp 330–332.

[Seymour82] Seymour, W., *Yours to Reason Why—Decision in Battle*, St. Martin's Press, New York, 1982.

[Wall82] Wall, R. & Rissland, E., "Scenarios as an Aid to Planning", *Proceedings of the National Conference on Artificial Intelligence 1982 (AAAI-82)*, Pittsburg, Pennsylvania, 1982, pp 176–180.

[Wall83] Wall, R., *The Theory and Use of Scenarios*, Technical Report 82-31, Computer and Information Science Dept., University of Massachusetts at Amherst, 1982 (Ph. D. Dissertation).

[Wall87] Wall, R., "Case-Based Reasoning for Command and Control", *Proceedings of the DARPA Knowledge-Based Planning Workshop*, Austin, TX, December, 1987.

Learning to Program by Examining and Modifying Cases *

Robert S. Williams
Department of Computer and Information Science
University of Massachusetts
Amherst, MA 01003, USA
(413) 545-2440

March 31, 1988

Abstract

This paper describes a system called **TA**, which learns how to program by maintaining a case base of previously encountered programs and modifying those cases in attempts to solve new programming problems. TA uses three case bases: one for programs, one for patches to code, and one for bugs that have been encountered in previous programming sessions. As TA writes correct programs, they are added to the program case base. If bugs are encountered in the process of arriving at a correct program, these (and the patches that TA uses to fix the buggy code) are added to the appropriate case bases. Thus, as TA writes more programs, its skill at finding similar programs increases, as does its ability to find and fix bugs.

---

*This is an expanded version of a paper to appear in the proceedings of the Fifth International Conference on Machine Learning. This research was supported by the Office of Naval Research, under a University Research Initiative Grant, Contract #N00014-86-K-0764; by NSF Presidential Young Investigators Award NSFIST-8351863; and by DARPA contract N00014-87-K-0238.

1 Introduction

Writing programs seems a natural thing to want a computer to do, and indeed there have been many attempts at automatic synthesis of programs (e.g., [Balzer et al., 1978], [Barstow, 1979], [Manna and Waldinger, 1981]). Most of these attempts, however, have assumed a static corpus of programming knowledge — the programming systems have all their knowledge present at all times.[1]

In addition, these attempts have ignored two important aspects of the programming task as it is carried out by people:

- Most automatic programmers produce an artifact (the program) that is complete and correct. In contrast, most people produce a program that is incorrect, and then must modify it to yield a correct program. As people gain experience with programming, they tend not to make the same kinds of mistakes that they made early on.

- Even though the result of the programming process is a formal object, the process that people go through to arrive at that result is complex and not easily formalized.

We feel that these two aspects make the task of programming (as people do it) a good candidate for techniques in machine learning. First, the fact that people make mistakes, from which they can learn, indicates that programming is indeed an area where learning is a key component. Second, the fact that the process of programming is complex and not easily formalizable makes the task an interesting "real-world" problem. Finally, since the results of programming *are* easily formalizable, they lend themselves to evaluation of the performance of the system.

This paper will discuss a system called **TA**, which uses a *case-based* approach to learning programming ([Bradtke and Lehnert, 1988], [Rissland and Ashley, 1987], [Lehnert, 1987], [Hammond, 1986]); i.e., it learns how to program by maintaining a case base of previously encountered programs and modifying those cases in attempts to solve new programming problems. TA's memory organization allows it to reap the benefits of memories based on generalization hierarchies (e.g., [Kolodner, 1984] or [Lebowitz, 1986]), but without some of the costs: since generalizations are not stored explicitly, case base size and case retrieval time are kept small.

In the following sections, we will describe the general approach taken by TA, give some details about its architecture, describe how cases are indexed in TA, show an example of TA at work, and discuss planned extensions to TA.

2 The General Approach

We are interested in understanding how knowledge about programming is acquired by novice programmers. We would like to start out with a system having very little knowledge

---

[1]There are exceptions — for instance, [Anderson, 1986] describes how his ACT system can be applied to learning how to program.

about programming, and have that system learn programming concepts through experience with writing programs. In particular, we would like to start our system out with the kind of knowledge contained in the first chapter of [Friedman, 1974], and have the system learn how to write the kinds of programs contained in the remainder of that text.

We assume that programming cannot be learned in a vacuum: a system that is able to learn how to write programs must be able to understand what the programs it writes are supposed to do. This may seem obvious, but what does it mean to "understand what a program is supposed to do?" We believe that this kind of understanding involves three skills:

- Given sample input, one should be able to predict the output that a correct version of the program would produce (without actually writing the program). We call this an **emulation** skill.

- When asked how this output was produced, one should be able to describe the steps taken to to produce the output (and similarly, when faced with a program that produces incorrect output, one should be able to point to incorrect parts of the program). This **explanatory** skill may be weak at first, but should improve as experience in writing programs increases.

- Given a specification for a program, one should be able to find specifications for other programs that are similar. This can be thought of as an **analogical** skill. This skill should also improve as experience with writing programs increases.

Thus, writing a program will involve the following steps:

1. Use the analogical skill to find a program with a similar specification.

2. Given sample input, use the emulation skill to compare the expected behavior of a correct program with the actual behavior produced by the similar program.

3. If the expected behavior does not match the actual behavior, use the explanatory skill to isolate fragments of the program that are not correct. Use the analogical skill to find correct code fragments.

Since TA is intended to be a computer model of a novice learning how to write programs, it is provided with the skills described above. Section 3 describes how this is done.

3 The System Architecture

TA represents knowledge about programming as networks of communicating entities, similar in spirit to Actors [Hewitt, 1977] or agents/agencies [Minsky, 1986]. Each individual entity, or node, represents some small piece of knowledge related to the programming endeavor. Each node can communicate with one or more other nodes in a network by passing messages. A computation is carried out by propagating messages through a network. The connectivity of the nodes determines which nodes receive which messages, and the manner in which a computation proceeds depends on how the nodes are connected to one another. Learning can ultimately be accomplished through a variety of means, including adding new nodes, changing connections between nodes, and modifying a node's preference for messages of a specific type. At present, learning in TA is accomplished only by adding new nodes.

There are two types of networks that occur in TA: **emulation** networks and **case** networks. These will each be described in turn.

3.1 Emulation networks

Emulation networks provide TA with a means of relating knowledge about programming with other kinds of knowledge, giving the system an emulation skill (as described in section 2). In particular, TA translates specifications for programs into an internal form which represents the system's understanding of what the specification is supposed to denote. This internal form is then used to create an emulation network which, when activated, will emulate a run of the specified program.

Let us look at an example. Consider a program that checks to see whether its input argument is a list of atoms. The specification as presented to TA is as follows: (∀ ?X ?L (ATOMIC ?X)).[2]

TA creates an internal representation for the above specification that is intended to reflect an understanding of that specification that is independent of any knowledge about programming per se.[3] In particular, TA understands the problem as a search problem, where the search space is a CONS named ?L, the search to be carried out is a specific type of search (a list search), the search can only terminate after each item has been examined, the test to be carried out for each item is a test for atomicity, etc. The complete internal representation of the specification is shown below.

```
(SEARCH  (SEARCH-SPACE-TYPE CONS)
         (SEARCH-SPACE ?L)
         (SEARCH-TYPE LIST-SEARCH)
         (SEARCH-ELEMENT ?X)
         (STOP-AFTER ALL-SEARCHED)
         (ON-TERMINATION SUCCEED)
         (TEST
            (TESTER (TEST (ISA ?X ATOM))
                    (ON-SUCCESS SUCCEED)
                    (ON-FAIL FAIL)))
```

---

[2] A literal reading of this specification might be: "For all x in the input argument l, x is an atom."

[3] It is assumed, however, that TA understands, e.g., what a list is and what an atom is. In other words, it is assumed that TA starts with an understanding of the concepts described in chapter 1 of [Friedman, 1974].

```
(ON-SUCCESS CONTINUE)
(ON-FAIL FAIL))
```

The above is essentially a frame representation. The specification is represented as a "search" frame, with slots "search-space-type," "search-space," "search-type," etc. The value of the "test" slot is itself a frame of type "tester," with slots "test," "on-success," and "on-fail."

From this internal representation, a network is constructed that "proceduralizes" the specification.[4] This network, when run, will produce the same output that a correct program (i.e., a program consistent with the specification) would produce.

It bears repeating that neither the above internal specification nor the network it generates by itself constitutes a program; rather, they make up an understanding of what a program following the external specification should do. Given a sample call of the specified program, the emulation network will allow TA to determine whether the call will fail or succeed; but neither the network nor the internal specification that generated it offers much insight into what a LISP program that embodies the specification will look like.[5]

3.2 Case networks

Case networks afford TA a mechanism for remembering previously encountered programs, patches and bugs. Each case is assigned to its own node in a case network. For retrieval, a current problem situation is communicated to each of the potentially relevant cases. The cases then decide individually (in parallel) how well they match the problem situation. These estimates are then sent to a collection of arbitration nodes, which decide which case is the best match for the purposes of solving the current problem.

There will, in general, be about the same number of arbitration nodes as cases. The arbitrators are arranged as an upside-down binary tree, with the leaves of the tree connected to at most two cases, and each internal node connected to at most two arbitrators (see figure 1 for an illustration). Estimates are sent from cases to the leaf arbitrators; these nodes identify the locally-best matches and send their results to their parent arbitrators. This process continues until the root arbitrator can suggest a globally-best match.

For a case base with n cases, the above scheme results in $O(\log n)$ parallel time performance, assuming only one message about the current problem situation is sent to each case. If k messages are sent to each case, the result is $O(k \cdot \log n)$ parallel time performance. Additionally, storage into such a case base can be done dynamically, with each new case to be stored taking $O(\log n)$ time (parallel or serial). As mentioned above, such a scheme takes up $O(n)$ space — about two nodes for each case.

---

[4]The details of how this proceduralization takes place are beyond the scope of this paper. The translation of internal specification to emulation network is somewhat similar to, e.g., the translation of PLASMA script to actor behavior in [Hewitt, 1977].

[5]In fact, the network offers no direct insight at all, since TA is not capable of examining the networks it creates, only of activating them and watching what happens. In a sense, the network is an executable version of the internal specification.

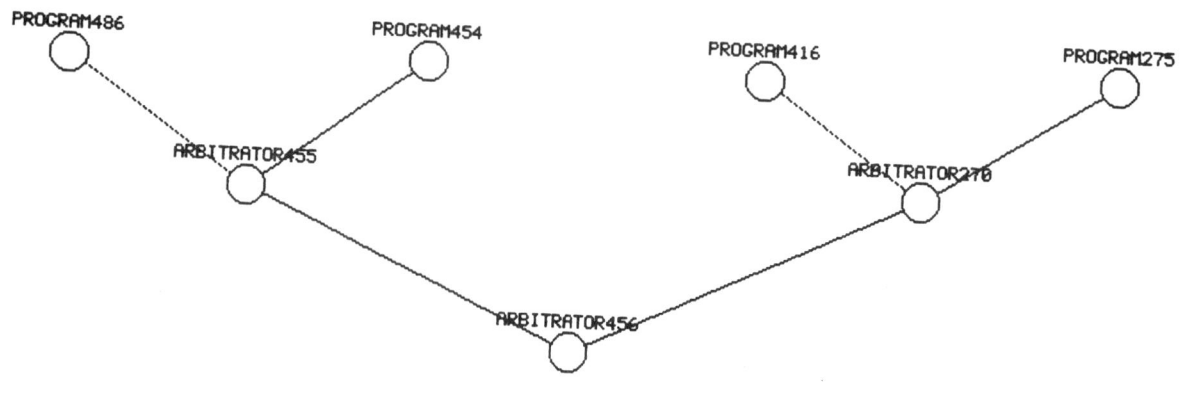

Figure 1: A case base for programs.

In the programming domain, the architecture described above is used to store knowledge about various aspects of programming. There are several case bases, each representing different types of knowledge:

- A **program** case base organizes programs that the system knows about (whether through "being told" or through actually writing them).

- A **patch** case base organizes patches that the system has discovered to turn buggy code fragments into working code fragments. Patches are stored as old code/new code pairs. The patch and program case bases give TA its analogical skill.

- A **debugging** case base organizes various bugs that the system has encountered in its attempts to write programs. A bug contains information about which parts of a buggy program were incorrect, e.g., "incorrect first question of COND clause." The debugging case base provides TA with its explanatory skill.

Each of these case bases is indexed by program specifications, though the details of how cases are indexed differ from case base to case base. In the program case base, cases are indexed by their actual specifications. Patches are indexed by differences in specification fragments; while bugs are indexed by generalized forms of differing specifications. [6]

For example, suppose the system has in its case base a program with the specification ($\forall$?X ?L (ATOMIC ?X)). Suppose further that it is presented with the following specification for which to write a program: ($\exists$?X ?L (ATOMIC ?X)). In the course of attempting to write a new program, the system discovers a bug brought about by trying to use the code for the first program as a solution to the new problem. It comes up with a patch to fix the

---

[6]In fact, the indices used are derived from the internal versions of the specifications, as will be explained in section 4. The external versions are used here for brevity.

bug, and it uses the patch in coming up with a new, bug-free program. The new program will be indexed by its original specification, (∃ ?X ?L (ATOMIC ?X)). The patch will be indexed by the differences between the old and new specifications:

old: (∀ . ?Z)
new: (∃ . ?Z)

The bug will be indexed by the generalization of the specifications: (?P ?X ?L (ATOMIC ?X)).

4 Indexing Cases in TA

In section 3.2, we treated cases as though they were indexed directly by external specifications; in fact, the indexing scheme is somewhat more involved.

Indices in TA are actually derived from the internal form of a specification. Each index is basically a "flattened" version of a corresponding line in the specification, including all surrounding slot names and frame types to provide context (though the order that symbols appear in the specification is reversed in the index). For example, in the specification shown in section 3.1, the line (ON-TERMINATION SUCCEED), in the "search" frame, would have the index (SUCCEED ON-TERMINATION SEARCH) derived from it. The entire set of indices for that specification is as follows:

(CONS SEARCH-SPACE-TYPE SEARCH),
(?L SEARCH-SPACE SEARCH),
(LIST-SEARCH SEARCH-TYPE SEARCH),
(?X SEARCH-ELEMENT SEARCH),
(ALL-SEARCHED STOP-AFTER SEARCH),
(SUCCEED ON-TERMINATION SEARCH),
(?X ISA TEST TESTER TEST SEARCH),
(ATOM ISA TEST TESTER TEST SEARCH),
(SUCCEED ON-SUCCESS TESTER TEST SEARCH),
(FAIL ON-FAIL TESTER TEST SEARCH),
(CONTINUE ON-SUCCESS SEARCH),
(FAIL ON-FAIL SEARCH).

Now, suppose that a program is stored in the case base, indexed by the above set of indices, and that TA is presented with the specification (∃ ?X ?L (ATOMIC ?X)). This specification has the internal form:

(SEARCH (SEARCH-SPACE-TYPE CONS)
        (SEARCH-SPACE ?L)
        (SEARCH-TYPE LIST-SEARCH)

```
(SEARCH-ELEMENT ?X)
(STOP-AFTER ALL-SEARCHED)
(ON-TERMINATION FAIL)
(TEST (TESTER
        (TEST (ISA ?X ATOM))
        (ON-SUCCESS SUCCEED)
        (ON-FAIL FAIL)))
(ON-SUCCESS SUCCEED)
(ON-FAIL CONTINUE))
```

Its index set is:

```
(CONS SEARCH-SPACE-TYPE SEARCH)
(?L SEARCH-SPACE SEARCH)
(LIST-SEARCH SEARCH-TYPE SEARCH)
(?X SEARCH-ELEMENT SEARCH)
(ALL-SEARCHED STOP-AFTER SEARCH)
(FAIL ON-TERMINATION SEARCH)
(?X ISA TEST TESTER TEST SEARCH)
(ATOM ISA TEST TESTER TEST SEARCH)
(SUCCEED ON-SUCCESS TESTER TEST SEARCH)
(FAIL ON-FAIL TESTER TEST SEARCH)
(SUCCEED ON-SUCCESS SEARCH)
(CONTINUE ON-FAIL SEARCH)
```

The case retrieval process will send these indices to the cases in the case base. The cases then count how many input indices match their own indices; normalized versions of these counts are then sent to the arbitration nodes described in section 3.2.[7] So, for the given set of search indices, the given case will find 9 matches (out of 12) and will send the number 3/4 to its arbitration node.

Indices for bugs and patches are created and used in an analogous manner to those for programs.

5 An Example

This section describes TA at work, showing how it builds up a small case-base of programs, patches, and bugs.

---

[7] Counts are normalized as follows: if the number of search indices is x, and the number of case indices is y, and the number of matching indices is m, the number sent to the arbitration node is $(m/x + m/y)/2$.

5.1 The initial configuration

Initially, let us assume that the patch and bug case bases are empty, and that the program case base contains the single program ISLAT, described in section 3.1. The code for this program is as follows:

```
(cond ((null ?l) t)
      ((atom (car ?l)) (islat (cdr ?l)))
      (t nil))
```

5.2 Learning a patch and a bug

Now, suppose TA is asked to write a program NO-ATOMS that tests whether each element in a list is *not* an atom: ($\forall$?X ?L ($\neg$ (ATOMIC ?X))). TA examines its program case base, and finds the code for ISLAT. It can't find any patches, since the patch case base is empty, so it begins testing phase. It is given the following sample call to test: (no-atoms '((a) (b))). It determines via its emulation network that this call should succeed, but the code fails when run. Since this is the first incorrect program that TA has come across, it does not know about any bugs; it therefore must resort to tracing the program a line at a time. The first line of the program contains the COND clause (null ?l). TA asks the user whether this code fragment is acceptable. Since it is, TA continues with the next line, which contains the code fragment (atom (car ?l)). At this point, the user points out that the correct code fragment is (not (atom (car ?l))). TA creates a patch:

```
old: (atom (car ?l))
new: (not (atom (car ?l)))
```

The patch is then entered into the patch case base, and applied to the buggy program. The resulting program is found to be correct, and is added to the program case base. The bug "incorrect second question in COND clause" is created and stored in the bug case base.

5.3 Using a bug

Next, suppose TA is asked to write a program ALL-ATOM-CAR which, given a list of lists, tests whether the first element of each sublist is an atom: ($\forall$?X ?L (ATOMIC (FIRST ?Y ?X))). TA searches its program case base, and again finds the code for ISLAT. When it then searches its patch case base, however, it still comes up empty, since the only patch it finds is not a close enough match to be usable. Upon testing, it is given the following call: (all-atom-car '((a) (b))). Once again, the emulation determines that the call should succeed, but the code indicates that the call fails. TA searches its bug case base, and finds the bug uncovered during testing of NO-ATOMS. Using this bug, TA is able to determine that the buggy line of code is the line containing the clause (atom (car ?l)); but it again must ask for the correct code fragment. Once the correct fragment is given, the following patch is created:

```
old: (atom (car ?l))
new: (atom (car (car ?l))))
```

This patch is stored in the patch case base. It is then applied to the code, resulting in a correct program which is stored in the program case base.

5.4 Using a patch

Finally, suppose TA is asked to write a program NO-ATOM-CAR that, given a list of lists, tests whether the first element of each sublist is *not* an atom: ($\forall$?X ?L ($\neg$ (ATOMIC (FIRST ?Y ?X)))). When TA searches its program case base, it now finds that the earlier program NO-ATOMS is the closest match. Further, when its patch case base is searched, it discovers that the patch created during the creation of ALL-ATOM-CAR is close enough to apply. This patch is applied, yielding the program:

```
(cond ((null ?l) t)
      ((not (atom (car (car ?l)))) (no-atom-car (cdr ?l)))
      (t nil))
```

This program is correct, and so the testing phase need not be entered and the program can be stored in the appropriate case base.

6 Further Work

The system as it stands now suffers from not being able to determine on its own whether a given code fragment is buggy. Further, once a buggy code fragment is found, the system is unable to determine what the correct fragment should be. To solve these problems, a method is needed to let TA learn to associate code fragments with specification fragments. In Friedman (1974), this type of goal is accomplished by tracing through programs (especially those that are correct) a step at a time, showing how each line of code contributes to a solution. We hope to extend our program along similar lines by introducing a case base that learns associations between code fragments and fragments of internal specifications.

For example, consider the program ISLAT, with program as shown in section 5 and internal specification as shown in section 3.1. We can see that, e.g., the clause (null ?l) can be associated with the fragment (STOP-AFTER ALL-SEARCHED), the clause (atom (car ?l)) can be associated with the fragment (TEST (ISA ?X ATOM)), etc.[8] With a case base of these kinds of associations, TA should be able both to determine incorrect code fragments for itself, and to figure out what the correct code fragments should be.

---

[8] Note that nothing guarantees that there will be a one-one mapping between between code fragments and specification fragments; thus, some code fragments might map to more than one spec fragment, and vice versa. If, however, it is the case that a code fragment maps to no spec fragments, this indicates either redundant code or an incomplete understanding of what the program was supposed to do.

Knowledge of the kind described above should also be useful in the actual writing of programs. For example, it may be that for a given program specification, there are no stored cases that match well enough to be useful. It may still be possible to use fragments from the internal specification to find code fragments that had been previously associated with them, and build a program from results obtained in this way. This seems somewhat similar in spirit to methods like Derivational Analogy [Carbonell, 1983], in that cases are searched for based on functional, rather than structural, similarities.

7 Conclusions

We feel that there is a great deal of insight to be gained from studying systems that acquire knowledge dynamically, as a student taking an introductory course in programming might acquire the knowledge. Though such a system does need general problem-solving knowledge, it needs very little knowledge about programming per se.

We have described a system, TA, that learns to write programs by retrieving and modifying cases of previous programs that it encountered. We feel that the combination of case base architecture and indexing scheme which we have described is a noteworthy contribution to case-based learning. In effect, this scheme gives us generalizations based on similarities "for free:" a current problem and a retrieved case can be thought of as being instances of the same general concept, but the generalization itself need not be stored. Since there is no explicit generalization hierarchy, the size of the case base is guaranteed to remain strictly proportional to the number of cases, and retrieval time for cases will remain small as well.

References

[Anderson, 1986] J.R. Anderson. Knowledge compilation: the general learning mechanism. In R. S. Michalski, J. G. Corbonell, and T. M. Mitchell, editors, *Machine Learning: An Artificial Intelligence Approach*, pages 289–310, Morgan Kaufmann, Los Altos, CA, 1986.

[Balzer et al., 1978] R. M. Balzer, N. Goldman, and D. Wile. Informality in program specifications. *IEEE Transactions on Software Engineering*, SE-4(2):94–103, 1978.

[Barstow, 1979] D. R. Barstow. An experiment in knowledge-based automatic programming. *Artificial Intelligence*, 12:73–119, 1979.

[Bradtke and Lehnert, 1988] S. Bradtke and W. Lehnert. Some experiments with case-based search. In *Proceedings of the 1988 Case-Based Reasoning Workshop*, Clearwater Beach, Florida, 1988.

[Carbonell, 1983] J. G. Carbonell. Derivational analogy and its role in problem solving. In *Proceedings of the Third National Conference on Artificial Intelligence*, pages 64–69, American Association for Artificial Intelligence, Morgan Kaufmann Publishers, Inc., 95 First Street, Los Altos, CA 94022, 1983.

[Friedman, 1974] D. Friedman. *The Little LISPer (First Edition)*. Science Research Associates, Inc., Chicago, 1974.

[Hammond, 1986] K. J. Hammond. Chef: a model of case-based planning. In *Proceedings of the Fifth National Conference on Artificial Intelligence*, pages 267–271, American Association for Artificial Intelligence, Morgan Kaufmann Publishers, Inc., 95 First Street, Los Altos, CA 94022, 1986.

[Hewitt, 1977] C. Hewitt. Viewing control structures as patterns of passing messages. *Artificial Intelligence*, 8:???, 1977.

[Kolodner, 1984] J. L. Kolodner. *Retrieval and Organizational Strategies in Conceptual Memory: A Computer Model*. Lawrence Erlbaum Associates, Hillsdale, NJ, 1984.

[Lebowitz, 1986] M. Lebowitz. Concept learning in a rich input domain: generalization-based memory. In R. S. Michalski, J. G. Corbonell, and T. M. Mitchell, editors, *Machine Learning: An Artificial Intelligence Approach*, Morgan Kaufmann, Los Altos, CA, 1986.

[Lehnert, 1987] W. G. Lehnert. Case-based problem solving with a large knowledge base of learned cases. In *Proceedings of the Sixth National Conference on Artificial Intelligence*, pages 301–306, American Association for Artificial Intelligence, Morgan Kaufmann Publishers, Inc., 1987. 95 First Street, Los Altos, CA 94022.

[Manna and Waldinger, 1981] Z. Manna and R. Waldinger. A deductive approach to program synthesis. In B. L. Webber and N. J. Nilsson, editors, *Readings in Artificial Intelligence*, pages 141–172, Tioga, Palo Alto, CA, 1981.

[Minsky, 1986] M. Minsky. *The Society of Mind*. Simon and Schuster, New York, New York, 1986.

[Rissland and Ashley, 1987] E. L. Rissland and K. D. Ashley. *HYPO: a Case-Based Reasoning System*. Technical Report CPTM-18, Department of Computer and Information Science, University of Massachusetts at Amherst, Amherst, MA, 01003, 1987.

Appendix
Bibliography on Case-Based Reasoning and Related Topics

1 Case-Based Reasoning

1. Alterman, R. (1985). Adaptive Planning: Refitting Old Plans to New Situations. *Proceedings of the Seventh Annual Conference of the Cognitive Science Society*, Irvine, CA.

2. Alterman, R. (1987). The Operational Level of a Commonsense Planner. *Proceedings of the Ninth Annual Conference of the Cognitive Science Society*, Seattle, WA.

3. Ashley, K. (1985). Reasoning by Analogy: A Survey of Selected A.I. Research with Implications for Legal Expert Systems. *Computing Power and Legal Reasoning*, Charles Walter (ed.), West Publishing Co., St. Paul, MN.

4. Ashley, K. (1986). Knowing What to Ask Next and Why: Asking Pertinent Questions Using Cases and Hypotheticals. *Proceedings of the Eighth Annual Conference of the Cognitive Science Society*, Amherst, MA.

5. Ashley, K. D. (1987). *Modelling Legal Argument: Reasoning with Cases and Hypotheticals.* Ph.D. Dissertation, COINS Technical Report No. 88–01, Department of Computer and Information Science, University of Massachusetts, Amherst.

6. Ashley, K. D. (1988). Arguing by Analogy in Law: a Case-Based Model. *Analogical Reasoning: Perspectives of Artificial Intelligence, Cognitive Science, and Philosophy*, Helman, D. (Ed.), D. Reidel.

7. Ashley, K. and Rissland, E. L. (1987). Compare and Contrast: A Test of Expertise. *Proceedings of AAAI-87.*

8. Ashley, K. D. and Rissland, E. L. (1988). *A Case-Based Approach to Modeling Legal Expertise.* Counselor Project Technical Memorandum No. 23, Department of Computer and Information Science, University of Massachusetts, Amherst. To appear in *IEEE Expert*, Summer, 1988.

9. Bain, W. (1984). *Toward a Model of Subjective Interpretation.* Technical Report No. 324, Dept. of Computer Science, Yale University, New Haven, CT.

10. Bain, W. (1986). *Case-Based Reasoning: A Computer Model of Subjective Assessment.* Ph.D. Thesis, Dept. of Computer Science, Yale University, New Haven, CT.

11. Carbonell, J. G. (1981). A Computational Model of Analogical Problem Solving. *Proceedings of IJCAI-7*, Vancouver, B.C., Canada.

12. Carbonell, J.G. (1982). Experiential Learning in Analogical Problem Solving. *Proceedings of AAAI-82*, Pittsburgh, PA.

13. Carbonell, J.G. (1983). Learning by Analogy: Formulating and Generalizing Plans from Past Experience. *Machine Learning: An Artificial Intelligence Approach*, R. Michalski, J. Carbonell and T. Mitchell (Eds.), Tioga, Palo Alto, CA.

14. Carbonell, J.G. (1986). Derivational Analogy: A Theory of Reconstructive Problem Solving and Expertise Acquisition. *Machine Learning, An Artificial Intelligence Approach, Vol. 2*, R. Michalski, J. Carbonell and T. Mitchell (Eds.), Morgan Kaufmann, Los Altos, CA.

15. Collins, G. (1987). *Plan Creation: Using Strategies as Blueprints.* Ph.D. thesis. Department of Computer Science, Yale University, New Haven, CT.

16. Cullingford, R.E. and Kolodner, J.L. (1986). Interactive Advice Giving. *Proceedings of the 1986 IEEE International Conference on Systems, Man, and Cybernetics.*

17. Hammond, K. (1986). *Case-based Planning: An Integrated Theory of Planning, Learning and Memory.* Ph.D. Thesis, Yale University, New Haven, CT.

18. Hammond, K. (1986). CHEF: A Model of Case-Based Planning. *Proceedings of AAAI-86*, Philadelphia, PA.

19. Hammond, K. (1986). Learning to Anticipate and Avoid Planning Problems through the Explanation of Failures. *Proceedings of AAAI-86*, Philadelphia, PA.

20. Hammond, K. (1986). The Use of Remindings in Planning. *Proceedings of the Eighth Annual Conference of the Cognitive Science Society*, Amherst, MA.

21. Hammond, K. (1987). Explaining and Repairing Plans that Fail. *Proceedings of IJCAI-87.*

22. Kass, A. (1986). Modifying Explanations to Understand Stories. *Proceedings of the Eighth Annual Conference of the Cognitive Science Society*, Amherst, MA.

23. Kolodner, J. L. (1982). The Role of Experience in Development of Expertise. *Proceedings of AAAI-82.*

24. Kolodner, J. L. (1983). Towards an Understanding of the Role of Experience in the Evolution from Novice to Expert. *International Journal of Man-Machine Studies*, Vol. 19.

25. Kolodner, J.L. (1985). *Experiential Processes in Natural Problem Solving.* Technical Report No. GIT-ICS-85/23. School of Information and Computer Science, Georgia Institute of Technology, Atlanta, GA.

26. Kolodner, J.L. (1986). Some Little-Known Complexities of Case-Based Inference. *Proceedings of the 1986 Conference on Theoretical Issues in Conceptual Information Processing* (unpublished), Philadeplphia, PA.

27. Kolodner, J.L. (1987). Capitalizing on Failure Through Case-Based Inference. *Proceedings of the Ninth Annual Conference of the Cognitive Science Society.*

28. Kolodner, J. L. (1987). Extending Problem Solving Capabilities Through Case-Based Inference. *Proceedings of the Fourth International Machine Learning Workshop.*

29. Kolodner, J.L. and Cullingford, R.E. (1986). Towards a Memory Architecture that Supports Reminding. *Proceedings of the Eighth Annual Conference of the Cognitive Science Society*, Amherst, MA.

30. Kolodner, J. L. and Kolodner, R. M. (1987). Using Experience in Clinical Problem Solving: Introduction and Framework. *IEEE Transactions on Systems, Man, and Cybernetics.*

31. Kolodner, J.L. and Riesbeck, C.K. (1986). *Experience, Memory and Reasoning.* Lawrence Erlbaum Associates, Hillsdale, NJ.

32. Kolodner, J.L. and Simpson, R.L. (1984). Experience and Problem Solving: A Framework. *Proceedings of the Sixth Annual Conference of the Cognitive Science Society*, Boulder, CO.

33. Kolodner, J. L. and Simpson, R. L. (1988). *The MEDIATOR: A Case Study of a Case-Based Reasoner.* Technical Report No. GIT-ICS-88/11. School of Information and Computer Science. Georgia Institute of Technology. Atlanta, GA.

34. Kolodner, J.L., Simpson, R.L. and Sycara, K. (1985). A Process Model of Case-Based Reasoning in Problem Solving. *Proceedings of IJCAI-85*, Los Angeles, CA.

35. Leake, D. and Owens, C. (1986). Organizing Memory for Explanations. *Proceedings of the Eighth Annual Conference of the Cognitive Science Society*, Amherst, MA.

36. Lehnert, W.G. (1986). *Utilizing Episodic Memory for the Integration of Syntax and Semantics.* Counselor Project Technical Memo No. 15, Univ. of Massachusetts, Amherst, MA.

37. Lehnert, W.G. (1987). Learning to Integrate Syntax and Semantics. *Proceedings of the Fourth International Machine Learning Workshop.*

38. Lehnert, W.G. (1987). Case-Based Problem Solving with a Large Knowledge Base of Learned Cases. *Proceedings of AAAI-87*, Seattle, WA.

39. Lehnert, W. G. (1987). Word Pronunciation as a Problem in Case-Based Reasoning. *Proceedings of the Ninth Annual Conference of the Cognitive Science Society.*

40. Lehnert, W. (1987). *Case-Based Reasoning as a Paradigm for Heuristic Search.* Technical Report No. 87-107, Department of Computer and Information Science, University of Massachusetts.

41. Mark, W. and Barletta, R. (1987). *Case-Based Reasoning in Manufacturing.* Manuscript, Lockheed AI Center, Palo Alto, CA.

42. Riesbeck, C. K. (1981). Failure-Driven Reminding for Incremental Learning. it Proceedings of IJCAI-81, Vancouver, B.C., Canada.

43. Riesbeck, C.K. (1983). *Knowledge Organization and Reasoning Style.* Technical Report 270, Dept. of Computer Science, Yale University, New Haven, CT.

44. Rissland, E. L. (1980). Example Generation. *Proceedings of the Third National Conference of the Canadian Society for Computational Studies of Intelligence*, Victoria, B.C., Canada.

45. Rissland, E. L. (1981). *Constrained Example Generation.* Technical Report 81-24, University of Massachusetts, Amherst, MA.

46. Rissland, E. L. (1983). Examples in Legal Reasoning: Legal Hypotheticals. *Proceedings of IJCAI-83*, Karlsruhe, West Germany.

47. Rissland, E. L., and Ashley, K. (1986). Hypotheticals as Heuristic Device. *Proceedings of AAAI-86*, Philadelphia, PA.

48. Rissland, E. and Ashley, K. (1987). HYPO: A Case-Based Reasoning System. *Proceedings of IJCAI-87*, Milan, Italy.

49. Rissland, E. and Ashley, K. (1987). A Case-Based System for Trade Secrets Law. *Proceedings, First International Conference on Artificial Intelligence and Law.*

50. Rissland, E. L. and Ashley, K. D. (in press). HYPO: A Precedent-Based Case-Based Reasoning System, *Advanced Issues of Law and Information Technology*, G. Vandenberghe (Ed.), Kluwer.

51. Rissland, E.L. and Collins, R.T. (1986). The Law as a Learning System. *Proceedings of the Eighth Annual Conference of the Cognitive Science Society*, Amherst, MA.

52. Rissland, E. L., Valcarce, E. M., Ashley, K. (1984). Explaining and Arguing with Examples. *Proceedings of AAAI-84*, Austin, Texas.

53. Schank, R. (1982). *Dynamic Memory: A Theory of Learning in Computers and People*, Cambridge University Press, New York, NY.

54. Schank, R. (1986). *Explanation Patterns: Understanding Mechanically and Creatively.* Lawrence Erlbaum Associates, Hillsdale, NJ.

55. Simpson, R.L. (1985). *A Computer Model of Case-Based Reasoning in Problem Solving: An Investigation in the Domain of Dispute Mediation.* Ph.D. Thesis. Technical Report No. GIT-ICS-85/18, School of Information and Computer Science, Georgia Institute of Technology, Atlanta, GA.

56. Sycara, E.P. (1987). *Resolving Adversarial Conflicts: An Approach to Integrating Case-Based and Analytic Methods*. Ph.D. Thesis. Technical Report No. GIT-ICS-87/26, School of Information and Computer Science, Georgia Institute of Technology, Atlanta, GA.

57. Turner, R. (1986). A derivational approach to plan refinement for advice giving. *Proceedings of the 1986 IEEE International Conference on Systems, Man, and Cybernetics*, Atlanta, GA.

58. Turner, R. (1987). *Issues in the Design of Advisory Systems: The Consumer Advisor System*. Technical Report No. GIT-ICS-87/19. School of Information and Computer Science. Georgia Institute of Technology. Atlanta, GA.

59. Turner, R. (1987). Modifying Previously Used Plans to Fit New Situations. *Proceedings of the Ninth Annual Conference of Cognitive Science Society*.

60. Wall, R. and Rissland, E. (1982). Scenarios as an Aid to Planning. *Proceedings of AAAI-82*, Pittsburgh, PA.

2 Analogical Problem Solving and Learning Through Analogy

1. Burstein, M.H. (1983). A Model of Learning by Incremental Analogical Reasoning and Debugging. it Proceedings of AAAI-83, Washington, D.C.

2. Burstein, M. (1986). Concept Formation by Incremental Analogical Reasoning and Debugging. it Machine Learning: An Artificial Intelligence Approach, Vol. 2, R. Michalski, J. Carbonell and T. Mitchell (Eds.), Morgan Kaufmann, Los Altos, CA.

3. Burstein, M. (1987). Combining Analogies in Mental Models. *Analogical Reasoning*, D. Halman (Ed.), D. Reidel Publishing Co.

4. Collins, A. and Gentner, D. (1982). Constructing Runnable Mental Models. *Proceedings of the Fourth Annual Conference of the Cognitive Science Society*, Ann Arbor, MI.

5. Forbus, K.D. and Gentner, D. (1986). Learning Physical Domains: Toward a Theoretical Framework. *Machine Learning: An Artificial Intelligence Approach, Vol. 2*, R. Michalski, J. Carbonell and T. Mitchell (Eds.), Morgan Kaufmann, Los Altos, CA.

6. Gentner. D. (1983). Structure-Mapping: A Theoretical Framework for Analogy. *Cognitive Science*, Vol. 7, No. 2.

7. Gentner, D. (1987). The Mechanisms of Analogical Learning. *Similarity and Analogical Reasoning*, S. Vosniadou and A. Ortony (Eds.), Cambridge University Press, New York, NY.

8. Gick and Holyoak, K. (1980). Analogical Problem Solving. *Cognitive Psychology*, Vol. 12.

9. Holyoak, K.J. (1985). The Pragmatics of Analogical Transfer. *The Psychology of Learning and Motivation*, G. Bower (Ed.), Academic Press, New York, NY.

10. Holyoak, K. and Thagard, P.R. (1985). Rule-Based Spreading Activation and Analogical Transfer. *Proceedings of Analogica*, Rutgers University, New Brunswick, NJ.

11. Ross, B.H. (1986). Remindings in Learning: Objects and Tools. *Similarity and Analogical Reasoning*, S. Vosniadou and A. Ortony (Eds.), Cambridge University Press, New York, NY.

12. Spiro, R. J. (1979). *Prior Knowledge and Story Processing: Integration, Selection and Variation.* Technical Report No. 138. Center for the Study of Reading, University of Illinois at Urbana-Champaign, IL.

13. Spiro, R. J., Feltovitch, P. J., Coulson, R. L. and Anderson, D. K. (1987). *Multiple Analogies for Complex Concepts: Antidotes for Analogy-Induced Misconception in Advanced Knowledge Acquisition.* Technical Report No. 2. Conceptual Knowledge Research Project, Southern Illinois University School of Medicine, Springfield, Illinois.

14. Thagard, P. and Holyoak, K. (1985). Discovering the Wave Theory of Sound: Inductive Inference in the Context of Problem Solving. *Proceedings of IJCAI-85*, Los Angeles, CA.

15. Winston, P. (1980). Learning and Reasoning by Analogy. *Communications of the ACM*, Vol. 23, No. 12.

16. Winston, P. (1982) Learning New Principles from Precedents and Exercises. *Artificial Intelligence*, Vol. 19.

17. Winston, P. (1984). Learning Physical Descriptions from Functional Definitions, Examples and Precedents. *Proceedings of AAAI-83*, Pittsburgh, PA.

3 Generalization Methods

1. DeJong, G. (1981). Generalizations Based on Explanations. *Proceedings of IJCAI-81*, Vancouver, B.C., Canada.

2. DeJong, J. (1983). Acquiring Schemata Through Understanding and Generalized Plans. *Proceedings of IJCAI-83*, Karlsruhe, West Germany.

3. DeJong, J. (1983). An Approach to Learning From Observation. *Proceedings of the Second International Machine Learning Workshop*, University of Illinois, Monticello, IL.

4. DeJong, G. (1985). A Brief Overview of Explanatory Schema Acquisition. *Proceedings of the Third International Machine Learning Workshop.* Rutgers University, New Brunswick, N.J.

5. DeJong, G. and Mooney, R. (1986). Explanation-based learning: An alternative view. *Machine Learning*, Vol. 1.

6. Lebowitz, M. (1983). Generalization from Natural Language Text. *Cognitive Science*, Vol. 7, No 1.

7. Lebowitz, M. (1983). RESEARCHER: An overview. *Proceedings of AAAI-83*, Washington, D.C.

8. Lebowitz, M. (1986). Concept Learning in a Rich Input Domain: Generalization-Based Memory. *Machine Learning: An Artificial Intelligence Approach, Vol. 2*, R. Michalski, J. Carbonell, and T. Mitchell (Eds.), Morgan Kaufmann, Los Altos, CA.

9. Michalski, R., Carbonell, J., and Mitchell, T. (Eds.) (1983). *Machine Learning: An Artificial Intelligence Approach*, Tioga, Palo Alto, CA.

10. Michalski, R., Carbonell, J., and Mitchell, T. (Eds.) (1986). *Machine Learning: An Artificial Intelligence Approach, Vol 2*, Morgan-Kaufmann Publishers, Palo Alto, CA.

11. Mitchell, T. (1983). Learning and Problem Solving. *Proceedings of IJCAI-83*, Karlsruhe, West Germany.

12. Mitchell, T. M., Kellar, R. M. and Kedar-Cabelli, S. T. (1986). Explanation based learning: An unifying view. *Machine Learning*, Vol. 1.

4 Memory-Based Reasoning

1. Stanfill, C., and Waltz, D. (1986). Toward Memory-Based Reasoning. *Communications of the ACM*, Vol. 29, No.12.

5 Organizing and Retrieving Cases

1. Hammond, K. (1984). *Indexing and Causality: The organization of plans and strategies in memory.* Technical Report No. 351. Dept. of Computer Science, Yale University, New Haven, CT.

2. Kolodner, J.L. (1983). Maintaining Organization in a Dynamic Long-Term Memory. *Cognitive Science*, Vol. 7, No. 4.

3. Kolodner, J.L. (1983). Reconstructive Memory: A Computer Model. *Cognitive Science*, Vol. 7, No 4.

4. Kolodner, J.L. (1984). *Retrieval and Organization Strategies in Conceptual Memory: A Computer Model.* Lawrence Erlbaum Associates, Hillsdale, NJ.

5. Kolodner, J.L and Barsalou, L. (1982). Psychological Issues Raised by an AI Model of Reconstructive Memory. *Proceedings of the Fourth Annual Conference on Cognitive Science*, Ann Arbor, MI.

6. Kolodner, J.L. and Cullingford, R.E. (1986). Towards a Memory Architecture that Supports Reminding. *Proceedings of the Eighth Annual Conference of the Cognitive Science Society*, Amherst, MA.

7. Leake, D. and Owens, C. (1986). Organizing Memory for Explanations. *Proceedings of the Eighth Annual Conference of the Cognitive Science Society*, Amherst, MA.

8. Lebowitz, M. (1983). Generalization from Natural Language Text. *Cognitive Science*, Vol. 7, No 1.

9. Lebowitz, M. (1983). RESEARCHER: An overview. *Proceedings of AAAI-83*, Washington, D.C.

10. Lebowitz, M. (1986). Concept Learning in a Rich Input Domain: Generalization-Based Memory. *Machine Learning: An Artificial Intelligence Approach, Vol. 2*, R. Michalski, J. Carbonell, and T. Mitchell (Eds.), Morgan Kaufmann, Los Altos, CA.

11. Riesbeck, C.K. (1986). Direct Memory Access Parsing. *Experience, Memory and Reasoning*, Kolodner, J.L. and Riesbeck, C.K. (Eds.) Lawrence Erlbaum Associates, Hillsdale, NJ.

12. Schank, R. (1982). *Dynamic Memory: A Theory of Learning in Computers and People*, Cambridge University Press, New York, NY.

13. Schank, R. and Abelson, R. (1977). *Scripts, Plans, Goals and Understanding*, Lawrence Erlbaum Associates, Hillsdale, NJ.

6 Related Problem Solving Literature

1. Simmons, R. and Davis, R. (1987). Generate, Test and Debug: Combining Associational Rules and Causal Models. *Proceedings of IJCAI-87*.

2. Sussman, G. (1975). *A Computer Model of Skill Acquisition.* American Elsevier, New York.